Connect Government is an application-based assignment platform containing engaging, user-friendly tools that help students better understand and connect with the concepts and language used in the American Government course. Political Scientists have reported deeper critical thinking, improved student performance, and increased classroom efficiency as a result of using Connect Government, which includes innovative tools that are often auto-gradable, such as:

SmartBook®

Described as a "textbook for the 21st century" by a political scientist, SmartBook gives students a road map to success through an adaptive reading experience that changes the way students read. It creates a personalized, interactive reading environment by highlighting important concepts, while helping students identify their strengths and weaknesses. This ensures that he or she is focused on the content needed to close specific knowledge gaps, while it simultaneously promotes long-term learning.

NewsFlash

Responding to the need for currency in the American Government course, this new Connect assignment pairs fresh content on a rolling basis with auto-grade questions that allow instructors to assess student understanding of the important news of the day.

Applied Critical Thinking

Nicknamed ACT!, these new activities encourage students to apply critical thinking skills to core course content through political research and reflection. First, students assess their understanding of content, then gather applicable political research, and lastly, critically reflect on the results.

Practice Government Missions

Practice Government, McGraw-Hill's educational game focused on the American political system, can now be played inside of Connect American Government! Two introductory missions have now been paired with auto-grade and critical thinking questions that harness the power of "learning by doing" right within Connect. Additional missions are available through mhpractice.com.

Concept Clips

Expanded to now include audio, Concept Clips are engaging videos that walk students through the more difficult concepts in the American government course (such as the Electoral College, Supreme Court procedures, or how to evaluate a public opinion poll).

Interactive Data Analysis

Help your students consume political data in a meaningful way. Students in the American government course now have the ability to interact with political data visualizations to gain insight into important factors that shape our political process. Students can review electoral turnout over time or study how demographic shifts in the American population might affect future elections. These interactive charts and maps are paired with auto-grade and critical thinking questions to enhance student understanding.

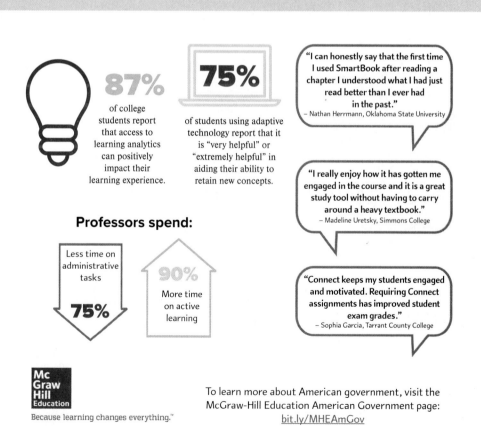

87% of college students report that access to learning analytics can positively impact their learning experience.

75% of students using adaptive technology report that it is "very helpful" or "extremely helpful" in aiding their ability to retain new concepts.

"I can honestly say that the first time I used SmartBook after reading a chapter I understood what I had just read better than I ever had in the past."
– Nathan Herrmann, Oklahoma State University

"I really enjoy how it has gotten me engaged in the course and it is a great study tool without having to carry around a heavy textbook."
– Madeline Uretsky, Simmons College

Professors spend:

Less time on administrative tasks **75%**

More time on active learning **90%**

"Connect keeps my students engaged and motivated. Requiring Connect assignments has improved student exam grades."
– Sophia Garcia, Tarrant County College

Mc Graw Hill Education
Because learning changes everything.™

To learn more about American government, visit the McGraw-Hill Education American Government page:
bit.ly/MHEAmGov

WE THE PEOPLE

AN INTRODUCTION TO AMERICAN GOVERNMENT

THIRTEENTH EDITION

THOMAS E. PATTERSON

Bradlee Professor of Government and the Press
John F. Kennedy School of Government
Harvard University

WE THE PEOPLE: AN INTRODUCTION TO AMERICAN GOVERNMENT,
THIRTEENTH EDITION

Published by McGraw-Hill Education, 2 Penn Plaza, New York, NY 10121. Copyright © 2019 by McGraw-Hill Education. All rights reserved. Printed in the United States of America. Previous editions © 2017, 2015, and 2013. No part of this publication may be reproduced or distributed in any form or by any means, or stored in a database or retrieval system, without the prior written consent of McGraw-Hill Education, including, but not limited to, in any network or other electronic storage or transmission, or broadcast for distance learning.

Some ancillaries, including electronic and print components, may not be available to customers outside the United States.

This book is printed on acid-free paper.

1 2 3 4 5 6 7 8 9 LCR 22 21 20 19

ISBN 978-1-259-91240-5 (bound edition)
MHID 1-259-91240-X (bound edition)
ISBN 978-1-260-16575-3 (loose-leaf edition)
MHID 1-260-16575-2 (loose-leaf edition)

Portofolio Manager: *Jason Seitz*
Product Development Manager: *Dawn Groundwater*
Senior Product Developer: *Sarah Colwell*
Marketing Manager: *Will Walter*
Content Project Managers: *Rick Hecker, George Theofanopoulos*
Buyer: *Laura Fuller*
Design: *Egzon Shaqir*
Content Licensing Specialist: *Ann Marie Jannette*
Cover Image: *©Steve Heap/Shutterstock*
Compositor: *Aptara®, Inc.*

All credits appearing on page or at the end of the book are considered to be an extension of the copyright page.

Library of Congress Cataloging-in-Publication Data

Names: Patterson, Thomas E.
Title: We the people / Thomas E. Patterson, Bradlee Professor of Government
    and the Press, John F. Kennedy School of Government, Harvard University.
Description: Thirteenth edition. | New York, NY : McGraw-Hill Education, [2019]
Identifiers: LCCN 2018041814 | ISBN 9781259912405 (alk. paper) | ISBN
    125991240X (alk. paper)
Subjects: LCSH: United States—Politics and government.
Classification: LCC JK276 .P38 2019 | DDC 320.473—dc23 LC record available at
    https://lccn.loc.gov/2018041814

The Internet addresses listed in the text were accurate at the time of publication. The inclusion of a website does not indicate an endorsement by the authors or McGraw-Hill Education, and McGraw-Hill Education does not guarantee the accuracy of the information presented at these sites.

mheducation.com/highered

To My Son and Daughter.
Alex and Leigh

ABOUT THE AUTHOR

Courtesy of Thomas Patterson

Thomas E. Patterson is Bradlee Professor of Government and the Press in the John F. Kennedy School of Government at Harvard University. He was previously Distinguished Professor of Political Science in the Maxwell School of Citizenship at Syracuse University. Raised in a small Minnesota town near the Iowa and South Dakota borders, he attended South Dakota State University as an undergraduate and served in the U.S. Army Special Forces in Vietnam before enrolling at the University of Minnesota, where he received his PhD in 1971.

Since then, he has regularly taught introductory American government. In 2013 he was chosen as teacher of the year and adviser of the year by Harvard University's Kennedy School of Government students, the first time a member of its faculty has received both awards simultaneously.

He has authored numerous books and articles, which focus mainly on elections, the media, and citizenship. His most recent book, *Informing the News*, which was described as "superb" and "mesmerizing" in one review, examines the public misinformation resulting from the emergence of partisan outlets and the decline in citizens' attention to news. An earlier book, *The Vanishing Voter* (2002), describes and explains the long-term decline in voter participation. His book *Out of Order* (1994) received national attention when President Clinton urged every politician and journalist to read it. In 2002 *Out of Order* received the American Political Science Association's Graber Award for the best book of the past decade in political communication. Another of Patterson's books, *The Mass Media Election* (1980), received a Choice award as Outstanding Academic Title, 1980–1981. Patterson's first book, *The Unseeing Eye* (1976), was selected by the American Association for Public Opinion Research as one of the 50 most influential books of the past half century in the field of public opinion.

His research has been funded by major grants from the National Science Foundation, the Markle Foundation, the Smith-Richardson Foundation, the Ford Foundation, the Knight Foundation, The Carnegie Corporation, and the Pew Charitable Trusts.

CONTENTS

CHAPTER THREE

CHAPTER FIVE

EQUAL RIGHTS: STRUGGLING TOWARD FAIRNESS

CHAPTER SIX

PUBLIC OPINION AND POLITICAL SOCIALIZATION: SHAPING THE PEOPLE'S VOICE

CHAPTER NINE

INTEREST GROUPS: ORGANIZING FOR INFLUENCE

CHAPTER TEN

THE NEWS MEDIA AND THE INTERNET: COMMUNICATING POLITICS

CHAPTER ELEVEN

CONGRESS: BALANCING NATIONAL GOALS AND LOCAL INTERESTS

CHAPTER TWELVE

THE PRESIDENCY: LEADING THE NATION   360

CHAPTER THIRTEEN

THE FEDERAL BUREAUCRACY: ADMINISTERING THE GOVERNMENT

CHAPTER FOURTEEN

THE FEDERAL JUDICIAL SYSTEM: APPLYING THE LAW

CHAPTER FIFTEEN

ECONOMIC AND ENVIRONMENTAL POLICY: CONTRIBUTING TO PROSPERITY   463

CHAPTER SIXTEEN

CHAPTER SEVENTEEN

A LETTER FROM THE AUTHOR

Anyone who writes an introductory program on American government faces the challenge of explaining a wide range of subjects. One way is to pile fact upon fact and list upon list. It's a common approach to textbook writing, but it turns politics into a pretty dry subject. Politics doesn't have to be dry, and it certainly doesn't have to be dull. Politics has all the elements of drama plus the added feature of affecting the everyday lives of real people.

My goal has been to make this text the most readable one available. Rather than piling fact upon fact, the program relies on narrative. A narrative program weaves together theory, information, and examples in order to bring out key facts and ideas. The response to this approach has been gratifying. As a previous edition was being prepared, I received the following note from a longtime instructor:

> I read this book in about three days, cover to cover.... I have never seen a better basic government/politics textbook. I think reading standard textbooks is "boring" (to use a favorite student word), but this one overcomes that. Dr. Patterson has managed to do something that I heretofore thought could not be done.

When writing, I regularly reminded myself that the readers were citizens as well as students. For this reason, the text encourages "critical thinking," by which I mean the process through which an individual determines what can reasonably be believed and then applies reason and information to reach a thoughtful conclusion. Each chapter has five boxes that ask you to "think critically." Two of these—the "How the U.S. Differs" box and the "How the 50 States Differ" box—ask you to think critically about differences in governing systems. A third box—"Party Polarization"—asks you to critically analyze differences in the Republican and Democratic Parties. A fourth box—"Case Study"—discusses a political event and then asks you to analyze the outcome. The final box—"Fake or Fact?"—asks you to critically assess a factual claim. These boxes are rooted in the idea that critical thinking is a skill that can be nurtured and, once acquired, can help you become a more responsible citizen, whether in casting a vote, forming an opinion about a public policy, or contributing to a political cause.

Improving your ability to think critically is a primary goal of this text. If the only result of reading the text was to increase your factual knowledge of American government, I would judge it a failure. As Albert Einstein once noted, "The value of a college education is not the learning of many facts but the training of the mind to think." Political science courses, like those in other social science and humanities disciplines, should help students hone their critical thinking skills. As I indicated, the five boxes in each chapter are designed for this purpose. So, too, is the "Critical Thinking Zone" at the end of each chapter. This feature asks you to make use of the chapter's information through the application of the three skills—conceptualizing, synthesizing, and analyzing—that are the foundation of critical thinking.

Finally, in this program I have attempted to present American government through the analytical lens of political science but in a way that captures the vivid world of real-life politics. Only a tiny fraction of students in the introductory course are enrolled because they intend to pursue an academic career in political science. Most students take it because they are required to do so or because they have an interest in politics. I have sought to write a book that will deepen your political interest if you are the second type of student, and kindle your interest if you are the first type.

We the People has been in use in college classrooms for more than two decades. During this time, the program has been adopted at more than 1,000 colleges and universities. I am extremely grateful to all who have used it. I am particularly indebted to the many instructors and students who have sent me suggestions on how to strengthen it. As they have done for several editions now, the University of Northern Colorado's Steve Mazurana and his students graciously sent me detailed feedback that broadly informed this edition's revisions. If you have ideas you would like to share, please contact me at the John F. Kennedy School, Harvard University, Cambridge, MA 02138, or by e-mail: thomas_patterson@harvard.edu.

Thomas E. Patterson

PREFACE

RELEVANCY AND READABILITY TO ENGAGE TODAY'S STUDENT

Tom Patterson's *We the People* is a **concise** approach to American government, emphasizing **critical thinking** through **relevant** examples that appeal to today's students. This extremely **readable** text provides opportunities to **engage** with the political process through tools that help students **learn how to think about politics**, utilizing digital resources that connect students with the material in a highly **personalized** way.

BETTER DATA, SMARTER REVISION, IMPROVED RESULTS

Students helped inform the revision strategy:

STEP 1. Over the course of three years, data points showing concepts that caused students the most difficulty were collected anonymously from McGraw-Hill Education's Connect® American Government's SmartBook for *We the People.*

STEP 2. The data from SmartBook was provided to the author in the form of a *heat map,* which graphically illustrated "hot spots" in the text that impacted student learning (see image below).

STEP 3. The author used the *heat map* data to refine the content and reinforce student comprehension in the new edition. Additional quiz questions and assignable activities were created for use in Connect American Government to further support student success.

RESULT: Because the *heat map* gave the author empirically based feedback at the paragraph and even sentence level, he was able to develop the new edition using precise student data that pinpointed concepts that caused students the most difficulty.

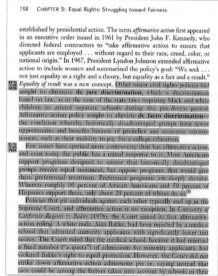

Heat map data also inform the activities and assessments in Connect American Government, McGraw-Hill Education's assignable and assessable learning platform. Where the heat map data indicates that students struggled with specific learning objectives or concepts, we created new Connect assets—Concept Clips, Applied Critical Thinking (ACT), and Newsflash current event activities—to provide another avenue for students to learn and master the content.

▊▊SMARTBOOK™

Fueled by LearnSmart, SmartBook is the first and only adaptive reading experience currently available.

Make It Effective. SmartBook creates a personalized reading experience by highlighting significant concepts that a student needs to learn at that moment. This ensures that every minute spent with SmartBook productively contributes to student learning.

Make It Informed. The reading experience continuously adapts by highlighting content based on what the student knows and doesn't know. Real-time reports quickly identify the concepts that require more attention from individual students—or the entire class. SmartBook detects the content a student is most likely to forget and resurfaces it to improve long-term retention.

New to this edition, SmartBook is now optimized for mobile and tablet and is accessible for students with disabilities. And as part of any American government course, SmartBook now focuses on the broader context for and building blocks of the political system. Specifically, it has been enhanced with improved learning objectives to ensure that students gain foundational knowledge while also learning to make connections for broader understanding of government institutions, events, and behavior. SmartBook personalizes learning to individual student needs, continually adapting to pinpoint knowledge gaps and focus learning on topics that need the most attention. Study time is more productive and, as a result, students are better prepared for class and coursework. For instructors, SmartBook tracks student progress and provides insights that can help guide teaching strategies.

INFORMING AND ENGAGING STUDENTS ON POLITICAL CONCEPTS

Using Connect American Government, students can learn the course material more deeply and study more effectively than ever before.

At the *remember* and *understand* levels of Bloom's taxonomy, **Concept Clips** help students break down key concepts in American government. Using easy-to-understand audio narration, visual cues, and colorful animations, Concept

Clips provide a step-by-step presentation that aids in student retention. New Concept Clips for this edition include the following:

- What are the Types of Government?
- Federalists and Antifederalists
- What is Devolution?
- Regulation of the Media
- Who Participates?
- Presidency: Going Public
- U.S. Foreign Policy

In addition to the concept-based clips, the new edition also offers several skills-based clips that equip students for work within and outside the classroom. These skills-based clips include the following:

- Evaluating the News
- Critical Thinking
- How to Read a Court Case
- How to Understand Charts and Graphs
- Political Cartoons
- How to Avoid Plagiarism

Also at the *remember* and *understand* levels of Bloom's taxonomy, **Newsflash** ties current news stories to key American government concepts and learning objectives. After evaluating a related news story, students are assessed on their ability to connect it to the course content. Examples include the 2018 midterm election results, 2017 tax reform legislation, and trade tariffs.

Deepen understanding of how politics happens in the real world by leveraging the most popular podcasts available with our new **Podcast Assignments.** These assignments allow you to bring greater context and nuance to your courses while engaging students through the storytelling power of podcasts.

At the *apply, analyze,* and *evaluate* levels of Bloom's taxonomy, **critical thinking activities** allow students to engage with the political process and learn by doing.

- Quiz: What Is Your Political Ideology?
- Poll: Americans' Confidence in the Police
- Research: Find Your Senator
- Infographic: Compare the Courts

Practice Government, McGraw-Hill's educational game focused on the American political system, is fully integrated inside of Connect American Government! A set of focused introductory missions are paired with auto-grade and critical thinking.

CONTENT CHANGES

In addition to thorough updates of the data and figures throughout the text, fresh new photographs and other images in every chapter, and a new "Fake or Fact?" boxed feature (individual boxes listed below) to help students negotiate misinformation in today's social media–driven and increasingly partisan media, the revisions to Chapters 6, 10, and 13 were guided by the student heat map data mentioned earlier.

Finally, *We the People*, Thirteenth Edition, includes the following specific chapter-by-chapter changes:

Chapter 1, Critical Thinking and Political Culture: Becoming a Responsible Citizen

- New introduction focused on the impact of the current wave of misinformation on Americans' beliefs (using the 2016 Edgar Maddison Welch "pizzagate" shooting and other examples) as an introduction to the book's strong emphasis on critical thinking
- Thoroughly revised "Learning to Think Critically" section (previously "Learning to Think Politically") emphasizing how the skill of critical thinking—and the avoidance of confirmation bias—is more important than ever in light of our current culture of misinformation
- New "Fake or Fact?" box ("Do Immigrants Commit More Crimes?") in the "Political Culture: Americans' Enduring Beliefs" section

Chapter 2, Constitutional Democracy: Promoting Liberty and Self-Government

- New introduction focused on John McCain's acceptance speech upon receiving the National Constitution Center's Liberty Medal as a segue into the chapter's focus on the idealism that has shaped America from its beginning
- New "Fake or Fact?" box ("Were Millions of Illegal Votes Cast in Favor of Hillary Clinton in the 2016 Election?") in the "Providing for Representative Government" section

Chapter 3, Federalism: Forging a Nation

- New introduction focused on the conflict between Donald Trump's immigrant deportation policy and the establishment of sanctuary cities as a segue into the chapter's focus on national versus state power
- New "Case Study" box ("The Power of Government") in the "Federalism: National and State Sovereignty" section
- New "Fake or Fact?" box ("Do States Have Final Authority over Marijuana Laws?") in the "Federalism: National and State Sovereignty" section

Chapter 4, Civil Liberties: Protecting Individual Rights

- New "Fake or Fact?" box ("Do You Have a Right to Speak Freely on Campus?") in the "Freedom of Expression" section
- New discussion of the Supreme Court ruling in the 2018 *Masterpiece Cakeshop v. Colorado Civil Rights Division* case in the "Freedom of Expression" section
- New discussion of the Supreme Court ruling in the 2018 *Carpenter v. United States* case in the "Rights of Persons Accused of Crimes" section

Chapter 5, Equal Rights: Struggling toward Fairness

- Reorganized and streamlined discussion of equal rights throughout the chapter
- New "Fake or Fact?" box ("Is Justice Color Blind?") in the "Equality through Law" section

Chapter 6, Public Opinion and Political Socialization: Shaping the People's Voice

- New chapter introduction focused on public opinion and the gun control debate in the wake of the Parkland school shooting
- Fully updated discussions of opinion dimensions (with marijuana legalization and Trump approval rating examples) and problems with polls in "The Measurement of Public Opinion" section
- New "Fake or Fact?" box ("Can the Polls Be Trusted?") in "The Measurement of Public Opinion" section
- New introduction to the "Political Socialization: The Origins of Americans' Opinions" section, focused on opinion regarding free trade, as well as updated discussion of national pride (including a fully revised "How the U.S. Differs" box)
- Updated discussions of religion and economic class group orientations in the "Frames of Reference: How Americans Think Politically" section
- Updated discussion of partisanship with new examples in "The Influence of Public Opinion of Policy" section

Chapter 7, Political Participation: Activating the Popular Will

- Updated discussion of midterm participation, voter ID laws, European voter participation, and the Hispanic vote in the "Voter Participation" section
- New "Fake or Fact?" box ("Are Our Attention Spans Shrinking?") in the "Voter Participation" section
- Thoroughly updated discussions of the Black Lives Matter, #MeToo, and anti-gun violence movements (as well as factors in the success of various political movements) in the "Unconventional Activism: Political Movements and Protest" section

Chapter 8, Political Parties, Candidates, and Campaigns: Defining the Voter's Choice

- New chapter introduction focused on the results of the 2018 midterm elections
- Expanded discussion of the history of party partisanship from the 1960s to today in the "Party Competition and Majority Rule" section
- New "Fake or Fact?" box ("Are Strong Partisans the Most Informed Citizens?") in the "Party Competition and Majority Rule" section

- Updated coverage of third parties, as well as fully revised discussion of the decline of moderate voters and the characteristics of Republican and Democratic voters in the "Electoral and Party Systems" section
- Fully revised and restructured section on "Parties and Candidates in the Campaign" (formerly "Party Organizations")
- Expanded discussion of voter accountability in the "Parties, Candidates, and the Public's Influence" section

Chapter 9, Interest Groups: Organizing for Influence

- New introduction discussing the unprecedented number of corporate lobbyists who sought a steep cut in the corporate tax rate during congressional deliberations on the 2017 Tax Cuts and Jobs Act
- New discussion of the power of the National Rifle Association as an example of outside lobbying in the "Outside Lobbying: Seeking Influence through Public Pressure" section
- New "Fake or Fact?" box ("Do 'the People' Decide?") in "The Group System: Indispensable but Biased in Favor of Economic Groups" section

Chapter 10, The News Media and the Internet: Communicating Politics

- New chapter title (formerly "The News Media: Communicating Political Images") reflecting the ever-increasing importance of the Internet as a source of political communication
- New chapter introduction focused on the extremely disparate messages coming from American news sources
- Fully revised (and newly titled) section on "Media Change: From the Nation's Founding to Today," with a new introduction, new organization, an expanded section on the rise of cable TV and partisan talk shows, and a new section on the rise of the Internet
- Fully revised (and newly titled) section on "The Media: Content and Functions," with a new introduction, new organization, a thoroughly revised section on information-centered communication, new discussion of Trump and tweeting, a new "How the U.S. Differs" box ("Russian Interference in Western Elections"), and a new section on partisan-centered communication
- New "Fake or Fact?" box ("Are the Traditional News Media Politically Biased?") in "The Media: Content and Functions" section
- Fully revised (and newly titled) section on "Media Audiences and Effects," with a new introduction, new organization, a new section on the traditional audience, and thoroughly revised sections on partisan and inattentive audiences

Chapter 11, Congress: Balancing National Goals and Local Interests

- New chapter introduction focused on bipartisan support of the 2018 budget bill
- Revised "Congress as a Career: Election to Congress" section, with updated and expanded discussions of gerrymandering, personal misconduct, and challenges to incumbents.
- Revised "Parties and Party Leadership" section, with expanded discussion of partisanship, new discussion of the Hastert Rule, and a new section on party leaders and their members
- New discussion of the effects of polarization in the "Committees and Committee Leadership" section
- Revised "Congress's Policymaking Role" section, with new discussions of partisanship in relation to immigration reform, policy deadlock, and the House Intelligence Committee's investigation into Russian meddling in the 2016 presidential election
- New "Fake or Fact?" box ("Are Policy Problems Simple and Easy to Fix?") in the "Congress: An Institution Divided" section

Chapter 12, The Presidency: Leading the Nation

- New introduction on the unprecedented nature of the first year of Trump's presidency
- Revised "Choosing the President" section, with new discussion of Democrats expected to run in the 2020 presidential election, the effects of Gary Johnson and Jill Stein on the 2016 presidential elections, and the total price tag for the 2016 presidential elections
- New discussion of the firing of Rex Tillerson in the "Staffing the Presidency" section
- Revised "Factors in Presidential Leadership" section, with new discussion of Trump's relationship with Congress during his first two years, Americans' approval of Trump's missile strikes on Syrian installations, and Trump's unprecedented media coverage
- New "Fake or Fact?" box ("Do Trump's Supporters Believe His Claims?") in the "Factors in Presidential Leadership" section

Chapter 13, The Federal Bureaucracy: Administering the Government

- New examples within the discussions of regulatory agencies and presidential commissions, as well as new discussion of the Department of Homeland Security in the "Origin and Structure of the Federal Bureaucracy" section
- New examples throughout "The Budgetary Process" section
- Updated discussion of clientele groups in the "Policy and Power in the Bureaucracy" section

- New "Fake or Fact?" box ("Is There a 'Deep State'?") in the "Policy and Power in the Bureaucracy" section
- Fully revised "Party Polarization" box ("The Politicization of the Bureaucracy") and updated discussions of the EPA and SES in the "Democracy and Bureaucratic Accountability" section

Chapter 14, The Federal Judicial System: Applying the Law

- Updated coverage of filibustering of Supreme Court nominees, the Neil Gorsuch and Brett Kavanaugh Supreme Court nominations, and women and minority appointees to the federal court in the "Federal Court Appointees" section
- New "Fake or Fact?" box ("Would Democracy Do Better If Presidents Could Ignore the Courts?") in "The Nature of Judicial Decision Making" section

Chapter 15, Economic and Environmental Policy: Contributing to Prosperity

- Updated discussion of partisan views on regulation in the "Government as Regulator of the Economy" section, focusing on the Democrat-supported 2010 Dodd-Frank Act and the Republican-supported 2018 Economic Growth, Regulatory Relief, and Consumer Protection Act
- New discussion of Trump's withdrawal from the Paris accord in the "Government as Protector of the Environment" section
- New discussion of the 2018 Supreme Court decision on mandatory union dues in the "Government as Promoter of Economic Interests" section
- New coverage of the 2017 Tax Cuts and Jobs Act in the "Fiscal Policy as an Economic Tool" section
- New "Fake or Fact?" box ("Would Eliminating Foreign Aid Balance the Budget?") in the "Fiscal Policy as an Economic Tool" section

Chapter 16, Income, Welfare, and Education Policy: Providing for Personal Security

- New introduction focused on the 2017 Tax Cuts and Jobs Act
- New discussion of Trump's withdrawal from the Trans-Pacific Partnership and corporate lobbying for the 2017 Tax Cuts and Jobs Act in the "Income Politics and Policies" section
- Updated coverage of entitlement programs in the "Welfare Politics and Policies" section
- New "Fake or Fact?" box ("Do Citizens Who Claim to Know the Most about Policy Issues Actually Know the Most?") in the "Education Politics and Policies" section

Chapter 17, Foreign Policy: Protecting the American Way

- New introduction focused on Trump's withdrawal from the Trans-Pacific Partnership
- Fully revised (and newly titled) "The Pattern of U.S. Foreign and Defense Policy" section, with reorganized and updated discussions of the Islamic State, Russia, and China
- New "Fake or Fact?" box ("Did Russia Try to Influence the 2016 Election?") in "The Pattern of U.S. Foreign and Defense Policy" section
- Updated "How the U.S. Differs" box and updated military spending data in "The Military Dimension of National Security Policy" section
- New discussion of Donald Trump's "America First" policy, a new "Case Study" box ("Trade with China"), and updated coverage of American foreign aid in "The Economic Dimension of National Security Policy" section

ACKNOWLEDGMENTS

Nearly two decades ago, when planning the first edition of *We the People,* my editor and I concluded that it would be enormously helpful if a way could be found to bring into each chapter the judgment of those political scientists who teach the introductory course year in and year out. Thus, in addition to soliciting general reviews from a select number of expert scholars, we sent each chapter to a dozen or so faculty members at U.S. colleges and universities of all types—public and private, large and small, two-year and four-year. These political scientists, 213 in all, had well over 1,000 years of combined experience in teaching the introductory course, and they provided countless good ideas.

Since then, several hundred other political scientists have reviewed subsequent editions. These many reviewers will go unnamed here, but my debt to all of them remains undiminished by time. For the thirteenth edition, I have benefited from the thoughtful advice of the many who responded to McGraw-Hill's online survey.

I also want to thank those at McGraw-Hill Education and who contributed to the thirteenth edition: Katie Stevens, Jason Seitz, Dawn Groundwater, Elisa Odoardi, Rick Hecker, Will Walter, Sarah Colwell, Kelly Heinrichs, and Ann Marie Jannette, as well as freelance product developer Bruce Cantley and photo researchers Steve Rouben and Danny Meldung at Photo Affairs, Inc. At Harvard, I had the ongoing support of Emily Roseman and Eric Singerman.

Thomas E. Patterson

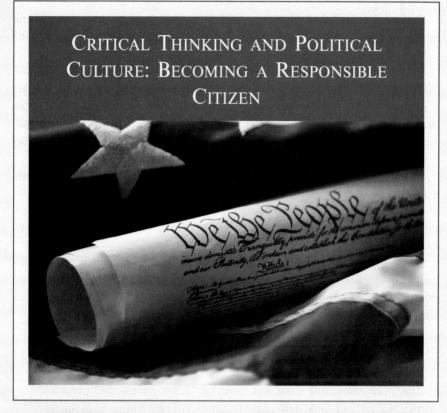

CRITICAL THINKING AND POLITICAL CULTURE: BECOMING A RESPONSIBLE CITIZEN

©Alan Crosthwaite/Alamy

❝ The worth of the state, in the long run, is the worth of the individuals composing it. ❞

JOHN STUART MILL[1]

It was a bright Sunday afternoon in the nation's capital when Edgar Maddison Welch walked into Comet Ping Pong pizza restaurant and, after telling customers to flee, searched the restaurant and opened fire. After his arrest, police recovered a pistol and an assault rifle at the scene and another gun in his pickup truck.

What prompted Welch to shoot up a pizzeria? He didn't have a grudge against a former boss or fellow employee. Welch had driven his truck from North Carolina to "self-investigate" a story he had seen online.[2] The fake story claimed that coded e-mails on Hillary Clinton's private server revealed the pizza shop was a front for a child sex-ring in which she and other top Democrats were involved. The victims were allegedly imprisoned in vaults hidden below the shop. As it turned out, there was no sex-ring, and the pizza shop didn't even have a basement.

1

As senseless as Edgar Maddison Welch's act might seem, he was not alone in his thinking. A poll taken after Welch's arrest found that a third of Americans thought the sex-ring allegation was "definitely" or "probably" true.[3]

In addition to its grim side, misinformation has its comic side. In one poll, 10 percent of respondents thought that Judith Sheindlin ("Judge Judy") holds a seat on the Supreme Court.[4] But the grim side is alarming. It's easy today to find policy issues on which millions of Americans are wildly misinformed. Never in the history of scientific opinion polls, which date to the 1930s, has misinformation clouded the minds of so many people.[5]

Some degree of political misinformation is to be expected. Politics is largely a second-hand experience—something we hear about from others. We would understand it better if we experienced it directly. A skier who has just smacked into a tree has a reality check denied to the citizen who's convinced that payments to welfare recipients account for half the federal budget.

Today's volume of misinformation is unprecedented. A full list of Americans' false beliefs would fill many pages. Here are just a few of the more prominent ones from recent years, along with the rough percentage of Americans who believed they were true at the time:

- Crime has gone up in the past decade (70 percent).[6]
- Donald Trump won the popular vote in the 2016 election (30 percent).[7]
- The 2010 Affordable Care Act included "death panels" (40 percent).[8]
- The federal budget deficit could be eliminated by cutting government waste and fraud (70 percent).[9]
- China owns more than half of U.S. debt (50 percent).[10]
- Social Security will go totally broke in my lifetime (50 percent).[11]

Early opinion polls revealed that Americans didn't know much about public affairs.[12] An alarming number of citizens couldn't answer simple questions like "What is the name of your state's governor?" Polls since then have found the same tendency, which has led analysts to question whether citizens are equipped to play the role that democracy asks of them. Political scientist James David Barber wrote that the uninformed "are dangerously unready when the time comes for choice."[13]

But whatever risks the uninformed pose, they pale alongside the risks posed by the misinformed. The uninformed know what they don't know, whereas the misinformed think they know something but don't know that they're wrong. It's the difference between ignorance and irrationality.[14] If large numbers of citizens are misinformed, and make policy and candidate choices on that basis, politics becomes aimless. Whether in forming an opinion or casting a vote,

People respond, not to the world as it is, but to the world as they *think* it is. That's as true today as during the time when people thought the world was flat and wouldn't sail out to sea because they feared sailing off the edge. Many of today's citizens hold opinions that are wildly at odds with reality. (*Source:* Swedish National Library)

citizens need to know what's at issue, so that they can make a reasoned judgment. When they lose touch with reality, such judgments are impossible.[15] The problem with misinformed voters is not their logic. Their decisions make perfect sense given what they believe. The problem is that they're living in an alternative world.

LEARNING TO THINK CRITICALLY

This book aims to help students, as citizens, learn to think critically about politics. Critical thinking is not the mere act of having an opinion. Critical thinking is defined instead by the process through which conclusions are reached. **Critical thinking** involves determining what can reasonably be believed and then using the information to reach a thoughtful conclusion. It enables citizens to act responsibly, whether in casting a vote, forming an opinion on a political issue, or contributing to a political cause. It involves the careful evaluation of information in the process of forming a judgment about the issue at hand. Opinions not reached in this way are likely to be incomplete at best, perhaps even wildly off base.[16]

Critical thinking requires a willingness to listen to alternative points of view and a desire to know the facts. Critical thinking takes effort. Citizens who make that effort will often reach different conclusions about what policies or leaders are best for the country. Critical thinking involves judging information in the context of one's values and interests, which differ from one citizen to the next and can lead reasonable people to make different choices. But sound judgment is blunted when the citizen is mired in misinformation or hears only what one side has to say. The true test of an opinion is not whether it seems solid but whether it holds up when judged against other views. "He who knows only his one side of the case knows little of that," philosopher John Stuart Mill wrote. "His reasons may be good, and no one may have been able to refute them. But if he is equally unable to refute the reasons of the opposite side, if he does not so much as know what they are, he has no ground for preferring either opinion."[17]

Democracy liberates the individual. Authoritarian governments suppress individuality, forcing people to think and act in prescribed ways or risk punishment. Democracy frees the mind, but the individual citizen determines how that freedom will be used. Citizens can develop the habit of critical thinking, or they can invent cockeyed visions of reality. There is nothing to stop them from thinking the world is flat rather than round, but in such cases they can only blame themselves for how their choices turn out. They will make choices—forming an opinion on this issue or that one, voting for this candidate or that one—but the result will not be what they expect. Consider that many Americans supported the 2003 invasion of Iraq because they thought the war would end in weeks, given that the Iraqi army was no match for the U.S. military. A decade later the war was still going on as a result of the ethnic and religious strife that was unleashed by the U.S. invasion. If a decade-long war might have been difficult to predict, the thought that the war would end in weeks was wishful thinking, not critical thinking.

Obstacles to Critical Thinking

The obstacles to critical thinking have increased in recent decades. Our media system has changed markedly, as first cable and then the Internet expanded our sources of information. Many of the newer sources are not to be trusted. Some talk-show hosts, bloggers, and website creators care little about the accuracy of the claims they make. They routinely slant or invent information to suit their purpose while hiding contradictory information. During the 2016 presidential campaign, for example, a fake story headlined "Pope Francis Shocks World, Endorses Donald Trump for President, Releases Statement" was widely circulated on the Internet. A poll found that three-fourths of Donald Trump's supporters and half of Hillary Clinton's supporters who had seen the story believed it,[18] although a moment's reflection should have told them otherwise.[19] Popes do not endorse political candidates, whether they're running for office in the United States or elsewhere.

Political leaders have also contributed to the rise in misinformation. Deception has always been part of our politics. During the Vietnam conflict, the

Johnson and Nixon administrations told Americans that the conflict was going well when in fact it was going poorly. Nevertheless, the public at an earlier time was less tolerant of deceptive claims, and leaders were less inclined to make them. In recent years, as our politics has become more heated and divisive, we've become more tolerant of leaders who slant the facts, and they've become more willing to do it.[20] For instance, during the 2016 presidential campaign, Donald Trump and Bernie Sanders claimed that free trade agreements were the major killer of factory jobs. Foreign trade has indeed cost America factory jobs, but it's not anywhere near the biggest job killer. It accounts for only one in eight lost factory jobs. Automation is the real killer. Since the 1950s, manufacturing has shed two-thirds of its jobs, but its productive output has increased sixfold because of automation.[21] And that problem will only worsen as advances in artificial intelligence enable machines to take over more and more jobs.

We're also behind the rise in misinformation. **Confirmation bias** refers to our tendency to interpret information in ways that reinforce what we already believe.[22] Given the same information, Republicans and Democrats will often construe it in ways that fit their partisan bias, which can lead them to false conclusions. For example, as the rumor spread that Democrat Hillary Clinton was part of a child sex-ring run out of a pizza shop (see the beginning of this chapter), Republicans were far more likely than Democrats to think it was true.[23] After 9/11, when it was rumored that Republican president George W. Bush

Critical thinking is what enables citizens to act responsibly and effectively when forming opinions and choosing candidates. The challenges to critical thinking have increased in recent years with the rise of misinformation. Many of the political messages that today's citizens see and hear are factually wrong. (©master_art/Shutterstock)

personally knew in advance of the terrorist attack and let it happen to further his geopolitical ambitions, Democrats were far more likely than Republicans to believe the false claim.[24]

Many citizens choose to immerse themselves in "echo chambers," where what they hear is what they want to hear. Conservative talk-show programs, for example, have an audience made up largely of conservatives, while liberal programs have a heavily liberal audience. On many of these programs, listeners are fed a distorted version of truth. "A sociopathic alternative reality" is one observer's description.[25] People who wouldn't consider asking their plumber to diagnose a persistent cough accept without thinking what a favorite talk-show host tells them about the intricacies of foreign policy. People who spend hours listening to partisan talk shows have the distinction of being among America's most misinformed citizens.[26]

What Political Science Can Contribute to Critical Thinking

This text will not try to tell you *what* to think politically. There is no correct way of thinking when it comes to the "what" of politics. People differ in their political values and interests and, thus, also differ in their political opinions.

Instead, this text will help you learn *how* to think critically by providing you with analytical tools that can sharpen your understanding of American politics. The tools are derived from **political science**—the systematic study of government and politics. Political science has developed largely through the work of scholars, but political practitioners and writers have also contributed. One of America's foremost political scientists was the chief architect of the U.S. Constitution and later a president. Even today, James Madison's essays on constitutional design (two of which can be found in this book's appendixes) are masterpieces of political science.

As a discipline, political science is descriptive and analytical—that is, it attempts to depict and explain politics. This effort takes place through various frameworks, including rational choice theory, institutional analysis, historical reasoning, behavioral studies, legal reasoning, and cultural analysis. Political science offers a set of analytical tools that can increase one's ability to think critically:

- Reliable information about how the U.S. political system operates
- Systematic generalizations about major tendencies in American politics
- Terms and concepts that precisely describe key aspects of politics

These tools will broaden your understanding of American politics and help you think critically about it.

Like any skill, critical thinking needs to be developed through practice. For this reason, each of the text's chapters includes boxes that ask you to think critically. Some boxes deal with perennial questions, such as about the president's war powers and the proper relation between the nation and the states. Other boxes ask you to think critically by comparing how politics in the United States and in your state differs from that of other nations and states. Still other boxes present cases of actual events and ask you to think critically by analyzing these developments. Other boxes provide information and ask you to assess whether the claim is fake or fact. Finally, some boxes deal with current controversies, including the rising level of party polarization in America.

POLITICAL CULTURE: AMERICANS' ENDURING BELIEFS

An understanding of U.S. politics properly begins with an assessment of the nation's political culture. Every country has its **political culture**—the widely shared and deep-seated beliefs of its people about politics.[27] These beliefs derive from the country's traditions and help define the relationship of citizens to their government and to each other.

Although every country has a distinctive political culture, the United States, as the British writer James Bryce observed, is a special case.[28] Americans' beliefs are the foundation of their national identity. Other people take their identity from the common ancestry that led them gradually to gather under one flag. Thus, long before there was a France, Germany, or Japan, there were French, German, and Japanese people, each a kinship group united through ancestry. Not so for Americans. They are a multitude of people from different lands—England, Germany, Ireland, Africa, Italy, Poland, Mexico, and China, to name just a few (see "How the U.S. Differs"). Americans are linked not by a shared ancestry but by allegiance to a common set of ideals. The French writer Alexis de Tocqueville was among the first to recognize how thoroughly certain beliefs were embedded in the American mind. "Habits of the heart" was how he described them.

America's core ideals are rooted in the European heritage of the first white settlers. They arrived during the Enlightenment period, when people were awakening to the idea of individual potential, which could be pursued with less difficulty in the more equal society of the New World than in the more stratified society—of nobles and commoners—of the Old World. Ultimately, the colonists overturned the European way of governing. The American Revolution was the first successful large-scale rebellion in human history driven largely by

HOW THE U.S. DIFFERS

CRITICAL THINKING THROUGH COMPARISONS

A Nation of Immigrants

The United States has been called a "nation of immigrants." Americans can trace their ancestral roots to nearly every country on earth. Even today, one in every seven Americans is an immigrant. If the children of immigrants are included, the figure is one in every four Americans.

Migrants make up a larger percentage of the population in the United States than they do in nearly every other country. Here are selected comparisons, based on the percentage of the population of high school age who are immigrants or the children of immigrants.

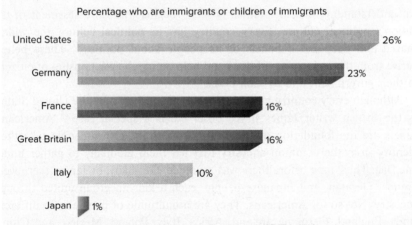

Percentage who are immigrants or children of immigrants

United States	26%
Germany	23%
France	16%
Great Britain	16%
Italy	10%
Japan	1%

Source: Organization for Economic Cooperation and Development (OECD), 2016.

Q: How might more recent U.S. immigrants differ from those who came to the United States earlier in its history?

A: The great majority of early immigrants to America came from Europe, which was due in part to restrictions on immigrants from other parts of the globe. Legislation was enacted in 1965 that eased restrictions on immigration from Latin America and Asia. Since then, most immigrants have come from those regions.

the desire to create a radically different form of society.[29] In the words of the Declaration of Independence:

> We hold these truths to be self-evident, that all men are created equal; that they are endowed by their Creator with certain unalienable rights; that among these are life, liberty, and the pursuit of happiness. That, to secure these rights, governments are instituted among men, deriving their just powers from the consent of the governed; that, whenever any form of government becomes destructive of these ends, it is the right of the people to alter or to abolish it, and to institute a new government, laying its foundation on such principles, and organizing its powers in such form, as to them shall seem most likely to effect their safety and happiness.

A decade later, in the drafting of the Constitution of the United States, some of these ideas were put into writing: Leaders would be required to govern within a set of rules designed to protect people's rights and interests.

Core Values: Liberty, Individualism, Equality, and Self-Government

An understanding of America's cultural ideals begins with recognition that the individual is paramount. Government is secondary. Its role is to serve the people, as opposed to a system where people are required to serve government. No clearer statement of this principle exists than the Declaration of Independence's reference to "unalienable rights"—freedoms that belong to each and every citizen and that cannot lawfully be taken away by government.

Liberty, individualism, equality, and self-government are widely regarded as America's core political ideals. **Liberty** is the principle that individuals should be free to act and think as they choose, provided they do not infringe unreasonably on the freedom and well-being of others.[30] Political liberty was nearly a birthright for early Americans. They did not have to accept the European system of absolute government when greater personal liberty was as close as the next area of unsettled land. Religious sentiments also entered into the thinking of the early Americans. Many of them had fled Europe to escape religious persecution and came to look upon religious freedom as part of a broader set of rights, including freedom of speech. Unsurprisingly, these early Americans were determined, when forming their own government, to protect their liberty. The Declaration of Independence rings with the proclamation that people are entitled to "life, liberty, and the pursuit of happiness." The preamble to the Constitution declares that the U.S. government was founded to secure "the Blessings of Liberty to ourselves and our Posterity."

Early Americans also enjoyed unprecedented economic opportunities. Unlike Europe, America had no hereditary nobility that owned virtually all the land. The New World's great distance from Europe and its vast stretches of open

Americans' cultural beliefs have their roots in the nation's formative years. The challenges and opportunities of North America's vast wilderness helped foster in settlers a commitment to liberty, equality, self-reliance, and self-determination. This 19th-century portrayal of frontier life is a hand-painted Currier & Ives lithograph created by Frances Flora Bond Palmer. She was one of the era's leading lithographic artists. (*Source:* Yale University Art Gallery)

territory gave ordinary people the chance to own property, provided they were willing to work hard enough to make it a success. Out of this experience grew a sense of self-reliance and a culture of "rugged individualism." **Individualism** is a commitment to personal initiative and self-sufficiency. Observers from Tocqueville onward have seen fit to note that liberty in America, as in no other country, is tied to a desire for economic independence. Americans' chief aim, wrote Tocqueville, "is to remain their own masters."[31]

A third American political ideal is **equality**—the notion that all individuals are equal in their moral worth and thereby entitled to equal treatment under the law. Europe's rigid system of aristocratic privilege was unenforceable in frontier America. It was this natural sense of personal equality that Thomas Jefferson expressed so forcefully in the Declaration of Independence: "We hold these truths to be self-evident, that all men are created equal." However, equality has always been America's most elusive ideal. Even Jefferson professed not to know its exact meaning. A slave owner, Jefferson distinguished between free citizens, who were entitled to equal rights, and slaves, who were not. After slavery was abolished, Americans continued to argue over the meaning of equality, and the debate continues today. Does equality require that wealth and opportunity be widely shared? Or does it merely require that artificial barriers to advancement be removed? Despite differing opinions about such questions, an insistence on equality is a distinctive feature of the American experience. Americans, said Bryce, reject "the very notion" that some people might be "better" than others merely because of birth or position.[32]

America's fourth great political ideal is **self-government**—the principle that the people are the ultimate source of governing authority and should have a voice in their governing. Americans' belief in self-government formed in colonial America. The Old World was an ocean away, and European governments had no option but to give the American colonies a degree of self-determination. Out of this experience came the vision of a self-governing nation that led tens of thousands of ordinary farmers, merchants, and tradesmen to risk their lives fighting the British during the American Revolution. "Governments," the Declaration of Independence proclaims, "deriv[e] their just powers from the consent of the governed." The Constitution of the United States opens with the words "We the People." Etched in a corridor of the Capitol in Washington, D.C., are the words Alexander Hamilton spoke when asked about the foundation of the nation's government: "Here, sir, the people govern."

The Limits and Power of Americans' Ideals

America's cultural beliefs are idealistic. They hold out the promise of a government of high purpose, in which power is widely shared and used for the common good, and where individuals are free, independent, and equal under the law.

Yet high ideals do not come with a guarantee that people will live up to them. The clearest proof in the American case is the human tragedy that began nearly four centuries ago and continues today. In 1619 the first black slaves were brought in chains to America. Slavery lasted 250 years. Slaves worked in the fields from dawn to dark (from "can see, 'til can't"), in both the heat of summer and the cold of winter. The Civil War brought an end to slavery but not to racial oppression. Slavery was followed by the Jim Crow era of legal segregation: Black people in the South were forbidden by law to use the same schools, hospitals, restaurants, and restrooms as white people. Those who spoke out against this system were subjected to beatings, firebombings, rapes, and murder—hundreds of African Americans were lynched in the early 1900s by white vigilantes. Today, African Americans have equal rights under the law, but in fact they are far from equal. Compared with white children, black children are twice as likely to live in poverty and to die in infancy.[33] There have always been two Americas, one for whites and one for blacks.

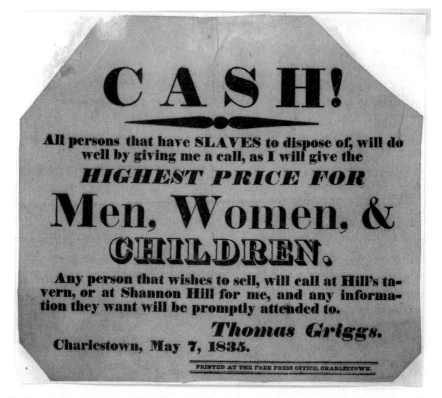

The largest stain on America's founding principles is the nation's treatment of its black citizens. For more than two centuries, they were bought and sold as slaves and, after being freed by the Civil War, were denied equal citizenship throughout the South. That legacy carries into today, as evidenced by the extraordinarily high levels of poverty and joblessness in the black community. For the nation's blacks, America's promise of equality has always been a hollow one. (*Source:* Library of Congress, Prints and Photographs Division [LC-USZ62-62799])

Despite the lofty claim that "all men are created equal," equality has never been an American birthright. In 1882, Congress suspended Chinese immigration on the assumption that the Chinese were an inferior people. Calvin Coolidge in 1923 asked Congress for a permanent ban on Chinese immigration, saying that people "who do not want to be partakers of the American spirit ought not to settle in America."[34] Not to be outdone, California enacted legislation prohibiting individuals of Japanese descent from purchasing property in the state. Not until 1965 was discrimination against the Chinese, Japanese, and other Asians eliminated from U.S. immigration laws. For more on America's conflicted relationship with immigrants (see "Fake or Fact? Do Immigrants Commit More Crimes?").

America's callous treatment of some groups is not among the stories that the American people like to tell about themselves. A University of Virginia

Detecting Misinformation

Do Immigrants Commit More Crimes?

America is portrayed as a nation that opens its arms to immigrants. At the base of the Statue of Liberty are the words of Emma Lazarus's oft-cited poem, "Give me your tired, your poor, your huddled masses yearning to breathe free."

©Everett Historical/Shutterstock

Yet, many Americans have opposed the entry of immigrants, particularly those with different backgrounds. In the mid-1800s, Catholic immigrants from Ireland and Germany were widely reviled by Protestants already here. In the late 1800s and early 1900s, hostility was directed at new arrivals from southern and eastern Europe—Italians, Greeks, Poles, Hungarians, Jews, Russians, and others. Congress in 1924 passed a law that largely blocked further immigration from southern and eastern Europe. Congress had earlier closed the nation's shores to immigrants from Asia.

An argument that was heard in those earlier periods, and is heard again today, is that immigrants are undesirable because they pose a threat to public safety. A Pew Research Center poll found that Americans by a ratio of seven to one believe that immigrants are more likely than native-born Americans to commit crimes.[35]

Is that claim fact, or is it fake?

Government in past times did not compile systematic statistics on crime, so there's no way to show conclusively whether earlier immigrants had unusually high crime rates. But we do know whether the claim is true today. There has been substantial research on the issue, including recent studies by the National Academy of Sciences and the conservative Cato Institute. The studies have found that immigrants are more law abiding than are native-born Americans. The 2017 Cato Institute study, for example, found that immigrants are 69 percent less likely to be incarcerated than are the native born. That's true also of illegal immigrants, who are 44 percent less likely than the native born to have been convicted of crime and imprisoned.[36]

survey found that American adults are far more likely to want children to be taught about the nation's achievements than its shortcomings. For example, more than four out of five of those surveyed said children should be taught that "with hard work and perseverance anyone can succeed in America," while less than three in five said the same about teaching children of the nation's "cruel mistreatment of blacks and American Indians." Selective memory can be found among all peoples, but the tendency to recast history is perhaps exaggerated in the American case because Americans' beliefs are so idealistic. How could a nation that claims to uphold the principle of equality have barred the Chinese, enslaved blacks, declared wives to be the "property" of their husbands,[37] and killed Indians in order to steal their lands?

Although America's ideals obviously do not determine exactly what people will do, they are far from empty promises. If racial, gender, ethnic, and other forms of intolerance constitute the nation's sorriest chapter, the centuries-old struggle of Americans to build a more equal society is among its finest. Few nations have battled so relentlessly against the insidious discrimination that stems from superficial human differences such as the color of one's skin. The abolition and suffrage movements of the 1800s and the more recent civil rights movements of black Americans, women, Hispanics, and the LGBTQ community testify to Americans' persistent effort to build a more equal society. In 1848, at the first-ever national convention on women's rights, the delegates issued the Declaration of Sentiments, which read in part: "We hold these truths to be self-evident: that all men and women are created equal." A century later, speaking at the Lincoln Memorial at the peak of the black civil rights movement, Martin Luther King Jr. said: "'We hold these truths to be self-evident, that all men are created equal.'"[38]

Americans' determination to build a more equal society can also be seen in its public education system. In the early 1800s, the United States pioneered the idea of a free public education for children—this at a time when education in Europe was reserved for children of the wealthy. Even today, the United States spends more heavily on public education than do European countries. Compared with Great Britain or France, for example, the United States spends about 30 percent more per pupil annually on its primary and secondary schools. The United States also has the world's most elaborate system of higher education, which includes roughly 4,000 two-year and four-year institutions. Although some of America's youth do not have a realistic chance of attending college, the nation's college system is a relatively open one. Nearly a third of Americans over the age of 25 have a college degree, which ranks second only to Canada worldwide. Even the American states with the lowest proportion of college graduates have a higher percentage of residents with a bachelor's degree than does the typical European country (see "How the 50 States Differ").

HOW THE 50 STATES DIFFER

CRITICAL THINKING THROUGH COMPARISONS

A College Education

Reflecting their belief in individualism and equality, Americans have developed the world's largest college system—comprising roughly 4,000 institutions. According to U.S. Census Bureau figures, nearly one in three Americans over the age of 25 is a college graduate. Even the lowest-ranking state—West Virginia with one in six—has a higher percentage of college graduates than do most European countries.

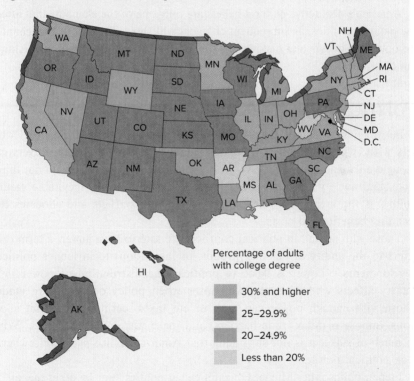

Percentage of adults with college degree

- 30% and higher
- 25–29.9%
- 20–24.9%
- Less than 20%

Q: Why do the northeastern and western coastal states have a higher percentage of adults with college degrees?

A: The northeastern and western coastal states are wealthier and more urbanized than most states. Accordingly, young people in these states can better afford the costs of college and are more likely to pursue careers that require a college degree.

The principle of self-government has also shaped American society. No country holds as many elections as does the United States, or has anywhere near as many publicly elected officials. There are roughly a half million American elected officials, everyone from the president of the United States to the local council member. The United States is also nearly the only country to use primary elections as the means of choosing party nominees.

The principles of liberty and individualism have also shaped American society. Few people have pursued their individual rights—ranging from freedom of expression to fair-trial protections—as relentlessly as have Americans. And there are few countries where individualism is as deeply ingrained as in the United States (see "Case Study: Social Welfare Policy"). Political analysts William Watts and Lloyd Free described the United States as "the country of individualism *par excellence.*"[39]

America's distinctive cultural beliefs are only one of the elements that affect the nation's politics, as subsequent chapters will show. The rest of this chapter introduces concepts and distinctions that are basic to an informed understanding of politics.

POLITICS AND POWER IN AMERICA

Political scientist Harold Lasswell described politics as a conflict over "who gets what, when, and how."[40] Politics would be a simple matter if everyone thought alike and could have everything they pleased. But people do not think alike, and society's resources are limited. Conflict is the inevitable result. **Politics** is the means by which society settles its conflicts and allocates the resulting benefits and costs.

Those who prevail in political conflicts are said to have **power,** a term that refers to the ability of persons, groups, or institutions to influence political developments.[41] Power is basic to politics. The distribution of power in a society affects who wins and who loses when policy decisions are made. Those with enough power can raise or cut taxes, permit or prohibit abortions, impose or relax trade barriers, and make war or declare peace. With so much at stake, it is not surprising that Americans, like people elsewhere, seek political power.

French philosopher Michel Foucault called politics "war by other means,"[42] a phrase that literally describes politics in some countries. An **authoritarian government** is one that openly represses its political opponents, mostly through intimidation and prohibitions on free expression but sometimes by brutalizing opposition leaders. Such regimes are backed by the country's police and armed forces, forego free and fair elections, and exert tight control over the media. The authoritarian regime in China, for example, blocks Facebook, Twitter,

C A S E
S T U D Y

Politics in Action

Social Welfare Policy

Americans' cultural beliefs distinguish them from people of other nations. An example is Americans' commitment to individualism. Although individualism is also part of European culture, it takes exaggerated form in the United States, as can be seen from a Pew Research Center survey. Respondents in four European countries and the United States were asked whether they thought "freedom to pursue life's goals" or making sure that "nobody is in need" was the more important value. Americans were easily the most likely to say that "freedom to pursue life's goals" was the more important.

Percentage who said "freedom to pursue life's goals"

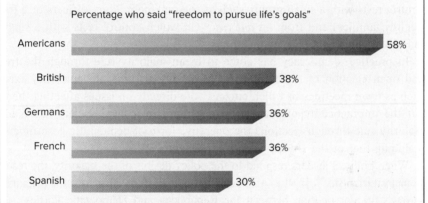

Americans	58%
British	38%
Germans	36%
French	36%
Spanish	30%

Source: Pew Research Center Global Attitudes & Trends survey, 2011.

The effect of these differences can be seen in welfare policy. The United States—though having a higher poverty rate than European countries—spends much less on programs for the poor. Americans are not necessarily less sympathetic with the poor. Compared with Europeans, they are twice as likely to donate to charities. But Americans are less inclined than Europeans to support welfare policies that could relieve people of the responsibility to care of themselves.

Q: Can you think of another major policy area where the United States and Europe differ as a result of the emphasis that their citizens place on individual achievement?

ASK YOURSELF: What activity gives you a monetary benefit? Which government policy affects how much of this benefit you get to keep and how much of it goes to the government?

YouTube, and other outlets—including those within the country—that convey messages contrary to what the Chinese government wants its people to hear.[43]

The United States operates by a different standard. It has "rules" designed to keep government in check. These rules—democracy, constitutionalism, and a free market—determine which side will prevail when conflict occurs, as well as what is off limits to the winning side (see Table 1-1).

A Democratic System

The word *democracy* comes from the Greek words *demos,* meaning "the people," and *kratis,* meaning "to rule." In simple terms, **democracy** is a form of government in which the people govern, either directly or through elected representatives. A democracy is thus different from an *oligarchy* (in which control rests with a small group, such as top-ranking military officers or a few wealthy families) and from an *autocracy* (in which control rests with a single individual, such as a king or dictator).

In practice, democracy has come to mean majority rule through the free and open election of representatives. More direct forms of democracy exist, such as town meetings in which citizens vote directly on issues affecting them, but the impracticality of such an arrangement in a large society has made majority rule through elections the operative form of democratic government, including that of the United States (see Chapter 2).

When political leaders respond to the policy desires of the majority, the result is **majoritarianism**.[44] In the American case, majoritarianism occurs primarily through the competition between the Republican and Democratic Parties (see "Party Polarization: Conflict between the Political Parties Has Intensified in Recent Years"). In the 2016 presidential campaign, for instance, Republican

table 1-1 GOVERNING SYSTEMS AND POLITICAL POWER	
System	**Description and Implications**
Democratic	A system of majority rule through elections; empowers majorities (majoritarianism), groups (pluralism), and officials (authority)
Constitutional	A system based on rule of law, including legal protections for individuals; empowers individuals by enabling them to claim their rights in court (legal action)
Free market	An economic system that centers on the transactions between private parties; empowers business firms (corporate power) and the wealthy (elitism)

nominee Donald Trump and Democratic nominee Hillary Clinton differed sharply in their positions on immigration, health care, the environment, and other major policy issues, giving voters a choice over the direction of national policy.

However, majoritarianism has its limits. The public as a whole takes an interest in only a few of the hundreds of policy decisions that officials make each year (see Chapter 6). Even if they wanted to, party leaders would have difficulty getting the majority to pay attention to most issues. Accordingly,

---

P A R T Y POLARIZATION

Conflicting Ideas

Conflict between the Political Parties Has Intensified in Recent Years

Conflict between America's two major parties—the Republicans and the Democrats—has intensified in the past few decades. Partisan divisions have surfaced on nearly every major issue, and the fights have been bitter and prolonged, so much so that the term **party (partisan) polarization** is used to characterize today's party politics. Subsequent chapters will examine various aspects of this polarization, but two things should be noted at the outset: The situation is much different than it was a few decades ago but is not very different from what it was during much of the nation's history.

A high level of bipartisanship—cooperation between the parties—marked the period from the end of World War II in 1945 until the late 1960s. Leaders and voters of both parties agreed on the need to contain Soviet communism. In addition, Republican leaders had largely abandoned their effort to turn back the New Deal policies of Democratic president Franklin Roosevelt, which had given the federal government a larger role in economic security (for example, the Social Security program) and economic regulation (for example, oversight of the stock market).

During much of their previous history, however, Americans disagreed strongly over policy and, in the case of the Civil War, took their fight to the battlefield. In fact, periods of bipartisanship are the exception rather than the rule. President George Washington's first years in office, the so-called Era of Good Feeling in the early 1800s, and the World War I and World War II periods are among the few times Americans have put partisan differences largely aside.

Q: Do you see any contradiction in the fact that Americans share a common set of ideals and yet often find themselves on opposite sides when it comes to party politics?

most policies are formulated in response to the groups with a direct interest in the issue. Farmers, for example, have more influence over agricultural sub-sidies than do other groups, even though these subsidies have far-reaching effects, including the price that shoppers pay for food. Some political scien-tists, like Yale's Robert Dahl, argue that democracies more often operate as pluralistic (multi-interest) systems than as majoritarian systems.[45] **Pluralism** holds that, on most issues, the preference of the special interest largely deter-mines what government does (see Chapter 9).

A democratic system also bestows another form of power. Although officials are empowered by the majority, they also exercise power in their own right as a result of the positions they hold. When President Trump decided in 2017 to withdraw the United States from the Paris Agreement on climate change, he did so despite polls that showed two-thirds of Americans wanted the United States to honor its commitment.[46] In making the decision, Trump was exercis-ing his constitutional authority as chief executive. Such grants are a special kind of power. **Authority** is the recognized right of officials to exercise power. Members of Congress, judges, and bureaucrats, as well as the president, rou-tinely make authoritative decisions, only some of which are a response to power asserted by the majority or special interests.

Authority is a term for the recognized right of officials to exercise power. The President of the United States, for example, exercises authority through the powers granted the office by the Constitution. That authority includes, for example, the power to implement the laws, to veto acts of Congress, and to appoint high-ranking executive officials. (*Source:* Official White House Photo by Shealah Craighead)

A Constitutional System

In a democracy, the votes of the majority prevail over those of the minority. If this principle were unlimited, the majority could treat the minority in any manner of its choosing, including depriving it of its liberty and property. As fanciful as this possibility might seem, it preoccupied the writers of the U.S. Constitution. The history of democracies was filled with examples of majority tyranny, and the nation's early experience was no exception. In 1786, debtors had gained control of Rhode Island's legislature and made paper money a legal means of paying debts, even though contracts called for payment in gold. Creditors were then hunted down and held captive in public places so that debtors could come and pay them in full with worthless paper money. A Boston newspaper wrote that Rhode Island ought to be renamed Rogue Island.

To guard against oppressive majorities, the writers of the Constitution devised an elaborate system of checks and balances, dividing authority among the legislative, executive, and judicial branches so that each branch could check the power of the others (see Chapter 2). The Bill of Rights was added to the Constitution a few years later as a further check on the majority. For example, Congress was prohibited from enacting laws that abridge freedom of speech, press, or religion. These limits reflect the principle of **constitutionalism**—the idea that there are lawful restrictions on government's power. Officials are obliged to act within the limits of the law, which include the protection of individual rights.

The Bill of Rights in combination with an independent judiciary and a firm attachment to private property have made **legal action**—the use of the courts as a means of asserting rights and interests—a channel through which ordinary citizens exercise power. Americans have an expansive view of their rights and turn more readily to the courts to make their claims than do people elsewhere (see Chapters 4 and 5).[47] A handwritten note by a penniless convict, for example, triggered the U.S. Supreme Court's landmark *Gideon v. Wainwright* ruling.[48] Clarence Gideon had been made to stand trial in Florida without the aid of a lawyer for breaking into a pool hall. When he appealed his conviction, the Supreme Court concluded that his constitutional right to counsel had been violated. The ruling established a new policy: If the accused is too poor to hire a lawyer, the government must provide one.

A Free-Market System

Politics is not confined to the halls of government. Many of society's costs and benefits are allocated through the private sector, although economic systems differ in the degree of government intervention. Under *communism,* which characterized the former Soviet Union and is practiced most fully today in North Korea, the government owns most or all major industries and also takes responsibility for overall management of the economy, including production quotas, supply points, and pricing. Under *socialism,* as it is practiced today in Sweden and other countries, government does not attempt to manage the overall economy, but owns a number of major industries and guarantees every individual a minimal standard of living. In contrast, a **free-market system** operates mainly on private transactions. Firms are largely free to make their own production, distribution, and pricing decisions, and individuals depend largely on themselves for economic security.

The U.S. economy is chiefly a free-market system. It has millions of small businesses as well as a corporate sector that includes large firms like Google, Ford, and Bank of America. **Corporate power**–the influence of business firms on public policy–has been a defining feature of American politics since the late 1800s. Corporate power can be seen today in the fact that roughly two-thirds of all lobbyists in the nation's capital represent business firms, which also contribute heavily to political candidates. Corporate power can also be seen in the workplace, where U.S. firms have greater control over wages and working conditions than do firms in other Western democracies. The annual

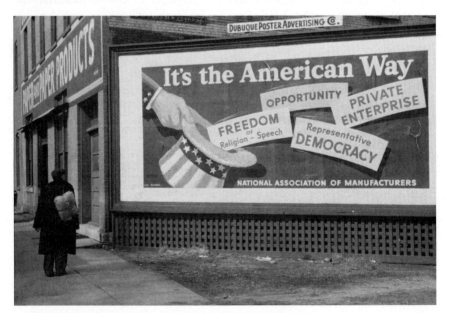

As C. Wright Mills and other theorists have noted, corporate elites must be taken into account in assessing how power in America is distributed and used. The influence of the nation's major corporations goes beyond the workplace. Through advertising and public relations efforts, they seek to build public support for the private enterprise system. (*Source:* Library of Congress, Prints and Photographs Division [LC-USF33-T01-001695-M4])

income of a minimum-wage worker, for instance, is roughly $15,000 in the United States, compared with roughly $18,000 in France and $22,000 in Great Britain.[49]

Wealth is also the foundation of **elitism,** which refers to the power exercised by well-positioned and highly influential individuals.[50] Sociologist C. Wright Mills concluded that corporate elites, operating behind the scenes, have greater control over economic policy than do elected officials.[51] Some scholars contend that Mills overstated the power of elites, while overlooking the fact that some elites are motivated to serve society's interests as well as their own.[52] Few scholars, however, dispute the claim that corporate elites have more political power in America than they do in most Western democracies.

Who Governs?

This text's perspective is that a full explanation of American politics requires an accounting of all these forms of power—as exercised by the majority, interest groups, elites, corporations, individuals through legal action, and those in positions of governing authority. In fact, a defining characteristic of American politics is the widespread sharing of power. Few nations have as many competing interests and institutions as does the United States.

THE TEXT'S ORGANIZATION

American politics operates within a constitutional system that defines how power is to be obtained and exercised. This system is the focus of the next few chapters, which examine how, in theory and practice, the Constitution defines the institutions of governments and the rights of individuals. The discussion then shifts to the political role of citizens and of the intermediaries that enable citizens to act together and connect them to government. These subjects are explored in chapters on public opinion, political participation, political parties, interest groups, and the news media. The functioning of governing officials is then addressed in chapters on the nation's elective institutions—the Congress and the presidency—and its appointive institutions—the federal bureaucracy and the federal courts. These chapters describe how these institutions are structured but aim chiefly to explain how their actions are affected by internal and external factors, as well as by the constitutional system in which they operate.

Throughout the text, but particularly in the concluding chapters, attention is given to **public policies,** which are the decisions of government to pursue particular courses of action. No aspect of a nation's politics is more revealing of how it is governed than are its policies—everything from how it chooses to educate its children to how it chooses to use its military power.

Underlying the text's discussion of American politics and policy is the recognition of how difficult it is to govern effectively and how important it is to try. It cannot be said too often that the issue of governing is the most difficult issue facing a democratic society. It also cannot be said too often that governing is a quest rather than a resolved issue. Political scientist E. E. Schattschneider said it clearly: "In the course of centuries, there has come a great deal of agreement about what democracy is, but nobody has a monopoly on it and the last word has not been spoken."[53]

SUMMARY

Critical thinking is the careful gathering and sifting of information in the process of forming knowledgeable views of political developments. Critical thinking is a key to responsible citizenship, but many citizens avoid it by virtue of paying scant attention to politics. The tools of political science can contribute to the critical thinking process.

The United States is a nation that was formed on a set of ideals. Liberty, individualism, equality, and self-government are foremost among these ideals. These ideals became Americans' common bond and today are the basis of their political culture. Although imperfect in practice, these ideals have guided what generations of Americans have tried to achieve politically.

Politics is the process by which it is determined whose values will prevail in society. The basis of politics is conflict over scarce resources and competing values. Those who have power win out in this conflict and are able to control governing authority and policy choices. In the United States, no one faction controls all power and policy. Majorities govern on some issues, while other issues are dominated by groups, elites, corporations, individuals through legal action, or officials who hold public office.

Politics in the United States plays out through rules of the game that include democracy, constitutionalism, and free markets. Democracy is rule by the people, which in practice refers to a representative system of government in which the people rule through their elected officials. Constitutionalism refers to rules that limit the rightful power of government over citizens. A free-market system assigns private parties the dominant role in determining how economic costs and benefits are allocated.

©gangliu10/Getty Images

CRITICAL THINKING ZONE

KEY TERMS

authoritarian government (*p. 16*)

authority (*p. 20*)

confirmation bias (*p. 5*)

constitutionalism (*p. 21*)

corporate power (*p. 22*)

critical thinking (*p. 3*)

democracy (*p. 18*)

elitism (*p. 23*)

equality (*p. 10*)

free-market system (*p. 22*)

individualism (*p. 10*)

legal action (*p. 21*)

liberty (*p. 9*)

majoritarianism (*p. 18*)

party (partisan) polarization (*p. 19*)

pluralism (*p. 20*)

political culture (*p. 7*)

political science (*p. 6*)

politics (*p. 16*)

power (*p. 16*)

public policies (*p. 23*)

self-government (*p. 11*)

APPLYING THE ELEMENTS OF CRITICAL THINKING

Conceptualizing: Distinguish between political power (generally) and authority (as a special kind of political power).

Synthesizing: Contrast the American political culture with that of most Western democracies. What in the American experience has led its people to derive their national identity from a set of shared political ideals?

Analyzing: Explain the types of power that result from each of America's major systems of governing—democracy, constitutionalism, and a free market.

EXTRA CREDIT

A Book Worth Reading: Gordon S. Wood, *The Idea of America: Reflections on the Birth of the United States* (New York: Penguin Press, 2011). A perceptive book by a Pulitzer Prize-winning historian, it explores the ideals, such as liberty and equality, that were the driving force behind the American Revolution.

PARTICIPATE!

Critical thinking is a key to responsible citizenship. As a prelude to preparing yourself to think critically, reflect on your current habits. From what sources do you get most of your political information? Are they reliable sources (that is, do they place a premium on accuracy)? How frequently do you encounter opposing arguments or opinions? How carefully do you listen to them? When forming political opinions, do you tend to reflect on your choices or do you tend to make snap judgments?

CHAPTER 2

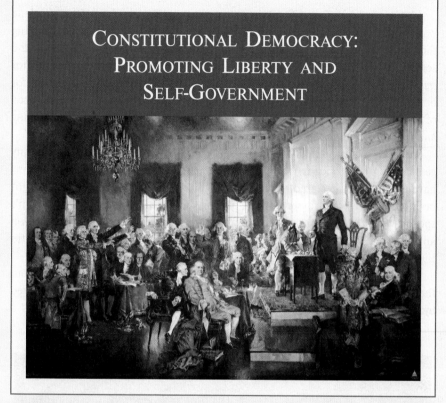

CONSTITUTIONAL DEMOCRACY: PROMOTING LIBERTY AND SELF-GOVERNMENT

Source: Architect of the Capitol

> ❝Why has government been instituted at all? Because the passions of man will not conform to the dictates of reason and justice, without constraint.❞
>
> ALEXANDER HAMILTON[1]

On October 16, 2017, the late John McCain stepped to the podium to accept the National Constitution Center's Liberty Medal for his lifetime of service to the nation. A six-term U.S. senator and the 2008 Republican presidential nominee, McCain thanked those in attendance for the award and then spoke of America's ideals. "We are," said McCain, "the land of the free, the land where anything is possible, the land of the immigrant's dream." He said that those among us who would "abandon our ideals" and pit us against each other are "unpatriotic." "We live in in a land made of ideals," said McCain. "We are the custodians of those ideals at home, and their champion abroad."

McCain, who endured five years as a prisoner of war when his navy plane was shot down during the Vietnam War, concluded his speech by recognizing the sacrifices of other Americans. Said McCain: "I've been inspired by the service of better patriots than me. I've seen Americans make sacrifices for our country and her causes and for people who were strangers to them but for our common humanity, sacrifices that were much harder than the service asked of me. And I've seen the good they have done, the lives they freed from tyranny and injustice, the hope they encouraged, the dreams they made achievable."

The ideas that guided McCain's speech would have been familiar to any generation of Americans. The same ideas have been invoked when Americans have gone to war, declared peace, celebrated national holidays, launched major policy initiatives, and asserted new rights.[2] The ideas expressed in McCain's speech were the same ones that shaped the speeches of George Washington and Abraham Lincoln, Susan B. Anthony, Franklin D. Roosevelt, Martin Luther King Jr., and Ronald Reagan.

The ideas were there at the nation's beginning, when Thomas Jefferson put them into words in the Declaration of Independence. They had been nurtured by the colonial experience in the New World, which offered the settlers a

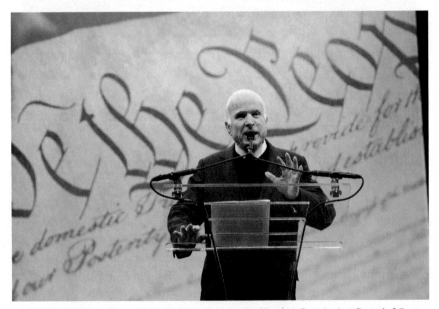

Shown here is the late Senator John McCain accepting the National Constitution Center's Liberty Medal. It's given annually to an individual who has furthered the ideals of freedom, democracy, and equality, often at great personal cost. Past recipients include presidents Jimmy Carter and George H. W. Bush, Supreme Court justices Thurgood Marshall and Sandra Day O'Connor, the Dalai Lama, and South Africa's Nelson Mandela. (©William Thomas Cain/Getty Images)

degree of liberty, equality, and self-government unimaginable in Europe. When the Revolutionary War settled the issue of American independence in the colonists' favor, they faced the question of how to turn their ideals into a system of government. The Constitution of the United States became the instrument of that goal. The framers of the Constitution sought to create a **limited government**—one that is subject to strict legal limits on the uses of power, so that it would not threaten the people's liberty. They also sought to establish a system of **representative government**—one in which the people would govern through the selection of their representatives.

The challenge facing the framers was that, although limited government and representative government can reinforce each other, they can also conflict. Representative government requires that the majority through its elected representatives has the power to rule. However, limited government requires that the majority's power stop at the point where it infringes on the lawful rights and interests of the minority. This consideration led the framers to forge a constitution that provides for majority rule but has built-in restrictions on the power of the majority and its elected representatives.

This chapter describes how the principles of representative government and limited government are embodied in the Constitution and explains the tension between them. It also indicates how these principles have been modified in practice in the course of American history. This chapter presents the following main points:

- *America during the colonial period developed traditions of limited government and representative government.* These traditions were rooted in governing practices, political theory, and cultural values.

- *The Constitution provides for limited government mainly by defining lawful powers and by dividing those powers among competing institutions.* The Constitution, with its Bill of Rights, also prohibits government from infringing on individual rights. Judicial review is an additional safeguard.

- *The Constitution in its original form provided for representative government mainly through indirect methods of electing representatives.* The framers' theory of representative government was based on the notion that political power must be separated from immediate popular influences if sound policies are to result.

- *The idea of popular government—in which the majority's desires have a more direct and immediate impact on governing officials—has gained strength since the nation's beginning.* Originally, the House of Representatives was the only institution subject to direct vote of the people. This mechanism has been extended to other institutions and, through primary elections, even to the nomination of candidates for public office.

BEFORE THE CONSTITUTION: THE COLONIAL AND REVOLUTIONARY EXPERIENCES

Early Americans' admiration for limited government stemmed from their British heritage. Unlike other European governments of the time, Britain did not have an absolute monarchy. Parliament was an independent body with law-making power and local representation. Many of the colonial charters conferred upon Americans "the rights of Englishmen," which included, for example, the right to trial by jury. The colonies also had experience in self-government. Each colony had an elected representative assembly.

The American Revolution was partly a rebellion against Britain's failure to uphold the colonies' established traditions. After the French and Indian War (1754-1763), during which colonists fought alongside British soldiers to drive the French out of the western territories, the British government for the first time imposed heavy taxes on the colonies. The war with France, which was also waged in Europe, had created a budget crisis in Britain. Taxing the colonies was a way to reduce the debt, so Parliament levied a stamp tax on colonial newspapers and business documents. The colonists were not represented in Parliament, and they objected. "No taxation without representation" was their rallying cry.

Although Parliament backed down and repealed the Stamp Act, it then passed the Townshend Act, which imposed taxes on all glass, paper, tea, and lead sold in the colonies. The colonists again objected, and Parliament again backed down, except for the tax on tea, which Britain retained to show that it was still in charge of colonial affairs. The tea tax sparked an act of defiance that became known as the Boston Tea Party. In December 1773, under the cover of darkness, a small band of patriots disguised as Native Americans boarded an English ship in Boston Harbor and dumped its cargo of tea overboard. When the British demanded that the city pay for the tea, and Boston refused, the British navy blockaded its port.

In 1774, the colonists met in Philadelphia at the First Continental Congress to formulate their demands on Britain. They asked for their own councils for the imposition of taxes, an end to the British military occupation, and a guarantee of trial by local juries. (British authorities had resorted to shipping "troublemakers" to London for trial.) King George III rejected their demands, and British troops and Massachusetts minutemen clashed at Lexington and Concord on April 19, 1775. Eight colonists died on the Lexington green in what became known as "the shot heard 'round the world." The American Revolution had begun.

At daybreak on April 19, 1775, colonial militiamen fought for the first time against British troops. The battle on the village green in Lexington, Massachusetts, marked the start of the Revolutionary War. (*Source:* Library of Congress, Prints and Photographs Division [LC-DIG-pga-00995])

The Declaration of Independence

Although grievances against Britain were the immediate cause of the American Revolution, ideas about the proper form of government also fueled the rebellion.[3] Building on the writings of Thomas Hobbes,[4] John Locke claimed that government is founded on a **social contract.** Locke asserted that people living in a state of nature enjoy certain **inalienable (natural) rights,** including those of life, liberty, and property, which are threatened by individuals who steal, kill, and otherwise act without regard for others. To protect against such individuals, people agree among themselves to form a government (the social contract). They submit to the government's authority in return for the protection it can provide, but, in doing so, they retain their natural rights, which the government is obliged to respect. If it fails to do so, Locke contended, people can rightfully rebel against it.[5]

Thomas Jefferson declared that Locke "was one of the three greatest men that ever lived, without exception." Jefferson paraphrased Locke's ideas in passages of the Declaration of Independence, including those asserting that "all men are created equal," that they are entitled to "life, liberty, and the pursuit of happiness," that governments derive "their just powers from the consent of the governed," and that "it is the right of the people to alter or abolish" a tyrannical government. The Declaration was a call to revolution rather than a framework for a new form of government, but the ideas it contained—liberty, equality, individual rights, self-government, lawful powers—became the basis, eleven years later, for the Constitution of the United States.

(The Declaration of Independence and the Constitution are reprinted in their entirety in this book's appendixes.)

The Articles of Confederation

A **constitution** is the fundamental law that defines how a government will legitimately operate—the method for choosing its leaders, the institutions through which these leaders will work, the procedures they must follow in making policy, and the powers they can lawfully exercise. The U.S. Constitution is exactly such a law; it is the highest law of the land. Its provisions define how power is to be acquired and how it can be used.

The first government of the United States, however, was based not on the Constitution but on the Articles of Confederation. The Articles, which were adopted during the Revolutionary War, created a very weak national government that was subordinate to the states. Under the Articles, each state retained its full "sovereignty, freedom, and independence." The colonies had always been governed separately, and their people considered themselves Virginians, New Yorkers, Pennsylvanians, and so on, as much as they thought of themselves as Americans. Moreover, they were wary of a powerful central government.

John Adams, Roger Sherman, Robert Livingston, Thomas Jefferson, and Benjamin Franklin present their draft of the Declaration of Independence to the Continental Congress. Jefferson (tallest of the three men standing directly in front of the desk) was its principal author. Jefferson's bold declaration that "all men are created equal" was contradicted by the fact that he, like several of the signers, was a lifelong slaveholder. (©John Parrot/Stocktrek Images/Getty Images)

The American Revolution was sparked by grievances against the arbitrary policies of King George III, and Americans were in no mood to replace him with a strong national authority of their own making.

Under the Articles of Confederation, the national government had no judiciary and no independent executive. All authority was vested in the Congress, but it was largely a creature of the states. Each of the 13 states had one vote in Congress, and each state appointed its congressional representatives and paid their salary. Legislation could be enacted only if 9 of the 13 state delegations agreed to it. The rule for constitutional amendments was even more imposing. The Articles of Confederation could be amended only if each state agreed.

The Articles prohibited Congress from levying taxes, so it had to ask the states for money. It was slow to arrive, if it arrived at all. During one period, Congress requested $12 million from the states but received only $3 million. By 1786, the national government was so desperate for funds that it sold the navy's ships and cut the army to less than 1,000 soldiers—this at a time when Britain had an army in Canada and Spain had one in Florida. Congress was also prohibited from regulating the states' trade policies, so it was powerless to forge a national economy. Free to do as they wanted, states enacted policies designed to protect their manufacturers from competitors in nearby states. Connecticut, for example, placed a higher tariff on goods built in neighboring Massachusetts than on the same goods manufactured in England.

The American states had stayed together out of necessity during the Revolutionary War. They would have lost to the British if each state had tried to fend for itself. Once the war ended, however, the states felt free to go their separate ways. In a melancholy letter to Thomas Jefferson, George Washington wondered whether the United States deserved to be called "a nation."

A Nation Dissolving

In late 1785 at his Mount Vernon home, Washington met with leaders of Virginia and Maryland to secure an agreement between the two states on commercial use of the Potomac River. During the meeting, they decided on the desirability of a commerce policy binding on all the states, which would require an amendment to the Articles of Confederation.

A revolt in western Massachusetts added urgency to the situation. A ragtag army of 2,000 farmers armed with pitchforks marched on county courthouses to prevent foreclosures on their land. Many of the farmers were veterans of the Revolutionary War; their leader, Daniel Shays, had been a captain in the American army. They had been given assurances during the Revolution that their land, which sat unplowed because they were away at war, would not be confiscated for unpaid debts and taxes. They were also promised the back pay owed to them for their military service. (Congress had run out of money during the Revolution.) Instead, they received no back pay, and heavy new taxes were levied on their farms. Many farmers faced not only losing their property but also being sent to prison for unpaid debts.

Shays' Rebellion frightened wealthy interests, who called on the governor of Massachusetts to put down the revolt. He in turn asked Congress for help, but it had no army to send. Although Shays' Rebellion was quashed by a private militia hired by wealthy merchants, the rebellion exposed the weaknesses of the national government, which led Virginia and Maryland to invite the other 11 states to meet in Annapolis to propose amendments to the Articles of Confederation. Only five states sent delegates to the Annapolis Convention, which meant no formal steps could be taken. However, James Madison and Alexander Hamilton convinced the delegates to adopt a resolution calling for a constitutional convention. Congress agreed and called for it to be held in Philadelphia. Congress placed a restriction on the convention: It was to meet for "the sole and express purpose of revising the Articles of Confederation."

NEGOTIATING TOWARD A CONSTITUTION

The delegates to the Philadelphia constitutional convention ignored the instructions of Congress, instead drafting a constitution for an entirely new form of government. Prominent delegates (among them George Washington, Benjamin Franklin, and James Madison) were determined from the outset to create a stronger central government. They had come to understand the foolishness of the claim that small government is always the best form of government. The lesson of the Articles of Confederation was that government must be granted the amount of power that is necessary for it to carry out its responsibilities effectively.

The Great Compromise: A Two-Chamber Congress

Debate at the constitutional convention of 1787 began over a plan put forward by the Virginia delegation, which was dominated by strong nationalists. The **Virginia Plan** (also called the *large-state plan*) included separate judicial and executive branches as well as a two-chamber Congress that would have supreme authority in all areas "in which the separate states are incompetent," particularly defense and interstate trade. Members of the lower chamber would be chosen by the voters, while members of the upper chamber would be selected by members of the lower chamber from lists of nominees provided by their respective state legislatures. In both chambers, the heavily populated states would have more representatives than would the lightly populated ones. Small states such as Delaware and Rhode Island would be allowed only one representative in the lower chamber, while large states such as Massachusetts and Virginia would have more than a dozen.

The Virginia Plan was sharply attacked by delegates from the smaller states. They rallied around a counterproposal made by New Jersey's William Paterson. The **New Jersey Plan** (also called the *small-state plan*) called for a stronger national government than that provided for by the Articles of Confederation. It would have the power to tax and to regulate commerce among the states. In most other respects, however, the Articles would remain in effect. Congress would have a single chamber in which each state, large or small, would have a single vote.

The debate over the two plans dragged on for weeks before the delegates reached what is now known as the **Great Compromise.** It provided for a bicameral (two-chamber) Congress. One chamber, the House of Representatives, would be apportioned on the basis of population. States with larger populations would have more House members than states with smaller populations, although each state would have at least one representative. The other chamber, the Senate, would be apportioned on the basis of an equal number of senators (two) for each state. This compromise was critical. The small states would have refused to join a union in which their vote was always weaker than that of large states, a fact reflected in Article V of the Constitution: "No state, without its consent, shall be deprived of its equal suffrage in the Senate."

The Three-Fifths Compromise: Issues of Slavery and Trade

Differences between the interests of northern states and southern states forced a second major compromise, this time over the issues of slavery and trade. The South's delegates were concerned that northern representatives in Congress would tax or even bar the importation of slaves. A decade earlier, at the insistence of southern states, a statement critical of slavery had been deleted from Jefferson's initial draft of the Declaration of Independence, and southern delegates to the Philadelphia convention were determined to block any attempt to end slavery through a new constitution.

The southern delegates were also concerned that the North, which included more states and had a larger population, would use its numerical majority in the House and Senate to enact tax policies injurious to the South. Most of the nation's manufacturing was based in the North, and if Congress sought to protect it by placing a heavy tax (tariff) on manufactured products imported from Europe, the higher cost of these imports would be borne by the South, which was more dependent on them. If Congress also imposed a heavy tariff on the export of agricultural goods, which would make them more expensive and therefore less attractive to foreign buyers, the South would again bear most of the tax burden because it provided most of the agricultural goods shipped abroad, such as cotton and tobacco.

After extended debate, a compromise was reached. Congress would have the authority to tax imports but not exports, and would be prohibited until 1808 from passing laws to end the slave trade. However, the most controversial trade-off was the so-called **Three-Fifths Compromise,** which was proposed by Madison, who was a slaveholder. For purposes of apportionment of taxes other seats in the U.S. House of Representatives, each slave was to count as less than a full person. Northern delegates had argued against the counting of slaves because they did not have legal rights. Southern delegates wanted to count them as full persons for purposes of apportioning House seats (which would have the effect of increasing the number of southern representatives) and to count them as nonpersons for purposes of apportioning taxes (which would have the effect of decreasing the amount of federal taxes levied on the southern states). The delegates finally settled on a compromise that included both taxation and apportionment but counted each slave as three-fifths of a person, which was the ratio necessary to give the southern states nearly half of the House seats. If slaves had not been counted at all, the southern states would have had only about a third of the House seats. If they had been counted as full persons, southern states would have had a slight majority of House members, even though slaves would have had no say in their election.

These compromises have led critics to claim that the framers of the Constitution had no objections to slavery. In fact, most of the delegates were deeply troubled by it, recognizing the stark inconsistency between the practice of slavery and the nation's professed commitment to liberty and equality. "It is inconsistent with the principles of the Revolution," said Maryland's Luther Martin.[6] Benjamin Franklin and Alexander Hamilton were among the delegates who were involved in antislavery organizations.

Nevertheless, the southern states' dependence on slavery was a reality that had to be confronted if there was to be a union of the states. The northern states had few slaves, whereas the southern economies were based on slavery (see Figure 2-1). John Rutledge of South Carolina asked during the convention debate whether the North regarded southerners as "fools." Southern delegates insisted that their states would form a separate union rather than join one that banned slavery.

A Strategy for Ratification

The compromises over slavery and the structure of the Congress took up most of the four months that the convention was in session. Some of the other

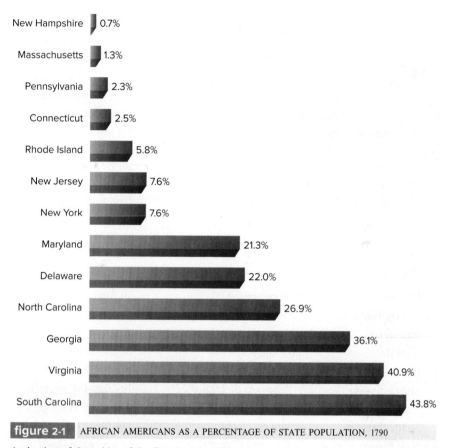

figure 2-1   AFRICAN AMERICANS AS A PERCENTAGE OF STATE POPULATION, 1790

At the time of the writing of the Constitution, African Americans (most of whom were slaves) were concentrated in the southern states. (*Source:* U.S. Census Bureau.)

issues were the subject of remarkably little debate. Decisions on the structure of the federal judiciary and bureaucracy, for example, were largely delegated to Congress.

The last issue that had to be decided was a process for ratifying the proposed constitution. The delegates realized that all their work would amount to nothing if the states could not be persuaded to adopt the new constitution. In authorizing the Philadelphia convention, Congress had stated that any proposed change in the Articles of Confederation would have to be "agreed to in Congress" and then "confirmed by [all] the states."

In a bold move, the delegates ignored Congress's instructions and established their own ratification process. The document was to be submitted to the states, where it would become law if approved by at least nine states in

P A R T Y POLARIZATION

Conflicting Ideas

The Fight over the Ratification of the Constitution

The intense partisanship that typifies today's politics also marked the debate over the Constitution's ratification. Angry exchanges took place between proponents of a stronger national government and those arguing for a state-centered union. Although the pro-Constitution side won easily in most states, the balloting in New York and Virginia was so close that it took the promise of a bill of rights to secure the votes for ratification. North Carolina and Rhode Island (the latter had refused even to send delegates to the Philadelphia convention) initially rejected the Constitution, ratifying it only after the other states began to form a union without them. Here is the breakdown of the ratifying vote in each state:

State	Date of Ratification	Vote Totals
Delaware	December 7, 1787	30 for, 0 against
Pennsylvania	December 12, 1787	46 for, 23 against
New Jersey	December 18, 1787	38 for, 0 against
Georgia	January 2, 1788	26 for, 0 against
Connecticut	January 9, 1788	128 for, 40 against
Massachusetts	February 6, 1788	187 for, 168 against
Maryland	April 28, 1788	63 for, 11 against
South Carolina	May 23, 1788	149 for, 73 against
New Hampshire	June 21, 1788	57 for, 47 against
Virginia	June 25, 1788	89 for, 79 against
New York	July 26, 1788	30 for, 27 against
North Carolina	November 21, 1789	194 for, 77 against
Rhode Island	May 29, 1790	34 for, 32 against

Q: If historians are correct in concluding that the American public as a whole was evenly split over ratification of the Constitution, why might the pro-Constitution side have prevailed in so many states and so easily in some states?

A: State and local governments were in charge of selecting the delegates to the state ratifying conventions. For the most part, they chose prominent leaders to serve as delegates, with the result that wealthy merchants, large landholders, and top public officials dominated the conventions. These groups were more supportive of the Constitution than were other groups, including small farmers, craftspeople, and shopkeepers.

special ratifying conventions of popularly elected delegates. It was a masterful strategy. There was little hope that all 13 state legislatures would approve the Constitution, but 9 states through conventions might be persuaded to ratify it. Indeed, North Carolina and Rhode Island were steadfastly opposed to the new union and did not ratify the Constitution until the other 11 states had ratified it and begun the process of forming the new government (see "Party Polarization: The Fight over the Ratification of the Constitution").

The Ratification Debate

The debate over ratification was historic. The **Anti-Federalists** (as opponents of the Constitution were labeled) raised arguments that still echo in American politics. They claimed that the national government would be too powerful and would threaten self-government in the separate states and the liberty of the people. Many Americans had an innate distrust of centralized power and worried that the people's liberty could be eclipsed as easily by a distant American government as it had been by the British king.

The fact that the Constitution contained no bill of rights heightened this concern. Did its absence indicate that the central government would be free to define for itself what the people's rights would be? Patrick Henry expressed outrage at the omission, saying: "The necessity of a Bill of Rights appears to be greater in this government than ever it was in any government before."

The Anti-Federalists worried that the national government would fall under the control of a political elite. They admired state governments for having legislatures in which the members were not greatly different in wealth from the voters who elected them. New York's Melancton Smith argued that such representatives are "more competent" than "those of a superior class" whose concerns were far removed from the reality of most people's lives. "I am convinced," Smith said, that members of Congress will become "the natural aristocracy of the country. . . . The government will fall into the hands of the few and the great. This will be a government of repression."[7]

The presidency was another source of contention. The office of chief executive did not exist under the Articles of Confederation, and some worried that it would degenerate into an American monarchy. The fact that the president would be chosen by electors appointed by the states (the Electoral College) lessened but did not eliminate this concern.

The Anti-Federalists acknowledged the need for more economic cooperation between the states and for a stronger common defense, but they opposed the creation of a strong national government as the mechanism, arguing that a revision of the Articles of Confederation could accomplish these goals without the risk of establishing an overly powerful central government. (The Anti-Federalist argument is discussed further in Chapter 3.)

The **Federalists** (as the Constitution's supporters called themselves) responded with a persuasive case of their own. Their strongest arguments were set forth by James Madison and Alexander Hamilton, who along with John Jay wrote a series of essays (*The Federalist Papers*) that were published in a New York City newspaper under the pen name Publius. Madison and Hamilton argued that the government of the Constitution would correct the defects of the Articles; it would have the power necessary to forge a secure and prosperous union. At the same time, because of restrictions on its powers, the new government would endanger neither the states nor personal liberty. In *Federalist* Nos. 47, 48, 49, 50, and 51, for example, Madison explained how the separation of national institutions was designed both to empower and to restrict the federal government. (The Federalist argument is discussed further in Chapter 3.)

Whether the ratification debate changed many minds is unclear. Historical evidence suggests, however, that a majority of ordinary Americans opposed the Constitution's ratification. But their voice in the state ratifying conventions was smaller than that of wealthier interests, which in the main supported the change. The pro-ratification forces were also bolstered by the assumption that George Washington, the country's most trusted and popular leader, would become the first president. In the view of historians, this assumption, and the fact that Washington had presided over the Philadelphia convention, tipped the balance in favor of ratification.

Delaware was the first state to ratify the Constitution, and Connecticut, Georgia, and New Jersey soon followed, an indication that the Great Compromise had satisfied some of the small states. In the early summer of 1788, New Hampshire became the ninth state to ratify. The Constitution was law. But neither Virginia nor New York had ratified it, and a stable union without them was almost unthinkable. As large in area as many European countries, Virginia and New York conceivably could have survived as independent nations. In fact, they nearly did choose their own paths. In both states, the Constitution passed only after Federalists said they would support amending it to include a bill of rights.

The Framers' Goals

The Englishman James Bryce ranked America's Constitution as its greatest contribution to the practice of government. The Constitution offered the world a new model of government in which a written document defining the government's lawful powers was a higher authority than the dictates of any political leader or institution.

New York and Virginia voted narrowly in favor of ratification of the Constitution. They were the key to whether the United States could survive as a nation. New York and Virginia were each large enough and wealthy enough to be independent nations. If they had chosen that path, the United States would have been split into three parts—New England, mid-Atlantic, and southern. It's doubtful that the nation would have lasted for long in that form. (©North Wind Picture Archives/Alamy)

The Constitution embodied the framers' vision of a proper government for the American people (see Table 2-1). One of the framers' primary goals was the creation of a national government strong enough to meet the nation's needs, particularly in the areas of defense and commerce. Another basic goal

table 2-1	PRIMARY GOALS OF THE FRAMERS OF THE CONSTITUTION

1. A government strong enough to meet the nation's needs—an objective sought through substantial grants of power to the federal government in areas such as defense and commerce
2. A government that would not threaten the existence of the separate states—an objective sought through federalism and through a Congress tied to the states through elections
3. A government that would not threaten liberty—an objective sought through an elaborate system of checks and balances
4. A government based on popular consent—an objective sought through provisions for the direct and indirect election of public officials

was to preserve the states as governing entities. Accordingly, the framers established a system of government (federalism) in which power is divided between the national government and the states. Federalism is discussed at length in Chapter 3, which also explains how the Constitution laid the foundation for a strong national government.

The framers' other two primary goals will be the focus of the rest of this chapter. These goals were, first, to establish a national government that was restricted in its lawful uses of power (limited government) and, second, to create a national government that gave the people a voice in their governance (representative government).

PROTECTING LIBERTY: LIMITED GOVERNMENT

The framers of the Constitution sought a national government that could act decisively, but not one that would act irresponsibly. History had taught them to mistrust unrestricted majority rule. In times of stress or danger, popular majorities had often acted recklessly, trampling on the liberty of others. In fact, **liberty**—the principle that individuals should be free to act and think as they choose, provided they do not infringe unreasonably on the freedom and well-being of others—was the governing ideal that the framers sought most to uphold. Americans enjoyed an unparalleled level of personal freedom as a result of their open society, and the framers were determined that it not be sacrificed to either European-style monarchy or mob-driven democracy.

The threat to liberty was inherent in government because of its coercive power. Government's unique characteristic is that it alone can legally arrest, imprison, or even kill people who violate its directives. Force is not the only basis by which government maintains order, but without it, lawless individuals would prey on innocent people. The dilemma is that government itself can use force to intimidate or brutalize its opponents. "It is a melancholy reflection," James Madison wrote to Thomas Jefferson shortly after the Constitution's ratification, "that liberty should be equally exposed to danger whether the government has too much or too little power."[8]

Grants and Denials of Power

The framers chose to limit the national government in part by confining its scope to constitutional **grants of power** (see Table 2-2). Congress's lawmaking powers are specifically listed in Article I, Section 8, of the Constitution. Seventeen in number, these listed powers include, for example, the powers to tax, establish an army and navy, declare war, regulate commerce among the states, create a national currency, and borrow money. Powers *not* granted to the government by the Constitution are in theory denied to it. In a period when other governments had unrestricted powers, this limitation was remarkable.

The framers also used **denials of power** as a means to limit government, prohibiting certain practices that European rulers had routinely used to oppress political opponents. The French king, for example, could imprison a subject indefinitely without charge. The U.S. Constitution prohibits such action: Citizens have the right to be brought before a judge under a writ of

table 2-2	CONSTITUTIONAL PROVISIONS FOR LIMITED GOVERNMENT
Mechanism	**Purpose**
Grants of power	Powers granted to the national government; accordingly, powers not granted it are denied it unless necessary and proper to carry out granted powers.
Separated institutions	Division of national government's power among three power-sharing branches, each of which acts as a check on the powers of the other two.
Federalism	Division of political authority between national government and the states, enabling the people to appeal to one authority if their rights and interests are not respected by the other authority.
Denials of power	Powers expressly denied to the national and state governments by the Constitution.
Bill of Rights	First 10 amendments to the Constitution, which specify rights of citizens that the national government must respect.
Judicial review	Power of courts to declare governmental action null and void when it violates the Constitution.
Elections	Power of voters to remove officials from office.

habeas corpus for a determination of the legality of keeping them in jail. The Constitution also forbids Congress and the states from passing ex post facto laws, under which citizens can be prosecuted for acts that were legal at the time they were committed.

Although not strictly a further denial of power, the framers made the Constitution difficult to amend, thereby making it hard for those in office to increase their power by changing the rules. An amendment could be proposed only by a two-thirds majority in both chambers of Congress or by a national constitutional convention called by two-thirds of the state legislatures. A proposed amendment would then become law only if ratified by three-fourths of state legislatures or state conventions. (Over the course of the nation's history, all amendments have been proposed by Congress and only one amendment—the Twenty-First, which repealed the prohibition on alcohol—was ratified by state conventions. The others were ratified by state legislatures.)

Using Power to Offset Power

Although the framers believed that grants and denials of power could act as controls on government, they had no illusion that written words alone would suffice. As a consequence, they sought to limit government by dividing its powers among separate branches.[9]

Decades earlier, the French theorist Montesquieu had argued that the power of government could be controlled by dividing it among separate branches rather than investing it entirely in a single individual or institution. His concept of a **separation of powers** was widely admired in America, and when the states drafted new constitutions after the start of the Revolutionary War, they built their governments around the ideal. Pennsylvania was an exception, and its experience only seemed to prove the necessity of separated powers. Unrestrained by an independent judiciary or executive, Pennsylvania's all-powerful legislature ignored basic rights and freedoms: Quakers were disenfranchised for their religious beliefs, conscientious objectors to the Revolutionary War were prosecuted, and the right of trial by jury was eliminated.

In *Federalist* No. 10, Madison asked why governments often act according to the interests of overbearing majorities rather than according to principles of justice. He attributed the problem to "the mischiefs of faction." People, he argued, are divided into opposing religious, geographic, ethnic, economic, and other factions. These divisions are natural and desirable in that free people have a right to their personal opinions and interests. Yet if a faction gains full power, it will seek to use government to advance itself at the expense of all others. (*Federalist* No. 10 is widely regarded as the finest political essay ever written by an American.)

Out of this concern came the framers' special contribution to the doctrine of the separation of powers. They did not believe that it would be enough, as Montesquieu had proposed, to divide the government's authority strictly along institutional lines, granting all legislative power to the legislature, all judicial power to the courts, and all executive power to the president. This total separation would make it too easy for a single faction to exploit a particular type of political power. A faction that controlled the legislature, for example, could enact laws ruinous to other interests. A safer system would be one in which each branch had the capacity to check the power of the others.[10]

Separated Institutions Sharing Power: Checks and Balances

Political scientist Richard Neustadt devised the term **separated institutions sharing power** to describe the framers' governing system.[11] The separate branches are interlocked in such a way that an elaborate system of **checks and balances** is created (see Figure 2-2). No institution can act decisively without the support or acquiescence of the other institutions. Legislative, executive, and judicial powers in the American system are divided in such a way that they overlap: Each of the three branches of government checks the others' powers and balances those powers with powers of its own.

As natural as this system now might seem to Americans, most democracies are of the parliamentary type, with executive and legislative power combined in a single institution rather than vested in separate ones. In a parliamentary system, the majority in the legislature selects the prime minister, who then serves as both the legislative leader and the chief executive (see "How the U.S. Differs").

Shared Legislative Powers   Under the Constitution, Congress has legislative authority, but that power is partly shared with the other branches and thus is checked by them. The president can veto acts of Congress, recommend legislation, and call special sessions of Congress. The president also has the power to execute—and thereby interpret—the laws Congress makes.

The Supreme Court has the power to interpret acts of Congress that are disputed in legal cases. The Court also has the power of judicial review: It can declare laws of Congress void when it finds that they are not in accord with the Constitution.

Within Congress, there is a further check on legislative power: For legislation to be passed, a majority in each chamber of Congress is required. Thus, the Senate and the House of Representatives can block each other from acting.

The Supreme Court over the President:
May declare executive action unlawful because it is not authorized by legislation; (by tradition) may declare presidential action unconstitutional.

**The Supreme Court—
Judiciary Branch**

**The White House—
Executive Branch**

The President over the Supreme Court:
Nominates federal judges; may pardon those convicted in court; executes court decisions and thereby affects their implementation.

Congress over the President:
May impeach and remove the president; may override presidential veto; may investigate presidential action; must approve treaties and executive appointments; enacts the budget and laws within which presidential action occurs.

The Supreme Court over Congress:
Has the power to interpret legal disputes arising under acts of Congress and (by tradition) may declare acts of Congress unconstitutional.

**The Capitol—
Legislative Branch**

Congress over the Supreme Court: Decides the size of the federal court system, the number of Supreme Court justices, and the appellate jurisdiction of the Supreme Court; may impeach and remove federal judges; may rewrite legislation that courts have interpreted and may initiate constitutional amendments; confirms judicial nominees.

The President over Congress:
May veto acts of Congress, recommend legislation, and call Congress into special session; executes, and thereby interprets, laws enacted by Congress.

figure 2-2   SEPARATE BRANCHES SHARING POWER

The U.S. Constitution separates power among the legislative, executive, and judicial branches but assigns each branch part of the power of the other two branches so that it can act as a check on their power. (*Source:* Richard Neustadt, *Presidential Power*, New York: Macmillan, 1986, 33.)

Shared Executive Powers   Executive power is vested in the president but is constrained by legislative and judicial checks. The president's power to make treaties and appoint high-ranking officials, for example, is subject to Senate approval. Congress also has the power to impeach and remove the president from office. In practical terms, Congress's greatest checks on executive action

HOW THE U.S. DIFFERS

CRITICAL THINKING THROUGH COMPARISONS

Checks and Balances

Although all democracies place constitutional limits on the power of government, the United States is an extreme case in that its government rests on an elaborate system of constitutional checks and balances. The system employs a separation of powers among the executive, legislative, and judicial branches. Most democracies have parliamentary systems, which invest both executive and legislative leadership in the office of prime minister. Great Britain, for example, has this type of system. If the British Parliament under the prime minister's leadership enacts a bill, it automatically becomes law. It is not subject to veto by a president, as in the case in the United States.

Q: The framers of the Constitution saw checks and balances as a means of fostering political moderation. Is there a relationship between the number of checks and balances Western democracies have and their tendency toward political moderation?

A: There is no clear relationship. Great Britain, for example, is often cited as an example of political moderation although it lacks an elaborate system of checks and balances. By contrast, Mexico, which has such a system, is often held up as an example of political extremes. This fragmentary evidence does not mean that checks and balances are ineffective in controlling power, but the evidence does suggest that other factors, such as a country's political traditions, must also be taken into account in a full explanation of political moderation.

are its lawmaking and appropriations powers. The executive branch cannot act without laws that authorize its activities or without the money that pays for these activities.

The judiciary's major check on the presidency is its power to declare an action unlawful because it is not authorized by the laws that the executive claims to be implementing.

Shared Judicial Powers   Judicial power rests with the Supreme Court and with lower federal courts, which are subject to checks by the other branches of the federal government. Congress is empowered to establish the size of the federal court system, to restrict the Supreme Court's appellate jurisdiction in some circumstances, and to impeach and remove federal judges from office. More important, Congress can rewrite legislation that the courts have misinterpreted and can initiate amendments when it disagrees with court rulings on constitutional issues.

The president has the power to appoint federal judges with the consent of the Senate and to pardon persons convicted in the courts. The president also is responsible for executing court decisions, a function that provides opportunities to influence the way rulings are carried out.

The Bill of Rights

Although the delegates to the Philadelphia convention discussed the possibility of placing a list of individual rights (such as freedom of speech and the right to a fair trial) in the Constitution, they ultimately decided that such a list was unnecessary because of the doctrine of expressed powers: Government could not lawfully engage in actions, such as the suppression of speech, that were not authorized by the Constitution. Moreover, the delegates argued that a bill

The U.S. political system is based on separation of power between the executive, legislative, and judicial branches, with each branch having a check on the power of the other two. Such a check occurred in early 2017 when federal courts blocked implementation of President Donald Trump's executive order that immediately banned travel to the United States from six predominantly Muslim countries. President Trump subsequently issued a modified executive order that was upheld by the Supreme Court. (*Source:* Official White House Photo by Stephanie Chasez)

of rights was undesirable because government might feel free to disregard any right that was inadvertently left off the list or that might emerge in the future.

These arguments failed to convince those who favored a bill of rights. They worried that the Constitution, unlike the Articles of Confederation, granted the federal government direct authority over individual citizens and yet did not contain a list of their rights. "A bill of rights," Jefferson argued, "is what the people are entitled to against every government on earth, general or particular, and what no just government should refuse or rest on inference." Jefferson had included a bill of rights in the constitution he wrote for Virginia at the outbreak of the Revolutionary War, and all but four states had followed Virginia's example.

Ultimately, the demand for a bill of rights led to its addition to the Constitution. Madison himself introduced a series of amendments during the First Congress, 10 of which were quickly ratified by the states. These amendments, traditionally called the **Bill of Rights,** include free-expression rights such as freedom of speech and due process protections such as the right to a jury trial. (These rights, termed *civil liberties,* are discussed in Chapter 4.)

The Bill of Rights is a precise expression of the concept of limited government. In consenting to be governed, the people agree to accept the authority of government in certain areas but not in others; the people's constitutional rights cannot lawfully be denied by government.

Judicial Review

The writers of the Constitution both empowered and limited government. But who was to decide whether officials were operating within the limits of their constitutional powers? The framers did not specifically entrust this power to a particular branch of government, although they did grant the Supreme Court the authority to decide on "all cases arising under this Constitution." Moreover, at the ratifying conventions of at least 8 of the 13 states, it was claimed that the judiciary would have the power to nullify actions that violated the Constitution.[12]

Nevertheless, because the Constitution did not explicitly grant the judiciary this authority, the principle had to be established in practice. The opportunity arose with an incident that occurred after the election of 1800, in which John Adams lost his bid for a second presidential term after a bitter campaign against Jefferson. Between November 1800, when Jefferson was elected, and March 1801, when he was inaugurated, the Federalist-controlled Congress created 59 additional lower-court judgeships, enabling Adams to appoint loyal Federalists to the positions before he left office. However, Adams's term expired before his secretary of state could deliver the judicial commissions to all the appointees. Without this authorization, an appointee could not take office. Knowing this, Jefferson told his secretary of state, James Madison, not

Politics in Action

The Watergate Scandal

On a June night in 1972, a security guard at the Watergate complex noticed that the latch on the door to the Democratic Party's national headquarters had been taped open. He removed the tape and went away. Coming back later, he noticed the door had been taped open again. He called police, who caught five men inside, installing hidden microphones ("bugs") in the phones and ceilings. As it turned out, the men had links to President Richard Nixon's reelec-

Source: Richard Nixon Presidential Library and Museum

tion campaign. Nixon denied that anyone at the White House had knowledge of the break-in. In truth, the Watergate break-in was part of a large effort—including the stealing of documents—aimed at ensuring Nixon's reelection.

A turning point in the Watergate scandal occurred during a Senate investigative hearing when a White House assistant revealed that Nixon had tape-recorded his Oval Office conversations. Nixon at first refused Congress's demand that he turn over the tapes. As pressure mounted, he released transcripts of what he claimed were "all the relevant" ones. When Congress demanded additional material, Nixon refused. Congress then filed suit to get the tapes. In a unanimous decision, the U.S. Supreme Court, which included four Nixon appointees, ordered Nixon to turn them over. They were incriminating. Nixon was heard telling his assistants to cover up the Watergate break-in, including using the CIA to block the FBI from investigating it. With that, the House of Representatives began impeachment proceedings.

At that point, Nixon resigned his office, the first and only president to do so. Despite holding what is often called "the most powerful office on earth," Nixon was powerless to stop Congress and the Supreme Court from acting. The framers of the Constitution had established them as separate and independent branches, and they acted in exactly that way.

Continued

> **Q:** Can you think of situations where the separation of powers would fail to prevent unconstitutional action?
>
> **ASK YOURSELF:** Are there situations where all three branches of government have been in agreement that unconstitutional action is required? (In this context, you might consider the forced internment of Japanese Americans during World War II.) What about the case where one political party controls both the presidency and Congress? (In the Watergate case, President Nixon was a Republican and Democrats controlled the House and the Senate.)

to deliver the commissions. William Marbury was one of those who did not receive his commission, and he asked the Supreme Court to issue a writ of mandamus (a court order directing an official to perform a specific act) that would force Madison to deliver it.

Marbury v. Madison (1803) became the foundation for judicial review by the federal courts. Chief Justice John Marshall wrote the *Marbury* opinion, which declared that Marbury had a legal right to his commission. The opinion also said, however, that the Supreme Court could not issue him a writ of mandamus because it lacked the constitutional authority to do so. Congress had passed legislation in 1789 that gave the Court this power, but Marshall noted that the Constitution prohibits Congress from expanding the Supreme Court's authority except through a constitutional amendment. That being the case, Marshall argued, the legislation that provided the authorization was constitutionally invalid.[13] In striking down this act of Congress, the Court asserted its power of **judicial review**—that is, the power of the judiciary to decide whether a government official or institution has acted within the limits of the Constitution and, if not, to declare its action null and void. (Not every court case involves judicial review. It refers only to judgments of whether government officials or institutions have acted within the boundaries of their constitutional power.)

Marshall's decision was ingenious because it asserted the power of judicial review without creating the possibility of its rejection by either the executive or the legislative branch. In declaring that Marbury had a right to his commission, the Court in effect said that President Jefferson had failed in his constitutional duty to execute the laws faithfully. However, because it did not order Jefferson to deliver the commission, he was deprived of the opportunity to disobey the Court's ruling. At the same time, the Court reprimanded Congress for passing legislation that exceeded its constitutional authority. But Congress also had no way to retaliate. It could not force the Court to accept the power to issue writs of mandamus if the Court itself refused to issue them.

PROVIDING FOR REPRESENTATIVE GOVERNMENT

"We the People" is the opening phrase of the Constitution. It expresses the idea that in the United States the people will have the power to govern themselves. In a sense, there is no contradiction between this idea and the Constitution's provisions for limited government, because individual *liberty* is an essential element of *representative government.* If people cannot express themselves freely, they cannot be truly self-governing. In another sense, however, the contradiction is clear: Restrictions on the power of the majority are a denial of its right to govern society as it sees fit.

The framers believed that the people deserved and required a voice in their government, but they worried that the people could become inflamed by a passionate issue or fiery demagogue and act rashly. To the framers, the great risk of popular government was **tyranny of the majority:** the people acting as an irrational mob that tramples on the rights of the minority. The history of unfettered democracies was not encouraging, leading James Madison to say in *Federalist* No. 10 that they "have ever been spectacles of turbulence and contention; have ever been found incompatible with personal security or the rights of property; and have in general been as short in their lives as they have been violent in their deaths."

Democracy versus Republic

No form of representative government could eliminate the possibility of majority tyranny, but the framers believed that the risk would be greatly diminished by creating a republican government as opposed to a democratic one.[14] Today, the terms *democracy, republic,* and *representative government* are often used interchangeably to refer to a system of government in which political power rests with the people through their ability to choose representatives in free and fair elections. To the writers of the Constitution, however, a democracy and a republic were different forms of government.

By the term **democracy,** the framers meant a government in which the majority, either directly or through its representatives, has absolute power. The law is whatever the majority declares it to be. If the majority decides to rule in the interest of all, it has the power to do so. But if the majority decides instead to trample on the rights and interests of the minority, it has the power to do that as well. In a democracy, as the framers defined it, there are no limits on the majority's power.

By the term **republic,** the framers meant a government that has limits on its power. The people have rights that are beyond the reach of government, guaranteed by a constitution and protected through carefully designed institutions. Governing institutions are structured in ways that foster deliberation and provide checks against action that would deprive the minority of its rights. The majority has power, but its power is subject to constitutional and institutional limits.[15]

Limited Popular Rule

To ensure that the government they created would be a republic and not a democracy, the framers created a system of representation that placed most federal officials beyond the direct control of the voters (see Table 2-3).

The House of Representatives was the only institution that would be based on direct popular election—its members would be elected to serve for two years by a vote of the people. Frequent and direct election of House members was intended to make government responsive to the concerns of popular majorities.

U.S. senators would be appointed by the legislatures of the states they represented. Because state legislators were popularly elected, the people would be choosing their senators indirectly. Every two years, a third of the senators would be appointed to six-year terms. The Senate, by virtue of the less frequent and indirect election of its members, was expected to be less responsive to popular pressure and thereby serve as a check on the House.

Presidential selection was an issue of considerable debate at the Philadelphia convention. Direct election of the president was twice proposed and twice rejected because it would link executive power directly to popular majorities. The framers finally chose to have the president selected by the votes of electors (the so-called **Electoral College**). Each state would have the same number of **electoral votes** as it had members in Congress and could select its electors by a method of its choosing. The president would serve four years and be eligible for reelection.

The framers decided that federal judges and justices would be appointed rather than elected. They would be nominated by the president and confirmed through approval by the Senate. Once confirmed, they would "hold their

table 2-3	METHODS OF CHOOSING FEDERAL OFFICIALS	
Office	**Method of Selection**	**Term of Service**
President	Electoral College	4 years
U.S. senator	State legislature, changed in 1913 to popular election	6 years (one-third of senators' terms expire every 2 years)
U.S. representative	Popular election	2 years
Federal judge	Nominated by president, approved by Senate	Indefinite (subject to "good behavior")

offices during good behavior." In effect, they would be allowed to hold office for life unless they committed a crime. The judiciary was an unelected institution that would uphold the rule of law and serve as a check on the elected branches of government.[16]

These differing methods of selecting national officeholders would not prevent a determined majority from achieving unchecked power, but control could not be attained quickly. Unlike the House of Representatives, institutions such as the Senate, presidency, and judiciary would not yield to an impassioned majority in a single election. The delay would reduce the chance that government would degenerate into mob rule driven by momentary passions.

Altering the Constitution: More Power to the People

The framers' conception of representative government was at odds with what the average American in 1787 would have expected.[17] Self-government was an ideal that had led tens of thousands of ordinary farmers, merchants, and tradesmen to risk their lives fighting the British in the American Revolution. The ensuing state constitutions had put the ideal into practice. Every state but South Carolina held annual legislative elections, and several states also chose their governors through direct annual election.

Not long after ratification of the Constitution, Americans began to challenge the Constitution's restrictions on majority rule, an effort that would extend into the early 1900s.

Jeffersonian Democracy: A Revolution of the Spirit   Thomas Jefferson was among the prominent Americans who questioned the Constitution's limited provisions for self-government. In a letter to Madison, he objected to its system of representation, voicing the Anti-Federalist's fear that federal officials would lose touch with the people and ignore their interests. His concern intensified when John Adams became president after Washington's retirement. Under Adams, the national government increasingly favored the nation's wealthy interests. Adams publicly stated that the Constitution was designed for a governing elite and hinted that he might use force to suppress dissent.[18] Jefferson asked whether Adams, with the aid of a strong army, intended to deprive ordinary people of their rights. Jefferson challenged Adams in the next presidential election and, upon defeating him, hailed his victory as the "Revolution of 1800."

Although Jefferson was a champion of the common people, he had no clear vision of how a popular government might work in practice. He saw Congress, not the presidency, as the institution better suited to representing majority opinion.[19] He also had no illusions about the ability of a largely uneducated population

THE MODERN BALAAM AND HIS ASS.

Andrew Jackson revolutionized American politics by appealing to the "common man." He sought to reduce the power of the banks, fought for eliminating the property requirement for voting, argued for tying electoral votes to the popular vote, and appointed ordinary citizens to public office. This 1837 lithograph is the first time the donkey was used to symbolize the Democratic Party. It has been the party's symbol ever since. (*Source:* Library of Congress, Prints and Photographs Division [LC-DIG-ppmsca-15775])

to play a substantial governing role and feared what would happen if the people were incited to rise up against the rich. Jeffersonian democracy was mostly a revolution of the spirit. Jefferson taught Americans to look on national government institutions as belonging to all, not just to the privileged few.[20]

Jacksonian Democracy: Linking the People and the Presidency   Not until the election of Andrew Jackson in 1828 did the nation have a powerful president who was willing and able to involve the public more fully in government. Jackson carried out the constitutional revolution that Jeffersonian democracy had foreshadowed.

Jackson recognized that the president was the only official who could legitimately claim to represent the people as a whole. Unlike the president, members of Congress were elected from separate states and districts rather than from the entire country. Yet the president's claim to popular leadership was weakened by the fact that the president was chosen by electors rather than by the voters. To connect the presidency more closely to the people, Jackson

Detecting Misinformation

Were Millions of Illegal Votes Cast in Favor of Hillary Clinton in the 2016 Election?

Under the Constitution, the president is chosen by the votes of electors (the so-called Electoral College). The states grant their electoral votes to the candidate who gets the most popular votes in the states. Because electoral votes are decided state-by-state, it's possible for a candidate to win the national popular vote and yet get fewer electoral votes and thereby lose the election. That happened in 2016. Although Hillary Clinton had 2.9 million more popular votes nationally

©Hill Street Studios/Blend Images

than did Donald Trump, she had fewer electoral votes (227 to 304). Narrow victories in the states of Pennsylvania, Michigan, and Wisconsin provided Trump with the electoral vote margin he needed to win the election.

After the election, Trump claimed that he, and not Clinton, had actually won the popular vote. Trump tweeted: "I won the popular vote, if you deduct the millions of people who voted illegally." A *Politico* poll found that 28 percent of Americans, and 47 percent of Republicans, believed Trump's claim. Were millions of illegal votes cast for Clinton in 2016?

Is that claim fact, or is it fake?

After the election, the states reviewed their votes and none of them found evidence of widespread illegal voting. Scholars also studied the vote returns and found no indication of massive vote fraud. In May 2017, President Trump created a commission—the Presidential Advisory Commission on Election Integrity, headed by Vice President Mike Pence—to investigate illegal voting. The commission found it difficult to gather the relevant information and was disbanded after eight months without producing any evidence that would support the notion that millions of ineligible individuals cast votes in the 2016 election.

urged the states to award their electoral votes to the candidate who wins the state's popular vote. Soon thereafter, nearly all states adopted this method. This arrangement, still in effect, places the selection of the president in the voters' hands in most elections. The candidate who gets the most popular votes nationally is also likely to finish first in enough states to win a majority of the electoral votes. Since Jackson's time, four candidates—Rutherford B. Hayes in 1876, Benjamin Harrison in 1888, George W. Bush in 2000, and Donald Trump in 2016—have won the presidency after losing the popular vote. (The Electoral College is discussed further in Chapter 12.)

The Progressives: Senate and Primary Elections   The Progressive Era of the early 1900s brought another wave of democratic reforms. The Progressives sought to weaken the influence of large corporations and political party bosses by placing power more directly in the hands of the people.[21] They succeeded in changing the way some state and local governments operate. Progressive reforms at state and local levels included the initiative and the referendum, which enable citizens to vote directly on legislative issues (see "How the 50 States Differ").

The Progressives also instigated two changes in federal elections. One was the **primary election** (also called the *direct primary*), which gives ordinary voters the power to select party nominees. In the early 1900s, nearly all states adopted the primary election as a means of choosing nominees for at least some federal and state offices. Prior to this change, nominees were selected by party leaders. The second change was the direct election of U.S. senators, who before the ratification of the Seventeenth Amendment in 1913 were chosen by state legislatures and were widely perceived as agents of big business (the Senate was nicknamed the "Millionaires' Club"). Senators who stood to lose their seats in a direct popular vote had blocked earlier attempts to amend the Constitution. However, as a result of several developments, including revelations that several senators owed their seats to corporate bribes, the Senate was finally persuaded to back the amendment.

The Progressive Era even spawned attacks on the framers. A prominent criticism was laid out in historian Charles S. Beard's *An Economic Interpretation of the Constitution.*[22] Arguing that the Constitution grew out of wealthy Americans' fears of the debtor rebellions, Beard claimed that the Constitution's elaborate systems of power and representation were devices for keeping power in the hands of the rich. As evidence, Beard cited the Constitution's protections of property and referred to Madison's notes on the Philadelphia convention, which showed that property concerns were high on the framers' agenda. Beard also noted that most of the delegates were wealthy. Not one was a laborer or small farmer.

Beard's thesis was challenged by other historians, and he later acknowledged that he had not taken into account the framers' full array of motives. Their conception of separation of powers, for example, was a governing principle that had earlier been incorporated into state constitutions. Nevertheless, Beard

HOW THE 50 STATES DIFFER

CRITICAL THINKING THROUGH COMPARISONS

Direct Democracy: The Initiative and the Popular Referendum

By gathering enough signatures on a petition, citizens in some states can place legislation of their own choosing on the ballot (the initiative) or place an act of the state legislature on the ballot (the popular referendum). The voters can then choose to accept or reject what's being proposed. A popular referendum is different from a legislative referendum, in which the state legislature itself places a proposal on the ballot for the voters to accept or reject. All states have a form of the legislative referendum, but only some states, as indicated by the accompanying map, allow the initiative or popular referendum.

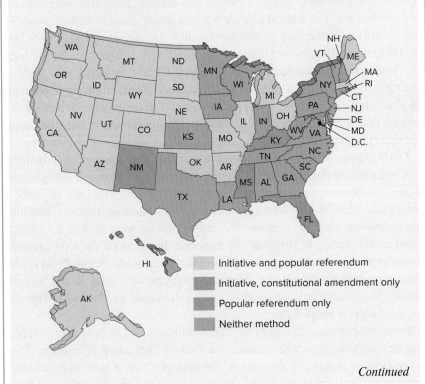

Initiative and popular referendum

Initiative, constitutional amendment only

Popular referendum only

Neither method

Continued

Q: Why are northeastern and southern states less likely than other states to have the initiative and popular referendum?

A: The initiative and popular referendum were introduced in the early 1900s by the Progressives, who sought to weaken the power of political bosses and give voters more influence. In the Northeast, party machines had enough strength in state legislatures to block their enactment. In the South, the white establishment blocked enactment out of fear that blacks and poor whites might use them to gain power.

held onto his claim that the Constitution was designed to protect the interests of the wealthy rather than to promote the interests of the broad public.

Beard's claim has some validity, but to say that the framers were foes of democracy is inaccurate. Although they did not have great trust in popular rule, they were determined to balance the need to create a system of self-government with the need to create a system of limited government. Convinced that unchecked majority rule was likely to devolve into tyranny, the framers devised institutions that were responsive to majority opinion without being captive to it.

CONSTITUTIONAL DEMOCRACY TODAY

The type of government created in the United States in 1787 could accurately be called a **constitutional democratic republic.** It is constitutional in its requirement that power gained through elections be exercised in accordance with law and with due respect for individual rights; democratic in its provisions for majority influence through elections; and a republic in its multiple institutions (presidency, Congress, and the courts), each of which checks the power of the others.[23]

By some standards, the American system of today is a model of *representative government.*[24] The United States schedules the election of its larger legislative chamber (the House of Representatives) and its chief executive more frequently than does any other democracy. In addition, it is the only major democracy to rely extensively on primary elections rather than party organizations for the selection of party nominees. The principle of direct popular election to office, which the writers of the Constitution regarded as a method to be used sparingly, has been extended further in the United States than anywhere else.

By other standards, however, the U.S. system is less democratic than some. Popular majorities must work against the barriers to power devised by the framers—divided branches, staggered terms of office, and separate constituencies. In fact, the link between an electoral majority and a governing majority is less direct in the American system than in many democratic systems. In the European parliamentary democracies, for example, legislative and executive power is not divided, is not subject to close check by the judiciary, and is acquired through the winning of a legislative majority in a single national election. The framers' vision was a different one, dominated by a concern with liberty and therefore with controls on political power. It was a response to the experiences they brought with them to Philadelphia in the summer of 1787.

SUMMARY

The Constitution of the United States is a reflection of the colonial and revolutionary experiences of the early Americans. Freedom from abusive government was a reason for the colonies' revolt against British rule, but the English tradition also provided ideas about government, power, and freedom that were expressed in the Constitution and, earlier, in the Declaration of Independence.

The Constitution was designed in part to provide for a limited government in which political power would be confined to proper uses. The framers wanted to ensure that the government they were creating would not itself be a threat to freedom. To this end, they confined the national government to expressly granted powers and also denied it certain specific powers. Other prohibitions on government were later added to the Constitution in the form of stated guarantees of individual liberties in the Bill of Rights. The most significant constitutional provision for limited government, however, was a separation of powers among the three branches. The powers given to each branch enable it to act as a check on the exercise of power by the other two, an arrangement that during the nation's history has in fact served as a barrier to abuses of power.

The Constitution, however, made no mention of how the powers and limits of government were to be judged in practice. In its historic ruling in *Marbury v. Madison,* the Supreme Court assumed the authority to review the constitutionality of legislative and executive actions and to declare them unconstitutional and thus invalid.

The framers of the Constitution, respecting the idea of self-government but distrusting popular majorities, devised a system of government that they felt would temper popular opinion and slow its momentum so that the public's "true interest" (which includes a regard for the rights and interests of the minority) would guide public policy. Different methods were advanced for selecting the president, the members of the House and the Senate, and federal judges as a means of insulating political power against momentary majorities.

Since the adoption of the Constitution, the public gradually has assumed more direct control of its representatives, particularly through measures that affect the way officeholders are chosen. Presidential popular voting (linked to the Electoral College), direct election of senators, and primary elections are among the devices aimed at strengthening the majority's influence. These developments are rooted in the idea, deeply held by ordinary Americans, that the people must have substantial direct influence over their representatives if government is to serve their interests.

©gangliu10/Getty Images

CRITICAL THINKING ZONE

KEY TERMS

Anti-Federalists (*p. 39*)
Bill of Rights (*p. 49*)
checks and balances (*p. 45*)
constitution (*p. 32*)
constitutional democratic
 republic (*p. 59*)
democracy (according to the
 framers) (*p. 52*)
denials of power (*p. 43*)
Electoral College (*p. 53*)
electoral votes (*p. 53*)
Federalists (*p. 40*)
grants of power (*p. 43*)
Great Compromise (*p. 35*)
inalienable (natural) rights (*p. 31*)

judicial review (*p. 51*)
liberty (*p. 42*)
limited government (*p. 29*)
New Jersey (small-state) Plan (*p. 35*)
primary election (direct
 primary) (*p. 57*)
representative government (*p. 29*)
republic (*p. 52*)
separated institutions sharing
 power (*p. 45*)
separation of powers (*p. 44*)
social contract (*p. 31*)
Three-Fifths Compromise (*p. 36*)
tyranny of the majority (*p. 52*)
Virginia (large-state) Plan (*p. 34*)

APPLYING THE ELEMENTS OF CRITICAL THINKING

Conceptualizing: Define the concept of judicial review. How does a court decision involving judicial review differ from an ordinary court decision, such as a ruling in a case involving robbery?

Synthesizing: Contrast the original system for electing federal officials with the system of today, noting in each case how voters acquired a more direct voice in the election process than was originally the case.

Analyzing: Why is it more accurate to say that the United States has a system of "separated institutions sharing power" rather than a system of "separated powers"? Provide examples of how shared power can act to check and balance the power of each institution.

EXTRA CREDIT

A Book Worth Reading: Robert A. Dahl, *How Democratic Is the American Constitution?* 2nd ed. (New Haven, Conn.: Yale University Press, 2003). A short, readable book by a preeminent political scientist that explores the question of whether the U.S. Constitution is suited to today's governing needs.

A Website Worth Visiting: **www.archives.gov** The National Archives is the repository of America's important documents. Its site includes, for example, an in-depth history of the writing of the Declaration of Independence.

PARTICIPATE!

The classroom provides an everyday opportunity to develop a skill that is basic to effective citizenship—the ability to speak clearly and persuasively. To the Greek philosopher Aristotle, rhetoric was the defining skill of citizenship. Aristotle did not define rhetoric in the way it is often used today, as a derisive term for speech that is long on words and short on reason. Rather, he saw rhetoric as a tool in the search for truth, a form of persuasion that flourishes when people exchange ideas. The college classroom is a good place to develop rhetorical skills. Speak up in the classroom when you have a point to make and can support it. Rhetorical skills are honed only through practice, and few settings offer more opportunities for practice than does the classroom.

3
CHAPTER

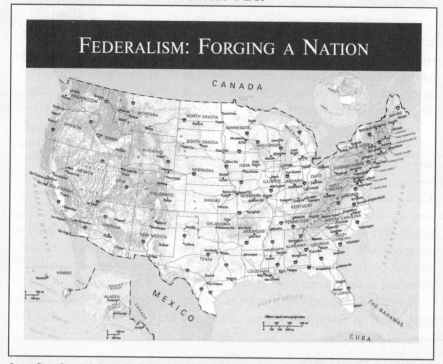

FEDERALISM: FORGING A NATION

Source: Perry-Castañeda Library Map Collection, University of Texas Libraries

> ❝ The question of the relation of the states to the federal government is the cardinal question of our Constitutional system. It cannot be settled by the opinion of one generation, because it is a question of growth, and each successive stage of our political and economic development gives it a new aspect, makes it a new question. ❞
>
> WOODROW WILSON[1]

On his fourth day as president of the United States, Donald Trump issued sweeping directives aimed at deporting undocumented immigrants. Citing federal control over immigration, Trump ordered an increase in the number of immigration enforcement officers, expanded the list of targeted classes of deportees, and established an expedited process for deporting those who were apprehended. Trump asked state and local officials for help in identifying undocumented aliens and, if they detained such individuals, to hold them until federal officials could take them into custody.

Some states and cities cooperated with the Trump administration, but others declared themselves "sanctuaries" for undocumented immigrants. They instructed their officials not to cooperate with federal immigration officers, citing a Supreme Court ruling that says state and local officials cannot be "commandeered" by the federal government to assist in the enforcement of federal directives.[2] Trump then threatened to withhold federal grants-in-aid to sanctuary cities and states. In turn, they cited a Supreme Court ruling that says the federal government cannot use grants-in-aid to "coerce" states and localities into carrying out a particular action unless Congress, in setting up the grant program, listed that action as a condition for receipt of the grant.[3]

The conflict surrounding the Trump administration's deportation policy is one of thousands of disagreements over the course of American history that have hinged on whether national or state authority will prevail. Americans possess what amounts to dual citizenship: They are citizens both of the United States and of the state where they reside. The American political system is a *federal system*, in which constitutional authority is divided between a national government and state governments. Each government is assumed to derive its powers directly from the people and therefore to have sovereignty (final authority) over the policy responsibilities assigned to it. The federal system consists of states and nation, separate yet indivisible.[4]

The relationship between the states and the nation was the most pressing issue when the Constitution was written and has been a divisive issue ever

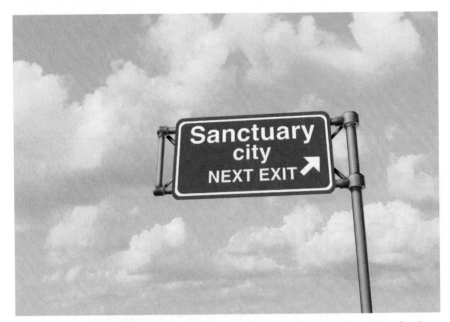

Early in his presidency, Donald Trump issued orders aimed at increasing the deportation of undocumented immigrants. A number of cities and states refused to cooperate in the federal effort, declaring themselves to be sanctuaries for the undocumented. The resulting conflict between federal power, on the one hand, and state and local power, on the other, is but one of many such episodes over the course of the nation's history. (©wildpixel/Getty Images)

since. In one case, the Civil War, it nearly caused the dissolution of the United States. Throughout the nation's history, federalism has been a source of contention between the Republican and Democratic Parties, although they have shifted sides when it has served their political goals. This chapter examines federalism—its creation through the Constitution, its evolution during the nation's history, and its current status. This chapter presents the following main points:

- *The power of government must be equal to its responsibilities.* The Constitution was needed because the nation's preceding system (under the Articles of Confederation) was too weak to accomplish its expected goals, particularly those of a strong defense and an integrated economy.

- *Federalism—the Constitution's division of governing authority between two levels, nation and states—was the result of political bargaining.* Federalism was not a theoretical principle, but rather a compromise made necessary in 1787 by the prior existence of the states.

- *Federalism is not a fixed principle for allocating power between the national and state governments, but rather a principle that has changed over time in response to political needs and partisan ideology.* Federalism has passed through several distinct stages in the course of the nation's history.

- *Contemporary federalism tilts toward national authority, reflecting the increased interdependence of American society.*

FEDERALISM: NATIONAL AND STATE SOVEREIGNTY

At the time of the writing of the Constitution, some of America's top leaders were dead set against the creation of a stronger national government. When rumors began to circulate that the Philadelphia convention was devising just such a government, Virginia's Patrick Henry said that he "smelt a rat." His fears were confirmed when he obtained a copy of the draft constitution. "Who authorized them," he asked, "to speak the language of 'We, the People,' instead of 'We, the States'?"

The question of "people versus states" was precipitated by the failure of the Articles of Confederation. It had created a union of the states, and they alone had authority over the people (see Chapter 2). The national government could not tax or conscript citizens, nor could it regulate their economic activities. Its directives applied only to the states, and they often ignored them. Georgia and North Carolina, for example, contributed no money at all to the national treasury between 1781 and 1786, and the federal government had no way to force

"GIVE ME LIBERTY, OR GIVE ME DEATH !"

PATRICK HENRY delivering his great speech on the Rights of the Colonies, before the Virginia Assembly.

Patrick Henry was a leading figure in the American Revolution ("Give me liberty or give me death!"). He later opposed ratification of the Constitution on grounds that the national government should be a union of states and not also a union of people. (*Source:* Library of Congress, Prints and Photographs Division [LC-USZC2-2452])

them to pay. The only feasible solution to this problem was to give the federal government direct authority over the people. If individuals are ordered to pay taxes, most of them will do so rather than accept the alternative—imprisonment or confiscation of their property.

At the same time, the writers of the Constitution wanted to preserve the states. The states had their own constitutions and a governing history extending back to the colonial era. Although their residents thought of themselves as Americans, many of them identified more strongly with their states. When Virginia's George Mason said that he would never agree to a constitution that abolished the states, he was speaking for nearly all the delegates.

These two realities—the need to preserve the states and the need for a national government with direct authority over the people—led the framers to invent an entirely new system of government. Before this point in history, **sovereignty** (supreme and final governing authority) had been regarded as indivisible. By definition, a government cannot be sovereign if it can be overruled by another government. Nevertheless, the framers divided sovereignty between the national government and the states, a system now known as **federalism.** Each level—the national government and the state governments—directly governs the residents within its assigned territory. Each level has authority that is not subject to the other's approval. And each level is constitutionally protected. The national government cannot abolish a state, and the states cannot abolish the national government.

In 1787, other nations in the world were governed by a **unitary system,** in which sovereignty is vested solely in the national government (see "How the U.S. Differs"). Local or regional governments in a unitary system do not have sovereignty. They have authority only to the degree that it is granted by the national government, which can also withdraw any such grant. (This situation applies to America's local governments. They are not sovereign, but instead derive their authority from their respective state governments, which can, though it occurs rarely, even choose to abolish a local unit of government.)

HOW THE U.S. DIFFERS

CRITICAL THINKING THROUGH COMPARISONS

Federal Systems

Federalism involves the division of sovereignty between a national government and subnational (state) governments. The United States was the first federal government and, today, about two dozen countries have a federal system. Most countries instead have a unitary system, which vests sovereignty solely in the national government.

In federal systems, the national legislature has two chambers—one apportioned by population (as in the case of the U.S. House of Representatives) and the other by geographic area (as in the case of the U.S. Senate). The U.S. Senate is a pure federal institution in the sense that each state has the same number of senators. In some federal systems, including Germany's and Canada's, the states are not equally represented even in the legislative chamber apportioned on the basis of geography rather than population.

Q: Federal systems have a two-chamber legislature, whereas some unitary systems have only one chamber. Why the difference?

A: In a unitary system, there is no constitutional need for a second legislative chamber based on geographic subdivisions (states), as is the case with a federal system.

Federalism is also different from a **confederacy,** which was the type of government that existed under the Articles of Confederation. In a confederacy, the states alone are sovereign. They decide the authority, even the continuing existence, of the central government. Confederacies have been rare in human history, but the government of the Articles was not the first. The ancient Greek city-states and medieval Europe's Hanseatic League were of this type. (Despite its name, the Confederate States of America—the South's Civil War government—had a federal constitution rather than a confederate one. Sovereignty was divided between the central and state governments.)

The federal system established in 1787 divides the responsibilities of government between the nation and the states (see Figure 3-1). The system gives states the power to address local issues in ways of their choosing; they have primary responsibility, for example, for public education and police protection. The national government, by contrast, is responsible for matters of national scope, such as military defense and the currency. The national and state governments also have some concurrent powers (that is, powers exercised over the same policy areas). Each of them has, for example, the power to raise taxes and borrow money.

The Argument for Federalism

The strongest argument for federalism in 1787 was that it would correct the defects in the Articles. Two of the defects were particularly troublesome: The national government had neither the power to tax nor the power to regulate commerce among the states. Without money from taxes, the national

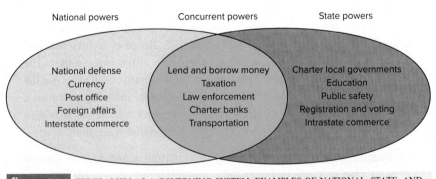

National powers	Concurrent powers	State powers
National defense	Lend and borrow money	Charter local governments
Currency	Taxation	Education
Post office	Law enforcement	Public safety
Foreign affairs	Charter banks	Registration and voting
Interstate commerce	Transportation	Intrastate commerce

figure 3-1   FEDERALISM AS A GOVERNING SYSTEM: EXAMPLES OF NATIONAL, STATE, AND CONCURRENT POWERS

The American federal system divides sovereignty between a national government and the state governments. Each is constitutionally protected in its existence and authority, although their powers overlap somewhat even in areas granted to one level (for example, the federal government has a role in education policy).

government lacked the financial means to maintain an army strong enough to prevent encroachment by European powers or to maintain a navy strong enough to protect America's merchant ships from harassment and attack by foreign navies and pirates. And without the ability to regulate commerce, the national government could neither promote the general economy nor prevent trade wars between the states. New York and New Jersey were among the states that imposed taxes on goods shipped into their state from other states (see "Case Study: The Power of Government").

Although it is sometimes claimed that "the government which governs least is the government that governs best," the Articles proved otherwise. The problems with the too-weak national government were severe: public disorder, economic

---

**C A S E
S T U D Y**

Politics in Action

The Power of Government

America's original constitution was the Articles of Confederation. Ratified during the American Revolution, it vested final (sovereign) authority in the states. The national government had only those powers granted it by the states and was dependent on them for funding. It did not have the power to tax. Lacking this power, as well as not having the power to regulate commerce among the states, the national government was unable after the Revolution to enact policies that would encourage the states to work together in their common interest. It didn't even have the funds necessary to establish an army and navy capable of defending the nation.

Q: What does the example of the Articles of Confederation tell you about the power of government? Some people say that "the best government is the least government." Does that claim make sense?

A R T I C L E S

o f

CONFEDERATION

A N D

PERPETUAL UNION

BETWEEN THE

S T A T E S

O F

©Everett Historical/Shutterstock

ASK YOURSELF: Is the question of government power a simple question of more power or less power? Or is it a question of whether government has the power necessary to carry out its responsibilities?

THE

FEDERALIST:

A COLLECTION OF

E S S A Y S,

WRITTEN IN FAVOUR OF THE

NEW CONSTITUTION,

AS AGREED-UPON BY THE

FEDERAL CONVENTION,

SEPTEMBER 17, 1787.

America's most noted essays were written to urge ratification of the Constitution. Penned mostly by James Madison and Alexander Hamilton, but written anonymously under the pen name Publius, they appeared in serial in two New York City papers. A year later, they were published together as *The Federalist.* More than a century elapsed before they came to be called *The Federalist Papers,* which is the common reference today. (*Source:* Library of Congress, Prints and Photographs Division [LC-USZ62-70508])

chaos, and an inadequate defense. Although the problems were widely recognized, many Americans in 1787 feared that a strong central government would eventually swallow up the states. An outspoken Anti-Federalist (as opponents of the Constitution were called) proclaimed: "[The states] will eventually . . . have power over little else than yoking hogs or determining the width of cart wheels."[5]

The challenge of providing a response to the Anti-Federalists fell to James Madison and Alexander Hamilton. During the ratification debate, they argued in a series of essays (the so-called *Federalist Papers*) that a federal system would protect liberty and moderate the power of government.

Protecting Liberty   Although theorists such as John Locke and Montesquieu had not proposed a division of power between national and local authorities as a means of protecting liberty, the framers argued that federalism was a part of the system of checks and balances.[6] Alexander Hamilton wrote in *Federalist* No. 28 that the American people could shift their loyalties back and forth between the national and state governments in order to keep each under control. "If [the people's] rights are invaded by either," Hamilton wrote, "they can make use of the other as the instrument of redress."

Moderating the Power of Government   To the Anti-Federalists, the sacrifice of the states' power to the nation was unwise. They argued that a distant national government could never serve the people's interests as well as the states could. Liberty *and* self-government, the Anti-Federalists argued, were enhanced by state-centered government. To support their case, they turned to the French theorist Montesquieu, who had claimed that a small republic is more likely than a large one to serve people's interests. When government encompasses a smaller area, he argued, its leaders are in closer touch with the people.

In *Federalist* No. 10, James Madison took issue with this claim. He argued that whether a government serves the common good is a function not of its size but of the range of interests that share political power. The problem with a small republic, Madison claimed, is that it can have a dominant faction—whether it be landholders, financiers, an impoverished majority, or some other group—that is strong enough to control government and use it for selfish purposes. A large republic is less likely to have an all-powerful faction. If financiers are strong in one area of a large republic, they are likely to be weaker elsewhere. The same will be true of farmers, merchants, laborers, and other groups. A large republic, Madison argued, would make it difficult for a single group to gain full control, which would force groups to share in the exercise of power. In making this claim, Madison was arguing not for central authority but for limited government, which he believed would result if power were shared widely. "Extend the sphere," said Madison, "and you take in a greater variety of parties and interests; you make it less probable that a majority of the whole will have a common motive to invade the rights of other citizens."

The Powers of the Nation and the States

The U.S. Constitution addresses the lawful authority of the national government, which is provided through *enumerated and implied powers.* Authority that is not granted to the national government is left—or "reserved"—to the states. Thus, the states have *reserved powers.*

Enumerated Powers and the Supremacy Clause   Article I of the Constitution grants to Congress 17 **enumerated (expressed) powers.** These powers were intended to establish a government strong enough to forge a union that was secure in its defense and stable in its economy. Congress's powers, for example, to regulate commerce among the states, to create a national currency, and to borrow money would provide a foundation for a sound national economy. Its power to tax, combined with its authority to establish an army and navy and to declare war, would enable it to provide for the common defense.

In addition, the Constitution prohibits the states from actions that would encroach on national powers. Article I, Section 10, prohibits the states from making treaties with other nations, raising armies, waging war, printing money, or entering into commercial agreements with other states without the approval of Congress.

The writers of the Constitution recognized that the lawful exercise of national authority would at times conflict with the laws of the states (see "Fake or Fact? Do States Have Final Authority over Marijuana Laws?"). In such instances, national law was intended to prevail. Article VI of the Constitution grants this dominance in the so-called **supremacy clause**, which provides that "the laws of the United States . . . shall be the supreme law of the land."

Implied Powers: The Necessary and Proper Clause   The writers of the Constitution recognized that government, if it was to be effective, had to be capable of adjusting to change. A weakness of the Articles was that the national government was prohibited from exercising powers not expressly granted it, which limited its ability to meet the country's changing needs after the end of the Revolutionary War. To avoid this problem with the new government, the framers included in Article I of the Constitution the **"necessary and proper" clause** or, as it later came to be known, the *elastic clause*. It gives Congress the power "to make all laws which shall be necessary and proper for carrying into execution the foregoing [enumerated] powers." This clause gives the national government **implied powers:** powers that are not listed in the Constitution but that are related to the exercise of listed powers.

Reserved Powers: The States' Authority   The supremacy and "necessary and proper" clauses were worrisome to the Anti-Federalists. The two clauses stoked their fear of an overly powerful national government because they provided a constitutional basis for expanding federal authority. Such concerns led them to demand a constitutional amendment that would protect states' rights and interests. Ratified in 1791 as the Tenth Amendment to the Constitution, it reads: "The powers not delegated to the United States by the Constitution, nor prohibited by it to the States, are reserved to the States." The states' powers under the U.S. Constitution are thus called **reserved powers**.

At the time of ratification, the Tenth Amendment was seen as strong protection of the states. It turned out to be something less. The logic of the Constitution is that the states control only those policies not controlled by the federal government. As a result, the constitutional issue in federal–state disputes is the limit on federal power. If an action is within the lawful power of the federal

Detecting Misinformation

Do States Have Final Authority over Marijuana Laws?

In recent years, numerous states have decriminalized the use of marijuana. More than half the states allow its use for medical purposes, although the medical conditions that qualify vary from one state to the next. A sixth of the states have authorized the recreational use of marijuana, and other states have downgraded marijuana possession in limited amounts from a felony to a misdemeanor or citation. States would appear from these examples to have final authority over the regulation of marijuana use.

©Emilio100/Shutterstock

Is that claim fact, or is it fake?

States do have final authority over marijuana use in a limited respect. The courts have held that, if a state decriminalizes marijuana, individuals cannot be convicted in state court for possession or use of marijuana that complies with state law—for example, possession of an amount of marijuana that does not exceed the state limit. However, marijuana use and possession are prohibited by federal law. The U.S. government classifies marijuana as an illegal controlled substance, and the Supreme Court in Gonzales v. Raich (2005) upheld that classification as a valid exercise of Congress's commerce power. Because of the Constitution's supremacy clause, federal law supersedes conflicting state law. Accordingly, residents of a state that has legalized marijuana could be charged with violating federal drug law. Nevertheless, the federal government has seldom pursued cases of marijuana use and possession where an individual is in compliance with state law. Law enforcement officers have what's called prosecutorial discretion. They have leeway in deciding which criminal offenses will get their attention and resources. Personal marijuana use is regarded as a low priority relative to other types of federal crime.

government, it's permissible. If it's outside the federal government's lawful power, it's not. This feature of the Constitution, as will be discussed later in the chapter, has enabled the national government to intrude on policy areas initially reserved to the states. Over time, there's been a **nationalization**[7] of America's federal system—a gradual shift in power from the states to the national government.

FEDERALISM IN HISTORICAL PERSPECTIVE

Since ratification of the Constitution over two centuries ago, no aspect of it has provoked more frequent or bitter conflict than federalism. By establishing two levels of sovereign authority, the Constitution created two centers of power and ambition, each of which was sure to claim disputed areas as belonging to it. Ambiguities in the Constitution have also contributed to conflict between the nation and the states. For example, the document does not specify the dividing line between *inter*state commerce (which the national government is empowered to regulate) and *intra*state commerce (which is reserved for regulation by the states).

Not surprisingly, federalism has been a contentious system, its development determined less by constitutional language than by the strength of the contending interests and the country's changing needs. Federalism can be viewed as having progressed through three historical eras, each of which has involved a different relationship between the nation and the states. At the same time, each era has ended with a national government that was stronger than at the start of the era.

An Indestructible Union (1789–1865)

The issue during the first era—which lasted from the time the Constitution went into effect (1789) until the end of the Civil War (1865)—was the Union's survival. Given America's state-centered history before the Constitution, it was inevitable that the states would dispute national policies that threatened their interests.

The Nationalist View: McCulloch v. Maryland   An early dispute over federalism arose when President George Washington's secretary of the treasury, Alexander Hamilton, proposed that Congress establish a national bank. Hamilton and his supporters claimed that because the federal government had constitutional authority to regulate currency, it had the "implied power" to establish a national bank. Thomas Jefferson, Washington's secretary of state, opposed the bank on the grounds that its activities would enrich the wealthy at the expense of ordinary people. Jefferson claimed the bank was unlawful because the Constitution did not expressly authorize it. Jefferson said: "I consider the foundation of the Constitution as laid on this ground that 'all powers not delegated to the United States by the Constitution, nor prohibited by it to the states, are preserved to the states or to the people.'"

Hamilton's argument prevailed, and Congress in 1791 established the First Bank of the United States, granting it a 20-year charter. Although Congress did not renew the bank's charter when it expired in 1811, Congress decided in 1816 to establish the Second Bank of the United States. State and local

Born in the West Indies and orphaned as a child, Alexander Hamilton was the most influential of the early American leaders who did not serve as president. As secretary of treasury in the Washington administration, he was the architect of the nation's early economic policies. He created a system of tariffs, established a national bank, encouraged manufacturing, and promoted trade among the states and with Europe. Hamilton's policies provided the foundation for America's economic prosperity. A French diplomat called Hamilton the greatest leader of his era, ranking him ahead even of Washington and Napoleon. This portrait was painted by John Trumbull, a contemporary of Hamilton, who was called "The Painter of the Revolution." (*Source:* Yale University Art Gallery)

banks did not want competition from a national bank and sought protection from their state legislatures. Several states, including Maryland, levied taxes on the national bank's operations within their borders, hoping to drive it out of existence by making it unprofitable. James McCulloch, who was in charge of the Maryland branch of the national bank, refused to pay the Maryland tax and the resulting dispute was heard by the Supreme Court.

The chief justice of the Supreme Court, John Marshall, was a nationalist, and in *McCulloch v. Maryland* (1819) the Court ruled decisively in favor of national authority. It was reasonable to infer, Marshall concluded, that a government with powers to tax, borrow money, and regulate commerce could establish a bank in order to exercise those powers effectively. Marshall's argument was a clear statement of *implied powers*—the idea that through the "necessary and proper" clause, the national government's powers extend beyond a narrow interpretation of its enumerated powers.

Marshall's ruling also addressed the meaning of the Constitution's supremacy clause. The state of Maryland had argued that, even if the national government had the authority to establish a bank, a state had the authority to tax it. The Supreme Court rejected Maryland's position, concluding that valid national law overrides conflicting state law. Because the national government had the power to create the bank, it also could protect the bank from state actions, such as taxation, that might destroy it.[8]

The *McCulloch* decision served as precedent for later rulings in support of national power. In *Gibbons v. Ogden* (1824), for example, the Marshall-led Court rejected a New York law granting one of its residents a monopoly on a ferry that operated between New York and New Jersey, concluding that New York had encroached on Congress's power to regulate commerce among the states. The Court asserted that Congress's commerce power was not limited to trade between the states, but to all aspects of that trade, including the transportation of goods. The power over commerce, the Court said, "is vested in Congress as absolutely as it would be in a single government."[9]

Marshall's opinions asserted that legitimate uses of national power took precedence over state authority and that the "necessary and proper" clause and the commerce clause were broad grants of power to the national government. As a nationalist, Marshall provided a legal basis for expanding federal power in ways that fostered the development of the United States as a nation rather than as a collection of states. As Justice Oliver Wendell Holmes Jr. noted a century later, the Union could not have survived if each state had been allowed to decide for itself which national laws it would obey.[10]

The States' Rights View: The Dred Scott Decision   Although John Marshall's rulings strengthened national authority, the issue of slavery posed a growing threat to the Union's survival. Westward expansion and immigration into the northern states were tilting power in Congress toward the free states, which increasingly signaled their determination to outlaw slavery at some future time. Fearing the possibility, southern leaders did what others have done throughout American history: They developed a constitutional interpretation fitted to their political purpose. John C. Calhoun declared that the United States was founded upon a "compact" between the states. The national government, he said, was "a government of states . . . not a government of individuals."[11] This line of reasoning led Calhoun to his famed "doctrine of nullification," which declared that a state has the constitutional right to nullify a national law.

In 1832, South Carolina invoked the doctrine, declaring "null and void" a national tariff law that favored northern interests. President Andrew Jackson called South Carolina's action "incompatible with the existence of the Union," a position that gained strength when Congress gave Jackson the authority to take military action against South Carolina. The state backed down after Congress agreed to changes in the tariff act. The dispute foreshadowed the

Civil War, a confrontation of far greater consequence. Although war would not break out for another three decades, the dispute over states' rights was intensifying.

The Supreme Court's infamous *Dred Scott* decision (1857), written by Chief Justice Roger Taney, an ardent states'-rights advocate, inflamed the dispute. Dred Scott, a slave who had lived in the North for four years, applied for his freedom when his master died, citing a federal law—the Missouri Compromise of 1820—that made slavery illegal in a free state or territory. The Supreme Court ruled against Scott, claiming that slaves were not citizens and therefore had no right to have their case heard in federal court. The Court also invalidated

Shown here is a slave auction house in Atlanta, Georgia. Conflict over the issue of slavery dominated the early decades of American federalism. Attempts, including the Missouri Compromise of 1820, to contain the issue did not succeed in preventing the outbreak of the Civil War. It was one of the bloodiest conflicts the world had yet known. Ten percent of fighting-age males died in the four-year war, and uncounted others were wounded. The death toll—618,000 (360,000 from the North, 258,000 from the South)—exceeded that of the number of Americans killed in World War I, World War II, the Korean War, and the Vietnam War combined. (*Source:* Library of Congress, Prints and Photographs Division [LC-DIG-stereo-1s02513])

the Missouri Compromise by holding that slaves were property, not people. Accordingly, since the Constitution prohibited Congress from interfering with owners' property rights, Congress lacked the power to outlaw slavery in any state.[12]

The Taney Court's decision provoked outrage in the North and contributed to a sectional split in the nation's majority party, the Democrats. In 1860, the Democratic Party's northern and southern wings nominated separate candidates for the presidency, which split the Democratic vote, enabling the Republican candidate, Abraham Lincoln, to win the presidency with only 40 percent of the popular vote. Lincoln had campaigned on a platform that called, not for an immediate end to slavery, but for its gradual abolition through payments to slaveholders. Nevertheless, southern states saw Lincoln's election as a threat to their way of life. By the time Lincoln took office, seven southern states, led by South Carolina, had left the Union. Four more states followed. In justifying his decision to wage war on the South, Lincoln said, "The Union is older than the states." In 1865, the superior strength of the Union army settled by force the question of whether national authority is binding on the states.

Dual Federalism and Laissez-Faire Capitalism (1865–1937)

Although the North's victory in the Civil War preserved the Union, new challenges to federalism were surfacing. Constitutional doctrine held that certain policy areas, such as interstate commerce and defense, belonged exclusively to the national government, whereas other policy areas, such as public health and intrastate commerce, belonged exclusively to the states. This doctrine, known as **dual federalism,** was based on the idea that a precise separation of national and state authority was both possible and desirable. "The power which one possesses," said the Supreme Court, "the other does not."[13]

American society, however, was in the midst of changes that raised questions about the suitability of dual federalism as a governing concept. The Industrial Revolution had given rise to large business firms, which were using their economic power to dominate markets and exploit workers. Government was the logical counterforce to this economic power. Which level of government—state or national—would regulate business?

Dual federalism became a barrier to an effective response by either level. From the 1860s through the 1930s, the Supreme Court held firm to the idea that a sharp dividing line existed between national and state authority and that neither level of government would be allowed to substantially regulate business. The era of dual federalism was characterized by business supremacy in commerce policy.

The Fourteenth Amendment and State Discretion   Ratified after the Civil War, the Fourteenth Amendment was intended to protect the newly freed slaves from discriminatory action by state governments. A state was prohibited from depriving "any person of life, liberty, or property without due process of law," from denying "any person within its jurisdiction the equal protection of the laws," and from abridging "the privileges or immunities of citizens of the United States."

Supreme Court rulings in subsequent decades, however, undermined the Fourteenth Amendment's promise of liberty and equality for all. In 1873, for example, the Court held that the Fourteenth Amendment did not substantially limit the power of the states to determine the rights to which their residents were entitled.[14] Then, in *Plessy v. Ferguson* (1896), the Court issued its infamous "separate but equal" ruling. A black man, Homer Adolph Plessy, had been convicted of violating a Louisiana law that required white and black citizens to ride in separate railroad cars. The Supreme Court upheld his conviction, concluding that state governments could force blacks to use separate facilities as long as the facilities were "equal" in quality to those reserved for use by whites. "If one race be inferior to the other socially," the Court argued, "the Constitution of the United States cannot put them on the same plane." The lone dissenting justice in the case, John Marshall Harlan, had harsh words for his colleagues: "Our Constitution is color-blind and neither knows nor tolerates classes among citizens. . . . The thin disguise of 'equal' accommodations . . . will not mislead anyone nor atone for the wrong this day done."[15]

With its *Plessy* decision, the Supreme Court endorsed government-based racial segregation in the South. Black children were forced into separate public schools that had few teachers. Public hospitals for blacks had few doctors and almost no medical supplies. The *Plessy* ruling had become a justification for the separate and *unequal* treatment of black Americans.[16]

Judicial Protection of Business   After the Civil War, the Supreme Court also gave nearly free rein to business. A majority of the Court's justices favored laissez-faire capitalism (which holds that business should be "allowed to act" without interference) and interpreted the Constitution in ways that restricted government's attempts to regulate business activity. In 1886, for example, the Court decided that corporations were "persons" within the meaning of the Fourteenth Amendment, and thereby were protected from substantial regulation by the states.[17] In other words, a constitutional amendment that had been enacted to protect newly freed slaves from being treated as second-class persons was ignored for that purpose but used instead to protect fictitious persons—business corporations.

The Court also weakened the national government's regulatory power by narrowly interpreting its commerce power. The Constitution's **commerce clause** says that Congress shall have the power "to regulate commerce" among the states. However, the clause does not spell out the economic activities included in the grant of power. When the federal government invoked the Sherman Antitrust Act (1890) in an attempt to break up the monopoly on the manufacture of sugar (a single company controlled 98 percent of it), the Supreme Court blocked the action, claiming that interstate commerce covered only the "transportation" of goods, not their "manufacture."[18] Manufacturing was deemed part of intrastate commerce and thus, according to the dual federalism doctrine, subject to state regulation only. However, because the Court had previously ruled that the states' regulatory powers were limited by the Fourteenth Amendment, the states were largely prohibited from regulating manufacturing.

Although some business regulation was subsequently allowed, the Court remained an obstacle to efforts to curb business practices. An example is the case of *Hammer v. Dagenhart* (1918), which arose from a 1916 federal law that prohibited the interstate shipment of goods produced by child labor. The law had public support in that factory owners were exploiting children, working them for long hours at low pay. Nevertheless, the Court invalidated the law, ruling that the Tenth Amendment gave the states, and not the federal government, the power to regulate factory practices.[19] However, in an earlier case, *Lochner v. New York* (1905), the Court had blocked states from regulating labor practices, concluding that such action violated factory owners' property rights.[20]

In effect, the Court had negated the principle of self-government. Neither the people's representatives in Congress nor those in the state legislatures were allowed to regulate business. America's corporations, with the Supreme Court as their protector, had control over economic policy.[21]

National Authority Prevails   The Democratic Party with its working-class base attacked the Court's position, and its candidates increasingly called for greater regulation of business and more rights for labor. Progressive Republicans like Theodore Roosevelt also fought against uncontrolled business power, but the Republican Party as a whole was ideologically committed to unregulated markets and to a small role for the federal government. Accordingly, when the Great Depression began in 1929, Republican president Herbert Hoover refused at first to use federal authority to put people back to work. Adhering to his party's free-market philosophy, Hoover argued that the economy would quickly rebound on its own and that government intervention would only delay the recovery.

In the 1932 election, voters elected as president the Democratic candidate, Franklin D. Roosevelt, who recognized that the economy had become a national one. More than 10 million workers (compared to 1 million in 1860) were employed by industry, whose products were marketed throughout the nation. Urban workers typically were dependent on landlords for their housing, on farmers and grocers for their food, and on corporations for their jobs. Farmers were more independent, but they too were increasingly a part of a larger economic network. Farmers' income depended on market prices and shipping and equipment costs.[22] Economic interdependence meant that, when the Great Depression hit in 1929, its effects could not be contained. At the depths of the Depression, one-fourth of the nation's workforce was jobless.

The states had responsibility for helping the poor, but they were nearly penniless because of declining tax revenues and the high demand for welfare assistance. Franklin Roosevelt's New Deal programs were designed to ease the hardship. The 1933 National Industrial Recovery Act (NIRA), for example, established a federal jobs program and enabled major industries to coordinate

The Great Depression cost a fourth of workers their jobs. States lacked the resources to meet the needs of the unemployed and the national government stepped in, resulting in a permanent shift of power within the American federal system. Shown here is a soup kitchen in Chicago set up to feed the unemployed. This particular kitchen was opened and funded by Chicago mob boss Al Capone as a way to enhance his public image. (*Source:* National Archives and Records Administration (541927))

their production decisions. Economic conservatives opposed such programs, accusing Roosevelt of leading the country into socialism. They found an ally in the Supreme Court. In *Schechter Poultry Corp. v. United States* (1935), just as it had done in previous New Deal cases, the Supreme Court in a 5-4 ruling declared the NIRA to be unconstitutional.[23]

Frustrated by the Court's rulings, Roosevelt in 1937 sought to exploit the fact that the Constitution gives Congress the power to determine the number of Supreme Court justices. Although the number had stayed at nine justices for seven decades, there was no constitutional barrier to increasing the number, which, in fact, had been altered several times in the nation's early years. Roosevelt asked Congress to pass legislation that would allow a president to nominate a new justice whenever a seated member passed the age of 70 1/2. Since some of the justices had already reached that age, the legislation would enable Roosevelt to appoint enough new justices to swing the Court to his side. Congress hesitated to do so, but the attempt ended with the "switch in time that saved nine." For reasons that have never been fully clear, Justice Owen Roberts switched sides on New Deal cases, giving the president a 5-4 majority on the Court.

Within months, the Court upheld the 1935 National Labor Relations Act, which gave employees the right to organize and bargain collectively.[24] In passing the legislation, Congress claimed that disputes between labor and management disrupted the nation's economy and therefore could be regulated through the commerce clause. In upholding the act, the Supreme Court endorsed Congress's reasoning.[25] In a subsequent ruling, the Court declared that Congress's commerce power is "as broad as the needs of the nation."[26] Congress would be allowed to regulate *all* aspects of commerce.

The Supreme Court had finally acknowledged the obvious: that an industrial economy is not confined by state boundaries and must be subject to national regulation. It was a principle that business also increasingly accepted. The nation's banking industry, for example, was saved from almost complete collapse in the 1930s by the creation of a federal regulatory agency, the Federal Deposit Insurance Corporation (FDIC). By insuring depositors' savings against loss, the FDIC stopped the panic withdrawals that had already ruined thousands of the nation's banks.

During the 1930s, the Supreme Court also loosened its restrictions on Congress's taxing and spending power.[27] In *United States v. Butler* (1936), the Court held that the Constitution's taxing and spending clause confers a grant of power that is "limited only by the requirement that it shall be exercised to provide for the general welfare of the United States."[28] General welfare is a very broad category, so broad in fact that Congress has used its spending power to involve itself in policy areas traditionally controlled by the states, as will be explained later in the chapter.[29]

CONTEMPORARY FEDERALISM (SINCE 1937)

Since the 1930s, relations between the nation and the states have changed so fully that dual federalism is no longer an accurate description of the American system. An understanding of today's federalism requires the recognition of two countervailing developments. The larger trend is a long-term *expansion* of national authority that began in the 1930s and continues to this day. The national government now operates in many policy areas that were once almost exclusively within the control of states and localities. The national government does not dominate in these policy areas, but it does play a significant role.

Many of the federal initiatives trace to the 1960s as part of President Lyndon Johnson's Great Society program. A Democrat in the mold of Franklin Roosevelt, Johnson believed that federal power should be used to assist the economically disadvantaged. However, unlike Roosevelt's New Deal, which dealt mostly with the economy, Johnson's Great Society dealt mostly with social welfare issues, which have an indirect constitutional basis. The Constitution does not grant Congress the power to regulate "social welfare." However, Congress may tax and spend for that purpose, which was the basis of the Great Society. Johnson's presidency was marked by dozens of new federal assistance grants to states for programs in health care, public housing, nutrition, public assistance, urban development, education, and other policy areas traditionally reserved to states and localities. Johnson's initiatives were both creative and coercive: creative in the large number of new federal programs and coercive in the restrictions placed on states and localities as a condition of their receipt of federal funds.

A smaller and more recent development is the attempt to "pass down" authority from the national level to the state and local levels in selected areas. Known as *devolution,* this development peaked in the 1990s. Although it has since receded, devolution remains a component of contemporary federalism, as is discussed later in the chapter.

Interdependency and Intergovernmental Relations

Interdependency is a reason national authority has increased substantially. Modern systems of transportation, commerce, and communication transcend local and state boundaries. These systems are national—and even international—in scope, which means that problems affecting Americans living in one part of the country will affect Americans living elsewhere. This situation has required Washington to assume a larger policy role. National problems typically require national solutions.

Interdependency has also encouraged national, state, and local policymakers to work together to solve policy problems. This collaborative effort has been described as **cooperative federalism**.[30] The difference between the older dual federalism and cooperative federalism has been likened to the difference between a layer cake, whose levels are separate, and a marble cake, whose levels flow together.[31]

Cooperative federalism is based on shared policy responsibilities rather than sharply divided ones. An example is the Medicaid program, which was created in 1965 as part of President Johnson's Great Society initiative and provides health care for the poor. The Medicaid program is jointly funded by the national and state governments, operates within eligibility standards set by the national government, and gives states some latitude in determining recipient eligibility and benefits. The Medicaid program is not an isolated example. Literally hundreds of policy programs today are run jointly by the national and state governments. In many cases, local governments are also involved. These programs have the following characteristics:

- Jointly funded by the national and state governments (and sometimes by local governments)
- Jointly administered, with the states and localities providing most of the direct service to recipients and a national agency providing general administration
- Jointly determined, with both state and national governments (and sometimes local governments) having a say in eligibility and benefit levels and with federal regulations, such as those prohibiting discrimination, imposing a degree of uniformity on state and local efforts

Cooperative federalism should not be interpreted to mean that the states are powerless and dependent.[32] States have retained most of their traditional authority in areas such as education, health, public safety, and roadways. In the area of public schools, for example, states determine the length of the school year, teachers' qualifications, and graduation requirements. Nevertheless, the federal government's involvement in policy areas traditionally reserved for the states has increased its policy influence and diminished state-to-state policy differences.

Government Revenues and Intergovernmental Relations

The interdependency of American society—the fact that developments in one area affect what happens elsewhere—is one of three major reasons the federal government's policy role has expanded greatly since the early 20th century. A second reason is that Americans expect government help. Whenever an area of the country is hit by a natural disaster, for example, its residents seek relief

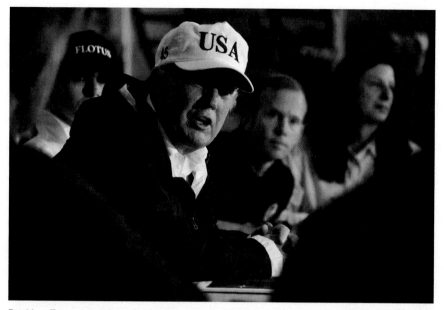

President Trump is being briefed by Coast Guard officials during a visit to Texas in the aftermath of Hurricane Harvey, which devastated parts of the Gulf Coast in 2017. Federal, state, and local officials worked together in the relief effort. *Cooperative federalism* is a term used to describe such joint efforts. (*Source:* Coast Guard photo by Petty Officer 1st Class Patrick Kelley)

from Washington. Moreover, whenever a federal program, such as student loans or farm supports, has been established, its recipients will fight to keep it. As a consequence, federal programs rarely end while new ones get added each year. A third reason is the federal government's superior taxing capacity. States and localities are in a competitive situation with regard to taxation. A state with high corporate and personal income taxes will lose firms and people to states with lower taxes. By contrast, firms and people are less likely to move to another country in search of lower taxes. The result is that the federal government raises more tax revenue than do all 50 states and the thousands of local governments combined (see Figure 3-2).

Fiscal Federalism   The federal government's revenue-raising advantage has made money a basis for relations between the national government and the states and localities. **Fiscal federalism** refers to the expenditure of federal funds on programs run in part through state and local governments.[33] The federal government provides some or all of the money through **grants-in-aid** (cash payments) to states and localities, which then administer the programs. The pattern of federal assistance to states and localities is shown in Figure 3-3. Federal grants-in-aid have increased dramatically since the mid-1950s. Roughly one in every five dollars spent by local and state governments in recent decades

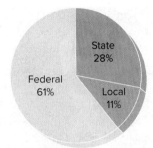

figure 3-2   FEDERAL, STATE, AND LOCAL SHARES OF GOVERNMENT TAX REVENUE

The federal government raises more tax revenues than do all state and local governments combined. (*Source:* Tax Policy Center, 2018.)

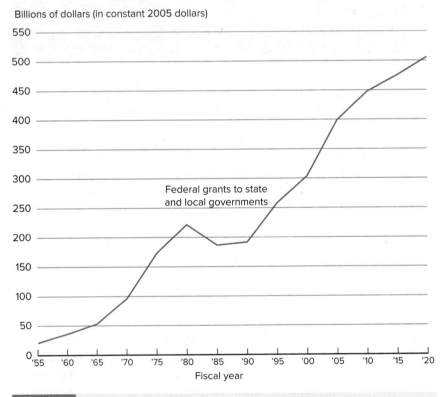

figure 3-3   FEDERAL GRANTS TO STATE AND LOCAL GOVERNMENTS

Federal aid to states and localities has increased dramatically since the 1950s. (*Source:* Office of Management and Budget (OMB), FY2017. Figures are based on constant (2005) dollars to control for effects of inflation. Figure for each year shown in graph is the average per year for previous five years. Figure for 2020 is based on OMB estimates) has been raised not by them, but by the federal government in Washington (see "How the 50 States Differ").

Cash grants to states and localities increase Washington's policy influence. State and local governments can reject a grant-in-aid, but if they accept it they must spend it in the way specified by Congress. Money designated for a school lunch program, for example, cannot be used for school construction or to pay teachers' salaries. Also, because most grants require states to contribute matching funds, the federal programs in effect determine how states will allocate some of their own tax dollars.

Nevertheless, federal grants-in-aid also serve the policy interests of state and local officials. Although they often complain that federal grants contain too many restrictions and infringe too much on their authority, most of them are eager to have the money because it permits them to offer services they could not otherwise afford. In 2015, for example, Congress passed a transportation bill that granted billions of dollars to states and localities to improve their roadways and mass transit systems. Said one observer about federal grants: "For governors, it's free money—they get the benefits and they don't have to pay the costs of raising the revenues."[34]

Categorical and Block Grants   State and local governments receive two major types of assistance—categorical grants and block grants—which differ in the degree to which Washington restricts their use. **Categorical grants,** the more restrictive type, can be used only for a designated activity. An example is Medicaid funds. They must be used to provide medical care to lower-income individuals. The funds can't be diverted to other health-related activities, such the training of medical students. **Block grants** are less restrictive. The federal government specifies the general area in which the funds must be used, but state and local officials select the specific projects. A block grant targeted for the education area, for example, might give state and local officials the authority to decide whether to use the money for school construction, computer equipment, teacher training, or some other education-related activity.

State and local officials prefer federal money that comes with fewer strings attached and thus favor block grants. In contrast, members of Congress have typically preferred categorical grants, because it gives them more control over how the money is spent. Most grants are of the categorical type, but block grants have increased in frequency since the 1980s as a result of a movement known as devolution.

Devolution

Devolution embodies the idea that American federalism can be strengthened by a partial shift in power from the federal government to state and local governments.[35] Devolution rests on a belief—held more strongly by Republicans

HOW THE 50 STATES DIFFER

CRITICAL THINKING THROUGH COMPARISONS

Federal Grants-in-Aid to the States

Federal assistance accounts for a significant share of general state revenue, but the variation is considerable. Mississippi, which gets 45 percent of its general revenue from the federal government, is at one extreme. Alaska, at 20 percent, is at the other extreme.

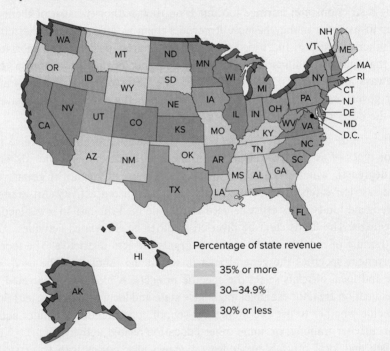

Percentage of state revenue

35% or more

30–34.9%

30% or less

Source: U.S. Census Bureau, 2016.

Q: Why do states in the South, where anti-Washington sentiment is higher than in most parts of the country, get more of their revenue from the federal government than do most other states?

A: Many federal grant programs are designed to assist low-income people, and poverty is more widespread in the South. Moreover, because southern states traditionally have provided fewer government services, federal grants constitute a larger proportion of their budgets.

than Democrats—that federal authority has intruded too far into areas belonging to state and local governments.

The expansion of the federal government's domestic policy role from the 1930s onward was largely initiated by Democratic lawmakers, with strong backing from the public. The New Deal and Great Society programs had broad public support at the outset. After the 1960s, however, public support for federal domestic spending declined. Some of the programs, particularly those providing welfare benefits to the poor, were widely seen as too costly, too bureaucratic, and too lax—there was a widespread perception that many welfare recipients were getting benefits they neither needed nor deserved. Republican leaders increasingly questioned the effectiveness of the programs, a position that meshed with the party's ideology of lower taxes and local control.

Upon taking office in 1981, Republican president Ronald Reagan proposed a "new federalism" that would give more control to states and localities. In issuing an executive order to initiate the change, Reagan said: "Federalism is rooted in the knowledge that our political liberties are best assured by limiting the size and scope of national government." Reagan advocated the use of block grants as opposed to categorical grants and prohibited federal agencies from submitting to Congress legislative proposals that would "regulate the states in ways that would interfere" with their "traditional governmental functions."

The Republican Revolution   When the Republican Party scored a decisive victory in the 1994 congressional elections, Speaker of the House Newt Gingrich declared that "1960s-style federalism is dead." Republican lawmakers proposed to cut some federal programs, but, even more, they sought to devolve power to the state and local levels. The GOP-controlled Congress grouped a

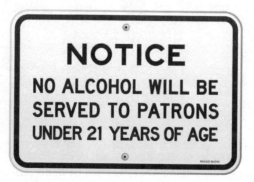

This familiar sign illustrates the power of fiscal federalism. In half the states until the 1980s, persons younger than 21 could legally buy alcohol. The policy changed when Congress enacted legislation requiring states to set the drinking age at 21 in order to receive their full allotment of federal highway funds. Although the states complained, the financial stakes were too high for them to maintain a lower age limit. (©Vitezslav Valka/Alamy)

number of categorical grants into block grants in order to give states more control over how the federal money would be spent. Congressional Republicans also passed legislation to reduce *unfunded mandates*–federal programs that require action by states or localities but provide no or insufficient funds to pay for it. The Clean Air Act of 1963, for example, required states to comply with national air quality standards but did not provide them the funds necessary to implement their plans.

The most significant change occurred in 1996, when Congress enacted the sweeping Welfare Reform Act. Opinion polls at the time indicated that a majority of Americans felt that government was spending too much on welfare and that too many welfare recipients were abusing the system. The Welfare Reform Act tightened spending and eligibility. The legislation's key element, the Temporary Assistance for Needy Families (TANF) block grant, ended the decades-old federal program that granted cash assistance to poor families with children. TANF restricts a family's eligibility for federal assistance to five years and gives states wide latitude in setting benefit levels. TANF also places states in charge of developing training programs that have the goal of moving people

In the 1990s, some policy responsibilities were shifted from the federal government to the states, a policy called devolution. The trend stalled after 2000 for several reasons, including the terrorist attacks of September 11, 2001, which required a national response. Included was a larger role for the federal government in domestic security. Shown here is a scene familiar to air travelers. Federal officers rather than state or local police are in charge of screening airline passengers. (©David R. Frazier Photolibrary, Inc.)

off welfare and into jobs. (TANF and other aspects of the 1996 welfare reform legislation are discussed further in later chapters.)[36]

The Continuing Issue of National Power   Proponents of devolution had some success but were unable to substantially shift power back to the states or stop the flow of power to the federal government. After the terrorist attacks on New York and Washington on September 11, 2001, there was an expansion of federal authority, including creation of the Department of Homeland Security, a cabinet-level federal agency with policing and emergency responsibilities traditionally belonging to states and localities. It was established during the presidency of George W. Bush, a Republican.

Then, in 2010, the Democrat-controlled Congress enacted the Affordable Care Act (ACA), which is one of the largest expansions of federal authority since the 1960s. Among its provisions is the requirement that business firms of a certain size provide their employees with health insurance or pay a penalty.

P A R T Y POLARIZATION

Conflicting Ideas

The Power of the Federal Government

Although the Republican and Democratic Parties have had opposing views on the power of the federal government since the 1930s, the difference has widened in recent years. Republicans have sought to roll back federal power, resisted at nearly every turn by Democrats. A recent example is the health care reform act that the Democrat-controlled Congress enacted in 2010 and that Republican lawmakers have since sought to overturn.

Differing opinions on federal power are not confined to lawmakers. As indicated by the graph below, Americans who identify with the Republican Party are far more likely than Democratic identifiers to believe that the federal government "has too much power."

Percentage who think federal government has "too much power"

Republicans	77%
Democrats	36%

Source: Gallup polls. Figures are averages for surveys conducted between 2009 and 2015.

Q: Can you think of a policy area in which Republicans are more likely than Democrats to support higher federal spending?

In its original form, it also required individuals to have insurance or pay a penalty, but the Republican-controlled Congress removed that provision in 2017. Before the ACA was enacted, states had charge of health insurance, controlling everything from the coverage plans that insurance companies could offer to the rates they could charge.

The partisan fight over the scope of federal power will continue, but one thing is certain: American federalism is, and will remain, a vastly different system than it was before the 1930s. The demands of contemporary life—a complex and integrated economy, a public that is insistent on its rights and accustomed to government services, and a global environment filled with challenges and opportunities—have combined to give the federal government a bigger role in federal-state relations. The change can be seen even in the structure of the federal government. Five cabinet departments—Health and Human Services, Housing and Urban Development, Transportation, Education, and Homeland Security—were created after the 1930s to administer federal programs in policy areas traditionally reserved to the states.

THE PUBLIC'S INFLUENCE: SETTING THE BOUNDARIES OF FEDERAL-STATE POWER

Public opinion has had a decisive influence on the ebb and flow of federal power during the past century. Every major change in federalism has been driven by a major shift in public support toward one level of government or the other.

During the Great Depression, when it was clear that the states would be unable to help, Americans turned to Washington for relief. For people without jobs, the fine points of the Constitution were of little consequence. President Roosevelt's New Deal programs, which offered both jobs and income security, were a radical departure from the past, but quickly gained public favor. A 1936 Gallup poll indicated, for example, that 61 percent of Americans supported Roosevelt's Social Security program, whereas only 27 percent opposed it.[37] The second great wave of federal social programs—Lyndon Johnson's Great Society—was also driven by public demands. Income and education levels had risen dramatically after World War II, and Americans wanted more and better services from government.[38] When the states were slow to respond, Americans pressured federal officials to act. The Medicare and Medicaid programs, which provide health care for individuals who are elderly and poor, respectively, are examples of the Johnson administration's response. A 1965 Gallup poll indicated that two-thirds of Americans approved of federal involvement in the provision of medical care, despite the fact that health was traditionally the states' responsibility.

Public opinion was also behind the rollback of federal authority in the 1990s. Polls showed that a majority of Americans had come to believe that the federal government had become too large and intrusive. Americans' dissatisfaction with federal programs and spending provided the springboard for the Republican takeover of Congress in the 1994 midterm elections, which led to policies aimed at devolving power to the states, including the widely popular 1996 Welfare Reform Act.[39]

The public's role in determining the boundaries between federal and state power would come as no surprise to the framers of the Constitution. For them, federalism was a pragmatic issue, one to be decided by the nation's needs rather than by inflexible rules. Alexander Hamilton suggested that Americans would shift their loyalties between the nation and the states according to whichever level seemed more likely to serve their immediate needs. James Madison said much the same thing in predicting that Americans would look to whichever level of government was more responsive to their interests. Indeed, each succeeding generation of Americans has seen fit to devise a balance of federal and state power suited to its needs.

SUMMARY

A leading feature of the American political system is its division of authority between a national government and state governments. The first U.S. government, established by the Articles of Confederation, was essentially a union of the states.

In establishing the basis for a stronger national government, the U.S. Constitution also made provision for safeguarding state interests. The result was the creation of a federal system (federalism) in which sovereignty was vested in both national and state governments. The Constitution enumerates the general powers of the national government and grants it implied powers through the "necessary and proper" clause. Other powers are reserved to the states by the Tenth Amendment.

From 1789 to 1865, the nation's survival was at issue. The states found it convenient at times to argue that their sovereignty took precedence over national authority. In the end, it took the Civil War to cement the idea that the United States was a union of people, not of states. From 1865 to 1937, federalism reflected the doctrine that certain policy areas were the exclusive responsibility of the national government, whereas responsibility in other policy areas belonged exclusively to the states. This constitutional position validated the laissez-faire doctrine that big business was largely beyond governmental control. It also allowed the states to discriminate against African Americans in their public policies. Federalism in a form recognizable today began to emerge in the 1930s.

In the areas of commerce, taxation, spending, civil rights, and civil liberties, among others, the federal government now plays an important role, one that is the inevitable consequence of the increasing complexity of American society and the interdependence of its people. National, state, and local officials now work closely together to solve the nation's problems, a situation known as cooperative federalism. Grants-in-aid from Washington to the states and localities have been the chief instrument of national influence. States and localities have received billions in federal assistance; in accepting federal money, they also have accepted both federal restrictions on its use and the national policy priorities that underlie the granting of the money.

Throughout the nation's history, the public through its demands on government has influenced the boundaries between federal and state power. The expansions of federal authority in the 1930s and the 1960s, for example, were driven by Americans' increased need for government assistance, whereas the devolutionary trend of the 1990s was sparked by Americans' sense that a rollback in federal power was desirable.

©gangliu10/Getty Images

CRITICAL THINKING ZONE

KEY TERMS

block grants (*p. 87*)
categorical grants (*p. 87*)
commerce clause (*p. 80*)
confederacy (*p. 68*)
cooperative federalism (*p. 84*)
devolution (*p. 87*)
dual federalism (*p. 78*)
enumerated (expressed) powers (*p. 71*)
federalism (*p. 67*)
fiscal federalism (*p. 85*)

grants-in-aid (*p. 85*)
implied powers (*p. 72*)
nationalization (*p. 73*)
"necessary and proper" clause (elastic clause) (*p. 72*)
reserved powers (*p. 72*)
sovereignty (*p. 66*)
supremacy clause (*p. 72*)
unitary system (*p. 67*)

APPLYING THE ELEMENTS OF CRITICAL THINKING

Conceptualizing: Distinguish between a federal system, a unitary system, and a confederacy. What circumstances led the framers of the Constitution to create a federal system?

Synthesizing: Contrast dual federalism and cooperative federalism. Is the distinction between a layer cake and a marble cake helpful in understanding the difference between dual federalism and cooperative federalism?

Analyzing: How have the federal government's superior taxing policy and the economic interdependency of the American states contributed over time to a larger policy role for the national government? What role have federal grants-in-aid played in the expansion of federal authority?

EXTRA CREDIT

A Book Worth Reading: Ron Chernow, *Alexander Hamilton* (New York: Penguin, 2005). Written by a Pulitzer Prize-winning historian, this biography examines the life of Alexander Hamilton, including the role of his economic policies in America's development.

A Website Worth Visiting: http://avalon.law.yale.edu/subject_menus/fed.asp. This Yale Law School site includes a documentary record of the *Federalist Papers*, the Annapolis convention, the Articles of Confederation, the Madison debates, and the U.S. Constitution.

PARTICIPATE!

The U.S. federal system of government offers an array of channels for political participation. Vital governing decisions are made at the national, state, and local levels, all of which provide opportunities for citizens to make a difference and also to build skills—such as public speaking and working with others—that will prove valuable in other areas of life. You have a participatory arena close at hand: your college campus. Most colleges and universities support a variety of activities in which students can engage. Student government is one such opportunity; another is the student newspaper. Most colleges and universities also offer a wide range of groups and sponsored programs, from debate clubs to fraternal organizations. If you are not now active in campus groups, consider joining one. If you join—or if you already belong to—such a group, take full advantage of the participatory opportunities it provides.

4
CHAPTER

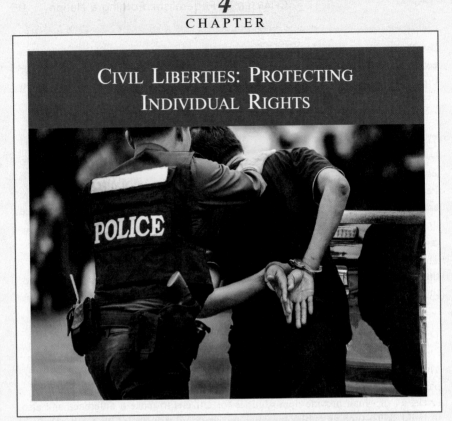

CIVIL LIBERTIES: PROTECTING INDIVIDUAL RIGHTS

❝ A bill of rights is what the people are entitled to against every government on earth, general or particular, and what no just government should refuse, or rest on inference. **❞**

THOMAS JEFFERSON[1]

Without a warrant from a judge, the police and the FBI had secretly attached a GPS tracking device to Antoine Jones's car and knew exactly where it was at any time of the day or night. For a month, they monitored the car's every turn. They subsequently arrested Jones on charges of conspiracy to sell drugs. The evidence obtained through the tracking device helped prosecutors convict him, and he was sentenced to life in prison.

Jones appealed his conviction and won a temporary victory when a federal appellate court—noting that individuals are protected by the Fourth Amendment from "unreasonable searches and seizures"—concluded that the officers should have sought a warrant from a judge, who would have decided whether they had sufficient cause to justify a search of Jones's possessions, much less the placing of a tracking device on his car.

In a unanimous 9-0 vote, the Supreme Court in *United States v. Jones* (2012) upheld the lower court's ruling. The Court rejected the government's argument that attaching a small device to a car's undercarriage was too trivial an act to constitute an "unreasonable search." The government had also claimed that anyone driving a car on public streets can expect to be monitored, even continuously in some circumstances—after all, police had legally been "tailing" suspects for decades. The Court rejected those arguments, though the justices disagreed on exactly why the Constitution prohibits what the officers had done. Five justices said that the Fourth Amendment's protection of "persons, houses, papers, and effects" reasonably extends to private property such as an automobile. For them, the fact that the officers had placed a tracking device on the suspect's property without a warrant invalidated the evidence. Four justices went further, saying that the officers' actions intruded not only on the suspect's property rights but also on his "reasonable expectation of privacy." At its core, they said, the Fourth Amendment "protects people, not places."[2]

As the case illustrates, issues of individual rights have become increasingly complex. The framers of the Constitution could not possibly have envisioned a time when technology would have enabled authorities to electronically track people's locations. The framers understood that authorities would sometimes be tempted to snoop on people, which is why they wrote the Fourth Amendment. At the same time, the amendment protects Americans not from *all* searches but from *unreasonable* searches. The public would be unsafe if law officials could never track a suspect. Yet citizens would forfeit their privacy if police could track at will anyone of their choosing. The challenge for a civil society is to establish a level of police authority that meets the demands of public safety without infringing unduly on personal freedom. The balance point, however, is always subject to dispute. In this particular case, the Supreme Court sided with the accused. In other cases, it has sided with law enforcement officials.

This chapter examines issues of **civil liberties**—specific individual rights, such as the right to a fair trial, that are constitutionally protected against infringement by government. Although the term *civil liberties* is sometimes used interchangeably with the term *civil rights,* they differ. Civil rights (which will be examined in Chapter 5) are a question of whether members of differing groups—racial, sexual, religious, and the like—are treated equally by government and, in some cases, by private parties. By contrast, civil liberties refer to individual rights, such as freedom of speech and the press. Civil liberties are the subject of this chapter, which focuses on these points:

• *Freedom of expression is the most basic of democratic rights, but like all rights, it is not unlimited.*

- *"Due process of law" refers to legal protections (primarily procedural safeguards) designed to ensure that individual rights are respected by government.*
- *Over the course of the nation's history, Americans' civil liberties have been expanded in law and been more fully protected by the courts.* Of special significance has been the Supreme Court's use of the Fourteenth Amendment to protect individual rights from action by state and local governments.
- *Individual rights are constantly being weighed against the collective interests of society.* All political institutions are involved in this process, as is public opinion, but the judiciary plays a central role and is the institution that is typically most protective of civil liberties.

THE BILL OF RIGHTS, THE FOURTEENTH AMENDMENT, AND SELECTIVE INCORPORATION

As was explained in Chapter 2, the Constitution's failure to enumerate individual freedoms led to demands for the **Bill of Rights**. Ratified in 1791, these first 10 amendments to the Constitution list a set of rights that the federal government is obliged to protect. Among them are freedoms of speech, press, assembly, and religion (First Amendment); the right to bear arms (Second Amendment); protection against unreasonable search and seizure (Fourth Amendment); protection against self-incrimination and double jeopardy (Fifth Amendment); right to a jury trial, to an attorney, and to confront witnesses (Sixth Amendment); and protection against cruel and unusual punishment (Eighth Amendment).

At the time the Bill of Rights was adopted, it applied only to action by the federal government and not to action by the states, a position the Supreme Court affirmed a few decades later.[3] Today, however, most of the rights contained in the Bill of Rights are also protected from action by the state governments, a development resulting from adoption of the Fourteenth Amendment in the aftermath of the Civil War.

Soon after the war, several southern states enacted laws that denied newly freed slaves their rights, including the right to own property and to travel freely. Congress responded by proposing a constitutional amendment designed to protect their rights. The former Confederate states, with the exception of Tennessee, refused to ratify it. Congress then passed the Reconstruction Act, which placed the southern states under military rule until they did so. In 1868, the Fourteenth Amendment was ratified. It includes a **due process clause** that says "No State shall . . . deprive any person of life, liberty, or property, without due process of law."

Initially the Supreme Court largely ignored the due process clause, allowing states to decide for themselves what rights their residents would have. In 1925, however, the Court changed course by invoking the Fourteenth Amendment in a case involving state government. Although the Court upheld New York's law making it illegal to advocate the violent overthrow of the U.S. government, it ruled in *Gitlow v. New York* that states do not have total control over what their residents can legally say. The Court said: "For present purposes we may and do assume that freedom of speech and of the press—which are protected by the First Amendment from abridgement by Congress—are among the fundamental personal rights and 'liberties' protected by the due process clause of the Fourteenth Amendment from impairment by the states."[4]

The ruling marked a fundamental shift in constitutional doctrine. In essence, the Court had concluded that a right protected by the Bill of Rights from action by the federal government was now also protected from action by individual states. Shortly thereafter, the Court in a series of cases applied the new doctrine to other First Amendment rights. The Court invalidated state laws restricting expression in the areas of speech (*Fiske v. Kansas*), press (*Near v. Minnesota*), religion (*Hamilton v. Regents, University of California*), and assembly and petition (*DeJonge v. Oregon*).[5] The *Near* decision is the best known of these rulings. Jay Near was the publisher of a Minneapolis weekly newspaper that regularly made defamatory statements about blacks, Jews, Catholics, and labor union leaders. His paper was closed down on the basis of a Minnesota law banning "malicious, scandalous, or defamatory" publications. Near appealed to the Supreme Court, which ruled in his favor, saying that the Minnesota law was "the essence of censorship."[6]

Three decades later, the Supreme Court extended the principle to include the rights of the criminally accused. The breakthrough case was *Mapp v. Ohio* (1961). Police had forcibly entered the home of Dollree Mapp, saying they had a tip she was harboring a fugitive. They didn't find the suspect but handcuffed her anyway and rummaged through her possessions, where they found obscene photographs. Mapp was convicted of violating an Ohio law prohibiting the possession of such material. The Supreme Court overturned her conviction, ruling that police had acted unconstitutionally, citing the Fourth Amendment prohibition on unreasonable searches and seizures. The Court held that evidence acquired through an unconstitutional search cannot be used to obtain a conviction in state courts.[7]

During the 1960s, the Court also ruled that defendants in state criminal proceedings must be provided a lawyer in felony cases if they cannot afford to hire one,[8] cannot be compelled to testify against themselves,[9] have the right to remain silent and to have legal counsel at the time of arrest,[10] have the right to confront witnesses who testify against them,[11] must be granted a speedy trial,[12] have the right to a jury trial in criminal proceedings,[13] and cannot be subjected to double jeopardy.[14]

In these various rulings, the Court was applying what came to be called the doctrine of **selective incorporation**—the use of the Fourteenth Amendment to apply selected provisions of the Bill of Rights to the states. In its *Mapp* ruling, for example, the Court incorporated the Fourth Amendment protection against unreasonable search and seizure into the Fourteenth Amendment, thereby

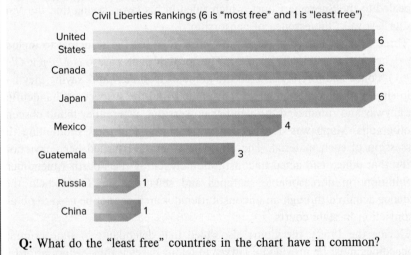

HOW THE U.S. DIFFERS
CRITICAL THINKING THROUGH COMPARISONS

Civil Liberties

Individual rights are basic to the American governing system. The government's ability to restrict free expression is limited, and the individual's right to a fair trial is protected by substantial due process guarantees, such as the right to an attorney. According to Freedom House, an independent organization that tracks civil liberties, the United States is among the "most free" nations. Freedom House bases its rankings on four areas: free expression, organizational rights, rule of law, and personal autonomy. The chart shows the latest Freedom House rankings of selected countries.

Civil Liberties Rankings (6 is "most free" and 1 is "least free")

Country	Ranking
United States	6
Canada	6
Japan	6
Mexico	4
Guatemala	3
Russia	1
China	1

Q: What do the "least free" countries in the chart have in common?

A: The "least free" countries in the chart are characterized by one-party rule.

protecting it from infringement by states and localities. (The incorporation process is selective in that the Supreme Court has chosen to protect some Bill of Rights guarantees from state action but not others. Even today, for example, the Seventh Amendment right to a jury trial in civil cases is not required of the states.)

Selective incorporation through the Fourteenth Amendment's due process clause has been of utmost importance. Because states and localities bear most of the responsibility for maintaining public order and safety, they are the authorities most likely to act in ways that infringe on people's rights. If they were allowed to determine for themselves what these rights mean in practice—for example, how far local police can go in interrogating suspects—Americans' rights would be at risk or, in some locations, ignored. As it stands, nearly all freedoms in the Bill of Rights are now national rights and under the protection of the federal courts.

In the sections that follow, the law and practice of Americans' civil liberties will be examined, starting with rights protected by the First Amendment.

FREEDOM OF EXPRESSION

The First Amendment provides for **freedom of expression**—the right of individual Americans to communicate thoughts of their choosing (see Table 4-1). Some forms of expression are not protected by the First Amendment because the courts have concluded that they fall outside the civic realm. Some forms of "commercial speech" are of this type. For example, pharmaceutical companies in their public advertising are required by law to disclose the harmful side

table 4-1 BILL OF RIGHTS: A SELECTED LIST OF FIRST AMENDMENT PROTECTIONS
First Amendment
Speech: You are free to say almost anything except that which is obscene, slanders another person, or has a high probability of inciting others to take imminent lawless action.
Press: You are free to write or publish almost anything except that which is obscene, libels another person, seriously endangers military action or national security, or has a high probability of inciting others to take imminent lawless action.
Assembly: You are free to assemble, although government may regulate the time and place for reasons of public convenience and safety, provided such regulations are applied evenhandedly to all groups.
Religion: You are protected from having the religious beliefs of others imposed on you, and you are free to believe what you like.

effects of drugs. Obscene forms of sexual expression—child pornography as an example—also do not have First Amendment protection.[15]

The First Amendment had an inauspicious beginning. Although it prohibits Congress from abridging freedom of expression, Congress ignored the restriction in passing the Sedition Act of 1798, which made it a crime to print harshly critical newspaper stories about the president or other national officials. Thomas Jefferson called the Sedition Act an "alarming infraction" of the Constitution and, upon replacing John Adams as president in 1801, pardoned those who had been convicted under it. However, the Sedition Act was not ruled on by the Supreme Court, which left open the question of whether Congress had the power to restrict free expression and, if so, how far its power extended.

Today, free expression is vigorously protected by the courts. Like other rights, it is not absolute in practice. Free expression does not entitle individuals to say whatever they want to whomever they want. Free expression can be denied, for example, if it endangers national security, wrongly damages the reputation of others, or deprives others of their basic rights. Nevertheless, in nearly every circumstance Americans can freely express their political views without fear of government interference or retribution.

Free Speech

Until the 20th century, free expression was rarely at issue in the United States. However, as the country began to get enmeshed in world affairs and face threats from abroad, the government started to restrict expression that it believed was a danger to national security. A first restriction was the 1917 Espionage Act, which prohibited forms of dissent that could have harmed the nation's effort in World War I.

The legislation became the object of the first-ever Supreme Court free-expression decision. In *Schenck v. United States* (1919), the Supreme Court upheld the conviction of defendants who had distributed leaflets urging draft-age men to refuse induction into the military service. Writing for a unanimous Court, Justice Oliver Wendell Holmes upheld the constitutionality of the Espionage Act, saying that Congress had the authority to restrict expression that posed "a clear and present danger" to the nation's security. In a famous passage, Holmes argued that not even the First Amendment would permit a person to falsely yell "Fire!" in a crowded theater and create a panic that could kill or injure innocent people.[16]

Although the *Schenck* decision upheld a law that limited free expression, it also established a constitutional standard—the **clear-and-present-danger test**—for determining when government could legally do so. To meet the test, the government has to clearly demonstrate that spoken or written expression presents a clear and

In this U.S. Army recruitment poster from the World War I, an ape in a German helmet and with the German word *Kultur* on his club is shown clutching Lady Liberty (the Statue of Liberty figure). During the war, the U.S. government placed limits on forms of expression deemed a threat to the war effort. Ever since, the balance between individual rights and national security has been a source of controversy. A recent dispute is the National Security Agency (NSA) surveillance program that collects metadata on Americans' phone calls and e-mails in order to detect signs of terrorist activity. (*Source:* Library of Congress, Prints and Photographs Division [LC-DIG-ds-03216])

present danger before it can prohibit the expression. (The use of a "test" to judge the limits of government's authority is a common practice of the Supreme Court.)

In the early 1950s, the Court applied the clear-and-present-danger test in upholding the convictions of 11 members of the U.S. Communist Party who had been prosecuted under a federal law (the Smith Act of 1940) that made it illegal to advocate the forceful overthrow of the U.S. government.[17] The Court concluded that "the gravity of the 'evil' . . . justifies such invasion of free speech as necessary to avoid the danger."

By the late 1950s, Americans had come to realize that fears of a communist takeover of the U.S. government had been greatly exaggerated. The Supreme Court abruptly switched its position, concluding that words alone were not a threat to the nation's security.[18] Ever since, it has held that national security must be clearly and substantially endangered before government can lawfully prohibit citizens from speaking out. Because the spoken word does not ordinarily pose that kind of threat, Americans are largely free to say what they want about politics. Over the past six decades, which includes the Vietnam and Iraq Wars, not a single individual has been convicted solely for criticizing the government's war policies. (Some dissenters have been found guilty on other grounds, such as for assaulting a police officer.)

In addition to curbing the federal government's attempts to limit free speech, the Supreme Court has moved to protect speech from actions by the states. A defining case was *Brandenburg v. Ohio* (1969). In a speech at a Ku Klux Klan rally, Clarence Brandenburg said that "revenge" might have to be taken if the national government "continues to suppress the white Caucasian race." He was convicted under an Ohio law, but the Supreme Court overturned the conviction, saying a state cannot prohibit speech that advocates the unlawful use of force unless it meets a two-part test: First, the speech must be "directed at inciting or producing imminent lawless action" and, second, it must be "likely to produce such action."[19] This test—the likelihood of **imminent lawless action**—is an imposing barrier to any government attempt to restrict speech. It is extremely rare for words alone to lead others to engage in rioting or other immediate forms of lawless action.

The imminent lawless action test gives Americans the freedom to express nearly any political opinion they want, including "hate speech." In a unanimous 1992 opinion, the Court struck down a St. Paul, Minnesota, ordinance making it a crime to engage in speech likely to arouse "anger or alarm" on the basis of "race, color, creed, religion or gender." The Court said that the First Amendment prohibits government from "silencing speech on the basis of its content."[20] (This protection of hate *speech* does not extend to hate *crimes,* such as assault, motivated by racial or other prejudice. A Wisconsin law that allowed lengthier sentences for hate crimes was challenged as a violation of the First Amendment. In a unanimous 1993 opinion, the Court said that the law was aimed, not at free speech, but at "conduct unprotected by the First Amendment.")[21]

Few cases illustrate more clearly the extent to which Americans are free to speak their minds than does *Snyder v. Phelps* (2011). Pastor Fred Phelps of the Westboro Baptist Church (WBC) led a protest demonstration at the funeral of Matthew Snyder, a U.S. Marine killed in Iraq. Like their protests at other military funerals, WBC's protest at Snyder's funeral service was directed at what WBC claims is America's tolerance of gays and lesbians. Displaying signs such as "Fag troops" and "Thank God for dead soldiers," the protesters were otherwise orderly and stayed three blocks away from the memorial service. Snyder's father sued WBC for "emotional distress" and was awarded $5 million in a federal trial. In an 8–1 decision, the Supreme Court overturned the award, holding that WBC's protest, although "hurtful," was protected by the First Amendment.[22]

The Supreme Court's protection of **symbolic speech** (action, not words) has been nearly as substantial as its protection of verbal speech. In 1989, for example, the Court ruled that the symbolic burning of the American flag is a lawful form of expression. The ruling came in the case of Gregory Lee Johnson, who had set fire to a flag outside the hall in Dallas where the 1984 Republican National Convention was being held. The Supreme Court rejected the state of Texas's argument that flag burning is, in every instance, an imminent danger to public safety. "If there is a bedrock principle underlying the First Amendment," the Court said, "it is that the Government may not prohibit the expression of an idea simply because society finds the idea itself offensive or disagreeable."[23]

In general, the Supreme Court has held that government regulation of the *content* of a message is unconstitutional. In the flag-burning case, for example, Texas was regulating the content of the message—contempt for the flag and

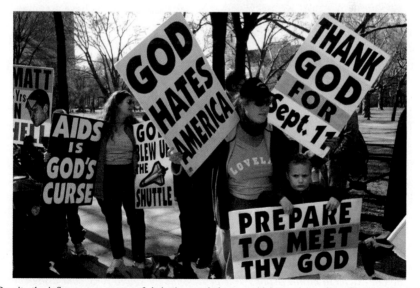

Despite the inflammatory nature of their signs and slogans, which members of the Westboro Baptist Church have displayed at numerous military funerals and other events, the Supreme Court has ruled that their actions are protected by the First Amendment. (©Enigma/Alamy)

the principles it represents. Texas could not have been regulating the act itself, for the Texas government's own method of disposing of worn-out flags is to burn them.

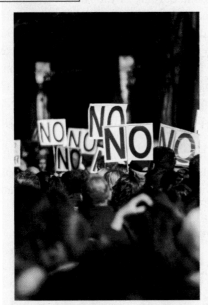

F A K E	**Detecting Misinformation**
or	
F A C T	

Do You Have a Right to Speak Freely on Campus?

The Supreme Court holds that there are few limits on government's ability to limit free expression. Government is not allowed to regulate the content of speech—your opinion has as much protection as anyone else's. At many colleges, both public and private, there have been instances when students have sought to prevent invited speakers from delivering a talk because they disagree with what the speaker represents or is likely to say. Some students have assumed that their right of free expression includes the right to shout down or disrupt a speaker with whom they disagree.

©Eric Crama/Shutterstock

Is that claim fact, or is it fake?

Students have substantial free speech rights, but they're not as broad as in some settings. The Supreme Court has ruled that speech in a school setting can be limited if it is disruptive of "the educational mission." Moreover, students are governed by their college's code of conduct. Speech that violates the code is not typically protected. Students who violate it can be subject to disciplinary action by their college, though they have due process rights, including the right to be informed of the charge and the basis for it, as well as an opportunity to contest it. Finally, even free speech rights that are protected in a campus setting do not extend to hostile actions. It is permissible for you to voice your disagreement with the opinions of others but not to physically threaten them.

Free Assembly

In a key case involving freedom of assembly, the U.S. Supreme Court in 1977 upheld a lower-court ruling against local ordinances of Skokie, Illinois, that had been invoked to prevent a parade there by the American Nazi Party.[24] Skokie had a large Jewish population, including survivors of Nazi Germany's concentration camps. The Supreme Court held that the right of free assembly takes precedence over the mere *possibility* that the exercise of that right might have undesirable consequences. Before government can lawfully prevent a speech or rally, it must demonstrate that the event will likely cause harm and must show that it lacks an alternative way (such as assigning police officers to control the crowd) to prevent the harm from happening.

The Supreme Court has recognized that freedom of speech and assembly may conflict with the routines of daily life. Accordingly, individuals do not have the right to hold a public rally at a busy intersection during rush hour or the right to turn up the volume on loudspeakers to the point where they can be heard miles away. The Court allows public officials to regulate the time, place, and conditions of public assembly, provided the regulations are reasonable and are applied fairly to all groups, whatever their issue.[25]

Press Freedom and Libel Law

Freedom of the press also receives strong judicial protection. In *New York Times Co. v. United States* (1971), the Court ruled that the *Times*'s publication of the "Pentagon Papers" (secret government documents revealing that officials had deceived the public about aspects of the Vietnam War) could not be blocked by the government, which claimed that publication would harm the war effort. The documents had been obtained illegally by antiwar activists, who gave them to the *Times*. The Court ruled that "any system of prior restraints" on the press is unconstitutional unless the government can provide a compelling reason why the material should not be published.[26]

The unacceptability of **prior restraint**—government prohibition of speech or publication before it occurs—is basic to the current doctrine of press freedom. The Supreme Court has said that attempts by government to prevent expression carry "a 'heavy presumption' against its constitutionality."[27] One exception is wartime reporting; in some circumstances, the government can censor news reports that contain information that could compromise a military operation or risk the lives of American troops.

The constitutional right of free expression is not a legal license to avoid responsibility for the impact of what is said or written. Although news outlets and individuals cannot ordinarily be stopped from speaking out, they can be held responsible for the consequences of what they say. If false information harmful to a person's reputation is published (**libel**) or spoken (**slander**), the injured party can sue for damages. Nevertheless, slander and libel laws in the United States are based on the assumption that society has an interest in encouraging news organizations and citizens to express themselves freely. Accordingly, public officials can be criticized nearly at will without fear that the writer or speaker will have to pay them damages for slander or libel. (The courts are less protective of the writer or speaker when allegations are made about a private citizen. What is said about private individuals is considered to be less basic to the democratic process than what is said about public officials.)

The Supreme Court has held that factually accurate statements, no matter how damaging to a public official's reputation, are a protected form of expression.[28] Even false statements enjoy considerable legal protection. In *New York Times Co. v. Sullivan* (1964), the Supreme Court overruled an Alabama state court that had found the *New York Times* guilty of libel for publishing an advertisement that claimed Alabama officials had mistreated civil rights activists. Although only some of the allegations were true, the Supreme Court backed the *Times,* saying that libel of a public official requires proof of actual malice, which was defined as a knowing or reckless disregard for the truth.[29] It is hard to prove that a news outlet recklessly or deliberately published a false accusation. In fact, no federal official has won a libel judgment against a news outlet in the more than five decades since the *Sullivan* ruling.

FREEDOM OF RELIGION

Free religious expression is the forerunner of free political expression, at least within the English tradition of limited government. England's Glorious, or Bloodless, Revolution of 1689 resulted in the Act of Toleration, which gave members of Protestant sects the right to worship freely and publicly. The First Amendment reflects this tradition; it protects religious freedom, as well as political expression.

In regard to religion, the First Amendment reads: "Congress shall make no law respecting an establishment of religion, or prohibiting the free exercise thereof." Two clauses are contained in those words, one referring to the "establishment of religion" (the establishment clause) and one referring to the "free exercise" of religion (the free-exercise clause).

The Establishment Clause

The **establishment clause** has been interpreted by the Supreme Court to mean that government may not favor one religion over another or support religion over no religion. (This position contrasts with that of a country such as England, where Anglicanism is the official, or "established," state religion, though no religion is prohibited.)

To this end, the Court has largely prohibited religious practices in public schools. A leading case was *Engel v. Vitale* (1962), which held that the establishment clause prohibits the reciting of prayers in public schools.[30] A year later, the Court struck down Bible readings in public schools.[31] Efforts to bring religion into the schools in less direct ways have also been invalidated. For example, an Alabama law attempted to circumvent the prayer ruling by permitting public schools to set aside one minute each day for silent prayer or meditation. In 1985, the Court declared the law unconstitutional, ruling that "government must pursue a course of complete neutrality toward religion."[32]

Families have different beliefs about religion, which is a reason the Supreme Court has blocked schools from imposing particular religious beliefs on children, who are more vulnerable than adults to what those in authority tell them is true. The Court has been less strict about the expression of religious messages in other contexts. Congress and state legislatures, for example, open their sessions with a prayer, which the Court accepts as a long-standing tradition.

The Court also takes tradition into account in determining whether religious displays on public property will be allowed. Because of the prominence of religion in American life, many public buildings display religious symbols. For instance, a statue of Moses holding the Ten Commandments stands in the rotunda of the Library of Congress building, which opened in 1897. Legal challenges to such displays have rarely succeeded.[33] In contrast, the Supreme Court in 2005 ordered the removal of displays of the Ten Commandments on the walls of two Kentucky courthouses. The displays were recent and had initially hung alone on the courtroom walls. Only after county officials were sued did they place a few historical displays alongside the religious ones. The Supreme Court concluded that the officials had a religious purpose in mind when they erected the displays and had to remove them.[34]

Although the Court can be said to have applied the *wall of separation doctrine* (a strict separation of church and state) in these rulings, it has also relied upon what is called the *accommodation doctrine*. This doctrine allows government to aid religious activity if no preference is shown toward a particular religion and if the assistance is of a nonreligious nature. In applying the doctrine, the Court at times has used a test articulated in *Lemon v. Kurtzman* (1971), a case involving state funding of the salaries of religious school instructors who teach secular subjects, such as math and English. In its ruling, the Court articulated a three-point test that has come to be known as the **Lemon** test. Government policy must meet all three conditions for it to be lawful: First, the policy must have a nonreligious purpose; second, its principal or primary effect must be one that neither advances nor inhibits religion; finally, the policy must not foster "an excessive government entanglement with religion."[35]

In the *Lemon* case, the Court held that state funding of the salaries of religious school teachers failed the test. The Court concluded that such payments involve "excessive government entanglement with religion" because an instructor, even though teaching a subject such as math or science, could use the classroom as a time to engage in religious teaching. In contrast, the Court in another case allowed states to pay for math, science, and other secular textbooks used in church-affiliated schools, concluding that the textbooks contained little if any religious content.[36]

The Supreme Court's biggest departure from its wall-of-separation doctrine came in a 2002 decision (*Zelman v. Simmons-Harris*), which upheld an Ohio law that allows students in Cleveland's failing public schools to receive a tax-supported voucher to attend a private or religious school. Even though 90 percent of the vouchers were being used to attend religious schools, the Court's majority said that the program did not violate the establishment clause because students had a choice between secular and religious education. Four members of the Court voted against the ruling. Justice John Paul Stevens said the ruling went beyond accommodation and had in effect removed a "brick from the wall that was once designed to separate religion from government."[37]

The Free-Exercise Clause

The First and Fourteenth Amendments also prohibit government interference with the free exercise of religion. The **free-exercise clause** has been interpreted to mean that Americans are free to hold religious beliefs of their choosing. Americans are not always free, however, to act on their beliefs. The Supreme Court has allowed government interference when the exercise of religious beliefs conflicts with otherwise valid law. An example is court-ordered medical care for gravely ill children whose parents have denied them treatment on religious grounds.

In a potentially far-reaching free-exercise decision (*Burwell v. Hobby Lobby Stores*), the Supreme Court in 2014 held that "closely held" companies (those with only a few owners) are not required, if the owners object on religious grounds, to include contraceptives in their employees' health insurance coverage. The case stemmed from the 2010 Affordable Care Act, which required companies that provide employee health insurance to include contraceptives. The Court's majority said the requirement violates the owners' free-exercise rights if the use of contraceptives contradicts their religious beliefs. In a strongly worded dissent, Justice Ruth Bader Ginsburg criticized the majority's opinion as a radical rewriting of corporation rights, saying it opened the door for business firms to challenge numerous other laws on religious grounds.[38]

In a 2018 ruling, *Masterpiece Cakeshop v. Colorado Civil Rights Commission*, the Supreme Court sided with a bakery that had refused to provide a wedding cake for the marriage of a same-sex couple, concluding that the civil rights commission had violated the baker's free exercise rights by showing religious hostility toward him in its deliberations. The Court chose not to issue a broad ruling on the intersection of anti-discrimination laws and the free exercise of religion, thus leaving open the question of how far a business can go in invoking religious freedom as a reason for denial of goods or services.[39]

In some instances, the free exercise of religion clashes with the prohibition on the establishment of religion, and the Supreme Court is forced to choose between them. In 1987, for example, the Court overturned a Louisiana law that required creationism (the Bible's account of how God created life in seven days about 10,000 years ago) to be taught along with the theory of evolution (the scientific account of how life evolved over millions of years) in public school science courses. The Court held that creationism is a religious doctrine, not a scientific theory, and that its inclusion in public school curricula violates the establishment clause by promoting a religious belief.[40] Many Christians believe in creationism (see Figure 4-1), and the Court's ruling is seen by some of them as a violation of the free-exercise clause because it forces students who believe in creationism to study a version of creation—evolution—that conflicts with their religious beliefs.

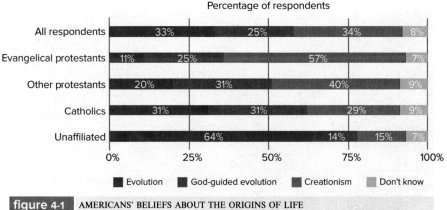

figure 4-1   AMERICANS' BELIEFS ABOUT THE ORIGINS OF LIFE

Some Americans believe that life originated millions of years ago through a natural process; other Americans accept evolutionary theory but say evolution was guided by God; and still others reject evolutionary theory, holding that life was created by God in its present form about 10,000 years ago. People's beliefs on this issue, as the figure shows, vary by religious affiliation. These differences have been a source of political conflict. Those who believe life was created by God in its present form have argued that their version (creationism) should be taught in public school science classes where the theory of evolution is taught. The Supreme Court has rejected that position, holding that creationism is a religious theory and that teaching it in public schools would violate the First Amendment ban on the establishment of religion. (*Source:* Pew Research Center, Religion Landscape Study, 2014.)

THE RIGHT TO BEAR ARMS

The Second Amendment to the Constitution says: "A well regulated Militia, being necessary to the security of a free State, the right of the people to keep and bear Arms shall not be infringed." The amendment is widely understood to prevent the federal government from abolishing state militias (such as National Guard units), but there has been disagreement over whether the amendment also gives individuals the right to possess weapons outside their use in military service.

Remarkably, more than two centuries passed before the Supreme Court squarely addressed the issue of how the Second Amendment is to be interpreted. The decision came in *District of Columbia v. Heller* (2008). In its ruling, the Court said that "the Second Amendment protects an individual right to possess a firearm unconnected with service in a militia, and to use that arm for traditionally lawful purposes, such as self-defense within the home." The ruling struck down a District of Columbia law that had banned the possession of handguns but not rifles or shotguns within the district's boundaries. Writing for the 5-4 majority, Justice Antonin Scalia said that the justices were "aware of the problem of handgun violence in this country." But Scalia concluded: "The enshrinement of constitutional rights necessarily takes certain policy

The Supreme Court has ruled that gun ownership is a protected constitutional right, although the Court has not said precisely how far that protection extends. (©Moodboard/Image Source)

choices off the table. These include the absolute prohibition of handguns held and used for self-defense in the home."[41] In a sharply worded dissent, Justice John Paul Stevens said the majority had devised a ruling that fit its partisan agenda rather than what the framers intended. Stevens declared: "When each word in the text is given full effect, the Amendment is most naturally read to secure to the people a right to use and possess arms in conjunction with service in a well-regulated militia. So far as it appears, no more than that was contemplated by its drafters."

The District of Columbia is federal territory, so the *Heller* ruling applied only to the federal government. However, in a 2010 decision, *McDonald v. Chicago,* the Supreme Court through selective incorporation applied the same standard to state and local governments in striking down a Chicago ordinance that banned handgun possession.[42] In this and the *Heller* ruling, the Court did not prohibit all gun restrictions, such as bans on gun ownership by former felons. However, the Court did not list all of the allowable restrictions, leaving the issue to be decided in future cases.

THE RIGHT OF PRIVACY

Until the 1960s, Americans' constitutional rights were confined largely to those listed in the Bill of Rights. This situation prevailed despite the Ninth Amendment, which reads, "The enumeration of the Constitution, of certain rights, shall not be construed to deny or disparage others retained by the people." In 1965, however, the Supreme Court added to the list of individual rights, declaring that Americans have "a right of privacy." This judgment derived from the case of *Griswold v. Connecticut,* which challenged a state law prohibiting the use of condoms and other birth control devices, even by married couples. The Supreme Court struck down the law, concluding that a state has no business dictating a married couple's method of birth control. Rather than invoking the Ninth Amendment, the Court's majority reasoned that the freedoms in the Bill of Rights imply an underlying **right of privacy**. The Court held that individuals have a "zone of [personal] privacy" that government cannot lawfully invade.[43]

Although the right of privacy has not been applied broadly by the Supreme Court, it has been invoked in two major areas—a woman's right to choose an abortion and consensual relations among same-sex adults.

Abortion

The right of privacy was the basis for the Supreme Court's ruling in *Roe v. Wade* (1973), which gave women full freedom to choose abortion during the first three months of pregnancy. In overturning a Texas law banning abortion except to save the life of the mother, the Court said that the right of privacy is "broad enough to encompass a woman's decision whether or not to terminate her pregnancy."[44]

The *Roe* decision was met with praise by some Americans and condemnation by others, provoking a still-continuing debate. Americans are sharply divided over the abortion issue and have been throughout the more than four decades since *Roe* (see "Party Polarization: Pro-life versus Pro-choice").

After the *Roe* ruling, anti-abortion activists sought a constitutional amendment that would ban abortion, but failed in that effort, prompting them to

---

P A R T Y
POLARIZATION

Conflicting Ideas

Pro-life versus Pro-choice

Since the Supreme Court ruled in *Roe v. Wade* (1973) that a woman has a constitutional right to choose abortion, every Republican Party national platform has expressed opposition to abortion. In the same period, every Democratic Party national platform has had a pro-choice plank. A sharp divide over the abortion issue also exists between self-identified Democratic and Republican voters, as the following graph shows.

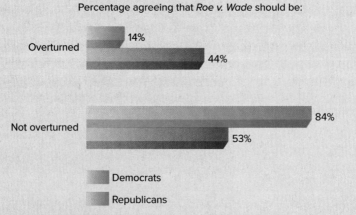

Percentage agreeing that *Roe v. Wade* should be:

Overturned — 14% / 44%

Not overturned — 84% / 53%

Democrats
Republicans

Source: Pew Research Center for the People and the Press, 2016.

Q: Do you think there is a "middle ground" that could bring Republicans and Democrats together on the abortion issue? Or is the moral and political divide over the issue so great that no compromise is possible?

pursue alternatives. They persuaded the Missouri legislature to pass a law that prohibited abortions from being performed in the state's publicly funded medical facilities, a policy that the Supreme Court upheld in *Webster v. Reproductive Health Services* (1989).[45] Then in *Planned Parenthood v. Casey* (1992), the Court upheld a Pennsylvania law that requires a minor to have parental or judicial consent before obtaining an abortion. Any such restriction, the Court said, is constitutional as long as it does not impose an "undue burden" on the woman.[46] The Court has used the "undue burden" test in subsequent decisions related to laws that would limit women's access to abortion.

In *Gonzales v. Carhart* (2007), the Supreme Court for the first time upheld a ban on a particular type of abortion. At issue was the federal Partial-Birth Abortion Ban Act, passed by Congress in 2003. The law provides for a fine and a prison term for physicians who perform an abortion when the mother is giving birth even if her life or health is in danger. Writing for the 5–4 majority, Justice Anthony Kennedy said that the federal act did not place an "undue burden" on women. In a dissenting opinion, Justice Ruth Bader Ginsburg, who at the time was the lone woman on the Court, said the decision put women's lives and health at risk.[47]

In 2016, the Supreme Court issued what observers called the most important abortion ruling since the 1990s. The case centered on a Texas law that required abortion clinics to meet the standards of hospital-based surgical centers and required doctors who perform abortions to have admitting privileges at a local hospital. The law, if upheld, would have forced nearly every Texas abortion clinic to close. In a 5–3 decision, the Supreme Court rejected the state of Texas's claim that the law was aimed at protecting women's health, concluding that its main purpose was to interfere with a woman's right to seek an abortion. The Court held that "the surgical center requirement, like the admitting-privileges requirement, provides few, if any, health benefits for women, poses a substantial obstacle to women seeking abortions, and constitutes an 'undue burden' on their constitutional right to do so."[48]

Consensual Sexual Relations among Same-Sex Adults

Although the Supreme Court's 1965 *Griswold* ruling on contraceptive use was widely said to have taken "government out of people's bedrooms," an exception remained. Every state prohibited sexual relations between consenting adults of the same sex. Over the next two decades, many states eliminated this prohibition and others stopped enforcing it. Nevertheless, in a 1986 Georgia case, *Bowers v. Hardwick,* the Supreme Court held that the right of privacy did not extend to consensual sexual relations among adults of the same sex.[49]

In *Lawrence v. Texas* (2003), the Court in a 6–3 decision reversed its position, ruling that sodomy laws violate "the right of privacy" implied by the grant of liberty in the Fourteenth Amendment's due process clause.[50] The Court held that states cannot lawfully ban sexual relations between consenting same-sex adults. (In 2015, the Supreme Court legalized marriage between same-sex couples, a subject discussed in Chapter 5.)

RIGHTS OF PERSONS ACCUSED OF CRIMES

Due process refers to legal protections that have been established to preserve the rights of individuals. The most significant of these protections is **procedural due process**; the term refers primarily to procedures that authorities must follow before a person can lawfully be punished for an offense. No system of justice is foolproof. Even in the most careful systems, innocent people have been wrongly accused, convicted, and punished with imprisonment or death. But the scrupulous application of procedural safeguards, such as a defendant's right to legal counsel, greatly increases the likelihood of a fair trial. "The history of liberty has largely been the history of the observance of procedural guarantees," said Justice Felix Frankfurter in *McNabb v. United States* (1943).[51]

The U.S. Constitution offers procedural safeguards designed to protect a person from wrongful arrest, conviction, and punishment. The Fifth and Fourteenth Amendments provide generally that no person can be deprived of life, liberty, or property without due process of law. Specific procedural protections for the accused are listed in the Fourth, Fifth, Sixth, and Eighth Amendments.[52] (See Table 4-2.)

Suspicion Phase: Unreasonable Search and Seizure

In 1766, Parliamentary leader William Pitt forcefully expressed a principle of English common law: "The poorest man may, in his cottage, bid defiance to all the forces of the Crown. It may be frail; its roof may shake; the wind may blow through it; the rain may enter; but the King of England may not enter; all his force dares not cross the threshold."[53] In the period immediately preceding the American Revolution, few things provoked more anger among the colonists than Britain's disregard for the sanctity of the home. British soldiers regularly forced their way into colonists' houses, looking for documents or other evidence of anti-British activity.

The Fourth Amendment was included in the Bill of Rights to prohibit such actions by the U.S. government. The Fourth Amendment reads: "The right of the people to be secure in their persons, houses, papers, and effects, against

table 4-2	BILL OF RIGHTS: A SELECTED LIST OF DUE PROCESS PROTECTIONS
Fourth Amendment	**Sixth Amendment**
Search and seizure: You are protected from unreasonable searches and seizures, although you forfeit that right if you knowingly waive it. **Arrest:** You are protected from arrest unless authorities have probable cause to believe that you have committed a crime.	**Counsel:** You have a right to be represented by an attorney and can demand to speak first with an attorney before responding to questions from law enforcement officials. **Prompt and reasonable proceedings:** You have a right to be arraigned promptly, to be informed of the charges, to confront witnesses, and to have a speedy and open trial by an impartial jury.
Fifth Amendment	**Eighth Amendment**
Self-incrimination: You are protected against self-incrimination, which means that you have the right to remain silent and to be protected against coercion by law enforcement officials. **Double jeopardy:** You cannot be tried twice for the same crime if the first trial results in acquittal. **Due process:** You cannot be deprived of life, liberty, or property without proper legal proceedings.	**Bail:** You are protected against excessive bail or fines. **Cruel and unusual punishment:** You are protected from cruel and unusual punishment, although this provision does not protect you from the death penalty or from a long prison term for a minor offense.

unreasonable searches and seizures, shall not be violated, and no Warrants shall issue, but upon probable cause, supported by Oath or affirmation, and particularly describing the place to be searched, and the persons or things to be seized."

The Fourth Amendment protects individuals against arbitrary police action. Although a person caught in the act of a crime can be arrested (seized) and searched for weapons and incriminating evidence, the police ordinarily cannot search an individual merely on the basis of suspicion. In such instances they have to convince a judge that they have "probable cause" (sufficient evidence) to believe that a suspect is engaged in criminal activity. If the judge concludes that the evidence is strong enough, the police will be granted a search warrant. The Court has also held that police must have a search warrant to investigate a suspect using modern technology, such as a listening or thermal-imaging device.[54]

In a unanimous 2014 decision, the Supreme Court delivered what many legal experts consider a landmark ruling. At issue were two cases, one from California and the other from Massachusetts, in which police without a warrant searched a suspect's cell phone after an arrest. In each case, they found information implicating the suspect. In *Riley v. California* and *United States v. Wurie,* the Court noted that, although police upon making an arrest can normally search a suspect and seize relevant physical items (such as weapons or drugs), cell phones and similar electronic devices are different in kind in that they contain large amounts of personal information (see "Case Study: *Riley v. California* (2014)"). The Court noted that "a cell phone search would typically expose to the government far more than the most exhaustive search of a house." The Court acknowledged that its ruling would make the work of police more difficult but said the protection of Americans' constitutional rights took priority. "We cannot deny that our decision today will have an impact on the ability of law enforcement to combat crime," said the Court. "Privacy comes at a cost."[55]

| C A S E | **Politics in Action** |
| S T U D Y | |

Riley v. California (2014)

The Fourth Amendment says: "The right of the people to be secure in their persons, homes, papers, and effects, against unreasonable searches and seizures, shall not be violated." However, the Constitution does not distinguish between "unreasonable" search and seizure, which is prohibited, and "reasonable" search and seizure, which is permitted.

The Supreme Court addressed that issue in a key 2014 case, *Riley v. California*. David Riley had been pulled over by San Diego police in 2009 for having an expired vehicle registration tag. As it turned out, he also had a suspended driver's license, which, under California law, requires the vehicle to be towed. In such instances, officers must list the vehicle's contents to prevent the owner from later claiming that property had been stolen from it. In doing the inventory, police found two loaded handguns hidden under the vehicle's hood. Riley was a known gang member and having a loaded

Source: Photographs in the Carol M. Highsmith Archive, Library of Congress, Prints and Photographs Division [LC-DIG-highsm-15438]

Continued

handgun in a car is a criminal offense in California. Police arrested Riley, took his cell phone, and downloaded information from it that implicated him in a gang shooting. He was convicted of the shooting.

Riley appealed his conviction, arguing that police had violated his right to protection against unreasonable search and seizure. In a 9-0 ruling, the Supreme Court ruled in Riley's favor. The Court noted that cell phones and similar electronic devices can contain a significant amount of personal information. The Court said that to equate such devices to physical objects like weapons "is like saying a ride on horseback is materially indistinguishable from a flight to the moon." The Court likened a cell phone to a home, saying that both contain large amounts of personal information. Since police cannot normally search a person's home without getting a search warrant from a judge, a warrant is also required in *most* circumstances before a cell phone search. Police had failed to seek a warrant in Riley's case, and the Supreme Court held that the evidence gathered from his cell phone could not be used against him at trial.

Q: Do you agree with the Court's reasoning in the *Riley* case? Can you think of circumstances in which police could lawfully search a suspect's cell phone without first getting a warrant?

ASK YOURSELF: Is a suspect's cell phone fundamentally different in kind from physical items such as drugs found on a suspect? What about a situation in which police have solid reason to believe the suspect's cell phone has information that could prevent an imminent criminal act, such as a terrorist attack or bank robbery, by the suspect's accomplices? Would a warrantless search be legal in that type of situation?

The Supreme Court extended digital-age search and seizure protection in *Carpenter v. United States* (2018). At issue was a warrantless search in which police obtained from a suspect's cell phone provider a record of the locations from which he had placed calls. The locations matched those where the individual was suspected of having committed crimes, which contributed to his conviction. In a 5-4 decision, the Court held that government violates the Fourth Amendment when it accesses records of the physical locations of a cellphone without a search warrant.[56]

The Supreme Court allows warrantless searches in some circumstances. For example, the Court has generally given school administrators wide latitude to search students for drugs and weapons on the grounds that administrators bear responsibility for the safety of other students.[57] The Court has also held, for example, that police roadblocks to check drivers for signs of intoxication are legal as long as the action is systematic and not arbitrary (for example, stopping only young drivers would be unconstitutional, whereas stopping all drivers is acceptable). The Court justified this decision by saying that roadblocks serve an important highway safety objective.[58] However, the Court does not allow police roadblocks to check for drugs. The Court has held that narcotics roadblocks serve a general law enforcement purpose rather than one specific to highway safety and thereby violate the Fourth Amendment's requirement that police have suspicion of wrongdoing before they can search an individual's auto.[59]

Arrest Phase: Protection against Self-Incrimination

The Fifth Amendment says, in part, that an individual cannot "be compelled in any criminal case to be a witness against himself." This provision is designed to protect individuals from the age-old practice of coerced confession. Trickery, torture, and the threat of an extra-long prison sentence can lead people to confess to acts they did not commit.

At the time of arrest, police cannot legally begin their interrogation until the suspect has been warned that his or her words can be used as evidence. This warning requirement emerged from *Miranda v. Arizona* (1966), which centered on Ernesto Miranda's confession to kidnapping and rape during police questioning. The Supreme Court overturned his conviction on the grounds that police had not informed him of his right to remain silent and to have legal assistance. The Court reasoned that suspects have a right to know their rights.[60] The Court's ruling led to the formulation of the "Miranda warning" that police are now required to read to suspects: "You have the right to remain silent. . . . Anything you say can and will be used against you in a court of law. . . . You have the right to an attorney." (Miranda was subsequently retried and convicted on the basis of evidence other than his confession.)

The Court strengthened the Miranda precedent in *Missouri v. Siebert* (2004). This ruling came in response to a police strategy of questioning suspects before informing them of their Miranda rights and then, after telling them of their rights, questioning them a second time. In such instances, suspects who admitted wrongdoing in the first round of questioning often did so also in the second round. The Court concluded that the police strategy was intended "to undermine the Miranda warnings" and was a violation of suspects' rights.[61]

Trial Phase: The Right to a Fair Trial

The right to a fair trial is basic to any reasonable notion of justice. If the trial process is arbitrary or biased against the defendant, justice is denied. It is sometimes said the American justice system is based on the principle that it

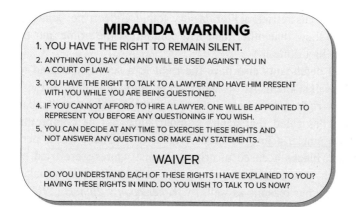

MIRANDA WARNING

1. YOU HAVE THE RIGHT TO REMAIN SILENT.

2. ANYTHING YOU SAY CAN AND WILL BE USED AGAINST YOU IN A COURT OF LAW.

3. YOU HAVE THE RIGHT TO TALK TO A LAWYER AND HAVE HIM PRESENT WITH YOU WHILE YOU ARE BEING QUESTIONED.

4. IF YOU CANNOT AFFORD TO HIRE A LAWYER. ONE WILL BE APPOINTED TO REPRESENT YOU BEFORE ANY QUESTIONING IF YOU WISH.

5. YOU CAN DECIDE AT ANY TIME TO EXERCISE THESE RIGHTS AND NOT ANSWER ANY QUESTIONS OR MAKE ANY STATEMENTS.

WAIVER

DO YOU UNDERSTAND EACH OF THESE RIGHTS I HAVE EXPLAINED TO YOU? HAVING THESE RIGHTS IN MIND. DO YOU WISH TO TALK TO US NOW?

Shown here is a reproduction of the Miranda warning card that FBI agents carry. Agents are required in most instances to read suspects their rights before interrogating them. The Miranda warning includes the Fifth Amendment right to remain silent and the Sixth Amendment right to have an attorney.

is better to let one hundred guilty parties go free than to convict one innocent person. The system does not actually work that way. Once a person has been arrested and charged with a crime, prosecutors are determined to get a conviction. Defendants in such instances have fair-trial guarantees that are designed to protect them from wrongful conviction.

Legal Counsel and Impartial Jury   Under the Fifth Amendment, suspects charged with a *federal* crime cannot be tried unless indicted by a grand jury. The grand jury hears the prosecution's evidence and decides whether it is strong enough to allow the government to try the suspect. (This protection has not been incorporated into the Fourteenth Amendment. As a result, states are not required to use grand juries, although roughly half of them do so. In the rest of the states, the prosecutor usually decides whether to proceed with a trial.)

The Sixth Amendment provides a right to legal counsel before and during trial. But what if a person cannot afford a lawyer? For most of the nation's history, poor people had no choice but to serve as their own attorneys. In *Johnson v. Zerbst* (1938), the Supreme Court held that criminal defendants in federal cases must be provided a lawyer at government expense if they cannot afford one.[62] The Court extended this requirement to include state cases with its ruling in *Gideon v. Wainwright* (1963). This case centered on Clarence Gideon, who had been convicted in a Florida court of breaking into a pool hall. He had asked for a lawyer, but the trial judge denied the request, forcing Gideon to act as his own attorney. He appealed his conviction, and the Supreme Court overturned it on grounds that he did not have adequate legal counsel.[63] (In his retrial, a Florida jury found Gideon not guilty. His lawyer was able to show that other men had committed the crime and then lied to say Gideon had done it.)

Criminal defendants also have the right to a speedy trial and to confront witnesses against them. At the federal level and sometimes at the state level, they have a right to jury trial, which is to be heard by an "impartial jury." The Court has ruled that a jury's impartiality can be compromised if the prosecution stacks a jury by race or ethnicity.[64] There was a period in the South when blacks accused of crimes against whites were tried by all-white juries, which invariably returned a guilty verdict. The jury's makeup can be an issue for other reasons as well. In *Witherspoon v. Illinois* (1968), for example, the Supreme Court invalidated Illinois's policy of allowing the prosecution to challenge an unlimited number of potential jurors in capital cases. The prosecution used the challenges to remove from the jury anyone who expressed doubt about sentencing the defendant to death if found guilty. To allow that practice, the Court ruled, is to virtually guarantee "a verdict of death" by a "hanging jury."[65]

The Exclusionary Rule   An issue in some trials is the admissibility of evidence obtained in violation of the defendant's rights. The **exclusionary rule** bars the use of such evidence in some circumstances. The rule was formulated on a limited basis in a 1914 Supreme Court decision and was devised to deter police from violating people's rights. If police know that illegally obtained evidence will be inadmissible in court, they presumably will be less inclined to obtain it. As the Court wrote in *Weeks v. United States* (1914): "The tendency of those who execute the criminal laws of the country to obtain convictions by means of unlawful searches and enforced confessions . . . should find no sanction in the judgment of the courts."[66]

In the 1960s, the liberal-dominated Supreme Court expanded the exclusionary rule to the point where illegally obtained evidence was almost never admissible in court. Opponents accused the Court of "coddling criminals," and the appointment of more conservative justices to the Court led to the creation of exceptions to the exclusionary rule. One such exception emerged from *United States v. Leon* (1984), where the Court ruled that evidence discovered under a faulty warrant was admissible because the police had acted in "good faith."[67] The **good faith exception** holds that otherwise inadmissible evidence can be used in trial if police honestly believed they were following proper procedures.

A second instance in which tainted evidence can be admitted is the **inevitable discovery exception**. It was developed in the case of *Nix v. Williams* (1984). An eyewitness account had led police to believe that Williams had kidnapped a young girl. While being transported by police, despite assurances to his lawyer that he would not be questioned en route, Williams was interrogated and told police where the girl's body could be found. When Williams appealed his conviction, the Court acknowledged that his rights had been violated but concluded that police had other evidence that would have led them to the girl's body. "Exclusion of physical evidence that would have inevitably been discovered adds nothing to either the integrity or fairness of a criminal trial," the Court said.[68]

A third instance is the **plain view exception**. In a key 1996 case, *Whren v. United States,* the Court upheld the conviction of a man stopped for a minor traffic infraction who had drugs sitting in plain view in the front seat of his car.[69] The ruling reaffirmed an earlier decision upholding the admissibility of evidence found in plain sight even when the evidence relates to an infraction other than the one for which the individual was stopped.[70]

As some observers see it, the Court has weakened the exclusionary rule almost to the point where it applies only to extreme forms of police misconduct. Some Court rulings would support that contention. On the other hand, the Court's recent rulings on cell phones and tracking devices indicate it is unwilling to give police broad latitude in the use of modern technology, recognizing that it can easily be applied in ways that abridge constitutional rights.

Sentencing Phase: Cruel and Unusual Punishment

Most issues of criminal justice involve *procedural* due process. However, adherence to proper procedures does not necessarily produce reasonable outcomes. The Eighth Amendment was designed to address this issue. It prohibits "cruel and unusual punishment" of those convicted of crime. The Supreme Court has applied several tests in determining whether punishment is cruel and unusual, including whether it is "disproportionate to the offence," violates "fundamental standards of good conscience and fairness," and is "unnecessarily cruel."

However, the Supreme Court has typically let Congress and the state legislatures determine the appropriate penalties for crime (see "How the 50 States Differ"). For example, the Court upheld a conviction under California's "three strikes and you're out" law that sent a twice previously convicted felon to prison for life without parole for shoplifting videotapes worth $100.[71]

At the same time, the Supreme Court has recently employed the Eighth Amendment's "cruel and unusual punishment" clause to ban the death penalty for juveniles and the mentally ill and to ban life sentences without parole for juveniles.[72] In 2016, the Court extended the ban on life-without-parole for juveniles to individuals convicted before the ban was established. The Court said that such prisoners must be resentenced or have the opportunity to apply for parole.[73]

HOW THE 50 STATES DIFFER

CRITICAL THINKING THROUGH COMPARISONS

Incarceration Rates

Most crimes in the United States are governed by state law rather than federal law, and states differ widely in their crime rates and sentencing practices. As a result, there is wide variation in the size of state prison populations. Louisiana has the highest incarceration rate: 1,380 inmates for every 100,000 residents. Maine has the lowest rate: 380 inmates per 100,000 residents.

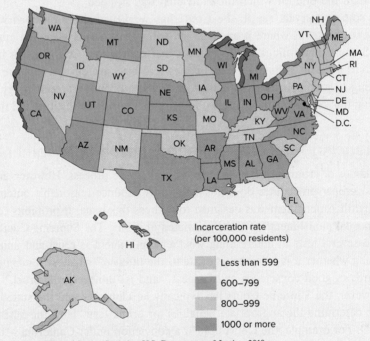

Incarceration rate
(per 100,000 residents)

■ Less than 599

■ 600–799

■ 800–999

■ 1000 or more

Source: Office of Justice Statistics, U.S. Department of Justice, 2018.

Q: What do many of the low-incarceration states have in common?

A: Most of them rank high on levels of education and income. Studies indicate that individuals who are college educated and those with higher incomes are less likely than others to engage in crime and, if convicted, less likely to receive a lengthy sentence.

Appeal: One Chance, Usually

The Constitution does not guarantee an appeal after conviction, but the federal government and all states permit at least one appeal. The Supreme Court has ruled that the appeal process cannot discriminate against poor defendants. At a minimum, government must provide indigent convicts with the legal resources to file a first appeal.

Prisoners who believe their constitutional rights have been violated by state officials can appeal their conviction to a federal court. With a few exceptions, the Supreme Court has held that prisoners have the right to have their appeal heard in federal court unless they had "deliberately bypassed" the opportunity to first make their appeal in state courts.[74] Under a law enacted in 1996 to prevent inmates from filing frivolous and multiple appeals, they typically are allowed only a single appeal. The Supreme Court has ruled that, except in unusual cases, it is fair to ask inmates to first pursue their options in state courts and then to limit themselves to a single federal appeal.[75]

Crime, Punishment, and Police Practices

Although the exclusionary rule has been weakened, there has not been a return to the lower procedural standards that existed prior to the 1960s. Most of the precedents established in that decade remain in effect, including the most important one: the principle that procedural protections guaranteed to the accused by the Bill of Rights must be observed by states and localities as well as by the federal government.

Supreme Court rulings have changed police practices. Most police departments, for example, require their officers to read suspects the Miranda warning before questioning them. Nevertheless, constitutional rights are applied unevenly. An example is the use of *racial profiling,* which is the targeting of individuals from minority groups, particularly blacks, Hispanics, and Muslims. Research indicates that such individuals are more likely than other Americans to be arbitrarily stopped, searched, and detained by police on everything from traffic infractions to public intoxication.[76] Such individuals are also more likely to be victims of police violence, an issue that became front-page news in 2014 when an unarmed black teenager, Michael Brown, was shot to death by a police officer in Ferguson, Missouri. His killing brought other police shootings to public attention, sparking "Black Lives Matter"—a movement aimed at ending racial disparities in police practices.

Sentencing policies are also an issue. Political candidates who are "tough on crime" are popular with some voters, which led state legislatures in the 1990s to enact stiffer penalties for crime while also limiting the ability of judges to reduce sentences for nonviolent crimes committed by first-time

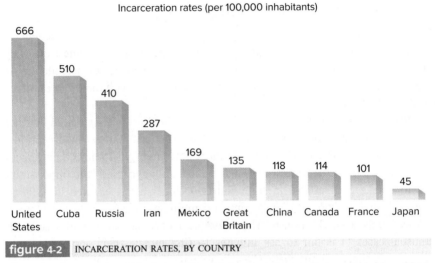

Incarceration rates (per 100,000 inhabitants)

666 — United States
510 — Cuba
410 — Russia
287 — Iran
169 — Mexico
135 — Great Britain
118 — China
114 — Canada
101 — France
45 — Japan

figure 4-2   INCARCERATION RATES, BY COUNTRY

The United States is the world leader in terms of the number of people it places behind bars. More than half of the people in U.S. prisons were convicted of nonviolent offenses, such as drug use or property theft. (*Source:* International Centre for Prison Studies, 2018.)

offenders. As a result, the number of prison inmates more than doubled after the 1990s. In fact, on a per-capita basis, the United States has the largest prison population in the world (see Figure 4-2). Cuba and Russia are the only countries that are even close to the United States in terms of the percentage of its citizens who are behind bars.

The human and financial costs of keeping so many people in prison have prompted some states to change their sentencing laws and implement early-release programs, primarily for those convicted of nonviolent drug-related offenses. Some states have even set up treatment programs as an alternative to prison for some drug-related offenses, a policy that's in line with the practice of many Western democracies.

RIGHTS AND THE WAR ON TERRORISM

In time of war, the courts have upheld government policies that would not be permitted in peacetime.[77] After the Japanese attack on Pearl Harbor in 1941, for example, President Franklin D. Roosevelt ordered the forced relocation of tens of thousands of Japanese Americans living on the West Coast to detention camps in Arizona, Utah, and other inland locations. Congress endorsed the policy, and the Supreme Court upheld it in *Korematsu v. United States* (1944).[78] After the terrorist attacks of September 11, 2001, George W. Bush's administration invoked such precedents in declaring that customary legal protections would not be afforded to individuals it deemed to have engaged in terrorist activity.

Detention of Enemy Combatants

The Bush administration soon announced its policy for handling captured "enemy combatants"—individuals judged to be engaged in, or in support of, hostile military actions against U.S. military forces. Some of these prisoners were sent to a detention facility created at the U.S. naval base at Guantánamo Bay on the tip of Cuba. Others were imprisoned in Afghanistan, Iraq, and elsewhere. Some prisoners were subjected to abusive treatment, including torture, although the practice was denied by U.S. officials until photographic and other evidence surfaced.

In 2004, the Supreme Court issued its first ruling on these practices, holding that the Guantánamo Bay detainees have the right to challenge their detention in court. The Court reasoned that the naval base, though in Cuba, is on land leased to the United States and therefore under the jurisdiction of U.S. courts.[79] In a second 2004 case, the Court ruled that one of the Guantánamo Bay detainees, who was a U.S. citizen by virtue of having been born in the United States though he was raised in Saudi Arabia, had the right to be heard in U.S. courts. The Court said that the government has a legitimate interest in detaining individuals who pose a threat to the nation's security but that "an unchecked system of detention carries the potential to become a means of oppression and abuse of others who do not present that sort of threat."[80]

Two years later, the Supreme Court issued its sharpest rebuke of the Bush administration's detention policies. In a ruling nearly unprecedented in its challenge to a president's wartime authority, the Court held that the detainees were protected both by the U.S. Uniform Code of Military Justice and by the Geneva Conventions. At issue was the Bush administration's use of secret military tribunals to try detainees. In *Hamdan v. Rumsfeld* (2006), the Court ruled that the tribunals were unlawful because they did not provide even minimal protections of detainees' rights, including the right to see the evidence against them. The Court said that the detainees were entitled to trial by a court that upholds rights "which are recognized as indispensable by civilized peoples."[81]

Surveillance of Suspected Terrorists

After the September 11 terrorist attacks, Congress passed the USA Patriot Act, which gave the government additional tools for combating terrorism, including expanded surveillance power. The National Security Agency launched a program that collected Americans' phone records as a means of detecting activity that might be terrorist related. If a pattern of phone calls or e-mails suggested the possibility of terrorist activity, the NSA had to obtain a warrant from a federal judge before it could eavesdrop on a person's actual conversations.

The NSA program became public in 2013 when Edward Snowden, an NSA contractor, leaked documents about the program to the press. The documents showed that the NSA had collected data on nearly every call made by Americans and had actually listened in on the calls of some foreign leaders, including German chancellor Angela Merkel.

The NSA program was challenged in court and a federal appellate court ruled it unlawful, not on grounds that it violated the Fourth Amendment protection against unreasonable search and seizure, but because it had not been explicitly authorized by Congress. In 2015, after heated debate and a close vote in the Senate, Congress passed legislation authorizing the program, while putting limits on it. For example, the legislation requires phone data to be

Major national security threats can lead government to take actions that intrude on citizens' liberties. The war on terrorism is particularly challenging because the threat is not confined to overseas areas but includes the U.S. homeland. Concern about terrorist attacks on U.S. soil is the basis for the NSA's surveillance program, which collects data on Americans' phone calls and e-mails, particularly when the other party is elsewhere in the world. The courts have upheld the constitutionality of the program because the NSA, although it collects data on communication traffic, must have a court warrant to examine the actual content of any message. Nevertheless, the NSA program involves a level of personal surveillance beyond anything Americans experienced in the past. (©Morakot Kawinchan/Shutterstock)

stored with telecommunications companies rather than the NSA and to be available to the NSA only if it obtains a warrant. In 2018, Congress reauthorized the program, extending it for a period of six years.

THE COURTS AND A FREE SOCIETY

The United States was founded on the idea that individuals have an innate right to liberty—to speak their minds, to worship freely, to be secure in their homes and persons, to be assured of a fair trial. Americans embrace these freedoms in the abstract. In particular situations, however, many Americans think otherwise. A 2010 CNN survey found, for example, that more than two in five Americans think that individuals arrested by police on suspicion of terrorism should not be read their Miranda rights.

The judiciary is not isolated from the public mood. Judges inevitably must balance society's need for security and public order against the rights of the individual. Nevertheless, relative to elected officials, police officers, or the general public, judges are more protective of individual rights. How far the courts will go in protecting a person's rights depends on the facts of the case, the existing status of the law, prevailing social needs, and the personal views of the judges (see Chapter 14). Nevertheless, most judges and justices regard the protection of individual rights as their constitutional duty, which is the way the framers saw it. The Bill of Rights was created to transform the abstract idea that individuals have a right to life, liberty, and happiness into a set of specified constitutional rights, thereby bringing them under the protection of courts of law.[82]

SUMMARY

The Bill of Rights was added to the Constitution shortly after its ratification. These amendments guarantee certain political, procedural, and property rights against infringement by the national government.

The guarantees embodied in the Bill of Rights originally applied only to the national government. Under the principle of selective incorporation of these guarantees into the Fourteenth Amendment, the courts extended them to state governments, though the process was slow and uneven. In the 1920s and 1930s, First Amendment guarantees of freedom of expression were given protection from infringement by the states. The states continued to have wide discretion in criminal proceedings until the early 1960s, when most of the fair-trial rights in the Bill of Rights were given federal protection.

Freedom of expression is the most basic of democratic rights. People are not free unless they can freely express their views. Nevertheless, free expression may conflict with the nation's security needs during times of war and insurrection. The courts at times have allowed government to limit expression substantially for purposes of national security. In recent decades, however, the courts have protected a wide range of free expression in the areas of speech, press, and religion. They have also established a right of privacy, which in some areas, such as abortion, remains a source of controversy and judicial action.

Due process of law refers to legal protections that have been established to preserve individual rights. The most significant form of these protections consists of procedures designed to ensure that an individual's rights are upheld (for example, the right of an accused person to have an attorney present during police interrogation). A major controversy in this area is the breadth of the exclusionary rule, which bars illegally obtained evidence from being used in trials.

The war on terrorism that began after the attacks on September 11, 2001, has raised new issues of civil liberties, including the detention of enemy combatants, the use of harsh interrogation techniques, and warrantless surveillance. The Supreme Court has not ruled on all such issues but has generally held that the president's war-making power does not include the authority to disregard provisions of statutory law, treaties (the Geneva Conventions), and the Constitution.

Civil liberties are not absolute but must be judged in the context of other considerations (such as national security or public safety) and against one another when different rights conflict. The judicial branch of government, particularly the Supreme Court, has taken on much of the responsibility for protecting and interpreting individual rights. The Court's positions have changed with time and conditions, but the Court is typically more protective of civil liberties than are elected officials or popular majorities.

©gangliu10/Getty Images

CRITICAL THINKING ZONE

KEY TERMS

Bill of Rights (*p. 98*)

civil liberties (*p. 97*)

clear-and-present-danger test (*p. 102*)

due process clause (of the Fourteenth Amendment) (*p. 98*)

establishment clause (*p. 108*)

exclusionary rule (*p. 122*)

freedom of expression (*p. 101*)

free-exercise clause (*p. 110*)

good faith exception (*p. 122*)

imminent lawless action test (*p. 104*)

inevitable discovery exception (*p. 122*)

Lemon test (*p. 109*)

libel (*p. 108*)

plain view exception (*p. 123*)

prior restraint (*p. 107*)

procedural due process (*p. 116*)

right of privacy (*p. 113*)

selective incorporation (*p. 100*)

slander (*p. 108*)

symbolic speech (*p. 105*)

APPLYING THE ELEMENTS OF CRITICAL THINKING

Conceptualizing: Distinguish between the establishment clause and the free-exercise clause of the First Amendment. To which one does the *Lemon* test apply, and what are the components of that test?

Synthesizing: Assume that an individual has been arrested and is eventually brought to trial. Identify the procedural due process rights that the individual has at each step in the legal process. How might the exclusionary rule affect the outcome?

Analyzing: What is the process of selective incorporation, and why is it important to the rights Americans have today?

EXTRA CREDIT

A Book Worth Reading: Anthony Lewis, *Gideon's Trumpet: How One Man, a Poor Prisoner, Took His Case to the Supreme Court—and Changed the Law of the United States* (New York: Vintage, 1964). Written by a two-time Pulitzer Prize winner, this best-selling book recounts the story of how James Earl Gideon got the Supreme Court to accept his case, which led to a constitutional ruling requiring government to provide the poor with legal counsel.

A Website Worth Visiting: **www.sentencingproject.org/** The Sentencing Project works on issues and policies relating to criminal justice reform.

PARTICIPATE!

Although their right of free expression is protected by law, Americans often choose not to exercise this right for fear of social pressure or official reprisal. Yet constitutional rights tend to wither when people fail to exercise them. The failure of citizens to speak their minds, Alexis de Tocqueville said, reduces them "to being nothing more than a herd of timid and industrious animals of which government is the shepherd." Think of an issue that you care about but that is unpopular on your campus or in your community. Consider writing a letter expressing your opinion to the editor of your college or local newspaper. (Practical advice: Keep the letter short and to the point; write a lead sentence that will get readers' attention; provide a convincing and courteous argument for your position; and be sure to sign the letter and provide a return address so that the editor can contact you if there are questions.)

5
CHAPTER

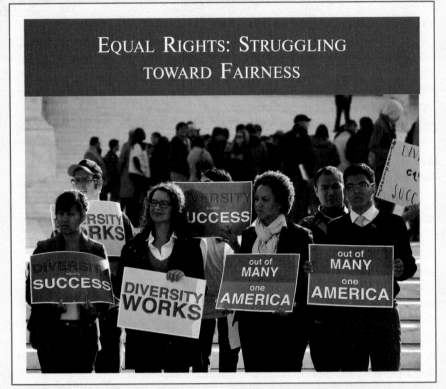

EQUAL RIGHTS: STRUGGLING TOWARD FAIRNESS

©Mark Wilson/Getty Images

❝The assertion that 'all men are created equal' was of no practical use in effecting our separation from Great Britain, and it was placed in the Declaration not for that, but for future use. ❞

ABRAHAM LINCOLN[1]

The Urban Institute paired up a large number of male college students. The students in each pair had similar majors, grades, work records, speech patterns, and physical builds. The students then responded to hundreds of classified job advertisements in Chicago and Washington, D.C. Within each pair, one type consistently got more interview invitations and job offers than the other type. What was the difference in the two types? Well, in each pair, one of the students was white and the other was black. The white students were far more likely than the black students to get interviews and jobs. As the Urban Institute study concluded: "The level of reverse discrimination [favoring blacks over whites] that we found was limited, was certainly far lower than many might have been led to fear, and was swamped by the extent of discrimination against black job applicants."[2]

The Urban Institute study suggests why some Americans still struggle for equality. Although Americans in theory have equal rights, they are not now equal, nor have they ever been. African Americans, women, Hispanic Americans, individuals with disabilities, Jews, Native Americans, Catholics, Mormons, Asian Americans, LGBTQ people, and members of other minority groups have been victims of discrimination in fact and in law.

This chapter focuses on **equal rights (civil rights)**—terms that refer to the right of every person to equal protection under the laws and equal access to society's opportunities and public facilities. As Chapter 4 explained, civil liberties refer to specific *individual* rights, such as freedom of speech, that are protected from infringement by government. Equal rights, or civil rights, are a question of whether individual members of differing *groups,* such as racial, gender, and ethnic groups, are treated equally by government and, in some instances, by private parties.

Although the law refers to the rights of individuals first and to those of groups in a secondary and derivative way, this chapter concentrates on groups because the history of civil rights has been largely one of group claims to equality. The catchphrase of nearly every group's claim to a more equal standing in American society has been "equality under the law." When secure in their legal rights, people are positioned to pursue equality in other arenas, such as the economic sector. This chapter examines the major laws relating to equality and the conditions that led to their adoption. The chapter concludes with a brief look at some of the continuing challenges facing America's historically disadvantaged groups. The chapter emphasizes these points:

- *Americans have attained substantial equality under the law.* In purely legal terms, although not always in practice, they have equal protection under the laws, equal access to accommodations and housing, and an equal right to vote.

- *Legal equality for all Americans has not resulted in de facto equality.* African Americans, women, Hispanic Americans, and other traditionally disadvantaged groups have a disproportionately small share of America's opportunities and benefits. However, the issue of what, if anything, government should do to deal with this problem is a major source of contention.

- *Disadvantaged groups have had to struggle for equal rights.* African Americans, women, Native Americans, Hispanic Americans, Asian Americans, and a number of other groups have had to fight for their rights in order to achieve a fuller measure of equality.

EQUALITY THROUGH LAW

Equality has always been the least developed of America's founding concepts. Not even Thomas Jefferson, who wrote the words, believed that a precise meaning could be given to the claim of the Declaration of Independence that "all men are created equal."[3] Nevertheless, the promise contained in that phrase has placed history on the side of those seeking greater equality. Every civil rights movement, from suffrage for males without property in the 1830s to LGBTQ rights today, has derived moral strength from the nation's pledge of equality for all. Those efforts have led to policies that have made Americans more equal in law.

The Fourteenth Amendment: Equal Protection

The Fourteenth Amendment, which was ratified in 1868 after the Civil War, declares in part that no state shall "deny to any person within its jurisdiction the equal protection of the laws." The **equal-protection clause** was designed to require states to treat their residents equally, but the Supreme Court at first refused to interpret it that way. As discussed in Chapter 3, the Court in *Plessy v. Ferguson* (1896) ruled that "separate" public facilities for black citizens did not violate the Constitution as long as the facilities were "equal."[4] The *Plessy* decision became a justification for the separate and *unequal* treatment of African Americans. Black children were forced, for example, to attend separate schools that rarely had libraries or enough teachers.

These practices were challenged through legal action, but not until the late 1930s did the Supreme Court begin to respond. In a first ruling, the Court held that blacks must be allowed to use public facilities reserved for whites in cases where the states had not created separate facilities. When Oklahoma, which had no law school for blacks, was ordered to admit Ada Sipuel as a law student in 1949, it created a separate law school for her—she sat alone in a roped-off corridor of the state capitol building. The white students, meanwhile, continued to meet at the University of Oklahoma's law school in Norman, 20 miles away. The Supreme Court then ordered the law school to admit her to regular classes. The law school did so but roped off her seat from the rest of the class and stenciled the word *colored* on it. In her memoir, Sipuel wrote that, although law school administrators did not try to help her, several law students did assist, including those who gave her notes from the classes she missed while sitting alone at the capitol building.[5]

Segregation in the Schools   Substantial judicial intervention on behalf of African Americans finally occurred in 1954 with *Brown v. Board of Education of Topeka* (see "Case Study: Brown v. Board of Education (1954)"). The case

During the Jim Crow era of racial segregation in the South, black citizens were forbidden by law from using the same public facilities as whites. Included in the ban were universities, schools, transportation facilities, and hospitals. Even public drinking fountains were segregated, as can be seen in this photo. (*Source:* Library of Congress, Prints and Photographs Division [LC-DIG-fsa-8a03228])

began when Linda Carol Brown, a black child in Topeka, Kansas, was denied admission to an all-white elementary school that she passed every day on her way to her all-black school, which was nearly a mile farther away. In a unanimous decision, the Court invoked the Fourteenth Amendment's equal-protection clause, declaring that racial segregation of public schools "generates [among black children] a feeling of inferiority as to their status in the community that may affect their hearts and minds in a way unlikely ever to be undone. . . . Separate educational facilities are inherently unequal."[6]

Although the *Brown* decision banned forced segregation in the public schools, it did not require states to take active steps to integrate their schools. Most children attended neighborhood schools, and because most residential neighborhoods were racially segregated, so too were the schools. Even as late as 15 years after *Brown,* 95 percent of black children were attending schools that were mostly or entirely black.

In *Swann v. Charlotte-Mecklenberg County Board of Education* (1971), the Supreme Court upheld the busing of children out of their neighborhoods for the purpose of achieving racially integrated schools.[7] Forced busing produced angry demonstrations in Charlotte, Detroit, Boston, and dozens of other cities,

C A S E S T U D Y	**Politics in Action**

Brown v. Board of Education (1954)

The Fourteenth Amendment, ratified after the Civil War to protect newly freed slaves, declared that no state shall "deny to any person within its jurisdiction the equal protection of the laws." Nevertheless, southern states soon established a two-race system. Black residents were prohibited from using the same public schools, hospitals, and other facilities as white residents. In 1896, the Supreme Court held that separate facilities for whites and blacks were legal as long as they were

Source: Library of Congress, Prints and Photographs Division [LC-USF34-046235-D]

"equal," ignoring both the intent of the Constitution and the fact that facilities reserved for blacks were vastly inferior.

The South's two-race system crumbled when the Supreme Court in 1954 voided the policy of separate public schools. In its unanimous decision in *Brown v. Board of Education*, the Court said: "Separate educational facilities are inherently unequal [and violate] the equal protection of the laws guaranteed by the Fourteenth Amendment."

A 1954 Gallup poll indicated that a sizable majority of southern whites opposed the *Brown* decision, and billboards were erected along southern roadways that called for the impeachment of Chief Justice Earl Warren. In the so-called Southern Manifesto, southern members of Congress urged their state governments to "resist forced integration by any lawful means." Rioting broke out in 1957 when Arkansas's governor called out the state's National Guard to prevent black students from entering Little Rock's high school. They achieved entry only after President Dwight D. Eisenhower used his power as commander in chief to place the Arkansas National Guard under federal control.

The Supreme Court's *Brown v. Board of Education* decision became precedent for rulings that over the years have extended equal protection to other groups. Indeed, *Brown* is widely regarded as one of the Supreme Court's most important decisions, ranking alongside such rulings as *Marbury v. Madison* (1803), *McCulloch v. Maryland* (1819), *Schenck v. United States* (1919), and *Mapp v. Ohio* (1961).

Continued

Q: What is the major limit on the Fourteenth Amendment as a means of preventing discrimination?

ASK YOURSELF: Who or what is prohibited by the Fourteenth Amendment from discriminating against individuals on the basis of their race, creed, or ethnicity? Who or what is not? If an individual is denied service in a restaurant because of race, creed, or ethnicity, would that person be entitled to sue the owner on grounds that his or her Fourteenth Amendment rights have been violated? Why or why not?

and the policy had mixed results. Studies found that busing improved school children's racial attitudes and improved minority children's performance on standardized tests without diminishing the performance of white classmates.[8] But the policy forced many children to spend long hours each day riding buses to and from school. Busing also contributed to white flight to the suburbs, which were protected by a 1974 Supreme Court decision that prohibited busing across school district lines except where district boundaries had been deliberately drawn to keep the races apart.[9] The declining number of white students in city schools made it harder, even with the use of busing, to create racially balanced classrooms.

In 2007, the Supreme Court in a decision involving the Seattle, Washington, and Louisville, Kentucky, school systems effectively ended forced busing. The Court ruled that it violated the equal-protection rights of students who were required to attend a distant school.[10] As a result of the end of racial busing and white flight to private and suburban schools, America's schools have become less racially diverse. In fact, America's schools are now more racially segregated than they were when busing began.[11]

Judicial Tests of Equal Protection   The Fourteenth Amendment's equal-protection clause does not require government to treat all groups or classes of people equally in all circumstances. The judiciary allows inequalities that are "reasonably" related to a legitimate government interest. In applying this **reasonable-basis test**, the courts require government only to show that a particular law is reasonable. For example, 21-year-olds can legally drink alcohol but 20-year-olds cannot. The courts have held that the goal of reducing fatalities from alcohol-related accidents involving young drivers is a valid reason for imposing an age limit on the purchase and consumption of alcohol.

The reasonable-basis test does not apply to racial or ethnic classifications (see Table 5-1). Any law that treats people differently because of race or ethnicity is subject to the **strict-scrutiny test**, which presumes that the law is

table 5-1	LEVELS OF COURT REVIEW FOR LAWS THAT TREAT AMERICANS DIFFERENTLY	
Test	**Application**	**Standard Used**
Strict scrutiny	Race, ethnicity	Suspect category—assumed unconstitutional in the absence of an overwhelming justification
Intermediate scrutiny	Gender	Almost suspect category—assumed unconstitutional unless the law serves a clearly compelling and justified purpose
Reasonable basis	Other categories (such as age and income)	Not suspect category—assumed constitutional unless no sound rationale for the law can be provided

unconstitutional unless government can provide a compelling basis for it. The Supreme Court's position is that race and national origin are **suspect classifications**—in other words, laws that classify people differently on the basis of their race or ethnicity are assumed to have discrimination as their purpose.

Although the notion of suspect classifications was implicit in earlier cases, including *Brown,* the Court did not use those words until *Loving v. Virginia* (1967). The state of Virginia had a law that prohibited white residents from marrying a person of a different race. When Richard Loving, a white man, and Mildred Jeter, a woman of African American and Native American descent, went to Washington, D.C., to get married and then returned home to Virginia, police invaded their home and arrested them. The state of Virginia claimed that its ban on interracial marriage did not violate the equal-protection clause because the penalty for the offense—a prison sentence of one to five years—was the same for both the white and the nonwhite spouse. The Supreme Court ruled otherwise, saying the Virginia law was "subversive of the principle of equality at the heart of the Fourteenth Amendment." The Court concluded that the law was based solely on "invidious racial discrimination" and that any such "classification" was unconstitutional.[12]

When women began to assert their rights more forcefully in the 1970s, some observers thought the Supreme Court would expand the scope of strict scrutiny to include gender. Instead, the Court held that men and women can be treated differently if the policy in question is "substantially related" to the achievement of "important governmental objectives."[13] The Court thus placed gender classifications in an intermediate (or almost suspect) category. Gender classifications were to be scrutinized more closely than some others

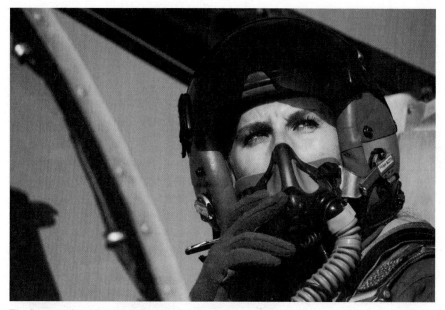

The Supreme Court has ruled that government cannot treat men and women differently in law unless it has a compelling justification for doing so. One such law excludes women from being drafted involuntarily into the military, although they can volunteer for military duty. Shown here is an A-10 Thunderbolt pilot assigned to the U.S. Air Force's 74th Expeditionary Fighter Squadron. (*Source:* U.S. Air Force photo by Staff Sgt. Joe W. McFadden/Released)

(for example, income or age) but were constitutionally valid if government could clearly show why men and women should be treated differently. In *Rostker v. Goldberg* (1980), the Court upheld such a classification, ruling that the male-only draft registration law served the important objective of excluding women from *involuntary* combat duty.[14]

Since then, however, the Supreme Court has struck down nearly every gender-based law it has reviewed. A leading case is *United States v. Virginia* (1996), in which the Court invalidated the male-only admissions policy of Virginia Military Institute (VMI), a 157-year-old state-supported college. In its ruling, the Court said that Virginia had failed to provide an "exceedingly persuasive" argument for its policy.[15]

The Civil Rights Act of 1964

The Fourteenth Amendment prohibits discrimination by government but not by private parties. As a result, for a long period in American history, private employers could freely discriminate in their hiring practices, and owners of restaurants, hotels, theaters, and other public accommodations could legally bar black people from entering. That changed with passage of the 1964 Civil

Rights Act. Based on Congress's power to regulate commerce, the legislation entitles all persons to equal access to public accommodations. The legislation also bars discrimination on the basis of race, color, religion, sex, or national origin in the hiring, promotion, and wages of employees of medium-size and large firms. A few forms of job discrimination are still lawful under the Civil Rights Act. For example, a church-related school can take religion into account in hiring teachers.

F A K E
     or
F A C T

Detecting Misinformation

Is Justice Color Blind?

Over the past half-century, the United States has made progress in upholding the ideal of "equal justice under the law."

Supreme Court rulings based on the Fourteenth Amendment's due process and equal-protection clauses have boosted the legal standing of black Americans and other historically disadvantaged groups. But does the reality of daily life match the legal gains?

©Michael Matthews/Police Images/Alamy

Most black Americans say no. A NBC poll found, for example, that only 12 percent of blacks believe that their community's police officers treat white and blacks equally.[16]

Is that claim fact, or is it fake?

There are communities where police do treat white and black residents equally, but research indicates that this pattern is not typical. Studies show that black residents are more likely than white residents to be ticketed or arrested for engaging in the same acts.[17] They are also more likely to be convicted and receive a stiffer sentence when charged with comparable crimes.[18] A U.S. Department of Justice study found, for example, that among persons convicted of drug crimes in state courts, half of black defendants received a prison sentence, compared with a third of white defendants.[19]

The Civil Rights Act proved effective in reducing discrimination in access to public accommodations because it's fairly easy to prove discrimination when a person is denied service at a restaurant or hotel that has available space. The act proved less effective in the area of job discrimination, where it's harder to prove that an individual has been the victim of discrimination. This situation led to the creation of affirmative action programs, a topic is discussed in a later section.

The Voting Rights Act of 1965

Free elections are the bedrock of American democracy, but the right to vote has only recently become a reality for many Americans, particularly African Americans. Although the 1870 Fifteenth Amendment granted blacks the right to vote, southern whites invented an array of devices such as whites-only primaries to keep blacks from registering and voting. In the mid-1940s, for example, there were only 2,500 registered black voters in the entire state of Mississippi, even though its black population numbered half a million.[20]

Racial barriers to voting began to crumble in the mid-1940s when the Supreme Court declared that whites-only primary elections were unconstitutional.[21] Ratification of the Twenty-Fourth Amendment in 1964 outlawed the poll tax, which was a fee that an individual had to pay in order to register to vote. Two years later, the Supreme Court banned the use of literacy tests as a condition for being allowed to register to vote.[22]

Nevertheless, the major policy change was the Voting Rights Act of 1965, which prohibited discrimination in voting and registration. The legislation empowered federal agents to register voters in states and localities with a history of voter discrimination. The Voting Rights Act had an immediate impact on black participation. In the ensuing presidential election, black turnout in the South jumped by 20 percentage points.

In *Shelby County v. Holder* (2013), the Supreme Court invalidated the provision (Section 4) of the Voting Rights Act that included the formula for determining which states and counties were subject to federal oversight. The formula included factors such as an area's use of various devices to keep black citizens from voting. Designated states and counties were required by the preclearance provision (Section 5) of the Voting Rights Act to obtain permission from federal officials before they made changes—such as redrawing electoral districts or altering registration requirements—that might adversely affect a minority group. In its *Shelby County* decision, the Court's majority held that the formula for identifying the states and counties subject to federal oversight was based on "obsolete statistics" and that Congress would need to update it before a formula could be used.[23]

The practical effect of the *Shelby County* ruling is to eliminate the requirement that some states and counties receive federal permission before they can change their voting process. Once changes are made, however, they can be challenged on grounds they are discriminatory. Some of these challenges have been upheld. In 2017, for instance, the Supreme Court struck down the boundaries of two North Carolina congressional districts on grounds they had been drawn in a way deliberately designed to reduce the power of black voters.[24]

SAMPLE   SAMPLE

(46)

"B"

1. Can you be imprisoned, under Alabama law, for a debt? No

2. In addition to becoming a U. S. citizen by birth, a person may become a citizen by:

   _____ immigration

   ___X___ naturalization

   _____ voting

3. Name one person by name or title who is part of the judicial branch of government in Alabama. Chief Justice Livingston.

4. The first sentence of the United States Constitution is called the Preamble. True

----

"C"

1. In what year did the Congress gain the right to prohibit the migration of persons to the states? 1808

2. Who is the commander-in-chief of the army and navy of the United States? The President

3. Which of the Parts above, of the United States Constitution, deals with the federal government's authority to call the state militia into federal service? Part 1

4. The president is forbidden to exercise his authority of pardon in cases of impeachment.

Until literacy tests were banned in the 1960s, they were used by some states as a way to keep black citizens (and sometimes poor white citizens) from registering to vote. To register, a citizen had to pass a literacy test that often contained questions on obscure topics. The questions in this example are from a portion of the 1965 Alabama literacy test. (*Source:* Civil Rights Movement Veterans, www.crmvet.org)

The Civil Rights Act of 1968

In 1968, Congress passed civil rights legislation designed to prohibit discrimination in housing. A building owner cannot refuse to sell or rent housing because of a person's race, religion, ethnicity, or sex. An exception is allowed for owners of small multifamily dwellings who reside on the premises.

Despite legal prohibitions on discrimination, housing in America remains highly segregated. Only a third of African Americans live in a neighborhood that is mostly white. One reason is that the annual income of most black families is substantially below that of most white families. Another reason is banking practices. At one time, banks contributed to housing segregation by *redlining*—refusing to grant mortgage loans in certain neighborhoods, typically those with large black populations. Since buyers could not get a mortgage, homeowners had to lower the selling price to sell their home. As home values dropped, white families increasingly left these neighborhoods, which had the

Until prohibited by the 1968 Civil Rights Act, redlining was a common banking practice in many cities. It involved the blanket denial of mortgages in certain neighborhoods, usually those with large black populations. The effect was to drive down housing prices, which contributed to white flight from these neighborhoods, resulting in increasingly segregated cities with blacks concentrated in certain neighborhoods and whites in others. (*Source:* National Archives and Records Administration II RG 195 Entry 39 Folder "Richmond, VA Master File–Security Map and Area Descriptions" Box 141. Image provided by LaDale Winling, www.urbanoasis.org.)

effect of increasing the percentage of black families. The 1968 Civil Rights Act prohibits redlining, but many of the segregated neighborhoods it helped create still exist. Moreover, minority status continues to affect the lending practices of some banks. Studies indicate that Hispanics and African Americans have more difficulty obtaining mortgages than do white applicants with comparable incomes.[25]

Affirmative Action

Changes in the law seldom have large or immediate effects on how people behave. For example, although the 1964 Civil Rights Act prohibited job discrimination on the basis of race, color, religion, sex, or national origin, many employers continued to favor white male employees. Other employers maintained employment procedures that kept women and minorities at a disadvantage. Membership in many union locals, for example, was handed down from father to son. Moreover, the Civil Rights Act did not require employers to prove that their employment practices were fair. Instead, the burden of proof was on the woman or minority-group member who was denied a job. It was costly and usually difficult for an individual to prove in court that gender or race was the reason for not being hired or promoted. Moreover, a victory in court applied only to the individual in question; it did not help other women and minorities faced with job discrimination.

Affirmative action programs were devised as a remedy for such problems. **Affirmative action** refers to deliberate efforts to provide full and equal opportunities in employment, education, and other areas for members of traditionally disadvantaged groups. Affirmative action applies only to organizations—such as universities, agencies, and construction firms—that receive federal funding or contracts. These organizations are required to establish programs designed to ensure that all applicants are treated fairly. They also bear a burden of proof. If an organization grants a disproportionate share of opportunities to white males, it must show that the pattern is the result of necessity (such as the nature of the job or the locally available labor pool) and not the result of systematic discrimination.

Equality of result, which was the aim of affirmative action, was a new concept. Other major civil rights policies had sought to eliminate **de jure discrimination**, which is discrimination based on law, as in the case of state laws requiring black and white children to attend separate schools during the pre-*Brown* period. Affirmative action policy sought to alleviate **de facto discrimination**—the condition whereby historically disadvantaged groups have fewer opportunities and benefits because of prejudice and economic circumstance, such as their inability to pay for a college education.

Few issues have sparked more controversy than has affirmative action, and even today the public has a mixed response to it. Most Americans support programs designed to ensure that historically disadvantaged groups receive equal treatment, but oppose programs that would give them preferential treatment. A Gallup poll found, for example, that only 4 percent of white Americans believed race and ethnicity should be a "major factor" in college admission decisions, while 67 percent said race and ethnicity should count "not at all" in such decisions.[26]

Policies that pit individuals against each other over jobs, college admissions, and the like typically end up in the Supreme Court, and affirmative action is no exception. In *University of California Regents v. Bakke* (1978), the Court issued its first affirmative action ruling, holding that a California medical school had violated the equal-protection rights of Alan Bakke, a white male applicant, by reserving a fixed number of admissions ("a quota") for minority applicants. The Court struck down the use of quotas but did not invalidate affirmative action per se, holding instead that race could be among the factors taken into account by schools in their effort to create a diverse student body.[27]

The Court later narrowed the scope of affirmative action. In the key case of *Adarand v. Peña* (1995), for example, the Court invalidated a federal policy that had reserved 10 percent of federally funded construction projects for

In 2016, the Supreme Court ruled on a key affirmative action case involving the University of Texas at Austin (pictured here). The case centered on the university's discretionary admissions policy, which, in addition to academic achievement, was based on such things as athletic ability, extracurricular activities, musical talent, and ethnic and racial background. The University of Texas case was not unprecedented. Several key affirmative action rulings have centered on college admissions policies, including the first ever affirmative action ruling, *Regents of the University of California v. Bakke* (1978). (©dszc/Getty Images)

minority-owned firms. The Court held that such firms cannot benefit from the fact that minority-owned firms had been discriminated against in the past.[28]

Opponents of affirmative action thought that the *Adarand* decision might lead the Supreme Court to abolish it completely. However, in *Grutter v. Bollinger* (2003), the Court upheld the University of Michigan law school's admissions policy, which took into account race (along with other factors such as work experience and extracurricular activities) in admissions decisions. The Court concluded that Michigan's program was being applied sensibly and that it fostered Michigan's "compelling interest in obtaining the educational benefits that flow from a diverse student body."[29]

The Court reaffirmed that position in 2016 in *Fisher v. University of Texas*. At issue was the university's policy for admitting students who were not in the top 10 percent of their Texas high school graduating class. Whereas applicants at the top of their class are admitted automatically, other applicants are admitted or rejected based on a "holistic" evaluation that includes their high school grades, standardized test scores, and other factors, including extracurricular activities, special skills (such as musical talent or athletic ability), and race or ethnicity. The Supreme Court held that the university's use of race and ethnicity as factors in admissions decisions was permissible, noting that it served the university's compelling interest in creating a diverse student body while also noting that it was narrowly tailored in that it gave only a slight advantage to minority students. The Court said that "[c]onsiderable deference is owed to a university in defining those intangible characteristics, like student body diversity, that are central to its identity and educational mission."[30]

The Michigan and Texas cases clarified the test that the Supreme Court applies in affirmative action cases. For affirmative action to be upheld, it must, first, serve a "compelling governmental interest." At root, it must serve a critical interest as opposed to something that is merely desired. A diverse student body, for example, can be justified because it enhances learning and promotes understanding, which are central to a university's educational mission. Second, to be upheld affirmative action must be "narrowly tailored" to achieve the desired goal. What this means, in effect, is that overly broad actions cannot be justified. That part of the test was what led the Supreme Court to strike down the 10 percent rule for government contracts. The awarding of contracts to minority firms merely because other such firms had been discriminated against in the past was not narrowly tailored to fit the current situation.

THE STRUGGLE FOR EQUALITY

American history indicates that disadvantaged groups have never achieved greater equality without a struggle.[31] The policies that protect these groups today are the result of sustained political action that forced entrenched interests to relinquish or share their privileged status. Progress has been made toward a more equal America, but civil rights problems involve deeply rooted conditions, habits, and prejudices. The following discussion describes the struggles these groups faced historically and some of the struggles they face today.

Black Americans

The impetus behind the 1964 Civil Rights Act was the black civil rights movement. Without it, the legislation would have come later and possibly have been less sweeping.

During World War II, African American soldiers fought against Nazi racism only to return to an America where racial discrimination was legal and oppressive.[32] Demands for change intensified after an incident in Montgomery, Alabama, on December 1, 1955. Upon leaving work that day, Rosa Parks boarded a bus for home, taking her seat as required by law in the section reserved for blacks. When all the seats for white passengers were occupied, the bus driver ordered Parks to give her seat to a white passenger. She refused and was arrested. A young pastor at a local Baptist church, Dr. Martin Luther King Jr., led a boycott of Montgomery's bus system, which spread to other cities. The black civil rights movement was under way and would continue for more than a decade. A peak moment occurred in 1963 with the March on Washington for Jobs and Freedom, which attracted 250,000 marchers, one of the largest gatherings in the capital's history. In a riveting speech to the massive crowd, King expressed his dream of a better America, one where people are judged by the quality of their personal character rather than by the color of their skin.[33]

The momentum of the March on Washington carried over into Congress, where major civil rights legislation was languishing in House committee. Although opponents employed every possible legislative maneuver in an effort to block it, it finally cleared the House the following February. Senate maneuvering and debate—including a 55-day filibuster—took another four months. Finally, in early July, President Lyndon Johnson signed into law the Civil Rights Act of 1964.

Martin Luther King Jr.'s dream of an equal society for black Americans remains elusive.[34] Poverty is a persistent problem in the black community, affecting everyone from the very old to the very young. The median net worth of households headed by retired black people is less than $20,000, compared with roughly $200,000 for retired white people. Among adults of employment age, the jobless rate of African Americans is twice that of white Americans.

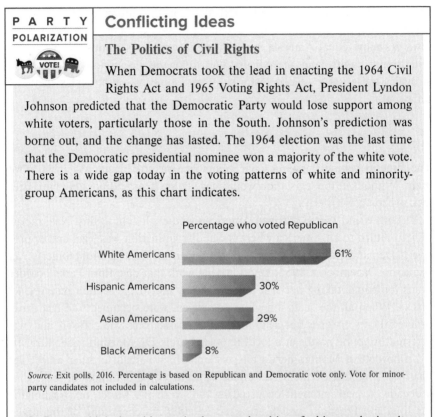

PARTY
POLARIZATION

Conflicting Ideas

The Politics of Civil Rights

When Democrats took the lead in enacting the 1964 Civil Rights Act and 1965 Voting Rights Act, President Lyndon Johnson predicted that the Democratic Party would lose support among white voters, particularly those in the South. Johnson's prediction was borne out, and the change has lasted. The 1964 election was the last time that the Democratic presidential nominee won a majority of the white vote. There is a wide gap today in the voting patterns of white and minority-group Americans, as this chart indicates.

Percentage who voted Republican

White Americans	61%
Hispanic Americans	30%
Asian Americans	29%
Black Americans	8%

Source: Exit polls, 2016. Percentage is based on Republican and Democratic vote only. Vote for minor-party candidates not included in calculations.

Q: Do you think the wide gap in the party loyalties of whites and minority-group members makes it easier or harder for Republicans and Democrats to bridge their other differences?

Black children are particularly disadvantaged. Roughly 35 percent of them live below the government-defined poverty line, compared with about 12 percent of white children. In addition, more than half of black children grow up in a single-parent family, and about 1 in 10 grow up in a home where neither parent is present. Children who grow up in a single-parent household are much more likely to have inadequate nutrition, not finish high school, not attend college, be unemployed as an adult, and spend time in prison.[35]

An area in which African Americans have made substantial progress is elective office. Although the percentage of black elected officials is still far below the proportion of African Americans in the population, it has risen in recent decades.[36] There are now roughly 400 black mayors and 40 black members of Congress. Barack Obama's election to the presidency in 2008 marked the first time an African American was chosen to fill the nation's highest office.

Women

The black civil rights movement inspired other disadvantaged groups to demand their rights. Women were the most vocal and successful of these groups.

The United States carried over from English common law a political disregard for women, forbidding them to vote, hold public office, or serve on juries.[37] Upon marriage, a woman essentially lost her identity as an individual and could not own and dispose of property without her husband's consent. Even a wife's body was not fully hers. A wife's adultery was declared by the Supreme Court in 1904 to be a violation of the husband's property rights.[38]

The first large and well-organized attempt to promote women's rights came in 1848 in Seneca Falls, New York. Lucretia Mott and Elizabeth Cady Stanton had been barred from the main floor of an antislavery convention and decided to organize a women's rights convention. Thereafter, the struggle for women's rights became closely aligned with the abolitionist movement. However, when Congress wrote the Fifteenth Amendment after the Civil War, women were not included in its provisions despite promises to the contrary. The Fifteenth Amendment declared only that the right to vote could not be abridged on account of race or color. Not until passage of the Nineteenth Amendment in 1920 did women acquire the right to vote.

The Nineteenth Amendment's ratification encouraged women's leaders in 1923 to propose a constitutional amendment granting equal rights to women. Congress rejected the proposal but 50 years later approved the Equal Rights Amendment (ERA) and submitted it to the states for ratification. The ERA failed by three states to receive the required three-fourths majority.[39] Women did succeed in other efforts, however. Among the congressional measures were the Equal Pay Act of 1963, which prohibits sex discrimination in salary and wages by some categories of employers; Title IX of the Education Amendment of 1972, which prohibits sex discrimination in education; and the Equal Credit Act of 1974, which prohibits sex discrimination in the granting of financial credit.

In recent decades, increasing numbers of women have entered the job market. They are six times more likely today than a half-century ago to work outside the home and have made inroads in male-dominated occupations. For example, roughly half of all graduating lawyers and physicians are women. The change in women's work status is also reflected in general education statistics. A few decades ago, more men than women were enrolled in college. Today, the reverse is true. A recent U.S. Education Department report showed that

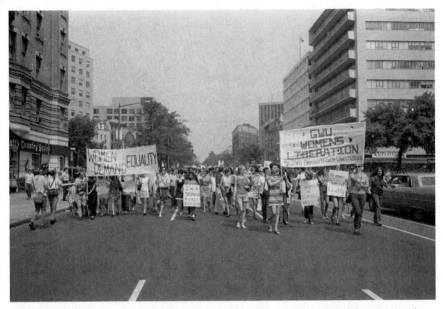

Historically disadvantaged groups awoke in the mid-20th century to their second-class status and pressed for change. Pictured here is a women's rights march that took place in Washington in 1970. The women's rights movement helped prompt legislation that prohibits sexual discrimination in areas such as employment and financial credit. (*Source:* Library of Congress, Prints and Photographs Division [LC-U9-23117-25])

women are ahead of men in more than just college enrollment; they are also more likely on average to complete their degree, do so in a shorter period, and get better grades.[40]

Nevertheless, women have not achieved job equality. Women increasingly hold managerial positions, but, as they rise through the ranks, they can encounter the so-called glass ceiling, which refers to the invisible but nonetheless real barrier that some women face when firms choose their top executives. Of the 500 largest U.S. corporations, only about 7 percent are headed by women. Women also earn less than men: The average hourly pay for full-time female employees is about 82 percent of that for full-time male employees. Many of the jobs traditionally held by women, such as office assistant, pay less than many of the jobs traditionally held by men, such as truck driver. Women's groups have had only limited success in persuading courts and employers to institute *comparable worth policies* that would give women and men equal hourly pay for jobs that require a similar level of training and education.[41]

Women gained a major victory in the workplace in 1993 when Congress passed the Family and Medical Leave Act. It provides for up to 12 weeks of unpaid leave for employees to care for a new baby or a seriously ill family

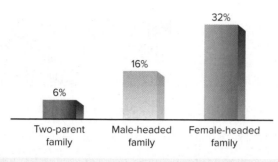

figure 5-1   PERCENTAGE OF FAMILIES LIVING IN POVERTY, BY FAMILY COMPOSITION

Poverty is five times higher among female-headed households than among two-parent households. (*Source:* U.S. Census Bureau, 2016)

member. Upon return from leave, the employee ordinarily must be given the original or an equivalent job position with equivalent pay and benefits. These provisions apply to men as well as women, but women were the instigating force behind the legislation and are the primary beneficiaries because they usually bear most of the responsibility for newborn or sick family members.

Most single-parent families are headed by women, and about one in three of these families live below the poverty line, which is five times the level of two-parent families (see Figure 5-1). The situation has been described as "the feminization of poverty." Especially vulnerable are single-parent families headed by women who work in a nonprofessional field. Women without a college education or special skills often cannot find jobs that pay significantly more than the child-care expenses they incur if they work outside the home.

Women, too, have made substantial gains in the area of appointive and elective offices. In 1981, President Ronald Reagan appointed the first woman to serve on the Supreme Court, Sandra Day O'Connor. When the Democratic Party in 1984 chose Geraldine Ferraro as its vice presidential nominee, she became the first woman to run on the national ticket of a major political party. When Hillary Clinton won the 2016 Democratic presidential nomination, she became the first woman to head a major party's national ticket. Nevertheless, women are still a long way from attaining political parity.[42] Women hold less than one in four congressional seats (see "How the U.S. Differs").

Hispanic Americans

Hispanic Americans—that is, people of Spanish-speaking background—are one of the nation's oldest ethnic groups. Hispanics helped colonize California, Texas, Florida, New Mexico, and Arizona before those areas were annexed by the United States. Most Hispanics, however, are immigrants or the children or grandchildren of immigrants.

HOW THE U.S. DIFFERS

CRITICAL THINKING THROUGH COMPARISONS

Women's Representation in National Legislatures

Women today hold far more congressional seats than at earlier times in American history, but they are still far from achieving parity with men. Moreover, the United States ranks substantially below European democracies in terms of the percentage of women lawmakers, as the chart indicates.

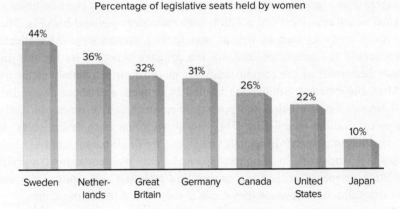

Percentage of legislative seats held by women

Source: Inter-parliamentary Union, 2018. Based on seats in the single or lower legislative chamber, which is the House of Representatives in the case of the United States.

Q: How might differences in the U.S. and European electoral systems contribute to differences in the number of women legislators? (Most European democracies rely on a proportional representation system, where the parties get seats in proportion to the number of votes they receive in the election. In contrast, U.S. candidates are elected singly in legislative districts.)

A: In a proportional representation system, each party lists its candidates in priority order before the election. By placing women high on its list, a party can ensure that they will receive a certain proportion of the legislative seats it wins in an election. In contrast, the U.S. system rests on the preferences of voters in individual contests, which makes it harder for a political party to control who gets its legislative seats. (The proportional and single-member district systems are explained more fully in Chapter 8.)

Hispanics are the fastest-growing minority in the United States and recently surpassed African Americans as the nation's largest racial or ethnic minority group. More than 50 million Hispanics live in the United States—twice the number of two decades ago. They have emigrated to the United States primarily from Mexico and the Caribbean islands, mainly Cuba and Puerto Rico. About half of all Hispanics in the United States were born in Mexico or claim a Mexican ancestry. Hispanics are concentrated in their states of entry. Florida, New York, and New Jersey have large numbers of Caribbean Hispanics, whereas California, Texas, Arizona, and New Mexico have many Mexican immigrants. Hispanics, mostly of Mexican descent, constitute more than half of the population of Los Angeles.

An early civil rights action by Hispanics occurred in California in the late 1960s when Hispanic farm laborers, most of whom were migrant workers, went on strike over labor rights. Migrants were working long hours for low pay, were living in shacks without electricity or plumbing, and were unwelcome in many local schools and hospitals. Farm owners at first refused to bargain with the workers, but a well-organized national boycott of California grapes and lettuce forced the state to pass a law giving migrant workers the right to bargain collectively. The strikes were led by Cesar Chavez, who had grown up in a Mexican American migrant family. Chavez's tactics were copied with less success in other states, including Texas.[43]

Recent Hispanic civil rights action has centered on undocumented immigrants, individuals who have entered the country illegally or stayed after their visa expired. Estimates of the number of undocumented immigrants run as high as 12 million people, most of whom are Hispanic. Although polls show that most Americans favor providing them a path to citizenship,[44] they've periodically been the target of heightened legislative or law enforcement efforts aimed at their deportation. Such efforts have been resisted by the Hispanic community and, in some instances, have sparked mass demonstrations. The largest such demonstrations came in response to a bill passed by the Republican-controlled House of Representatives that, if it had been passed by the Senate, would have led to the arrest and deportation of millions of undocumented immigrants.

Hispanics' average annual income is substantially below the national average, but the effect is buffered somewhat by the fact that the family is integral to Hispanic culture. As compared with black Americans, Hispanics are nearly twice as likely to live in a two-parent family, often a two-income family. As a result, fewer Hispanic than black families live below the poverty line. Health researchers have concluded that family structure helps account for the fact that Hispanics are healthier and have longer life expectancy than would be predicted on the basis of their education and income levels.

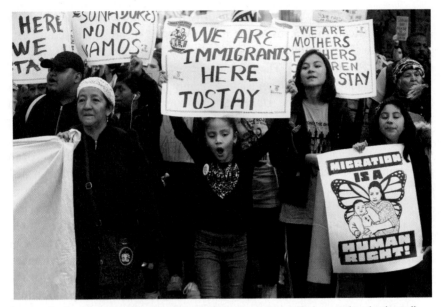

Immigration has been one of President Donald Trump's top issues. He has sought a border wall running the length of the U.S.-Mexico border to control illegal immigration and has expanded efforts to detain and deport undocumented immigrants. Polls indicate that Hispanic Americans are the group most opposed to the policies. (©a katz/Shutterstock)

More than 4,000 Hispanic Americans hold public office. Hispanics have been elected to statewide office in several states, including New Mexico and Arizona, and nearly three dozen Hispanic Americans currently serve in the House of Representatives. In 2009, Sonia Sotomayor was appointed to serve on the U.S. Supreme Court, becoming the first Hispanic to do so. In 2016, senators Marco Rubio and Ted Cruz were top contenders for the Republican presidential nomination—the first time any Hispanic had that level of success. At present, only about half of all Hispanics are registered to vote, limiting the group's political power. Nevertheless, the sheer size of the Hispanic population in states such as Texas, Florida, and California will make the group a potent political force in the years to come (see Chapter 8).

Native Americans

When white settlers first arrived, an estimated 5 to 10 million Native Americans lived in what is now the United States. By 1900, they numbered less than a million. In the whole of recorded history, no people had suffered such a huge population decline in such a short period. Smallpox and other diseases brought by white settlers took the heaviest toll, but wars and massacres also contributed. As part of a policy of westward expansion, settlers and U.S. troops

HOW THE 50 STATES DIFFER

CRITICAL THINKING THROUGH COMPARISONS

Minority Group Populations in the States

Black Americans, Hispanics, and Asian Americans constitute about 40 percent of the U.S. population; by 2050, they will constitute a majority. Minorities are already in the majority in Hawaii, California, New Mexico, and Texas. The upper Midwest states have the smallest minority-group populations.

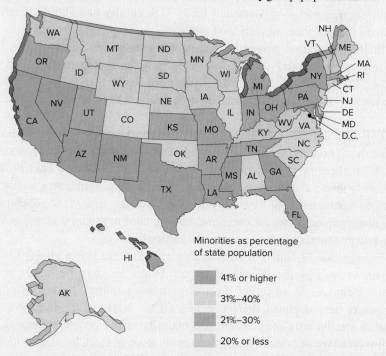

Minorities as percentage of state population

- 41% or higher
- 31%–40%
- 21%–30%
- 20% or less

Q: What factors might explain the high proportion of minorities in some states?

A: Southern states have large black populations, a legacy of slavery. Southwestern states owe their high minority populations to their proximity to the Mexican border, which has been a major point of entry for immigrants from Mexico and Central and South America. In the North, the more heavily industrialized states tend to have larger minority populations than the more rural states. During the 20th century, large numbers of black Americans left the South for jobs in northern cities (the so-called Great Migration).

mercilessly drove the eastern Indians from their ancestral lands to the Great Plains and then seized most of the territory there as well. Until Congress changed the policy in 1924, Native Americans by law were denied citizenship, which meant they lacked even the power to vote.

At first, Native Americans were not part of the 1960s civil rights movement. That changed in 1972 when Native American leaders organized the "Trail of Broken Treaties," a caravan that journeyed from California to Washington, D.C., to protest federal policy. The next year, armed Native Americans took control of the village of Wounded Knee on a Sioux reservation in South Dakota; over the next two months they exchanged sporadic gunfire with U.S. marshals that left two Native Americans dead and one marshal paralyzed. Eight decades earlier at Wounded Knee, U.S. cavalry had shot to death 300 disarmed Sioux men, women, and children.

In 1974, Congress passed legislation that granted Native Americans living on reservations greater control over federal programs affecting them. Six years earlier, Congress had enacted the Indian Civil Rights Act, which gives Native Americans on reservations constitutional guarantees similar to those held by other Americans.

Full-blooded Native Americans, including Alaska Natives, currently number more than two million, about half of whom live on or close to reservations set aside for them by the federal government. State governments have no direct authority over federal reservations, and the federal government's authority is defined by the terms of its treaty with the particular tribe. U.S. policy toward the reservations has varied over time, but the current policy is aimed at fostering self-government and economic self-sufficiency.[45]

Preservation of Native American culture is another policy goal.[46] Children in schools run by the Bureau of Indian Affairs can now be taught in their native language. At an earlier time, English was required. Nevertheless, tribal languages have declined sharply in use. Of the larger tribes, the Navajo and Pueblo are the only ones in which a majority of the people still speak their native language at home. Ninety percent or more of the Cherokee, Chippewa, Creek, Iroquois, and Lumbee speak only English.

In recent years, a number of tribes have erected gaming casinos on reservation land. The world's largest casino, Foxwoods, is operated by the Mashantucket Pequots in Connecticut. Casinos have brought economic opportunities. The employment level of Native Americans living on or near the reservations where casinos are located has increased by a fourth.[47] However, the casinos have also brought controversy—traditionalists argue that the casinos are creating a gaming culture that, whatever its economic benefits, is eroding tribal traditions.[48]

Although casino gambling has raised Native Americans' average income level, it is still far below the national average. Native Americans are a disadvantaged group by other indicators as well. For example, they are less than half as likely as other Americans to have completed college, and their infant mortality rate is nearly twice that of white Americans.[49]

Asian Americans

Chinese and Japanese laborers were brought to the western states during the late 1800s to work in mines and to build railroads. When the need for this labor declined, Congress in 1892 suspended Asian immigration on grounds that Asians were inferior people. Over the next seven decades, laws and informal arrangements blocked residents of most Asian countries, including China and Japan, from coming to the United States. In 1965, as part of its broader civil rights agenda, Congress lifted restrictions on Asian immigration. Strict limits on Hispanic immigration were also lifted at this time, and since then, most immigrants have come from Latin America and Asia (see Figure 5-2).

Asian Americans were not politically active to any great extent during the 1960s, but their rights were expanded by the 1964 Civil Rights Act and other policies adopted in response to action by other minority groups. However, in *Lau v. Nichols* (1974), a case initiated by a Chinese American family, the Supreme Court ruled unanimously that placing public school children for whom English is a second language in regular classrooms without special assistance violates the Civil Rights Act because it denies them the opportunity to obtain a proper education.[50] The Court did not mandate bilingual instruction, but the *Lau* decision prompted many schools to implement it.

Asian Americans now number about 12 million, or roughly 4 percent of the total U.S. population. Most Asian Americans live on the West Coast, particularly in California. China, Japan, Korea, India, Vietnam, and the Philippines are the ancestral homes of most Asian Americans.

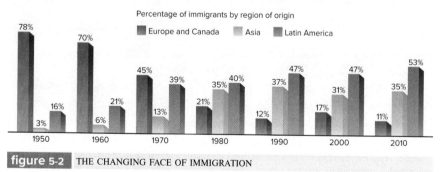

figure 5-2   THE CHANGING FACE OF IMMIGRATION

Until 1965, immigration laws were biased in favor of European immigrants. The laws enacted in 1965 increased the proportion of immigrants from Asia and Latin America. Percentages are totals for each decade; for example, the 2010 figures are for the 2001–2010 period. (*Source:* U.S. Immigration and Naturalization Service, 2016)

Asian Americans are an upwardly mobile group.[51] Most Asian cultures emphasize family-based self-reliance, which, in the American context, includes educational achievement as a means of getting ahead. Asian Americans now make up a disproportionately large share of students at the nation's top universities, which base admission primarily on high school grades and standardized test scores.[52]

Asian Americans have the highest percentage of two-parent families of any racial group, which, in combination with educational attainment, has led to their emergence in the past two decades as the group with the highest median family income. The median Asian American family's income exceeds $60,000, which is about $10,000 more than that of the median non-Hispanic white family and almost double that of the median black or Hispanic family.

Nevertheless, Asian Americans are underrepresented in certain areas of the workplace. According to U.S. government figures, Asian Americans account

Asian Americans have faced discrimination throughout their history. During World War II, for example, Japanese Americans living on the West Coast were relocated to inland detention camps on grounds they might assist America's enemy, Japan. Ironically, Japanese Americans were allowed to fight in Europe and made up the entirety of the U.S. Army's 442nd Regimental Combat Team. The 442nd became the most decorated unit of its size, not just in World War II, but in the entire history of the U.S. Army. Twenty-one of its soldiers won the Congressional Medal of Honor—the nation's highest award for valor. (*Source:* National Archives and Records Administration Archives (26-G-3422))

for about 5 percent of professionals and technicians, which is slightly more than their percentage of the population. Yet they have not attained a proportionate share of top business positions; they hold less than 3 percent of managerial jobs. They hold a larger proportion of such positions in the tech sector but, even there, they are underrepresented relative to the number of Asian Americans who work in the tech sector.[53]

Asian Americans are also underrepresented politically, even by comparison with Hispanics and blacks.[54] Only a dozen Asian Americans currently serve in Congress. Not until 1996 was an Asian American elected governor of a state other than Hawaii, and not until 2000 did an Asian American hold a presidential cabinet position.

Other Disadvantaged Groups

The Civil Rights Act of 1964 classified women and minorities as legally protected groups, which has made it easier for them to pursue their claims in federal court. Other disadvantaged groups do not have the same degree of legal protection, but have benefited from particular policies. For example, the Age Discrimination Act of 1975 and the Age Discrimination in Employment Act of 1967 prohibit discrimination against older workers in hiring for jobs in which age is not a critical factor in job performance. More recently, mandatory retirement ages for most jobs have been eliminated by law. Nevertheless, the courts have given government and employers some leeway in establishing age-based policies.[55] Forced retirement for reasons of age is permissible if justified by the nature of a particular job or the performance of a particular employee. Commercial airline pilots, for instance, are required by law to retire at 65 years of age and must pass a rigorous physical examination to continue flying after they reach the age of 60.

Individuals with disabilities are also protected through laws. In 1990, for example, Congress passed the Americans with Disabilities Act, which grants employment and other protections to this group. Government agencies are required, for instance, to take reasonable steps, such as installing access ramps, to make public buildings and services available to the disabled.[56] Earlier, through the Education for All Handicapped Children Act of 1975, Congress required that schools provide all children, however severe their disability, with a free and appropriate education. Before the legislation, four million children with disabilities were getting either no education or an inappropriate one (as in the case of a blind child who is not taught braille).

No disadvantaged group has gained more legal protection in the past decade than has the LGBTQ community. Not that long ago, they were subject to unchecked discrimination. They could, for example, be fired from a job if their sexual orientation became known. Such prohibitions no longer exist, and the legal protections in some jurisdictions now extend to transgender people's access to the public restroom corresponding to their gender identity. Until recently, the LGBTQ community's struggle for equal rights focused on marriage rights. In 2004, Massachusetts became the first state to permit same-sex marriage. The effort spread to other states and, in *Obergefell v. Hodges* (2015), the Supreme Court expanded the right to include all states, holding that bans on same-sex marriage violated the Fourteenth Amendment's guarantees of equal protection and due process.[57]

Public opinion was a driving force behind the change. Rarely in the history of polling has public opinion on a major issue changed so dramatically and so quickly as in the case of same-sex marriage (see Figure 5-3). Two decades ago, less than 30 percent of Americans expressed support for same-sex marriage. Today more than 60 percent do so. The support level is particularly high among younger adults—three-fourths of them say same-sex couples should be allowed to marry. Within all age groups, however, the support level has risen substantially. Among Americans over 65 years of age, for example, more than two in every five are now in favor of same-sex marriage, compared with only one in every seven two decades ago.

Other groups could have been described in this section. The United States has, for example, a long history of religious discrimination, targeted at various times and places against Catholics, Jews, Mormons, Muslims, various Protestant sects, and others. Numerous ethnic groups, including the Irish, the Italians, and the Poles, have likewise faced severe discrimination. Space precludes the discussion of the many forms of discrimination in America, but the point

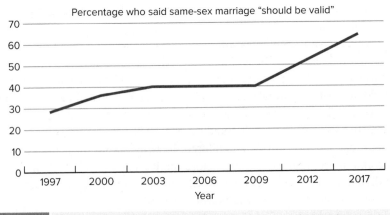

figure 5-3　OPINIONS ON SAME-SEX MARRIAGE

Twenty years ago, a majority of Americans opposed same-sex marriage. Today, a majority support it. (*Source:* Gallup poll, 2017) of any such discussion would be the same: Equality has been America's most elusive ideal.

DISCRIMINATION: SUPERFICIAL DIFFERENCES, DEEP DIVISIONS

In 1944, Swedish sociologist Gunnar Myrdal gained fame for his book *An American Dilemma,* whose title referred to deep-rooted racism in a country that idealized equality.[58] Equality is a difficult idea in practice because it requires people to shed preconceived notions about how other people think, behave, and feel. People have difficulty looking beyond superficial differences—whether those differences relate to skin color, national origin, religious preference, gender, age, disability, or lifestyle.[59] Myrdal called discrimination "America's curse." He could have broadened the generalization. Discrimination is civilization's curse, as is clear from the thousands of ethnic, national, and religious conflicts that have marred human history. But America carries a special responsibility because of its high ideals. In the words of Abraham Lincoln, the United States is a nation "dedicated to the proposition that all men are created equal."

SUMMARY

During the past half-century, the United States has undergone a revolution in the legal status of its traditionally disadvantaged groups, including African Americans, women, Native Americans, Hispanic Americans, and Asian Americans. Such groups are now provided equal protection under the law in areas such as education, employment, and voting. Discrimination by race, sex, and ethnicity has not been eliminated from American life, but it is no longer substantially backed by the force of law. This advance was achieved against strong resistance from established interests, which only begrudgingly and slowly responded to demands for equality in law.

Traditionally disadvantaged Americans have achieved fuller equality primarily as a result of their struggle for greater rights. The Supreme Court has been an instrument of change for disadvantaged groups. Its ruling in *Brown v. Board of Education* (1954), in which racial segregation in public schools was declared a violation of the Fourteenth Amendment's equal-protection clause, was a major breakthrough in equal rights. Through its affirmative action and other rulings, such as those providing equal access to the vote, the Court has also mandated the active promotion of social, political, and economic equality. However, because civil rights policy involves large issues concerned with social values and the distribution of society's opportunities and benefits, civil rights have also been advanced through legislative and administrative action. The history of civil rights includes landmark legislation, such as the 1964 Civil Rights Act and the 1965 Voting Rights Act.

In more recent decades, civil rights issues have receded from the prominence they had during the 1960s. The scope of affirmative action programs has narrowed, and the use of forced busing to achieve racial integration in America's public schools has been largely eliminated.

The legal gains of disadvantaged groups over the past half-century have not been fully matched by material gains. Although progress in areas such as education, income, and health care has been made, it has often been slow and incomplete. Tradition, prejudice, and the sheer difficulty of social, economic, and political progress stand as formidable obstacles to achieving a more equal America.

©gangliu10/Getty Images

CRITICAL THINKING ZONE

KEY TERMS

affirmative action (*p. 144*)
de facto discrimination (*p. 144*)
de jure discrimination (*p. 144*)
equal-protection clause (*p. 134*)

equal rights (civil rights) (*p. 133*)
reasonable-basis test (*p. 137*)
strict-scrutiny test (*p. 137*)
suspect classifications (*p. 138*)

APPLYING THE ELEMENTS OF CRITICAL THINKING

Conceptualizing: Distinguish between de jure discrimination and de facto discrimination. Why is the latter form of discrimination more difficult to overcome?

Synthesizing: Using material in this chapter and the previous one, contrast the Fourteenth Amendment's due process clause with its equal-protection clause. What level of government in America's federal system is governed by the two clauses?

Analyzing: What role have political movements played in securing the legal rights of disadvantaged groups?

EXTRA CREDIT

A Book Worth Reading: Ta-Nehisi Coates, *Between the World and Me* (New York: Spiegel & Grau, 2015). Winner of the 2015 National Book Award for Nonfiction, the book recounts the history of violence directed at black Americans.

A Website Worth Visiting: www.cawp.rutgers.edu The Center for American Women and Politics at Rutgers University tracks women's political participation. Its website has state-by-state information on the subject.

PARTICIPATE!

Think of a disadvantaged group that you would like to assist. It could be one of the federal government's designated groups (such as Native Americans), one of the other groups mentioned in the chapter (such as people with disabilities), or some other group (such as individuals who are homeless). Contact a college, community, national, or international organization that seeks to help this group, and volunteer your assistance. (The Internet provides the names of thousands of organizations, such as Habitat for Humanity, that are involved in helping those who are disadvantaged.)

6
CHAPTER

PUBLIC OPINION AND POLITICAL SOCIALIZATION: SHAPING THE PEOPLE'S VOICE

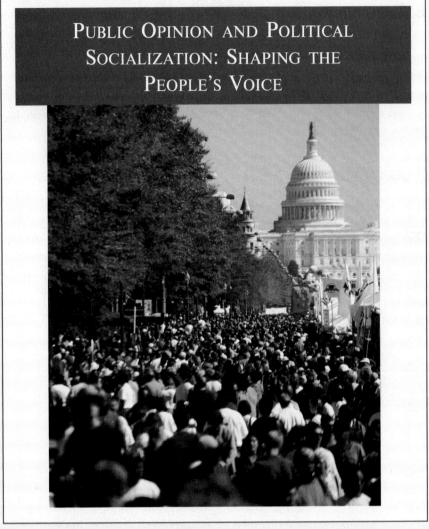

©Photodisc/PunchStock

> **❝** Towering over Presidents and [Congress] . . . public opinion stands out, in the United States, as the great source of power, the master of servants who tremble before it. **❞**
>
> JAMES BRYCE[1]

On the afternoon of February 14, 2018, a gunman walked into Marjory Stoneman Douglas High School in Parkland, Florida, and opened fire, killing fourteen students and three staff members, as well as wounding more than a dozen others. It was the eighth school shooting in less than two months, and the deadliest since the massacre of twenty-six children and teachers at Connecticut's Sandy Hook Elementary School in 2012.

The Parkland shooting, like earlier ones, brought calls for stricter gun control. But this time, the response was more substantial. The surviving Marjory Stoneman Douglas High School students were vocal in their demand that lawmakers take action to stop school violence. They went on television to voice their concerns, held public demonstrations, and traveled to the state capital and Washington to pressure lawmakers. Polls showed a rise in support for gun control measures. Two-thirds of Americans said there should be a ban on assault rifles—the type of weapon used in the Parkland shooting. More than 90 percent wanted tighter background checks on gun buyers.[2]

Nevertheless, in the ensuing months, few policies were enacted to limit guns. Congress took no action. That was also true of most state legislatures. However, some states, including Florida, did enact limited policies, including laws that allowed for "extreme risk protection orders." Such laws, popularly called "red flag" laws, give law enforcement officers the authority to temporarily take firearms from individuals who are deemed likely to harm other people or themselves.

Gun control is a telling example of the influence of public opinion on government. Public opinion is not something that public officials can ignore, but it is also not something that forces them to take a specific course of action. They have latitude in deciding what to do.

Students from Marjory Stoneman Douglas High School in Parkland, Florida, speak in support of gun control after fourteen of their classmates and three staff members were shot to death by a former student. Their efforts placed pressure on lawmakers to address the problem of gun violence in America's schools. (©Shawn Thew/EPA-EFE/REX/Shutterstock)

This chapter discusses public opinion and its influence on U.S. politics. In this text, **public opinion** is defined as the politically relevant opinions held by ordinary citizens that they express openly. That expression can be verbal, as when citizens voice an opinion to a neighbor or respond to a question asked in an opinion poll. But expression can take other forms—for example, participating in a protest demonstration or casting a vote in an election. The key point is that people's private thoughts become public opinion when they are revealed to others.

A major theme of the chapter is that public opinion is a powerful yet inexact force.[3] The policies of the U.S. government cannot be understood apart from public opinion; at the same time, public opinion is not a precise determinant of public policies. The chapter makes the following main points:

- *Public opinion consists of those views held by ordinary citizens that are openly expressed.* Public officials have various means of gauging public opinion but increasingly use public opinion polls for this purpose.

- *Public opinion is characterized by its direction (whether people hold a pro or con position on an issue), its intensity (how strongly people feel about their issue position), and its salience (how high a particular issue ranks in people's minds relative to other issues).*

- *The process by which individuals acquire their political opinions is called political socialization.* This process begins during childhood, when, through family and school, people acquire many of their basic political values and beliefs. Socialization continues into adulthood, during which time the news media, peers, and political leaders are important influences.

- *Americans' political opinions are shaped by several frames of reference, including partisanship, ideology, and group attachments.*

- *Public opinion has an important influence on government but ordinarily does not determine exactly what officials will do.*

The Measurement of Public Opinion

Woodrow Wilson once said that he had spent much of his adult life in government and yet had never seen "a government." What Wilson was saying, in effect, was that government is a system of relationships. A government is not tangible in the way that a building is. So it is with public opinion. No one has ever seen "a public opinion," and thus it cannot be measured directly. It must be assessed indirectly.

Election returns are a traditional method for assessing public opinion. Politicians routinely draw conclusions about what citizens are thinking by studying how they vote. Letters to the editor in newspapers and the size of crowds at mass demonstrations are among the other means of judging public opinion. All these indicators are useful guides for policymakers. Each of them, however, is a limited guide to what is on people's minds. Election returns indicate how many votes each party or candidate received but do not indicate why voters acted as they did. As for letter writers and demonstrators, research indicates that their opinions are more intense and usually more extreme than those of most citizens.[4]

Public Opinion Polls

Today, opinion polls or surveys are the primary method for estimating public sentiment.[5] In a **public opinion poll**, a relatively few individuals—the **sample**—are interviewed in order to estimate the opinions of a whole **population**, such as the residents of a city or country.

How is it possible to measure the thinking of a large population on the basis of a relatively small sample of that population? How can interviews with, say, 1,000 Americans provide a reliable estimate of what millions of them are thinking? The answer is found in the laws of probability. Consider the hypothetical example of a huge jar filled with a million marbles, half of them red and half of them blue. If a blindfolded person reaches into the jar, the probability of selecting a marble of a given color is 50-50. And if 1,000 marbles are chosen in this random way, it is likely that about half of them will

Public opinion is not directly observable. In times past, election returns, letters to the editor, and other measures were used as indicators of what citizens were thinking. In more recent times, public opinion polls have become the preferred method of assessing what's on people's minds. (©Iculig/123RF)

be red and about half will be blue. Opinion sampling works in the same way. If respondents are chosen at random from a population, their opinions will approximate those of the population as a whole.

Random selection is the key to scientific polling, which is theoretically based on *probability sampling*—a sample in which each individual in the population has a known probability of being chosen at random for inclusion. Individuals do not step forward to be interviewed; they are selected at random to be part of the sample. A scientific poll is thereby different from an Internet survey that invites visitors to a site to participate. Any such survey is biased because it includes only individuals who use the Internet, who happen for one reason or another to visit the particular site, and who have the time and inclination to complete the survey.

The science of polling is such that the size of the sample, as opposed to the size of the population, is the key to the poll's accuracy. Although it might be assumed that a much larger sample would be required to poll accurately the people of the United States as opposed to, say, the residents of Georgia or San Antonio, the sample requirements are nearly the same. Consider again the example of a huge jar filled with marbles, half of them red and half of them blue. If 1,000 marbles were randomly selected, about half would be red and about half would be blue, regardless of whether the jar held 1 million, 10 million, or 100 million marbles. By contrast, the size of the sample—the number of marbles selected—would matter. If only 10 marbles were drawn, it might happen that 5 would be of each color but, then again, it would not be unusual for 6 or 7 of them to have the same color. In fact, the odds are about 1 in 20 that eight or more would be the same color. However, if 1,000 marbles were drawn, it's highly unlikely for 600 of the marbles, much less a greater number, to be of the same color. The odds of drawing 600 of the same color are about 1 in 100,000.

The accuracy of a poll is expressed in terms of **sampling error**—the error that results from using a sample to estimate the population. A sample provides an estimate of what the population is thinking, and sampling error is a measure of how accurate that estimate is likely to be. As would be expected, the larger the sample, the smaller the sampling error. A sample of 1,000 respondents would be expected to be more accurate than one of 200 respondents if the surveys were otherwise conducted in the same way.

Sampling error is usually expressed as a plus-or-minus percentage. For example, a properly drawn sample of 1,000 individuals has a sampling error of roughly plus or minus 3 percent. Thus, if 55 percent of a sample of 1,000 respondents say they intend to vote for the Republican presidential candidate, there is a high probability that between 52 and 58 percent (55 percent plus or minus 3 percent) of all voters actually plan to vote Republican. It should be noted that if the poll had found that the candidates were separated by one percentage point, it would be mathematically incorrect to claim that one of them is "leading." The one-point difference in their support is smaller than the poll's three-point sampling error.

Opinion Dimensions

In studying public opinion, scholars and pollsters focus on various dimensions of people's opinions. One dimension is **direction**, which refers to whether people have a pro or con position on a topic. A 2017 Gallup poll, for example, asked respondents whether "the use of marijuana should be made legal." Sixty-four percent of the respondents said it should; 32 percent said it should not.

A second dimension of people's opinions is **intensity**, which refers to how strongly people feel about their opinion. At the one-year mark of Donald Trump's presidency, for example, an NBC News/*Wall Street Journal* poll asked respondents whether they approved or disapproved of the job he was doing, and how strongly they felt about it. Fifty-seven percent of respondents said they disapproved of his job performance, with 51 percent saying they "strongly" disapproved. Thirty-nine percent said they approved of the job he was doing, with 26 percent saying they "strongly" approved.[6] Intensity is an indicator of the likelihood that people will act on an opinion. Voters who feel strongly about a particular issue, for example, are more likely to take that issue into account when deciding which candidate to support.

People's opinions differ in important ways, one of which is intensity. On virtually every issue, some people feel more strongly about it than do others. Politicians are typically more attentive to intense opinions than lightly held ones, knowing that those who hold intense views are more likely to act on them. (©Andrius Repsys/Shutterstock)

A third opinion dimension is **salience**, which refers to how important people think an issue is relative to other issues. Salience is related to intensity—the more strongly people feel about something, the more likely they are to think that it's important. But the two attributes are not identical. For example, an individual might have an intense opinion about genetically modified food but see it as less salient than a number of other issues, such as unemployment and terrorism. In polls, salience is typically measured by asking respondents what they regard as the country's most important issue. An issue's salience can affect how officials respond. They don't ordinarily risk much by ignoring a low-salience issue, but they can get in trouble by ignoring one that a lot of people view as important. People expect elected officials to respond to pressing issues (see "Case Study: Gun Control").

C A S E STUDY	## Politics in Action

Gun Control

Issue opinions have several dimensions—direction, intensity, and salience—that can affect the response of elected officials. A case in point is gun control.

The United States has more gun-related deaths per capita than nearly every other country, which has led to calls for gun control. Some federal laws have been enacted, such as those banning gun sales to felons and individuals who are mentally ill. But calls to ban military-style assault weapons, which have

©Zoonar GmbH/Alamy

been used in mass killings, have not materialized. They had been banned in 1994 but when the ban came up for renewal in 2004, Congress voted against it.

Now what's been the pattern of gun control opinions over the past two decades? In terms of *direction,* Americans have been split on the issue, although the majority has been on the side of stricter control of guns. However, opinions have split along party lines—Democrats are more supportive of gun control than are Republicans. In terms of *intensity,* gun rights advocates tend to be more committed to their position than are gun

Continued

control advocates. Those who favor gun rights are far more likely than those who favor gun control to give money or contact a public official in an effort to influence gun policy.[7] Finally, in terms of *saliency,* gun control has ranked relatively low on the public's list of top issues, except in periods immediately following mass shootings. In most Gallup polls over the past two decades, 1 percent of respondents or fewer have named gun violence when asked what they regard as the nation's "most important problem."

Q: How might the dimensions of public opinion—its direction, intensity, and salience—help explain why Congress has not taken decisive action to curb gun violence?

ASK YOURSELF: What importance do you attach to the fact that opinions on gun control divide sharply along partisan lines? What's the significance of the fact that those who oppose gun control have more intense opinions and are more likely to act on them? Does the relatively low salience of the issue give lawmakers leeway in terms of deciding whether to take action on the issue?

Problems with Polls

Although pollsters assume that their samples are drawn from a particular population, such as all citizens of adult age, pollsters rarely have a list of all individuals in the population from which to sample. An expedient alternative is a sample based on telephone numbers. Pollsters use computers to randomly pick telephone numbers (now also including cell phone numbers), which are dialed by interviewers to reach households. Within each of these households, a respondent is then randomly selected. Because the computer is as likely to pick one telephone number as any other, a sample selected in this way is assumed to be representative of the whole population. Nevertheless, some Americans do not have phones, and many of those who are called will not be home or refuse to participate. Such factors reduce the accuracy of telephone polling. Indeed, pollsters are concerned about the future of telephone polling. The refusal rate has increased sharply in recent decades.

The accuracy of polling is also diminished when respondents are asked about unfamiliar issues. Although respondents may answer the question anyway in order not to appear uninformed, their responses cannot be regarded as valid. Scholars label such responses "nonopinions." In other instances, respondents will have an opinion but choose to hide it. Respondents are not always truthful, for example, when it comes to expressing opinions that relate to race,

FAKE or FACT

Detecting Misinformation

Can the Polls Be Trusted?

On the eve of the 2016 presidential election, pollsters were predicting that Hillary Clinton would finish first. Of the thirteen major national polls conducted during the election's last week, only one had Donald Trump in the lead. When he won the election, Trump ridiculed the polls for underestimating his strength and tweeted that they were not to be trusted—"fake polls." In a *New Republic* article entitled "After 2016, Can We Ever Trust the Polls Again?" Nicole Narea wrote: "America's divisions were in plain sight. But pollsters and political analysts alike portrayed Hillary Clinton's victory as an inevitability, failing to realize the precariousness of their own models' assumptions and to communicate any sense of uncertainty."

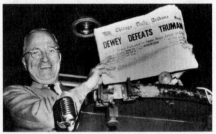

©Bettmann/Getty Images

Is that claim fact, or is it fake?

National polls measure voter intention in order to estimate the candidates' popular support. In 2016, the 13 major national polls conducted within a week of Election Day gave Hillary Clinton a three-percentage-point lead over Donald Trump. She won the popular vote by a margin of two percentage points, which was only one point off the polling average and well within the sampling error for a national poll. So why did some pundits claim that the polls had erred badly? They failed to account for the fact that a president is elected through the Electoral College rather than directly through the national popular vote. Trump gained his electoral vote victory by winning in Pennsylvania, Michigan, and Wisconsin by a combined total of less than 100,000 votes.

Polls are not infallible, but they have a remarkable accuracy record. Within their margin of error, polls have accurately predicted the popular vote outcome of nearly every presidential election of the past seven decades. The most embarrassing miss came during the early years of polling. In 1948, a Gallup poll taken several weeks before the election showed Harry Truman trailing badly. Gallup stopped polling at that point in the campaign and missed a late shift in the vote that carried Truman to a four-point victory.

gender, or ethnicity. A recent study that compared poll results and online behavior, for example, concluded that racism is far more prevalent in the United States than opinion polls suggest.[8]

Question wording can also affect poll results. A recent poll, for example, used a variety of questions to measure Americans' opinions on immigration policy. When respondents were asked whether "ties to family members in the United States" should be taken into account in deciding who to admit, 60 percent said it should be. When they were then asked whether "professional or academic achievement" should factor in, 54 percent said yes. Responses to those two questions would suggest that Americans place family ties ahead of achievement as an immigration criterion. Yet, when respondents were asked later in the same poll whether immigration policy should place "greater emphasis on an applicant's job skills over their ties to family members," 56 percent agreed while 42 percent disagreed, suggesting that Americans place achievement ahead of family ties as a criterion.[9]

Despite such issues, polls remain the best available indicator of people's opinions. If the questions are worded carefully and proper procedures are followed, polls can portray what the public is thinking.

POLITICAL SOCIALIZATION: THE ORIGINS OF AMERICANS' OPINIONS

People's opinions form in response to events, issues, and problems that draw their interest. But people's opinions are also a response to their prior attitudes. A striking example is Republicans' opinions on free trade. In 2015, Republicans had a more favorable view of free-trade agreements than did Democrats. Roughly 60 percent of Republicans said that such agreements are good for the country. Barely more than a year later, they had switched sides on the issue. Now less than 30 percent of Republicans expressed support for free-trade agreements.[10] Why the change? It was due to Donald Trump's presidential candidacy. He was a vocal opponent of free-trade agreements, and Republicans lined up behind him on the issue.[11]

Partisanship is a learned response. People are not born as Democrats or as Republicans, but instead they acquire these attachments. This learning is called **political socialization**. Just as language, a religion, or an athletic skill is acquired through a learning process, so too are people's political orientations.

Broadly speaking, the process of political socialization has two distinguishing characteristics. First, although socialization continues throughout life, most people's political outlooks are influenced by childhood learning. Basic ideas about which political party is better, for example, are often formed uncritically in childhood, in much the same way that belief in the superiority of a particular religion—typically, the religion of one's parents—is acquired.

A second characteristic of political socialization is that its effect is cumulative. Early learning affects later learning because people's beliefs affect how new information is interpreted. Prior attitudes serve as a psychological screen through which new information is filtered, as in the case of the change in Republicans' opinions on free trade.

The political socialization process takes place through **agents of socialization**. They can be divided between primary and secondary agents. *Primary agents* interact closely and regularly with the individual, usually early in life, as in the case of the family. *Secondary agents* have a less intimate connection with the individual and are usually more important later in life, as in the case of work associates. It is helpful to consider briefly how various primary and secondary agents affect political learning.

Primary Socializing Agents: Family, School, and Church

The family is a powerful primary agent because it has a near-monopoly on the attention of the young child, who places great trust in what a parent says. By the time children reach adulthood, many of the beliefs and values that will stay with them throughout life are firmly in place. Indeed, as sociologist Herbert Hyman concluded from his research: "Foremost among agencies of socialization into politics is the family."[12] Many adults are Republicans or Democrats today almost solely because their parents backed that party. They can give all sorts of reasons for preferring their party to the other, but the reasons came later in life. The family also contributes to basic orientations that, although not directly political, have political significance. American children, for example, often have a voice in family decisions, contributing to a sense of social equality.[13]

The school, like the family, affects children's basic political beliefs. Teachers at the elementary level praise the country's political institutions and extol the exploits of national heroes such as George Washington, Abraham Lincoln, and Martin Luther King Jr.[14] Although teachers in the middle and high school grades present a more nuanced version of American history, they tend to emphasize the nation's great moments—for example, its decisive role in the two world wars. U.S. schools are more instrumental in building support for the nation and its cultural beliefs than are the schools in most other democracies. The Pledge of Allegiance, which is recited daily in many U.S. schools, has no equivalent in Europe. Schools there do not open the day by asking students to take a pledge of national loyalty.

Grade school is a primary agent of political socialization, serving to introduce students to American ideals, customs, and historical heroes. (©McGraw-Hill Education/Jill Braaten)

Religious organizations are a powerful socializing agent for some children. Although many American children do not experience religion or do so only fleetingly, others attend church regularly. Scholars have not studied the influence of religion on childhood political socialization as closely as they have studied the influence of families or schools.[15] Nevertheless, religion can have a formative influence on children's attitudes, including beliefs about society's obligations to the poor and the unborn.

Secondary Socializing Agents: Peers, Media, Leaders, and Events

With age, additional socializing agents come into play. An individual's peers—friends, neighbors, coworkers, and the like—become sources of opinion. Research indicates that many individuals are unwilling to deviate too far politically from what their peers think. In *The Spiral of Silence,* Elisabeth Noelle-Neumann shows that individuals tend to withhold opinions that are at odds with those of the people around them. If nearly everyone in a group favors legalizing same-sex marriage, for example, a person who believes otherwise is likely to remain silent. As a result, the group's dominant opinion will appear to be more widely held than it actually is, which can persuade those with lightly held opinions to adopt the group opinion as their own.[16]

The mass media are also a powerful socializing agent. Politics for the average citizen is a secondhand affair, observed mainly through the media rather than directly. In the words of journalist Walter Lippmann, "the pictures in our heads of the world outside" owe substantially to how that world is portrayed for us by the media.[17] For example, heavy exposure to crime on television, whether through news or entertainment, can lead people to believe that their community is more dangerous than it actually is.[18]

Individuals in positions of authority are also sources of opinion.[19] In the American case, no authority figure has more influence on public opinion than does the president. After the terrorist attacks of September 11, 2001, for example, many Americans were confused about who the enemy was and how America should respond. Their opinions became firmer a few days later when President George W. Bush in a nationally televised speech identified al Qaeda members as the perpetrators and declared that America would attack Afghanistan if it continued to provide them sanctuary. Polls indicated that 9 of every 10 Americans supported Bush's stance on Afghanistan. At the same time, political leaders' ability to influence public opinion depends on their standing. After President Bush led America into a costly war in Iraq on the erroneous claim that it had weapons of mass destruction, his political support weakened, as did his ability to persuade Americans that the war in Iraq was worth fighting.

Finally, no accounting of the political socialization process would be complete without considering the impact of major events. The Great Depression, World War II, the Vietnam War, and the 2001 terrorist attacks are examples of events that had a lasting influence on Americans' opinions. The effect in each case was strongest on younger citizens. They are more responsive to disruptive events because their political beliefs are less fixed.[20] Slow, long-term developments can also produce changes in people's political views. Over the past few decades, for example, partisanship has intensified to the point where Democratic and Republican lawmakers fight over nearly every issue. Each party has usually been strong enough to block the other from acting and rarely strong enough to act decisively on its own. Urgent policy problems have worsened for lack of government action. In the words of one scholar, the U.S. political system "has become appallingly dysfunctional."[21] The situation has affected Americans' pride in their democracy. As recently as 2002, 90 percent of Americans said they were proud "of the way democracy works in America."[22] Now, less than 65 percent feel that way.[23] (See "How the U.S. Differs" for more on the subject of national pride.)

HOW THE U.S. DIFFERS

CRITICAL THINKING THROUGH COMPARISONS

National Pride

Political socialization in the United States is not the rigid program of indoctrination that some countries impose on their people. Nevertheless, Americans are told of their country's greatness in many ways, everything from the Pledge of Allegiance that American children recite at the beginning of the school day to the flying of the flag on American homes and businesses. Such practices are uncommon in other democracies and contribute to Americans' comparatively high degree of national pride. At the same time, Americans' pride in their nation has been declining in response to rising partisan hostility and other factors. In polls over the past decade, there has not been a single month in which the number of respondents who thought the country was heading in "the right direction" exceeded the number of those who thought it was on "the wrong track." Not surprisingly, as the accompanying figure shows, the number of Americans who say they are "proud" of "the way democracy works in America" has been declining.

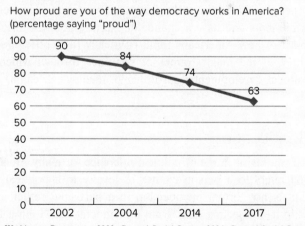

How proud are you of the way democracy works in America? (percentage saying "proud")

Sources: Washington Post survey, 2002; General Social Survey, 2004; General Social Survey, 2014; Washington Post-University of Maryland survey, 2017.

Q: Why might words and symbols of the nation's greatness be more important to Americans than to people of most countries? Why might the recent decline in Americans' pride in their political system be a worrying development?

Continued

A: The unifying bond in most countries is a common ancestral heritage. The French and Chinese, for example, have ancestral ties that go back centuries. In contrast, Americans come from many different countries and depend more heavily on national symbols and ceremonies as a common bond. As a result, when the bond weakens, Americans' commitment to the nation's collective well-being could diminish. When citizens lose their sense of being "one people," they can slip into selfishness and the scapegoating of those with whom they differ.

FRAMES OF REFERENCE: HOW AMERICANS THINK POLITICALLY

Through the socialization process, citizens acquire frames of reference (or schemas) that serve as reference points by which they evaluate issues and developments. These frames of reference are important for two reasons. First, they provide an indication of how people think politically. Second, they are a basis for common cause. The opinions of millions of Americans would mean almost nothing if everyone's opinions were different from those of all others. If enough people share the same frame of reference, however, they have strength in numbers and have a chance of exerting political influence.

The subject of how Americans think politically fills entire books. Outlined here are three of the major frames of reference through which Americans evaluate political developments: partisanship, ideological leanings, and group attachments.

Party Identification

Partisanship is a major frame of political reference for many Americans. **Party identification** refers to a person's sense of loyalty to a political party. Party identification is not formal membership in a party but rather an emotional attachment to it—the feeling that "I am a Democrat" or "I am a Republican." Scholars and pollsters typically have measured party identification with a question of the following type: "Generally speaking, do you think of yourself as a Republican, a Democrat, an independent, or what?" Most adults call themselves either Democrats or Republicans (see Figure 6-1). Even those who call themselves independents are less independent than might be assumed. When independents are asked if they lean toward the Republican or Democratic Party, about two in three independents say they lean toward one of the parties.

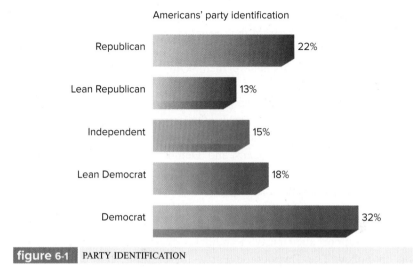

figure 6-1 PARTY IDENTIFICATION

Most Americans say they identify with the Republican or Democratic Party. Among those who call themselves independents, most say they "lean" toward a party and typically vote for that party's candidates. (*Source:* Gallup poll, January 2018)

Most of these independents vote in the direction they lean. In fact, they are nearly as likely to support their party's candidates as voters who call themselves Republicans or Democrats.

Early studies of party identification concluded that it was highly stable and seldom changed over the course of adult life.[24] Subsequent studies have shown that party loyalty is more fluid than originally believed; it can be influenced by the issues and candidates of the moment.[25] Nevertheless, many adults remain lifelong Republicans or Democrats even if their personal lives change in ways that might reasonably lead them to identify with the other party. Historically, major shifts in the party attachments of large numbers of Americans have occurred only in the context of a momentous upheaval. Even then, the shift has usually been concentrated among younger adults because their partisanship tends to be less firmly rooted. During the Great Depression, for example, Franklin Roosevelt's New Deal prompted many younger Republicans, but relatively few older ones, to change their loyalty to the Democratic Party.

Once acquired, partisanship affects what people "see." *Selective perception* is the process whereby people selectively choose from incoming information those aspects that support what they already believe. During the 2016 presidential election, Donald Trump was heard saying on *Access Hollywood* tapes that he groped women at will—"when you're a star, they let you do it." Trump's opponents thought his behavior was misogynistic. Trump's supporters accepted his explanation that it was only "locker room talk."[26] When more than a dozen women then came forward to accuse Trump of sexual impropriety, the vast majority of non-Trump voters said they believed the women's claims. A majority of Trump's supporters said the women were lying, and most of the rest said they weren't sure whether to believe them. Only 1 in 10 said the women's claims were credible.[27]

In the everyday world of politics, no source of opinion divides Americans more clearly than does their partisanship. On nearly every major issue, Republicans and Democrats have contrasting opinions. A recent Pew Research Center poll found that Republicans and Democrats have sharply different views of the nation's policy priorities. For example, Democrats rate climate change and poverty assistance more highly, whereas Republicans rate military spending and budget deficit reduction more highly (see Figure 6-2).

For most people, partisanship is not blind faith in their party. Although they typically support their party's candidates, their party loyalty usually has it roots in policy. The Democratic Party, for example, has promoted the nation's social welfare and workers' rights policies, whereas the Republican

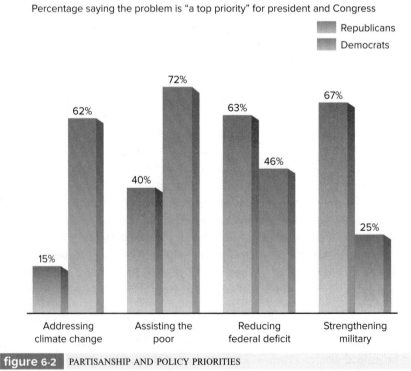

Percentage saying the problem is "a top priority" for president and Congress

■ Republicans
■ Democrats

- Addressing climate change: 15% / 62%
- Assisting the poor: 40% / 72%
- Reducing federal deficit: 63% / 46%
- Strengthening military: 67% / 25%

figure 6-2 PARTISANSHIP AND POLICY PRIORITIES

Republicans and Democrats differ in their opinions on the nation's policy priorities. (*Source:* Pew Research Center poll, 2017)

Party has spearheaded the nation's pro-business and tax reduction policies. The fact that most union workers are Democrats and most people in business are Republicans is hardly a coincidence.[28] (Partisanship is examined in additional detail at various points later in this book, particularly in Chapters 7, 8, 11, and 12.)

Political Ideology

Karl Marx's collaborator, Friedrich Engels, said that he saw no real chance of communism taking root in the United States. Writing in 1893, Engels said America's workers lacked sufficient class consciousness, being concerned instead about getting ahead on their own.[29] In broader historical terms, Americans did not embrace any of the large 20th-century ideologies—communism, fascism, or socialism—that captured the imagination of many Europeans. Historian Daniel Boorstin argued that most Americans are pragmatists at heart, driven less by allegiance to ideology than by a desire to find workable solutions to problems.[30]

Of course, political ideology does not have to take extreme forms, as it did in the case of Soviet communism and German fascism. In simplified form, an **ideology** can be defined as a general belief about the role and purpose of government.[31] Some Americans believe, for instance, that government should use its power to help people who are economically disadvantaged. Such individuals can be labeled **economic liberals**. Other Americans believe that the government should leave the distribution of economic benefits largely to the workings of the free market. They can be described as **economic conservatives**. Americans differ also in their views on government's role in regard to social and cultural issues, such as abortion and the legalization of marijuana. **Cultural (social) liberals** would leave lifestyle choices to the individual. In contrast, **cultural (social) conservatives** would use government to promote traditional values—for example, through laws banning abortion.

Although it is sometimes said that liberals believe in big government while conservatives believe in small government, this claim is inaccurate, as the foregoing discussion would indicate. Conservatives prefer a smaller role for government on economic issues but want to use the power of government to uphold cultural traditions. The reverse is true of liberals. Each group wants government to be active or inactive, depending on which approach serves its policy goals.

There is no logical reason, of course, why an economic liberal also has to be a cultural liberal. Although most economic liberals are also cultural liberals, some are not. The term **populist** (although some analysts prefer the term *communitarian*) is used to describe an individual who is an economic liberal and a cultural conservative. Similarly, some economic conservatives are cultural liberals. They believe government should refrain from undue intervention in the economic marketplace *and* in people's private lives. The term **libertarian** is used to characterize someone with this set of beliefs.

Group Orientations

Many Americans see politics through the lens of a group affinity. Their identity or self-interest is tied to the group, and they respond accordingly when a policy issue arises that affects it. Issues surrounding Social Security, for example, usually evoke a stronger response from senior citizens than from younger adults. Later chapters examine group tendencies more fully, but it is useful here to describe briefly a few groupings—religion, economic class, region, race and ethnicity, gender, and age.

Religion   Religious beliefs have long been a source of solidarity among group members and a source of conflict with outsiders. As Catholics came to America in large numbers in the 19th and early 20th centuries, they faced hostility from the Protestant majority. Religious hatred sparked the rebirth of the Ku Klux Klan, which resurrected itself in the early 1900s as anti-Catholic, as well as anti-Jewish, anti-Mormon, and anti-Black. At the Klan's peak in the 1920s, one in every six Protestant adult males—4 million in total—was a Klan member.[32] It took the nation's all-out effort in World War II to convince the Protestant majority that Catholics weren't their enemy.

Today, Catholics, Protestants, and Jews hold similar opinions on many policy issues. Nevertheless, important religious differences remain, although the alignment shifts as the issue shifts.[33] Fundamentalist Protestants and Roman Catholics are more likely than mainline Protestants and Jews to oppose legalized abortion, a split that partly reflects differing religious beliefs about whether human life begins at conception or later in the development of the fetus. Religious beliefs also affect opinions on poverty programs. Support for such programs is higher among Catholics and Jews than among Protestants. An obligation to help the poor is a central theme of Catholic and Jewish teachings, whereas self-reliance is a central theme in the teachings of some Protestant denominations.

The most powerful religious force in today's politics is the so-called religious right, which consists mostly of white evangelical Protestants (see "Party Polarization: Religion and Politics"). Their opinions on issues such as gay rights, abortion, and school prayer differ significantly from those of the population as a whole. A 2017 Pew Research Center survey, for example, found that white evangelical Protestants were more than twice as likely as other Americans to oppose same-sex marriage.[34]

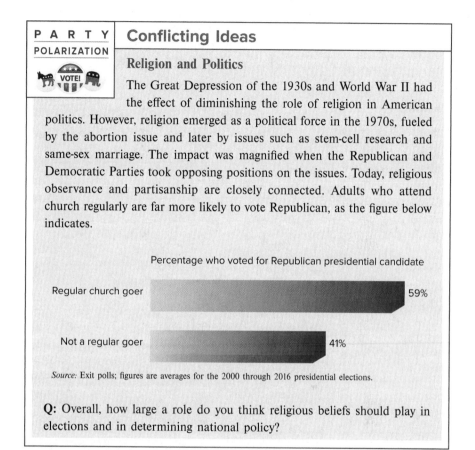

PARTY
POLARIZATION

Conflicting Ideas

Religion and Politics

The Great Depression of the 1930s and World War II had the effect of diminishing the role of religion in American politics. However, religion emerged as a political force in the 1970s, fueled by the abortion issue and later by issues such as stem-cell research and same-sex marriage. The impact was magnified when the Republican and Democratic Parties took opposing positions on the issues. Today, religious observance and partisanship are closely connected. Adults who attend church regularly are far more likely to vote Republican, as the figure below indicates.

Percentage who voted for Republican presidential candidate

Regular church goer — 59%

Not a regular goer — 41%

Source: Exit polls; figures are averages for the 2000 through 2016 presidential elections.

Q: Overall, how large a role do you think religious beliefs should play in elections and in determining national policy?

Economic Class   Economic class has less influence on political opinion in the United States than in Europe, but income and education levels do affect Americans' opinions on some issues. Welfare assistance programs and business regulation, for example, have more support among lower-income Americans, whereas higher-income Americans are more supportive of tax cuts.

An obstacle to class-based politics in the United States, particularly among those of lower income, is that they have different ideas about how to get ahead economically. Support for collective bargaining, for example, is higher among factory workers than among small farmers, white-collar workers, and workers in the skilled crafts, even though the average income of each of these groups is similar. Class-based action is also blunted by racial and ethnic differences. In *Strangers in Their Own Land*, Arlie Russell Hochschild describes how working-class whites see themselves as having waited patiently in line for a piece of the American Dream only to see working-class minorities and immigrants cut the line, ushered there by affirmative action and other policy initiatives.[35]

Although working-class whites are better off economically than minorities, they see themselves as being held back so that minorities can get ahead.[36] The interplay of class and opinion is examined more closely in Chapter 9, which discusses interest groups.

Region   For a period in U.S. history, region was the defining dimension in American politics. The North and South were divided over the issues of race and states' rights. Racial progress has shrunk the regional divide, as has the relocation to the South of millions of Americans from the less conservative Northeast and Midwest. Nevertheless, regional differences continue to exist on some issues, including social welfare and civil rights. The differences are large enough that when analysts talk about "red states" (Republican bastions) and "blue states" (Democratic bastions), they are generally referring to regions. The red states are clustered in the South, Great Plains, and Rocky Mountains, whereas the blue states are found mostly in the Northeast, the northern Midwest, and the West Coast (see "How the 50 States Differ").

Race and Ethnicity   As was discussed in Chapters 4 and 5, race and ethnicity affect opinions on civil rights and civil liberties issues. Blacks and Hispanics, for example, are generally more supportive of affirmative action and less trusting of police and the judicial system than are non-Hispanic whites. Blacks and Hispanics also tend to differ from non-Hispanic whites on social welfare spending, although this difference largely reflects differences in their income levels.

HOW THE 50 STATES DIFFER

CRITICAL THINKING THROUGH COMPARISONS

Party Loyalties in the States

The states differ widely in the number of residents who identify with the Republican and Democratic Parties. In classifying states by party, the Gallup organization lists a state as solid Republican or Democratic if a party has an advantage in party identifiers of five percentage points or higher. States in which the advantage is less than five points are judged as competitive. By Gallup's indicator, Republican strength is concentrated in the Plains and Rocky Mountains and Democratic strength is found in the Northeast and West Coast. The six most heavily Republican states are, in order, Wyoming, North Dakota, Utah, Idaho, Alaska, and South Dakota,

Continued

while Massachusetts, Maryland, New York, Vermont, Hawaii, and California (in that order) are the six most heavily Democratic states.

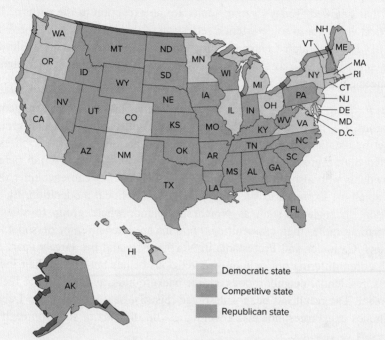

Democratic state

Competitive state

Republican state

Q: Why might several southern states be classified as "competitive" even though Republicans dominate their elections?

A: In these states, Republicans are more likely than Democrats to vote and to support their party's candidates when they do vote.

Gender Although men and women think alike on many issues, they diverge on others.[37] Polls have found, for example, that women have more liberal opinions than men on education and social welfare issues, reflecting their greater economic vulnerability and greater role in child care. Women also differ from men on the use of military force. Polls taken during the past decade have consistently found women to be less supportive than men of U.S. involvement in the Afghan, Iraqi, and Syrian conflicts.[38]

Generations and Age As a generation comes of age, it encounters a different political environment than its predecessors, with the result that its political views will differ somewhat from those of earlier generations. Those Americans who came of age during World War II, for example, acquired a

sense of civic duty unmatched by the preceding generation or by any generation since. By contrast, those who came of age during the Vietnam War era
were more mistrustful of government than the generation before them or the
one that followed. Today's young adults are no exception to the pattern. Their
political views are to some extent a reflection of their generation's experiences.
A 2017 Pew Research Center poll, for example, found that young adults were
substantially more likely than senior citizens to support same-sex marriage and
stronger environmental regulations.[39]

Crosscutting Groups   Although group loyalties have an impact on people's
opinions, the influence is diminished when identification with one group is
offset by identification with other groups. In a pluralistic society such as the
United States, groups tend to be "crosscutting"—that is, each group includes
individuals who also belong to other groups, where they can encounter different opinions. Exposure to such opinions fosters political moderation. By comparison, in societies such as Northern Ireland, where group loyalties are
reinforcing rather than crosscutting, opinions are intensified by personal interactions. Catholics and Protestants in Northern Ireland live largely apart from
each other, differing not only in their religious beliefs but also in their income
levels, residential neighborhoods, ethnic backgrounds, and loyalties to the government. The result has been widespread mistrust between Northern Ireland's
Catholics and Protestants and a willingness on the part of some on each side
to resort to violence.

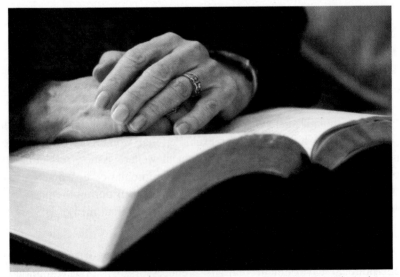

Religion is a socializing force in American life. Churches, synagogues, mosques, and temples are
places where Americans acquire values and beliefs, which can influence their opinions on political
issues. (©Kristy-Anne Glubish/Design Pics)

In the past few decades in the United States, the overlap between groups has diminished. Although the situation is still far different than in a place like Northern Ireland, Americans today interact less with those of a different background. Residential neighborhoods, for example, are now less diverse. Workplaces are also less diverse today than in the past. Many office workers and professionals, for example, spend their workday interacting almost entirely with others of the same occupation. Even Americans' "virtual" interaction has narrowed. Until the 1980s, Americans were exposed through television to a version of news that included Republican and Democratic arguments in roughly equal amount. Today, many Americans get their news from a cable outlet or Internet site that plays up one side of the partisan debate while dismissing the other side (see Chapter 10).

It's also the case that three of America's deepest divides—race, religion, and geography—are now more tightly tied to partisanship.[40] White Americans, the religious minded, and suburban and rural residents now lean strongly toward the Republican Party, while minorities, the secular minded, and urban residents lean heavily Democratic. The party polarization that defines today's politics thus goes beyond ideological differences between liberals and conservatives. The dividing line now also separates Americans by how they look and where they live, which has made partisan conflict a question of identity as well as a question of issues.[41] Partisan differences are sharper and harder to bridge when group and party loyalties are intertwined (see "Party Polarization" boxes throughout the book).

THE INFLUENCE OF PUBLIC OPINION ON POLICY

Observers disagree on the impact public opinion *should* have on policy. One view holds that representatives should act as their constituents' **delegate**—acting in response to what constituents say they want. This perspective was expressed by George Gallup, a pioneer in the field of polling. Said Gallup, "The task of the leader is to decide how best to achieve the goals set by the people."[42] An opposing view was put forth by 18th-century English theorist Edmund Burke who argued that representatives should act as their constituents' **trustee**—taking their concerns into account but exercising judgment about the policies that will best serve their interest. "Effective government," journalist Walter Lippmann wrote, "cannot be conducted by legislators and officials who, when a question is presented, ask themselves first and last not what is . . . the right and necessary course, but 'What does the Gallup Poll say'?"[43]

There is also disagreement over the impact of public opinion on government. It is not a simple matter to pinpoint the influence of public opinion, as will now be explained.

Limits on the Public's Influence

Even if officials were intent on governing by public opinion, they would face obstacles, including contradictions in what citizens say. In the entire history of polling, there has never been a national survey in which a majority of respondents said their taxes should be raised significantly.[44] In a 2015 Gallup poll, for example, 51 percent of respondents claimed that taxes were too high, and only 3 percent said taxes were too low. Yet, when respondents are asked in polls whether they would support steep cuts in Social Security, defense, and other costly spending programs in order to pay for a large tax cut, a majority say no.

What then would they cut? The policy that normally ends up at the top of their list is foreign aid. Polls show that most Americans believe that 20 to 30 percent of the federal budget is spent on foreign aid, which leads them to believe that slashing foreign aid would dramatically reduce the federal budget and the taxes required to fund it.[45] The problem here is that foreign aid actually accounts for less than 1 percent of the budget. Even if all foreign aid programs were eliminated, the savings would not fund a major tax cut or come anywhere close to eliminating the budget deficit. That example points to a problem with basing policy on public opinion—people's poor understanding of issues. Poll after poll over the past decades has shown that most citizens are not well informed about politics and some are badly misinformed.[46]

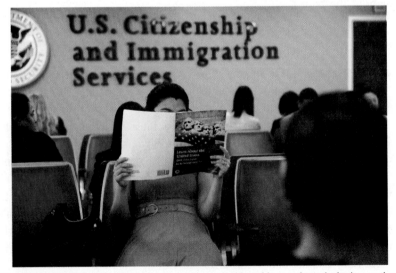

To become an American citizen, immigrants must pass a citizenship test that asks basic questions about the U.S. political system. Ironically, when the test is given to a cross-section of Americans who are already citizens, many of them fail it. Citizens' lack of information serves to limit the impact of public opinion on policy. (©John Moore/Getty Images)

Of course, citizens do not have to be well informed to have a reasonable opinion on some issues.[47] Knowing only that the economy is performing poorly, a citizen could reasonably expect government to take action to fix it, and judge officials by their response.[48] It's also the case that information is not a prerequisite for judgment on some policy issues. Opinions on the abortion issue, for example, are largely a question of people's values and beliefs.

Nevertheless, the public's weak understanding of issues can make it difficult for policymakers to respond to public opinion, even in those cases where they're inclined to do so. The problem has become more acute with the rise in misinformation. When citizens lose touch with reality, lawmakers face an impossible task. Even if they wanted to act in accord with public opinion, it makes no sense for them to do so when citizens hold absurd ideas about the nature of the world.

In addition, there are many issues on which there is no general public opinion that could serve as a guide to policymakers. These issues have such low salience that most people haven't thought about them and might not even be aware that they exist.[49] Agricultural conservation programs, for example, are of keen interest to some farmers, hunters, and environmentalists but of little or no concern to most people.[50] In deciding such issues, policymakers tend to be responsive to those who do care about them (see Chapter 9). A recent study by political scientists Martin Gilens and Benjamin Page examined nearly 1,800 policy issues and concluded that "economic elites and organized groups representing business interests" have far more influence on most policies than do "average citizens."[51]

The influence of public opinion is also limited by leaders' efforts to influence people's views, a process that linguist Noam Chomsky calls "manufactured consent."[52] Officials often go to great lengths to win public support for their policies.[53] If they succeed, policy and opinion will coincide, but the result speaks more to the power of leaders than to the power of public opinion. A case in point is the period leading up to the U.S. invasion of Iraq in 2003. Although Americans had been hearing about Iraqi leader Saddam Hussein for years and had concluded that he was a tyrant, they were unsure whether an attack on Iraq made sense. Polls indicate that many Americans preferred to have UN inspectors investigate Iraq's weapons program before an invasion decision was made. Other Americans expressed support for an invasion only if the United States had the backing of its European allies. Still others thought that if a war were launched, it should be conducted entirely through the air. However, over the course of a roughly six-month period, the Bush administration pressed the case for a ground invasion, which led to a gradual increase in public support for that action.[54] When the war began, polls showed that President Bush's decision to conduct an all-out assault on Iraq had the backing of 70 percent of Americans.

The Iraq invasion is an extreme example in terms of its policy consequences but not in terms of how presidents tend to operate. In *Who Governs?*, political scientists James Druckman and Lawrence Jacobs studied internal White House documents to show that presidents typically pursue their own agenda rather than one that closely matches public opinion. Rather than seeing public opinion as something to be followed, presidents in most instances see it as something that they can influence.[55]

Public Opinion and the Boundaries of Action

Although there are clear limits to the influence of public opinion, it nevertheless affects the choices that officials make. For one thing, it limits their options. As political scientist V. O. Key noted, officials typically must operate within the boundary of what the public will accept.[56] Social Security is a prime example. During his second presidential term, George W. Bush attempted to privatize a part of Social Security, only to back down in the face of determined opposition from senior citizens. The founder of Social Security, Franklin D. Roosevelt, understood that public opinion would act to preserve the program. Because Social Security benefits are funded by payroll taxes, workers feel they have earned their retirement benefits and will fight to keep them. "No damn politician," Roosevelt said, "can ever scrap my social security program."[57]

The public also sets boundaries on officials' actions in another way. Sweeping changes in public opinion invariably lead to lasting and substantial changes in the direction of national policy. During the Great Depression of the 1930s, for example, a massive shift in popular support from the Republican Party to the Democratic Party ushered in a three-decade period of Democratic dominance of American politics, as well as a host of major policies, including Social Security, the minimum wage, and Medicare. Then, in the 1970s, the American public began to question the scope of federal power and spending, which led to a range of policy changes, including major tax cuts and a tightening of the eligibility rules for welfare assistance. Public opinion was also behind the tougher crime and sentencing laws enacted in the 1990s, which led to a sharp increase in the nation's prison population. As a congressman said at the time, "Voters were afraid of criminals, and politicians were afraid of voters."[58]

Abrupt shifts in opinion on a salient issue can change the boundaries of acceptable action. As mentioned earlier, until Donald Trump ran for the presidency on a platform that called for an end to free-trade agreements, Republican members of Congress were strong advocates of free trade. Over 90 percent of Senate and House Republicans had voted in 2011 to enact the three most

Public opinion places boundaries on what public officials will do. Republican lawmakers were strong supporters of free-trade agreements until Republican voters, following the lead of Donald Trump, shifted from being pro-free trade to anti-free trade. (©David H. Carriere/Getty Images)

recent such agreements—bilateral arrangements with Colombia, Panama, and South Korea. However, when Republican voters in response to Trump's candidacy flipped from being pro-free trade to anti-free trade, most congressional Republicans quickly backed away from their free-trade position.

Nowhere is the impact of public opinion felt more clearly than in Congress. Members of Congress are career politicians who want to keep their jobs, which requires them to hold on to their support in their home state or district. When in doubt about whether a legislative vote could cost them support, they tend to side with the opinion of the voters who hold the key to their reelection.[59] "Running scared" is how political scientist Anthony King describes their strategy.[60] In 2014, Eric Cantor, the House majority leader and next in line to become Speaker, lost in his district's Republican primary to a right-wing political unknown. Cantor had said that Republicans should give legal status to "dreamers"—those who came to the country illegally as children. For anti-immigration voters in his district, Cantor's stand amounted to treachery. The lesson of Cantor's defeat was not lost on House Republicans. "Immigration reform, any hope of it, just basically died," said a Republican insider.[61]

The immigration issue illustrates what is broadly true about the power of public opinion. When an issue is highly salient and people feel intensely about their position, elected officials tend to follow public opinion. That conclusion is supported by numerous studies. Although scholars have reached conflicting conclusions about many aspects of public opinion, they largely agree on one thing: The power of public opinion is clearest on issues of high salience that people care about.[62]

SUMMARY

Public opinion can be defined as those opinions held by ordinary citizens that they openly express. Public officials have many ways of assessing public opinion, such as the outcomes of elections, but they have increasingly come to rely on public opinion polls. There are many possible sources of error in polls, and surveys sometimes present a misleading portrayal of the public's views. However, a properly conducted poll can be an accurate indication of what the public is thinking. Polls are typically used to measure three dimensions of people's policy opinions: direction (whether they favor or oppose a particularly policy), intensity (how strongly they feel about their position on a policy), and salience (how important they think a policy issue is relative to other issues).

The process by which individuals acquire their political opinions is called political socialization. During childhood, the family, schools, and church are important sources of basic political attitudes, such as beliefs about the parties and the nature of the U.S. political and economic systems. Many of the basic orientations that Americans acquire during childhood remain with them in adulthood, but socialization is a continuing process. Adults' opinions are affected mostly by peers, the news media, and political leaders. Events themselves also have a significant short-term influence on opinions.

The frames of reference that guide Americans' opinions include political ideology, although most citizens do not have a strong and consistent ideological attachment. In addition, individuals develop opinions as a result of group orientations—notably, religion, economic class, region, race and ethnicity, gender, and age. Partisanship is the main source of political opinions; Republicans and Democrats differ in their voting behavior and views on many policy issues.

Public opinion has a significant influence on government but seldom determines exactly what government will do in a particular instance. Public opinion serves to constrain the policy choices of officials but also is subject to their efforts to influence what the public is thinking. Evidence indicates that officials are particularly attentive to public opinion on highly visible and controversial issues of public policy.

©gangliu10/Getty Images

CRITICAL THINKING ZONE

KEY TERMS

agents of socialization (*p. 174*)
cultural (social) conservatives (*p. 181*)
cultural (social) liberals (*p. 181*)
delegate (*p. 187*)
direction (of an opinion) (*p. 169*)
economic conservatives (*p. 181*)
economic liberals (*p. 181*)
ideology (*p. 181*)
intensity (of an opinion) (*p. 169*)
libertarian (*p. 182*)
party identification (*p. 178*)

political socialization (*p. 173*)
population (*p. 167*)
populist (*p. 181*)
public opinion (*p. 166*)
public opinion poll (*p. 167*)
salience (of an opinion) (*p. 170*)
sample (*p. 167*)
sampling error (*p. 168*)
trustee (*p. 187*)

APPLYING THE ELEMENTS OF CRITICAL THINKING

Conceptualizing: *Population, sample,* and *sampling error* are terms associated with public opinion polling. Explain each term and how it relates to the others.

Synthesizing: Contrast the views of conservatives and liberals on how far government should go to help individuals who are economically disadvantaged, and then contrast their views on how far government should go to promote traditional social (cultural) values. Note that each group wants government to be active or inactive, depending on which approach serves its policy goals.

Analyzing: What factors limit the influence of public opinion on the policy choices of public officials?

EXTRA CREDIT

A Book Worth Reading: Christopher H. Achen and Larry M. Bartels, *Democracy for Realists: Why Elections Do Not Produce Responsive Government* (Princeton, N.J.: Princeton University Press, 2016). Written by leading political scientists, this book argues that voters base their decisions on social identities and partisan loyalties, not on the basis of their preferences on policy issues.

A Website Worth Visiting: www.people-press.org The Pew Research Center for the People and the Press is an independent, nonprofit institute. Its website includes recent and past poll results, including cross-national comparisons.

PARTICIPATE!

Studies have regularly found that Americans, in relative and in absolute terms, are substantially uninformed about the issues affecting their state, their nation, and the world. As a result, Americans' opinions about policy issues and problems are not as informed as they could and should be. Citizenship entails responsibilities, one of which is to stay informed about problems and developments that affect the community, the state, and the nation. As an informed citizen, you will be better able to make judgments about policy issues, to choose wisely when voting during elections, and to recognize situations that call for greater personal involvement. Fortunately, you have access to one of the most substantial news systems in the world. News about public affairs is virtually at your fingertips—through your computer, on television, and in the newspaper. Spending only a small amount of time each day following the news from a reliable source will help you be a more effective and involved citizen.

7
CHAPTER

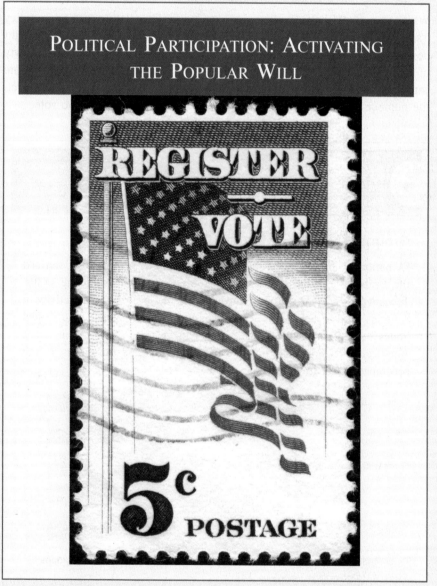

POLITICAL PARTICIPATION: ACTIVATING THE POPULAR WILL

©Sergey Kohl/Shutterstock

❝ We are concerned in public affairs, but immersed in our private ones. ❞

WALTER LIPPMANN[1]

At stake in the 2018 midterm elections was control of the House and the Senate. Which political party would have the larger say on legislation relating to domestic issues like gun control, health care, immigration, and wage stagnation?

Which one would have the larger say on legislation relating to foreign policy issues like trade and the war on terrorism? With so much at stake, it might be thought that Americans would have rushed to the polls to vote for the party of their choice. Yet, even though both parties waged intensive get-out-the-vote campaigns, millions of eligible voters did not bother to go to the polls. In fact, the number of nonvoters outnumbered those who took the time to vote.

HOW THE U.S. DIFFERS

CRITICAL THINKING THROUGH COMPARISONS

Groups: "A Nation of Joiners"

"A nation of joiners" is how Frenchman Alexis de Tocqueville described the United States during his writing tour of this country in the 1830s. Tocqueville said that Europeans would find the level of group activity in America hard to believe. "The political activity that pervades the United States," said Tocqueville, "must be seen to be understood." Even today, Americans are more fully involved in groups than are Europeans, as the accompanying chart shows.

	No group	1–3 groups	4 or more groups
United States	18%	63%	19%
Germany	33%	60%	7%
Great Britain	46%	45%	9%
Italy	59%	40%	←1%
France	61%	35%	4%

Percentage belonging to: ▮ No group ▮ 1–3 groups ▮ 4 or more groups
Source: World Values Survey Association, 2012.

Q: How does the nature of community life in the United States contribute to Americans' tendency to participate in groups?

A: Compared with Europeans, Americans have a stronger tradition of public education and religious practice. Schools and churches are a primary source of Americans' group activity, through everything from parent-teacher associations to religious auxiliary groups.

Voting is a form of **political participation**—involvement in activities intended to influence public policy and leadership. Political participation involves other activities in addition to voting, such as joining political groups, writing to elected officials, demonstrating for political causes, and giving money to political candidates.

Democracies are distinguished by their emphasis on citizen participation. Self-government would be an empty promise if citizens could not participate in public affairs. It would also be an empty promise without *meaningful* opportunities—ones that make a difference in how the country is governed. It would also be empty if those opportunities were reserved for the few. It is one thing if political participation is like attendance at a rock concert, which is mostly a matter of personal interest, and another thing if participation is like attendance at an elite prep school, which is mostly a matter of social privilege. Barriers to participation must be low, and they must be low for all citizens.

As this chapter will show, the United States provides citizens with abundant opportunities for meaningful participation while at the same time having structures that work against full participation by some citizens, particularly those of lower income and education. The chapter will also show that the pattern of participation in the United States differs from that of most Western democracies. It has a relatively low level of voter participation while having a relatively high level of other types of participation, including volunteer work in local communities. The chapter's main points are the following:

- *Voter turnout in U.S. elections is low in comparison with that of other Western democracies.* The reasons include U.S. election laws, particularly those pertaining to registration requirements and the scheduling of elections.

- *Most citizens do not participate actively in politics in ways other than voting.* Only a minority of Americans can be classified as political activists. Nevertheless, Americans are more likely than citizens of other democracies to contribute time and money to political and community organizations.

- *Most Americans distinguish between their personal lives and public life.* This outlook reduces their incentive to participate and contributes to a pattern of participation dominated by citizens of higher income and education.

VOTER PARTICIPATION

In its original form, the Constitution gave states control over voting, granting state legislatures the power to decide the "Times, Place, and Manner of holding elections" for federal office.

The states chose to limit **suffrage**—the right to vote—to property-owning males, a practice that Benjamin Franklin saw fit to ridicule. Observing that a man whose only item of property was a jackass would lose his right to vote if the jackass died, Franklin asked, "Now tell me, which was the voter, the man or the jackass?" Fifty years elapsed before the property restriction was lifted in all states.

African Americans appeared to have gained suffrage after the Civil War with passage of the Fifteenth Amendment, which says that a state cannot abridge the right to vote "on account of race, color, or previous condition of servitude." Nevertheless, African Americans were disenfranchised throughout the South by intimidation and electoral trickery, including rigged literacy tests as a precondition of being allowed to register to vote. The tests contained questions so difficult that often the examiner had to look up the answers. If that was not enough of an obstacle, the names of those who took the test were sometimes published in the local newspaper so that employers, the local police, and even the KKK would know the names of the "troublemakers." The extreme case was Mississippi. Even as late as the 1950s, only about 1 in 25 of its black residents was registered to vote (see Figure 7-1). Not until the 1960s did Congress and the courts sweep away the last legal barriers to equal suffrage for African Americans (see Chapter 5).

Women did not secure the vote until 1920, with the ratification of the Nineteenth Amendment. Decades earlier, Susan B. Anthony had tried to vote in her hometown of Rochester, New York, claiming that as a U.S. citizen she had a right to vote. She was arrested for "illegal voting" and told that her proper place was in the home. By 1920, men had run out of excuses for denying the vote to women. As Senator Wendell Phillips observed, "One of two things is true: either woman is like man—and if she is, then a ballot based on brains belongs to her as well as to him. Or she is different, and then man does not know how to vote for her as she herself does."[2]

The nation's youngest adults are the most recent beneficiaries of a suffrage amendment. Ratified during the Vietnam War—a time when the military draft was in full swing and the minimum voting age in nearly every state was

Percentage of adults registered to vote

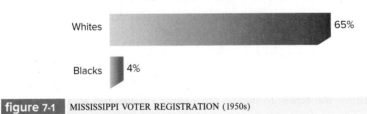

Whites   65%

Blacks   4%

figure 7-1   MISSISSIPPI VOTER REGISTRATION (1950s)

Through intimidation, poll taxes, and rigged literacy tests, the state of Mississippi kept all but a small number of its black residents from registering to vote. (*Source:* Estimated by author from multiple sources.)

21 years—the Twenty-Sixth Amendment lowered the voting age to 18 years. "If you're old enough to die, you're old enough to vote" was the rallying cry of its proponents.

Factors in Voter Turnout: The United States in Comparative Perspective

Nearly all Americans embrace the symbolism of the vote, saying that they have a duty to vote in elections. Nevertheless, many Americans shirk their duty. Millions choose not to vote regularly, a tendency that sets Americans apart from citizens of most other Western democracies. In the past two decades, **voter turnout**—the proportion of adult citizens who actually vote in a given election—has averaged roughly 60 percent in presidential elections. In other words, about three in five eligible citizens have gone to the polls in recent presidential elections while two in five have stayed away.

Although turnout in presidential elections is not particularly high, it is significantly higher than the turnout in the midterm congressional elections that

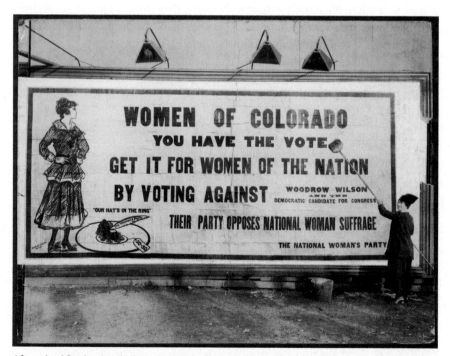

After a hard-fought, decades-long campaign, women across the nation finally won the right to vote in 1920. Fifteen states, most of them located west of the Mississippi River, had earlier granted suffrage to women. Wyoming in 1869 was the first to do so. Colorado in 1893 was the second. (*Source:* Library of Congress, Manuscript Division [159016])

take place between presidential elections. Midterm turnout has not reached 50 percent since 1920 and has averaged roughly 40 percent in recent decades. There was a surge in voting in the 2018 midterm elections. It increased by several percentage points over the previous midterm, but was still short of the 50 percent level. Turnout in local elections is lower yet. In many places, only about 20 percent of eligible citizens—one in five—bother to vote.

Voter participation is lower in the United States than in nearly every other democracy (see Figure 7-2). Compared with the 60 percent turnout level in U.S. presidential elections, turnout in national elections is, for example, 85 percent in Belgium and more than 70 percent in Germany and Italy.[3]

Registration Requirements   America's lower turnout level owes partly to its more demanding registration requirement. Before Americans are allowed to vote, they must make the effort to register—that is, they need to get their name on the official list of eligible voters. **Registration** began around 1900 as a way of preventing voters from casting more than one ballot on Election Day. Multiple balloting had become a tactic of big-city party machines—"vote early and often" was their motto. Although registration reduced illegal voting, it also placed a burden on honest citizens. Because they were required to register beforehand, citizens who forgot or otherwise failed to do so were unable to vote. Turnout in U.S. elections declined after registration began.

Although other democracies also require registration, most of them place the responsibility on government. When someone moves to a new address, for example, the postal service will notify registration officials of the change. The

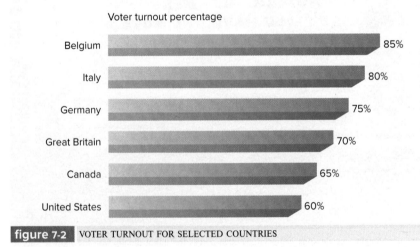

Voter turnout percentage

Country	Percentage
Belgium	85%
Italy	80%
Germany	75%
Great Britain	70%
Canada	65%
United States	60%

figure 7-2 VOTER TURNOUT FOR SELECTED COUNTRIES

The United States ranks near the bottom among the world's democracies in terms of the percentage of its eligible citizens who vote. (*Source:* Developed by author from multiple sources. Percentages are rounded averages of recent national elections.)

United States—in keeping with its individualistic culture—is one of the few democracies in which registration is the individual's responsibility. Moreover, registration is largely controlled by the state governments. Although the 1993 Motor Voter Act requires them to allow people to register when they apply for a driver's license or public assistance,[4] some states make little effort otherwise to inform citizens about registration times and locations.[5] Scholars estimate that turnout would be roughly ten percentage points higher in the United States if it had European-style registration.[6]

States with more convenient registration laws have higher turnout than other states. About 10 states, including Idaho, Maine, and Minnesota, allow people to register at their polling places on Election Day. Their turnout rates are more than ten percentage points above the national average. States with the most restrictive registration laws—for example, those that require residents to register at least two weeks before Election Day and make it difficult to cast an absentee ballot—have turnout rates well below the national average. Indiana, Mississippi, and Alabama are among the states in this category.

Some states have recently enacted laws requiring their residents to have a government-issued photo ID, such as a passport or driver's license, before they are allowed to register to vote. In 2008, the Supreme Court upheld Indiana's photo ID law, which had been challenged on grounds it discriminated against the poor. The Court held that states have a "valid interest" in taking steps to deter voter fraud. (©Brand X Pictures)

A recent device, voter identification cards, serves to discourage voter turn-out. Legislatures in more than half the states have enacted laws requiring citizens to have documented evidence of citizenship, such as a driver's license, passport, or certified birth certificate, in order to register and vote. Proponents of these laws say a government-issued document is needed to prevent voter fraud. In every state with a government-issued ID requirement, except Rhode Island and Hawaii, the law was passed by a Republican-controlled state legislature. Opponents of the law, most of whom are Democrats, say the voter ID requirement is a thinly disguised effort to keep low-income voters, many of whom don't have a driver's license or passport, from voting (see "Case Study: Party Strategy and Voter Registration").

CASE STUDY

Politics in Action

Party Strategy and Voter Registration

Because citizens cannot vote unless they are registered to vote, voter registration has long been a source of partisan maneuvering. If registration is eased, the number of voters expands. If it is made harder, the number of voters shrinks.

The Democratic Party has pressed to make voter registration easier, most notably through the 1993 Motor Voter Act. It requires states to offer voter registration to individuals who apply for a driver's license or public assistance. The legislation was first passed by the Democratic-controlled Congress

©Rob Crandall/Shutterstock

in 1991 but was vetoed by Republican president George H. W. Bush. Congress passed the bill again in 1993, when a fellow Democrat, Bill Clinton, was president. Clinton signed the bill into law. In the Senate, only three Republicans voted for the bill, while all Democratic senators did so. Voting in the House also divided sharply along party lines, with Republican members overwhelmingly opposed and Democratic members overwhelmingly in favor.

For their part, Republican lawmakers have sought to make voter registration harder, most notably at the state level through voter ID laws. In strictest form, such laws require a citizen to have a government-issued ID, such

Continued

as a driver's license or passport, in order to register to vote. A weaker form permits individuals to register if they can otherwise prove they are citizens. One of the first such laws was passed in 2005 by Indiana's Republican-controlled legislature. Today, more than 30 states have such laws. In every state with a voter ID requirement, except Rhode Island and Hawaii, the law was enacted by a Republican-controlled legislature.

The figure below indicates the percentage of people in various groups who do not have a government-issued photo ID.

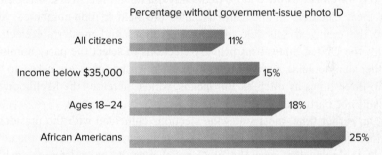

Percentage without government-issue photo ID

All citizens	11%
Income below $35,000	15%
Ages 18–24	18%
African Americans	25%

Source: Based on Brennan Center for Justice, New York University School of Law, 2018

Q: Why do Democratic lawmakers tend to favor less restrictive voter registration requirements while Republican lawmakers tend to prefer more restrictive ones?

ASK YOURSELF: Which groups tend to vote Democratic? Which groups tend to vote Republican? Which groups have the highest percentage of individuals on public assistance and thereby are advantaged by the Motor Voter Act? Which groups have the fewest individuals with a driver's license or passport and thereby are disadvantaged by voter ID laws?

In 2008, the U.S. Supreme Court ruled on a case involving Indiana's voter identification card law. Writing for the Court's 6–3 majority, Justice John Paul Stevens said states have a "valid interest" in improving election procedures and deterring fraud. The Court acknowledged that Indiana's Republicans had a partisan interest in enacting the law but argued that the law "should not be disregarded simply because partisan interests may have provided one motivation for the votes of individual legislators."[7] However, the courts have not allowed the states complete freedom when it comes to voter ID laws. In 2017, for example, the Supreme Court upheld a lower federal court ruling that invalidated North Carolina's voter ID law. Enacted by the state's Republican legislation after a surge in registration and voting by the state's black residents, the law required a registrant to have a government-issued photo ID. The lower federal court ruled that the law had "discriminatory intent," concluding that its purpose was to suppress the black vote.[8]

Frequency of Elections   Just as America's registration system places a burden on voters, so too does its election schedule. The United States holds elections more often than other nations. No other democracy has elections for the lower chamber of its national legislature (the equivalent of the U.S. House of Representatives) as often as every two years, and no democracy schedules elections for chief executive more frequently than every four years.[9] In addition, most local elections in the United States are held in odd-numbered years, unlike the even-year schedule of federal elections and most state elections. Finally, the United States uses primary elections to select the party nominees. In other democracies, party leaders pick them. Americans are asked to vote two to three times as often as Europeans, which increases the likelihood that they will not participate every time.[10]

At an earlier time, most statewide elections coincided with the presidential election, when turnout is highest. This scheduling usually worked to the advantage of the party that won the presidential race—its candidates got a boost from the strong showing of its presidential nominee. In an effort to eliminate "presidential coattails" that might help the weaker party in their state, states began in the 1930s to hold their gubernatorial elections in nonpresidential years. Over three-fourths of the states have adopted this schedule, and two states—Virginia and New Jersey—elect their governors in odd-numbered years, insulating them even further from the turnout effects of federal elections.

Why Some Americans Vote and Others Do Not

Even though turnout is lower in the United States than in other major Western democracies, some Americans vote regularly while others seldom or never vote. Among the explanations for these individual differences are education and income, age, civic attitudes, and political interest and partisanship.

Education and Income   College-educated and upper-income Americans have above-average voting rates. They have the financial resources and communication skills that encourage participation and make it personally rewarding. Nevertheless, the United States is unusual in the degree to which education and income are related to voter participation. Europeans with less education and income vote at only slightly lower rates than other citizens. By comparison, Americans with a college degree or high income are substantially more likely to vote in a presidential election than are those who did not finish high school or have a low income.

Detecting Misinformation

Are Our Attention Spans Shrinking?

Democracy affords citizens a chance to participate in politics. But participation by itself is not the standard of good citizenship. That standard is informed participation, where the citizen when forming an opinion or casting a vote understands what's actually at stake. Studies indicate that Americans' understanding of politics is declining. On average, citizens know less about politics than they did a few decades ago and are more likely to have bizarre notions of reality. Analysts have suggested

©DGLimages/Shutterstock

that the change is attributable to a decline in attention to traditional news sources and an increase in attention to less reliable sources, such as talk show hosts and bloggers. Some analysts have also suggested that the digital age, with its onslaught of short messages, has shortened our attention spans, which makes learning harder.

Is that claim fact, or is it fake?

A 2015 Microsoft study used surveys and electroencephalograms (EEGs) to study the length of people's attention spans, finding that individuals lose their concentration after 8 seconds on average. When the study was conducted in 2000, the average was 12 seconds, leading the research team to conclude that today's fast-paced digital environment is reducing our ability to learn. And just how short is an 8-second attention span? Before the 2015 study was conducted, the baseline for comparisons was the goldfish, which has a 9-second attention span.[11]

Why the great difference between the United States and Europe? For one thing, Europeans with less income and education are encouraged to participate by the presence of class-based organizations. Labor unions are stronger in Europe, and most European democracies have a major socialist or labor party that is dedicated to the interests of lower-income voters. The United States has never had a major socialist or labor party. In addition, Europeans do not have the imposing voter registration requirements that some U.S. states place on their residents. Americans with less income and education are the individuals most adversely affected by the country's registration system. Many of them do not own cars or homes and are thus less likely to be registered in advance of an election or have the documentation that some states require as a condition for registration. They are also less familiar with registration locations and times.[12]

Age   Young adults are substantially less likely than middle-aged and older citizens to vote. For one thing, younger adults are less likely to live in the same residence from one election to the next, in which case they have to register again in order to retain their eligibility to vote. Even senior citizens, despite the infirmities of old age, have a much higher turnout rate than do voters under the age of 30. The difference is more pronounced in midterm congressional elections than in presidential elections. In recent years, the voter turnout rate of young adults in midterm elections has been roughly half the level that it is in presidential elections.

Civic Attitudes   People differ in their attitudes toward politics, which affects the likelihood they will exercise their right to vote.

Apathy—a lack of interest in politics—typifies some citizens. They rarely if ever vote. Just as some people would not attend the Super Bowl even if it was free and being played across the street, some Americans care so little about politics that they would not bother to vote even if a ballot were delivered to their door.

Still other Americans refrain from voting because of **alienation**—a feeling of powerlessness rooted in the belief that government ignores their interests. The Hispanic vote was expected to surge in the 2016 presidential election as a result of the prominence of immigration as a campaign issue The surge did not materialize. Some Hispanics had concluded, after years of government inaction on immigration reform, that their votes didn't make a difference.[13]

By contrast, some Americans have a keen sense of **civic duty**—a belief that they ought to participate in public affairs. Citizens who hold this belief tend to vote more regularly. Civic duty and apathy are attitudes that are usually acquired from one's parents. When parents vote regularly and take an active interest in politics, their children usually grow up thinking they have a duty to participate. When parents never vote and show no interest in public affairs, their children are likely to be politically apathetic as adults.

Political Interest and Partisanship   Finally, the likelihood that citizens will vote varies with their interest in politics. As would be expected, citizens with a strong or moderate interest in politics are much more likely to vote than those with little or no interest. What makes this fact noteworthy is that political interest is largely a consequence of partisanship. Although "independents" are sometimes idealized in high school civics classes, they have much lower voting rates than citizens who identify with a political party.

Party loyalists are more likely to vote than independents in part because they are more familiar with the policy differences between the parties and therefore are more likely to understand an election's consequences. Moreover, party loyalty is like people's other loyalties—it deepens their commitment. Although some NFL football fans, for example, have no team loyalty, they are few and far between. Loyalty to a team heightens interest in watching NFL football on television. So it is with politics. Loyalty to a political party heightens interest in voting (see "Party Polarization: Ideology and Voter Turnout").

P A R T Y
POLARIZATION

Conflicting Ideas

Ideology and Voter Turnout

The heightened level of party polarization in recent years includes a widening ideological divide. Americans who identify with the Republican Party have increasingly called themselves conservatives, whereas those who identify with the Democratic Party have increasing labeled themselves as liberals.

The ideological divide is exaggerated in elections because conservatives and liberals are more likely than moderates to vote. That's the case in all elections and is especially true in primaries and midterm congressional elections. Following are the percentages of adults who say they "always vote" by whether they are conservative, liberal, or moderate in their political beliefs.

Percentage who say they "always vote"

- Conservatives — 68%
- Liberals — 51%
- Moderates — 39%

Source: Pew Research Center poll, 2014

Q: How might higher voter turnout among liberals and conservatives affect what happens in Congress?

A: Higher turnout among liberals and conservatives results in an increase in the number of ideologues nominated and elected to Congress. Their presence in Congress results in intensified partisan conflict over bills, which can lead to legislative deadlock.

CONVENTIONAL FORMS OF PARTICIPATION OTHER THAN VOTING

No form of political participation is as widespread as voting. Nevertheless, voting is a limited form of participation. Citizens have the opportunity to vote only at a particular time and only for the choices listed on the ballot. Fuller opportunities for participation exist, including contributing time and money to political and civic causes.

Campaign and Lobbying Activities

Compared with voting, working for a candidate is more time-consuming. Not surprisingly, only a small percentage of citizens engage in such activities. Nevertheless, the number is substantially higher in the United States than in Europe. A study that compared Americans with citizens in several European countries found, for example, that Americans were about five times more likely to take an active part in political campaigns and were twice as likely to converse with other people about their preferred candidate or party.[14]

Why the reversal? Why are Americans more likely than Europeans to take part in election activity even though they are less likely to show up at the polls on Election Day? The explanation rests in part on differences in American and European election campaigns. Just as a more imposing registration system reduces voter turnout in the United States, a more extensive electoral structure produces higher campaign involvement in the United States. For one thing, American campaigns last much longer than those in Europe, where many start and end within a few weeks. Because the United States has primary elections, candidates launch their campaigns months in advance of Election Day, offering citizens plenty of time to join in. Then, too, the United States is a federal system with campaigns for national, state, and local offices. A citizen who wants to participate can easily find an opportunity at one level of office or another. Most of the European governments are unitary in form (see Chapter 3), which means that there are many fewer elective offices and thus many fewer campaigns in which to participate.

Americans are also more likely than citizens elsewhere to support the activities of political groups. This support usually takes the form of a monetary contribution but also includes more active forms, such as contacting lawmakers or attending public rallies. Among the hundreds of groups that depend on citizen contributions are Greenpeace, Common Cause, AARP (formerly known as the American Association of Retired Persons), the Christian Coalition of America, and the National Conservative Political Action Committee. (Lobbying groups are discussed further in Chapter 9.)

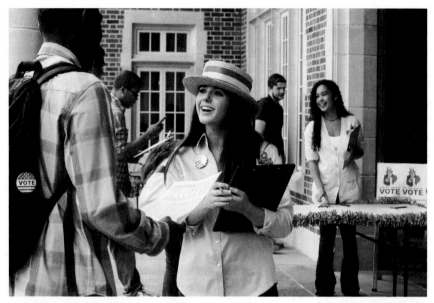

Although Americans are less likely than Europeans to vote, they are more likely than Europeans to participate actively in political campaigns. Most Americans are not active participants, but many do get involved by working for a candidate or party, contributing to a favorite candidate, or, as in the case of those pictured here, encouraging people to register and vote. (©Ariel Skelley/Blend Images)

Virtual Participation

The introduction of the World Wide Web in the 1990s opened up an entirely new venue for political participation—the Internet. It has created previously unimaginable participation possibilities. Although this participation is "virtual" rather than face-to-face, much of it involves contact with friends, acquaintances, and activists through Facebook, Twitter, e-mail, and other social media. Internet participation peaks during presidential campaigns and now easily outstrips conventional participation.

Internet fundraising is also flourishing. Although the donors who contribute millions of dollars to campaigns get most of the attention in the news, the Internet has made it easy for small donors to contribute. In 2016, Democrat Bernie Sanders's presidential nominating campaign alone received online contributions from more than 5 million donors—the average donation was about $30.[15]

Many groups have built extensive online organizations. MoveOn.org, for example, has a network of more than 3 million "online activists" that it mobilizes in support of liberal causes. In the run-up to the 2016 presidential election, MoveOn launched a grassroots effort to draft Senator Elizabeth Warren of

Massachusetts to run for the Democratic presidential nomination. Failing in that effort, MoveOn put its weight behind Sanders's candidacy. Its endorsement of Sanders resulted from a poll of MoveOn's supporters who voted overwhelming to back him rather than Hillary Clinton. "MoveOn members are feeling the Bern," said Ilya Sheyman, MoveOn's political action executive director, in announcing the Sanders endorsement.[16] (The Internet is discussed further in Chapter 10.)

Community Activities

Political participation extends beyond campaigns and elections to involvement in the community. Citizens can join community groups, work to accomplish community goals, and let officials know their opinions on community matters. Such contacts generate what Harvard University's Robert Putnam has labeled **social capital**—the face-to-face interactions between people that contribute to a sense of community and foster civic cooperation.

The chief obstacle to participation is not opportunities, which are abundant, but the motivation to join in. Most people choose not to get involved, particularly when it comes to time-consuming activities. Nevertheless, many Americans are involved in community affairs through local organizations such as parent–teacher associations, neighborhood groups, business clubs, and church-affiliated groups (see "How the 50 States Differ").

The number of such participants is difficult to estimate precisely, but the U.S. Department of Labor puts it at roughly 25 percent of adults annually, which is a total of about 60 million people. Their volunteer activity takes many forms, but more than 70 percent of this participation takes place through church-related groups, school-related groups, and civic organizations.[17]

Americans' community involvement is substantially higher than that of Europeans. One reason is that religion plays a larger role in American society. Americans are more than twice as likely as Europeans to attend church regularly, which increases the likelihood they will engage in church-related community activity. Then, too, compared with cities and towns in Europe, those in the United States have greater control over local policy, which provides residents an incentive to participate in local affairs. The same is true of American schools. Local control and parental involvement in schools are stronger traditions in the United States than in Europe. Overall, Americans are more than twice as likely as Europeans to participate in community groups.[18]

HOW THE 50 STATES DIFFER

CRITICAL THINKING THROUGH COMPARISONS

Volunteer Activity

Although community volunteering is a tradition in every state, the rate varies considerably, as indicated by a recent study by the Corporation for National and Community Service. Utah has the highest volunteer rate: 43 percent of its residents 16 years of age or older are engaged yearly in community volunteer work. Louisiana, at 18 percent, ranks lowest.

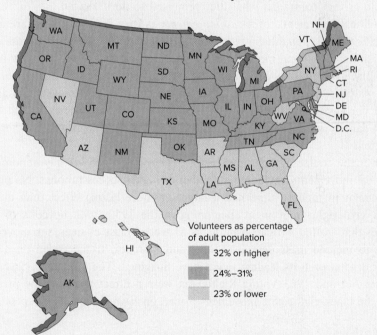

Volunteers as percentage of adult population

- 32% or higher
- 24%–31%
- 23% or lower

Source: Corporation for National and Community Service, 2018

Q: Why might the more northern states that lie west of the Mississippi River have higher than average volunteer rates?

A: Many residents of these states live in smaller communities with relatively stable populations. People in such communities are more likely to know each other and work together on community activities. In addition, these states were identified by political scientist Daniel Elazar as having participatory cultures as a result of their settlement by immigrant groups, Scandinavians particularly, who came from European countries that had a tradition of civic engagement.

UNCONVENTIONAL ACTIVISM: POLITICAL MOVEMENTS AND PROTESTS

During the pre-democratic era, people resorted to protest as a way of expressing displeasure with their rulers. Tax and food riots were the typical forms of protest. When democratic governments came into existence, citizens had a regular and less disruptive way to express themselves—through their votes. Voting is double-edged, however. Although the vote gives citizens control over government, *the vote also gives government control over citizens.*[19] Because they have been elected by the voters, public officials can claim to be constitutionally empowered even if they pursue policies that are opposed by a majority of the people or that contradict what they promised to do if elected.

Political movements, or *social movements* as they are also called, are a way for citizens disenchanted with government policy to actively express their opposition.[20] Political movements, as political scientist Sidney Tarrow notes, take place largely outside established institutions in the form of protest rallies, marches, and the like. Thus, participation in political movements differs from participation through interest groups or political parties, which takes place largely within established institutions, such as legislative bodies and elections.[21]

Over the course of American history, there have been literally hundreds of political movements, including a number of highly successful ones. No protest movement in modern time had a larger or more lasting effect than did the black civil rights movement. Beginning in the 1950s with boycotts of businesses that treated African Americans as second-class citizens, the movement grew to include mass demonstrations and marches. It succeeded on a level beyond what even its leaders might have imagined. The landmark 1964 Civil Rights Act and 1965 Voting Rights Act were a direct result of the pressure that the black civil rights movement placed on lawmakers (see Chapter 5).

Recent Protest Movements and Their Success

Recent years have witnessed a rise in protest activity. Among the reasons is the widening partisan divide. As Republicans and Democrats have moved apart, the issues that divide them have intensified and in some cases spilled over into protest activity. As well, because of partisan deadlock in Washington, many policy problems have been neglected, compounding the anxiety and frustration that result when problems get worse rather than better. In any case, Americans have increasingly looked outside established political channels to make their voices heard. The following discussion highlights some of the more recent protest movements and their success in achieving their goals.

Tea Party Movement   The Tea Party came to the public's attention on April 15, 2009—the date that federal income taxes were due. The timing was not a coincidence, nor was the movement's name. Like the participants in the legendary Boston Tea Party, those who took to the streets in hundreds of cities and towns on that April day were expressing their opposition to high taxes. In Washington, D.C., the protesters hurled tea bags over the White House fence. Tea Party advocates called for sharp reductions in federal spending, saying in their "Contract for America": "Our moral, political, and economic liberties are inherent, not granted by our government. It is essential to the practice of these liberties that we be free from restriction over our peaceful political expression and free from excessive control over our economic choices."

Occupy Wall Street   When the Occupy Wall Street (OWS) movement emerged in 2011, it began small—a single encampment in New York City's Zuccotti Park, adjacent to Wall Street. Within a few weeks, however, it had spread to dozens of American cities. OWS was sparked by anger at the government's bailout of the financial industry and its failure to hold bankers accountable for their role in the financial crisis that occurred in 2008. Unlike the Tea Party, OWS's target was private wealth. OWS's core issue was the widening income gap between rich and poor, which had been exacerbated by

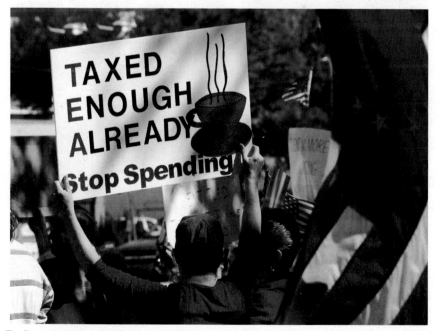

Tea Party protestors stage a rally at the Capitol against federal spending and taxes. (©Cheryl Casey/ Shutterstock)

the Bush-era tax policies that benefited the wealthiest 1 percent of Americans. "We are the 99%" was the movement's slogan.

Black Lives Matter   Sparked by the killing of unarmed young black men by police officers in several cities, including Baltimore, Chicago, and Ferguson, Missouri, the Black Lives Matter movement sought to change not just the behavior of law enforcement officers but also the public agenda broadly. Many local governments, for example, provide inferior services in black neighborhoods. Through public demonstrations, marches, and the reenactment of police killings, the movement has sought to highlight disparities in how white and black citizens are treated by local officials.

The #MeToo Movement   In 2017, #MeToo spread virally as a social media hashtag to show the extent to which women are subjected to sexual assault and harassment. Popularized by actress Alyssa Milano, the hashtag was used 200,000 times the day she proposed it and was subsequently posted millions of times, often accompanied by the sender's personal story. It contributed to the firing or resignation of a large number of powerful men, including Hollywood

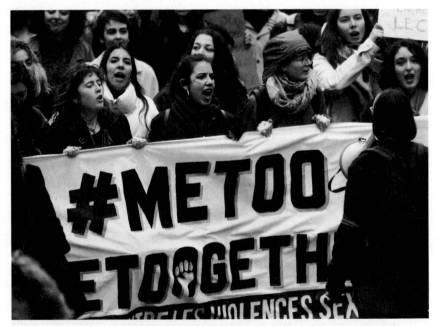

The #MeToo movement emerged rapidly in 2017 as thousands of women used social media to say that they, too, had been the victim of sexual assault or harassment. Within a relatively few weeks, powerful men in media, politics, and business who were credibly accused of sexual misconduct had been fired or resigned. The movement sought to raise public awareness of sexual misconduct and get firms and organizations to establish policies to prevent such abuses. (©Mustafa Sevgi/SIPA/Newscom)

producer Harvey Weinstein, television host Charlie Rose, casino magnate Steve Wynn, and U.S. representative John Conyers. The movement's larger goal was to raise awareness of the extent of sexual misconduct, show its devastating effect on victims, and encourage firms and organizations to adopt policies aimed at stopping the practice.

Movement against Gun Violence   The movement against gun violence had a relatively low profile until the 2018 mass killing at Marjory Stoneman Douglas High School in Parkland, Florida. The school's students responded with an impassioned plea for an end to school shootings. Their action captured the nation's attention. It led to National School Walkout Day and March for Our Lives demonstrations in hundreds of cities and towns. The movement's goal aimed at pressuring lawmakers at the national, state, and local levels to enact tougher gun control measures, including a rigorous background check for gun buyers and a ban on military-style assault rifles, which had been used in several recent mass killings, including the Parkland shooting.

Factors in the Success of Social Movements   Most political movements in the nation's history have failed to achieve their goals. Some of them, like the anarchists and communist movements, had goals that were so at odds with American values that they failed to attract a sizeable following. Others failed because they lacked the resources to sustain the effort. Typically, a lengthy period of intense and sustained action is required for a movement to succeed. Finally, movements can fail if they are unable to institutionalize their goals through legal, political, or social change. If the black civil rights movement, for example, had not succeeded in getting some of its goals institutionalized through the 1964 Civil Rights Act and the 1965 Voting Rights Act, its long-term impact would have been far more limited.

Recent political movements differ in their level of success. All of them were able to draw attention to their core issue, but they otherwise differed in one or more ways. To date at least, the Tea Party is the most successful of the recent movements. It was able to transform itself from a movement to a permanent force within the Republican Party, which provided it an institutional base from which to pursue its goal of cutting taxes and government spending. At one point, nearly 150 congressional Republicans called themselves a Tea Party member or sympathizer. In contrast, Occupy Wall Street protesters rejected the idea of developing institutional links, which meant, when their encampments were disbanded, they didn't have an organization through which to pursue their goals. OWS later tried to resurrect itself through a website but failed to attract a significant following. However, OWS's issue of income inequality was at the core of Bernie Sanders's bid for the Democratic presidential nomination in 2016.

It's too early to say with certainty whether Black Lives Matter, the #MeToo movement, and the movement against gun violence will achieve substantial institutional and policy gains. Each movement has had an impact. Black Lives Matter prompted some cities and towns to change their policing policies, the #MeToo movement got some firms and organizations to establish policies aimed at curbing sexual misconduct, and the movement against gun violence led to a few policies aimed at curbing the sale and possession of particular types of firearms and accessories. But none of these movements, as of yet, has succeeded in bringing about wholesale policy change. The history of the black civil rights movement suggests that any judgment on the success of these movements could come years from now. It took several decades before the black civil rights movement was able to get lawmakers to enact the landmark legislation that is now its lasting legacy.

The Public's Response to Protest Activity

Protest politics has a long history in America. Indeed, the United States was founded on a protest movement that sparked a revolution against Britain. Despite this tradition, protest activity is less common today in the United States than in many Western democracies. Spain, France, Germany, Sweden, and Mexico are among the countries that have higher rates of protest participation.

Public support for protest activity depends on what's at issue. When the protesters' grievance is widely shared and seen as legitimate, the public is supportive. By contrast, when U.S. military action has been the object of protest, public support has at times been weak. The Vietnam War protests, which in some cases were accompanied by the burning of the American flag, had only marginal public support. When unarmed student protesters at Kent State University and Jackson State University were shot to death in May 1970 by members of the National Guard, most American polls faulted the students. In a *Newsweek* poll, 58 percent of respondents blamed the Kent State killings on the student demonstrators, while only 11 percent said the guard soldiers were at fault. The Iraq war protest in 2003 had a higher level of public support. Three in every five Americans said they saw the protests as "a sign of a healthy democracy." Still, almost two in five poll respondents said that "opponents of the war should not hold antiwar demonstrations" and half of them said that antiwar demonstrations should be outlawed.

In short, although most Americans recognize that protest is part of America's tradition of free expression, they do not embrace it as fully as they do voting. Many Americans would prefer that people voice their discontent through elections rather than by taking to the streets. In this sense, protest is seen by most Americans as something to be accepted but not always something to be admired.

PARTICIPATION AND THE POTENTIAL FOR INFLUENCE

Most Americans are not highly active in politics. One reason is the emphasis that the American culture places on individualism. Most Americans under most conditions expect to solve their problems on their own rather than through political action. "In the United States, the country of individualism *par excellence,*" William Watts and Lloyd Free write, "there is a sharp distinction in people's minds between their own personal lives and national life."[22]

Paradoxically, although they have more need for government help, lower-income Americans are the least likely to engage in collective action. Lower-income individuals tend to have less education, less access to transportation, less access to permanent housing, and less understanding of how to get involved in politics—all of which work to reduce their level of political participation.[23] Indeed, Americans in the bottom fifth in terms of income are a third less likely to be registered to vote than those in the top fifth (see Figure 7-3). As a consequence, their political influence is relatively limited. In *Unequal Democracy,* political scientist Larry Bartels demonstrates that elected officials are much less responsive to the concerns of their less affluent constituents than to their wealthier ones.[24]

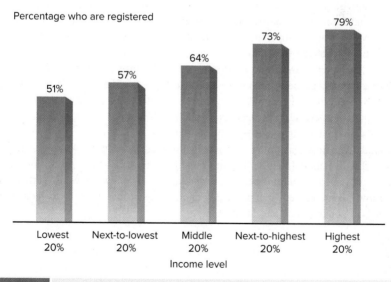

Percentage who are registered

Lowest 20%	Next-to-lowest 20%	Middle 20%	Next-to-highest 20%	Highest 20%
51%	57%	64%	73%	79%

Income level

figure 7-3   VOTER REGISTRATION AND INCOME LEVEL

Americans of lower income are much less likely to be registered to vote than those of higher income. (*Source:* U.S. Census Bureau, 2017)

In sum, the pattern of political influence in the United States parallels the distribution of economic influence. Those who have the least power in the marketplace also have the least power in the political arena. However, the issue of individual participation is only one piece of the larger puzzle of how power in America is distributed. Subsequent chapters will furnish additional pieces.

SUMMARY

Political participation is involvement in activities designed to influence public policy and leadership. A main issue of democratic government is the question of who participates in politics and how fully they participate.

Voting is the most widespread form of active political participation among Americans. Yet voter turnout is significantly lower in the United States than in other democratic nations. The requirement that Americans must personally register in order to become eligible to vote is one reason for lower turnout among Americans; other democracies place the burden of registration on government officials rather than on the individual citizens. The fact that the United States holds frequent elections also discourages some citizens from voting regularly.

Only a minority of citizens engage in the more demanding forms of political activity, such as work on community affairs or on behalf of a candidate during a political campaign. Nevertheless, the proportion of Americans who engage in these more demanding forms of activity exceeds the proportion of Europeans who do so. Most political activists are individuals of higher income and education; they have the skills and material resources to participate effectively and tend to take a greater interest in politics. More than in any other Western democracy, political participation in the United States is related to economic status.

Social movements are broad efforts to achieve change by citizens who feel that government is not properly responsive to their interests. These efforts typically take place outside established channels; demonstrations, picket lines, and marches are common means of protest. Despite America's tradition of free expression, protest activities do not always have a high level of public support.

Overall, Americans are only moderately involved in politics. Although they are concerned with political affairs, they are mostly immersed in their private pursuits, a reflection in part of a cultural belief in individualism. The lower level of participation among low-income citizens has particular significance in that it works to reduce their influence on public policy and leadership.

CRITICAL THINKING ZONE

KEY TERMS

alienation (*p. 206*)
apathy (*p. 206*)
civic duty (*p. 206*)
political (social) movements (*p. 212*)
political participation (*p. 197*)

registration (*p. 200*)
social capital (*p. 210*)
suffrage (*p. 197*)
voter turnout (*p. 199*)

APPLYING THE ELEMENTS OF CRITICAL THINKING

Conceptualizing: How do alienation, apathy, and civic duty differ?

Synthesizing: Compare voting rates in the United States with those in Europe. Why are they lower in the United States? Then compare community participation rates in the United States with those in Europe. Why are they higher in the United States?

Analyzing: Why does economic status—differences in Americans' education and income levels—make such a large difference in their level of political participation? Why does it make a larger difference in the United States than in Europe?

EXTRA CREDIT

A Book Worth Reading: Thomas Paine, *The American Crisis* (Scotts Valley, Calif.: CreateSpace, 2017). A compilation of Thomas Paine's pamphlets, including his famed *Common Sense,* written between 1776 and 1783. The pamphlets have a message for citizens: Get involved in politics; there's a lot at stake.

A Website Worth Visiting: www.votesmart.org. Project Vote Smart is a nonpartisan, nonprofit organization. Its website includes helpful information for voters on the backgrounds and policy positions of Republican and Democratic candidates for office.

PARTICIPATE!

If you are not currently registered to vote, consider registering. You can obtain a registration form from the election board or clerk in your community of residence. Several websites contain state-by-state registration information. One such site is http://turbovote.org. If you are already registered, consider participating in a registration or voting drive on your campus. Although students typically register and vote at relatively low rates, they will often participate if encouraged by other students to do so.

8
CHAPTER

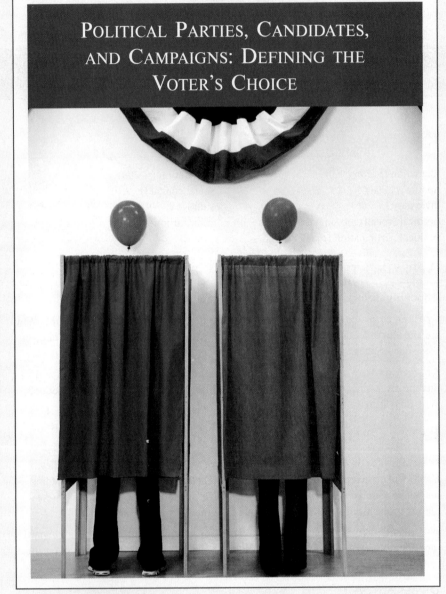

POLITICAL PARTIES, CANDIDATES, AND CAMPAIGNS: DEFINING THE VOTER'S CHOICE

©Hill Street Studios/Getty Images

❝ Political parties created democracy and . . . modern democracy is unthinkable save in terms of the parties. ❞

E. E. SCHATTSCHNEIDER[1]

$\mathbf{T}$oe-to-toe, they slugged it out in states and districts across the breadth of America, each side claiming it had the answers to America's problems. One side promised to raise the minimum wage, reduce student loan obligations, enhance the status of women, widen access to health care, protect immigrants, and tighten gun controls. The other side pointed to tax cuts it had enacted into law, its tough action on illegal immigration, its buildup of the military, and its efforts to improve the nation's trade imbalance. The scene of this showdown was the 2018 midterm elections. The opposing sides were the Democratic Party and the Republican Party, each with its slate of House and Senate candidates who carried its message to voters across America.

Political parties are in the business of offering voters a choice. A **political party** is an ongoing coalition of interests joined together in an effort to get its candidates for public office elected under a common label.[2] By offering a choice between policies and leaders, parties give voters a chance to influence the direction of government. "It is the competition of [parties] that provides the people with an opportunity to make a choice," political scientist E. E. Schattschneider wrote. "Without this opportunity popular sovereignty amounts to nothing."[3]

This chapter examines political parties and the candidates who run under their name. U.S. campaigns are **party centered** in the sense that the Republican and Democratic Parties compete across the country election after election. Yet campaigns are also **candidate centered** in the sense that individual candidates devise their own strategies, choose their own issues, and form their own campaign organizations. The following points are emphasized in this chapter:

- *Political competition in the United States has centered on two parties, a pattern that is explained primarily by America's single-member district system of elections.* Minor parties exist in the United States but have been unable to attract enough votes to win legislative seats.

- *To win an electoral majority, candidates of the two major parties must appeal to a large number of voters.* This can lead them to advocate moderate policies, although in recent years they've increasingly positioned themselves away from the political center because of party polarization and a decline in the number of competitive states and districts.

- *U.S. party organizations play an important role in campaigns, although one that is less substantial than in their heyday.* The introduction of primary elections and the emergence of televised campaigning gradually shifted primary control of elections from the parties to the candidates. Nevertheless, party organizations at the local, state, and national levels are major players in election campaigns.

- *Presidential and congressional campaigns are largely candidate centered.* These campaigns are based on money and media and utilize the skills of professional consultants.

PARTY COMPETITION AND MAJORITY RULE

Through their numbers, citizens can exert influence, but it cannot be realized unless they act together. Parties give them that capacity. Parties are **linkage institutions;** they serve to connect citizens with government. When Americans go to the polls, they have a choice between candidates representing the Republican and Democratic Parties. This **party competition** narrows voters' options to two and in the process enables people with different backgrounds and opinions to act in unison. In casting a majority of its votes for one party, the electorate chooses that party's candidates, philosophy, and policies over those of the opposing party.

The history of democratic government is inseparable from the history of parties. When the people of Eastern Europe gained their freedom from the Soviet Union in the early 1990s, one of their first steps toward democracy was the formation of political parties. When the United States was founded over two centuries ago, the formation of parties was also a first step toward building its democracy. The reason is simple: It is the competition among parties that gives popular majorities a choice over how they will be governed.[4] If there were no mechanism like the party to enable citizens to act as one, they would be powerless—each too weak to influence government.

The First Parties

Many of America's early leaders mistrusted parties. George Washington in his farewell address warned the nation of the "baneful effects" of parties, and James Madison likened parties to special interests. However, Madison's misgivings about parties slowly gave way to grudging admiration. He came to realize that parties were the best way for like-minded leaders and citizens to work together to accomplish their common goals.

America's first parties originated in the rivalry between Alexander Hamilton and Thomas Jefferson, who opposed Hamilton's attempts to strengthen the federal government through national commerce. To advance his goal, Hamilton organized his followers into the Federalist Party, taking the name from the faction that had spearheaded the ratification of the Constitution (see Figure 8-1). Jefferson responded by creating the Democratic-Republican Party. The name harkened to the spirit behind the Declaration of Independence and reflected the party's strength among small farmers and states' rights advocates. The Federalists' preoccupation with commercial and moneyed interests fueled

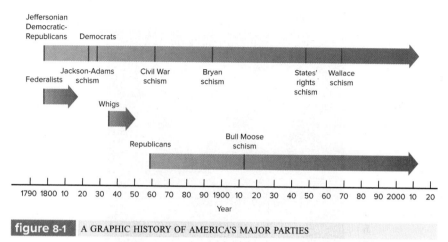

figure 8-1   A GRAPHIC HISTORY OF AMERICA'S MAJOR PARTIES

The U.S. party system has been remarkable for its continuity. Competition between two major parties has been a persistent feature of the system.

Jefferson's claim that they were bent on establishing a government of the rich and wellborn. After Jefferson in the election of 1800 defeated John Adams, who had succeeded Washington as president, the Federalists never again controlled the White House or Congress.

During the so-called Era of Good Feeling, when James Monroe ran unopposed in 1820 for a second presidential term, it appeared as if the political system might operate without competing parties. Yet by the end of Monroe's second term, policy differences had split the Democratic-Republicans. The dominant faction, under the leadership of Andrew Jackson, embraced Jefferson's commitment to the common people and adopted the label "Democrats." Thus, the Democratic-Republican Party of Jefferson is the forerunner of today's Democratic Party rather than of today's Republican Party.

Andrew Jackson and Grassroots Parties

Jackson's goal was to wrest political power from the established elite—the previous presidents had all come from old-line Virginia and Massachusetts families. Jackson saw a reorganized Democratic Party as the vehicle for change. Whereas Jefferson's party had operated largely at the leadership level, Jackson sought a **grassroots party**. As such, it was organized chiefly at the local level and was open to all citizens. The efforts of the local party organizations, along with the extension of voting rights to citizens without property, contributed to a nearly fourfold rise in election turnout during the 1830s.[5] Writing at the peak of Jacksonian democracy, Alexis de Tocqueville claimed that "The People reign in the American political world as the Deity does in the universe."[6]

Although largely forgotten, the Whig Party was once one of America's two major parties. Four Whigs served as president—William Henry Harrison, John Tyler, Zachary Taylor, and Millard Fillmore. The party came into being in the early 1830s and lasted into the 1850s before being replaced by the newly created Republican Party. (*Source:* Library of Congress, Prints and Photographs Division [LC-DIG-pga-09004])

During this period, a new opposition party—the Whig Party—emerged to challenge the Democrats. The Whigs were united less by a governing philosophy than by their opposition for one reason or another to Jackson and his followers. However, competition between the Whigs and the Democrats was relatively short-lived. During the 1850s, the slavery issue began to tear both parties apart. The Whig Party disintegrated, and a northern-based new party, calling itself Republican, emerged as the Democrats' main challenger. In the 1860 presidential election, the Democratic Party's northern faction nominated Stephen A. Douglas, who held that the question of whether slavery would be allowed in a new state was for its voters to decide, while the southern faction nominated John C. Breckinridge, who called for legalized slavery in all states. The Democratic vote split sharply along regional lines between these two candidates—with the result that the Republican nominee, Abraham Lincoln, who had called for the gradual elimination of slavery, was able to win the presidency with only 40 percent of the popular vote. Lincoln's election prompted the southern states to secede from the Union.

The Civil War was the first and only time in the nation's history that the party system failed to peacefully settle Americans' political differences. The issue of slavery was simply too explosive to be settled through electoral competition.[7]

Republicans versus Democrats: Realignments and the Enduring Party System

After the Civil War, the nation settled into the pattern of competition between the Republican and Democratic Parties that has lasted through today. The durability of the two parties is due not to their ideological consistency but to their ability to change during periods of crisis. By abandoning at these crucial times their old ways of doing things, the Republican and Democratic Parties have reorganized themselves—with new bases of support, new policies, and new public philosophies.

These periods of extraordinary party change are known as **party realignments**. A realignment typically involves three basic elements:

1. The emergence of unusually powerful and divisive issues
2. An election contest or contests in which the voters shift their partisan support
3. An enduring change in the parties' policies and coalitions

Realignments are rare. They do not occur simply because one party takes control of government from the other in a single election. Realignments result in deep and lasting changes in the party system that affect subsequent elections as well. By this standard, there have been four realignments since the 1850s.

The first was a result of the nation's Civil War and worked to the advantage of the Republicans. Called the "Union Party" by many, the Republicans dominated elections in the larger and more populous North, while the Democrats acquired a stronghold in what became known as "the Solid South." During the next three decades, the Republicans held the presidency except for Grover Cleveland's two terms in office and had a majority in Congress for all but four years.

The 1896 election also resulted in realignment. Three years earlier, a banking crisis had caused a severe depression. The Democrat Cleveland was president when the crash happened, and people blamed him and his party. In the aftermath, the Republicans made additional gains in the Northeast and Midwest, solidifying their position as the nation's dominant party. During the four decades between the 1890s realignment and the next one in the 1930s, the Republicans held the presidency except for Woodrow Wilson's two terms and had a majority in Congress for all but six years.

The Great Depression of the 1930s triggered a third realignment. The Republican Herbert Hoover was president when the stock market crashed in 1929, and many Americans blamed Hoover, his party, and its business allies for the crisis. When the Democratic Party won the presidency in 1932 and gained the confidence of the American people through its economic recovery programs, it set itself up to be the nation's dominant party for years to come. Franklin D. Roosevelt's election as president began a 36-year period of Democratic presidencies that was interrupted only by Dwight D. Eisenhower's two terms in the 1950s. In this period, the Democrats also dominated Congress, losing control only in 1947–1948 and 1953–1954.

Franklin D. Roosevelt's election in 1932 signaled a party realignment that enabled the Democratic Party to dominate U.S. politics for the next three decades. (*Source:* Franklin D. Roosevelt Presidential Library and Museum)

Like earlier ones, the New Deal realignment led to fundamental changes in national policy. Before the 1930s, the Democrats were widely seen as the party of states' rights, reflecting its solid base of support in the South. In the 1930s, however, Democratic lawmakers used national power to offset the power of private wealth and big business. Their platform included business regulation, Social Security, higher taxes on the rich, the minimum wage, and collective bargaining rights. The Democratic Party was no longer the states' rights party but instead had become the party of federal power. It was during this period that the term *liberal* came into use as a description of the Democratic Party's governing philosophy.

Party realignments have a lasting effect because they are powered by changes in people's long-term party loyalties. Young voters in particular embrace the newly ascendant party, giving it a solid base of support for years to come. First-time voters in the 1930s came to identify with the Democratic Party by a two-to-one margin (see Figure 8-2). They retained their loyalty to the Democratic Party, enabling it to dominate national politics into the 1960s.[8]

The Democratic Party that was built during the New Deal era was made up largely of low- and moderate-income groups—blue-collar workers, inner-city dwellers, minority-group members, small farmers, and the like. Democrats prided themselves on being "the party of the little man." In contrast, the Republican Party in this period was dominated by middle- and upper-income groups, including businesspeople, merchants, well-to-do farmers, and professionals.

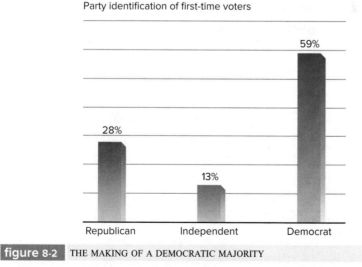

Party identification of first-time voters

figure 8-2   THE MAKING OF A DEMOCRATIC MAJORITY

During the Great Depression, first-time voters strongly backed the Democratic Party, positioning it to dominate national politics for the next three decades. (*Source:* Kristi Andersen, *The Creation of a Democratic Majority, 1928-1936* (Chicago: University of Chicago Press, 1979), 63. Based on first-time eligible voters in 1932, 1936, and 1940.)

The Nature and Origins of Today's Party Alignment

A party realignment gradually loses strength as the issues that gave rise to it decline in importance. By the late 1960s, with the Democratic Party divided over the Vietnam War and civil rights, it was apparent that the era of New Deal politics was ending.[9]

The change was most dramatic in the South. The region had been solidly Democratic at all levels since the Civil War, but the Democratic Party's leadership on civil rights alienated white conservatives. In the 1964 presidential election, five southern states voted Republican, an indicator of what was to come. The South gradually became the most heavily Republican region in the country. The region now delivers most of its electoral votes to the Republican presidential nominee, and Republicans dominate the South's state governments. The shift to Republican control can also be seen in the distribution of seats in the U.S. House of Representatives (see Figure 8-3). Whereas Democrats controlled most of the South's House seats in the 1960s, they are today largely in Republican hands. Meanwhile, the Northeast and West Coast have shifted toward the Democrats, most dramatically in the New England states (Connecticut. Maine, Massachusetts, New Hampshire, Rhode Island, and Vermont). They were once the stronghold of the Republican Party's moderate wing. As southern conservatives became an ever larger force within Republican ranks, the GOP moved to the right, distancing itself from many of its moderate voters.[10] Today, New England is a Democratic bastion. It is a reliable source of electoral votes for Democratic presidential candidates, and most of the region's top elected officials are Democrats.

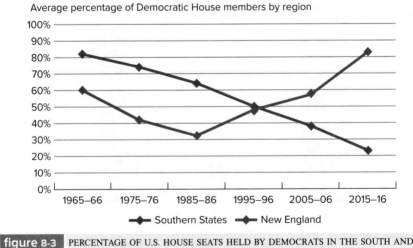

Average percentage of Democratic House members by region

◆ Southern States   ◆ New England

 figure 8-3   PERCENTAGE OF U.S. HOUSE SEATS HELD BY DEMOCRATS IN THE SOUTH AND NEW ENGLAND

In elections to the U.S. House of Representatives in recent decades, the southern states have increasingly voted Republican while the New England states have increasingly voted Democratic.

The net result of these and other regional changes has been a party realignment. Rather than occurring abruptly in response to a disruptive issue, as happened with the earlier realignments, the change took place gradually and is the product of several issues rather than of an overriding one. Civil rights was the triggering issue, but it was soon followed by what analysts Richard Scammon and Ben Wattenberg called the "social issue"—a loose set of controversies including crime, abortion, drugs, school prayer, and changing sexual and family norms.[11] Conservative Christians were the ones most alarmed by the changes, solidifying Republican gains in the southern and border states, particularly among white evangelicals. Ronald Reagan's presidency completed the transformation. President Johnson's Great Society programs, which included programs like Medicare and Medicaid, had expanded the federal government's social welfare role and increased federal spending. Conservatives felt the government was spending way too much and doing far too many things that were better left to the states. Reagan gave voice to their concerns, vowing to cut welfare, trim the federal budget, and devolve power to the states.

Although America's parties had realigned themselves without going through the sudden shock of a single realigning election, the change was dramatic. The

Democratic president Lyndon Johnson signs into law the 1964 Civil Rights Act, which gave black Americans equal access to restaurants, hotels, and other public accommodations. In much of the South, these accommodations had previously had a "whites only" policy. In signing the bill, Johnson said to an aide, "We [the Democratic Party] have lost the South for a generation." Johnson's prediction proved to be accurate. Within a few elections, the South had changed from being a heavily Democratic region to a heavily Republican one, changing the shape of the U.S. party system. (*Source:* LBJ Library photo by Cecil Stoughton)

parties emerged from the realignment with coalitions and philosophies differ-ent from their previous ones.[12] The extent of the change can be seen in the ideological transformation of the Republican Party. Although it began under Lincoln as the party of national power, it is today more clearly the states' rights party—an advocate of devolving power from Washington to the states (see Chapter 3).

F A K E
or
F A C T

Detecting Misinformation

Are Strong Partisans the Most Informed Citizens?

Decade after decade, opinion polls indicated that most Americans were not well informed about public affairs. Many of them were unable to answer even simple questions about current affairs or the nation's political system. Yet, there was a silver lining. Strong partisans were the ones most likely to vote and also the ones most likely to be relatively well informed. Because of their stronger interest in politics, they were the citizens who, on aver-age, were the most attentive to news about public affairs. It might be assumed that what was once true is also true today—that strong partisans are typically better informed than are other citizens.

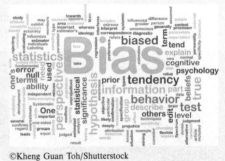

©Kheng Guan Toh/Shutterstock

Is that claim fact, or is it fake?

The picture today is a mixed one. It's still the case, on some issues, that strong partisans are more likely than other citizens to have their facts straight. On other issues, however, strong partisans are the most misinformed. Strong par-tisans are more likely than weak partisans or independents to pay attention to information sources, such as partisan blogs, talk shows, and the like, that promote false realities to further their partisan aims. As well, strong partisans are the citizens most likely to interpret information in ways that confirm what they'd like to believe—a tendency that scholars call "confirmation bias." Party polarization has had the effect, not only of widening the divide between the policy positions of Democrats and Republicans, but also of increasing the tendency of partisans to twist information to fit their preexisting beliefs. On issues ranging from climate change to health care policy, strong partisans are today the citizens most likely to hold views that are at odds with reality.[13]

The divide between the parties that began with civil rights continued after Reagan's presidency.[14] The parties today are polarized. There's barely an issue on which Democrats and Republicans see eye-to-eye. During the Reagan years, less than 10 percentage points separated Republicans and Democrats on the issue of legalized abortion.[15] Thirty-two percentage points separate them today.[16] On the question of human-caused climate change, a gap of 4 percentage points has widened to 37 points.[17] In terms of a ban on assault weapons, the divide has doubled from 13 points to 25 points.[18]

The shift in Congress has been even more pronounced. By the 112th Congress (2011–12), the middle had been hollowed out. As measured by roll-call votes, the least conservative Republican in the House or Senate was more conservative than the least liberal Democrat. Four decades earlier, roughly a fourth of House and Senate members were out of step with their party's majority—more conservative in the case of Democrats and more liberal in the case of Republicans.[19]

Parties and the Vote

The power of party is at no time clearer than when, election after election, Republican and Democratic candidates reap the vote of their party's identifiers. It is relatively rare—in congressional races as well as in the presidential race—for a party nominee to get less than 80 percent of the partisan vote.

The power of partisanship can be seen in the tendency of most voters to cast a *straight ticket*—meaning that they uniformly support their party's candidates. Most voters who cast a ballot for the Republican or Democratic presidential candidate also vote for that party's congressional candidate. Less than 20 percent of today's voters cast a *split-ticket,* voting for one party's presidential candidate and for the other party's congressional candidate (see "Party Polarization: Voting a Straight Ticket").

ELECTORAL AND PARTY SYSTEMS

Throughout nearly all of its history, the United States has had a **two-party system**: Federalists versus Jeffersonian Democratic-Republicans, Whigs versus Democrats, Republicans versus Democrats. A two-party system, however, is the exception rather than the rule (see "How the U.S. Differs"). Most democracies have a **multiparty system**, in which three or more parties have the capacity to gain control of government, separately or in coalition. Why the difference? Why are there three or more major parties in most democracies but only two major parties in the United States?

The Plurality (Single-Member-District) System of Election

America's two-party system is largely the result of the nation's method of choosing its officials. They are elected by winning a plurality of the votes in

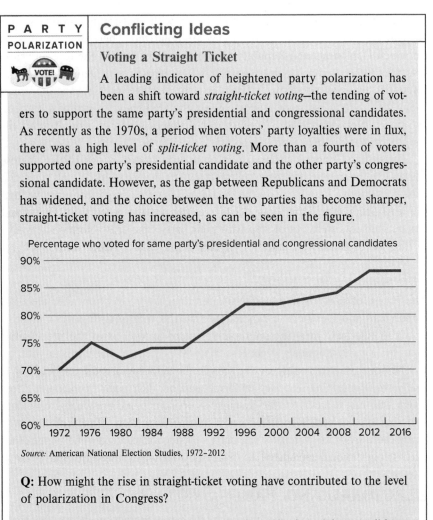

PARTY POLARIZATION

Conflicting Ideas

Voting a Straight Ticket

A leading indicator of heightened party polarization has been a shift toward *straight-ticket voting*—the tending of voters to support the same party's presidential and congressional candidates. As recently as the 1970s, a period when voters' party loyalties were in flux, there was a high level of *split-ticket voting*. More than a fourth of voters supported one party's presidential candidate and the other party's congressional candidate. However, as the gap between Republicans and Democrats has widened, and the choice between the two parties has become sharper, straight-ticket voting has increased, as can be seen in the figure.

Percentage who voted for same party's presidential and congressional candidates

Source: American National Election Studies, 1972–2012

Q: How might the rise in straight-ticket voting have contributed to the level of polarization in Congress?

A: Because voters have become less inclined to split their ticket, candidates have had less incentive to moderate their positions in order to appeal to voters of the other party. As a result, fewer moderates have been elected to Congress. The decline in the number of congressional moderates is a reason that Republican and Democratic lawmakers have found it harder to reach compromise positions on legislative issues.

single-member districts. Each constituency elects a single member to a particular office, such as U.S. senator or state representative; the candidate with the most votes (*the plurality*) in a district wins the office. The **plurality system** (sometimes called the *winner-take-all* system) discourages minor parties by reducing their chances of winning anything, even if they perform well by minor-party standards. Assume, for example, that a minor party receives exactly 20 percent of the vote in each of America's 435 congressional races. Even though one in five voters nationwide backed the minor party, it would not win

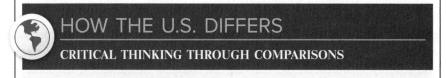

HOW THE U.S. DIFFERS
CRITICAL THINKING THROUGH COMPARISONS

Party and Electoral Systems

Since 1860, electoral competition in the United States has centered on the Republican and Democratic Parties. By comparison, most democracies have a multiparty system, in which three or more parties receive substantial support from voters.

Whether a country has a two-party or a multiparty system depends on several factors, but particularly its electoral system. The United States has a single-member, plurality district system in which only the top vote getter in a district is elected. This system is biased against smaller parties; even if they have some support in a great many races, they win nothing unless one of their candidates places first in an electoral district. By comparison, proportional representation systems enable smaller parties to compete; each party acquires legislative seats in proportion to its share of the total vote. Nearly every democracy with proportional representation, which includes most European countries, has at least three competitive parties, usually more than that number.

Q: Like the United States, Canada and Great Britain have the single-member-district system of election. Yet, unlike the United States, they have more than two parties. Why?

A: Canada's third parties have stemmed from regional differences and resentments. French-speaking Quebec has a strong regional party and strong regional parties have appeared from time to time in Canada's western provinces. Britain's strongest third party (currently the Liberal Democrats) has been able to survive because the British House of Commons is much larger than the U.S. House of Representatives (650 seats versus 435 seats) and the population of Britain is much smaller than that of the United States. As a result, British election districts have only about a tenth as many voters as U.S. House districts. Britain's Liberal Democrats have enough concentrated strength in some of these districts to win the seat.

any seats in Congress because none of its candidates would have placed first in any of the 435 single-member-district races. The winning candidate in each race would be the major-party candidate with the larger share of the remaining 80 percent of the vote.

By comparison, most European democracies use some form of a **proportional representation system**, in which seats in the legislature are allocated according to a party's percentage of the popular vote. This type of electoral system enables smaller parties to compete for power. In Germany's 2017 election, for example, the Green Party received 9 percent of the national vote and thereby won roughly 9 percent of the seats in the German parliament. If the Greens had been competing under America's electoral rules, they would not have won any seats.

Politics and Coalitions in the Two-Party System

The overriding goal of a major American party is to gain power by getting its candidates elected to office. Because there are only two major parties, however, the Republicans or Democrats can win consistently only by attracting majority support. If either party confines its support to too narrow a slice of voters, it forfeits its chance of victory.

Seeking the Center, without Losing the Support of the Party Faithful A two-party system usually requires the major parties to avoid positions that will carry them too far from the political center. The **median voter theorem** holds that, if there are two parties, the parties can maximize their vote only if they position themselves at the location of the median voter—the voter whose preferences are exactly in the middle.[20]

Although hypothetical, the median voter theorem helps explain the risk a party faces if it moves too far from the center, leaving it open to the other party. In 1964, the Republican nominee, Barry Goldwater, proposed the elimination of mandatory Social Security and suggested he might be open to the use of small nuclear weapons in the Vietnam conflict—extreme positions that cost him many votes. Eight years later, the Democratic nominee, George McGovern, took positions on Vietnam and income security that alarmed many voters; like Goldwater, he was buried in one of the biggest landslides in presidential history.

Although voters in the political center can hold the balance of power in an election, they are less important in the parties' strategies than they once were. As a result of party polarization, most voters today are positioned to the right or left of center.[21] If candidates move too close to the center, they risk alienating their party's core voters.

In addition, there are fewer competitive states and districts than in the past. The party realignment of recent decades took place along geographical lines with the effect that most states and congressional districts are now so lopsidedly Republican or Democratic that the stronger party is virtually certain to win the general election.[22] In these cases, the critical election is the stronger party's primary election. Primaries have relatively low turnout, and the voters who do show up are disproportionately the party's most committed voters. These voters, rather than the moderates, are the key to victory in a primary. Thus, rather than positioning themselves toward the political center, candidates take positions away from the center in order to appeal to their party's hardcore voters. It's a reason that Congress has far fewer moderate members today than in the past.

Party Coalitions   The groups and interests that support a party are collectively referred to as the **party coalition**. The Republican and Democratic coalitions differ in their composition (see Figure 8-4).

The Republican Party is made up largely of white Americans. Nine out of every 10 votes that Republicans received in the 2016 election were cast

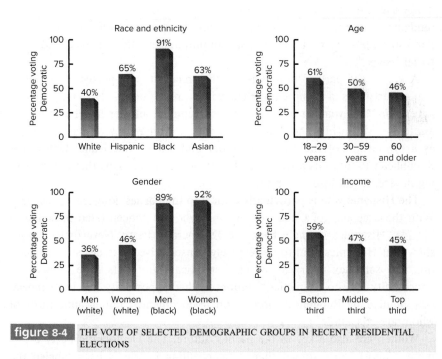

figure 8-4   THE VOTE OF SELECTED DEMOGRAPHIC GROUPS IN RECENT PRESIDENTIAL ELECTIONS

Although the Democratic and Republican coalitions overlap substantially, there are important differences, as illustrated by the Democratic Party's percentage of the two-party vote among some major demographic groups in recent elections.

by non-Hispanic white voters.[23] Not since Lyndon Johnson's landslide victory in the 1964 election has the Democratic presidential nominee won a majority of the white vote. White evangelical or born-again Christians are the largest Republican voting bloc, accounting for more than a third of the party's vote. They vote about three-to-one Republican.[24] By smaller margins, most males, older adults, and higher-income Americans vote Republican.[25]

The Democratic Party coalition is more diverse. Although non-Hispanic white voters constitute a majority of Democrats, roughly two-fifths of the party's vote comes from minority-group members. Black Americans vote roughly nine-to-one Democratic. Hispanics and Asian Americans vote nearly two-to-one Democratic. Women, younger voters, and lower-income Americans also vote disproportionately Democratic.

The party coalitions are a reflection of the parties' platforms. The Democratic Party has initiated nearly every major public assistance and civil rights program, which has attracted the support of minorities and lower-income Americans. For its part, the Republican Party has promoted tax cuts, business incentives, reduced federal spending, and traditional values, which has gained it the support of social conservatives and upper-income Americans. White fundamentalist Christians, for example, have been attracted to the Republican Party by its positions on abortion, school prayer, same-sex marriage, and other social issues.[26]

A key to the parties' futures is whether recent trends persist. The Democratic Party has a significant edge with three groups— Hispanics, Asian Americans, and younger adults—who are becoming an ever larger part of the electorate. Meanwhile, the Republican's edge is with groups who are declining as a proportion of the electorate—older and white Americans. Unless the Republican Party finds a way to make inroads on the groups that are increasing in size, it will lose out in the long run.[27]

The Hispanic vote is particularly critical to the parties' long-term prospects. With the exception of Cuban Americans, who are concentrated in southern Florida, Hispanics strongly back the Democratic Party. Nevertheless, polls show that Hispanics tend to be relatively conservative on issues such as abortion and same-sex marriage, which Republican strategists have seen as an opportunity to woo Hispanics.[28] However, that opportunity has been repeatedly blunted by Republican attacks on undocumented immigrants, most of whom are Hispanic.[29]

Women are also a key to the parties' future. The Democratic Party draws more support from women than men, resulting in what's been labeled the **gender gap**. The gap is widest among white voters. In 2016, the Democratic vote among white women was 22 percentage points higher than it was for

America's two-party system is dominated by the Republican and Democratic Parties. Their competition for power has persisted for more than 150 years. (©lightwise/123RF)

white men.[30] On a number of policy issues, including education and social welfare, white women hold opinions that are on average more liberal than those held by white men.[31] The gender gap is a challenge for both parties. To improve their long-term chances, Republicans need to find ways to increase their appeal to white women while Democrats need to make inroads among white men.

Minor (Third) Parties

Although the U.S. electoral system discourages the formation of minor parties (or, as they are sometimes called, third parties), the nation has always had them—more than 1,000 over its history.[32] Even the more successful ones have usually been short lived. If a minor party starts to gain a following, one of the major parties is likely to pick up its issue, at which time it will begin to lose support. Another problem for minor parties is that their candidates rarely win office. Most voters don't want to waste their ballot on what they know will be a losing cause. Only one minor party, the Republican Party, has achieved majority status.

Minor parties were at their peak in the 19th century, when the party system was still in flux.[33] Many of these parties were *single-issue parties* formed around a lone issue of overriding interest to their followers. Examples are the Free Soil Party, which fought the extension of slavery into new territories, and the Greenback Party, which sought a currency system based on paper money rather than gold and silver. The role that single-issue parties played in the 19th century is now played by single-issue interest groups (see Chapter 9).

The most important minor parties of the 20th century were *factional parties* that resulted from a split within one of the major parties. Although the Republican and Democratic Parties are usually successful at managing internal conflict, it has sometimes led the dissidents to break away and form their own party. The States' Rights Party in 1948 and George Wallace's American Independent Party in 1968 are examples of these factional parties. They were formed by white southern Democrats angered by northern Democrats' support of black civil rights. The most electorally successful factional party was the Bull Moose Party in 1912.[34] Four years earlier,

THE CROWD AS IT LOOKS TO THEODORE

Although the United States has long had a two-party system, numerous minor parties have surfaced. The most electorally successful was the Bull Moose Party, a factional party that split from the Republican Party. Headed by former president Theodore Roosevelt, it garnered 27 percent of the popular vote. The Republican nominee, incumbent William Howard Taft, came in third with 25 percent of vote. The Democratic nominee, Woodrow Wilson, won the presidency with 42 percent of the vote. (*Source:* Library of Congress, Prints and Photographs Division [LC-DIG-ppmsca-38463])

Theodore Roosevelt had declined to seek another presidential term, but he became disenchanted with the conservative policies of his handpicked successor, William Howard Taft, and challenged him for the 1912 Republican nomination. After losing out in the nominating race, Roosevelt formed the progressive Bull Moose Party (a reference to Roosevelt's claim that he was "as strong as a bull moose"). Roosevelt won 27 percent of the presidential vote to Taft's 25 percent, which enabled the Democratic nominee, Woodrow Wilson, to win the 1912 presidential election with 42 percent of the vote.

Some minor parties have been "anti-parties" in the sense that they arose out of a belief that partisan politics is a corrupting influence. The strongest of these *reform parties* was the Progressive Party, which in the early 1900s successfully pressured a number of states and localities into adopting primary elections, recall elections, nonpartisan elections, initiatives, and popular referendums (see Chapter 2). A more recent reform party was titled just that–the Reform Party. Created by Texas business executive Ross Perot after he garnered an astonishing 19 percent of the vote in 1992 as an independent presidential candidate (second only to Roosevelt's 27 percent in 1912), the Reform Party virtually disappeared after a divisive internal fight over its 2000 presidential nomination.

Other minor parties have been characterized by a commitment to a broad and noncentrist ideological position, such as redistribution of wealth. The strongest ideological party was the Populists, whose 1892 presidential nominee, James B. Weaver, won 9 percent of the national vote and carried six western states on a radical platform that included a call for government takeover of the railroads.[35] The strongest ideological parties today are the Libertarian Party, which calls for less government intervention in the marketplace and individuals' lives, and the Green Party, which promotes social equality and environmentalism. In the 2016 presidential election, the Libertarian Party's Gary Johnson and the Green Party's Jill Stein received a combined 4 percent of the popular vote. Some analysts have argued that, if they had not been in the race, most of their votes would have gone to Hillary Clinton, perhaps by a margin large enough to give her the victory.[36]

PARTIES AND CANDIDATES IN THE CAMPAIGN

The Democratic and Republican Parties have organizational units at the national, state, and local levels. These **party organizations** concentrate on the contesting of elections. A century ago, party organizations enjoyed nearly complete control of elections. Two developments–the introduction of primary elections and changes in the media system–served to gradually shift control to the candidates. Today, they have the lead role in presidential and congressional elections.[37]

Primary Elections and Candidate Control

Nomination refers to the selection of the individual who will run as the party's candidate in the general election. Until the early 20th century, the party organizations picked the nominees, who, if elected, were expected to share with it the spoils of office—government jobs and contracts. The party built its organization by giving the jobs to loyalists and by granting contracts to donors. Bribes and kickbacks were part of the process in some locations. New York City's legendary Boss Tweed once charged the city 20 times what a building had actually cost, amassing a personal fortune before winding up in prison. Reform-minded Progressives invented primary elections as a way to deprive party bosses of their power over nominations (see Chapter 2).

A **primary election** (or *direct primary*) gives control of nominations to the voters (see Chapters 2 and 12). The candidate with the most votes in a party's primary gets its nomination for the general election. In some states, the nominees are chosen in *closed primaries,* where participation is limited to voters registered with the party. Registered voters of the other party are not allowed to "cross over" to vote in the primary. The logic of a closed primary is that a party's voters should have the power to choose its general election candidate. In contrast, some states use *open primaries,* which allow independents and sometimes voters of the other party to vote in the party's primary (although they cannot vote simultaneously in both parties' primaries). The logic of the open primary is that it gives all voters a say in the choices they will have in the general election. California, Louisiana, Nebraska, and Washington conduct *top-two primaries.* Candidates are listed on the primary ballot without regard to party; the top two finishers become the general election candidates (see "How the 50 States Differ").

Primaries serve to shift control of campaigns from parties to the candidates. In Europe, where there are no primary elections, the parties are stronger. They control their nominations, and their candidates are expected to support the party's national platform. A candidate or officeholder who fails to do so is likely to be denied renomination in the next election. In the United States, however, candidates can seek nomination on their own by entering the party's primary. Primary elections require candidates to organize and run their campaigns. They raise the funds, hire the staff, and pick the issues on which they'll run. And once in office, they have an incentive to maintain contact with the donors and voters who backed their campaign.

HOW THE 50 STATES DIFFER

CRITICAL THINKING THROUGH COMPARISONS

Primary Elections

All states hold primary elections, but they differ in the type of primary they hold. Roughly a third of them have *open primaries,* which allow any registered voter to vote in the primary. Another third have *closed primaries,* which are limited to voters registered as members of the party holding the primary, or *partially closed primaries*, which give the parties the option of conducting a closed primary. Other states have *partially open primaries* that allow independents but not registered voters of the other party to partici-pate. Finally, four states—California, Louisiana, Nebraska, and Washing-ton—employ *top-two primaries* in which candidates of both parties are on the same ballot and the top-two finishers compete in the general election.

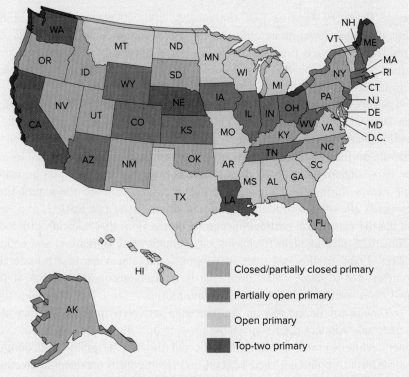

Closed/partially closed primary

Partially open primary

Open primary

Top-two primary

Source: National Council of State Legislatures, 2014.

Continued

Q: The top-two primary is relatively new. What do you think are the chief arguments for and against this type of primary?

A: Proponents argue that top-two primaries give independent voters a larger say in the selection of nominees and may result is the selection of more moderate nominees. Opponents say that this type of primary hurts the state's weaker party and can limit voters' choice in the general election to two candidates of the same party.

The Parties' Role in Campaigns

Although the parties have less control over campaigns than in their heyday, they retain a key role.[38] They provide a permanent organizational base for party activists and candidates. Moreover, certain activities, such as get-out-the-vote efforts on Election Day, affect all of a party's candidates and are done most efficiently through party organizations.

Local Political Parties   Of the roughly 500,000 elective offices in the United States, fewer than 500 are contested statewide and only two—the presidency and vice presidency—are contested nationally. The rest are local offices; not surprisingly, at least 95 percent of party activists work within local organizations.

Local parties vary greatly in their activities. Only a few of them, including the Democratic organizations in Philadelphia and Chicago, bear even a faint resemblance to the fabled old-time party machines that were able to deliver the vote on Election Day. In many urban areas, and in most suburbs and towns, the party organizations today do not have enough volunteers to play an active role except during the campaign period, at which time—to the extent their resources allow—they conduct registration drives, hand out leaflets, and help get out the vote. Local parties concentrate on elections that coincide with local boundaries, such as races for mayor, city council, state legislature, and county offices. Local parties take part in congressional, statewide, and presidential contests, but in these cases, their role is typically secondary to that of the candidates' personal campaign organizations.

Although candidates rely on the parties to get voters to the polls, they also increasingly conduct their own get-out-the-vote operations, making use of computer technology and information collected through telephone and door-to-door efforts to construct their contact lists. In the 2016 presidential election, the Clinton and Trump campaigns spent millions of dollars to amass huge voter lists, which were used to raise funds as well as to get out the vote.

State Party Organizations   The parties also have organizational units at the state and national levels, although there is no chain of command that connects them. The national party organization cannot tell the state organizations what to do, and, in turn, the state organizations cannot tell the local organizations what to do. The Texas state Democratic Party, for example, does not take orders from the national Democratic Party and does not give orders to the state's local Democratic party organizations, whether in a large city like Dallas or Houston or in a smaller one like McAllen or Amarillo. Each party organization is free to act as it wants. Nevertheless, party organizations at all levels have a shared stake in their party's success and thus have an incentive to work together to get the party's candidates elected to office and to build up a loyal base of voters.[39]

At the state level, each party is headed by a central committee made up of members of local party organizations and local and state officeholders. State central committees do not meet regularly and provide only general guidance to the state party organization, which is directed by a chairperson, who is a full-time, paid employee. The state party organizations engage in activities, such as fundraising and voter registration, that can improve their candidates' chances of success. State party organizations concentrate on statewide races, including those for governor and U.S. senator, and also focus on races for the state legislature. They play a smaller role in campaigns for national or local offices, and in most states, they do not endorse candidates in statewide primaries.[40]

National Party Organizations   The national Republican and Democratic party organizations, which are located in Washington, D.C., are structured much like those at the state level: They have a national committee and a national party chairperson. Neither the Democratic National Committee (DNC) nor the Republican National Committee (RNC) has great power. The RNC (with more than 150 members) and the DNC (with more than 300 members) are too large and meet too infrequently to actually run the national organization. Their power is largely confined to setting organizational policy, such as determining the site of the party's presidential nominating convention and deciding the rules governing the selection of convention delegates. They have no power to pick nominees or to dictate candidates' policy positions.

The national party's day-to-day operations are directed by a national chair chosen by the national committee, although the committee defers to the president's choice when the party controls the White House. The national parties run training programs for candidates and their staffs, raise money, seek media coverage of party positions and activities, conduct issue and group research, and send field representatives to help state and local parties with their operations. In some cases, the national parties also try to recruit potentially strong candidates to run in House and Senate races.

The national parties' major role in campaigns is raising money. Although the RNC and the DNC spend most of the money they raise to fund their own operations, they give some of it to the party's House and Senate candidates, who also get funding from campaign committees that the parties have formed in the House and Senate. In any case, the amount of money that a party committee can give directly to a candidate is limited by law—$5,000 for House candidates and $47,400 for Senate candidates. However, the total amount of money raised and spent by national party organizations is substantial. It easily exceeded $1 billion in the 2018 midterm elections.[41]

Media Changes and Candidate Control

Primaries are not the only reason for the shift in control of election campaigns from parties to candidates. Changes in the media also contributed. When primaries were introduced in the early 1900s, the party organizations remained strong enough to pick most of the nominees. Although it was possible for candidates to run and win on their own in primaries, it was difficult. They could buy newspaper ads to promote their candidacy, but newspaper advertising wasn't a solid foundation on which to base a campaign.[42]

Rise of Television   The introduction of television in the 1950s provided candidates with the tool they needed to take greater control of their campaigns. Televised ads proved to be an effective way to promote their candidacies, and television quickly became the principal medium of election campaigning.

Candidates now spend heavily on televised political advertising, which enables them to communicate directly—and on their own terms—with voters. *Air wars* is the term that political scientist Darrell West applies to candidates' use of televised ads.[43] Modern production techniques enable well-funded candidates to get new ads on the air within a few hours' time, which allows them to rebut attacks and exploit fast-breaking developments, a tactic known as *rapid response.* The production and airing of televised political ads accounts for roughly half of all campaign spending, and an even larger proportion in presidential campaigns (see Figure 8-5). Indeed, televised ads are the main reason for the high cost of U.S. campaigns. In most democracies, televised campaigning takes place through parties, which receive free air time to make their pitch. Many democracies, including France and Great Britain, prohibit the use of televised political ads.

Candidates also use the press to get their message across, although the amount of news coverage they get varies widely by location and office. Many House candidates are almost completely ignored by local news media. The

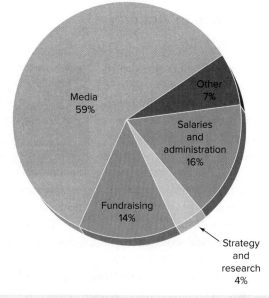

figure 8-5   PRESIDENTIAL CAMPAIGN SPENDING, 2016

Media expenditures, mostly for televised advertising, account for the largest share of presidential campaign spending. (*Source:* Figure based on author estimates from multiple sources.)

New York City media market, for example, includes more than a score of House districts in New York, New Jersey, Pennsylvania, and Connecticut, and candidates in these districts get little or no coverage from the New York media. They also get little exposure through televised ads because it is too expensive to buy ads in a metropolitan area where the congressional district is only a small fraction of the audience. Such candidates campaign the old-fashioned way, through leafleting, door-to-door canvassing, and the like. In contrast, presidential candidates get daily coverage from both national and local media. Between these extremes are Senate races, which always get some news coverage and, if hotly contested, typically get close coverage.[44]

Debates are also part of the media campaign. Although many House candidates find it impossible to convince local television stations to carry debates, they are routine occurrences in Senate and presidential races. Debates can be risky encounters because they give viewers a chance to compare the candidates directly. A weak or bumbling performance can hurt a candidate. Yet debates typically serve to reinforce voters' candidate preferences.

Rise of the Internet   New communication technology usually makes its way into campaign politics, and the Internet is no exception. Nearly all of the congressional candidates in the 2018 midterm elections had websites dedicated

| C A S E |
| S T U D Y |

Politics in Action

Donald Trump's Media Strategy

Donald Trump's presidential campaign began with a theatrical ride down the escalator in Trump Tower. Hired actors were at the bottom, cheering wildly as he arrived. Before long, news outlets were doing the cheering. He was a ratings hit. A Harvard University study found that, during every month of his presidential

©Jose More/agefotostock/SuperStock

campaign, Trump received by far the most heavy news coverage, allowing him to define his opponents—"Lying Ted," "Little Marco," "Crooked Hillary."[45]

Trump had no political experience, no political organization, and no deep-pocket backers when he launched his presidential bid. Strong candidates have traditionally had all of those things in place before running for president and have organized their campaigns around televised political advertising. Trump relied on so-called "free media"—the news coverage provided by news organizations. In the past, journalists had reserved their heavy coverage for candidates who ranked high in the polls. Trump ranked low in the polls when he announced his campaign. What Trump had in his favor was a flamboyant way of talking about issues, which he used to attract attention. Trump's insight was that attention equals power. In an information system that overloads us with messages, there are few things more powerful than the ability, as Trump said, "to keep people interested." "And that gives you power," he said. "It's not the polls. It's the ratings."[46]

Trump stayed with his media strategy throughout the 2016 campaign. Although he made use of televised political ads and other forms of paid outreach to voters, he spent far less on paid media than did his opponent, Hillary Clinton. From his years as a reality-TV host, Trump had come to understand that if you can attract people's attention, the news media will shower you with free coverage. "If you get good ratings," he said, "you'll be on all the time. . . . It's a very simple business. Very simple."[47]

Q. Could future presidential candidates follow Trump's strategy and expect to be successful?

ASK YOURSELF: How important was Trump's experience as a reality-TV host in his understanding of how the media operate? Did his name recognition as a TV host affect audience interest in the beginning stage of his candidacy? How unique was Trump's personality and agenda—could the typical candidate replicate the type of campaign that Trump conducted?

to providing information, generating public support, attracting volunteers, and raising money.

Although television is still the principal medium of election politics, some analysts believe that the Internet will eventually overtake it. Internet messaging is much less expensive than television advertising. Because it is a targeted medium, the Internet could become the channel through which candidates reach specific voting groups. However, the Internet also has some disadvantages relative to television, especially in the greater control that individual users have over the message. With television, when a brief political ad appears during a favorite program, many viewers will sit through it. An unsolicited message on the Internet is more easily ignored or deleted. So far, the Internet has shown itself to be the better medium for fundraising and mobilizing supporters, whereas television has proven to be the better medium for building name recognition and reaching less-interested voters.[48]

Rise of Campaign Money   As candidates increasingly based their campaigns on television, political consultant Joe Napolitan labeled it "the election game."[49] The game requires money—lots of it. Campaigns for high office are expensive, and the costs keep rising. In 1980, about $250 million was spent by Senate and House candidates in the general election. The figure had jumped to more than $400 million by 1990. In 2018, the figure exceeded $2 billion—eight times the 1980 level.[50] As could be expected, incumbents have a distinct advantage in fundraising. They have contributor lists from past campaigns and the policy influence that donors seek. House and Senate incumbents outspend their challengers by more than two to one.[51]

Because of the high cost of campaigns, candidates spend much of their time raising funds, which come primarily from individual contributors, political parties, and interest groups (through PACs, discussed in Chapter 9). The **money chase** is relentless.[52] A U.S. senator must raise nearly $20,000 a week on average throughout the entire six-year term in order to raise the minimum $5 million it takes to run a competitive Senate campaign in even a small state. A Senate campaign in a larger state can easily cost far more than that amount. In the 2016 Texas Senate race, incumbent Ted Cruz and his Democratic challenger, Beto O'Rourke, combined to spend more than $100 million, making it one of the most expensive Senate races ever. House campaigns are less costly, but expenditures of $1 million or more are now common. As for presidential elections, the numbers are astronomical. In 2016, Hillary Clinton and Donald Trump spent a combined total of more than $1 billion, with Clinton having a sizable edge in fundraising.[53]

The money that candidates raise from political parties, individuals, and interest groups is subject to legal limits (for example, $2,500 from an individual

American political campaigns last longer and are more costly than campaigns in other democracies. The United States is almost alone in using primary elections as the means of selecting party nominees, which extends the campaign period. Moreover, U.S. campaigns are candidate centered rather than party centered, which requires each candidate to conduct a separate campaign, driving up election costs. (©miker/Shutterstock)

contributor and $5,000 from a group per election). These contributions are termed **hard money**—the money is given directly to the candidate and can be spent as he or she chooses.

Candidates are also the beneficiaries (and sometimes the casualties) of spending by super PACs, which are organizations that can raise and spend money freely on campaigns as long as they do not coordinate their efforts with those of the candidate they support. Super PACs spent roughly $1 billion on the 2018 midterm elections. (Super PACs are discussed at greater length in Chapter 9.)

Rise of Political Consultants   The key operatives in today's campaigns—congressional as well as presidential—are highly paid *political consultants*. They include campaign strategists who help the candidate plot and execute a game plan. Over the years, some of these strategists, including James Carville and Roger Ailes, developed legendary reputations. Fundraising specialists are also part of the new politics. They are adept at tapping donors and interest groups that regularly contribute to election campaigns. The consultant ranks also include pollsters, whose surveys are used to identify issues and messages that will resonate with voters. Media consultants are another staple of the modern campaign. They are adept at producing televised political advertising, generating news coverage, and developing Internet-based strategies.

Campaign consultants are skilled at **packaging** a candidate—highlighting those aspects of the candidate's policy positions and personality that are thought most attractive to voters. Packaging is not new to politics. Andrew Jackson's self-portrayal in the 19th century as "the champion of the people" is an image that any modern candidate could appreciate. What is new is the need to fit the image to the requirements of a world of sound bites, 30-second ads, televised debates, and internet messages. In the old days, it was sometimes enough for candidates to drive home the point that they were a Republican or a Democrat, playing on the tendency of voters to choose a candidate on that basis. Party appeals are still critical, but today's voters also expect to hear about a candidate's personal life and policy proposals.

Over the course of a campaign, voters usually hear more about the candidates' weaknesses than about their strengths.[54] Of course, negative campaigning is as old as American politics. Thomas Jefferson, Andrew Jackson, and Abraham Lincoln were subjected to vicious attacks. Lincoln was portrayed as "a hick" and "a baboon" for his gangly looks and backwoods roots. But today's version of attack politics is unprecedented in its reach and scale. Negative television ads were once the exception, but they have increased to the point where they are now the majority.[55] Many of the ads are "badly misleading," according to FactCheck.org, which monitors ads and assesses their accuracy.[56]

How Much Difference Do Campaigns Make?   Because they consist of primary and general elections, American campaigns are lengthy affairs. Congressional campaigns go on for months, and the presidential campaign lasts longer than a year.

Given the amount of money and public attention they consume, it might be thought that campaigns determine who wins and who loses. That's not the case in most races. Less than half the states are considered competitive in the sense that either party has a reasonable chance of winning. The other states are so heavily Republican or Democratic that only in unusual circumstances does the weaker party's candidate win. It can happen, but it's rare. In the 2017 special election to fill Alabama's vacant Senate seat, Republicans nominated Judge Roy Moore, who was accused of having sexually molested teenage girls when he was in his 30s. Moore was defeated in the general election, the first time in a generation that the Democratic nominee won a Senate race in Alabama.

House races are even less competitive than Senate races. Of the the 435 House seats, only about 75 could conceivably be won by either party. Realistically, the number is much smaller. The average party turnover in recent elections has been about 25 seats. Moreover, when parties do lose seats, it's often

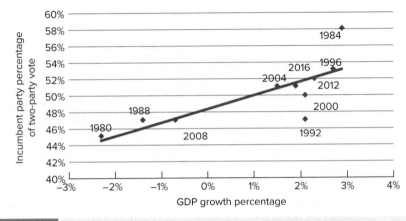

figure 8-6 ECONOMIC GROWTH AND PRESIDENTIAL ELECTION OUTCOMES

When the economy is growing, the party holding the presidency typically gets a larger share of the two-party presidential vote than it does when the economy is weakening. (*Source:* Adapted from John Sides and Lynn Vavreck, "What Really Decided the 2012 Election, in 10 Graphs," *Washington Post*, October 14, 2013.)

because of national conditions rather than what happens during the campaign. Nothing so tips the balance in close races as voters' satisfaction with the party that holds power. Although some voters are swayed by what candidates promise to do if elected (a form of voting known as *prospective voting*), a greater number respond to past performance (*retrospective voting*). National economic conditions are particularly important in voters' judgments in presidential elections. An analysis by political scientists John Sides and Lynn Vavreck found that the in-party nearly always loses votes when the economy is weak and nearly always gains votes when it's strong[57] (see Figure 8-6).

Although the candidates' campaigns do not determine the outcome of most races, each political party has a stake in conducting a strong campaign. If a party can win enough seats in the House or Senate, or get the votes needed to win the presidency, it acquires political power. The difference between being the majority party or minority party in Washington is the difference between being in or out of power. That's incentive enough for the parties and their candidates to mount large-scale campaign efforts.[58]

PARTIES, CANDIDATES, AND THE PUBLIC'S INFLUENCE

Candidate-centered campaigns have some distinct advantages. First, they can infuse new blood into electoral politics. Candidate recruitment is typically a slow process in party-centered systems. Would-be officeholders pay their dues by working in the party and, in the process, tend to adopt the outlook of those already there. By comparison, a candidate-centered system is more open and provides opportunities for newcomers to gain office quickly. Donald Trump is a case in point. He had never held, or even run for, political office before entering the race for the 2016 Republican presidential nomination. His public profile was based almost entirely on his real estate dealings and his role as host of a reality-TV show. Nevertheless, in a field of more than a dozen Republican candidates, most of whom had held high office, Trump easily prevailed. Trump's quick rise to political prominence would be almost unthinkable in a party-centered system.

Candidate-centered campaigns also encourage national officeholders to be responsive to local interests. In building personal followings among their state or district constituents, members of Congress respond to local needs. Nearly every significant domestic program enacted by Congress is adjusted to accommodate the interests of states and localities that otherwise would be hurt by the policy. Where strong national parties exist, national interests take precedence over local concerns. In both France and Britain, for example, the pleas of legislators from underdeveloped regions have often gone unheeded by their party's majority.

In other respects, candidate-centered campaigns have distinct disadvantages. They provide abundant opportunities for powerful interest groups to shower money on the candidates. The role of campaign money, and the influence it buys, has long been an issue in American politics and has achieved new heights as a result of the Supreme Court's *Citizens United* decision (see Chapters 1 and 9). In no other Western democracy does money play as large a role as it does in American elections.

Candidate-centered campaigns also weaken accountability by making it easier for officeholders to deny personal responsibility for government's actions. If national policy goes awry, an incumbent can always say that he or she represents only one vote out of many and that the real problem resides with "others" in Congress. The problem of accountability is apparent from surveys that have asked Americans about their confidence in Congress. Most citizens have a low opinion of Congress as a whole but say they have confidence in their local representative in Congress. This paradoxical attitude is so prevalent that the large majority of incumbents are reelected time and again (see Chapter 11).

As a result of party polarization, America's parties are subject to greater voter accountability than in the past. The parties are sharply divided on many issues, which has made it easier for voters to distinguish between them and to support or oppose candidates on the basis of what the parties represent. Nevertheless, America's candidate-centered campaigns allow candidates to evade responsibility for government performance in ways that Europe's party-centered campaigns do not. In Europe, voters tend to hold the majority party responsible when things go badly and vote large numbers of its members out of office. When things go badly in the United States, the majority party nearly always loses congressional seats in the next election but a far greater number of its party's candidates will escape unscathed. They survive in part as a result of the personal loyalties they've built among the voters in their state or district and in part because their state or district is one-sided enough in its party loyalties that they can manage a victory even if their level of support drops somewhat. (Congressional and presidential campaigns are discussed further in Chapters 11 and 12, respectively.)

SUMMARY

Political parties serve to link the public with its elected leaders. In the United States, this linkage is provided by the two-party system. Only the Republican and Democratic Parties have a realistic chance of winning control of government. The fact that the United States has only two major parties is explained in large part by an electoral system (single-member districts) that favors large parties and makes it difficult for smaller parties (minor or third parties) to win legislative seats in an election.

For more than 150 years, competition in America's two-party system has centered on the Republican and Democratic Parties. The remarkable endurance of these two parties is due to their ability to adapt to change. They have undergone several realignments, emerging each time with somewhat different coalitions and philosophies. The most recent realignment began in the 1960s over the issue of civil rights and progressed further in response to social issues such as abortion and the issue of the size of the federal government. The realignment led to party polarization—a widening divide between Republicans and Democrats, at the level of both elected officials and voters.

Because the United States has only two major parties, each of which seeks to gain majority support, their candidates traditionally have taken moderate positions in order to attract support from voters in the political center. However, as a result of party polarization and an increase in the number of states and districts that strongly favor the Republic or Democratic Party, candidates have increasing appealed to their party's more ideologically extreme voters, who turn out more heavily than do moderate voters in primary elections.

At one time, America's party organizations largely controlled campaigns—picking the nominees, choosing the issues, and conducting the campaign. Candidates gradually came to the forefront in campaigns, largely because of primary elections, which allow them to gain nomination directly from the voters rather than going through the party organization, and changes in the media, which allow them to pitch their appeals directly to the voters. Nevertheless, party organizations continue to play a key role in elections. Local party organizations build support for the party's candidates and conduct get-out-the-vote efforts on Election Day. The state and national party organizations help the party's candidates through fundraising, issue research, media training, and other activities.

American political campaigns, particularly those for higher office, are candidate centered. Presidential and congressional candidates spend much of their time fundraising and creating personal campaign organizations built around pollsters, media producers, fundraisers, and campaign managers. Strategy and image making are key components of the modern campaign, as is televised political advertising, which accounts for half or more of all spending in presidential and congressional races.

The advantages of candidate-centered politics include heightened responsiveness to new leadership and local concerns. Yet this form of politics can result in campaigns that are personality driven, depend on powerful interest groups, and blur responsibility for what government has done.

©gangliu10/Getty Images

CRITICAL THINKING ZONE

KEY TERMS

candidate-centered campaigns (*p. 221*)

gender gap (*p. 236*)

grassroots party (*p. 223*)

hard money (*p. 248*)

linkage institution (*p. 222*)

median voter theorem (*p. 234*)

money chase (*p. 247*)

multiparty system (*p. 231*)

nomination (*p. 240*)

packaging (of a candidate) (*p. 249*)

party-centered campaigns (*p. 221*)

party coalition (*p. 235*)

party competition (*p. 222*)

party organizations (*p. 239*)

party realignment (*p. 225*)

plurality (winner-take-all) system (*p. 232*)

political party (*p. 221*)

primary election (direct primary) (*p. 240*)

proportional representation system (*p. 234*)

single-member districts (*p. 232*)

two-party system (*p. 231*)

APPLYING THE ELEMENTS OF CRITICAL THINKING

Conceptualizing: Explain the difference between proportional representation and single-member districts as methods of electing candidates to office. Why is the first method more likely than the second to foster a multiparty system?

Synthesizing: Contrast the pattern of earlier political party realignments (such as the realignment brought about by the Great Depression) with the pattern of the most recent party realignment.

Analyzing: Why are elections conducted so differently in the United States than in European democracies? Why are American campaigns more expensive and more candidate centered?

EXTRA CREDIT

A Book Worth Reading: James E. Campbell, *Polarized: Making Sense of a Divided America* (Princeton, N.J.: Princeton University Press, 2016). This well-written book explores the forces behind the widening divide between Republicans and Democrats.

A Website Worth Visiting: **www.gop.org** or **www.democrats.org** These are the websites of the Republican Party and the Democratic Party, respectively. Each site has information on the party's issue positions, as well as information on how to become a party volunteer.

PARTICIPATE!

Consider becoming a campaign or political party volunteer. The opportunities are numerous. Parties and candidates at every level from the national on down seek volunteers to assist in organizing, canvassing, fundraising, and other activities. As a college student, you have communication and knowledge skills that would be valuable to a campaign or party organization. You might be pleasantly surprised by the tasks you are assigned.

9
CHAPTER

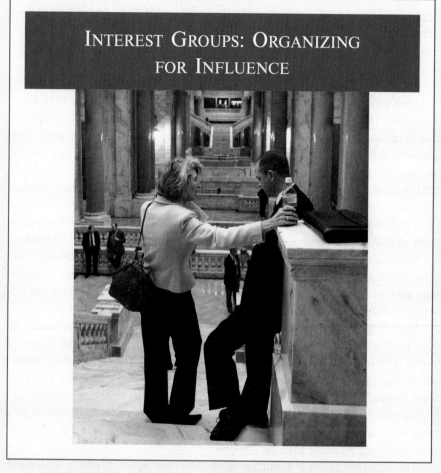

INTEREST GROUPS: ORGANIZING FOR INFLUENCE

©James Crisp/AP Photo

66 The flaw in the pluralist heaven is that the heavenly chorus sings with a strong upper-class bias. **99**

E. E. SCHATTSCHNEIDER[1]

As the 2017 Tax Cuts and Jobs Act was making its way through Congress, lobbyists were working feverishly. Public Citizen, a government watchdog group, found that 6,000 lobbyists were trying to influence the legislation—11 lobbyists for every member of Congress. Most of the lobbyists represented corporations and trade associations, which were seeking a steep cut in the corporate tax rate. The Chamber of Commerce alone had 100 lobbyists working on the tax issue, while 20 corporations and trade associations each had at least 50 lobbyists dedicated to the issue. "The mind-boggling number of lobbyists corporate America has hired to reshape the tax code is of almost biblical proportions," said Lisa Gilbert, Public Citizen's legislative affairs vice president.[2] When the bill passed, the corporate tax rate had indeed been slashed, reduced from 35 percent to 21 percent.

Corporate lobbyists' efforts to shape the 2017 tax cut bill suggest why interest groups are both necessary and unloved. Business firms have legitimate interests that are affected by public policy. It is perfectly appropriate for them to lobby on policy issues. The same can be said of farmers, consumers, minorities, college students—indeed, of virtually every interest in society. In fact, the *pluralist* theory of American politics (see Chapter 1) holds that society's interests are represented most effectively through groups.

Yet groups can wield too much power, getting their way at an unreasonable cost to the rest of society. Did the 2017 tax bill make too many concessions to business firms? Or did it have the effect of protecting workers' jobs by making American products more competitive in world markets? Opinions differ on the answers to such questions, but there is no doubt that groups have considerable influence over public policy.

Indeed, group influence has increased significantly in recent decades, as has the amount of money spent on lobbying activities. The United States is often singled out for the high cost of its election campaigns. Yet the amount of money spent on electioneering is less than the amount spent on lobbying (see Figure 9-1). And the official figures understate the difference. Many lobbying expenditures go unreported. The Center for Responsive Politics estimates that when all spending is taken into account, lobbying spending exceeds election spending by more than two to one.

The situation raises a perennial issue, one that James Madison addressed in his famous essay *Federalist* No. 10. Madison warned against "the dangers

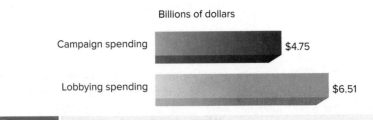

Billions of dollars

Campaign spending $4.75

Lobbying spending $6.51

figure 9-1 LOBBYING AND CAMPAIGN SPENDING

Although spending on lobbying gets less public attention than does election spending, far more money is spent on lobbying than on electioneering. (*Source:* Center for Responsive Politics. Figure based on preliminary estimates of federal campaign spending in the 2017–2018 election cycle and federal lobbying expenditures during the same two years.)

of faction," by which he meant a polity where factions (groups) become so powerful that they trample on the legitimate interests of other groups and society as a whole. Madison acknowledged that society has an obligation to protect the right of groups to freely organize but also said that society suffers if groups become overly powerful.

An **interest group**—also called a "faction," "pressure group," "special interest," "organized interest," or "lobbying group"—can be defined as any organization that actively seeks to influence public policy.[3] Interest groups are similar to political parties in some respects but differ from them in important ways.[4] Like parties, groups are a linkage mechanism: They serve to connect citizens with government. However, political parties address a broad range of issues so as to appeal to diverse blocs of voters. Above all, parties are in the business of trying to win elections. Groups, by contrast, concentrate on policies directly affecting their interests. A group may involve itself in elections, but its major purpose is to influence the policies of concern to it.

This chapter examines the degree to which various interests in American society are represented by organized groups, the process by which interest groups exert influence, and the costs and benefits of group politics. The chapter makes the following main points:

- *Although nearly all interests in American society are organized to some degree, those associated with economic activity, particularly business activity, are by far the most thoroughly organized.* Their advantage rests on their superior financial resources and on the private goods (such as wages and jobs) they provide to those in the organization.

- *Groups that do not have economic activity as their primary function often have organizational difficulties.* These groups pursue public or collective goods (such as a safer environment) that are available even to individuals who are not group members, so individuals may free ride, choosing not to pay the costs of membership.

- *Lobbying and electioneering are the traditional means by which groups communicate with and influence political leaders.* Recent developments, including grassroots lobbying and political action committees, have heightened interest groups' influence.

- *The interest-group system overrepresents business interests and fosters policies that serve a group's interest more than the society's broader interests.* Thus, although groups are an essential part of the policy process, they also distort that process.

THE INTEREST-GROUP SYSTEM

In the 1830s, the Frenchman Alexis de Tocqueville wrote that the "principle of association" was nowhere more evident than in America.[5] His description still holds. No other nation has as many organized interest groups as does the United States. The country's tradition of free association makes it natural for Americans to join together for political purposes, and their diverse interests give them reason to pursue policy influence through group action.

The nation's political structure also contributes to group action. Because of federalism and the separation of powers, groups have multiple points of entry through which to influence policy. At the federal level, lobbying groups can target the House, the Senate, the executive branch, and even the courts. Each of the 50 states provides a similar set of targets. Few political systems offer as many paths for group influence as does the American system (see "How the U.S. Differs").

The structure of the American system even contributes to a type of lobbying that is sometimes overlooked. Although the vast majority of organized interests represent private interests, some represent governments. Most states and major cities have at least one Washington lobbyist. Intergovernmental lobbying also occurs through groups such as the Council of State Governments, the National Governors Association, the National Association of Counties, the National League of Cities, and the U.S. Conference of Mayors. These organizations sometimes play a major role in national policy debates. For example, as Congress was preparing in 2017 to enact a sweeping tax reform bill, the National Governors Association lobbied to protect the deduction for state taxes.[6] Even foreign governments lobby in Washington. Arms sales, foreign aid, immigration, and trade practices are among the U.S. policies they target.[7]

The extraordinary number of interest groups in the United States does not mean that the nation's various interests are equally well organized. Groups develop when people with a shared interest have the opportunity and the incentive to join together. Some individuals or organizations have the skills, money, contacts, or time to participate in group politics; others do not. Moreover, some groups are inherently more attractive to potential members than others and thus find it easier to organize. Groups also differ in their financial resources and thus in their capacity for political action.

Therefore, a first consideration in regard to group politics in America is the issue of how thoroughly various interests are organized. Interests that are highly organized stand a good chance of having their views heard by policymakers. Those that are poorly organized run the risk of being ignored.

HOW THE U.S. DIFFERS
CRITICAL THINKING THROUGH COMPARISONS

Lobbying Groups

Washington, D.C., has roughly 11,500 registered lobbyists. An even larger number of individuals lobby informally or support the efforts of those who are registered. Registered lobbyists are required periodically to report their spending and their lobbying contacts.

No other national capital has anywhere near as many lobbyists as does Washington. Germany's capital, Berlin, has an estimated 5,000 lobbyists. France's capital, Paris, has an estimated 1,000 lobbyists. In fact, most democracies do not require lobbyists to register. Lobbying is not the large-scale enterprise that it is in the United States, and most democracies have not yet seen a need to regulate lobbying activities.

Q: How does the structure of the U.S. government contribute to the proliferation of lobbying groups in America?

A: Because of federalism and the separation of powers, the American system offers numerous points at which groups can try to influence public policy. If unsuccessful with legislators, groups can turn to executives or to the courts. If thwarted at the national level, groups can turn to state and local governments. Most democracies offer fewer pathways for group influence. France's unitary system, for example, concentrates power at the national level.

Economic Groups

No interests are more fully or effectively organized than those that have economic activity as their primary purpose. Corporations, labor unions, farm groups, and professional associations, among others, exist primarily for economic purposes—to make profits, provide jobs, improve pay, or protect an occupation. For the sake of discussion, we will call such organizations **economic groups.** Almost all such organizations engage in political activity as a means of promoting and protecting their economic interests. An indicator of this is the fact that Washington lobbyists who represent economic groups outnumber those of all other groups by two to one.

Among economic groups, the most numerous are *business groups.* Writing in 1929, political scientist E. Pendleton Herring noted, "Of the many organized groups maintaining offices in [Washington], there are no interests more fully, more comprehensively, and more efficiently represented than those of American industry."[8] Although corporations do not dominate lobbying as thoroughly as they once did, Herring's general conclusion still holds (see Figure 9-2). More than half of all groups formally registered to lobby Congress are business organizations. Virtually all large corporations and many smaller ones are politically active. Business firms are also represented through trade associations. Some of these "organizations of organizations" seek to advance the broad interests of business. One of the oldest associations is the National Association of Manufacturers, which was formed in 1894 and today represents 14,000 manufacturers. Another large business association is the U.S. Chamber of Commerce, which represents nearly 3 million businesses of all sizes. Other business associations, such as the American Petroleum Institute and the National Association of Home Builders, are confined to a single trade or industry.

Economic groups also include those associated with organized labor. *Labor groups* seek to promote policies that benefit workers in general and union members in particular. Although there are some major independent unions, such as the United Mine Workers of America and the Teamsters, the dominant

Lobbying groups in Washington, D.C.

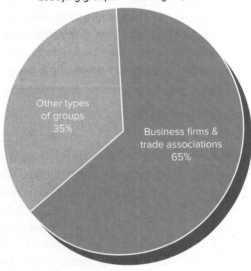

figure 9-2   TYPES OF LOBBYING GROUPS

Roughly two-thirds of lobbying groups in Washington, D.C., are associated with business. Every large corporation has its lobbyists, as do business-related trade associations such as the National Association of Manufacturers. (*Source:* Compiled by author from multiple sources.)

labor group is the AFL-CIO, which has its national headquarters in Washington, D.C. The AFL-CIO has roughly 12 million members in its 55 affiliated unions, which include, for example, the International Brotherhood of Electrical Workers and the American Federation of Teachers.

At an earlier time, about a third of the U.S. workforce was unionized. Today, only about one in nine workers is a union member. Historically, skilled and unskilled laborers constituted the bulk of organized labor, but their numbers have decreased as the economy has changed, while the number of professionals, technicians, and service workers has increased. Professionals have shown little interest in union organization, perhaps because they identify with management or consider themselves economically secure. A mere 2 percent of professionals are union members. Service workers and technicians can also be difficult for unions to organize because they work closely with managers and, often, in small offices. Nevertheless, unions have made inroads in their efforts to organize service and public employees. In fact, most union members today work in the public sector, despite the fact that it has only a fifth as many workers as does the private sector. The most heavily unionized employees are those who work for local government, such as teachers, police officers, and firefighters—roughly 40 percent of them are union members. State and federal employees are also heavily unionized. All told, more than 30 percent of public-sector workers are union members, compared with less than 10 percent of private-industry workers. Even the construction industry, which ranks high by comparison with most private-sector industries, has a unionization rate of less than 15 percent.[9]

Farm groups represent another large economic lobby. The American Farm Bureau Federation is the largest of the farm groups, with more than 4 million members. The National Farmers Union, the National Grange, and the National Farmers Organization are smaller farm lobbies. Agricultural groups do not always agree on policy issues. For instance, the Farm Bureau sides with agribusiness and owners of large farms, while the Farmers Union promotes the interests of smaller "family" farms. There are also numerous specialty farm associations, including the National Association of Wheat Growers, the American Soybean Association, and the Associated Milk Producers. Each association acts as a separate lobby, seeking to obtain policies that will serve its members' particular interests.

Most professions also have lobbying associations. Among the most powerful of these *professional groups* is the American Medical Association (AMA), which includes more than 250,000 physicians. Other professional groups include the American Bar Association (ABA) and the American Association of University Professors (AAUP).

This 1873 lithograph illustrates the benefits of membership in the National Grange, an agricultural interest group. Throughout their history, Americans have organized to influence government policy. (*Source*: Library of Congress, Prints and Photographs Division [LC-DIG-ppmsca-02956])

Citizens' Groups

Economic groups do not have a monopoly on lobbying. There is another category of interest groups—**citizens' groups** (or *noneconomic groups*). Group members in this category are joined together not by a *material incentive*—such as jobs, higher wages, or profits—but by a *purposive incentive,* the satisfaction of contributing to what they regard as a worthy purpose.[10] Whether a group's purpose is to protect the environment, return prayer to the public schools, or feed the poor at home or abroad, there are citizens who are willing to participate simply because they believe the cause is a worthy one.

Nearly every conceivable issue or problem has its citizens' group, often several of them. Some citizens' groups work to advance the interests of a particular social grouping; examples are the National Association for the Advancement of Colored People (NAACP), the National Organization for

Women (NOW), and La Raza, which is the largest Hispanic American lobbying group. Other citizens' groups have a broad agenda that derives from an ideological or moral position. The American Conservative Union (ACU) is the largest conservative organization and lobbies on issues like taxation and national defense. Americans for Democratic Action (ADA) is a liberal counterpart to the ACU. Another example is the Christian Coalition of America, which describes itself as "America's leading grassroots organization defending our godly heritage." The group addresses a wide range of issues, including school prayer, abortion, and television programming. Ideology is also a component of the state-level Public Interest Research Groups (PIRGs), such as NYPIRG (New York), CALPIRG (California), and TexPIRG (Texas). Almost every state has a PIRG, which usually has chapters on college campuses. Drawing on their network of researchers, students, and advocates, they approach issues from a public interest perspective. Ideological groups on both the left and the right have increased substantially in number since the 1960s (see "Party Polarization: Ideological Interest Groups").

Most citizens' groups, however, have an issue-specific policy agenda. *Single-issue groups* have risen sharply in number in the past half-century and now pressure government on almost every conceivable policy, from nuclear arms to drug abuse. Notable current examples are the National Rifle Association and the various right-to-life and pro-choice groups. Most environmental groups can also be seen as single-issue organizations in that they seek to influence public policy in a specific area, such as pollution reduction, wilderness preservation, or wildlife protection. The Sierra Club, one of the oldest environmental groups, was formed in the 1890s to promote the preservation of scenic areas. In contrast, the Environmental Defense Fund, established in 1967, concentrates on environmental problems, such as air and water pollution. Since 1960, membership in environmental groups has more than tripled in response to increased public concern about the environment.[11]

Citizens' groups are difficult to classify precisely because they differ so widely in their focus and goals. Some single-issue groups, for example, are ideological whereas others are pragmatic. A simple but precise way to describe citizens' groups is that they are "groups anyone can join." This does not mean that everyone would want to join a particular group. A conservative would not choose to join the ADA, just as a liberal would not join the ACU. But there is no barrier to joining a citizens' group if one is willing to contribute the required time or money. In this way, citizens' groups are distinct from business firms, which are closed to all but their employees, and distinct also from labor groups, farm groups, and professional associations, whose members have a particular type of training or occupation.[12]

P A R T Y POLARIZATION	Conflicting Ideas

Ideological Interest Groups

After the Watergate scandal in the early 1970s, Congress enacted campaign finance reforms that opened the door to a larger funding role for interest groups by reducing restrictions on political action committees (PACs). Many of the citizen-based PACs that formed were more ideological than were the parties or most voters. At first, these PACs concentrated on general election races, but then they also became heavily involved in primary election contests, working to defeat moderate candidates within their party. Their efforts have contributed to the election of senators and representatives who hold uncompromising conservative or liberal views, which has contributed to the party polarization in Congress in recent years. Examples of such groups are Emily's List, which supports liberal candidates, and the Family Research Council, which supports conservative candidates. In recent elections, Emily's List has given virtually 100 percent of its PAC contributions to Democratic candidates, while the Family Research Council has given virtually 100 percent of its PAC contributions to Republican candidates. The tendency of ideological groups to support one side of the partisan divide can also be seen in the figures below, which show how ideological PACs in a few areas divide their money between Republican and Democratic candidates.

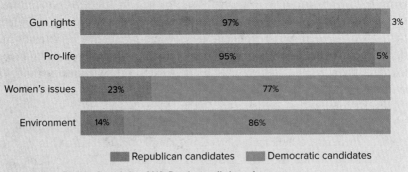

Source: Federal Election Commission, 2018. Based on preliminary data.

Q: Why do you think politically active citizen groups are generally more ideological—whether conservative or liberal—than is the society as a whole? Are citizens with strong views somehow more attracted to organized political activity than those with moderate opinions?

The Organizational Edge: Economic Groups versus Citizens' Groups

Although the number of citizens' groups has mushroomed in recent decades, they are substantially outnumbered by economic groups. The predominance of economic interests was predicted in *Federalist* No. 10, in which James Madison declared that property is "the most common and durable source of factions." Stated differently, nothing seems to matter quite so much to people as their economic self-interest. Several factors (summarized in Table 9-1) give economic groups an organizational advantage, including their resources and their size.

Unequal Access to Resources   One reason for the abundance of economic groups is their access to financial resources. Political lobbying is not cheap. If a group is to make its views known, it typically must have a headquarters, an expert staff, and communication facilities. Economic groups pay for these things with money generated by their economic activity. Corporations have the greatest built-in advantage. They do not have to charge membership dues or conduct fundraisers to support their lobbying. Their political money comes from their business profits.

table 9-1	ADVANTAGES AND DISADVANTAGES HELD BY ECONOMIC AND CITIZENS' GROUPS
Economic Groups	**Citizens' Groups**
Advantages	*Advantages*
Economic activity provides the organization with the resources necessary for political action.	Members are likely to support leaders' political efforts because they joined the group in order to influence policy.
Individuals are encouraged to join the group because of economic benefits they individually receive (such as wages).	*Disadvantages*
	The group has to raise funds, especially for its political activities.
In the case of firms within an industry, their small number encourages organization because the contribution of each firm can make a difference.	Potential members may choose not to join the group because they get collective benefits even if they do not join (the free-rider problem).
Disadvantages	Potential members may choose not to join the group because their individual contribution may be too small to affect the group's success one way or the other.
Members may not support the group's political efforts because they didn't join for political reasons.	

Some economic groups rely on dues rather than profits to support their lobbying, but they have something of economic value to offer in exchange. Labor unions, for example, provide their members access to higher-paying jobs in return for the dues they pay. Such groups offer what is called **private (individual) goods**—benefits, such as jobs, that are given directly to particular individuals. An important feature of private goods is that they can be held back. If an individual is unwilling to pay organizational dues, the group can withhold the benefit.

Citizens' groups do not have these inherent advantages. They do not generate profits or fees as a result of economic activity. Moreover, the incentives they offer prospective members are not exclusive. As opposed to the private or individual goods provided by many economic groups, most noneconomic groups offer **collective (public) goods** as an incentive for membership. Collective goods are, by definition, goods that belong to all; they cannot be granted or withheld on an individual basis. The air that people breathe and the national forests they visit are examples of collective goods. These goods are available to one and all, those who do not pay dues to a clean-air group or a wilderness preservation group as well as those who do.

The shared characteristic of collective goods creates what is called the **free-rider problem:** Individuals can obtain the good even if they do not contribute to the group's effort. National Public Radio (NPR) is an example. Although NPR's programs are funded primarily through listeners' donations, those who do not contribute are free to listen to the programs. They are free riders, getting the benefit of NPR's productions without helping to pay for them. A mere 1 in 10 listeners donate to NPR.[13]

In a purely economic sense, as economist Mancur Olson noted, it's not rational for an individual to contribute to a group when its benefit can be obtained for free.[14] Moreover, the dues paid by any single member are too small to affect the group's success one way or another. Why pay dues to an environmental group when any improvements in the air, water, or wildlife from its lobbying efforts are available to everyone and when one's individual contribution is too small to make a real difference? Although many people do join such groups anyway, the free-rider problem is one reason citizens' groups are organized less fully than economic groups.

In recent decades the free-rider problem has been lessened, but not eliminated, by advances in technology. Computer-assisted direct mail, e-mail, and social networks have greatly eased citizen groups' efforts to contact prospective donors. For some individuals, a contribution of $25 to $50 annually represents no great sacrifice and offers the satisfaction of supporting a cause in which they believe. "Checkbook members" is how political scientist Theda Skocpol describes such contributors.[15]

Business interests dominate the lobbying sector. Their advantage stems largely from the fact that they can use their profits to fund their lobbying activities. Citizens groups are in a weaker financial position. They depend on voluntary contributions to fund their lobbying efforts. (©achinthamb/Shutterstock)

The Advantages and Disadvantages of Size   Although citizens' groups have proliferated in recent decades, the organizational muscle in American politics rests primarily with economic groups. Business interests in particular have an advantage that economist Mancur Olson calls "the size factor."[16] Although it might be thought that groups with large memberships would typically prevail over smaller groups, the reverse is often true. Olson notes that small groups are ordinarily more united on policy issues and often have more resources, enabling them to win out against large groups. Business groups in a specific industry are usually few in number and have an incentive to work together to influence government on issues of joint interest. The U.S. automobile industry, for example, has its "Big Three"—General Motors, Ford, and Chrysler. Although they compete for car sales, they usually work together on policy issues. They have succeeded at times, for example, in persuading government to delay or reduce higher fuel efficiency and safety standards, which has meant billions in additional profits for them at an incalculable cost to car owners, who are many in number but are not an organized group.

Business associations testify to the advantage of small size. The business sector is divided into numerous industries, most of which include only a small number of major firms. Virtually every one of these industries, everything from oil to cereals, has its own trade association. More than 1,000 trade associations are represented in Washington, and they spend hundreds of millions of dollars annually on lobbying.

Their situation is far different from that of, say, taxpayers, who number in the tens of millions. Although taxpayers would be enormously powerful if they all joined together in a single cohesive group, most taxpayers have no real interest in paying dues to a taxpayers' group that would lobby on their behalf. In 2017, these differences came together in ways that conceivably hurt taxpayers while helping corporations. At issue was the largest overhaul of the tax code since the 1980s. When the legislation was passed, corporations saw their income tax rate reduced from 35 percent to 21 percent. Most taxpayers also got a cut but it was only a few percentage points. Moreover, whereas the corporate tax cut had no time limit, the individual tax cut will end in 10 years, at which time a fourth of taxpayers will be paying a higher rate than they would have if the old tax law had still been in effect.[17] Getting millions of taxpayers to work together to influence policy is infinitely more difficult than getting top corporations to collaborate. "[T]he larger the group," Olson wrote, "the less it will further its common interests."[18]

Nevertheless, there can be strength in numbers. No group illustrates this better than AARP (formerly known as the American Association of Retired Persons). Although not every retired person belongs to AARP, its annual dues are so low ($16) that it has more than 35 million members. AARP has a staff of more than 1,000 and is a formidable lobby on Social Security, Medicare, and other issues affecting retirees. Congress receives more mail from members of AARP than it does from members of any other group. A *Fortune* magazine survey of 2,200 Washington insiders, including members of Congress and their staffs, ranked AARP as the nation's most powerful lobbying group.[19]

INSIDE LOBBYING: SEEKING INFLUENCE THROUGH OFFICIAL CONTACTS

Modern government is involved in so many issues—business regulation, income maintenance, urban renewal, cancer research, and energy development, to name only a few—that barely any interest in society could fail to benefit from having influence over federal policies or programs. Moreover, officials are more inclined to solve problems than to ignore them. When Hurricane Harvey flooded Houston, Beaumont, Port Arthur, and other communities along the Gulf Coast in 2017, the federal government provided grants and loans for the cleanup and rebuilding effort.

Groups seek government's support through **lobbying,** a term that refers broadly to efforts by groups to influence public policy through contact with public officials.[20] Interest groups rely on two main lobbying strategies, which have been called *inside lobbying* and *outside lobbying.*[21] This section discusses **inside lobbying,** which is based on group efforts to develop and maintain close ("inside") contacts with policymakers. (Outside lobbying is described in the next section.)

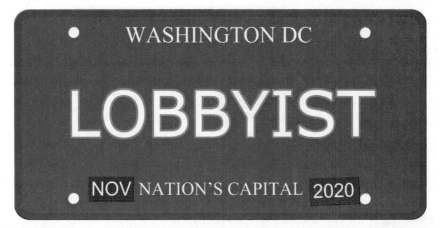

Washington, D.C., has the highest concentration of lobbyists of any of the world's capitals. (©Keith Bell/123RF)

Acquiring Access to Officials

Through inside lobbying, groups seek to gain direct access to officials in order to influence their decisions. Lobbying once depended significantly on tangible payoffs, including bribes. Such incidents are rare today. Bribery is illegal, and lobbying behavior is regulated more closely than in the past. Lobbyists are required by law to register and to file detailed reports on their lobbying expenditures.

Modern lobbying rests primarily on the skillful use of information. Lobbyists concentrate on providing lawmakers with arguments and evidence backing their position. Their goal is to persuade officials that what they want done is the best course of action.[22] "If I don't explain what we do . . . Congress will make uninformed decisions without understanding the consequences to the industry," said one lobbyist.[23]

Inside lobbying is directed at policymakers who are inclined to support the group rather than at those who have opposed it in the past. This tendency reflects both the difficulty of persuading opponents to change long-held views and the advantage of working through trusted officials. Thus, union lobbyists work mainly with pro-labor officeholders, just as corporate lobbyists work mainly with pro-business policymakers.

For lobbyists to be effective, they need to understand the policy process as well as the issue under consideration. It's a reason for the "revolving door" between lobbying firms and government. Many lobbyists worked previously in government, and some top officials were once lobbyists. Upon retirement, many members of Congress join lobbying firms. Although prohibited by law

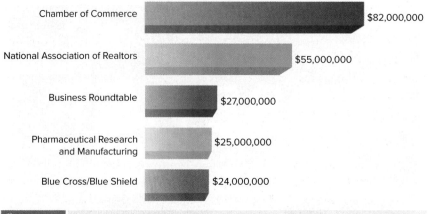

figure 9-3 THE FIVE TOP-SPENDING LOBBYING GROUPS

Lobbying is big business in two ways. First, huge sums of money are spent each year on lobbying. Second, most of the money is spent by business lobbies. (*Source:* Center for Responsive Politics, 2018. Data are 2017 spending amounts.)

from lobbying Congress for a set period of time after leaving office, they are free to do so thereafter and usually lobby in policy areas they handled during their time in Congress.[24]

Money is a key element in inside-lobbying efforts. Many groups have a Washington office and a professional staff of lobbyists and public relations specialists. Roughly 11,500 registered lobbyists work in Washington, along with a greater number who lobby informally or assist those who are registered.[25] The amount of money spent on lobbying is staggering. The Center for Responsive Politics divided the amount of money spent on lobbying by the number of hours Congress was in session to dramatize the extent of lobbying. The figure turned out to be a more than $1 million per hour.[26] Consistently among the top spenders is the U.S. Chamber of Congress with an annual lobbying budget exceeding $75 million (see Figure 9-3). Other groups get by on much less, but it is hard to lobby effectively on a tiny budget. Given the costs of maintaining a Washington lobby, the domination by corporations and trade associations is understandable. They have the money to retain high-priced lobbyists, while many other interests do not.

Lobbying Congress   The targets of inside lobbying are officials of all three government branches—legislative, executive, and judicial. The benefits of a close relationship with members of Congress are the most obvious. With support in Congress, a group can obtain the legislative help it needs to achieve its policy goals. By the same token, members of Congress benefit from ties to lobbyists. The volume of legislation facing Congress is heavy, and members rely on trusted lobbyists to identify bills that deserve their attention. When

Republican lawmakers took control of the House of Representatives in 2011, they consulted closely with corporate lobbyists on legislative issues affecting business. Congressional Democrats complained, but Republicans said they were merely getting advice from those who best understood business's needs and noted that Democrats had worked closely with organized labor when they were in power.

Lobbyists' effectiveness depends in part on their reputation for playing it straight. Said one member of Congress, "If any [lobbyist] gives me false or misleading information, that's it—I'll never see him again."[27] Bullying is also frowned upon. During the debate over the North American Free Trade Agreement in 1993, the AFL-CIO threatened to campaign against congressional Democrats who supported the legislation. The backlash from Democrats on both sides of the issue was so intense that the union withdrew its threat. The safe lobbying strategy is the aboveboard approach: Provide information, rely on trusted allies in Congress, and push steadily but not aggressively for favorable legislation.

Lobbying the Executive Branch   As the range of federal policy has expanded, lobbying of the executive branch has grown in importance. Some of this lobbying is directed at the president and presidential staff, but they are less accessible than top officials in the federal agencies, who are the chief targets.

Group influence is particularly strong in the regulatory agencies that oversee the nation's business sectors. Pharmaceutical companies, for example, provide much of the scientific evidence used by the Food and Drug Administration (FDA) in deciding whether a new drug is safe to market. The potential for influence is high, as are the stakes. After the FDA approved its marketing, the arthritis drug Vioxx generated $2.5 billion a year in sales for Merck, the pharmaceutical company that developed it. As it turned out, Vioxx was unsafe. Its users suffered an abnormally high number of strokes and heart attacks. A review panel concluded that the FDA had been lax in accepting Merck's assessments of the drug's safety.[28]

The FDA example illustrates what's called *agency capture.* The capture theory holds that regulatory agencies sometimes side with the industries they are supposed to regulate rather than with the public, which they are supposed to protect. Studies have found that capture theory explains some group-agency relationships, but not all of them. Agency officials are aware that they can lose support in Congress, which controls agency funding, if they show too much favoritism toward an interest group.[29] In response to the Vioxx controversy, as well as problems with other new drugs, Congress passed legislation in 2007 that forced the FDA to tighten its safety tests.

Washington, D.C., is a lobbyist's dream. Congress has two chambers, and all of its 535 members have the power to introduce legislation. The executive branch has scores of agencies. Even the judiciary offers lobbyists a channel through which they can exert influence. (*Source:* Library of Congress, Prints and Photographs Division [LC-DIG-highsm-01901])

Lobbying the Courts   Judicial rulings in areas such as education and civil rights have made interest groups recognize that they can sometimes achieve their policy goals through the courts.[30] Interest groups have several judicial lobbying options, including efforts to influence the selection of federal judges. Right-to-life groups have pressured Republican administrations to make opposition to abortion a prerequisite for nomination to the federal bench. Democratic administrations have in turn faced pressure from pro-choice groups in their judicial nominations.[31] Judicial lobbying also includes lawsuits. For some organizations, such as the American Civil Liberties Union (ACLU), legal action is the primary means of lobbying. The ACLU often takes on unpopular causes, such as the free-speech rights of fringe groups. Such causes have little chance of success in legislative bodies but may prevail in a courtroom.

As interest groups have increasingly resorted to legal action, they have often found themselves facing one another in court. Environmental litigation groups such as the Environmental Defense Fund have fought numerous court battles with oil, timber, and mining corporations. Even when groups are not a direct party to a lawsuit, they sometimes get involved through amicus curiae ("friend of the court") briefs. An amicus brief is a written document in which a group explains to a court its position on a case under review.

Webs of Influence: Groups in the Policy Process

To get a fuller picture of how inside lobbying works, it is helpful to consider two policy processes—iron triangles and issue networks—in which many groups are enmeshed.

Iron Triangles   An **iron triangle** consists of a small and informal but relatively stable set of bureaucrats, legislators, and lobbyists who seek to develop policies beneficial to a particular interest. The three "corners" of one such triangle are the Department of Agriculture (bureaucrats), the agriculture committees of Congress (legislators), and farm groups such as the Associated Milk Producers and the Association of Wheat Growers (lobbyists). Together they determine many of the policies affecting farmers. Although the support of the president and a majority in Congress is needed to enact new policies, they often defer to the judgment of the agricultural triangle, whose members are intimately familiar with farmers' needs.

Groups embedded in iron triangles have an inside track to well-positioned legislators and bureaucrats. They can count on getting a full hearing on issues affecting them. Moreover, because they have something to offer in return, the triangular relationship tends to be clad in "iron." The groups provide lobbying support for agency programs and campaign contributions to members of Congress. Defense contractors, for instance, donate millions of dollars to congressional campaigns during each election cycle. Most of the money goes to the campaigns of House and Senate incumbents who sit on the committees dealing with the military. In the 2016 election, more than 60 percent of their donations went to these lawmakers, who constitute less than 20 percent of Congress's total membership.[32] Figure 9-4 summarizes the benefits that flow to each member of an iron triangle.

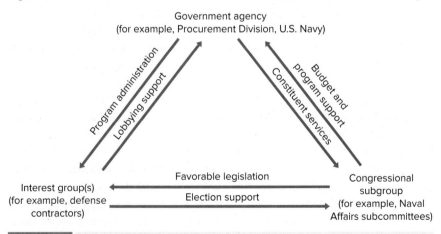

figure 9-4   HOW AN IRON TRIANGLE BENEFITS ITS PARTICIPANTS

An iron triangle works to the advantage of each of its participants—an interest group, a congressional subgroup, and a government agency.

Issue Networks   Iron triangles represent the pattern of influence in only certain policy areas and are less common now than in the past. A more frequent pattern of influence today is the **issue network**—an informal grouping of officials, lobbyists, and policy specialists (the "network") who come together *temporarily* around a policy problem (the "issue").

Issue networks are a result of the increasing complexity of policy problems. Participants must have a working knowledge of the issue at hand in order to address it effectively. Thus, unlike iron triangles, in which a participant's position is everything, an issue network is built around specialized interests and knowledge. On any given issue, the participants might come from a variety of executive agencies, congressional committees, interest groups, and institutions such as universities or think tanks. Compared to iron triangles, issue networks are less stable. As the issue develops, new participants may join the debate and old ones may drop out. Once the issue is resolved, the network disbands.[33]

An example of an issue network is the set of participants who would come together over the issue of whether a large tract of old forest should be opened to logging. A few decades ago, this issue would have been settled in an iron triangle consisting of the timber companies, the U.S. Forest Service, and relevant members of the House and Senate agriculture committees. But as forestlands have diminished and environmental concerns have grown, such issues can no longer be controlled by those who are linked through an iron triangle. Today, an issue network would form that includes logging interests, the U.S. Forest Service, House and Senate agriculture committee members, research scientists, and representatives of environmental groups, the housing industry, and animal-rights groups. Unlike the old iron triangle, which was confined to like-minded interests, this issue network would include opposing interests (for example, the loggers and the environmentalists). And unlike an iron triangle, the issue network would dissolve once the issue that brought the parties together was resolved.

In sum, issue networks differ substantially from iron triangles. In an iron triangle, a common interest brings the participants together in a long-lasting and mutually beneficial relationship. In an issue network, an immediate issue brings together the participants in a temporary network that is based on their ability to knowledgeably address the issue and where they play out their separate interests before disbanding once the issue is settled.

Despite these differences, iron triangles and issue networks do have one thing in common: They are arenas in which organized groups exercise influence. The interests of the general public may be taken into account in these webs of power, but the interests of the participating groups are the primary concern.

OUTSIDE LOBBYING: SEEKING INFLUENCE THROUGH PUBLIC PRESSURE

Although an interest group may rely solely on inside lobbying, this approach is more likely to be successful when the group can demonstrate that it represents an important constituency. Accordingly, groups also engage in **outside lobbying,** which involves bringing public ("outside") pressure to bear on policymakers (see Table 9-2).[34]

Constituency Advocacy: Grassroots Lobbying

Outside lobbying includes efforts, such as letter-writing campaigns or public demonstrations, aimed at convincing lawmakers that a group's policy position has popular support. A case in point is the 2000 legislation that resulted in the permanent normalization of trade relations with China. Most business lobbies supported the proposed legislation, and several of them launched grassroots lobbying efforts. Boeing Corporation, for example, asked its employees, subcontractors, and suppliers—more than 40,000 in all—to contact members of Congress.[35]

Few groups, however, are better at outside lobbying than is the National Rifle Association (NRA). Opposition from the NRA is a major reason the United States has lagged behind other Western societies in its gun control laws, despite opinion polls indicating that most Americans favor such laws.[36] Influential groups usually have one of two resources: either a lot of money or a committed membership. The NRA has both. It spends heavily on election campaigns. In 2016, it spent $50 million to support pro-gun candidates. And it is adept at mobilizing its 5 million members, most of whom reside in the South and Midwest. Candidates who advocate stricter gun laws are a target of the NRA and its members, who can be counted on to actively campaign against them.[37]

table 9-2	TACTICS USED IN INSIDE AND OUTSIDE LOBBYING EFFORTS	
Inside Lobbying	**Outside Lobbying**
Developing contacts with legislators and executives	Encouraging group members to contact their representatives
Providing information to key officials	Promoting their message through advertising and public relations
Forming coalitions with other groups	Supporting political candidates through money and endorsements

Electoral Action: Votes and Money

An "outside" strategy can also include election activity. "Reward your friends and punish your enemies" is a political adage that loosely describes how interest groups approach elections. One lobbyist said it directly: "Talking to politicians is fine, but with a little money they hear you better."[38] The possibility of campaign opposition from a powerful group can restrain an officeholder. In 2017, for example, AARP lobbied hard, and did so successfully, against a bill that would have imposed additional health care costs on older Americans.[39]

Political Action Committees (PACs)   A group's contributions to candidates are funneled through its **political action committee (PAC).** A group cannot give organizational funds (such as corporate profits or union dues) directly to candidates, but through its PAC a group can solicit voluntary contributions from members or employees and then donate this money to candidates. A PAC can back as many candidates as it wants but is legally limited in the amount it can contribute to a single candidate. The ceiling is $10,000 per candidate—$5,000 in the primary campaign and $5,000 in the general election campaign. (These financial limits apply to candidates for federal office. State and local campaigns are regulated by state laws, and some states allow PACs to make unlimited contributions to individual candidates.)

There are roughly 4,000 PACs, and they account for roughly a fifth of congressional campaign spending.[40] Their role is less significant in presidential campaigns, which are larger in scale and depend chiefly on donations from individual contributors.

More than 60 percent of all PACs are associated with businesses (see Figure 9-5). Most of these are corporate PACs, such as the Ford Motor Company Civic Action Fund, the Sun Oil Company Political Action Committee, and the Coca-Cola PAC. The others are tied to trade associations, such as RPAC (National Association of Realtors). The next-largest set of PACs consists of those linked to citizens' groups (that is, public-interest, single-issue, and ideological groups), such as the liberal People for the American Way and the conservative National Conservative Political Action Committee. Labor unions, once the major source of group contributions, constitute less than 10 percent of PACs.

PACs contribute roughly eight times as much money to incumbents as to their challengers. PACs recognize that incumbents are likely to win and thus to remain in positions of power. One PAC director, expressing a common view, said, "We always stick with the incumbent when we agree with them both."[41]

Super PACs   A few short years ago, the term *super PAC* was not part of the political lexicon. That changed when the Supreme Court ruled in *Citizens*

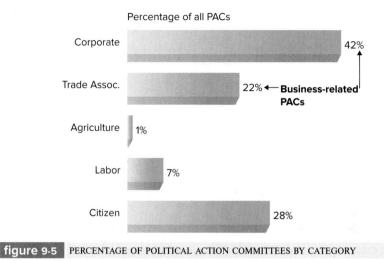

Percentage of all PACs

Corporate — 42%

Trade Assoc. — 22% ← **Business-related PACs**

Agriculture — 1%

Labor — 7%

Citizen — 28%

figure 9-5   PERCENTAGE OF POLITICAL ACTION COMMITTEES BY CATEGORY

Most PACs represent business. Corporate and trade association PACs make up roughly three out of every five PACs. (*Source:* Federal Election Commission, 2018.)

United v. Federal Election Commission (2010) that federal laws restricting campaign spending by corporations and unions violated their right of free expression. The Court held that corporations and unions can spend an unlimited amount of their funds on elections, as long as the spending is not directly coordinated with that of the candidate or party they're supporting (see Chapters 1 and 8).[42] In a follow-up case, a lower federal court ruled that political activists can form independent campaign committees to solicit and spend corporate, union, and individual contributions.

These rulings spawned **super PACs** or, as they are officially called, *independent-expenditure-only committees* (IEOCs). Super PACs are not allowed to give money directly to candidates or parties, but they are otherwise more or less free to spend as much as they want. By 2018, more than 2,400 super PACs had been created. They raised nearly $2 billion to influence the outcome of the 2016 election, roughly 20 times the amount in 2010, the first election after the *Citizens United* ruling (see Figure 9-6).

Super PACs have been a subject of intense debate. Critics have assailed the fact that super PACs can spend unlimited amounts of money and, unlike regular PACs, are not required to report their expenditures on a timely basis. Vermont Democratic senator Bernie Sanders is a critic of super PACs. Election outcomes, says Sanders, should represent "all of the people, and not just those wealthy individuals and corporations who can put millions into political campaigns."[43] Proponents of super PACs say they bring voices and views into the campaign that voters have a right to hear. Says Bradley Smith, a Republican

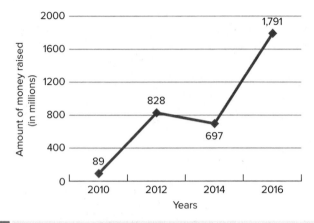

figure 9-6   CAMPAIGN FUNDS RAISED BY SUPER PACS

In its 2010 *Citizens United* ruling, the Supreme Court opened the door to super PACs, which can raise and spend unlimited amounts of money on elections provided that they do not coordinate their effort with that of the candidate they're supporting. Since the Court's ruling, super PACs have emerged as major players in U.S. federal elections. (*Source:* Center for Responsive Politics, 2018.)

who served as chair of the Federal Election Commission: "While people like to complain about political spending, research shows that increased spending improves voter knowledge of candidates and issues."[44]

THE GROUP SYSTEM: INDISPENSABLE BUT BIASED IN FAVOR OF ECONOMIC GROUPS

As noted in the chapter's introduction, pluralist theory holds that organized groups are a source of sound governance. On one level, this claim is indisputable. Groups are a means of getting government to pay attention to people's needs and interests. Yet the issue of representation through groups is also a question of whether the various interests in society are fairly represented, and here the pluralist argument is less persuasive.

The Contribution of Groups to Self-Government: Pluralism

Government does not exist simply to serve majority interests. The fact that most people are not retirees or union members or farmers or college students is not an indication that the interests of such "minorities" are unworthy of government's attention. What better instrument exists for promoting their interests than lobbying groups working on their behalf?

HOW THE 50 STATES DIFFER

CRITICAL THINKING THROUGH COMPARISONS

Lobbyists

Although Washington, D.C., has the largest concentration of registered lobbyists, they are also found in significant numbers in state capitals, as the accompanying map indicates. States decide many of the policies in areas such as education, health, social welfare, business, policing, and transportation. States are also in charge of licensing everything from doctors to liquor stores. All these policy areas are lobbying targets.

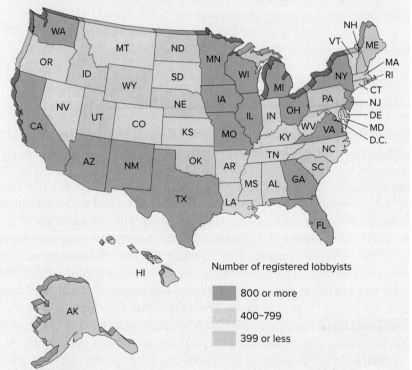

Number of registered lobbyists

- 800 or more
- 400–799
- 399 or less

Source: Center for Public Integrity, 2014.

Q: What do states with large numbers of lobbyists have in common?

A: Most of them have diverse economies and large populations, which result in high levels of policy activity. Most of them also have comparatively long legislative sessions, providing lobbyists with abundant opportunities to interact with lawmakers.

Some pluralists even question the usefulness of terms such as the *public interest*. If people disagree on society's goals and priorities, as they always do, how can anyone claim that their goal or priority represents the public interest? As an alternative, pluralists say that society is best seen as a collection of separate interests and is best served by a process that serves a wide array of these interests. Thus, if manufacturing interests prevail on one issue, environmentalists on another, farmers on a third, minorities on a fourth, and so on until a great many interests are served, the "public interest" will have been served. Pluralists also note that the promotion of the special interest often benefits others as well. Tax incentives for corporations that encourage research and capital investment, for example, can result in job creation and improved goods and services.

Finally, interest groups expand the range of issues that come to lawmakers' attention. Political parties sometimes shy away from controversial issues and, in any case, concentrate on those that have broad impact, which leaves hundreds of issues unaddressed through the party system. Interest groups advocate for and against many of these issues.[45]

Flaws in Pluralism: Interest-Group Liberalism and Economic Bias

Pluralist theory has questionable aspects. Political scientist Theodore Lowi points out that there is no concept of the public interest in a system that gives special interests the ability to determine the policies affecting them.[46] Nor can it be assumed that what a lobbying group receives is what the majority would also want. Consider the case of the federal law that required auto dealers to list the known defects of used cars on window stickers. The law was repealed after the National Association of Automobile Dealers contributed more than $1 million to the reelection campaigns of members of Congress. Auto dealers won another victory when their loans to car buyers were exempted from regulation by the new consumer protection agency that was created as part of the Dodd-Frank Act of 2010 (see Case Study: Dodd-Frank Act and the Auto Lobby).

Republican and Democratic lawmakers alike are in the habit of using government to promote group interests. Each party has its favorites—for example, business groups usually do better when Republicans are in power, and labor groups usually do better when Democrats are in power. Neither party has shown a reluctance to use the power of government on behalf of the groups it favors.

Another flaw in the pluralist argument resides in its claim that the group system is representative. Although pluralists acknowledge that well-funded interests have more clout, they say that the group process is relatively open and few interests are entirely left out. This claim contains an element of truth, but it is not the full story. As this chapter has shown, economic interests,

C A S E	**Politics in Action**
S T U D Y	

Dodd-Frank Act and the Auto Lobby

In 2008, the U.S. economy went into a deep recession as a result of reckless lending by the financial industry. Banks had given out huge numbers of mortgages to unqualified home buyers. When home prices then dropped sharply, many of the mortgages were "under water," meaning that the house was worth less than its mortgage. At this point, many of the buyers stopped making their monthly payments. Banks were left with vacant houses and mortgage defaults. It put many of them in the red, driving down their stock prices and sparking the financial crisis. Many banks survived only because they received bailout money from the federal government.

©Rainer Plendl/Getty Images

In 2010, Congress passed the Dodd-Frank Act in order to protect borrowers and end risky lending on everything from mortgages to credit cards to consumer loans. The legislation was named for its chief sponsors, Senator Christopher Dodd of Connecticut and Representative Barney Frank of Massachusetts.

As the Dodd-Frank bill was being drafted, more than 500 lobbyists from the auto industry—nearly one per member of Congress—went to Capitol Hill in an effort to get auto loans removed from the new regulations. They argued that auto loans do not pose the same risk as home mortgages. Failed mortgages, the lobbyists claimed, can bring down the economy but repossessed cars cannot. The auto industry succeeded in its effort. Members of Congress removed auto loans from the legislation. It was not the automobile lobby's first such victory. A few years earlier, it had persuaded Congress to repeal a law that required auto dealers to list on window stickers the known defects of the used cars they were selling.

Q: Why do you think the auto industry has so much influence in Congress?

Continued

> **ASK YOURSELF:** How many jobs, directly and indirectly, does the auto industry generate? How prominent are auto dealers in their communities? Are automobiles a commodity important to both labor and business and thus important to both Democratic and Republican lawmakers? What type of financial resources does the auto industry have to invest in lobbying and election campaigns?

particularly corporations, are the most highly organized and the most advantaged when it comes to exerting influence on policy.[47] Of course, economic groups do not dominate everything, nor do they operate unchecked. Most environmental groups, for example, work to shield the environment from threats posed by business activity. Activist government has also brought the group system into closer balance; the government's poverty programs have spawned groups that act to protect the programs. Nevertheless, the power of poverty-related groups is a pittance compared with the power of moneyed interests. Nearly two-thirds of all lobbying groups in Washington are business related, and their political clout is enormous.

A Madisonian Dilemma

James Madison recognized the dilemma inherent in group activity. Although he worried that interest groups would have too much political influence, he argued in *Federalist* No. 10 that a free society must allow the pursuit of self-interest. Unless people can promote the separate opinions that stem from differences in their needs, values, and possessions, they are not a free people.

Ironically, Madison's constitutional solution to the problem of factions is now part of the problem. Madison thought that the American system of checks and balances, with a separation of powers at its core, would prevent a majority faction from trampling on the interests of smaller groups. This same system, however, makes it relatively easy for minority factions—or, as they are called today, special-interest groups—to gain government support. Because of the system's division of power, they have numerous points at which to gain access and exert influence. Often, they need only to find a single ally, whether it is a congressional committee or an executive agency or a federal court, to get at least some of what they seek. And once they obtain a government benefit, it is likely to last. Benefits are hard to eliminate because concerted action by the executive branch and both houses of Congress is usually required. If a group has strong support in even a single institution, it can usually fend off attempts to eliminate a policy or program that serves its interest. Such support can be easy to acquire if the group has resources—information, money, and votes—that officeholders want. (Chapters 11 and 13 discuss further the issue of interest-group power.)

Detecting Misinformation

Do "the People" Decide?

Democracy is a system of government by the people, although in practice the people govern through their elected representatives. By implication, the major influence on representatives' decisions should be the voters' policy preferences.

©Brand X Pictures/PunchStock

Is that claim fact, or is it fake?

Political scientists Martin Gilens and Benjamin Page recently conducted a massive study to address the question of policy influence. They examined nearly 1,800 policy decisions between 1981 and 2002 on which there was related polling data on Americans' policy preferences. They then tested lawmakers' policy decisions against four possible explanations: whether their decisions aligned with the preferences of the majority of citizens ("majoritarian electoral democracy"), with the preferences of wealthier citizens ("economic-elite domination), with the preferences of mass-based interest groups ("majoritarian pluralism"), or with the preferences of business/professional interest groups ("biased pluralism").

Their analysis found that the preferences of the majority of citizens and those of mass-based interest groups did not have much influence of policy decisions. By contrast, the preferences of wealthy citizens and business/professional interest groups had a substantial influence.

Gilens and Page concluded: "majorities of the American public actually have little influence over the policies our government adopts. . . . policymaking is dominated by powerful business organizations and a small number of affluent Americans."[48] Other studies have found stronger evidence of majority influence,[49] but nearly all studies of policy influence have concluded that interest groups, particularly those associated with business, exert a powerful influence on the choices made by the people's elected representatives.

SUMMARY

A political interest group is composed of a set of individuals organized to promote a shared concern. Most interest groups owe their existence to factors other than politics. These groups form for economic reasons, such as the pursuit of profit, and they maintain themselves by making profits (in the case of corporations) or by providing their members with private goods, such as jobs and wages. Economic groups include corporations, trade associations, labor unions, farm organizations, and professional associations. Collectively, economic groups are by far the largest set of organized interests. The group system tends to favor interests that are already economically and socially advantaged.

Citizens' groups do not have the same organizational advantages as economic groups. They depend on voluntary contributions from potential members, who may lack interest and resources or who recognize that they will get the collective good from a group's activity even if they do not participate (the free-rider problem). Citizens' groups include public-interest, single-issue, and ideological groups. Their numbers have increased dramatically since the 1960s despite their organizational problems.

Organized interests seek influence largely by lobbying public officials and contributing to election campaigns. Using an inside strategy, lobbyists develop direct contacts with legislators, government bureaucrats, and members of the judiciary in order to persuade them to accept the group's perspective on policy. Groups also use an outside strategy, seeking to mobilize public support for their goals. This strategy relies in part on grassroots lobbying—encouraging group members and the public to communicate their policy views to officials. Outside lobbying also includes efforts to elect officeholders who will support group aims. Through political action committees (PACs), organized groups now provide nearly a fourth of all contributions received by congressional candidates. A more recent development is the emergence of super PACs. They are independent campaign committees that can raise and spend nearly unrestricted amounts of money on elections as long as they do not coordinate their efforts with those of the candidate they are supporting.

The policies that emerge from the group system bring benefits to many of society's interests and often serve the collective interest as well. But when groups can essentially dictate policies, the common good is rarely served. The majority's interest is subordinated to group (minority) interests. In most instances, the minority consists of business firms and individuals who already enjoy a substantial share of society's benefits.

©gangliu10/Getty Images

CRITICAL THINKING ZONE

KEY TERMS

citizens' (noneconomic) groups (*p. 262*)
collective (public) goods (*p. 266*)
economic groups (*p. 259*)
free-rider problem (*p. 266*)
inside lobbying (*p. 268*)
interest group (*p. 257*)
iron triangle (*p. 273*)

issue network (*p. 274*)
lobbying (*p. 268*)
outside lobbying (*p. 275*)
political action committee (PAC)
(*p. 276*)
private (individual) goods (*p. 266*)
super PACs (*p. 277*)

APPLYING THE ELEMENTS OF CRITICAL THINKING

Conceptualizing: How do iron triangles and issue networks differ?

Synthesizing: Contrast the methods of inside lobbying with those of outside lobbying.

Analyzing: Why are there so many more organized interest groups in the United States than in other Western democracies? Why are so many of these groups organized around economic interests, particularly business?

EXTRA CREDIT

A Book Worth Reading: Thomas T. Holyoke, *The Ethical Lobbyist: Reforming Washington's Influence Industry* (Washington, D.C.: Georgetown University Press, 2016). This brief, well-written book defines the principles for reforming lobbying in ways that would improve government.

A Website Worth Visiting: www.opensecrets.org. The Center for Responsive Politics is a nonpartisan, nonprofit organization. Its website includes up-to-date analysis and data on lobbying, PAC spending, and other interest-group activity.

PARTICIPATE!

Consider contributing to a citizens' interest group. Such groups depend on members' donations for operating funds. Citizens' groups cover the political spectrum from right to left and touch on nearly every conceivable public issue. You will not have difficulty locating a group through the Internet that has policy goals consistent with your beliefs and values. If you are interested in contributing your time instead, some citizens' groups (for example, PIRG) have college chapters that might provide opportunities for you to work on issues of personal interest.

CHAPTER *10*

THE NEWS MEDIA AND THE INTERNET: COMMUNICATING POLITICS

©Le Moal Olivier/123RF

❝ The press in America . . . determines what people will think and talk about, an authority that in other nations is reserved for tyrants, priests, parties, and mandarins.❞

THEODORE H. WHITE[1]

On March 8, 2018, President Donald Trump announced sweeping new tariffs on imported steel and aluminum. Were the tariffs a good idea, or a lousy one? America's news outlets offered sharply different answers to that question. *The Wall Street Journal* worried that the tariffs would drive up consumer prices, saying they could raise the cost of a new car by $300. *Breitbart News* praised the tariffs, claiming they would create 19,000 new jobs in the steel and aluminum industries. On her MSNBC talk show, Rachel Maddow criticized the tariffs, saying Trump was clueless about trade policy. On his Fox News talk show, Sean Hannity embraced the tariffs, saying they were part of Trump's efforts to "protect and build" America. *The Washington Post* described the tariffs as "stupid." CNN quoted a steel executive who said simply, "thank you, Mr. President."

The **news** is mainly an account of obtruding events, particularly those that are *timely* (new or unfolding developments rather than old or static ones),

287

dramatic (striking developments rather than commonplace ones), and *compelling* (developments that arouse people's emotions).[2] Trump's announcement on steel and aluminum tariffs fit that model. It was a sharp break from past policy with possibly far-reaching effects and was thus a dramatic and compelling development. At the same time, the news is not fixed in stone. News outlets differ in their reporting practices and thus in how they portray developments. Trump's announcement was big news in every outlet, but it was presented differently from one outlet to the next.

News outlets are a key intermediary between American citizens and their leaders. For nearly everyone, politics is a secondhand experience, something they hear about through the media rather than observe directly. However, the media are a different kind of intermediary than are political parties and interest groups. Parties and groups seek influence in order to promote particular leaders or policies. Some media outlets have that as their goal, but other media outlets seek primarily to inform the public about politics and still other media outlets use politics primarily as a way to entertain their audience. Most citizens are exposed in varying degrees to all three of these types of media outlets.

This chapter describes the media's role in American politics, starting with the history of the media and proceeding from there to a discussion of the media's functions. The chapter concludes with a look at the media audience. These are the main ideas presented in the chapter:

- *The American news media were initially tied to the nation's political party system (the partisan press) but gradually developed an independent position (the objective press).* In the process, the news shifted from a political orientation, which emphasizes political values and ideas, to a journalistic orientation, which stresses newsworthy information and events.

- *In recent decades, new forms of media have emerged—cable television shows, partisan talk shows, and Internet outlets.* Their norms and standards differ from each other, and from those of the traditional news media.

- *Media outlets seek to attract an audience by meeting people's information needs, playing to their partisan bias, or feeding their desire to be entertained.* All media outlets engage in each of these activities to a degree, but most outlets have one of the three as the primary focus.

- *The audience for public affairs has been fragmenting, largely as a result of the expanded number of media outlets created by the advent of cable television and the Internet.* Citizens have more choices than ever before and have tailored their choices to their information interests and partisan leanings.

President Donald Trump's announcement of tariffs on imported steel and aluminum launched a flurry of conflicting news reports and analyses. (*Source:* Official White House Photo by Joyce N. Boghosian)

MEDIA CHANGE: FROM THE NATION'S FOUNDING TO TODAY

The writers of the Constitution recognized a need to protect the press so as to ensure the free flow of information on which a self-governing nation depends.[3] The First Amendment guarantees freedom of the press, a right that the Supreme Court has vigorously upheld by limiting government's ability to interfere with publication efforts (see Chapter 4).

Press freedom has contributed to a robust American media system, although a system that has been shaped throughout the nation's history by technological change and by the need of political leaders to communicate with the public and the need for media outlets to secure the revenue required to stay in business.

Rise of the Partisan Press

America's early political leaders quickly recognized the value of newspapers in promoting their objectives. Alexander Hamilton persuaded John Fenno to start a newspaper, the *Gazette of the United States,* as a means of publicizing the policies of George Washington's administration. To finance the paper, Hamilton, as secretary of the treasury, granted it the Treasury Department's printing contracts. Hamilton's political rival, Thomas Jefferson, dismissed the *Gazette*'s reporting as "pure Toryism" and convinced Philip Freneau to start the *National Gazette* as an opposition paper. Jefferson, as secretary of state, gave Freneau the authority to print State Department documents.

Early newspapers were printed a page at a time on flat presses, a process that limited production and kept the cost of the newspaper copy beyond the reach of most citizens. Leading papers such as the *Gazette of the United States* had fewer than 1,500 readers and needed party patronage to survive. Not surprisingly, the "news" they printed was laced with partisanship.[4] In this era of the **partisan press,** most newspapers openly backed one party or the other.

The partisan press persisted for more than a century, although it was gradually weakened by technological change. As the telegraph came into widespread use in the middle of the 1800s, newspapers had access to breaking news about events outside the local area, which led them to substitute news reports for partisan commentary. The invention in the late 19th century of the power-driven printing press was equally important in that it enabled

Yellow journalism was built on sensationalism. William Randolph Hearst's *New York Journal* was among the newspapers that through their inflammatory reporting whipped up public support for a war in Cuba against Spain. Shown here awaiting burial at Arlington National Cemetery are the coffins of U.S. troops who died during the Spanish American War. The Washington Monument is visible in the distance. (*Source:* Library of Congress, Prints and Photographs Division [LC-USZ62-41746])

publishers to print the newspapers more cheaply and quickly. As circulations rose, so did advertising revenues, reducing newspapers' dependence on government patronage.

By 1900, some American newspapers had daily circulations in excess of 100,000 copies. The period marked the height of newspapers' power and the low point in their civic responsibility. A new style of reporting—"yellow journalism"—had emerged as a way of selling papers. It was "a shrieking, gaudy, sensation-loving, devil-may-care kind of journalism which lured the reader by any possible means."[5] A circulation battle between William Randolph Hearst's *New York Journal* and Joseph Pulitzer's *New York World* may have contributed to the outbreak of the Spanish-American War through sensational (and largely inaccurate) reports on the cruelty of Spanish rule in Cuba. A young Frederic Remington (who later became a noted painter and sculptor), working as a news artist for Hearst, planned to return home because Cuba appeared calm and safe, but Hearst allegedly cabled back: "Please remain. You furnish the pictures and I'll furnish the war."[6]

Rise of Objective Journalism

The excesses of yellow journalism led some publishers to devise ways of reporting the news more responsibly. One step was to separate the newspaper's advertising department from its news department, thus reducing the influence of advertisers on news content. A second development was **objective journalism,** which is based on the reporting of "facts" rather than opinions and is "fair" in that it presents both sides of partisan debate. An architect of the new model of reporting was Adolph Ochs of *The New York Times*. Ochs bought the *Times* in 1896, when its daily circulation was 9,000. Four years later, its readership had grown to 82,000. Ochs told his reporters that he "wanted as little partisanship as possible . . . as few judgments as possible."[7] The *Times* gradually acquired a reputation as the country's best newspaper. Objective reporting was also promoted through newly formed journalism schools, such as those at Columbia University and the University of Missouri. Within a few decades, objective journalism had become the dominant reporting model.

Until the 20th century, the print media were the only form of mass communication. By the 1920s, however, hundreds of radio stations were broadcasting throughout the nation. At first the government did not regulate radio broadcasting. The result was chaos. Nearby stations often used the same or adjacent radio frequencies, interfering with each other's broadcasts. Finally, in 1934, Congress passed the Communications Act, which regulated broadcasting and created the Federal Communications Commission (FCC) to oversee the process. Broadcasters had to be licensed by the FCC, and because broadcasting frequencies are limited in number, licensees were required to be impartial in their political coverage and were prohibited from selling or giving airtime to a political candidate without offering to sell or give an equal amount of airtime to other candidates for the same office. (An exception was later made for election debates; broadcasters can televise them even if third-party candidates are excluded.)

Television followed radio, and by the late 1950s, more than 90 percent of American homes had a TV set. In this period, the FCC imposed a second restriction on broadcasters, the Fairness Doctrine. It required broadcasters to "afford reasonable opportunity for the discussion of conflicting views of public importance." Broadcasters were prohibited from using their news coverage to promote one party or issue position at the expense of another. In effect, the objective-reporting model practiced voluntarily by the newspapers was imposed by law on broadcasters.

At peak in the 1970s, the evening newscasts of ABC, CBS, and NBC attracted a combined audience in excess of 50 million viewers. CBS had the largest audience. When asked in polls who was the "most trusted man" in America, respondents singled out CBS news anchor Walter Cronkite. (©CBS Photo Archive/Getty Images)

During the era of objective journalism, the news was not entirely devoid of partisanship. Although broadcasters were prohibited by law from editorializing, newspapers were not. Most of them backed one political party or the other on their editorial and opinion (op-ed) pages. Nevertheless, it was difficult to tell from a paper's news pages which party it backed editorially. Nearly all newspapers highlighted the same national stories each day, and if a high-ranking public official got embroiled in a scandal or policy blunder, they played it up, whether the official was a Republican or a Democrat.

Given that the United States had roughly 1,500 daily newspapers and 1,000 local television outlets, it might be thought that Americans would have been exposed to widely different versions of the news. But the objective model, with its emphasis on factual and balanced reporting, led journalists in different news outlets to cover political developments in similar ways. They did not always do so, but in their quest for balance they tended toward a common interpretation of political developments, as opposed to a Republican version or a Democratic version. In addition, most news outlets lacked the resources to gather news outside their own location and relied for this coverage on the wire services, particularly the Associated Press (AP), which had 3,000 reporters stationed throughout the country and the world to gather news stories and transmit them to subscribing news organizations. The AP, because it served the full range of American news outlets, studiously avoided partisanship in preparing its stories. Local television stations also depended on outside sources for their national news coverage. Television production is extremely expensive, which limited the ability of local stations to produce anything except local news. For their national coverage, they relied on video feeds from the broadcast television networks—ABC, CBS, and NBC.

The result was what scholars call *the information commons*—a shared set of facts and ideas transmitted to them through the news media.[8] Not every American derived the same meaning from the news they were getting, and the reporting had its blind spots.[9] But it was a balanced and common rendition of the news that fostered a shared understanding of the nation's politics.

Rise of Cable TV and Partisan Talk Shows

The information commons began to break apart in the 1980s. A major development occurred in 1987 when the FCC rescinded the Fairness Doctrine, claiming that the emergence of cable television and the expansion of FM radio had alleviated the problem of scarce frequencies. Radio stations quickly responded to the change in policy. They had previously been required to air public affairs content, which meant that even radio stations that featured rock or country music carried brief newscasts each hour. When the Fairness Doctrine was rescinded, most of them dropped their newscasts.

The elimination of the Fairness Doctrine also spawned partisan radio talk shows. The policy had discouraged the airing of such shows by requiring stations to offer a balanced lineup of liberal and conservative content. When the doctrine was eliminated in 1987, station owners no longer had to worry about carrying programs that ran counter to their political beliefs. Hundreds of radio stations shifted to talk shows, most of which had a conservative slant.[10] Partisan talk shows offered a version of politics radically different—more opinionated and less devoted to factual accuracy—than that of traditional news outlets. They quickly found an audience. In less than a decade, the number of weekly talk-show listeners jumped nearly 10-fold to almost 20 million people (see Figure 10-1).

During this same period, cable television came into existence. There were virtually no cable channels in the 1970s, but by 1990 half of American homes had cable access. Because cable television was transmitted by privately owned wire rather than through broadcasting, it was not subject to broadcasting regulations. Nevertheless, when media mogul Ted Turner in 1980 started CNN, the first of the cable news channels, he instructed his correspondents to use the objective model of reporting.

Turner's policy was not followed by Fox News, the second cable news channel. The success of conservative talk radio had convinced billionaire Rupert Murdoch to start Fox in 1996. Murdoch reasoned that conservatives, because of their distrust of the established networks, would embrace a channel that offered a conservative version of news. He hired Roger Ailes, a Republican political consultant, to run it. Ailes in turn hired a number of conservative

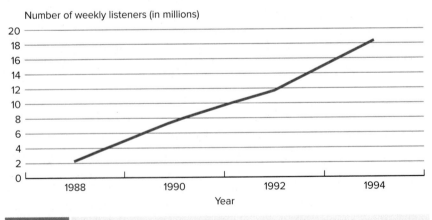

figure 10-1   THE RISE OF PARTISAN TALK RADIO

After the Fairness Doctrine was eliminated in 1987, partisan talk radio quickly became a major source of information for millions of Americans. (*Source:* Figures compiled by author from multiple sources.)

talk show hosts. Within a few years, propelled by a largely Republican audience, Fox News had become the nation's most heavily watched cable news network.

In the early 2000s, the third major cable news network, MSNBC, recast itself as the liberal alternative to Fox. It followed the Fox model, placing less emphasis on news reporting than on talk shows, building its early evening programming around its two biggest attractions, Rachel Maddow and Chris Matthews.

Partisanship also seeped into other cable programming, particularly comedy talk shows. Unlike partisan talk shows, where the top draws are conservative hosts like Rush Limbaugh, Sean Hannity, and Laura Ingraham, the top-rated partisan comedy talk shows have liberal hosts like Stephen Colbert, Bill Maher, John Oliver, and Samantha Bee.

Rise of the Internet

Cable television expanded Americans' media options. The Internet expanded them even further. Although the First Amendment protects each individual's right to press freedom, this right in practice has been confined to a tiny few. Journalist A. J. Liebling wrote that freedom of the press belonged to those with enough money to own a news outlet.[11] Today, because of the Internet,

Broadcast news dominated television until the advent of cable. Today, the ABC, CBS, and NBC newscasts compete with Fox News, CNN, and MSNBC for viewers. Cable news includes partisan organizations. Fox News pursues a politically conservative news agenda while MSNBC pursues a liberal one. (©Scott J. Ferrell/Congressional Quarterly/Alamy)

and its lower cost of entry, freedom of the press is actively enjoyed by a larger number of Americans than ever before.

Nevertheless, the Internet has not been the democratic instrument that some analysts expected. Although there are literally hundreds upon hundreds of websites where news is regularly displayed, news on the Internet is characterized by what analysts call "the long tail."[12] When news-based websites are arrayed by the number of visitors to each site, there are a few heavily visited sites on one end and thousands of lightly visited sites on the other end—the long tail.[13] Most of the heavily visited sites are those of the traditional media, including CNN.com and nytimes.com. Moreover, most of the other heavily visited sites, such as Yahoo News, carry news that was gathered and reported first by the established media. Audience concentration has also occurred for search engines and social media. Two-thirds of online users rely on Google as their core search engine and four-fifths of online users have a Facebook account.

Nevertheless, some outlets that started on the Internet have succeeded in attracting a large audience (see Table 10-1). The largest such website is the *Huffington Post,* which was started by liberal activist Arianna Huffington. Second is the alt-right *Breitbart News,* which was founded over a decade ago and is backed by conservative donor Robert Mercer. *Breitbart* attracts about 75 million visitors a month to its site.[14] Until his firing in 2017, one of *Breitbart's* key figures was Steve Bannon, who served for a time as President Trump's top political adviser. In addition to websites, the Internet has spawned thousands of bloggers, many of whom rely on YouTube to carry their messages. Those with the largest audiences are concentrated on the extreme right and have 100,000 or more followers.[15]

Most of the partisan messaging on the Internet is done by Americans, but foreign actors are also involved. During the 2016 presidential campaign, Russia alone is believed to have paid more than a thousand individuals to spread false information about Hillary Clinton.[16]

table 10-1	MONTHLY UNIQUE VISITORS TO THE 10 MOST POPULAR POLITICAL WEBSITES		
1. Huffington Post	80,000,000	6. Slate	18,000,000
2. Breitbart News	60,000,000	7. Daily Kos	15,000,000
3. Drudge Report	30,000,000	8. Info Wars	9,000,000
4. Politico	25,000,000	9. Salon	8,000,000
5. The Hill	20,000,000	10. The Blaze	7,700,000

Source: eBiz|MBA.com, "Top 15 Most Popular Political Websites, July 2017," http://www.ebizmba.com/articles/political-websites.

THE MEDIA: CONTENT AND FUNCTIONS

Media outlets act as *gatekeepers*. Among the countless message possibilities each day, they determine which ones will be transmitted to the public. In turn, their messages affect what citizens will see and hear, and thus what they will think and talk about.

What determines these selections? For one thing, messages are shaped by the need of media outlets to attract an audience.[17] Without advertising or other revenue sources, a media outlet would quickly go out of business. Media outlets typically attract attention by providing content that meets people's information needs, plays to their partisan bias, or feeds their desire to be entertained.

Information-Centered Communication

Media outlets, whether broadcast, print, cable, or on the Internet, that are in the business of creating and reporting original news stories are called the **news media (press).** They traditionally have performed three functions—the signaling, common-carrier, and watchdog functions—that contribute to the public's information needs. We'll look first at the signaling function.

The Signaling Function   The news media's responsibilities include a **signaling (signaler) function**—alerting the public to important developments as soon as possible after they happen. Occasionally, an event enters the news stream through social media, usually when someone on the scene captures it on a cellphone camera. Nevertheless, hundreds of news stories enter the news stream daily, and the great majority of them are generated by the news media.

In their capacity as signalers, the media have the power to focus the public's attention. The term **agenda setting** is used to describe the media's ability to influence what is on people's minds.[18] By covering the same events, problems, issues, and leaders—simply by giving them space or time in the news—the media place them on the public agenda. The press, as Bernard Cohen notes, "may not be successful much of the time in telling people what to think, but it is stunningly successful in telling them what to think about."[19]

A striking example occurred in the early 1990s when local television stations, in an attempt to bolster sagging news ratings, upped their crime coverage. "If it bleeds it leads" became the mantra of local TV news. Meanwhile, the national media were playing up several high-profile murder cases including the kidnap-murder of 12-year-old Polly Klaas in California. Crime was the most heavily reported national issue, overshadowing even coverage of the nation's struggling economy. The effect on public opinion was dramatic. In the previous decade, no more than 5 percent of Americans had believed at any time that crime was the country's biggest problem. By 1994, however, more than

The news media act as signalers, bringing important developments to the public's attention. When wildfires erupted in California in 2017 and 2018, news organizations helped alert residents to the dangers posed by the fires, which were the most extensive and costly wildfires on record in California. (©Paul Higley/Alamy)

40 percent of Americans said that crime was the top issue facing the nation. Lawmakers got caught up in the public's anxiety by enacting tough new sentencing policies and building new prisons at the fastest rate in the nation's history. The irony was that the level of crime in America was actually *declining* during this period. According to U.S. Justice Department statistics, the rate of violent crime dropped by 5 percent between 1990 and 1994.[20]

The Common-Carrier Function   The press also exercises a **common-carrier function,** serving as a conduit through which political leaders communicate with the public. The justification for this role is straightforward. Citizens cannot support or oppose a leader's plans and actions if they do not know about them, and leaders require news coverage if they are to get the public's attention and support.

In fact, national news focuses largely on the words and actions of top political leaders, particularly the president (see Chapter 12). More than two hundred reporters are assigned to cover the White House, where they receive daily briefings. The presidency gets substantially more coverage in the national press than does Congress and its 535 members.[21] That pattern was never more apparent than during Trump's early period as president, when he received more attention from the press than any president of the television age.[22] Even his frequent tweets prompted journalists to drop what they were covering and chase the latest one. Trump's tweets attracted a large audience, but it was not because people were glued to his Twitter feed. An estimated 99 percent of Americans' exposure to Trump's tweets was from hearing about them through stories generated by the news media.[23]

Although officials sometimes succeed in getting favorable coverage, two things blunt their efforts to manage the news. One is journalists' norm of partisan neutrality. Reporters depend heavily on official sources, but they often present the positions of leaders of both parties—the "he said, she said" style of reporting. If the president, secretary of defense, Senate majority leader, or other high-ranking official says something newsworthy, the news report often includes a contrary statement by another individual, usually of the opposite party.

Second, although news typically originates in the words and actions of political leaders, they do not monopolize the news, particularly on television.[24] In an effort to keep their viewers tuned in, television newscasts use a fast-paced format in which each story has multiple pieces woven together in story form, with the journalist acting as the storyteller. One indicator of this format is the "shrinking sound bite." In the 1960s, a newsmaker's sound bite (the length of time within a television story that a newsmaker speaks without interruption) was more than 40 seconds, on average.[25] Today, the average sound bite is less than 10 seconds, barely enough time for the newsmaker to utter a long sentence. It is the journalists, not the newsmakers, who do most of the talking on television news.[26]

The fact that journalists shape the content of their news stories is a major source of their power, **Framing** is the process by which journalists select particular aspects of situations and craft their stories around them.[27] In covering a congressional debate, for example, journalists could frame their stories in the context of the substance of the debate. Alternatively, they could frame their stories in the context of the partisan conflict over the proposed bill. As it happens, journalists typically frame their stories in the second way.[28] They portray politics largely as a fight for partisan advantage, which has what scholars call a priming effect.[29] **Priming** refers to the way in which the context established by media messages affects how people will interpret the information they receive.[30] When seeing or hearing something about politics, most people do not judge it by all that they know. They respond in terms of the thoughts that come most readily to mind. When the press consistently frames politicians as individuals who seek to win at all costs, people are "primed" to see politicians as self-serving. They'll ordinarily assume that what a politician has done is motivated by self-interest and judge the politician's actions through that lens.[31]

The Watchdog Function   The American press has assumed responsibility for exposing incompetent, hypocritical, and corrupt officials. In this **watchdog function,** the press exposes officials who violate accepted legal, ethical, or performance standards. The American news media have rightfully been called a fourth branch of government—part of the political system's checks on abuses by those in power.

Journalists are typically skeptical of politicians' motives and actions. A turning point was the Watergate scandal. Led by investigative reporters at *The Washington Post,* the press uncovered evidence that high-ranking officials in the Nixon administration had lied about their role in the 1972 burglary of the Democratic National Committee's headquarters and the subsequent cover-up. President Richard Nixon was forced to resign, as was his attorney general, John Mitchell.

Ever since Watergate, the press has been quick to pounce on any sign of public wrongdoing. After it became known that Hillary Clinton had sent and received e-mails as secretary of state from a private server rather than the Department of State's secure server, the news media called it a scandal and highlighted the story for months on end, contributing to the public's perception that Clinton was not trustworthy.[32] The controversy widened during the closing weeks of the 2016 presidential campaign when WikiLeaks made public thousands of e-mails hacked from the accounts of Clinton aides, including her campaign manager, John Podesta. The hacked e-mails included excerpts from speeches that Clinton had privately delivered to Wall Street firms and that contained statements at odds with some of her public remarks.

The release of Clinton's e-mails by WikiLeaks sparked another round of watchdog reporting when it was discovered that Russians had been the ones who hacked the e-mails, presumably to damage Clinton's campaign and promote Trump's campaign. As it became clear that Russian meddling extended into other areas of the campaign, news organizations launched investigations. *The Washington Post* and *The New York Times* alone published dozens of stories detailing what they had found (see "How the U.S. Differs").

Digital technology has enlarged the media's watchdog capacity. Nearly everything that public figures communicate through the Internet, and even some of what they say in private settings, is recorded in one way or another and can prove damaging if it becomes known. One such recording sent Donald Trump's 2016 campaign into temporary tailspin. Trump was caught on microphone making lewd comments and bragging about kissing and groping women

HOW THE U.S. DIFFERS

CRITICAL THINKING THROUGH COMPARISONS

Russian Interference in Western Elections

After the 2016 presidential election, Americans became aware of Russia's attempts to influence the outcome. What many Americans might not know is that Russia's activities were part of a larger pattern. In the past few years, Russia has used Internet messaging to disrupt elections in a dozen Western countries, including Germany, France, Great Britain, Norway, the Netherlands, and Austria.

Q: Is there a pattern to Russia's efforts?

A: A common element of Russia's disinformation efforts is to pit citizens against each other. A widely circulated fake story during the 2016 U.S. election, for instance, tried to stir up anger against Muslims. It falsely claimed that Muslim men in Michigan with multiple wives were collecting welfare checks for each of them.[33] Such messages seek to undermine the trust between citizens that's essential in a democracy. Russia has also tried to stir up resentments that could weaken Western alliances. In referendums in Britain and the Netherlands, for example, Russia's disinformation efforts aimed at undermining support for the European Union. Finally, Russia has tried to tilt popular support toward right-wing parties, on the assumption that such parties are more likely to take ultranationalist foreign policy positions rather than positions that would oppose Russia's efforts to expand its sphere of influence. That strategy was employed during the French, Austrian, and Bulgarian elections.

What was different about Russia's involvement in the 2016 U.S. election was the scale of the effort. It was more extensive than the meddling in other Western democracies. Facebook estimated that 150 million Americans, more than half of the adult population, received Russia-sponsored content during the election.

without their consent, saying that "when you're a star, they let you do it." Trump had made the claim in 2005 as he was arriving at a studio lot to make an appearance on a TV show, unaware that the microphone was open. The audio recording was provided by an anonymous source to *The Washington Post*, which quickly published it.

Partisan-Centered Communication

The **partisan function**–acting as an advocate for a particular viewpoint or interest–was traditionally the responsibility of political leaders, institutions, and organizations. Today, however, a large number of media outlets and programs operate in this way. They're in the business of promoting a partisan agenda by playing to their audience's partisan bias.

Radio and television partisan talk shows are the most visible form of this type of media. When talk shows emerged in the late 1980s, their hosts discovered through trial and error what listeners wanted to hear. Thoughtful give and take between guests turned out to be a ratings bust. What listeners liked best were rants about the opposing party, a discovery that, as Tufts University's Sarah Sobieraj and Jeffrey Berry found in their landmark study, has made partisan "outrage" the basis for their programming.[34]

Outrage is the selling card of conservative and liberal talk shows alike. They differ in their ideology but not in how in how they speak, the images they invoke, or the devices they use. Name calling, misrepresentation, mockery, character assassination, belittling, and imagined catastrophe are but a few of their tools. The goal is to make the target look stupid, inept, or dangerous.

MSNBC's Rachel Maddow is one of the best known partisan talk show hosts. Maddow offers a liberal slant on news developments. Like other high-profile talk show hosts, Maddow is one of the highest paid individuals in media today–an indication of the popularity and profitability of talk shows. (©Newsies Media/Alamy)

Senator Charles Schumer is "Up-Chuck," Hillary Clinton is a "feminazi," Tea Party members are "a bunch of greedy, water-carrying corporative-slave hypocrites," Obama supporters are "Obamatards," and Trump is "a clown" and "an orange-utan." As for the ordinary citizens who side with the other party, they're "fools" or "morons."[35] The partisan divide is the main point of attack for talk show hosts, but the cultural divide is a close second. Issues are played less as policy questions than as questions of cultural identity. On conservative talk shows, gun control isn't about trigger locks or background checks but instead about guns as cultural identity. Attempts to control guns are portrayed as a liberal plot to destroy a way of life that's been around since frontier days.[36]

Outrage is also the approach of most partisan Internet sites. They seek to inflame the partisan divide by nearly every conceivable means, including, in some cases, outright lies and distortions. The clearest example is *fake news*—entirely fictional stories that originate on the Internet and aim to undermine a political opponent. Even more extreme, however, are the operatives who offer uncompromising world views designed to demonize particular groups. One such operative, who calls himself "Black Pigeon Speaks," espouses a white nationalist ideology wherein Jewish bankers are trapping us in debt slavery, Muslim immigrants are plotting to impose Sharia law, and women are betraying their biological heritage by placing their careers above child-rearing. Black Pigeon Speaks said of women, "This half-century long experiment of women's liberation and political enfranchisement has ended in disaster for the West."[37]

Not all partisan programs fit the outrage model. In their newscasts, Fox and MSNBC, for example, stick largely to the objective journalism model, with its emphasis on factual accuracy. The newscasts on Fox and MSNBC differ primarily in the stories they choose to highlight, each playing up those that they think will work to the advantage of their side of the political divide. During Trump's first year in office, for example, conservative-leaning Fox played down the story of Russian meddling in the 2016 presidential election while playing up the rising stock market, while liberal-leaning MSNBC did just the opposite.[38]

Entertainment-Centered Communication

News has long included a dose of entertainment as a means of attracting a wider audience than would otherwise be the case. The legendary publisher William Randolph Hearst, who helped pioneer yellow journalism, said that an "editor has no objection to facts if they are also novel. But he would prefer a novelty that is not a fact to a fact that is not a novelty."[47]

The onset of cable increased the entertainment content in traditional news outlets. As cable spread into American homes in the 1980s and 1990s, the audience for traditional outlets began to shrink. Americans now had additional choices,

Detecting Misinformation

Are the Traditional News Media Politically Biased?

The traditional news media—the nation's daily papers and broadcast television outlets—say they report the news "objectively"—that they strive for factual accuracy and fair treatment of both sides of the partisan divide. Some Americans dispute that notion, claiming instead that the traditional media have a liberal bias.[39]

Is that claim fact, or is it fake?

Scholars have not found evidence of overwhelming liberal bias in the traditional media. Dozens of studies have investi-

©Andrew Cline/Shutterstock

gated the issue and, although there is evidence of a liberal bias, it's not anywhere on the scale that some Americans believe.[40] And partisan slant varies from one news outlet to the next. Those with more liberal audiences tend to offer more liberal content while those with more conservative audiences tilt conservative in their coverage, suggesting that marketing, rather than politics, drives much of the bias that exists.[41]

Nor is it true that the liberal side routinely gets the better coverage. Over the full course of the 2016 presidential campaign, for example, the candidate with the most negative coverage was Hillary Clinton, not Donald Trump. His coverage was 56 percent negative to 44 positive during the campaign, whereas her coverage was 62 percent negative to 38 percent positive.[42]

As the negative coverage of both Trump and Clinton might suggest, the real bias of the traditional press is not partisan in nature. Negativity is its true bias.[43] The news turned negative at the time of Watergate and has stayed that way. The networks' preference for "bad news" can be seen, for example, in their coverage of Congress. Congressional coverage has been steadily negative since the 1970s, regardless of which party controlled Congress or how much or little was accomplished. "Over the years," concluded scholar Mark Rozell, "press coverage of Congress has moved from healthy skepticism to outright cynicism."[44]

The traditional media's negativity helps explain why they are widely perceived as biased. Research indicates that negative news is perceived

Continued

differently by those who support and those who oppose the politician being criticized. Opponents tend to see the criticism as valid, whereas supporters tend to see it as unjustified and therefore biased.[45] It is not surprising, then, that Democrats during Bill Clinton's presidency thought that the networks favored the Republicans while Republicans during George W. Bush's presidency thought that the networks favored the Democrats. Such findings do not mean that the networks are completely unbiased, but they do indicate that much of the perceived bias is in the eye of the beholder.[46]

everything from HBO's movies to ESPN's sporting events. Soon thereafter a theatrical style of news emerged that was designed to compete with cable entertainment. It was aimed at the marginal news consumer—those with a weak interest in news who might stay tuned in if the news was made more entertaining. Celebrity gossip, hard-luck stories, good-luck tales, sensational crimes, scandals in high places, and other human interest stories became a larger part of the news mix. Such stories were labeled *soft news* to distinguish them from traditional *hard news* stories (breaking events involving public figures, major issues, or significant disruptions to daily routines).[48] A few news outlets, including *The New York Times*, *The Wall Street Journal*, and *The Washington Post*, stuck to the old way of doing things, but most outlets softened their news in an effort to attract a broader audience.[49]

Of the cable news networks, CNN is the one that most fully treats news as a form of entertainment. An example is CNN's coverage of Malaysian Airline Flight 370. The flight disappeared on March 8, 2014, while carrying 227 passengers and a crew of 12 on a scheduled route from Kuala Lumpur to Beijing. On the way, it turned westward and disappeared from radar, never to be found. CNN began its coverage reporting on a fatal accident before turning it into a global mystery story. Night after night for weeks on end, panels of "experts" offered competing theories on the location of Flight 370. One night, a caller asked whether the jetliner might have been sucked into a small black hole. The host suggested that the possibility deserved consideration before a guest informed him that "a small black hole would suck in our entire universe." CNN's coverage became the butt of jokes on late-night comedy shows, but CNN had the last laugh. Its ratings jumped dramatically and stayed high. CNN didn't cut back on the Flight 370 story until the ratings sagged.[50]

The feverish competition for audience resulting from the advent of cable and the Internet has led media outlets to search for ways to gain a competitive advantage. A service called CrowdTangle, for example, is used by hundreds of local newsrooms. It alerts them to topics that are trending on social media, a signal to begin producing stories on that topic until the traffic slows down.[51] Many of the newer digital publishers have embraced the entertainment strategy,

CASE
STUDY

Politics in Action

The Ebola Scare

The news media are a civic institution, protected by the First Amendment's free-press guarantee and charged with informing the public. But they're also business organizations that depend on advertising for revenue. Even serious subjects can get distorted by the media's desire to attract a large audience. In 2014, an Ebola epidemic broke out in West

Source: CDC/National Institute of Allergy and Infectious Diseases (NIAID)

Africa. When the first Ebola patient in the United States was diagnosed, many news outlets sensationalized the story. Some reports went so far as to speculate what would happen if Ebola, which is transmitted by direct contact with bodily fluids, went airborne and could be caught in the same way as a cold or the flu is caught. "Ebola in the Air? A Nightmare That Could Happen" is how CNN headlined one of its stories, which also warned that most people who get Ebola end up dead. In fact, however, there is *no* recorded case in the whole of human history in which a fluid-transmitted disease, like Ebola, has transformed itself into an airborne-transmitted disease. It might be theoretically possible, but, according to the World Health Organization, it has *never* happened.

"How worried are you that you or someone in your family will be exposed to the Ebola virus?"

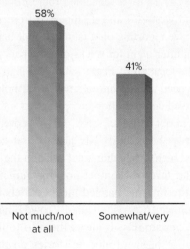

58%

41%

Not much/not at all   Somewhat/very

Continued

No one who contracted Ebola while in the United States died from it. But the sensationalized news coverage frightened millions of Americans, even those hundreds of miles from the nearest Ebola patient. Two in five Americans worried that they or a family member would catch the disease, as a Pew Research Center poll conducted early in the Ebola scare discovered.

Q: As a result of the special protections provided to the news media by the First Amendment, do they have an obligation to report the news in a responsible way, even if that results in smaller audiences?

ASK YOURSELF: Is the First Amendment intended to force individuals or organizations to act in a responsible way? Or is it intended to give them the freedom to act as they choose, free of government interference? Is hyped-up news a price that society must pay in order to receive the many positive benefits that come from having a free press?

doing little in the way of serious original reporting while letting readers' tastes drive what they display.[52] In posting its stories, *Upworthy* puts out a large sampling using a dozen or more versions of the headline. Whichever headline attracts the most attention—usually a variation of "You Won't Believe What Just Happened"—is then slapped on the rest of the feed.[53]

Nevertheless, the idea that news can be entertainment is clearest on the humor programs that focus on current affairs. One of the first was *The Daily Show*, hosted by Jon Stewart. Its format had the look of a conventional newscast, but its content aimed to entertain—its headlines were slanted, its news reports poked fun at those in power, it editorials blended satire with serious commentary. It was a ratings hit and helped spawn similar programs, many of which are carried on Comedy Central and other nontraditional news channels. The most frequent target of their jokes is whoever happens to be president at the moment. During his first hundred days in office, Trump set the record for a seated president. According to a study by the Center for Media and Public Affairs, there were 1,060 jokes on the humor talk shows mocking Trump's performance as president—roughly 10 jokes per day on average.[54]

MEDIA AUDIENCES AND EFFECTS

The media system is far different today than it was only a few decades ago, and the effects are substantial. America's earlier media system was a low-choice system. Most locations had a single daily newspaper and, for those who wanted to watch television at the dinner hour, the choices were limited to three—the

ABC, CBS, or NBC evening news, each of which had nearly the same lineup of stories told in much the same way. In contrast, Americans today have access to a **high-choice media system,** one in which they have a wide variety of alternatives.[55] As a result, people's exposure to politics and public affairs—what they see and hear, as well as what they choose not to see and hear—is largely within their control. A consequence is that the United States today has essentially three public affairs audiences—the traditional audience, the partisan audience, and, for lack of a better description, the inattentive audience.

The Traditional Audience

In the 1970s, news was the only available dinner-hour television programming and most viewers tuned in. More than 50 million viewers watched the network news each evening.[56] Newspaper circulation was also high. The combined daily circulation of morning and evening daily papers was roughly 60 million.[57] The introduction of cable television in the 1980s precipitated a decline in the audience of traditional news outlets. Today, the network evening newscasts draw roughly 25 million viewers each evening, while daily newspaper circulation is barely more than 30 million copies.[58]

The decline has not been as sharp as it might appear. Some newspaper readers now get their daily news online, and some television viewers rely on cable newscasts as their regular source of news. Nevertheless, the audience for traditional news outlets is significantly smaller than it was at peak. Although the traditional audience is still the largest one, it's been shrinking. So has the amount of time that people devote to traditional news. In the 1970s, the average reader devoted more than 30 minutes to reading the printed newspaper. It's now down to 16 minutes.[59] When people read a paper online, they spend even fewer minutes.[60]

Older Americans constitute the largest share of the traditional news audience. They came of age during the broadcast era and developed a habit of reading the print newspaper and watching newscasts at a scheduled time. In 1980, viewers of ABC, CBS, and NBC evening news were roughly 40 years of age, on average. Today, the average is roughly 60 years of age. Even the audience for cable news is aging—the average now exceeds 50 years of age.[61]

As a group, heavy consumers of traditional news are the best informed Americans. They are the citizens most likely to be aware of major developments. Newspaper reading in particular has been found to be correlated with a relatively high level of political knowledge.[62] Compared with other Americans, heavy consumers of traditional news also tend to hold relatively moderate political views as a result of their exposure to news that gives equal billing to the opposing parties.[63]

Nevertheless, most traditional news consumers fall short of being highly informed about politics. One reason is that citizens don't "study" the news, they "follow" it. Most of what people see and hear in the news is quickly forgotten. Moreover, issues do not figure all that prominently in the news. Issues are rooted in conditions that don't change much from week to week and thus don't yield the type of stories that journalists prize. That's true even of journalists in the top news outlets. During the closing weeks of the 2016 presidential election campaign, only 5 of 150 front-page *New York Times* articles compared Trump's and Clinton's policy stands and fewer than a dozen discussed their policy positions in detail.[64] Instead of issues, journalists focus on political conflict and strategy, which provide a constant source of fresh material.[65] Barely a day passes during an election when journalists don't cite a new opinion poll as proof that one side is getting the better of the other.[66]

In addition, the marketing strategy of blending soft news with hard news to broaden the appeal of news has diluted the coverage of public affairs. A study of broadcast evening news found, for example, that stories about government and politics has declined from about 70 percent of the newscast to roughly 50 percent.[67] Noting the shift in news content, New York University's Neil Postman warned about the consequences of treating news as a form of entertainment. "I am saying something far more serious than that we are being deprived of authentic information," wrote Postman. "I am saying we are losing our sense of what it means to be well informed. Ignorance is always correctable. But what shall we do if we take ignorance to be knowledge?"[68]

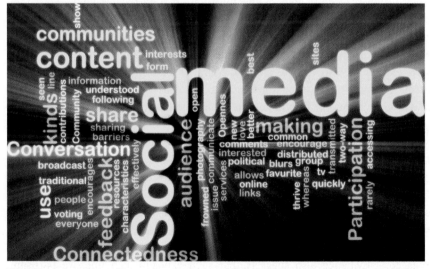

The Internet has changed the way many Americans get their information about public affairs. Even social media have become key links, although most of the news that circulates on social media originates with traditional news outlets. (©Kheng Guan Toh/Shutterstock)

The Partisan Audience

In the era of the information commons, partisan media outlets were few in number. Several weekly partisan magazines, such as *The Nation* and *The National Review*, were available. But when it came to daily news, there weren't any options in most locations. Today is different. On television, radio, the Internet, and social media, partisan outlets are readily available and easy to access.

Some Americans rely on partisan outlets as their primary information source.[69] They're still substantially outnumbered by those who prefer the traditional news media, but their numbers are growing.[70] And their choices are clear. They prefer sources that cater to what they already believe. Republicans are 13 times more likely than Democrats to say that Fox is their main source of news. Democrats are five times more likely than Republicans to cite MSNBC as their main news source.[71] The audience for *Breitbart News*'s website is 10-to-1 Republican over Democratic, while the audience for *Huffington Post*'s website is 3-to-1 Democratic over Republican.[72] The same pattern holds for talk shows. The audience of every conservative talk show is made up mostly of Republicans, while Democrats make up a majority of the audience of every liberal talk show.[73]

Most citizens who rely on partisan outlets also get news from traditional outlets, but an increasing number pay no attention to such outlets. Those who hold the most intense views, right or left, are the people most likely to do so. They reside in *echo chambers*—the information they receive aligns with their partisan loyalty. "We're increasingly able to choose our information sources based on their tendency to back up what we already believe," notes *Vox*'s Ezra Klein. "We don't even have to hear the arguments from the other side."[74]

Social media also serve as an echo chamber for some people. Because social media are used mainly for staying in touch with friends and associates, the messages that people encounter on social media are not as one-sided as on partisan blogs or talk shows. But Republicans are more likely to associate with other Republicans, while Democrats are more likely to associate with other Democrats.[75] As a result, when politics is discussed on social media, most people are hearing from those who share their point of view. Republicans and Democrats respond similarly to these messages, although Republicans are somewhat more likely to seek out supportive information while Democrats are somewhat more likely to "unfriend" those who express opposing views.[76]

Exposure to partisan outlets leads people to be more politically interested and engaged.[77] Evidence also suggests that such exposure can improve partisans' understanding of their own party's philosophy and policy positions.[78] At the same time, this type of exposure warps people's understanding of the opposing party

PARTY
POLARIZATION

Conflicting Ideas

Living in Different Worlds

In the 1970s, Americans' choice of TV news programs was limited to the three broadcast networks—ABC, CBS, and NBC. Each headlined the same stories and interpreted them in much the same way, while giving more or less equal coverage to the two major parties. The emergence of cable TV changed the pattern. Today, Americans have a range of choices, including outlets that heap praise on one party while attacking the other.

Americans who regularly consume partisan news typically prefer outlets aligned with their beliefs, as can be seen from the results of a recent Pew Research Center poll. Republicans have a preference for the conservative-leaning Fox News while Democrats' prefer the liberal-leaning MSNBC. Research has found that exposure to partisan news contributes to party polarization. Partisan news reinforces citizens' preexisting faith in their party while at the same time convincing them that the other party's positions lack merit.

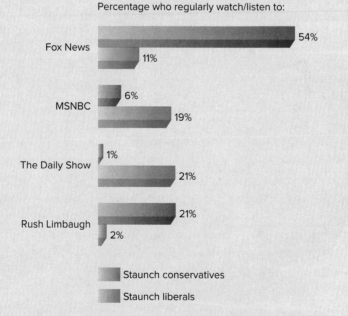

Percentage who regularly watch/listen to:

Fox News — 54% / 11%
MSNBC — 6% / 19%
The Daily Show — 1% / 21%
Rush Limbaugh — 21% / 2%

Staunch conservatives
Staunch liberals

Q: Do you find it troubling that partisan media outlets contribute to party polarization, or do you think they play a key role in clarifying the differences between the Republican and Democratic Parties? Do you personally rely more heavily on traditional news outlets or on partisan outlets?

and generates hostility toward those who identify with it.[79] Exposure to partisan outlets is also associated with extreme political opinions, although scholars differ on whether the correlation is a result of exposure or whether extremists are more likely to seek out reinforcing messages (see "Party Polarization: Living in Different Worlds").[80] Studies have also found that heavy exposure to partisan outlets fosters distrust of the traditional media and of political institutions generally.

The Inattentive Audience

In the period before cable TV, when the only viewing choice at the dinner hour was news, many of the viewers were "inadvertent viewers." They watched less out of a keen interest in news than because they were addicted to television viewing.[81] Even young adults, who generally pay less attention to news than older ones, were affected, as the research of political scientist Martin Wattenberg revealed. "There was little variation in news viewing habits by age," Wattenberg wrote. "TV news producers could hardly write off young adults, given that two out of three said they had watched such broadcasts every night."[82]

Inadvertent viewers are now few in number. Cable TV and the Internet have expanded the choices available at any hour. Movies, sports, and nearly everything else imaginable is available on demand. Those with a keen interest in

Attention to news has been declining. Americans have replaced some of the time formerly spent on news with exposure to the alternative content available through cable TV and the Internet. Accompanying the decline in attention to news has been a decline in Americans' factual knowledge of public affairs. (©Jupiterimages/Goodshoot/Alamy)

news can access it around the clock. Those without an interest have no difficulty finding other types of programs. The result has been a decline in news
consumption among all age groups, but particularly among young adults.[83]
Compared with adults over 50 years of age, those under 30 are only a third
as likely to follow public affairs closely through a newspaper, only half as likely
to watch television news regularly, and less likely even to consume news on
the Internet.[84]

Many Americans today pay only sporadic attention to news. They tune in
when something momentous occurs, such as the devastation that Hurricane
Harvey wreaked on the Gulf Coast in 2017. Otherwise, their news exposure is
hit or miss. They constitute what can be called "the inattentive audience."

Such citizens typically know very little about politics.[85] And much of what
they think they know about politics is inaccurate, based on what they've heard
from unreliable sources or inferred from fragments of information. They're also
more susceptible to disinformation or unfounded conspiracy theories than
other citizens. The best protection against being misled by false claims is having the facts. Accurate information actually does outweigh false information,
but only if you have it.[86]

There's another element to today's media system that works against an
informed public, and it affects even those who pay attention to news. It's the
distraction that results from the accelerated pace of media messages. As the
media have become an ever larger part of Americans' lives—the typical citizen
now devotes about 10 hours a day to media—the number of messages to which
people are exposed has multiplied (see "How the 50 States Differ").[87] The
typical American is exposed to hundreds of discrete messages every day, everything from the ads they see on television, to the social media messages they
receive, to the images and statements they encounter in news stories. Message
abundance might be thought to be a benefit. However, as Nobel Laureate
Herbert Simon noted, message abundance tends to create information overload, reducing people's ability to concentrate on any particular message.[88] Our
digital tools magnify the effect. Cognitive psychologist David Meyer calls
digital media a modern day "Skinner's box," a reference to psychologist B. F.
Skinner's famed stimulus-response studies of the 1930s.[89] Cell phones, TV
remotes, and other devices offer instant gratification, conditioning us to seek
more of it. The typical American sends more than 30 texts a day, up sharply
from just a few years ago and rising by the year.[90]

Media multitasking has magnified the "more is less" effect. While watching
TV, we surf the web, play a computer game, text our friends. "Media multitask-
ing" has more than doubled in the past two decades. MIT psychologist Sherry
Turkle found that people remember things less well when they multitask.
"When you multitask," Turkle says, "there's a degradation of function."[91]

HOW THE 50 STATES DIFFER

CRITICAL THINKING THROUGH COMPARISONS

Internet Access

The Internet has greatly expanded Americans' access to news and information, and most Americans have regular access to the Internet in their home or through their work. However, the percentage varies considerably by state. Eight in every 10 residents of Colorado, Minnesota, New Hampshire, and Washington—the states with the highest levels of Internet penetration—have regular access. In contrast, only 6 in every 10 residents of Arkansas, Mississippi, New Mexico, and Tennessee—the states with the lowest levels of Internet penetration—have access.

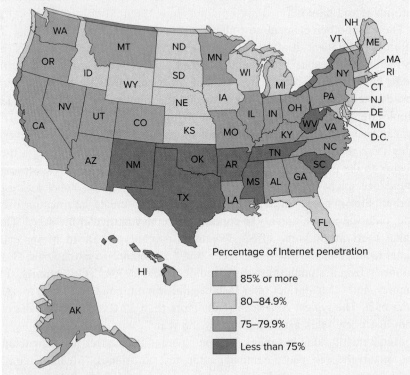

Percentage of Internet penetration

- 85% or more
- 80–84.9%
- 75–79.9%
- Less than 75%

Source: U.S. Census Bureau, 2014.

Continued

> **Q:** What might account for state-to-state differences in Internet penetration?
>
> **A:** States that are poorer and more rural have lower rates of Internet penetration. Less-affluent citizens are less able to afford the Internet, and Internet companies are less likely to offer it in rural areas because of the higher installation costs.

The onslaught of messages has diminished our capacity to concentrate and, thus, to learn about public affairs. During the era of the information commons, citizens got a degree of protection from information overload by the fact that the messages were mutually reinforcing. What citizens were seeing and hearing from media outlets was consistent. That's not the situation today. Our news sources offer different and conflicting messages, increasing the likelihood that confusion and misunderstanding will result from what we see and hear.

SUMMARY

In the nation's first century, the press was allied closely with the political parties and helped the parties mobilize public opinion. Gradually, the press freed itself from this partisan relationship and developed a form of reporting known as objective journalism, which emphasizes fair and accurate accounts of newsworthy developments. That model still governs the news reporting of the traditional media—daily newspapers and broadcasters—but does not hold for the newer media—radio talk shows, cable TV talk shows, and Internet outlets. Although some of them cover politics in the traditional way, many of them transmit news through a partisan lens. They slant information to favor their preferred party.

The traditional press performs three basic functions. First, in their signaling function, journalists communicate information to the public about breaking events and new developments. This information makes citizens aware of developments that affect their lives. However, because of the media's need to attract an audience, breaking news stories often focus on developments, such as celebrity scandals, that have little to do with issues of politics and government. Second, the press functions as a common carrier in that it provides political leaders with a channel for addressing the public. Increasingly, however, the news has centered nearly as much on the journalists themselves as on the newsmakers they cover. In a third function, that of watchdog, the press acts to protect the public by exposing deceitful, careless, or corrupt officials.

The news audience has changed substantially in the past few decades. Daily newspapers and broadcast news have lost audience to cable television and the Internet. Although most Americans continue to rely on traditional news outlets, an increasing number prefer partisan outlets, where they find support for what they already believe. And a larger number of Americans today pay little or no attention to news, preferring instead to use the media almost solely as a source of entertainment.

©gangliu10/Getty Images

CRITICAL THINKING ZONE

KEY TERMS

agenda setting (*p. 297*)
common-carrier function (*p. 298*)
framing (*p. 299*)
high-choice media system (*p. 308*)
news (*p. 287*)
news media (press) (*p. 297*)

objective journalism (*p. 291*)
partisan function (*p. 302*)
partisan press (*p. 290*)
priming (*p. 299*)
signaling (signaler) function (*p. 297*)
watchdog function. (*p. 300*)

APPLYING THE ELEMENTS OF CRITICAL THINKING

Conceptualizing: Define *high-choice media system*. How does it contribute to a less-informed public? To a more partisan public?

Synthesizing: Contrast the media's watchdog role with their common-carrier role. Is there a tension between these roles—does carrying out one of them work against carrying out the other?

Analyzing: What are the consequences of the fact that the press is charged with informing the public but at the same time needs to attract an audience in order to make a profit and fund its news-gathering operations?

EXTRA CREDIT

A Book Worth Reading: Diana Mutz, *In-Your-Face Politics: The Consequences of Uncivil Media* (Princeton, N.J.: Princeton University Press, 2015). This award-winning book explores the impact of the increasingly heated and partisan messaging in today's media.

A Website Worth Visiting: www.mediatenor.com. Media Tenor is a nonpartisan organization that analyzes U.S. and overseas news coverage on a daily basis. The site has information of interest to anyone curious about tendencies in news coverage, such as how various news outlets portray the president.

PARTICIPATE!

Before the Internet opened new channels of communication, freedom of the press, which is granted by the First Amendment to all Americans, was enjoyed for the most part only by the very few who owned or worked in the news media. With the Internet, the opportunity for citizen communication, though not unlimited, is greater than at any time in the nation's history. Take advantage of the opportunity. Meetup.com is one of literally thousands of Internet sites where you can participate in discussion forums about politics and issues. A more ambitious alternative is to start your own web log. Blogging is time-consuming, but it allows you to create an agenda of news, information, and opinion—an activity previously reserved for newspaper editors and broadcast producers. Either of these options will enable you to make your voice heard and also help you hone your citizenship skills—the ability to communicate, to defend your own views, and to learn the opinions of others.

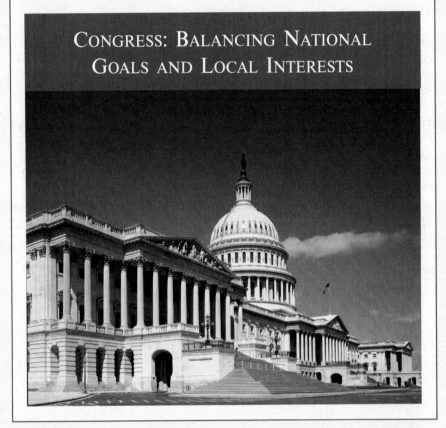

CONGRESS: BALANCING NATIONAL GOALS AND LOCAL INTERESTS

Source: Photographs in the Carol M. Highsmith Archive, Library of Congress, Prints and Photographs Division [LC-HS503- 1684]

❝ There are two Congresses. . . . The tight-knit complex world of Capitol Hill is a long way from [the member's district], in perspective and outlook as well as in miles.❞

ROGER DAVIDSON AND WALTER OLESZEK[1]

It was a budget bill the likes of which Washington had seldom seen in recent years. The deep partisan divide that had become characteristic of the lawmaking process had given way to bipartisanship. Republican lawmakers wanted a budget agreement that included significant increases in military spending while Democratic lawmakers were seeking a bill that had funding for health programs, including children's health, opioid treatment, and community health centers. There were also spending areas where Democratic and Republican lawmakers had overlapping interests, including infrastructure improvements and disaster relief, particularly for victims of Hurricanes Harvey, Irma, Maria, and Nate.

When the $300 billion budget bill was voted upon in early 2018, it passed by a 71-28 margin in the Senate and a 240-186 margin in the House. Unlike nearly every major bill that had come up for a vote in the previous year, the budget bill had strong bipartisan support. Large numbers of Republican and Democratic lawmakers voted in favor of the bill.

The story of the spending bill negotiations illustrates the dual nature of Congress. It is both a lawmaking institution for the country and a representative assembly for states and districts.[2] Members of Congress have a duty to serve both the interests of the nation as a whole and the interests of their individual constituencies. The budget bill addressed national policy concerns through an increase in military spending while also addressing local needs, including money for roads, bridges, community health centers, and disaster relief. The nation's needs are on the minds of lawmakers but so, too, are local needs because members' reelection depends on the support of the voters back home.[3]

The framers of the Constitution regarded Congress as the preeminent branch of the federal government and granted it the greatest of all the powers of government, the power to make the laws: "All legislative powers herein granted shall be invested in a Congress, which shall consist of a Senate and House of Representatives." Congress is granted the authority even to decide the form and function of the executive departments and the lower courts. No executive agency or lower court can exist unless authorized by Congress.

The positioning of Congress as the first among equals in a system of divided powers reflected the framers' trust in representative institutions. The framers' vision of a preeminent Congress has not fully stood the test of time, however. Over time, power has shifted from Congress to the presidency and, today, both institutions have a central role in lawmaking. This chapter emphasizes the following points:

- *Congressional elections usually result in the reelection of the incumbent.* Congressional office provides incumbents with substantial resources (free publicity, staff, and legislative influence) that give them (particularly House members) a major advantage in election campaigns.

- *Leadership in Congress is provided by party leaders, including the Speaker of the House and the Senate majority leader.* Party leaders are in a stronger position today than a few decades ago because the party caucuses in Congress are more ideologically cohesive than in the past.

- *Much of the work of Congress is done through its committees, each of which has its own leadership and its designated policy jurisdiction.*

- *Because of its fragmented structure, Congress is not well suited to take the lead on major national policies, which has allowed the president to assume this role. At the same time, Congress is well organized to handle policies of narrower scope.*

- *In recent decades, congressional Republicans have become more uniformly conservative and congressional Democrats have become more uniformly liberal. This has made it easier for each party's members to band together but harder for them to reach agreement with the other party's members, which has increased the frequency of legislative deadlock.*

- *Congress's policymaking role is based on three major functions: lawmaking, representation, and oversight.*

CONGRESS AS A CAREER: ELECTION TO CONGRESS

In the nation's first century, service in Congress was not a career for most of its members. Before 1900, at least a third of the seats in Congress changed hands at each election. Most members left voluntarily. Because travel was slow and arduous, serving in the nation's capital meant spending months away from one's family. Moreover, the national government was not the center of power that it is today; many politicians preferred to serve in state capitals.

The modern Congress is a different kind of institution. Most of its members are professional politicians, and a seat in the U.S. Senate or House is as high as most of them can expect to rise in politics. The pay (about $175,000 a year) is substantial, as is the prestige of their office. Most members of Congress seek to make it a career, which requires them to keep the voters happy. Members of Congress, says political scientist David Mayhew, are "single-minded seekers of reelection."[4] Most of them succeed in getting reelected (see Figure 11-1). **Incumbents** (as officeholders are called) have about a 90 percent probability of winning reelection.

Using Incumbency to Stay in Congress

The primary reason incumbents run so strongly is that many congressional districts and some states are so lopsidedly Democratic or Republican that candidates of the stronger party seldom lose. No more than 75 of the 435 House seats—about one in six—is competitive enough that each party has a realistic chance of victory. In any case, whether their constituency is lopsided or competitive, incumbents have substantial advantages over their challengers, as will now be explained.

figure 11-1   REELECTION RATES OF HOUSE AND SENATE INCUMBENTS

Congressional incumbents have a very good chance of winning another term, as indicated by the reelection rates of U.S. representatives and senators who sought reelection during the last five congressional elections. The actual chances of reelection are somewhat less than the rates indicate. Some incumbents, when faced with a reelection campaign that they might lose, chose to leave Congress voluntarily.

The Service Strategy: Taking Care of Constituents   Incumbents promote their reelection prospects by catering to their **constituency:** the people residing in their state or district. Members of Congress pay attention to constituency opinions when choosing positions on legislation, and they work hard to get their share of federal spending projects. Such projects are often derided as **pork** (or *pork-barrel spending*) by outsiders but are embraced by those who live in the state or district that gets a federally funded project, such as a new hospital, research center, or highway. Incumbents also respond to their constituents' individual requests, a practice known as the **service strategy.** Whether a constituent is seeking information about a government program or looking for help in obtaining a federal benefit, the representative's staff is ready to assist.

Congressional staffers spend most of their time not on legislative matters but on constituency service and public relations—efforts that can pay off on Election Day.[5] Each House member receives an annual office allowance of roughly $1 million with which to hire up to 18 permanent staff members.[6] Senators receive office allowances that range between $3 million and $5 million a year, depending on the population size of their state. Smaller-state senators have staffs of about 30 people whereas larger-state senators have staffs closer in number to 50 people.[7] Each member of Congress is also allowed free trips back to their home state and free mailings to constituent households (a privilege known as the "frank"). These trips and mailings, along with press releases and other public relations efforts, help incumbents build name recognition and constituent support—major advantages in their reelection campaigns.

It is noteworthy that legislators in other Western democracies do not have the large personal staffs or the travel and publicity budgets of members of Congress. A member of the House of Commons in Great Britain, for example, has a staff of three people.[8]

Campaign Fundraising: Raking in the Money   Incumbents also have a decided advantage when it comes to raising campaign funds. Congressional elections are expensive because of the high cost of TV advertising, polling, and other modern campaign techniques. Today the cost of running a successful House campaign in a competitive district exceeds a million dollars (see Figure 11-2). The price of victory in competitive Senate races is much higher, ranging from several million dollars in small states to $20 million or more in larger states. Rarely do incumbents have trouble raising enough money to conduct an effective campaign, whereas challengers usually fall far short of their fundraising needs.[9] In the most recent election cycle, House incumbents raised on average about $1.5 million in campaign funds—roughly six times the average amount raised by their challengers.[10]

Incumbents' past campaigns and constituent service provide them a ready list of potential contributors. Individual contributions, most of which are $200 or less, account for the single largest share of all funds received by congressional candidates and are obtained mainly through fundraising events, websites, and direct-mail

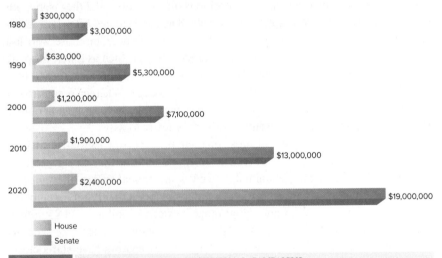

figure 11-2   THE RISING COST OF CONGRESSIONAL CAMPAIGNS

Each decade, the cost of running for congressional office has risen sharply as campaign techniques—TV advertising, opinion polling, and so on—have become more elaborate and sophisticated. The increase in spending can be seen from a comparison of the approximate average spending by both candidates per House or Senate seat at 10-year intervals, beginning in 1980. The figures for 2020 are projections based on the 2012–2018 congressional elections. (*Source:* Federal Election Commission.)

solicitation.[11] Incumbents also have an edge with political action committees (PACs), which are the fundraising arm of interest groups (see Chapter 9). Most PACs are reluctant to oppose an incumbent unless the candidate appears beatable. More than 85 percent of PAC contributions in recent elections have gone to incumbents (see Figure 11-3). "Anytime you go against an incumbent, you take a minute and think long and hard about what your rationale is," said Desiree Anderson, director of the Realtors PAC.[12] (A race without an incumbent—called an **open-seat election**—typically brings out a strong, well-funded candidate from each party when the parties are closely matched in a state or district.)

Redistricting: Favorable Boundaries for House Incumbents   House members, but not senators, have a final electoral advantage. Because incumbents are hard to unseat, they are always a force to be reckoned with, a fact that is apparent during redistricting. Every 10 years, after each population census, the 435 seats in the House of Representatives are reallocated among the states in proportion to their population. This process is called **reapportionment.** States that have gained population since the last census may acquire additional House seats, while those that have lost population may lose seats. After the 2010 census, for example, Texas and Florida were among the states that gained House seats and New York and Ohio were among those that lost seats.

States are required by law to have House districts that are as nearly equal in population as possible. As a result, they must redraw their district boundaries after each census to account for population shifts within the state during the previous 10 years. (The Senate is not affected by population change, because each state has two senators regardless of its size.) In most states, the responsibility for redrawing House election districts—a process called **redistricting**—rests with the respective state legislatures. The party that controls the legislature typically redraws the boundaries in a way that favors candidates of its party—a process called **gerrymandering.** (Among the few exceptions to this practice are Arizona, California, and Iowa, which entrust redistricting to an independent commission.)

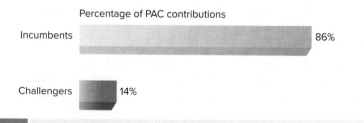

Percentage of PAC contributions

Incumbents   86%

Challengers   14%

figure 11-3   PAC CONTRIBUTIONS FAVOR INCUMBENTS

In allocating campaign contributions, PACs favor incumbent members of Congress over their challengers by a large margin. (*Source:* Center for Responsive Politics, 2018. Based on PAC contribution averages for the past five election cycles.)

C A S E S T U D Y	Politics in Action

The Veterans' Jobs Bill

For members of Congress concerned about reelection, a legislative bill offers risks and rewards. It can win friends or it can create enemies. So what type of legislation do members prefer? Ideally, it's a bill that offers a *concentrated benefit*, so that the recipients are aware of the benefit and might lend their support in the next election. And ideally, it's a bill that imposes a *diffuse cost*, so that those who are paying for it are unaware they are doing so.

A 2011 bill with these two features—a concentrated benefit and a diffuse cost—provides an example.

©nito/Shutterstock

At the time, Congress was deadlocked over budget issues, with Republicans seeking to cut government spending and Democrats seeking to increase taxes on upper incomes. Although Republicans and Democrats could not agree on anything else, they found time to pass a spending bill. The vote was 422-0 in the House and 95-0 in the Senate, meaning that every congressional Republican and Democrat voted for it.

So what was the nature of the bill? Well, it offered a concentrated benefit while diffusing the cost. The bill authorized the spending of $1.7 billion to help military veterans find jobs. The bill was "good politics" for a member of Congress. The benefit was concentrated—veterans alone would receive it and be thankful for it—while the cost was diffused across the entire taxpaying public so that its effect on any given taxpayer would be too small to be noticed.

The veterans' job bill is not an isolated example. Most of the bills passed by Congress include a concentrated benefit and a diffuse cost. Other types of bills are riskier. A bill with a diffuse benefit is less advantageous because the beneficiaries are unlikely to notice the benefit. Although Americans benefit, for example, from spending on diplomacy,

Continued

the average citizen is largely unaware of the benefit. There aren't many votes to be won from supporting legislation of that type. And a bill with a concentrated cost is risky because the group that is paying the cost will know it and might retaliate against members of Congress who vote for it. An example of such a bill is one that would require power plant owners to install expensive emissions-reduction equipment as a means of reducing their carbon emissions.

Incumbents typically benefit from gerrymandering. When redistricting, the majority party in the state legislature places enough of its party's voters in its incumbents' districts to ensure their reelection. Many of the minority party's incumbents are also awarded a safe district. If opposing incumbents have a strong base of support and would be difficult to defeat, the optimal strategy is to pack their district with as many voters of their party as possible, so that in effect the party "wastes" votes, reducing its competitiveness elsewhere in the state. Gerrymandering can have the effect of taking the choice of a representative out of the hands of the voters and giving it to the state legislature but, so far, the courts have not put substantial constraints on the practice.[13]

Although gerrymandering is widely thought to be the reason why so many House seats are not competitive, a more important reason is the increased geographic concentration of Republican and Democratic voters, a development that the writer Bill Bishop calls "The Big Sort."[14] In recent decades, most states have become more heavily Republican or Democratic. And within states, cities have become more heavily Democratic while suburban and rural areas have become more heavily Republican. A Rand Corporation study concluded that the geographic concentration of Republicans and Democrats accounts for far more one-sided districts than does gerrymandering.[15]

Most such policy issues also serve the reelection interests of members of Congress. The resulting legislation tends to be "distributive" in nature—that is, it confers a benefit on a particular group while spreading the cost across the taxpaying public (see "Case Study: The Veterans' Jobs Bill"). Distributive policies have a clear political advantage. The benefit is large enough that members of the recipient group will recognize and appreciate it, while the cost to each taxpayer is barely noticeable. Such policies are also the type that Congress, through its committee system, is organizationally best suited to handle. Most committees parallel a major constituent interest, such as agriculture, commerce, labor, or veterans.

Pitfalls of Incumbency

Incumbency is not without its risks. Senate and House incumbents can fall victim to disruptive issues, personal misconduct, turnout swings, strong challengers, and campaign money.

Disruptive Issues   Most elections are not waged in the context of disruptive issues, but when they are, incumbents are at greater risk. When voters are angry about existing political conditions, they are more likely to believe that those in power should be tossed from office. The 2018 congressional election, which was waged in the context of contentious issues like immigration, gun control, and income inequality, saw the retirement or defeat of an usually large number of incumbents. The majority of them were Republicans, which was the party in power at the time of the election.

Personal Misconduct   Life in Washington can be fast paced, glamorous, and expensive, and some members of Congress get caught up in influence peddling, sex scandals, and other forms of misconduct. "The first thing to being reelected is to stay away from scandal, even minor scandal," says political scientist John Hibbing.[16] More than a few members of Congress have lost their bid for reelection or been forced to resign their office as a result of personal scandal. Pennsylvania representative Tim Murphy, for example, resigned his seat in 2017 after it became public that Murphy, an abortion opponent, had pressured the woman with whom he was having an extramarital affair to abort a suspected pregnancy.

Turnout Variation: The Midterm Election Problem   In 21 of the last 25 **midterm elections**—those that occur midway through a president's term—the president's party has lost House seats. The 2018 midterm elections, when the Republican Party lost seats, fit the normal pattern. The pattern is partly attributable to the drop-off in turnout that accompanies a midterm election. Turnout in presidential elections is much higher than it is in the midterm elections. People who vote only in the presidential election tend to have weaker party ties and are more responsive to the issues of the moment. These issues typically favor one party, which contributes to the success not only of its presidential candidate but also of its congressional candidates. Two years later in the midterm elections, many of these voters stay home and those who do go to the polls vote largely along party lines. Accordingly, the congressional candidates of the president's party do not get the boost they enjoyed in the previous election, and House seats are lost as a result.[17] Moreover, some voters treat the midterm elections as a referendum on the president's performance. Presidents usually lose popularity during their term of office as a result of the policy decisions they make. As the president's support declines, so does voters' support of congressional candidates of the president's party.[18] Polls indicated that voters' discontent with President Donald Trump's performance contributed to the Democrats' big gains in the 2018 midterms, including its takeover of the U.S. House of Representatives.

Primary Election Challengers   Primary elections can also be a time of risk for incumbents, especially if they hold politically moderate views. If they are confronted with a strong challenger from the extreme wing of their party, they stand a chance of losing because strong partisans are more likely than party moderates to vote in primary elections.[19] Some moderate incumbents have responded by shifting their position toward the extreme wing of their party.[20] Others have risked the possibility of a primary challenger, and it has cost some of them their seats. In 2012, for example, Richard Luger, a six-term incumbent and widely respected member of the Senate, was beaten in Indiana's GOP primary by conservative Richard Mourdock, who portrayed Lugar as a moderate who was too much of a Washington insider.

Kevin de León represents the kind of challenger that congressional incumbents increasingly fear. De León, a Democrat and California state senator, challenged incumbent Democrat Dianne Feinstein in California's 2018 Senate race. De León portrayed Feinstein, a five-term U.S. senator, as being too moderate and overly willing to compromise with Republicans. Feinstein won their race by less than 10 percentage points. (©Brian Cahn/ZUMA Wire/Alamy)

General Election Challengers: A Problem for Senators   Incumbents, particularly those in the Senate, are also vulnerable to strong challengers. Senators often find themselves running against a high-ranking politician, such as the state's governor or attorney general. Such opponents have the voter base, campaign organization, fundraising ability, public recognition, and credentials to mount a strong campaign.

House incumbents are less likely to face strong challengers. A House seat is often not attractive enough to induce a prominent local politician, such as a mayor or state legislator, to risk losing to an incumbent.[21] As a result, most House incumbents face opponents who struggle to raise enough money to run a strong campaign. The scenario changes somewhat when conditions indicate that one or the other party has a strong chance of picking up House seats in the upcoming election. In that situation, the advantaged party finds it easier to convince strong challengers to enter the race. Polls in advance of the 2018 election, for example, indicated that voters were trending toward the Democratic Party, which enabled it to field an unusually strong set of candidates.[22]

A New Threat: Super PACs   Although incumbents ordinarily have a funding advantage over their challengers, the situation can change when they appear vulnerable. Contributors from outside the state or district may target the race and donate money to the challenger. Although this threat has existed for years, it has increased with the emergence of super PACs, which have the capacity to pour millions of dollars into a race (see Chapters 8 and 9). This scenario played itself out in the 2014 Senate race in North Carolina, which pitted the Democratic incumbent Kay Hagan against Republican Thom Tillis, the Speaker of North Carolina's House of Representatives. Their race turned out to be one of the most expensive campaigns in Senate history. More than $75 million was spent on the campaign with two-thirds of the money coming from super PACs. Hagan narrowly lost her reelection bid, falling to Tillis by less than 2 percentage points. In 2018, there were several dozen Senate and House races in which super PACs spent millions of dollars in an effort to influence the outcome.

Who Are the Winners in Congressional Elections?

The Constitution places only a few restrictions on who can be elected to Congress. House members must be at least 25 years of age and have been a citizen for at least 7 years. For senators, the age and citizenship requirements are 30 years and 9 years, respectively. Senators and representatives alike must be residents of the state from which they are elected.

But if the formal restrictions are minimal, the informal limits are substantial. Congress is not a microcosm of the population. Although lawyers constitute less than 1 percent of the population, they make up a fourth of the House and more than half of the Senate. Attorneys enter politics in large numbers in part because knowledge of the law is an asset in Congress and also because campaign publicity—even if a candidate loses—is a good way to build up a law practice. Along with lawyers, professionals such as business executives, educators, bankers, and journalists account for roughly 90 percent of congressional membership.[23] Blue-collar workers, clerical employees, and homemakers are seldom elected to Congress. Farmers and ranchers fare better; a number of House members from rural districts have an agricultural background.

Finally, members of Congress are disproportionately white and male. Although the number of women in Congress is 10 times that of a half century ago, they account for less than a fourth of the membership (see Chapter 5). Minorities account for about a fifth of the membership.

PARTIES AND PARTY LEADERSHIP

The U.S. Congress is a **bicameral legislature,** meaning it has two chambers, the House and the Senate. Both chambers are organized largely along party lines. At the start of each two-year congressional term, party members in each chamber meet to elect their **party leaders,** the individuals who will lead their party's efforts in the chamber. Party members also meet periodically in closed session, which is called a **party caucus,** to plan strategy, develop issues, and resolve policy differences. (Table 11-1 shows the party composition in Congress during the past decade.)

table 11-1	THE NUMBER OF DEMOCRATS AND REPUBLICANS IN THE HOUSE OF REPRESENTATIVES AND THE SENATE, 2011-2020				
	2011– 2012	2013– 2014	2015– 2016	2017– 2018	2019– 2020
House					
Democrats	192	197	184	194	229*
Republicans	243*	238*	251*	241	206
Senate					
Democrats	53	55	46	48	47
Republicans	47	45	54*	52	53

*Chamber not controlled by the president's party. Senate and House members who are independents are included in the total for the party with which they caucused. Figures are based on party totals that result from the congressional elections as opposed to subsequent totals that result, for example, because of the death or resignation of seated members.

Party Unity in Congress

Political parties are the strongest force within Congress. Parties are the primary source of unity among members of Congress, as well as the primary source of division.

The partisan divide in Congress has widened steadily in the past three decades. Earlier, congressional Republicans were divided almost evenly between the party's conservative and progressive wings, and congressional Democrats consisted of a liberal northern wing and a smaller conservative southern wing. Since then, the Republican Party's progressive wing and the Democratic Party's conservative southern wing have withered. In a recent study, political scientists Keith Poole and Howard Rosenthal found, for both the House and the Senate, that the least conservative Republican was more conservative than the most conservative Democrat.[24] As a result, each congressional party has attained a high level of **party unity**—in which members of a party band together on legislation and stand against the opposite party.[25]

The trend can be seen by looking at the party distribution on *roll-call votes* (these are votes on which each member's vote is officially recorded, as opposed to voice votes, where the members simply say "aye" or "nay" in unison and the presiding officer indicates which side prevails without tallying individual members' positions). Since the mid-1980s, party-line voting on roll calls has risen sharply (see "Party Polarization: Partisan Conflict in Congress"). The Tax Cuts and Jobs Act of 2017, for example, was enacted along party lines. Every House and Senate Democrat voted against it, while 98 percent of Republican senators and 95 percent of House Republicans voted for it.

As the partisan divide in Congress has widened, there has been a decline in the number of lawmakers in the political center. At an earlier time, congressional moderates were the key players. Their numbers were large enough for them to force other lawmakers to come to the middle to engage in the negotiation and compromise that can be necessary to get agreement on legislation. Today, there are too few moderates in Congress to force other members to come to the center.[26] A frequent result has been legislative deadlock. Republicans and Democrats have taken opposite positions on a bill, with neither side being willing to make the concessions that would produce the bipartisan support necessary to pass it. (The effects of heightened partisanship on the congressional process are discussed further in later sections of the chapter.)

Party Leadership in Congress

In both the House and the Senate, each party has leaders who are expected to promote the party's legislative agenda. But unlike the party leaders of most national legislatures, those in Congress cannot count on the backing of their

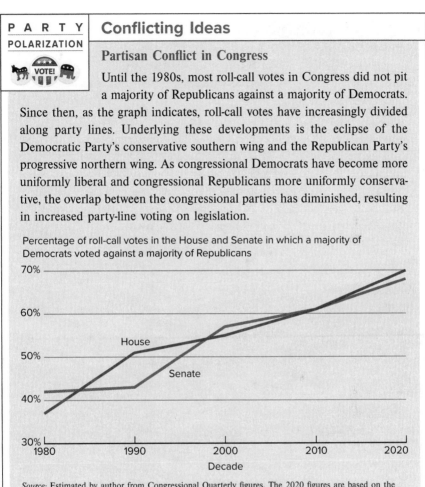

PARTY	Conflicting Ideas

POLARIZATION

Partisan Conflict in Congress

Until the 1980s, most roll-call votes in Congress did not pit a majority of Republicans against a majority of Democrats. Since then, as the graph indicates, roll-call votes have increasingly divided along party lines. Underlying these developments is the eclipse of the Democratic Party's conservative southern wing and the Republican Party's progressive northern wing. As congressional Democrats have become more uniformly liberal and congressional Republicans more uniformly conservative, the overlap between the congressional parties has diminished, resulting in increased party-line voting on legislation.

Percentage of roll-call votes in the House and Senate in which a majority of Democrats voted against a majority of Republicans

Source: Estimated by author from Congressional Quarterly figures. The 2020 figures are based on the average for 2010–2017 period. The figures for the other periods are the average for the previous decade.

Q: Some observers claim that heightened partisanship in Congress is crippling the institution as a policymaking body. Party disputes on everything from health care to tax policy have produced legislative deadlock and delay. Do you share the view that excessive partisanship is undermining the legislative process, or do you think members of Congress should stick to their partisan principles, whatever the consequences?

party's members. Members elsewhere can be denied nomination in the next election if they fail to support their party leaders' legislative agenda. In the United States, however, incumbents largely win election through their own efforts, which gives them the freedom to selectively support or oppose the party's legislative

HOW THE 50 STATES DIFFER

CRITICAL THINKING THROUGH COMPARISONS

Women in the State Legislatures

Women have had more success in gaining election to state legislatures than to Congress, partly because there is more turnover and less incumbency advantage at the state level, which creates more opportunities for newcomers to run and to win. More than one in five state legislators are women, a fourfold increase since 1970. Arizona and Vermont, with 40 percent each, have the highest proportion of women legislators. Wyoming, with 11 percent, has the lowest.

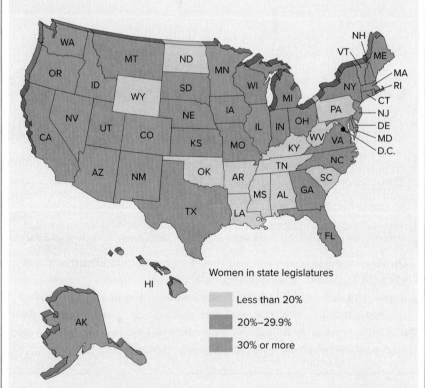

Women in state legislatures

- Less than 20%
- 20%–29.9%
- 30% or more

Source: Created from data gathered by the Center for the American Woman and Politics (CAWP); National Information Bank on Women in Public Office; and Eagleton Institute of Politics, Rutgers University, 2018.

Continued

Q: Why do southern states have the fewest women legislators?

A: One reason is that these states have a lower proportion of college-educated women in the workforce than do most other states. College-educated working women are more likely to run for public office and to actively support those who do run. Research also indicates that voters in southern states are more likely than voters elsewhere to hold traditional beliefs about the role of men and women in politics.

positions. Accordingly, party leaders in Congress can't assume that party members will automatically follow their lead. The challenge for congressional leaders is to craft legislative proposals that will attract their members' support.

House Leaders   The Constitution specifies that the House of Representatives will be presided over by a Speaker, elected by the vote of its members. Since the majority party has the largest number of members, it also has the most votes, and the Speaker has always been a member of the majority party.

Except for the president, the Speaker of the House has been described as the nation's most powerful elected national official. The Speaker's power owes primarily to the large size of the House. With 435 members, it requires strict rules to operate effectively, and the Speaker is in charge of many of the rules. The Speaker's formal powers include the right to speak first during House debate on legislation and the power to recognize members—that is, to grant them permission to speak from the floor. Because the House places a time limit on floor debate, only a relatively few members will get the chance to speak on a given bill, and the Speaker can sometimes influence legislation simply by exercising the power to decide who will speak. The Speaker also chooses the chairperson and the majority-party members of the powerful House Rules Committee, which controls the scheduling of bills. Bills that the Speaker wants passed are likely to reach the floor under conditions favorable to their enactment. The Speaker might, for example, ask the Rules Committee to delay sending a bill to the floor until there is sufficient support for its passage.

Although a powerful official, the Speaker is ultimately beholden to the party's members. Party members look to the Speaker for leadership on legislative issues, but the Speaker cannot force them to vote for or against a particular bill. As a result, the Speaker must take party members' views into account when devising the party's position on legislative issues. That's particularly true if the Speaker is a Republican. House Republicans operate by an informal agreement known as the **Hastert Rule,** also called the "majority of the majority" rule. Instituted in the late 1990s, it holds that, when Republicans are in the majority, the Speaker should bring a bill to the floor only if it's supported by a majority of House Republicans. A Republican Speaker is not literally bound by the rule—it's an informal directive—but Republican speakers have typically honored it, knowing that they could lose their position if they don't. In 2015, House Speaker John Boehner (R-Ohio) resigned his position after he ignored the rule on a few key bills and lost the support of his party's most conservative members. He was replaced by Paul Ryan (R-Wisc.), who pledged to abide by the rule.[27]

The minority party also has its House leaders. The House minority leader heads the party's caucus and plays the leading role in developing the party's legislative positions. The minority leader is assisted by a minority whip.

Senate Leaders   In the Senate, the most important party leadership position is that of the majority leader, who heads the majority-party caucus. The majority leader's role resembles that of the Speaker of the House in that the Senate majority leader formulates the majority party's legislative agenda. Like the Speaker, the Senate majority leader chairs the party's policy committee and acts as the party's voice in the chamber. The majority leader is assisted by the majority whip, who sees to it that members know when important votes are scheduled. The minority party in the Senate also has its leaders. The minority leader and minority whip have roles comparable to those of their House counterparts.

The House of Representatives with its 435 members is a very large legislative body that could not operate effectively without strict rules, such as a limit on the number of House members who are allowed to speak on a bill and for how long. Control over many of these rules rests with the Speaker of the House. (*Source:* Office of Photography, US House of Representatives)

The Senate majority leader's position is less powerful than that of the House Speaker. Unlike the House, where the Speaker directs the floor debate, the Senate has a tradition of unlimited debate. Ordinarily, any senator who wishes to speak on a bill can do so and for any length of time.*

Moreover, unlike the Speaker, the Senate majority leader does not strictly control the rules of debate on a bill. Through the House Rules Committee, the Speaker can introduce a bill under what's called a *closed rule*. This rule prohibits amendments to the bill. In contrast, the Senate allows its members to propose amendments to any bill. Such amendments are not even required to relate to the bill's content—for example, a senator could propose an antiabortion amendment to a bill dealing with defense expenditures. Such amendments are called *riders*. The House does not permit riders. Only amendments that relate directly to a bill's content are allowed in the House and, as noted, some House bills are debated under a closed rule, which prohibits amendments of any kind.

Because the Senate has only 100 members, it operates differently than the much larger House. Senators are allowed to speak on any bill, which serves to increase their power individually while diminishing the power of party leaders. The Senate majority leader has less control over Senate business than the House Speaker does over House business. (*Source:* United States Senate)

---

*Unlike the Speaker of the House, the Senate majority leader is not the chamber's presiding officer. The Constitution assigns this position to the vice president of the United States. But because the vice president is allowed to vote only in case of a tie, the vice president rarely attends Senate sessions. In the absence of the vice president, the president pro tempore (temporary president) has the right to preside over the Senate. By tradition, the president pro tempore is the majority party's most senior member, but the position is largely honorary. The Senate's presiding officer has no real power because any senator who wants to speak on a bill has the right to do so.

Finally, the Senate majority leader's power is limited by the fact that individual senators have more autonomy than do individual House members. The Senate is smaller in size—100 members versus 435 House members—which leads senators to act as coequals in a way that House members cannot. As well, senators serve six-year terms and do not face the unrelenting reelection pressures on House members, who serve two-year terms. Bob Dole of Kansas, who served as Republican Senate leader, remarked: "There's a lot of free spirits in the Senate. About 100 of them."[28]

Party Leaders and Their Members

Viewed from afar, party leaders can look very powerful. They're often in the news, and the high level of party unity on roll-call votes—Republicans lined up against Democrats—suggests that they're able to keep their fellow partisans in line. There's no question that party leaders have power or that their leadership at times is decisive in forging a bill that can make its way through Congress. Yet, they're less powerful than they might appear. It's not loyalty to the party leadership that holds party lawmakers together but instead that they have far more in common with each other than they do with lawmakers of the other party.

Moreover, members of Congress are more indebted to the hardcore partisan voters in their state or district, and to the wealthy donors who fund their campaigns, than they are to their party leaders. It can be uncomfortable for them to go against their party leaders on legislation, but it can be fatal to their reelection chances if they take positions that alienate their voters and donors. There's not much a party leader can offer that will persuade a lawmaker worried about angering diehard partisan voters or large donors. "Trying to be a leader where you have no sticks and very few carrots is dang near impossible," said former Senate Republican leader Trent Lott.[29]

COMMITTEES AND COMMITTEE LEADERSHIP

Most of the work in Congress is conducted through **standing committees,** which are permanent committees with responsibility for particular areas of public policy. At present there are 20 standing committees in the House and 16 in the Senate (see Table 11-2). Each chamber has, for example, a standing committee that handles foreign policy issues. Other important standing committees are those that deal with agriculture, commerce, the interior (natural resources and public lands), defense, government spending, labor, the judiciary, and taxation. House committees, which average about 35 to 40 members each, are about twice the size of Senate committees.

table 11-2	THE STANDING COMMITTEES OF CONGRESS
House of Representatives	**Senate**
Agriculture	Agriculture, Nutrition, and Forestry
Appropriations	Appropriations
Armed Services	Armed Services
Budget	Banking, Housing, and Urban Affairs
Education and the Workforce	Budget
Energy and Commerce	Commerce, Science, and Transportation
Ethics	Energy and Natural Resources
Financial Services	Environment and Public Works
Foreign Affairs	Finance
Homeland Security	Foreign Relations
House Administration	Health, Education, Labor, and Pensions
Judiciary	Homeland Security and Governmental Affairs
Natural Resources	Judiciary
Oversight and Government Reform	Rules and Administration
Rules	Small Business and Entrepreneurship
Science, Space, and Technology	Veterans' Affairs
Small Business	
Transportation and Infrastructure	
Veterans' Affairs	
Ways and Means	

Each standing committee has legislative authority in that it can draft and rewrite proposed legislation and can recommend to the full chamber the passage or defeat of the bills it handles. These are substantial sources of power that legislative committees in some democracies don't have. Their role is limited to advising party leaders on policy issues.

Most of the standing committees have subcommittees, each of which has a defined jurisdiction. The Senate Committee on Health, Education, Labor, and Pensions, for instance, has three subcommittees: Primary Health and Retirement Security, Children and Families, and Employment and Workplace Safety. Each House and Senate subcommittee has about a dozen members. These few individuals do most of the work and have a leading voice in the disposition of bills in their policy areas.

Congress could not manage its workload without the help of its committee system. About 10,000 bills are introduced during each two-year session of Congress. Even though a large majority of these bills do not get serious consideration, Congress would grind to a halt if its work was not divided among its standing committees, each of which has its own staff. Unlike the members' personal staffs, which concentrate on constituency relations, the committee staffs perform an almost entirely legislative function. They help draft legislation, gather information, and organize hearings.

In addition to its permanent standing committees, Congress also has a few *select committees* that have a designated responsibility but, unlike the standing committees, do not produce legislation. An example is the Senate Select Committee on Intelligence, which receives periodic classified briefings from the intelligence agencies. Congress also has *joint committees,* composed of members of both houses, which perform advisory functions. The Joint Committee on the Library, for example, oversees the Library of Congress, the largest library in the world. Finally, Congress has *conference committees*—joint committees formed temporarily to work out differences in House and Senate versions of a particular bill. The role of conference committees is discussed more fully later in the chapter.

Committee Jurisdiction

The 1946 Legislative Reorganization Act requires that each bill introduced in Congress be referred to the proper committee. An agricultural bill introduced in the Senate must be assigned to the Senate Agriculture Committee, a bill dealing with foreign affairs must be sent to the Senate Foreign Relations Committee, and so on. This requirement is a source of each committee's power. Even if a committee's members are known to oppose certain types of legislation, bills clearly within its **jurisdiction**—the policy area in which it is authorized to act—must be assigned to it.

Jurisdiction is not always clear-cut, however. Which House committee, for example, should handle a bill addressing the role of financial institutions in global commercial trade? The Financial Services Committee? The Energy and Commerce Committee? The Foreign Affairs Committee? All committees seek legislative influence, and each is jealous of its jurisdiction, so a bill that overlaps committee boundaries can provoke a "turf war" over which committee will handle it.[30] Party leaders can take advantage of these situations by assigning the bill to the committee that is most likely to handle it in the way they would like. But because party leaders depend on the committees for support, they cannot regularly ignore a committee that has a strong claim to a bill. At times, party leaders have responded by dividing up a bill, handing over some of its provisions to one committee and other provisions to a second committee.

Committee Membership

Each committee has a fixed number of seats, with the majority party holding most of them. The ratio of Democrats to Republicans on each committee is approximately the same as the ratio in the full House or Senate, but there is no fixed rule on this matter, and the majority party determines the ratio (mindful that at the next election it could become the chamber's minority party). Members of the House typically serve on only two committees. Senators often serve on four, although they can sit on only two major committees, such as the Finance Committee or the Foreign Relations Committee. Once appointed to a committee, the member can usually choose to stay on it indefinitely.

Each committee has a fixed number of seats, and a committee must have a vacancy before a new member can be appointed. Most vacancies occur after an election as a result of the retirement or defeat of committee members. Each party has a special committee in each chamber that decides who will fill the vacancies. A variety of factors influence these decisions, including members' preferences. Most newly elected members of Congress ask for and receive assignment to a committee on which they can serve their constituents' interests and at the same time enhance their reelection prospects. For example, when Joni Ernst was elected to the Senate in 2014 from Iowa, a state that depends

Most of the work in Congress is done through its standing committees, each of which has a policy jurisdiction and the authority to rewrite legislation, and hold hearings. Typically, bills reach the floor of the House or Senate after first being shaped and voted upon in committee. Pictured here is a House Ways and Means Committee hearing. (*Source:* Ways and Means Committee)

heavily on the farm sector, she asked for and received a seat on the Senate Agriculture Committee.

Some members of Congress prefer a seat on the most prestigious committees, such as the Senate Foreign Relations Committee or the House Ways and Means (taxation) Committee.[31] Although these committees do not align closely with constituency interests, they have responsibility for important policy issues. Factors such as party loyalty, level of knowledge, work ethic, and length of congressional service determine whether a member is granted a seat on a prestigious committee.*

Committee Chairs

Each committee (as well as each subcommittee) is headed by a chairperson. The position of committee chair is a powerful one. The chair schedules committee meetings, determines the order in which committee bills are considered, presides over committee discussions, directs the committee's majority staff, and can choose to lead the debate when a committee bill goes to the floor of the chamber for a vote.

Committee chairs are always members of the majority party and usually are the party member with the most **seniority** (consecutive years of service) on the committee. Seniority is based strictly on time served on a committee, not on time spent in Congress. Thus, if a member switches committees, the years spent on the first committee do not count toward seniority on the new one. The seniority system has advantages: It reduces the number of power struggles that would occur if the chairs were decided each time by open competition, it places committee leadership in the hands of experienced members, and it enables members to look forward to the reward of a position as chair after years of service on the same committee. The seniority system is not absolute, however, and is applied less uniformly than in the past, as the next section will explain.

Committee or Party: Which Is in Control?

In a sense, committees are an instrument of the majority party in that it controls most of each committee's seats and appoints its chair. In another sense, each committee is powerful in its own right. Committees have been described as "little legislatures," each secure in its jurisdiction and membership, and each wielding considerable influence over the legislation it handles.

---

*Subcommittee assignments are handled differently. The members of each party on a committee decide who among them will serve on each of its subcommittees. The member' preferences and seniority, as well as the interests of their constituencies, are key factors in subcommittee assignments.

Committees decentralize power in Congress and serve individual members' power and reelection needs. Less than a dozen members hold a party leadership position, but several hundred serve as committee or subcommittee chairs or are *ranking members,* the term for the minority party's committee and subcommittee leaders. In these positions, they can pursue local or personal policy agendas that may or may not coincide with the party leadership's goals.

Nevertheless, as a result of party polarization, the power of committees has been reduced somewhat. An effect of polarization has been to increase the number of issues on which Republicans and Democrats compete nationally. This development has led party leaders in Congress to seek greater control over the legislative agenda, including the bills in committee. The consolidation of control has been more pronounced among Republicans, who, for example, have placed a six-year limit on how long a member can chair a particular committee, which reduces the chair's ability to accumulate power over issues within the committee's jurisdiction.

Although the parties have more influence in Congress than they did a few decades ago, the balance between party power and committee power is an ongoing issue. Congress is at once a place where the parties pursue their national policy agendas and where the members pursue the policy interests of their local constituencies through their committee work. The balance of power has at times tipped toward the committees and at other times toward the party leaders. At all times, there has been an effort to strike a workable balance between the two. The distinguishing feature of congressional power is its division among the membership, with provision for added power—sometimes more and sometimes less—in the hands of the top party leaders.

How a Bill Becomes Law

Parties, party leaders, and committees are critical actors in the legislative process. Their roles and influence, however, vary with the nature of the legislation under consideration. The formal process by which bills become law is shown in Figure 11-4. A **bill** is a proposed legislative act. Many bills are prepared by executive agencies, interest groups, or other outside parties, but members of Congress also draft bills, and they alone can formally submit a bill for consideration by their chamber.

Committee Hearings and Decisions

When a bill is introduced in the House or the Senate, it receives a bill number and is sent to the relevant committee, which assigns it to one of its subcommittees.

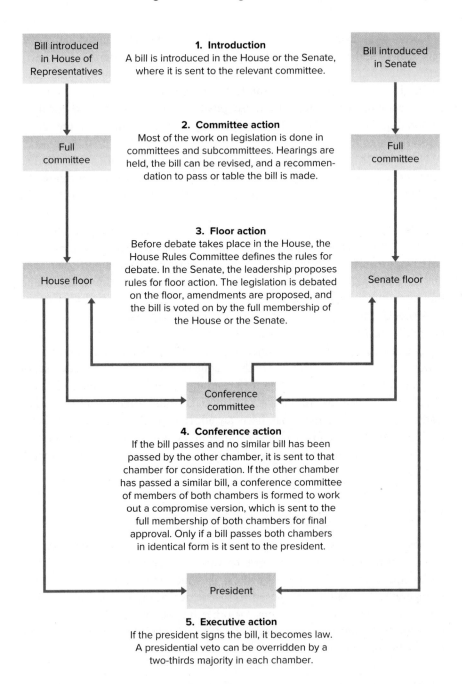

Bill introduced in House of Representatives

1. Introduction
A bill is introduced in the House or the Senate, where it is sent to the relevant committee.

Bill introduced in Senate

Full committee

2. Committee action
Most of the work on legislation is done in committees and subcommittees. Hearings are held, the bill can be revised, and a recommendation to pass or table the bill is made.

Full committee

House floor

3. Floor action
Before debate takes place in the House, the House Rules Committee defines the rules for debate. In the Senate, the leadership proposes rules for floor action. The legislation is debated on the floor, amendments are proposed, and the bill is voted on by the full membership of the House or the Senate.

Senate floor

Conference committee

4. Conference action
If the bill passes and no similar bill has been passed by the other chamber, it is sent to that chamber for consideration. If the other chamber has passed a similar bill, a conference committee of members of both chambers is formed to work out a compromise version, which is sent to the full membership of both chambers for final approval. Only if a bill passes both chambers in identical form is it sent to the president.

President

5. Executive action
If the president signs the bill, it becomes law. A presidential veto can be overridden by a two-thirds majority in each chamber.

figure 11-4 HOW A BILL BECOMES LAW

Although the legislative process can be short-circuited in many ways, this simplified diagram shows the major steps through which a bill becomes law.

Less than 10 percent of the bills referred to committee will get to the floor for a vote; the others are "killed" when committees decide they lack merit. The full House or Senate can overrule such decisions, but this rarely occurs. Most bills die in committee because they are poorly conceived or of little interest to anyone other than a few members of Congress. Some bills are not even supported by the members who introduce them. A member may submit a bill to appease a powerful constituent group and then quietly inform the committee to ignore it.

The fact that committees kill more than 90 percent of the bills submitted in Congress does not mean that they exercise 90 percent of the power in Congress. Committees do not operate in a vacuum. They rarely decide the fate of major bills that are of keen interest to other members. They also have to take into account the fact that their decisions can be reversed by the full chamber, just as subcommittees must recognize that the full committee can override their decisions.[32]

If a bill appears to have merit, the subcommittee will schedule hearings on it. After the hearings, if the subcommittee still feels that the legislation is needed, members will recommend the bill to the full committee, which might hold additional hearings. In the House, both the full committee and a subcommittee can *mark up* a bill—that is, they have the authority to change its content. In the Senate, mark up usually is reserved for the full committee.

From Committee to the Floor

If the majority on a committee vote to recommend passage of a bill, it is referred to the full chamber for action. In the House, the Rules Committee has the power to determine when the bill will be voted on, and how long the debate on it will last. On most House bills, only a small number of legislators are granted the opportunity to speak on the floor; in most cases, the bill's chief sponsor and one of the bill's leading opponents will choose the speakers. The Rules Committee also decides whether a bill will receive a "closed rule" (no amendments will be permitted), an "open rule" (members can propose amendments relevant to any of the bill's sections), or something in between (for example, only certain sections of the bill will be subject to amendment). The rules are a means by which the majority party controls legislation. When they had a majority in the House in the period before 1995, Democrats employed closed rules to prevent Republicans from proposing amendments to major bills, a tactic House Republicans said they would forgo when they took control in 1995. Once in control, however, the Republicans applied closed rules to a number of major bills. The tactic was too effective to ignore.

In the Senate, the majority leader, usually in consultation with the minority leader, schedules bills. Although the Senate has a rules committee, it doesn't set the terms of debate. All Senate bills are subject to unlimited debate unless

Shown here is Senator Rand Paul (R-Ky.). Paul is a critic of federal spending and frequently tries to filibuster spending bills. The filibuster affords senators an opportunity to delay or defeat a bill that they oppose. A three-fifths majority vote in the Senate is required to end a filibuster. (©AP Photo)

a three-fifths majority (60 of the 100 senators) vote for **cloture,** which limits debate to 30 hours. Cloture is a way of defeating a Senate **filibuster,** which is a procedural tactic whereby a minority of senators can block a bill by talking until other senators give in and the bill is withdrawn from consideration or altered to fit opponents' demands. (In 2013, the filibuster was eliminated for Senate votes on presidential nominees, though retained for legislation and the confirmation of Supreme Court justices. In 2017, it was eliminated for Supreme Court justices as well.)

Leadership and Floor Action

A bill that emerges from committee with the support of all or nearly all of its members is usually passed by an overwhelming majority of the full chamber. By contrast, when the committee vote is closely divided, other members may conclude that they need to give the bill a close look before deciding whether to support it. Other members are also less deferential to committee action on major bills and those that affect their constituents.

On major bills, the majority party's leaders (particularly in the House) have increasingly assumed the lead.[33] They shape the bill's broad content and work closely with the relevant committee during the committee phase. Once the bill clears the committee, they often direct the floor debate. In these efforts, they depend on the ongoing support of their party's members. To obtain it, they consult their members informally and through the party caucus. (The role of parties in Congress is discussed further in the section "The Representation Function of Congress".)

Conference Committees and the President

For a bill to pass, it must have the support of a simple majority (50 percent plus one) of the House or Senate members voting on it. To become law, however, a bill must first be passed in identical form by both the House and the Senate. About 10 percent of the bills that pass both chambers differ in important respects in their House and Senate versions. These bills are referred to conference committees to resolve the differences. Each **conference committee** is formed temporarily for the sole purpose of handling a particular bill. Its members are usually appointed from the House and Senate standing committees that drafted the bill. The conference committee's job is to develop a compromise version, which then goes back to the House and Senate floors for a final vote.

A bill passed in identical form by the House and the Senate is not yet a law. The president also has a say. If the president signs the bill, it becomes a **law.** If the president rejects the bill through use of the **veto,** the bill is sent back to Congress with the president's reasons for not signing it. Congress can override a veto by a two-thirds vote of each chamber; the bill then becomes law without the president's signature.*

CONGRESS'S POLICYMAKING ROLE

The framers of the Constitution expected that Congress, as the embodiment of representative government, would be the institution to which the people looked for policy leadership. During most of the 19th century, Congress had that stature. Aside from a few strong leaders such as Andrew Jackson and Abraham Lincoln, presidents did not play a major legislative role (see Chapter 12). However, as national and international forces combined to place greater policy demands on the federal government, the president assumed a central role in the legislative process. Today, Congress and the president share the legislative effort, although their roles differ.[34]

Congress's policymaking role revolves around its three major functions: lawmaking, representation, and oversight (see Table 11-3). In practice, the three functions overlap, but they are conceptually distinct.

---

*Although the large majority of bills are signed or vetoed by the president, a bill can also become law if the president fails to take action within 10 days (Sundays excepted). In that instance, the bill becomes law if Congress is still in session. However, if Congress has concluded its term and the president fails to sign a bill within 10 days, the bill does not become law. This last situation, called a pocket veto, forces Congress in its next term to start over from the beginning: The bill again must pass both chambers and again is subject to presidential veto.

table 11-3	THE MAJOR FUNCTIONS OF CONGRESS
Function	**Basis and Activity**
Lawmaking	Through its constitutional grant to enact law, Congress makes the laws authorizing federal programs and appropriating the funds necessary to carry them out.
Representation	Through its elected constitutional officers—U.S. senators and representatives—Congress represents the interests of constituents and the nation in its deliberations and its lawmaking.
Oversight	Through its constitutional responsibility to see that the executive branch carries out the laws faithfully and spends appropriations properly, Congress oversees and sometimes investigates executive action.

The Lawmaking Function of Congress

Under the Constitution, Congress is granted the **lawmaking function:** the authority to make the laws necessary to carry out the powers granted to the national government. The constitutional powers of Congress are substantial; they include the powers to tax, to spend, to regulate commerce, and to declare war. However, whether Congress takes the lead in the making of laws usually depends on the type of policy at issue.

Broad Issues: Fragmentation as a Limit on Congress's Role   Although Congress sometimes takes the lead on major national policy issues,[35] it often depends on the president to take the lead. One reason is that the structure of Congress is not well suited to tackling such issues. Congress is not one house but two, each with its own authority and constituency base. Neither the House nor the Senate can enact legislation without the other's approval, and the two chambers are hardly identical. California and North Dakota have exactly the same representation in the Senate (two senators each), but in the House, which is apportioned by population, California has 53 seats compared to North Dakota's one. Moreover, the House and the Senate are sometimes controlled by opposite parties, making agreement between the two chambers even harder to reach.

Congress also includes a lot of lawmakers: 100 members of the Senate and 435 members of the House. They come from different constituencies and represent different and sometimes opposing interests, which leads to disagreements, even among members of the same party. Most members of Congress, for example, say they are in favor of global free trade. Yet when it comes to specific trade issues, they may take the opposite position. Foreign competition means different things to manufacturers who produce automobiles, computer chips, or underwear; and it means different things to farmers who produce corn, sugar, or grapes. Because it means different things to different people in different parts of the country, members of Congress who represent these different areas will often have conflicting views on when free trade is advantageous.

As an institution, the presidency is better suited to the task of providing leadership on major national issues. First, whereas Congress's authority is divided, executive power is vested constitutionally in the hands of a single individual—the president. Unlike congressional leaders, who must bargain with their party's members when taking a stand on legislation, the president has less need to negotiate with other executive officials in taking a position. Second, whereas members of Congress often see issues from the perspective of their state or constituency, presidents have a national constituency and tend to look at policy from that perspective.

The president has one other noteworthy advantage over Congress when it comes to major legislative initiatives, especially those involving complex problems. The president, as will be explained in Chapter 12, is assisted by literally hundreds of policy specialists, both directly and through the executive agencies, such as the Departments of Treasury and Defense. These specialists have the expertise required for crafting intricate legislative initiatives. Congress does not have anywhere near the same level of access to knowledgeable experts.*

Presidential leadership on major policy issues means that Congress will listen to White House proposals, not that it will support them. It may reject a proposal outright, particularly when the president is from the opposing party. During President Obama's second term, most of his major legislative proposals were pronounced "dead on arrival" when they reached Congress. Republicans had the votes to block action on his proposals. By contrast, if a presidential proposal has enough congressional support, it becomes the starting point for negotiations, saving Congress the time and trouble of developing the legislation

---

*Congress's expertise is concentrated largely in its committee system, where members acquire policy knowledge in the policy area handled by the committees they serve on. Each committee also has a staff, some of whose members are hired for their expertise in the committee's policy area. Congress also has three agencies of its own, though they function as nonpartisan bodies rather than as policy bodies. One of these agencies is the Congressional Budget Office (CBO), which has a staff of 250 employees and provides Congress with estimates of government expenditures and revenues, which Congress uses in determining fiscal policy. A second congressional agency is the Government Accountability Office (GAO), with 3,000 employees. Its job is to determine whether executive agencies are complying with laws passed by Congress. The third agency is the Congressional Research Service (CRS) with 1,000 employees. The CRS functions as a research and information service for congressional members and committees. By law, it is prohibited from making policy recommendations.

Republican Susan Collins was first elected to the U.S. Senate from Maine in 1996. Collins is among the growing number of women who sit in the U.S. Congress. Collins won reelection to a fourth term in 2014. (©J. Scott Applewhite/AP Photo)

from scratch. (The legislative roles of Congress and the president are discussed further in Chapter 12.)

Congress in the Lead: Fragmentation as a Policymaking Strength
Congress's true strength as a legislative body is its ability to handle scores of small issues simultaneously. The great majority of the hundreds of bills that Congress considers each session deal with narrow issues, such as providing grants-in-aid to cities for their mass transit systems or authorizing a new weapons system for the navy. Such bills are handled largely through Congress's standing committees, each of which has policy expertise resulting from the fact that it concentrates on a particular policy area, such as taxation, agriculture, or military affairs. And because the standing committees operate somewhat independently of each other, the committee system as a whole can work simultaneously on a large number of bills. As political scientist James Sundquist noted, "Congress [is] organized to deal with narrow problems but not with broad ones."[36]

Most such policy issues also serve the reelection interests of members of Congress. The resulting legislation tends to be "distributive" in nature—that is, it confers a benefit on a particular group while spreading the cost across the taxpaying public. An example is the previously discussed $1.7 billion spending bill that was passed in 2011 to assist military veterans in finding jobs. Eligible veterans received assistance in getting a job, while the cost of the program fell on taxpayers as a whole. Distributive policies have a clear political advantage. The benefit is large enough that members of the recipient group will recognize and appreciate it, although the cost to each taxpayer is barely noticeable. Such policies are also the type that Congress, through its committee system, is organizationally best suited to handle. Most committees parallel a major constituent interest, such as agriculture, commerce, labor, or veterans.

The Representation Function of Congress

In the process of making laws, the members of Congress represent various interests within American society, giving them a voice in the national legislature. The proper approach to the **representation function** has been debated since the nation's founding. A recurrent issue is whether the representative should respond primarily to the interests of the nation as a whole or to those of his or her constituency. These interests overlap to some degree but do not coincide exactly. Policies that have broad benefits are not necessarily advantageous to particular localities. Free trade in steel is an example. Although U.S. manufacturers as a whole benefit from access to low-priced steel from abroad, domestic steel producers and the communities where they are located are hurt by it.

Representation of States and Districts   The choice between national and local interests is not a simple one, even for a legislator who is inclined toward one or the other orientation. To be fully effective, members of Congress must be reelected time and again, a necessity that compels them to pay attention to local demands. Yet they serve in the nation's legislative body and cannot ignore national needs. In making the choice, most members of Congress, on narrow issues at least, vote in a way that will not antagonize local interests.[37] Opposition to gun control legislation, for example, is stronger among members of Congress representing rural areas where hunting is prevalent than it is among those from urban areas where guns are more likely to be perceived as a threat to public safety.

Local representation occurs in part through the committee system. Although studies indicate that the policy positions of most committees are not radically different from those of the full House or Senate,[38] committee memberships roughly coincide with constituency interests. For example, farm-state legislators dominate the membership of the House and Senate Agriculture Committees. Committees are also the site of most *logrolling*—the practice of trading one's vote with another member's so that both get what they want, as in the case of agricultural committee members from corn-producing northern states trading votes with members from cotton-producing southern states.

Local representation also shapes how Congress distributes funds for federal programs. Members of Congress will often withhold their support unless their locality gets a share of the money, even if the effect is to make the program less efficient. An example is the State Homeland Security Program that helps states buy security equipment and train security personnel. Even though the threat of a terrorist attack is much higher in cities like New York, Washington, and Los Angeles, the act specifies that 40 percent of the money is to be spread across all the states.

Nevertheless, representation of constituency interests has its limits. Constituents have little awareness of most issues that come before Congress. Whether Congress appropriates a few million dollars in foreign aid to Chad or Bolivia is not the sort of issue that local residents will hear about. Moreover, members of Congress often have no choice but to go against the wishes of a significant portion of their constituency. The interests of workers and employers in a district or state, for example, can differ considerably. In such cases, members of Congress typically side with the interest that aligns with their party. When local business and labor groups take opposing sides on issues before Congress, for example, Republican members tend to back business's position, whereas Democratic members tend to line up with labor.

Representation of the Nation through Parties   When a vital national interest is at stake, members of Congress can be expected to respond to it. With the economy showing signs of a recession in early 2008, Congress enacted legislation that gave most taxpayers a rebate of several hundred dollars in the hope that they would spend it, thereby giving the economy a boost. The House voted 380–34 in favor of the tax rebate; the Senate vote was 81–16.

In most cases, however, members of Congress, though agreeing on a need for national action, disagree on the best course of action. Most lawmakers believe, for example, that the nation's immigration system needs to be overhauled. The nation has a need for immigrant labor and yet has roughly 11 million undocumented immigrants already here. The situation creates pressure for political action. But what action is necessary and desirable? Should the undocumented immigrants already here be given a path to citizenship? Should the immigration system favor immigrants with high skill levels or those with family members in the United States? What should be done to prevent additional individuals from entering the United States illegally?

There is no general agreement in Congress on such issues. Republican and Democratic lawmakers have different perspectives on national issues because their parties differ philosophically and politically. Differences in the parties' approaches to immigration policy, for example, have played out whenever an immigration bill has been debated, with Republicans pushing for more control over the nation's borders and Democrats pushing to accommodate the undocumented immigrants already in the country.

Partisan divisions have become more acute as a result of party polarization. As was discussed earlier, the overwhelming majority of congressional Democrats are liberal and the overwhelming majority of congressional Republicans are conservative, which has made it more difficult for the two sides to agree on legislation. Party polarization has also fostered a *nationalization* of congressional politics. When Republican and Democratic lawmakers vote in the same way as their fellow partisans, regardless of constituency differences, what else but a shift of issues to the national level would accurately describe what's taken place? Of course, local influences still matter in Congress but less so than in the past. On small and large issues alike, Republican and Democratic lawmakers have been deeply divided, even when they come from the same state or region.

A positive aspect of this development is that party differences are increasingly apparent to voters. At times in the past, many voters believed that the parties did not offer a clear choice. In the view of some political scientists, this situation was a barrier to accountability. They argue that America's voters deserve to have the choice between "responsible parties"—parties that take clear-cut and opposing policy positions and seek to enact them when in office so that voters can more easily hold them to account for their actions.[39]

Critics of this view say that it fails to account for the structure of U.S. institutions. In a European parliamentary system, the majority party has full control of legislative and executive power and can enact its agenda. At the next election, the voters can decide whether they approve or disapprove of what it has accomplished. In the American system, by contrast, executive and legislative powers are divided, and legislative power is further divided between the House and the Senate (see "How the U.S. Differs"). When the two parties are closely divided in strength, the division of powers enables each party to prevent the other from acting. The result can be policy deadlock and delay, even when the nation has a pressing policy needs.[40]

The fact that the parties are currently so closely matched has intensified the conflict between them. Each party sees the next election as a critical encounter that will determine whether it will control the House and the Senate. As a result, each party has an incentive to deny the other party any claim to legislative success. The minority party in Congress tries to block the policy initiatives of the party in power. In turn, the majority party does everything possible to marginalize the weaker party in order to destroy its credibility. Each party casts the other in stark terms—too extreme and too beholden to special interests to govern in the interests of ordinary Americans. As Frances Lee notes in *Insecure Majorities*, members of Congress are engaged in "messaging" rather than "governing.[41] In positioning themselves on bills, they are less concerned with whether their position will prevail in Congress than whether it will win them votes in the next election. Reflecting on the partisan fights and

HOW THE U.S. DIFFERS

CRITICAL THINKING THROUGH COMPARISONS

Legislative Structure

The U.S. House and Senate are equal in their legislative powers; without their joint agreement, no law can be enacted. This arrangement is unusual. Although most democracies have a bicameral (two-chamber) legislature, one chamber is usually more powerful than the other. In the Canadian parliament, for example, nearly all bills originate in the House of Commons with the Senate functioning more as a check on its actions than as a coequal body. Moreover, some democracies, including Sweden and Israel, have unicameral (one-chamber) legislatures. If the United States had an equivalent legislature, it would consist only of the House of Representatives.

Power in the U.S. Congress is divided in other ways as well: It has elected leaders with limited formal powers, a network of committees, and members who are free to follow or ignore other members of their party. It is not uncommon for a legislator to vote against the party's position on legislative issues. In contrast, European legislatures have a centralized power structure. Top leaders have substantial authority, the committees are weak, and the parties are unified. European legislators are expected to support their party unless granted permission to vote otherwise on a particular bill. If they defy the party leadership, they could be denied renomination in the next election.

Q: In terms of passing laws, what is the relative advantage and disadvantage of the way in which Congress is structured, compared with a national legislature with a single dominant chamber in which the majority party can count on its members to support its policy agenda?

A: A relative advantage of Congress is that it is structured in a way that slows the passage of legislation, which can be a safeguard against hastily prepared, ill-considered, or weakly supported bills. A relative disadvantage of Congress's structure is that it can result in legislative deadlock even on pressing national issues. The Senate filibuster can enable a determined minority to block legislation even if it has majority support within and outside Congress. And if one party controls the House and the other party controls the Senate, each party has the power to block the other from acting.

policy deadlock, a longtime congressional veteran recently said that Congress is no longer a place for debate over legislation. It's become, he said, "a campaign stage."[42]

As congressional partisanship has intensified, the public's image of Congress has plummeted (see Figure 11-5). In the 1980s, before partisan deadlock gripped Congress, roughly 6 in 10 Americans approved of how Congress was doing its job. Today, barely more than 2 in 10 approve.

The Oversight Function of Congress

In addition to enacting the laws, Congress has responsibility for seeing that its laws are carried out properly by the executive branch. This responsibility is known as Congress's **oversight function.**[43]

Oversight is carried out largely through the committee system of Congress, with each standing committee overseeing part of the executive branch. The House and Senate Agriculture Committees, for example, monitor the Department of Agriculture. The Legislative Reorganization Act of 1970 spells out each committee's responsibility for overseeing its parallel agency: "Each standing committee shall review and study, on a continuing basis, the application,

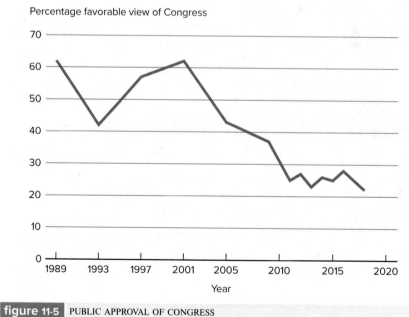

figure 11-5 PUBLIC APPROVAL OF CONGRESS

Partisan polarization in Congress has been accompanied by declining public approval of Congress. (*Source:* Pew Research Center for the People and the Press surveys.)

administration, and execution of those laws, or parts of laws, the subject matter of which is within the jurisdiction of that committee."

Oversight is a demanding task. The bureaucracy has hundreds of agencies and thousands of programs. Congress gets some leverage from the fact that federal agencies have their funding renewed each year, which provides an opportunity for congressional committees to review agency activities.[44] Nevertheless, because the task is so large, oversight is not pursued vigorously unless members of Congress are annoyed with an agency, have discovered that a legislative authorization is being abused, or are intending to modify an agency program.

When an agency is alleged to have acted improperly, committee hearings into the allegations can occur. Congress's investigative power is not listed in the Constitution, but the Supreme Court has upheld this power as a reasonable extension of Congress's power to make the laws. Except in cases involving *executive privilege* (the right of the executive branch to withhold confidential information affecting national security), executive branch officials are required to testify when called by Congress to do so. If they refuse, they can be cited for contempt of Congress, a criminal offense.

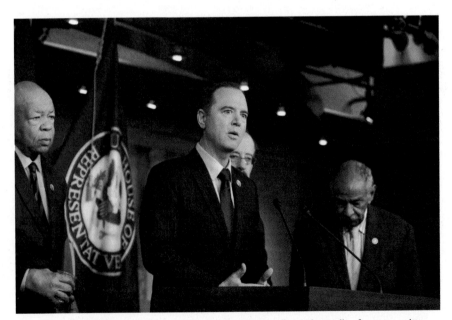

Adam Schiff (D-Calif.) of the House Intelligence Committee talks to the media after a committee hearing on Russian meddling in the 2016 presidential election. The high-profile hearings became a source of controversy, with Republican members accusing Democratic members of conducting "a witch hunt" aimed at harming President Trump while the Democrats accused the Republicans of engaging in "a cover-up" of Russia's election involvement. (©Jeff Malet Photography/Newscom)

Congress's interest in oversight diminishes when the White House is the target and the president is from the same party as the congressional majority. The House Intelligence Committee's investigation of Russian meddling in the 2016 presidential election, for example, sought to protect President Trump as much as it sought to examine Russian meddling. The committee's Republican majority refused to call key witnesses or subpoena those who refused to answer questions, and then it issued a report claiming that Russian meddling was inconsequential—a claim at odds with what the CIA, FBI, National Security Agency, and director of national intelligence had concluded in their investigations of the issue.[45]

CONGRESS: AN INSTITUTION DIVIDED

Congress is not an institution where majorities rule easily. Agreement within each chamber, and between the two chambers, is required to pass legislation. That can typically be achieved only if lawmakers are willing to act in a spirit of compromise. Such was the intention of the framers of the Constitution. They designed the institution to foster compromise, for the purpose of having the resulting legislation reflect the interests of many rather than of a powerful faction.

| F A K E | Detecting Misinformation |
| F A C T | |

(or)

Detecting Misinformation

Are Policy Problems Simple and Easy to Fix?

A recent poll found most people think "ordinary Americans" would do a better job than "elected officials" of "solving the country's problems."[46] That opinion dovetails with the findings of political scientists John Hibbing and Elizabeth Theiss-Morse in *Stealth Democracy*. They discovered that millions of Americans believe that our constitutional system's elaborate legislative process is a waste of time.[47] If, as these Americans think, policy problems are simple and easy to

©moodboard/Getty Images

fix, there's no reason for debate and deliberation. All that's required is for politicians to get out of the way and turn the job of legislating over to no-nonsense leaders.

Continued

Is that claim fact, or is it fake?

It's understandable that Americans would be frustrated by the failure of their elected leaders to address pressing national problems. Petty partisan feuds have prevented Congress from acting at a high level in recent years. At the same time, although policy issues may look simple, they seldom are. Foreign trade, for example, affects thousands of American businesses, some of which benefit from free trade and some of which don't. Moreover, foreign trade is not simply an economic issue. It's also a means of strengthening the ties between nations, which has implications for national security. As a result, the notion that America's trade problem, or any of its other major problems, is subject to an easy and simple fix is mistaken. Legislating requires the weighing of many considerations, some of which are complex and interrelated. It's the case, moreover, that policymaking in a democratic system must take into account a wide range of competing interests. Accommodating such interests requires negotiation and compromise. That's why the framers of the Constitution divided legislative power between two coequal chambers, apportioned differently and with different terms of office for each chamber. The framers recognized the importance of establishing a legislative process that would allow competing interests to make their voices heard, even though it would sometimes result in policy delay and deadlock.

What the writers of the Constitution did not fully anticipate was the degree to which intense partisanship could disrupt the workings of Congress. Party unity is the clearest way for the majority to overcome the obstacles to action inherent in Congress's fragmented structure. At the same time, party unity is the most direct way for the minority to block action. And because Congress's structure makes it easier to block legislation than to enact it, a determined minority party—if its members closely match in number those of the majority party—can act in ways that deadlock the institution, even in the face of urgent national problems.

SUMMARY

Members of Congress, once elected, are likely to be reelected. Members of Congress can use their office to publicize themselves, pursue a service strategy of responding to the needs of individual constituents, and secure pork-barrel projects for their states or districts. The fact that they hold a position in Congress also helps them attract campaign contributions from individual donors and PACs. Incumbency carries some risks. Members of Congress must take positions on controversial issues, may blunder into political scandal or indiscretion, must deal with changes in the electorate, or may face strong challengers. By and large, however, the advantages of incumbency far outweigh the disadvantages.

Congress is a fragmented institution. It has no single leader; rather, the House and the Senate have separate leaders, neither of whom can presume to speak for the other chamber. The chief party leaders in Congress are the Speaker of the House and the Senate majority leader. They share leadership power with committee and subcommittee chairpersons, who have influence on the policy decisions of their respective committees or subcommittees.

Congress's fragmentation is offset partially by partisanship, which serves as a common bond between members of the same party. In the past few decades, that bond has strengthened to the point where congressional Republicans and Democrats have regularly found themselves on the opposite sides of legislative issues. In some cases, the partisan gap has been so wide that compromise has failed, resulting in legislative delay and deadlock.

Committees are the locus of most of the day-to-day work of Congress. Each House and Senate standing committee has jurisdiction over bills in a particular area (such as agriculture or foreign relations), as does each of its subcommittees. In most cases, the full House and Senate accept committee recommendations about the passage of bills, although amendments to bills are not uncommon and committees are careful to take other members of Congress into account when making legislative decisions. On major bills, committees work closely with the party leaders, knowing that a bill will not win the necessary support if it's at odds with what party leaders and the party caucus are expecting.

The major function of Congress is to enact legislation. Yet the role it plays in developing legislation depends on the type of policy involved. Because of its divided chambers and committee structure, as well as the concern of its members with state and district interests, Congress, through its party leaders and caucuses, only occasionally takes the lead on broad national issues. Congress instead typically looks to the president for this leadership. Nevertheless, presidential initiatives are passed by Congress only if they meet its members' expectations and usually only after a lengthy process of compromise and negotiation. Congress is more adept at handling legislation that deals with problems of narrow interest. Legislation of this sort is decided mainly in congressional committees, where interested legislators, bureaucrats, and groups concentrate their efforts on issues of mutual concern.

A second function of Congress is the representation of various interests. Members of Congress are highly sensitive to the state or district on which they depend for reelection. They do respond to overriding national interests, but local concerns usually take priority. National or local representation often operates through party representation, particularly on issues that divide the Democratic and Republican Parties and their constituent groups, which is increasingly the case.

Congress's third function is oversight—the supervision and investigation of the way the bureaucracy is implementing legislatively mandated programs. Although oversight is a difficult and time-consuming process, it is one of the major ways that Congress exercises control over the executive branch.

©gangliu10/Getty Images

CRITICAL THINKING ZONE

KEY TERMS

bicameral legislature (*p. 329*)
bill (*p. 341*)
cloture (*p. 344*)
conference committee (*p. 345*)
constituency (*p. 321*)
filibuster (*p. 344*)
gerrymandering (*p. 323*)
Hastert Rule (*p. 333*)
incumbent (*p. 320*)
jurisdiction (of a congressional
  committee) (*p. 338*)
law (as enacted by Congress) (*p. 345*)
lawmaking function (*p. 346*)
midterm election (*p. 326*)

open-seat election (*p. 323*)
oversight function (*p. 353*)
party caucus (*p. 329*)
party leaders (*p. 329*)
party unity (*p. 330*)
pork (pork-barrel spending) (*p. 321*)
reapportionment (*p. 323*)
redistricting (*p. 323*)
representation function (*p. 349*)
seniority (*p. 340*)
service strategy (*p. 321*)
standing committees (*p. 336*)
veto (*p. 345*)

APPLYING THE ELEMENTS OF CRITICAL THINKING

Conceptualizing: Explain the lawmaking, representation, and oversight functions of Congress.

Synthesizing: Contrast the advantages that incumbents have in seeking reelection with the disadvantages they have. Which of these advantages and disadvantages apply only to House members? Which apply only to senators?

Analyzing:

1. How does the structure of Congress—for example, its two chambers and its committee system—affect its role in the making of policy on broad national issues, as compared with its role on narrower group-centered issues?

2. Compared with past times, there are now fewer conservative Democrats and fewer progressive Republicans in Congress. How has this development increased the importance of party and party leaders in Congress? How has it increased the chances of partisan deadlock on key legislative issues?

EXTRA CREDIT

A Book Worth Reading: Thomas E. Mann and Norman J. Ornstein, *It's Even Worse Than It Looks: How the American Constitutional System Collided with the New Politics of Extremism* (New York: Basic Books, 2012). A best-selling book that identifies the problems that have led Congress into deadlock and dysfunction.

A Website Worth Visiting: **www.house.gov** or **www.senate.gov.** The websites of the U.S. House of Representatives and the U.S. Senate, respectively. Each site has information on the chamber's party leaders, pending legislation, and committee hearings, as well as links to each member's office and website.

PARTICIPATE!

Each year, thousands of college students serve as interns in Congress or a state legislature. Many internships are unpaid, but students can ordinarily receive college credit for the experience. Internships are not always a great adventure. Many legislative interns envision themselves contributing ideas and research that might influence public policy, only to find that they are answering letters, developing mailing lists, or duplicating materials. Nevertheless, few interns conclude that their experience has been a waste of time. Most find it rewarding and ultimately memorable. Information about internships can be obtained from the American Political Science Association (www.apsanet.org). In addition, there are organizations in Washington that arrange internships in Congress and the executive agencies. These organizations frequently charge a fee for their services, so you might want to contact a legislative office or executive agency directly. It is important to make your request as early as possible in the college year, because some internship programs have deadlines and nearly all offices receive more requests than they can accommodate. You could also check with the student services office at your college or university. Some of these offices have information on internship opportunities.

12
CHAPTER

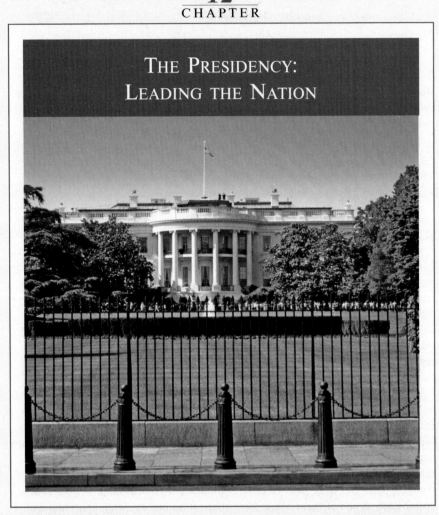

THE PRESIDENCY:
LEADING THE NATION

❝ [The president's] is the only voice in national affairs. Let him once win the admiration and confidence of the people, and no other single voice will easily overpower him.❞

WOODROW WILSON[1]

Donald Trump's presidency was expected to be different, but few predicted just how unprecedented it would be. Most presidents achieve a large number of their top policy goals during their first year in office. Trump was nearly at the end of his first year before he had his first major legislative success, the 2017 Tax Cut and Jobs Act. Most presidents in their first year establish strong relations with America's traditional allies. Trump downplayed the relationships. Early on, most presidents seek to create a stable team of cabinet members and policy advisers. Trump fired them at a record pace. When asked about it, he said, "I like conflict. . . . I like watching it, I like seeing it, and I think it's the best way to go."[2]

The presidency is America's least predictable institution. Lyndon Johnson's and Richard Nixon's dogged pursuit of the Vietnam War led to talk of "the imperial presidency," an office so powerful that constitutional checks and balances were no longer an effective constraint on it. Within a few years, because of the Watergate scandal and intractable international problems during the Ford and Carter presidencies, the watchword became "the imperiled presidency," an office too weak to meet the nation's need for executive leadership. Ronald Reagan's policy successes prior to 1986 renewed talk heard in the Roosevelt and Kennedy years of "a heroic presidency," an office that is the inspirational center of American politics. After the Iran-Contra scandal in 1986, Reagan was more often called a lame duck. George H. W. Bush's handling of the Gulf crisis—leading the nation in 1991 into a major war and emerging from it with a stratospheric public approval rating—bolstered the heroic conception of the office. A year later, Bush was defeated in his campaign for a second term. Bill Clinton overcame a fitful start to his presidency

President Trump at work in the Oval Office at the White House. The presidency is the most visible of America's political institutions but also the least predictable, not only from one president to the next but also during a president's term of office. (*Source:* Official White House Photo by Shealah Craighead)

to become the first Democrat since Franklin D. Roosevelt in the 1930s to win reelection. As Clinton was launching an aggressive second-term policy agenda, however, he got entangled in an affair with a White House intern, Monica Lewinsky, which led to his impeachment by the House of Representatives and weakened his claim to national leadership. After the terrorist attacks of September 11, 2001, George W. Bush's job approval rating soared to a record high. By the time he left office, Americans had turned against his economic and war policies and only a third of the public had a positive view of his leadership. Barack Obama in his first two years of office had a level of legislative success higher than any president since Johnson. In his last six years, his legislative success rate was the lowest of any president in six decades.

No other political institution has been subject to such varying characterizations as the modern presidency. One reason is that the formal powers of the office are relatively modest, so presidential power changes with political conditions and the personal capacity of the office's occupant. The American presidency is always a central office in that its occupant is a focus of national attention. Yet the presidency operates in a system of divided powers, which means that presidential power is conditional. It depends on the president's own abilities but even more on circumstances—on whether the situation demands strong leadership and whether there is public and congressional support for that leadership. When circumstances are favorable, the president exercises considerable power. When circumstances are unfavorable, the president struggles to exercise power effectively.

This chapter examines the roots of presidential power, the presidential selection process, the staffing of the presidency, and the factors associated with the success and failure of presidential leadership. The chapter covers the following main ideas:

- *Over time, the presidency has become a more powerful office.* This development owes largely to the legacy of strong presidents and to domestic and international developments that have increased the need for executive leadership.

- *The modern presidential campaign is a marathon affair in which self-selected candidates seek a strong start in the nominating contests and a well-run media campaign in the general election.*

- *The president could not control the executive branch without a large number of presidential appointees—advisers, experts, and skilled managers—but the sheer number of these appointees is itself a challenge to presidential control.*

- *The president's election by national vote and position as sole chief executive make the presidency the focal point of national politics.* Nevertheless, whether presidents are able to accomplish their goals depends on their personal capacity for leadership, national and international conditions, the stage of their presidency, the partisan composition of Congress, and whether the issue is foreign or domestic.

FOUNDATIONS OF THE MODERN PRESIDENCY

The framers of the Constitution knew what they wanted from the presidency—leadership in national affairs, command in time of war, direction in foreign affairs, implementation of the laws—but they did not have a clear sense of how the office would work in practice. Accordingly, they chose to describe the powers of the president in general terms. By comparison with the precise listing in Article I of Congress's powers, the provisions in Article II that define the president's authority are broadly worded (see Table 12-1).[3] The clause that provides for the president's executive authority, for example, says simply, "He

table 12-1 | THE CONSTITUTIONAL AUTHORITY FOR THE PRESIDENT'S MAJOR ROLES

Commander in chief: Article II, Section 2: "The President shall be commander in chief of the Army and Navy of the United States, and of the militia of the several states."

Chief executive: Article II, Section 2: "He shall have power, by and with the advice and consent of the Senate, to . . . appoint . . . judges of the Supreme Court, and all other officers of the United States, whose appointments are not herein otherwise provided for, and which shall be established by law."

Article II, Section 3: "He shall take care that the laws be faithfully executed, and shall commission all the officers of the United States."

Chief diplomat: Article II, Section 2: "He shall have power, and with the advice and consent of the Senate, to make treaties, provided two thirds of the senators present concur."

Article II, Section 2: "He shall . . . by and with the advice and the consent of the Senate . . . appoint ambassadors [and] other public ministers and consuls . . ."

Article II, Section 3: "He shall receive ambassadors and other public ministers."

Legislative leader: Article II, Section 3: "He shall from time to time give to the Congress information of the state of the Union, and recommend to their consideration such measures as he shall judge necessary and expedient." (Article I, Section 7, which defines the president's veto power, is also part of his legislative authority.)

shall take care that the laws be faithfully executed, and shall commission all the officers of the United States."

Over the course of American history, each of the president's constitutional powers has been expanded in practice beyond the framers' expectation. For example, the Constitution grants the president command of the nation's military, but only Congress can declare war. In *Federalist* No. 69, Alexander Hamilton wrote that a surprise attack on the United States was the only justification for war by presidential decree. Nevertheless, of the roughly 15 major wars the United States has fought, only 5 were formally declared by Congress.[4] None of America's most recent major conflicts—the Korean, Vietnam, Persian Gulf, Balkans, Afghanistan, and Iraq wars—were waged on the basis of a congressional declaration of war. Indeed, more than 80 percent of U.S. military engagements since World War II have been waged solely on presidential authority (see Figure 12-1).

The Constitution also empowers the president to act as diplomatic leader with the authority to appoint ambassadors and to negotiate treaties with other countries, subject to approval by a two-thirds vote of the Senate. The framers anticipated that Congress would define the nation's foreign policy objectives, while the president would oversee their implementation. However, presidents gradually took charge of U.S. foreign policy and today nearly every foreign policy initiative originates with the president.

The Constitution also vests "executive power" in the president. This power includes the responsibility to execute the laws faithfully and to appoint major administrators, such as the heads of federal agencies. In *Federalist* No. 76, Hamilton indicated that the president's real authority as chief executive was to be found in this appointive capacity. Presidents have indeed exercised power through their appointments, but they have also found their administrative authority—the power to execute the laws—to be significant because it enables them to decide how laws will be implemented. President Barack Obama used his executive power to *permit* the use of federal funds by family-planning clinics that offered abortion counseling. President Donald Trump exerted the same power to *prohibit* the use of federal funds for this purpose. The same act of

Percentage of military engagements

Authorized by president alone — 87%

Authorized by Congress, UN, or NATO — 13%

figure 12-1   AUTHORIZATION FOR WAR

Since World War II, the great majority of U.S. military engagements have been fought solely on the basis of the president's authority as commander in chief of the armed forces. (*Source:* Compiled by author from U.S, Department of Defense documents)

Congress was the basis for each of these decisions. The act authorizes the use of federal funds for family-planning services, but it neither requires nor prohibits their use for abortion counseling, enabling the president to decide the issue.

Finally, the Constitution provides the president with legislative authority, including use of the veto and the ability to propose legislation to Congress. The framers expected this authority to be used in a limited way. George Washington acted as the framers anticipated: He proposed only three legislative measures and vetoed only two acts of Congress. Modern presidents have assumed a more active legislative role. They regularly submit proposals to Congress and do not hesitate to veto legislation they dislike.

The Changing Conception of the Presidency

The presidency, for many reasons, is a more powerful office than the framers envisioned. But two features of the office in particular—*national election* and *singular authority*—have enabled presidents to make use of changing demands on government to claim national policy leadership. It is a claim that no other elected official can routinely make. Unlike the president, who is elected by nationwide vote and is the sole chief executive, members of Congress are elected from separate states or districts and operate in an institution where they share power with the other members.

The first president to forcefully assert a broad claim to national policy leadership was Andrew Jackson, who was elected in 1828 on a tide of popular support that broke the upper class's hold on the presidency (see Chapter 2). Jackson used his popular backing to challenge Congress's claim to national policy leadership, contending that he represented "the people's voice." Jackson's view, however, was not shared by his immediate successors. The nation's major issues were of a sectional nature (especially the North–South split over slavery) and were suited to action by Congress, which represented state interests. In fact, throughout most of the 19th century (the Civil War presidency of Abraham Lincoln was an exception), Congress jealously guarded its constitutional authority over national policy. James Bryce wrote in the 1880s that Congress paid no more attention to the president's policy recommendation than it did to the editorials of leading newspaper publishers.[5]

The 19th-century conception of the presidency was expressed in the **Whig theory,** which holds that the presidency is a limited office. According to this "weak presidency" theory, the president is primarily an administrator, charged with carrying out the will of Congress. "My duty," said President James Buchanan, a Whig adherent, "is to execute the laws . . . and not my individual opinions."[6]

Upon taking office in 1901, Theodore Roosevelt cast aside the Whig tradition.[7] He embraced what he called the **stewardship theory,** which calls for a "strong presidency" that is limited, not by what the Constitution allows, but by what it prohibits. The stewardship theory holds that presidents are free to act as they choose, as long as they do not violate the law. In his autobiography, Roosevelt wrote: "My belief was that it was not only [the president's] right but his duty to do anything that the needs of the nation demanded unless such action was forbidden by the Constitution or by the laws."[8] Acting on his belief, Roosevelt took on the job of breaking up the business monopolies that had surfaced during the nation's industrial revolution (see Chapter 3). He also opened world markets to American goods, using the navy and marines to project U.S. influence southward into the Caribbean and Latin America and westward toward Hawaii, the Philippines, and China (the "Open Door" policy). When congressional leaders objected, he forced a showdown, knowing that the American people would support the troops. Roosevelt said: "I have the money to send [the navy's ships] halfway around the world—let Congress bring them back."

Theodore Roosevelt's conception of a strong presidency was not shared by most of his immediate successors.[9] Herbert Hoover was slow to respond to

Theodore Roosevelt is widely regarded as the first of the "modern" presidents. Roosevelt ignored the nation's isolationist tradition and extended America's influence into Latin America and the Pacific. On the domestic front, he battled the business trusts, believing that unregulated capitalism was incompatible with social justice. Roosevelt held the presidency as a Republican from 1901 to 1908 and was defeated when he tried to recapture it as a third-party candidate in 1912. (*Source:* Library of Congress, Prints and Photographs Division [LC-DIG-pga-08163])

the human misery caused by the Great Depression, claiming that he lacked the constitutional authority to take strong action. His successor, Franklin D. Roosevelt (a distant cousin of Theodore Roosevelt), felt differently. His New Deal policies included unprecedented public works projects, social welfare programs, and economic regulatory actions (see Chapter 3). The New Deal effectively marked the end of the limited (Whig) presidency. FDR's successor, Harry S Truman, wrote in his memoirs: "The power of the President should be used in the interest of the people and in order to do that the President must use whatever power the Constitution does not expressly deny him."[10]

The Need for a Strong Presidency

Today the presidency is an inherently strong office, made so by the federal government's increased policy responsibilities. Although individual presidents differ in their capacity for leadership, the office they hold is one that requires active involvement in a broad range of policy areas.

Modern government consists of thousands of programs and hundreds of agencies. Congress is ill suited to directing and coordinating them. Congress is a fragmented institution that acts through negotiation, bargaining, and compromise. It is simply not structured in a way that would enable it to easily and regularly oversee government activity and develop comprehensive approaches to policy. The presidency is structured in a way that enables it to do so. Final authority rests with a single individual, the president, who is thereby able to direct the actions of others and to undertake large-scale planning.[11] As a result, major domestic policy initiatives since the New Deal era have usually come from the White House. When President Dwight D. Eisenhower took office in 1953 and didn't immediately put forth legislative initiatives, a House committee chair told him: "That's not the way we do things here—you draft the bills, and we work them over."[12]

The presidency has also been strengthened by the expanded scope of foreign policy. World War II fundamentally changed the nation's international role and the president's role in foreign policy. The United States emerged from the war as a global superpower, a giant in world trade, and the recognized leader of the noncommunist world—a development that had a one-sided effect on America's institutions.[13] Because of the president's constitutional authority as chief diplomat and military commander and the special demands of foreign policy leadership, the president, not Congress, assumed the dominant role.[14] Foreign policy requires singleness of purpose and, at times, fast action. The president, as sole head of the executive branch, can act quickly and speak authoritatively for the nation as a whole in its relations with other nations. Congress—a large, divided, and often unwieldy institution—is poorly suited to such a response. Congress's weakness was admitted begrudgingly by Senator William Fulbright, a leading critic of the Vietnam War.

Said Fulbright: "It has been circumstance rather than design which has given the executive its great predominance in foreign policy. The circumstance has been crisis, an entire era of crisis in which urgent decisions have been required again and again, decisions of a kind Congress is ill-equipped to make. . . . The President has the means at his disposal for prompt action; the Congress does not."[15]

CHOOSING THE PRESIDENT

As the president's policy and leadership responsibilities changed during the nation's history, so did the process of electing presidents. The public's role in selecting the president became ever more direct.[16] The United States in its history has had four systems of presidential selection, each more "democratic" than the previous one in the sense that it gave ordinary citizens a larger role in the president's election (see Table 12-2).

The delegates to the constitutional convention of 1787 feared that popular election of the president would make the office too powerful and accordingly devised an electoral vote system (the so-called Electoral College). The president was to be chosen by electors picked by the states, with each state entitled to one elector for each of its members of Congress (House and Senate combined). This system was modified after the election in 1828 of Andrew Jackson, who believed

table 12-2 THE FOUR SYSTEMS OF PRESIDENTIAL SELECTION

Selection System	Period	Features
1. Original	1788–1828	Party nominees are chosen in congressional caucuses.
		Electoral College members act somewhat independently in their presidential voting.
2. Party convention	1832–1900	Party nominees are chosen in national party conventions by delegates selected by state and local party organizations.
		Electoral College members cast their ballots for the popular-vote winner in their respective states.
3. Party convention, primary	1904–1968	As in system 2, except that a *minority* of national convention delegates are chosen through primary elections (the majority still being chosen by party organizations).
4. Party primary, open caucus	1972–present	As in system 2, except that a *majority* of national convention delegates are chosen through primary elections.

that the people's will had been thwarted four years earlier when he received the most popular votes but failed to get an electoral majority. Although Jackson failed to persuade Congress to pass a constitutional amendment to eliminate the Electoral College, he prodded the states to tie their electoral votes to the popular vote outcome in the state. Under Jackson's reform, which is still in effect today, the candidate who wins a state's popular vote is awarded its electoral votes (see Chapter 2). Thus, the popular vote for the candidates directly affects their electoral vote, and one candidate is likely to win both forms of the presidential vote. Since Jackson's time, Rutherford B. Hayes (in 1876), Benjamin Harrison (in 1888), George W. Bush (in 2000), and Donald Trump (2016) have won the presidency despite losing the national popular vote.

Jackson also championed the national party convention as a means of nominating presidential candidates (before this time, party nominees were chosen by party caucuses in Congress and in state legislatures). Jackson saw the national convention—where each state is represented by delegates who select the party nominee—as a way to tighten the connection between the presidency and the people. Since Jackson's time, all presidential nominees have been formally chosen at national party conventions.

Jackson's system of presidential nomination remained intact until the early 20th century, when the Progressives devised the primary election as a means of curbing the power of the party bosses (see Chapter 2). State party leaders had taken control of the nominating process by handpicking their states' convention delegates. The Progressives sought to give voters the power to select the delegates. Such a process is called an *indirect primary* because the voters are not choosing the nominees directly (as they do in House and Senate races) but rather are choosing delegates who in turn select the nominees. However, the Progressives were unable to persuade most states to adopt presidential primaries, which meant that party leaders continued to control a majority of the convention delegates.

That arrangement held until 1968, when Democratic Party leaders ignored the strength of anti-Vietnam War sentiment in the primaries and nominated Vice President Hubert Humphrey, who had not entered a single primary and was closely identified with the Johnson administration's Vietnam policy. After Humphrey narrowly lost the 1968 general election to Richard Nixon, reform-minded Democrats forced changes in the nominating process. The new rules gave the party's voters more control by requiring states to select their delegates through either primary elections or **open party caucuses** (meetings open to any registered party voter who wants to attend). Although the Democrats initiated the change, the Republicans also adopted it. Today it is the voters in state primaries and open caucuses who choose the Democratic and Republican presidential nominees.[17] (About 40 states choose their delegates through a primary election; the others use the caucus system.)

In sum, the presidential election system has changed from an elite-dominated process to one based on voter support. This arrangement has strengthened the presidency by providing the office with the added authority that the vote of the people confers. By virtue of having been chosen in a national election, the president has a claim to national leadership that no other U.S. official is positioned to make.

The Nominating Campaign: Primaries and Caucuses

The fact that voters pick the party nominees has opened the nominating races to nearly any prominent politician with the energy, resources, and desire to run. The competition is intense, except in the case of an incumbent president seeking renomination. The list of potential candidates is often quite long. A year in advance of the 2020 presidential election, analysts came up with a long list of potential candidates for the Democratic nomination, including Joe Biden, Cory Booker, Sherrod Brown, Steve Bullock, Andrew Cuomo, John Delaney, Eric Garcetti, Kirsten Gillibrand, Kamala Harris, John Hickenlooper, Jay Inslee, Amy Klobucher, Mitch Landrieu, Terry McAuliffe, Jeff Merkely, Seth Moulton, Chris Murphy, Deval Patrick, Bernie Sanders, and Elizabeth Warren. At that, analysts weren't sure that they had named them all and worried that they might have left the eventual nominee off the list.

Candidates for nomination have no choice but to start early and run hard. The year before the first contest in Iowa is a critical period, one that has been called the **invisible primary.** Although no votes are cast in this period, it is the time when candidates demonstrate through their fundraising ability, poll standing, and debate performance that they are serious contenders for the nomination. A candidate who fails to show strength in these areas is quickly dismissed as an also-ran. In fact, in nearly every nominating race of the past three decades, the winner has been the candidate who, before a single vote was cast, was ranked first in the national opinion polls.[18] The 2016 presidential nominating races were no exception. On the eve of the Iowa caucuses, Donald Trump was ahead in the national polls on the Republican side and Hillary Clinton led on the Democratic side.

Once the state caucuses and primaries get under way, a key to success is **momentum**—a strong showing in the early contests that contributes to voter support in subsequent ones. Nobody—not the press, not donors, not the voters—has an interest in candidates who are at the back of the pack. No candidate in recent decades has gotten off to a lousy start in the first few contests and then picked up enough steam to win the nomination. The advantage rests with the fast starters. They get more attention from the press, more money from contributors, and more consideration by the voters. It's not sur-

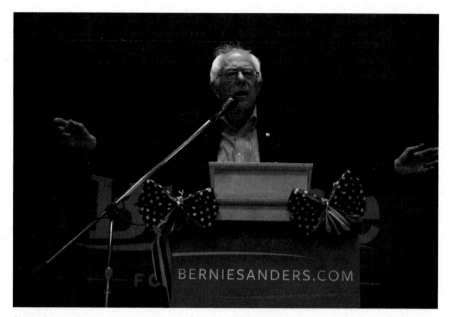

Shown here is Senator Bernie Sanders as he campaigns for the 2016 Democratic presidential nomination. He ran strongly against Hillary Clinton, particularly among young voters. Sanders' impressive showing in 2016 led analysts to speculate on whether he would run again in 2020. (©Frank Pearson/Alamy)

prising that presidential contenders strive to do well in the early contests, particularly the first caucus in Iowa and the first primary in New Hampshire.

After the early contests, the nominating races become a question of which candidates are going to acquire enough delegates in the primaries and caucuses to get the delegate majority needed for nomination. Money becomes a critical factor at this point. It takes a large amount of money to buy the televised ads and hire the staff to run a multistate campaign. In 2016, Clinton and her main Democratic rival, Senator Bernie Sanders, each spent upwards of $200 million on their nominating campaigns. Trump spent far less but, as noted in Chapter 10, he had less need for televised ads, given his huge edge over his Republican rivals in the amount of news coverage (the so-called free media) he received.*

---

*Until the 2000 election, primary-election candidates relied on federal funding to underwrite their nominating campaigns. Under the Federal Election Campaign Act of 1974 (as amended in 1979), a candidate qualifies for this funding by raising at least $5,000 in individual contributions in 20 or more states. In such cases, the government matches up to $250 per contributor, provided that the candidate agrees to limit campaign spending to a set amount in each state and overall (the overall limit for the 2016 election was roughly $50 million). In 2000, George W. Bush declined matching funds so that he could spend an unrestricted amount of money on his nominating campaign. He spent more than $100 million in winning the Republican nomination. Since then, with the exception of John McCain in 2008, all of the winning candidates, and some of the losers, have declined public funds.

The National Party Conventions

The summertime national party conventions mark the end of the nominating campaign. In an earlier era, the delegates from the various states actually bargained and negotiated over the choice of a presidential nominee. However, after the delegate selection process was changed in 1972, the strongest candidate in every case has acquired enough delegates through the primaries and caucuses to secure nomination in advance of the convention. Despite the lack of suspense, the convention is an important event. It brings together the delegates elected in the state caucuses and primaries, who approve a party platform and formally nominate the party's presidential and vice presidential candidates. It also serves as a time for the party to heal divisions created by the nominating race and to persuade the party faithful to rally behind its presidential candidate. Studies indicate that the conventions are a time when a large number of voters settle on their choice of a candidate, usually the one nominated by their preferred party.[19]

The convention is also the time when the parties choose their vice presidential nominees. By tradition, this choice rests with the presidential nominee. In 2016, Trump considered a number of possibilities before selecting as his running mate Governor Mike Pence of Indiana, a social and economic conservative.

The General Election Campaign

The winner in the November general election is nearly certain to be the Republican or the Democratic candidate. Two-thirds of the nation's voters identify with the Republican or Democratic Party, and most independents lean toward one or the other party. As a result, the major-party presidential nominees start the general election campaign with a large backing. Even Democrat George McGovern, whose level of party support was the lowest in the past half century, was backed in 1972 by 60 percent of his party's identifiers.

Because the Democratic and Republican nominees have a built-in advantage, a third-party candidate's chances of victory are remote. Nevertheless, some voters in every presidential election cast their ballots for a third-party candidate. In 2016, Clinton and Trump had unusually high unfavorable ratings, and the Libertarian Party nominee Gary Johnson and the Green Party nominee Jill Stein collectively received 4 percent of the popular vote. If they had not been in the race, polls indicated that most of their support would have gone to Clinton, although it's unclear whether it would have been enough to tip the Electoral College vote in her favor.[20]

Election Strategy   The candidates' strategies in the general election are shaped by several considerations, none more so than the Electoral College (see Chapter 2). Each state has two electoral votes for its Senate representation and a varying number of electoral votes depending on its House representation. Altogether, there are 538 electoral votes, including 3 for the District of Columbia, even though it has no voting representatives in Congress. To win the presidency, a candidate must receive at least 270 votes, an electoral majority. (If no candidate receives a majority, the election is decided in the House of Representatives. No president since John Quincy Adams in 1824 has been elected in this way.)

The importance of electoral votes is magnified by the **unit rule:** all states except Maine and Nebraska grant all their electoral votes as a unit to the candidate who wins the state's popular vote. For this reason, candidates are concerned with winning the most populous states, such as California, Florida, Illinois, Michigan, New York, Ohio, Pennsylvania, and Texas. California's winner, for example, gets all of its 55 electoral votes, which is roughly a fifth of the votes necessary to win the presidency.

Nevertheless, a larger strategic factor than a state's size is its competitiveness. Because of the unit rule, candidates have no incentive to campaign in a lopsidedly Republican or Democratic state because its electoral votes are not in doubt. As a result, the fall campaign becomes a fight to win the competitive states (see "How the 50 States Differ").

Although Trump lost the national popular vote in 2016 to Clinton by 2.9 million votes, he prevailed in the Electoral College through close wins in three toss-up states. He won Pennsylvania, Michigan, and Wisconsin by a combined total of less than 100,000 votes, which provided the margin that gave him a 304–227 edge in electoral votes.

Media and Money   The general election campaign is media centered. The Internet has become the foundation of the candidates' fundraising and get-out-the-vote efforts, while television remains the primary means through which candidates appeal for voters' support. Through appearances on news and interview programs, as well as through their televised advertising (which accounts for most of their spending), the nominees try to win over those voters who are undecided or wavering in their choice (see Chapter 8).[21] The televised presidential debates are part of the media effort. By the time of the debates, most voters have made their choice and find reason to stay with it even if their candidate doesn't perform all that well. Nevertheless, the debates sway some voters. In 2016, Clinton proved to be a stronger debater than Trump, and she picked up some vote support as a result.[22]

HOW THE 50 STATES DIFFER

POLITICAL THINKING THROUGH COMPARISONS

The Unit Rule and 2020 Electoral Vote Strategy

States have the authority to determine how their presidential electors are chosen. With two exceptions (Maine and Nebraska), the states give all their electoral votes to the popular-vote winner in the state–the so-called unit rule. This winner-take-all feature of the electoral vote system leads presidential candidates to focus on the competitive states–those that conceivably could be won by either party. One-sided states–those that are solidly Republican or Democratic–are more or less ignored during the fall campaign. The accompanying map is based on a state-by-state analysis derived from the Cook Political Report and other sources. Heading into the 2020 presidential election, the states are categorized as "Potential Battleground," "Leaning Republican," or "Leaning Democratic."

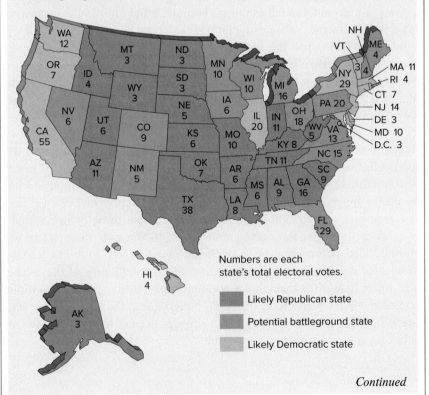

Numbers are each state's total electoral votes.

- Likely Republican state
- Potential battleground state
- Likely Democratic state

Continued

Q: Some state legislatures are considering an alternative to the unit rule. The alternative would allocate their state's electoral votes among the candidates in proportion to the popular votes they each receive. What's your view? Do you think the unit rule is the better way for states to distribute their electoral votes, or do you think a proportional distribution system would be better?

The presidential general election is marked by heavy spending. The total price tag for the 2016 campaign, including the primaries, was $2.4 billion.* The figure includes the amount spent by the candidates, the party organizations, and independent groups.[23] Clinton outspent Trump by a substantial amount during the general election period, but he had the edge in free media. Of the news coverage devoted to the two presidential candidates during the general election, Trump received 57 percent to Clinton's 43 percent.[24]

The presidential debates are a key moment of the general election campaign, although they rarely influence enough voters to tip the balance in the election. Polls after the 2016 presidential debates indicated that most viewers believed Hillary Clinton had bested Donald Trump in each of the three debates though, in the end, she lost the election. (©Xinhua/Alamy)

---

*Major-party candidates have the option of conducting their campaigns with a set amount of federal funds (the amount is roughly $100 million in 2020), provided that they limit their spending to the set amount. Barack Obama recognized that he could raise far more money for his 2008 campaign than the federal limit, and opted to do so. He spent three times as much as did his Republican opponent, John McCain, who accepted public funding. Since then, no presidential nominee has financed the general election campaign with federal funds. Minor-party and independent presidential candidates can qualify for federal funding if they receive at least 5 percent of the vote. Their funding is proportional to the votes they attract. If, for example, a third-party candidate receives half the number of votes as the average for the major-party nominees, that candidate would get half the federal funding that each of them was eligible to receive.

table 12-3	THE PATH TO THE WHITE HOUSE (SINCE 1901)		
President	**Years in Office**	**Highest Previous Office**	**Second Highest Office**
Theodore Roosevelt	1901–1908	Vice president*	Governor
William Howard Taft	1909–1912	Secretary of war	Federal judge
Woodrow Wilson	1913–1920	Governor	None
Warren G. Harding	1921–1924	U.S. senator	Lieutenant governor
Calvin Coolidge	1925–1928	Vice president*	Governor
Herbert Hoover	1929–1932	Secretary of commerce	War relief administrator
Franklin D. Roosevelt	1933–1945	Governor	Assistant secretary of navy
Harry S Truman	1945–1952	Vice president*	U.S. senator
Dwight D. Eisenhower	1953–1960	None (army general)	None
John F. Kennedy	1961–1963	U.S. senator	U.S. representative
Lyndon Johnson	1963–1968	Vice president*	U.S. senator
Richard Nixon	1969–1974	Vice president	U.S. senator
Gerald Ford	1974–1976	Vice president*	U.S. representative
Jimmy Carter	1977–1980	Governor	State senator
Ronald Reagan	1981–1988	Governor	None
George H. W. Bush	1989–1992	Vice president	Director, CIA
Bil Clinton	1993–2000	Governor	State attorney general
George W. Bush	2001–2008	Governor	None
Barack Obama	2009–2016	U.S. senator	State senator
Donald Trump	2017–	None	None

*Became president on death or resignation of incumbent.

The Winners   The Constitution specifies that the president must be at least 35 years old, be a natural-born U.S. citizen, and have been a U.S. resident for at least 14 years. Except for four army generals, nearly every president has served previously as vice president, a member of Congress, or state governor (see Table 12-3). Trump is the first businessman elected to the presidency who had not previously held public office. Until Obama's election in 2008, all presidents were white. Hillary Clinton in 2016 was the closest a woman has come to winning the presidency. Historians have devised rankings of the presidents, and their rankings reveal that there is no template for a successful presidency. Of the four army generals, for example, the presidencies of two of them (George Washington and Dwight D.

Eisenhower) are ranked high while the presidencies of the other two (Ulysses S. Grant and Zachary Taylor) are ranked low.

STAFFING THE PRESIDENCY

When Americans go to the polls on Election Day, they are electing more than a president. They are also picking a secretary of state, the director of the FBI, and hundreds of other federal executives. Each of them is a presidential appointee, and each one is an extension of the president's authority. Although the president cannot be in a hundred places at once, the president's appointees collectively can be. Not surprisingly, presidents typically appoint party loyalists who are committed to the administration's policy goals.

The Vice President

The vice president holds a separate elective office from the president but, in practice, is part of the presidential team. Because the Constitution assigns no executive authority to the office, the vice president's duties within the administration are determined by the president. At an earlier time, presidents largely ignored their vice presidents, who did not even have an office in the White House.

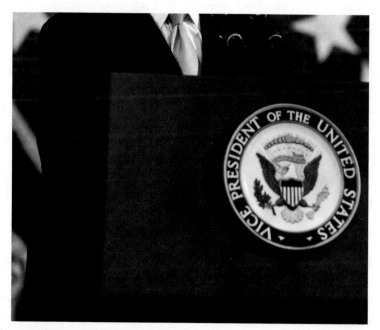

The vice presidency is a separately elected office. However, because the Constitution assigns it no authority other than to serve as president of the Senate and to cast a Senate vote only in case of a tie, the duties of the vice president are determined by the president. Recent presidents have assigned significant responsibilities to their vice presidents. Pictured here is the seal of the vice president of the United States. (*Source:* Lee Craker, USF-I Public Affairs)

A number of leading politicians, including Daniel Webster and Henry Clay, declined the chance to become vice president. Said Webster, "I do not propose to be buried until I am really dead."[25]

When Jimmy Carter assumed the presidency in 1977, he redefined the office by assigning important duties to his vice president and relocating him to an office in the White House, a practice followed by all presidents since Carter. Trump, for example, has assigned Vice President Mike Pence the task of deepening the administration's ties with other countries, which has included numerous trips abroad.

The Executive Office of the President (EOP)

The key staff organization is the Executive Office of the President (EOP), created by Congress in 1939 to provide the president with the staff necessary to coordinate the activities of the executive branch.[26] The EOP has since become the command center of the presidency. The EOP includes a number of units, including the White House Office (WHO), which consists of the president's closest personal advisers; the Office of Management and Budget (OMB), which consists of experts who formulate and administer the federal budget; the National Security Council (NSC), which advises the president on foreign and military affairs; and the National Economic Council (NEC), which assists the president on economic issues.

Most EOP units are staffed by policy specialists, including economists, legal analysts, and national security experts. An exception is the **White House Office (WHO),** which serves the president most directly. The WHO includes the Communications Office, the Office of the Press Secretary, and the Office of Legislative Affairs. As these labels suggest, the WHO consists of the president's personal assistants, including top political advisers and press agents. These individuals tend to be skilled at developing political strategy and communicating with the public, the media, and other officials. Because of their proximity to the president, they are among the most powerful individuals in Washington.

The Cabinet and Agency Appointees

The heads of the 15 executive departments, such as the Department of Defense and the Department of Agriculture, constitute the president's **cabinet.** They are appointed by the president, subject to confirmation by the Senate. Although the cabinet once served as the president's main advisory group, it has not played this role in nearly a century. As issues have grown in complexity, presidents have increasingly relied on presidential advisers for advice rather than seeking it from the cabinet as a whole. Nevertheless, cabinet members, as individuals who head major departments, are important figures in any administration. The president selects them for their prominence in politics, business, government, or the professions.[27] In every administration, a few of them, usually the attorney general or the secretary of state, defense, or treasury, become trusted advisers.

In addition to cabinet secretaries, the president appoints the heads and top deputies of federal agencies and commissions, as well as the nearly two hundred ambassadors. There are more than 2,000 full-time presidential appointees, a much larger number than are appointed by the chief executive of any other democracy.[28] About half of these appointees (including ambassadors and agency heads, but not the president's personal advisers) are subject to Senate confirmation. Reflecting the increased level of party polarization in Washington, presidential nominees in recent years had been increasingly blocked or slowed down by Senate filibusters. In 2013, the Senate Democratic majority prohibited the filibustering of presidential nominees, except in the case of Supreme Court justices. In 2017, Senate Republicans extended the prohibition to include Supreme Court nominees.

The Problem of Control

Although the president's appointees are a major asset, their large number poses a control problem for the president. President Truman kept a wall chart in the Oval Office that listed the more than one hundred officials who reported directly to him. He often told visitors, "I cannot even see all of these men, let alone actually study what they are doing."[29] Since Truman's time, the number of bureaucratic agencies has more than doubled, compounding the problem of presidential control over subordinates.[30]

The president's problem is most severe in the case of appointees who work in the departments and agencies. Their offices are located outside the White House, and their loyalty is sometimes split between a desire to promote the president's goals and an interest in advancing their own ideas. A year into his presidency, Donald Trump fired Rex Tillerson, his secretary of state, over personal and policy differences. Tillerson had allegedly called Trump "a moron" during a Pentagon meeting and had publicly expressed disagreement with Trump's positions on North Korea, Russia, and Iran.[31]

Lower-level appointees within the departments and agencies pose a different type of problem. The president rarely, if ever, sees them, and many of them are political novices (most have less than two years of government or policy experience). They are sometimes "captured" by the agency in which they work because they depend on the agency's career bureaucrats for advice and information.

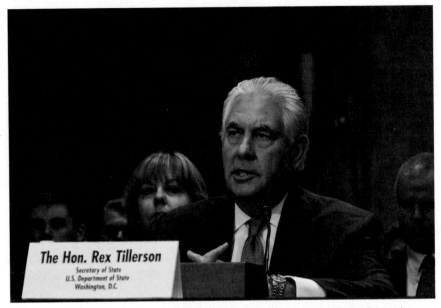

The Hon. Rex Tillerson
Secretary of State
U.S. Department of State
Washington, D.C.

Presidents' influence over the executive branch takes place largely through the efforts of those they appoint to head the various executive agencies. At the same time, presidents do not have time to oversee the work of all their appointees, some of whom will talk or act in ways inconsistent with the president's positions. In 2018, President Trump fired Rex Tillerson, his secretary of state, after Tillerson expressed disagreement with some of Trump's policies and actions. (©mark reinstein/Shutterstock)

In short, the modern presidential office is a mixed benefit. Although presidential appointees enable presidents to extend their influence into every executive agency, these appointees do not always act in ways that serve the president's interest. (The subject of presidential control of the executive branch is discussed further in Chapter 13.)

Factors in Presidential Leadership

All presidents are expected to provide national leadership, but not all presidents are equally adept at it.[32] Strong presidents have typically had a clear sense of where they want to lead the country and an ability to communicate that vision effectively.[33] Ronald Reagan had this capacity, which helped him alter the direction of domestic and foreign policy. Jimmy Carter lacked it. In what was arguably the most important speech of his presidency, Carter said that Americans were having "a crisis of confidence" and needed to adopt a more positive attitude. At a time when Americans were struggling with rising inflation and unemployment and wanted strong leadership, Carter criticized them for being pessimistic.

HOW THE U.S. DIFFERS

CRITICAL THINKING THROUGH COMPARISONS

Systems of Executive Leadership

The United States instituted a presidential system in 1789 as part of its constitutional checks and balances. This form of executive leadership was not copied in Europe. European democracies adopted parliamentary systems, in which the prime minister is both chief executive and head of the legislative branch.

The policy leadership of a president differs from that of a prime minister. As the head of a separate branch of government, presidents do not share executive authority but are dependent on Congress to enact their legislative proposals. In contrast, prime ministers share executive leadership with a cabinet, but once agreement within the cabinet is reached, they typically have the support that is required to enact legislation.

Q: Which executive leadership do you think is preferable—a presidential system, in which the chief executive heads only the executive branch, or a parliamentary system, in which the chief executive heads both the executive and the legislative branches? Why?

Although effective leadership is a key to presidential success, it is only one component. The president operates within a system of separate institutions that share power (see "How the U.S. Differs"). Significant presidential action typically depends on the approval of Congress, the cooperation of the bureaucracy, and sometimes the acceptance of the judiciary. Because other officials have their own priorities, presidents do not always get their way. Congress in particular—more than the courts or the bureaucracy—holds the key to presidential success. Without congressional authorization and funding, most presidential proposals are nothing but ideas, empty of action. Dwight D. Eisenhower, whose personal integrity made him perhaps the most trusted president of the 20th century, had a keen awareness of the need to win over Congress. "I'll tell you what leadership is," he said. "It's persuasion, and conciliation, and education, and patience. It's long, slow, tough work."[34]

Whether a president's initiatives succeed depends substantially on several factors, which will now be discussed.

The Force of Circumstance

During his first months in office and in the midst of the Great Depression, Franklin D. Roosevelt accomplished the most sweeping changes in domestic policy in the nation's history. Congress moved quickly to pass nearly every New Deal initiative he proposed. In 1964 and 1965, Lyndon Johnson pushed landmark civil rights and social welfare legislation through Congress on the strength of the civil rights movement, the legacy of the assassinated President Kennedy, and large Democratic majorities in the House and Senate. When Ronald Reagan assumed the presidency in 1981, inflation and high unemployment had greatly weakened the national economy and created a mood for change, enabling Reagan to persuade Congress to enact some of the largest taxing and spending changes in history.

From presidencies such as these has come the popular impression that presidents unilaterally decide national policy. However, each of these presidencies was marked by a special set of circumstances—a decisive election victory that gave added force to the president's leadership, a compelling national problem that convinced Congress and the public that bold presidential action was needed, and a president who was mindful of what was expected and pursued policies consistent with that expectation.

When conditions are favorable, the power of the presidency is remarkable. The problem for most presidents is that they serve at a time when conditions are not conducive to ambitious goals. Political scientist Erwin Hargrove suggests that presidential influence depends largely on circumstance.[35] Some presidents serve in periods when resources are scarce or when important problems are surfacing in American society but have not yet reached a critical stage. Such situations, Hargrove notes, work against the president's efforts to accomplish significant policy changes. In 1994, reflecting on budget deficits and other constraints beyond his control, President Bill Clinton said he had no choice but "to play the hand that history had dealt" him.

The Stage of the President's Term

If conditions conducive to great accomplishments occur irregularly, it is nonetheless the case that nearly every president has favorable moments. Most newly elected presidents enjoy a **honeymoon period** during which Congress, the press, and the public anticipate initiatives from the Oval Office and are more predisposed than usual to support them. Most presidents propose more new programs in their first year in office than in any subsequent year.[36] Later in their terms, presidents may have run out of good ideas or depleted their political resources; meanwhile, the momentum of their election is gone, and sources of opposition have emerged. Even successful presidents like Johnson and Reagan had weak records in their final years. Franklin D. Roosevelt began his presidency with a remarkable period of achievement—the celebrated "Hundred Days"—that he was unable to duplicate later in his presidency.

An irony of the presidency, then, is that presidents are often most powerful when they are least experienced—during their first months in office. These months can, as a result, be times of risk as well as times of opportunity. The slow start to Donald Trump's presidency owed in part to his inexperience in government. He didn't understand, for instance, the full importance of America's traditional military alliances. He wavered on the nation's commitment to NATO, which unnerved America's European allies. Trump eventually announced his full support of NATO, but his initial statements left European leaders wondering about the sincerity of his commitment.

The Nature of the Issue: Foreign or Domestic

In the 1960s, political scientist Aaron Wildavsky wrote that the nation has only one president but two presidencies: one domestic and one foreign.[37] Wildavsky had found that Congress since World War II had enacted almost twice as many presidential proposals in the foreign policy area as in the domestic policy area.

Wildavsky's finding is now regarded as a product of the postwar era, a time when Republican and Democratic leaders alike were agreed on a need to contain Soviet communism and strengthen America's diplomatic, military, and economic position in the world (see Chapter 17). Today, a president's legislative success in the foreign and domestic policy areas is affected by many of the same factors, such as the partisan makeup of Congress and the strength of competing lobby groups. Presidents still have a slight edge in the foreign policy area because Congress at times will defer to presidents' foreign policy proposals in order to maintain America's credibility abroad.[38] But the level of congressional deference today is nothing remotely like it was in the postwar era.

At the same time, presidents have considerable ability in the foreign policy area to act on their own, separate from what Congress might want. Presidents have the power, for example, to make treaty-like arrangements with other countries. The Supreme Court in 1937 ruled that *executive agreements*—which are formal agreements that presidents make on their own with foreign nations—are legally binding as long as they do not conflict with the Constitution or laws enacted by Congress.[39] A treaty requires Senate approval and cannot normally be voided by the president. In contrast, an executive agreement becomes law simply on the basis of the president's signature, although a subsequent president

Executive agreements   17,300

Treaties   1,100

figure 12-2   FORMAL AGREEMENTS WITH OTHER NATIONS

In the past eight decades, presidents have signed over 17,000 executive agreements with other countries—more than 15 times the number of treaties ratified by the Senate during the same period. Treaties require a two-thirds vote of Senate for ratification. Executive agreements require only the signature of the president. (*Source:* U.S. Department of State. Figure based on the 1939–2013 period.)

can void it. In the past eight decades, presidents have negotiated over 17,000 executive agreements—more than 15 times the number of treaties ratified by the Senate during the same period (see Figure 12-2).[40] These agreements span a wide range of policies, everything from military bases to cultural exchanges.

In no area, however, is the president's capacity for unilateral action clearer than in the use of military force. As was noted earlier in the chapter, the United States has engaged in military action roughly 150 times since the end of World War II. In the large majority of these case, presidents have taken the nation to war solely on their own authority. In some instances, Congress has been caught nearly by surprise. When President Ronald Reagan ordered the invasion of Grenada in 1983, for example, he waited until after the troops were on their way to tell congressional leaders. Speaker of the House Tip O'Neill was among those who were briefed by Reagan. "We weren't asked for advice," O'Neill said, "we were informed what was taking place."[41] Other members of Congress learned of the invasion through the media. They awakened to news that U.S. marines had landed in Grenada and were engaged in heavy fighting with the Cuban troops stationed there.

Presidents' ability to act on their own in the foreign policy arena is strengthened by their special relationship with the defense, diplomatic, and intelligence agencies. Other agencies are sometimes more responsive to Congress than to the president. The Department of Agriculture, for example, relies more heavily on the support of farm-state senators and representatives than on the president's backing. The defense, diplomatic, and intelligence agencies are different. Their missions closely parallel the president's constitutional authority as commander in chief and chief diplomat. In the period before the Iraq invasion in 2003, for example, U.S. intelligence agencies provided assessments that bolstered President Bush's assertion that Iraq's weapons systems threatened American interests. Only later did Congress discover that some of the intelligence assessments were tailored to support Bush's claims about Iraq's weaponry (see "Case Study: Invasion of Iraq").

C A S E	
S T U D Y	**Politics in Action**

Invasion of Iraq

Although the U.S. system is based on checks and balances, there is an area where one branch has the upper hand. Since World War II, the United States has engaged in military hostilities roughly 150 times, usually at the instigation of the president.

A case in point is the 2003 invasion of Iraq. The signal that President George W. Bush was targeting Iraq came in his 2002 State of the Union address, when he grouped Iraq with Iran and North Korea in what he called an "axis of evil." Later, Bush asked Congress for authorization to attack Iraq if it refused to turn over its weapons of

Source: US Department of Defense

mass destruction (WMDs). Bush claimed Iraq had WMDs and was preparing to use them. Citing intelligence reports, Bush said, "The evidence indicates that Iraq is reconstituting its nuclear weapons program."

During the congressional debate, Senator Robert Byrd (D-W. Va.) repeatedly asked the administration to reveal its intelligence reports, but few were forthcoming. The vote in Congress, which occurred a year after the 9/11 terrorist attacks—a time when Americans were still worried about the possibility of another such attack—was one-sided. The House vote was 297-133 in Bush's favor, while the Senate vote was 77-23.

When Bush first indicated the possibility of an invasion, opinion polls indicated that less than half the public thought it was a good idea. But Bush, as the figure below indicates, was able to use the news media to carry his message. Reporters were focused so intently on the White House that Bush administration sources were quoted roughly 10 times as often as were the war's congressional opponents. By the time of the invasion, 76 percent of respondents in a Gallup poll expressed approval—with four of every five of them expressing "strong approval."

Continued

Number of quoted statements in TV broadcast news in the period before Iraq invasion

Bush administration sources — 1,718

Congressional opponents of Iraq invasion — 150

Source: Estimated from Hayes, Danny and Guardino, Matt, "Whose Views Made News?" *Political Communication, vol.* 27, 2010, 73. Based on ABC, CBS, and NBC coverage, August 1, 2002–March 19, 2003.

As it turned out, the Bush administration's claim that Iraq had weapons of mass destruction was faulty. Although U.S. weapons inspectors searched high and low in Iraq for such weapons, they found none of consequence. But having started a war, the United States was caught up in it, and more than a decade later was still engaged in hostilities in the region.

Q. What checks are there on a president who is determined to take the nation to war? What are the conditions, if any, in which those checks might be powerful enough to dissuade the president from doing so?

ASK YOURSELF: What actions are available to Congress? When is Congress likely to invoke them? If the president were to order U.S. forces into combat in the face of congressional opposition, would Congress have any recourse? What about a situation where most Americans were opposed to the prospect of war? What costs would that impose on a president and the president's party? Are these costs significant enough to dissuade a president from acting?

Relations with Congress

Although the power of the presidency is not nearly as substantial as some Americans assume, the president's ability to set the national agenda is unrivaled. Whenever the president directs attention to a particular issue, members of Congress take notice. But will they take action? The answer is sometimes yes and sometimes no, depending in part on whether the president takes their interests into account.

Seeking Cooperation from Congress As the center of national attention, presidents can start to believe that their ideas should prevail over those of Congress. This reasoning invariably gets the president into trouble. Jimmy Carter had not held national office before he was elected president in 1976 and lacked a sense of how Washington operates.[42] Soon after taking office, Carter cut from his budget 19 public works projects that he regarded as a waste of taxpayers' money, ignoring the determination of members of Congress to obtain federally funded projects for their constituents. Carter's action set the tone for a conflict-ridden relationship with Congress.

To get the help of members of Congress, the president must respond to their interests.[43] The most basic fact about presidential leadership is that it takes place in the context of a system of divided powers. Although the president gets most of the attention, Congress has lawmaking authority, and presidents need its cooperation to achieve their legislative goals. Presidents can cajole members of Congress but cannot require them to act. President Truman expressed the situation in blunt terms: "The people can never understand why the President does not use his supposedly great power to make 'em behave. Well, all the President is, is a glorified public relations man who spends his time flattering, kissing and kicking people to do what they are supposed to do anyway."[44]

Even the president's most direct legislative tool, the veto, has limits. Congress can seldom muster the two-thirds majority in each chamber required to override a presidential veto, so the threat of a veto can make Congress bend to the president's demands. Yet, as presidential scholar Richard Neustadt argued, the veto is as much a sign of presidential weakness as it is a sign of strength, because it arises when Congress refuses to accept the president's ideas.[45] A case in point is President Obama's effort to overhaul the nation's agricultural policy. Obama promised it would be done in 2013, but the legislative battle dragged on into 2014, as members of Congress and lobbying groups with competing interests fought over the bill's particulars. Obama threatened to veto the bill unless Congress restored planned cuts in the bill's food stamp provisions. Congress restored some of the cuts but far fewer than Obama demanded. Yet, he signed the farm bill, recognizing that he had no chance of getting Congress to pass one that was more to his liking.

Congress is a constituency that all presidents must serve if they expect to gain its support. Neustadt concluded that presidential power, at base, is "the power to persuade."[46] Like any singular notion of presidential power, Neustadt's conception has limits. Presidents at times have the power to command and to threaten. They can also appeal directly to the American people as a means of pressuring Congress. But Congress can never be taken for granted. Theodore Roosevelt expressed the wish that he could "be the president and Congress too for just ten minutes." Roosevelt would then have had the power to enact as well as to propose legislation.

The State of the Union address, delivered annually in January by the president to the full Congress, symbolizes the president's dependence on Congress. As in the State of the Union, the president can propose legislation, but, in the end, Congress alone has the power to make laws and thereby decides whether the policies that the president wants take effect. Shown here is President John F. Kennedy delivering his 1963 State of the Union address. Behind him to the left in the photo is Vice President Lyndon Johnson, who would become president when Kennedy was assassinated on November 22, 1963. (*Source:* Cecil Stoughton. White House Photographs. John F. Kennedy Presidential Library and Museum, Boston)

Benefiting from Partisan Support in Congress   For most presidents, the next best thing to being "Congress, too" is to have a Congress loaded with members of their own party. The sources of division within Congress are many. Legislators from urban and rural areas, wealthier and poorer constituencies, and different regions of the country often have conflicting policy views. To obtain majority support in Congress, the president must find ways to overcome these divisions.

No source of support is more important to presidential success than whether the president's party controls Congress. Because the president, Senate, and House are elected separately, presidents are not guaranteed to have a Congress controlled by their party. When it is, a situation known as *unified government,* presidents have usually enjoyed considerable legislative success (see Figure 12-3). When the other party controls one or both houses, a situation known as *divided government,* presidents have had greater difficulty convincing Congress to follow their lead. During Obama's first two years in office, when Democrats controlled both the House and the Senate, more than 85 percent of the bills that he supported were enacted into law. In 2011, with Republicans holding

Percentage of bills backed by president that were passed by Congress

figure 12-3   PRESIDENTS' LEGISLATIVE SUCCESS

Presidents can endorse legislation, but it takes Congress to enact it. Although presidents have had considerable success in getting congressional support for bills they backed, they have fared much better when their party controlled Congress than when one or both congressional chambers were controlled by the other party. (*Source:* Calculated by author from Congressional Quarterly reports from 1952 to 2017.)

the House, it dropped to 32 percent and then fell to 20 percent in 2012, one of the lowest rates on record.

During his first year in office, Trump took the fewest positions on legislation of any recent president. Nevertheless, when he did take a position, Republican control of the House and the Senate worked to his advantage. On the average bill, roughly 95 percent of House and Senate Republicans supported his positions, enabling him to prevail more than 90 percent of the time.[47] Clearly, presidential power depends significantly on which party has the numerical majority in Congress. As the historian Arthur Schlesinger put it: "In the end, arithmetic is decisive."[48]

Colliding with Congress   On rare occasions, presidents have pursued their goals so zealously that Congress has taken steps to curb their use of power. Congress's ultimate sanction is its constitutional authority to impeach and remove the president from office. The House of Representatives decides by majority vote whether the president should be impeached (placed on trial), and the Senate conducts the trial and then votes on the president's case, with a two-thirds vote required for removal from office. In 1868, Andrew Johnson came within one Senate vote of being removed from office for his opposition to Congress's harsh Reconstruction policies after the Civil War. In 1974, Richard Nixon's resignation halted congressional proceedings on the Watergate affair that almost certainly would have ended in his impeachment and removal from office. In 1998, the House of Representatives impeached President Clinton on grounds he had lied under oath about a sexual relationship with intern Monica Lewinsky. The Senate acquitted Clinton, partly because polls indicated that most Americans did not think Clinton's behavior constituted "treason, bribery, or other high crimes and misdemeanors," which is what the Constitution defines as the grounds for removing a president from office.

The gravity of impeachment action makes it an unsuitable basis for curbing presidential action except in rare instances. More often, Congress has responded

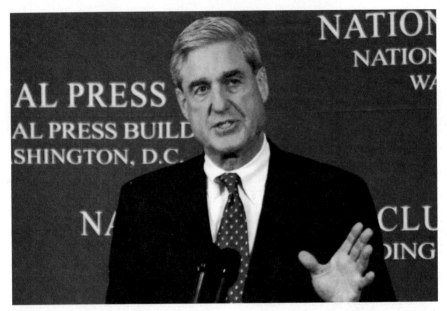

Speculation of possible impeachment proceedings surfaced early in Donald Trump's presidency around the question of whether his campaign colluded with the Russians to influence the 2016 presidential campaign. The appointment of former FBI director Robert Mueller (shown here) as special counsel to investigate the issue heightened that speculation, as did criminal charges that Mueller subsequently brought against top-ranking members of the Trump campaign, including his campaign manager Paul Manafort. Trump labeled the investigation "a witch hunt." (*Source:* Department of Justice)

with legislation aimed at limiting the president's discretion. An example is the Budget and Impoundment Control Act of 1974, which prohibits a president from indefinitely withholding funds that have been appropriated by Congress. The legislation grew out of President Nixon's practice of withholding funds from programs he disliked.

Congress's most ambitious effort to curb presidential power is the War Powers Act. During the Vietnam War, Presidents Johnson and Nixon misled Congress, supplying it with intelligence estimates that painted a falsely optimistic picture of the military situation. Having been told the war was being won, Congress regularly voted to provide the money to keep it going. However, congressional support changed abruptly in 1971 with publication in the *New York Times* of classified documents (the so-called Pentagon Papers) that revealed the White House had not been truthful about the war's progress.

In an effort to prevent future presidential wars, Congress in 1973 passed the War Powers Act. Nixon vetoed the measure, but Congress overrode his veto. The act does not prohibit the president from sending troops into combat, but it does require the president to consult with Congress whenever feasible before doing so and requires the president to inform Congress within 48 hours of the reason for the military action. Unless Congress approves an extension, the War Powers Act also requires hostilities to end within 60 days, although the president has an additional 30 days to withdraw the troops from hostile territory. Presidents have claimed that the War Powers Act infringes on their constitutional power as commander in chief, but the Supreme Court has not ruled on the issue, leaving open the question of whether it is a substantial constraint on the president's war-making powers.

In sum, the effect of presidential efforts to circumvent congressional authority has been to heighten congressional opposition. Even if presidents gain in the short run by acting on their own, they undermine their capacity to lead in the long run if they fail to keep in mind that Congress is a coequal branch of the American governing system.

Public Support

Presidential power rests in part on a claim to national leadership, and the strength of that claim is roughly proportional to the president's public support. **Presidential approval ratings** are usually high at the start of the president's time in office. When asked in polls whether they "approve or disapprove of how the president is doing his job," most Americans express approval during a president's first months in office. The honeymoon rarely lasts long, however. Difficult issues and adverse developments inevitably cut away at the president's public support, and more than half of post–World War II presidents have left office with an approval rating of less than 50 percent (see Table 12-4).

With public backing, the president's leadership cannot easily be dismissed by other Washington officials. When the president's public support sinks, however, officials are less inclined to accept that leadership. During his first two years in office, President George W. Bush was bolstered by public backing resulting from his handling of the terrorist attacks of September 11, 2001. In this period, Congress enacted 17 of his major initiatives, the second highest in such a short period among postwar presidents.[49] However, congressional opposition mounted as Bush's popularity fell in response to a deteriorating economy and a worsening of the Iraq conflict. Among the subsequent Bush initiatives rejected by Congress were his Social Security and immigration reform proposals.

Events and Issues   Public support for the president is conditioned by developments at home and abroad. International threats can result in a patriotic "rally around the flag" response that gives the president wider latitude in deciding policy. For example, polls show that most Americans oppose greater U.S. involvement in Syria's ongoing civil war. Yet in 2017 and again 2018, when it became known that the Syrian regime had used chemical weapons against civilian targets in violation of international law, public opinion momentarily

| table 12-4 | PERCENTAGE OF PUBLIC EXPRESSING APPROVAL OF PRESIDENT'S PERFORMANCE |

President	Years in Office	Average during Presidency (%)	First-Year Average (%)	Final-Year Average (%)
Harry S Truman	1945–1952	41	63	35
Dwight D. Eisenhower	1953–1960	64	74	62
John F. Kennedy	1961–1963	70	76	62
Lyndon Johnson	1963–1968	55	78	40
Richard Nixon	1969–1974	49	63	24
Gerald Ford	1974–1976	46	75	48
Jimmy Carter	1977–1980	47	68	46
Ronald Reagan	1981–1988	53	58	57
George H. W. Bush	1989–1992	61	65	40
Bill Clinton	1993–2000	57	50	60
George W. Bush	2001–2008	51	68	33
Barack Obama	2009–2016	51	58	51
Donald Trump	2017–		38	

Source: Averages compiled from Gallup polls.

shifted. When President Trump in each case ordered massive cruise-missile strikes on Syrian government targets, polls indicated that a majority of Americans approved of the strikes.

Economic conditions also play a part in a president's public support. Economic downturns invariably reduce public confidence in the president.[50] Ford, Carter, and the first President Bush lost their reelection bids when their popularity plummeted after the economy dipped. The irony, of course, is that presidents do not have all that much control over the economy. If they did, they would make sure the economy was strong when the time came to campaign for reelection.

The Televised Presidency An advantage that presidents have in their efforts to nurture public support is their access to the media, particularly television. Only the president can expect the networks to provide free airtime to address the nation, and in terms of the amount of news coverage, the presidency receives twice as much news coverage as Congress.

Political scientist Samuel Kernell calls it "going public" when the president bypasses bargaining with Congress and promotes "his policies by appealing to the American public for support."[51] Such appeals are at least as old as

P A R T Y	Conflicting Ideas

POLARIZATION

President of All the People, or Only Those from the Same Party?

Increasingly, Americans have diverged sharply in their opinions about the president's performance. As would be expected, Democrats are more likely to approve of the performance of a Democratic president and disapprove of that of a Republican president, while the reverse is true of Republicans. However, as indicated by Gallup polls, the gap in Democrats' and Republicans' opinions has widened significantly in recent years. During the three-decade period from Harry Truman's presidency in the late 1940s to Jimmy Carter's presidency in the late 1970s, the difference in the presidential approval level of Republicans and Democrats averaged roughly 35 percent. The difference now exceeds 60 percent, as can be seen in the following figure. As two *Washington Post* reporters said: "We are simply living in an era in which Democrats dislike a Republican president (and Republicans dislike a Democratic one) even before [the president] has taken a single official action."

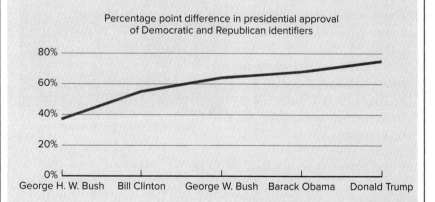

Percentage point difference in presidential approval of Democratic and Republican identifiers

Q: Why has the partisan approval gap widened?

A: The reasons are many, but one of them is that Democrats and Republicans are now further apart in their opinions on controversial policy issues. When it comes to these issues, presidents typically take positions that are in line with the prevailing view in their party. As a result, their positions please most of their party's followers while displeasing, even angering, most of the other party's followers.

Theodore Roosevelt's use of the presidency as a "bully pulpit," but they multiplied in number when television came into American homes in the 1950s. More recently, with cable TV's insatiable demand for news, presidents have had abundant opportunities to air their views. Through his frequent tweets, President Trump has taken the bully pulpit to new levels, garnering twice as much news attention during his first year in office as is typical for a president during that period.[52] As one writer noted of Trump's media visibility: "There was almost no other story in America."[53]

F	A	K	E	
		or		
F	A	C	T	

Detecting Misinformation

Do Trump's Supporters Believe His Claims?

In an assessment of President Donald Trump's statements during his first year as president, the *Washington Post* tallied over 2,000 false or misleading claims—an average of six a day.[57] The fabrications started with his claim that his inaugural crowd, which photos showed to be relatively sparse, was record breaking. "The audience was the biggest ever," Trump said. "This crowd was massive." Nevertheless, Trump's supporters continued to back him, leading some analysts to claim that many of Trump's supporters were too uninformed about the facts to recognize his false claims.

Source: Official White House Photo by Shealah Craighead

Is that claim fact, or is it fake?

Although some of Trump's supporters believed many of his false claims, research found that most of them knew he was stretching the truth. They were using a different test of "truth" in judging what he was saying. Authenticity, not factual accuracy, was their test. Was Trump ever going to build "a big, beautiful border wall as high as 55 feet" and "have Mexico pay for it"? The chances are remote. Trump himself, in a conversation with Mexican president Enrique Peña Nieto, said he didn't expect Mexico to pay for the wall. Trump's reference to a wall was his way of dramatizing his intent to crack down on illegal immigration. That's what Trump's supporters wanted, and, in Trump, they believed they'd finally found a politician who would act on his word.

At the same time, presidents are unable to control everything that reporters say about them. Journalists are adept at putting their own spin on what political leaders say and do, and they tend to play up the unfavorable aspects. During Trump's first year in office, his negative coverage outpaced his positive coverage by more than three to one.[54]

THE ILLUSION OF PRESIDENTIAL GOVERNMENT

Presidents have no choice but to try to counter negative press portrayals by putting their own spin on developments. Such efforts can carry a president only so far, however. No president can fully control his or her communicated image, and national conditions ultimately have the largest impact on a president's public support. No amount of public relations can disguise adverse developments at home or abroad. Indeed, presidents run a risk by building up their images through public relations. By thrusting themselves into the limelight, presidents contribute to the public's belief that they are in charge of the national government, a perception political scientist Hugh Heclo calls "the illusion of presidential government."[55] If they are as powerful as they project themselves to be, they will be held responsible for policy failures as well as policy successes.

Because the public's expectations are high, presidents get too much credit when things go well and too much blame when things go badly. Therein rests an irony of the presidential office. More than from any constitutional grant, more than from any statute, and more than from any crisis, presidential power derives from the president's position as the sole official who can claim to represent the entire American public. Yet because presidential power rests on a popular base, it erodes when public support declines. The irony is that the presidential office typically grows weaker as problems mount, which is the time when strong presidential leadership is needed most.[56]

SUMMARY

The presidency has become a much stronger office than the framers envisioned. The Constitution grants the president substantial military, diplomatic, legislative, and executive powers, and in each case the president's authority has increased measurably over the nation's history. Underlying this change is the president's position as the one leader chosen by the whole nation and as the sole head of the executive branch. These features of the office have enabled presidents to claim broad authority in response to the increased demands placed on the federal government by changing global and national conditions.

During the course of American history, the presidential selection process has been altered in ways intended to make it more responsive to the preferences of ordinary people. Today, the electorate has a vote not only in the general election but also in the selection of party nominees. To gain nomination, a presidential hopeful must win the support of the electorate in state primaries and open caucuses. Once nominated, the candidates are eligible to receive federal funds for their general election campaigns, which today are based on Internet and televised appeals.

Although the campaign tends to personalize the presidency, the responsibilities of the modern presidency far exceed any president's personal capacities. To meet their obligations, presidents have surrounded themselves with large staffs of advisers, policy experts, and managers. These staff members enable the president to extend control over the executive branch while at the same time providing the information necessary for policymaking. All recent presidents have discovered, however, that their control of staff resources is incomplete and that some things that others do on their behalf can work against what they are trying to accomplish.

As sole chief executive and the nation's top elected leader, presidents can always expect that their policy and leadership efforts will receive attention. However, other institutions, particularly Congress, have the authority to make presidential leadership effective. No president has come close to winning approval of all the programs he has placed before Congress, and presidents' records of success have varied considerably. The factors in a president's success include whether national conditions that require strong leadership from the White House are present and whether the president's party has a majority in Congress.

Presidential success stems from the backing of the American people. Recent presidents have made extensive use of the media to build public support for their programs, yet they have had difficulty maintaining that support throughout their terms of office. A major reason is that the public expects far more from its presidents than they can deliver.

©gangliu10/Getty Images

CRITICAL THINKING ZONE

KEY TERMS

cabinet (*p. 378*)
honeymoon period (*p. 382*)
invisible primary (*p. 370*)
momentum (in campaigns) (*p. 370*)
open party caucuses (*p. 369*)

presidential approval ratings (*p. 391*)
stewardship theory (*p. 366*)
unit rule (*p. 373*)
Whig theory (*p. 365*)
White House Office (WHO) (*p. 378*)

Applying the Elements of Critical Thinking

Conceptualizing: Define the *Whig theory* of the presidency and the *stewardship theory*. How did the increase in the federal government's policy responsibilities and the expanded role of the United States in world affairs contribute to the emergence of the powerful presidency suggested by the stewardship theory?

Synthesizing: Contrast the pre-1972 methods of selecting presidential nominees with the post-1972 method, noting particularly the public's increased role in the selection process.

Analyzing: Why is presidential power "conditional"—that is, why is it affected so substantially by circumstance, the nature of the issue, the makeup of Congress, and popular support? (The separation of powers should be part of your answer.)

Extra Credit

A Book Worth Reading: Richard E. Neustadt, *Presidential Power and the Modern Presidents* (New York: Free Press, 1990). A winner of multiple awards, this book is the classic analysis of the nature of presidential power. Although now somewhat dated in its arguments, it has had, as one leading political scientist put it, "a greater effect than any other book about a political institution."

A Website Worth Visiting: **www.ipl.org/div/potus.** A site that profiles the nation's presidents, their cabinet officers, and key events during their time in office.

Participate!

Consider writing a letter or sending an e-mail to the president or a top presidential appointee that expresses your opinion on an issue that is currently the object of executive action. You can inform yourself about the administration's policy or stance on the issue through the website of the White House (**www.whitehouse.gov**) or of the agency in question (for example, the State Department's site, **www.state.gov**).

13
CHAPTER

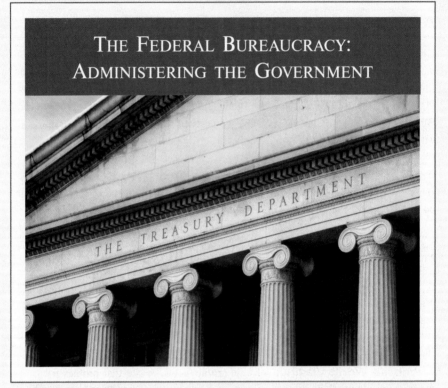

THE FEDERAL BUREAUCRACY: ADMINISTERING THE GOVERNMENT

©Ryan Rodrick Beiler/Shutterstock

    ❝ From a purely technical point of view, a bureaucracy is capable of attaining the highest degree of efficiency, and is in this sense formally the most rational known means of exercising authority over human beings.**❞**

MAX WEBER[1]

On April 20, 2010, as the *Deepwater Horizon* was drilling an exploratory oil well nearly a mile deep in the Gulf of Mexico, methane gas shot out from the drilling pipe and exploded, engulfing the oil platform in flames, killing 11 workers and forcing the rest to jump into the rig's lifeboats. Two days later, still aflame, the *Deepwater Horizon* sank, collapsing the drilling pipe, which sent oil from the well gushing into the Gulf. Nearly three months elapsed before the oil well could be capped, resulting in the worst environmental disaster in the nation's history. The resulting oil spill forced closure of much of the Gulf to fishing, damaged hundreds of miles of beaches and wetlands, and killed unknown quantities of marine life.

The U.S. government blamed the disaster on the oil firm BP, which owned the drilling rights and was supervising the ill-fated drilling operation. But the government itself had a hand in the disaster. Oversight of offshore drilling was the responsibility of the Minerals Management Service (MMS), a bureau within the Department of the Interior. MMS had been lax, or worse, in its responsibilities. Rather than closely regulating offshore drilling, top MMS managers had given oil companies wide latitude in meeting safety and environmental standards. When this information became known in the days following the sinking of the *Deepwater Horizon,* MMS's top officials were forced to resign and a reorganization of MMS was undertaken. In announcing this action, President Barack Obama said: "For a decade or more, the cozy relationship between the oil companies and the federal agency was allowed to go unchecked. That allowed drilling permits to be issued in exchange not for safety plans, but assurances of safety from oil companies. That cannot and will not happen anymore."

As was the case with MMS, government agencies are seldom in the headlines unless something goes wrong. Nor do federal agencies rank high in public esteem. Even though most Americans respond favorably to personal encounters with the federal bureaucracy (as, for example, when a senior citizen applies for Social Security), they have a low opinion of the bureaucracy as a whole. A recent poll found, for example, that roughly two-thirds of Americans see the bureaucracy as "inefficient and wasteful."[2]

Yet, ambitious programs like space exploration, Social Security, interstate highways, and the postal service would be impossible without the federal bureaucracy. In fact, the bureaucratic form of organization is found wherever there is a need to manage large numbers of people and tasks. Its usefulness is clear from the fact that virtually every large private organization is also a bureaucracy, although such organizations typically operate by a different standard than do most public organizations. Efficiency is the chief goal of private organizations but is only sometimes the goal of public organizations. The most efficient way to administer government loans to college students, for instance, would be to give money to the first students who apply and then shut down the program when the money runs out. College loan programs, like many other government programs, operate on the principles of fairness and need, which require that each application be judged on its merit.

In formal terms, **bureaucracy** is a system of organization and control that is based on three principles: hierarchical authority, job specialization, and formalized rules. These features are the reason bureaucracy, as a form of organization, is the most efficient means of getting people to work together on tasks of large magnitude. **Hierarchical authority** refers to a chain of command whereby the officials and units at the top of a bureaucracy have authority over those in the middle, who in turn control those at the bottom. Hierarchy speeds action by reducing conflict over the power to make decisions: those higher in the organization have authority over those below them. **Job specialization** refers to explicitly defined duties for each job position and to a precise division of labor within the organization. Specialization yields efficiency because each individual concentrates on a particular job and becomes proficient at the tasks it involves. **Formalized rules** are the established procedures and regulations by which a bureaucracy conducts its operations. Formalized rules enable workers to make quick and consistent judgments because decisions are based on preset rules rather than on a case-by-case basis.

The noted German sociologist Max Weber (1864–1920) was the first scholar to systematically analyze the bureaucratic form of organization. Weber admired the bureaucratic form of organization for its efficiency but recognized that the gain came at a price. Bureaucrats' actions are dictated by position, specialty, and rule. In the process, they can become insensitive to circumstance. They often stick to the rules even when it's clear that bending them would produce better outcomes. "Specialists without spirit," was Weber's unflattering description of the bureaucratic mindset.[3]

This chapter examines both the need for bureaucracy and the problems associated with it. The chapter describes the bureaucracy's responsibilities, organizational structure, and management practices. The chapter also explains the "politics" of

Burning oil from the *Deepwater Horizon* disaster spews fire into the air off the coast of Louisiana. Contributing to the disaster was the Minerals Management Service's lax oversight of the oil companies operating in the Gulf of Mexico. (*Source:* Coast Guard Photo by Petty Officer First Class John Masson)

the bureaucracy. Although the three constitutional branches of government impose a degree of accountability on the bureaucracy, its sheer size confounds their efforts to control it fully. The chapter presents the following main points:

- *Bureaucracy is an inevitable consequence of complexity and scale.* Modern government could not function without a large bureaucracy. Through authority, specialization, and rules, bureaucracy provides a means of managing thousands of tasks and employees.

- *Bureaucrats naturally take an "agency point of view," seeking to promote their agency's programs and power.* They do this through their expert knowledge, support from clientele groups (those that benefit from the agency's programs), and backing by Congress or the president.

- *Although agencies are subject to oversight by the president, Congress, and the judiciary, bureaucrats exercise considerable power in their own right.*

ORIGIN AND STRUCTURE OF THE FEDERAL BUREAUCRACY

The federal bureaucracy was initially small (3,000 employees in 1800, for instance). The federal government's role was confined largely to defense and foreign affairs, currency and interstate commerce, and the delivery of the mail. In the latter part of the 1800s, the bureaucracy began to grow rapidly in size, largely because economic growth was generating new demands on government. Farmers were among the groups clamoring for help, and Congress in 1889 created the Department of Agriculture. Business and labor interests also pressed their claims, and Congress in 1903 established the Department of Commerce and Labor. (A decade later, the department was split into separate commerce and labor departments.) The biggest spurt in the bureaucracy's growth, however, took place in the 1930s. Franklin D. Roosevelt's New Deal included creation of the Securities and Exchange Commission (SEC), the Social Security Administration (SSA), the Federal Deposit Insurance Corporation (FDIC), the Tennessee Valley Authority (TVA), and numerous other federal agencies. Three decades later, Lyndon Johnson's Great Society initiatives, which thrust the federal government into policy areas traditionally dominated by the states, resulted in the creation of additional federal agencies, including the Department of Transportation and the Department of Housing and Urban Development.

Although the federal bureaucracy is sometimes portrayed as an entity that grows larger by the year, the facts say otherwise. Federal employment today is at roughly the same level that it was 50 years ago (see Figure 13-1), despite the fact that the U.S. population has nearly doubled in size since then.

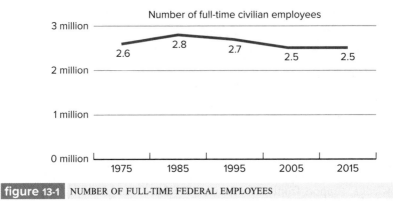

figure 13-1   NUMBER OF FULL-TIME FEDERAL EMPLOYEES

Despite the widespread view that the federal bureaucracy grows ever larger, the number of federal employees has been relatively stable since an expansion in the 1960s. One reason for the stability is improved technology. Many clerical tasks, for example, are now done with the help of computers. Also, the federal government has increasingly contracted out some of its tasks, particularly those for which there is a short-term need for additional workers. (*Source:* U.S. Bureau of the Census.)

Types of Federal Agencies

At present, the U.S. federal bureaucracy has roughly 2.5 million full-time employees, who have responsibility for administering thousands of programs. The president and Congress get far more attention in the news, but the federal bureaucracy has a more direct impact on Americans' daily lives. It performs a wide range of functions; for example, it delivers the mail, oversees the national forests, administers Social Security, enforces environmental protection laws, maintains the country's defense systems, provides foodstuffs for school lunch programs, and regulates the stock markets.

The U.S. federal bureaucracy is organized along policy lines. One agency handles veterans' affairs, another specializes in education, a third is responsible for agriculture, and so on. No two units are exactly alike. Nevertheless, most of them take one of five forms: cabinet department, independent agency, regulatory agency, government corporation, or presidential commission.

The leading administrative units are the 15 **cabinet (executive) departments** (see Figure 13-2). Except for the Department of Justice, which is led by the attorney general, the head of each department is its secretary (for example, the secretary of defense), who also serves as a member of the president's cabinet. Cabinet departments vary greatly in their size and budgets. The smallest, with a mere 4,000 employees, is the Department of Education. The Department of Defense has the largest budget and workforce, with more than 700,000 civilian employees (apart from the nearly 1.4 million uniformed active service members). The Department of Health and Human Services has the second largest budget, most of which goes for Medicaid and Medicare payments (but

figure 13-2 CABINET (EXECUTIVE) DEPARTMENTS

Each executive department is responsible for a general policy area and is headed by a secretary or, in the case of Justice, the attorney general, who serves as a member of the president's cabinet. Shown is each department's year of origin.

not Social Security payments, which are handled by the Social Security Administration, an independent agency).

The newest cabinet-level agency is the Department of Homeland Security (DHS), which was created in 2002 in response to the terrorist attacks on New York and Washington on September 11, 2001. The DHS has responsibility for coordinating domestic antiterrorism efforts, including securing the nation's borders, enhancing defenses against biological attacks, preparing emergency personnel (police, firefighters, and rescue workers) for their roles in responding to terrorist attacks, and coordinating efforts to stop domestic terrorism.[4]

Each cabinet department has responsibility for a general policy area, such as defense or law enforcement. This responsibility is carried out within each department by operating units that typically carry the label "bureau," "agency," "division," or "service." The Department of Justice, for example, has 13 such operating units, including the Federal Bureau of Investigation (FBI), the Civil Rights Division, the Tax Division, and the Drug Enforcement Administration (DEA).

Independent agencies resemble the cabinet departments but typically have a narrower area of responsibility. They include organizations such as the Central Intelligence Agency (CIA) and the National Aeronautics and Space Administration (NASA). The heads of these agencies are appointed by and report to the president but are not members of the cabinet. Some independent agencies exist apart from cabinet departments because their placement within a department would pose symbolic or practical problems. NASA, for example, could conceivably be located in the Department of Defense, but such positioning would suggest that the space program exists solely for military purposes and not also for civilian purposes, such as space exploration and satellite communication.

The largest independent agency is the U.S. Postal Service, with more than half a million career employees. Established at the nation's founding, the postal service delivers a first-class letter for the same low price to any postal address in the United States, a policy made possible by its status as a government agency. If the postal service were a private firm, the price of a first-class stamp would vary by location, with remote areas of states like Wyoming and the Dakotas paying extremely high rates.

Regulatory agencies have been created when Congress recognized a need for ongoing regulation of a particular economic activity. Examples of such agencies are the Securities and Exchange Commission (SEC), which oversees the stock and bond markets, and the Environmental Protection Agency (EPA), which regulates industrial pollution. In addition to their administrative function, regulatory agencies have a legislative function. They develop law-like regulations that regulated entities are required to follow. They also have a judicial function. They assess whether regulated entities are complying with legal requirements. They can impose fines and other penalties on entities that fail to comply. In 2017, for example, Volkswagen paid a $2.8 billion fine for use of illegal software to cheat on emissions tests in an effort to avoid compliance with the Clean Air Act.

Government corporations are similar to private corporations in that they charge for their services and are governed by a board of directors. However, government corporations receive federal funding to pay for some of their operating expenses, and their directors are appointed by the president with Senate approval. Government corporations include the Federal Deposit Insurance Corporation (FDIC), which insures personal savings accounts against bank failures, and the National Railroad Passenger Corporation (Amtrak), which provides passenger rail service.

Presidential commissions provide advice to the president. Some of them are permanent bodies; examples include the Commission on Civil Rights and the

HOW THE 50 STATES DIFFER

CRITICAL THINKING THROUGH COMPARISONS

The Size of State Bureaucracies

Although the federal bureaucracy is criticized as being "too big," it is smaller on a per-capita basis than every state bureaucracy. There are 83 federal employees for every 1,000 Americans. The Illinois bureaucracy, with 103 state employees per 1,000 residents, is the smallest. Hawaii has the largest—428 state employees per 1,000 residents.

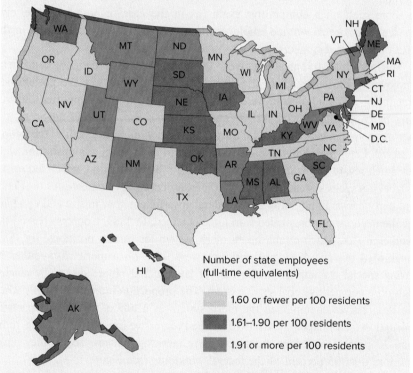

Number of state employees (full-time equivalents)

- 1.60 or fewer per 100 residents
- 1.61–1.90 per 100 residents
- 1.91 or more per 100 residents

Source: U.S. Census Bureau, 2014.

Q: What typifies the states with larger per-capita bureaucracies?

A: In general, the less populous states, especially those that cover a large geographic area, have larger bureaucracies on a per-capita basis. This pattern reflects the fact that a state, whatever its population or area, must provide basic services (such as highway maintenance and policing).

Commission on Fine Arts. Other presidential commissions are temporary. An example is the Presidential Advisory Commission on Election Integrity, which was created by President Trump in 2017 to investigate voting irregularities. It was disbanded in less than a year.

Federal Employment

The roughly 2.5 million full-time civilian employees of the federal government include professionals who bring their expertise to the problems involved in governing a large and complex society, service workers who perform such tasks as the typing of correspondence and the delivery of mail, and middle and top managers who supervise the work of the various federal agencies. Most civil servants are hired through the government's **merit system,** whereby they have to score high on a competitive exam (as in the case of postal service, civil service, and foreign service employees) or have specialized training (as in the case of lawyers, engineers, and scientists).*

The merit system is an alternative to the **patronage system** that governed federal employment during much of the 19th century. Patronage was the postelection practice of filling administrative offices with people who had supported the winning party. In the view of President Andrew Jackson, its chief advocate, the patronage system was a way to tie the administration of government to the people it served. Later presidents extended patronage to all levels of administration without much regard for its impact on the quality of administration, which led critics to label it a **spoils system**—a device for the awarding of government jobs to friends and party hacks. In any case, as the federal government grew in size and complexity, the need for a more skilled workforce emerged. In 1883, Congress passed the Pendleton Act, which established a merit system for certain positions. By 1885, roughly 10 percent of federal positions were filled on a merit basis—either by having special training, as in the case of lawyers and physicians, or by placing high on a competitive civil service exam. The proportion increased sharply when the Progressives championed the merit system as a way of eliminating partisan corruption (see Chapter 2). By 1920, as the Progressive Era was concluding, more than 70 percent of federal employees were merit appointees. Today, they make up more than 95 percent of the federal workforce (see Figure 13-3).[5]

The administrative objective of the merit system is **neutral competence.**[6] A merit-based bureaucracy is "competent" in the sense that employees are hired and retained on the basis of their ability, and it is "neutral" in the sense that employees are not partisan appointees and are expected to be of service to

---

*The merit system is overseen by two independent agencies. The Office of Personnel Management supervises the hiring and job classification of federal employees. The Merit Service Protection Board hears appeals from career civil servants who have been fired or face other disciplinary action.

Percentage of federal employees

figure 13-3   HOW FEDERAL EMPLOYEES GOT THEIR JOBS

In the 19th century, most federal workers were patronage appointees. Today, only a small percentage got their job through that route. The great majority are merit appointees, having obtained federal employment either by placing high on a competitive civil service exam or by having specialized training, such as a medical or engineering degree. (*Source:* Estimated by author from Office of Personnel Management data.)

everyone, not just those who support the incumbent president. Although the merit system contributes to impartial and proficient administration, it has its own biases and inefficiencies. Career bureaucrats tend to place their agency's interests ahead of those of other agencies and typically oppose efforts to trim their agency's programs. They are not partisans in a Democratic or Republican sense, but they are partisans in terms of protecting their own agencies, as will be explained more fully later in the chapter.

The large majority of federal employees have a GS (Graded Service) job ranking. The regular civil service rankings range from GS-1 (the lowest rank) to GS-15 (the highest). College graduates who enter the federal service usually start at the GS-5 level, which provides an annual salary of roughly $28,000 for a beginning employee. With a master's degree, employees begin at level GS-9 with a salary of roughly $42,000 a year. Federal employees' salaries increase with rank and length of service. Although higher-level federal employees are underpaid in comparison with their counterparts in the private sector, while those in some lower-level jobs are comparatively overpaid, federal workers receive better fringe benefits—including full health insurance, secure retirement plans, and substantial vacation time and sick leave—than do most private-sector employees.

Federal employees can form labor unions, but their unions by law have limited scope; the government has full control of job assignments, compensation, and promotion. Moreover, the Taft-Hartley Act of 1947 prohibits strikes by federal employees and permits the firing of striking workers. When federal air traffic controllers went on strike anyway in 1981, President Reagan fired them. There are also limits on the partisan activities of civil servants. The Hatch Act of 1939 prohibited them from holding key jobs in election campaigns. Congress relaxed this prohibition in 1993, although some high-ranking administrators are still barred from taking such positions.

THE BUDGETARY PROCESS

The Constitution mentions executive agencies but does not grant them authority. Their authority derives from grants of power to the three constitutional branches: Congress, the president, and the courts. Of special importance to executive agencies is the **budgetary process**—the process through which annual federal spending and revenue decisions are made. It is no exaggeration to say that agencies live and die by their budgets. No agency or program can exist without funding.

Agencies play an active role in the budgetary process, but the elected branches have final authority. The Constitution assigns Congress the power to tax and spend, but the president, as chief executive, also has a major role in determining the budget (see Chapter 12). The budgetary process involves give-and-take between Congress and the president as each tries to influence how federal funding will be distributed among various agencies and programs.[7] From beginning to end, the budgetary process lasts a year and a half (see Figure 13-4).

The President and Agency Budgets

The budgetary process begins in the executive branch when the president, in consultation with the Office of Management and Budget (OMB), establishes general budget guidelines. OMB is part of the Executive Office of the President (see Chapter 12) and takes its directives from the president. Hundreds of agencies are covered by the budget, and OMB uses the president's directives to issue guidelines for each agency's budget preparations. Each agency, for example, is assigned a budget ceiling that it cannot exceed in developing its budget proposal.

The agencies receive their guidelines in the spring and then work through the summer to create a detailed agency budget, taking into account their existing programs and new proposals. Agency budgets are then submitted to OMB in September for a full review that invariably includes further consultation with each agency and the White House. OMB then finalizes the agency budgets and combines them into the president's budget proposal.

figure 13-4   FEDERAL BUDGETARY PROCESS

The budget begins with the president's instructions to the agencies and ends when Congress enacts the budget. The entire process spans about 18 months. (*Source:* See Schick, Allen, *The Federal Budget: Politics, Policy, Process,* 3d ed., Washington, D.C.: Brookings Institution, 2007.)

The agencies naturally seek additional funding for their programs, whereas OMB has the job of matching the budget to the president's priorities. However, the president does not have any real say over most of the budget, about two-thirds of which involves mandatory spending. This spending is required by law, as in the case of Social Security payments to retirees. The president has no authority to suspend or reduce such payments. Accordingly, OMB focuses on the one-third of the budget that involves discretionary spending, which includes spending in areas such as defense, foreign aid, education, national parks, space exploration, and highways. In reality, even a large part of this spending is not truly discretionary. No president would slash defense spending to almost nothing or cut off funding for the national parks. The president, then, works on the margins of the budget. In most policy areas, the president will propose a modest spending increase or decrease over the previous year.

Presidents occasionally take bolder action. In his first budget proposal, President Trump called for cutting funding for the State Department and the U.S. Agency for International Development by roughly 25 percent, a reflection of his belief that diplomacy was not the most effective way to advance America's global interests.

Congress and the Agency Budgets

In January, the president's budget is submitted to Congress. During its work on the budget, the president's recommendations undergo varying degrees of change. Congress has constitutional authority over government spending, and its priorities are never exactly the same as the president's, even when the congressional majority is of the same political party. When it is of the opposite party, its priorities will differ substantially from those of the president.

Upon reaching Congress, the president's budget proposal goes to the House and Senate budget committees. Their job is to recommend overall spending and revenue levels. Once approved by the full House and Senate, the levels are a constraint on the rest of Congress's work on the budget.

The House and Senate appropriations committees take over at this point. As with the executive branch, these committees focus on discretionary spending programs, which are basically the only budget items subject to change. The House Appropriations Committee through its 12 subcommittees reviews the budget, which includes hearings with officials from each federal agency. Each subcommittee has responsibility for a particular substantive area, such as defense or agriculture. A subcommittee may cut an agency's budget if it concludes that the agency is overfunded or may increase the budget if it concludes that the agency is underfunded. The subcommittees' recommendations are

Congress has final authority over the budget, subject to a presidential veto. Shown here is a session of the House Appropriations Committee, which, through its 12 subcommittees, does most of Congress's work on budget details. (©Chine Nouvelle/SIPA/Newscom)

then reviewed by the House Appropriations Committee as a whole. The budget is also reviewed by the Senate Appropriations Committee and its subcommittees. However, the Senate is a smaller body, and its review of agency requests is less exacting than that of the House. To a degree, the Senate Appropriations Committee serves as a "court of last resort" for agencies that have had their funding requests cut by OMB or by the House Appropriations Committee. The Senate, for example, restored most of the cuts to the State Department budget that President Trump had proposed. Senator Lindsey Graham (R-S.C.) had declared Trump's proposal "dead on arrival" when it was announced, and, indeed, Congress overrode Trump's plan during its budget negotiations.[8]

Throughout the budgetary process, members of the House and the Senate rely on the Congressional Budget Office (CBO), which is the congressional equivalent of OMB. If CBO believes that OMB or an agency has miscalculated the amount of money needed to carry out its mandated programs, it will alert Congress to the discrepancy.

After the House and Senate appropriations committees have completed their work, they submit their recommendations to the full chambers for a vote. If approved by a majority in the House and in the Senate, differences in the Senate and House versions are then reconciled in conference committee (see Chapter 11). The reconciled version of the budget is then voted upon in the House and the Senate and, if approved, is sent to the president to sign or veto. The threat of a presidential veto can be enough to persuade Congress to accept many of the president's recommendations. In the end, the budget inevitably reflects both presidential and congressional priorities. Neither branch gets everything it wants, but each branch always gets some of what it seeks.

After the budget has been signed by the president, it takes effect on October 1, the starting date of the federal government's fiscal year. If agreement on the budget has not been reached by October 1, temporary funding legislation is required in order to maintain government operations. In 2017, Congress used temporary funding bills to avoid a government shutdown but failed to reach a timely agreement on another such bill in early 2018, resulting in a two-day shutdown of non-essential services.

POLICY AND POWER IN THE BUREAUCRACY

Administrative agencies' main task is **policy implementation**—that is, the carrying out of decisions made by Congress, the president, and the courts. When a directive is issued by Congress, the president, or the courts, the bureaucracy is charged with executing it. In implementing these decisions, the bureaucracy is constrained by the budget. It cannot spend money on an activity unless Congress has appropriated the necessary funds.

Some of what the bureaucracy does is fairly straightforward, as in the case of delivering the mail, processing government loan applications, and imprisoning those convicted of crime. Yet the bureaucracy sometimes has considerable discretion in implementing policy. Consider the example of the Consumer Financial Protection Bureau (CFPB) that Congress created in 2010 to protect consumers from financial institutions that exploit consumers in the granting of home mortgages, credit cards, and the like. The legislation that created the CFPB instructed the agency to do the following:

- Conduct rule-making, supervision, and enforcement for federal consumer financial protection laws.
- Restrict unfair, deceptive, or abusive acts or practices.
- Take consumer complaints.
- Promote financial education.
- Research consumer behavior.
- Monitor financial markets for new risks to consumers.

However, the legislation did not spell out in detail how the CFPB was to implement these tasks. What type of enforcement would it conduct? Which unfair practices would it restrict, and how would this be done? What action would be taken on consumer complaints? How would financial education occur? What consumer behaviors would be studied? How would financial markets be monitored and new risks identified? It was left to CFPB bureaucrats to formulate these policies. Such **rule-making**—determining how a law will work in practice—is the chief way administrative agencies exercise control over policy.[9]

The rule-making process is subject to checks. After an agency develops the initial rules for an activity, they are published in the *Federal Register* and are then subject to comments and objections by interested parties. When the agency then publishes the final rules, it cannot implement them for 60 days, during which time Congress can change them, although it seldom does so.

In the course of their work, administrators also develop policy ideas that they then propose to the White House or Congress. The origin of the Occupational Safety and Health Act is an example. A bureaucrat believed that worker safety was not receiving enough attention and encouraged his brother, a presidential speechwriter, to bring it to the attention of the White House. Department of Labor officials then picked up the issue, as did some labor unions and members of Congress. When the legislation was under consideration by congressional committees, bureaucrats who had pressed for the

Some government agencies are noteworthy for their performance. One of them is the U.S. Postal Service, which is regarded by many as the best entity of its kind anywhere. It delivers more mail to more addresses than any other postal service in the world, and it does so inexpensively and without undue delay. (©Photodisc/PunchStock)

creation of an occupational safety and health program were among those invited to testify.[10]

In sum, administrators initiate policy, develop it, evaluate it, apply it, and decide whether others are complying with it. The bureaucracy does not simply administer policy. It also *makes* policy.

The Agency Point of View

A key issue about bureaucratic policymaking is the perspective that bureaucrats bring to their decisions. Do they operate from the perspective of the president or do they operate from the perspective of Congress? The answer is that, although bureaucrats are responsive to both of them, they are even more responsive to the needs of the agency in which they work, a perspective called the **agency point of view.** This outlook comes naturally to most high-ranking civil servants. More than 80 percent of top bureaucrats reach their high-level positions by rising through the ranks of the same agency.[11] As one top administrator said when testifying before the House Appropriations

Committee, "Mr. Chairman, you would not think it proper for me to be in charge of this work and not be enthusiastic about it . . . would you? I have been in it for thirty years, and I believe in it."[12] One study found, for example, that social welfare administrators were twice as likely as other civil servants to believe that social welfare spending should be increased (see Figure 13-5).[13]

Professionalism also cements agency loyalties. High-level administrative positions have increasingly been filled by scientists, engineers, lawyers, educators, physicians, and other professionals. Most of them take a job in an agency whose mission they support, as in the case of the aeronautical engineers who work for NASA or the doctors who work for the National Institutes of Health (NIH).

Although the agency point of view distorts government priorities, bureaucrats have little choice but to look out for their agency's interests. The president and members of Congress differ in their constituencies and thus in the agencies to which they are most responsive. Republican and Democratic officials also differ in their priorities, a reality that is never more apparent than when party control of the presidency or Congress changes. Some agencies rise or fall in their level of political support for that reason alone. In sum, if an agency is to operate successfully in America's partisan system of divided power, it must seek support wherever it can find it. If the agency is a low priority for the president, it needs to find backing in Congress. If Republican lawmakers want to cut the agency's programs, it must turn to Democratic lawmakers for help. In other words, agencies are forced to play politics if they want to protect their programs.[14] An agency that sits on the sidelines while other agencies seek support from the White House and Congress is likely to lose out in budget negotiations.

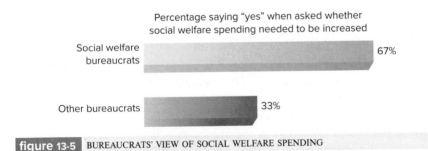

Percentage saying "yes" when asked whether
social welfare spending needed to be increased

Social welfare bureaucrats   67%

Other bureaucrats   33%

figure 13-5 BUREAUCRATS' VIEW OF SOCIAL WELFARE SPENDING

Bureaucrats in social welfare agencies are far more likely than bureaucrats in other agencies to think increased spending on social welfare is necessary. An "agency point of view" is prevalent in the federal bureaucracy. (*Source:* Adapted from Aberbach, Joel D., and Rockman, Bert A., "Clashing Beliefs within the Executive Branch," *American Political Science Review*, vol. 70, 1970, 461.)

Detecting Misinformation

Is There a "Deep State"?

In recent years, the claim that the United States is run by a "deep state" has gained increasing acceptance. The claim holds that high-ranking people in government agencies are able to control much of what government does, sepa-rate from the influence of the voters and elected officials. Many Americans have come to believe in the deep state's existence. In a recent ABC News/*Washington Post* poll, respon-dents were asked whether they agreed that "military, intelligence, and gov-ernment officials . . . secretly manipu-late government policy." Half of the

©Hisham F. Ibrahim/Getty Images

respondents agreed, while a third called the claim a "conspiracy theory," with the rest saying they were unsure. Republicans and Democrats were equally likely to believe in the deep state's existence, but there was a large difference among age groups. Young adults (ages 18–29) were the most likely (59 percent) to say the deep state was real, while senior citizens were the least likely (37 percent) to accept the claim.

Is that claim fact, or is it fake?

Investigations by journalists and others have failed to uncover any evidence of the deep state's existence. The origins of the claim would also lead one to question its validity. The idea of a deep state was initially pushed on the Internet by conspiracy theorists.

Although the deep state claim is unfounded, it is accurate to say that the interests of career government officials are sometimes at odds with those of elected officials and the voters. Career bureaucrats are committed to their agencies' programs, funding, and mission, and they try to protect them even when such action runs counter to what the people's representatives are advocating.

Sources of Bureaucratic Power

In promoting their agency's interests, bureaucrats rely on their specialized knowledge, the support of interests that benefit from their programs, and the backing of the president and Congress.

The Power of Expertise   Most of the policy problems confronting the federal government are extraordinarily complex. Whether the problem relates to space travel or hunger in America, a solution requires deep knowledge of the problem. Much of this expertise is provided by bureaucrats. They spend their careers working in a particular policy area, and many of them have had scientific, technical, or other specialized training (see "How the U.S. Differs").[15] Elected officials, by contrast, are generalists, none more so than the president, who must deal with dozens of issues. Members of Congress acquire some expertise through their committee work, but most of them lack the time, training, or inclination to become deeply knowledgeable of the issues they handle. It's not surprising that Congress and the president rely heavily on career administrators for policy advice.

All agencies acquire some influence over policy through their careerists' expertise. No matter how simple a policy issue may appear at first, it nearly always has layers of complexity. The recognition that the United States has a trade deficit with China, for example, can be the premise for policy change, but this recognition does not begin to address basic issues such as the form the new policy might take, its probable cost and effectiveness, and its links to other issues, such as America's standing in Asia. Among the officials most likely to understand these issues are the career bureaucrats in the Treasury Department, the State Department, the Commerce Department, and the Federal Trade Commission.

The Power of Clientele Groups   Most federal agencies were created for the purpose of promoting, protecting, or regulating a particular interest. Indeed, nearly every major interest in society—commerce, labor, agriculture, banking, and so on—has a corresponding federal agency. In most cases, these interests are **clientele groups** in the sense that they benefit directly from the agency's programs. As a result, clientele groups can be counted on to lobby Congress and the president on behalf of the agency when its programs and funding are being reviewed.[17] When President Trump in his 2018 budget proposed the elimination of grants for new mass transit projects, affected groups and local transit officials launched a lobbying effort to protect the grants, arguing that mass transit improvements were required if America's cities were to respond to the rising demand for modernized public transportation.[18]

The relationship between an agency and its clientele group is a reciprocal one. Just as a clientele group can be expected to protect its agency, the agency will work to protect the group.[19] The Department of Agriculture, for instance, is a dependable ally of farm interests year after year. The same cannot be said of the president or Congress as a whole, which must balance farmers' demands against those of other groups.

HOW THE U.S. DIFFERS

CRITICAL THINKING THROUGH COMPARISONS

Educational Backgrounds of Bureaucrats

In staffing its bureaucracy, the U.S. government tends to hire persons with specialized educations to hold specialized jobs. In contrast, Great Britain tends to recruit its top bureaucrats from the arts and humanities, on the assumption that a broad education is the best preparation. Germany takes a different approach, believing that a legal education is advantageous because of the part played by high-ranking bureaucrats in determining how laws will be implemented. These tendencies (see figure) were documented by political scientist Guy Peters in his comparative study of the college majors of senior civil servants.[16]

College major of senior civil servants

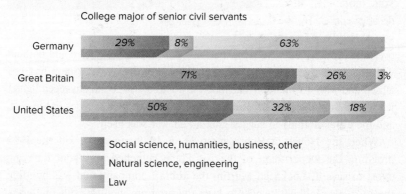

Germany: 29% | 8% | 63%

Great Britain: 71% | 26% | 3%

United States: 50% | 32% | 18%

■ Social science, humanities, business, other
■ Natural science, engineering
■ Law

Q: Why might the hiring pattern for the U.S. bureaucracy make it more likely that civil servants in the United States will take an agency point of view than will civil servants in some other democracies?

A: The U.S. bureaucracy has a high proportion of employees with a specialized education. They tend to take jobs in agencies where their specialty is particularly desirable, as in the case of the aeronautical engineers who work at NASA. Accordingly, their training would incline them to support their agency's mission—the agency point of view. European civil servants are more likely to have a type of education, as in the case of law or the humanities, that is less specific to the work of a particular agency, which presumably makes them less likely to deeply embrace their agency's mission.

C A S E S T U D Y	Politics in Action

The F-22 and the Department of the Air Force

In 1986, Congress authorized the construction of the F-22 fighter jet. Its chief advocate was the Department of the Air Force, which argued that the United States needed the F-22 to stay ahead of China and the Soviet Union. Opponents of the F-22 said it was unnecessary, noting that the F-22 was designed for air-to-air combat, a type of warfare that had not been fought since the Korean War, more than three decades earlier. By the late 1990s, cost

©Super Nova Images/Alamy

overruns on the F-22 were such that only half as many planes could be built with the funds that had been budgeted. Moreover, the Soviet Union had collapsed and with it so had the likelihood it would construct an advanced fighter jet. In addition, the Korean War was now more than four decades in the past, and there was nothing to suggest that an air war was likely.

When the House of Representatives in 1999 moved to kill the F-22 program, the Department of the Air Force launched an all-out lobbying effort to save it. Lockheed Martin, the aircraft company that was building the F-22, also lobbied heavily to keep the program, pointing out that components of the F-22 were being built by firms located in 48 of the 50 states. Lockheed Martin argued that, if Congress killed the F-22 program, it would be killing tens of thousands of well-paying jobs. When Congress passed the federal budget in 1999, funds for the F-22 program were included.

Ten years later, the F-22 was still in production, but the U.S. economy was in recession and Secretary of Defense Robert Gates concluded that the F-22 was an unnecessary expense. When the Department of the Air Force pushed back, Gates devised reasons to relieve the secretary of the air force and the air force chief of staff—two of the F-22's strongest advocates. Finally, in 2009, nearly a quarter of a century after the program was started, the F-22 failed to get enough support in Congress to keep the

Continued

program alive. But the vote was not overly one-sided. Forty-two senators—all from states where components of the F-22 were being built—voted to continue the funding.

Q: What can agency officials, interest groups, and members of Congress offer each other that would serve to protect an agency program, such as the Department of the Air Force's F-22 program?

ASK YOURSELF: What support can an interest group provide an agency when its budget comes up for review? What support can the group provide members of Congress? What support can members of Congress give an agency when its budget comes up for review? What support can congressional members give an interest group? What support can agency officials give an interest group that has a stake in its programs? What support can agency officials give members of Congress? (See Figure 9-4, "How an Iron Triangle Benefits Its Participants.")

The Power of Friends in High Places   Although the goals of the president or Congress can conflict with those of the bureaucracy, they need it as much as it needs them. An agency's resources—its programs, expertise, and group support—can help elected officials achieve their policy goals. When Barack Obama announced early in his presidency the goal of making the United States less dependent on foreign oil, he needed the help of the Department of Energy's experts to develop programs that would further that objective. At a time when other agencies were feeling the pinch of a tight federal budget, the Department of Energy's budget nearly doubled.

Agencies also have allies in Congress. Agencies with programs that benefit important key voting blocs are particularly likely to have congressional support. A prime example is the Department of Agriculture. Although the agricultural sector is just one of the president's many concerns, it is a primary concern of farm-state senators and representatives. They can typically be counted on to support Department of Agriculture funding and programs.

DEMOCRACY AND BUREAUCRATIC ACCOUNTABILITY

Studies have found that the U.S. federal bureaucracy compares favorably to government bureaucracies elsewhere. "Some international bureaucracies," Charles Goodsell writes, "may be roughly the same [as the U.S. bureaucracy] in quality of performance, but they are few in number."[20] The U.S. Postal

Service, for example, has an on-time and low-cost record that few national postal services can match.

Nevertheless, the federal bureaucracy's policy influence is at odds with democratic principles. The bureaucratic form of governing is the antithesis of the democratic form. Bureaucracy entails hierarchy, command, permanence of office, appointment to office, and fixed rules, whereas self-government involves equality, consent, rotation of office, election to office, and open decision making. The president and members of Congress are accountable to the people through elections. Bureaucrats are not elected and yet exercise a significant degree of independent power.

Their influence raises the question of **bureaucratic accountability**—the degree to which bureaucrats are held accountable for the power they exercise. To a small degree, they are accountable directly to the public. In some instances, for example, agencies are required to hold public hearings before issuing new regulations. For the most part, however, bureaucratic accountability occurs largely through the president, Congress, and the courts.[21]

Accountability through the Presidency

Periodically, presidents have launched broad initiatives aimed at making the bureaucracy more responsive. The most recent was the National Performance Review, which Bill Clinton began when he assumed the presidency in 1993. He had campaigned on the issue of "reinventing government" and assembled "reinventing teams" that produced 384 specific recommendations grouped into four broad imperatives: reducing red tape, putting customers first, empowering administrators, and eliminating wasteful spending.[22] Although different in its particulars, the National Performance Review was like earlier reform panels, including the Brownlow, Hoover, and Volcker commissions,[23] which sought with some success to improve the bureaucracy's efficiency, responsiveness, and accountability.

Presidents can also intervene more directly through *executive orders* to force agencies to pursue particular administrative actions. In the closing days of his presidency, for example, Bill Clinton ordered federal agencies to take the steps necessary to ensure that eligible individuals with limited English proficiency obtained full access to federal assistance programs.

Nevertheless, presidents do not have the time or knowledge to exercise personal oversight of the federal bureaucracy. It is far too big and diverse. Presidents rely instead on management tools that include reorganization, presidential appointees, and the executive budget.[24]

Reorganization   The bureaucracy's size—its hundreds of separate agencies—makes it difficult for presidents to coordinate its activities. Agencies pursue independent and even conflicting paths. For example, the United States spends more than $50 billion annually to gather intelligence on threats to the nation's security and does so through several agencies. Each of them has its own priorities and a desire to retain control of the intelligence information it has gathered. A lack of communication between the CIA and the FBI may have contributed to the failure to prevent the terrorist attacks on the World Trade Center and the Pentagon on September 11, 2001. Each agency had information that might have disrupted the attack if the information had been shared.

Presidents have sought to streamline the bureaucracy in an attempt to make it more accountable. After the intelligence breakdown in 2001, for example, President George W. Bush commissioned a study of the intelligence agencies that resulted in the creation of the Office of the Director of National Intelligence in 2004. Fifteen intelligence agencies, including the CIA and the FBI, now report directly to the director of national intelligence, who has responsibility for coordinating their activities. Like most reorganizations, this one improved agency performance, but not dramatically.[25] Although the various intelligence agencies now share more information than previously, they have continued to operate somewhat independently of each other—an indication of the tendency of agencies to protect their spheres of operation.

Presidents have had more success in controlling the bureaucracy by moving activities out of the agencies and into the Executive Office of the President (EOP). As explained in Chapter 12, the EOP is directly under White House

Some observers believe that, if the nation's various intelligence agencies had been more willing to share information, the terrorist attacks on U.S. soil on September 11, 2001, might have been prevented. Although they now share their information more fully, they still operate somewhat independently—a tendency that reflects agencies' determination to protect their turf.
(*Source:* Central Intelligence Agency)

control and functions to a degree as the president's personal bureaucracy. The EOP now makes some policy decisions that at an earlier time would have been made in the agencies. For example, the National Security Council staff, which is part of the EOP, has assumed some of the policy responsibility that once belonged to State and Defense department staffs.

Presidential Appointments   For day-to-day oversight of the bureaucracy, presidents rely on their political appointees. The president has roughly 2,000 full-time partisan appointees, twenty times the number appointed, for example, by the British prime minister.

The top positions in every agency are held by presidential appointees (see "Party Polarization: The Politicization of the Bureaucracy"). They are appointed by the president and can be removed from office at the president's discretion. Their influence is greatest in agencies that have substantial discretionary authority. Some agencies, like the Social Security Administration (SSA), operate within guidelines that limit what agency heads can do. Although the SSA has a huge budget and makes monthly payments to more than 40 million Americans, recipient eligibility is determined by fixed rules. The head of the SSA does not have the option, say, of granting a retiree an extra $100 a month because the retiree is facing financial hardship. At the other extreme are the regulatory agencies, which have considerable latitude in their decisions. For example, in the first year of the Trump administration, the Environmental Protection Agency (EPA) initiated 40 percent fewer cases for violation of pollution laws and imposed 65 percent fewer monetary penalties than the EPA did in the Obama administration's first year.[26]

Nevertheless, there are limits to what presidents can accomplish through their appointees. Many appointees lack detailed knowledge of the agencies they head, making them dependent on agency careerists. By the time they come to understand the agency's programs, they often leave. The typical presidential appointee stays on the job for only two years before moving on to other employment.[27]

OMB: Budgets and Rule-Making   Of the management tools available to the president, few are more direct than the Office of Management and Budget. Funding is the foundation of every agency, and OMB has substantial control over agency budgets.

OMB also reviews agency regulations before they go into effect. As noted earlier, rule-making is the chief way bureaucratic agencies create policy. Rules established by the agencies affect everything from how business will be regulated to how student loans will be administered. During the Reagan presidency, OMB was given the responsibility for reviewing proposed rules. In practice, OMB lacks the resources to review all such rules and closely examines fewer than a thousand out of the tens of thousands of rules proposed each year. A recent study found that OMB's rule-making oversight tends to be

PARTY POLARIZATION	Conflicting Ideas

The Politicization of the Bureaucracy

The top-level positions in the federal bureaucracy—the positions occupied by presidential appointees—have become increasingly partisan. Although presidents normally seek to appoint well-qualified individuals, they increasingly want them to be loyal to the president's policy agenda. More than any recent president, President Trump has used that standard in selecting his top administrators. Many of his cabinet-level appointments, for example, have been individuals with little or no experience with the programs and policies that their department is charged with administering.

The politicization of top administrators has been both praised and criticized. Some analysts say that the overriding principle of the bureaucracy should be neutral competence—impartial and expert administration. Other observers dismiss this claim, arguing that the bureaucracy needs to be responsive to partisan politics—that the will of the voters should be reflected in administrative staffing. They do not deny the need for competent administrators but argue that strong political leadership at the top—even if highly partisan—is the key to a more accountable and responsive bureaucracy.

Q: What's your view of the increased politicization of the bureaucracy? On balance, do you regard it as a favorable development? Would you have the same opinion if control of the presidency were to change to the other party?

reactive—triggered in most cases when a key interest complains about a proposed rule. "Reactive oversight," notes scholar William West, "allows the White House to focus its limited resources on agency initiatives that are problematic while ignoring the majority that are not."[28]

Accountability through Congress

A common misconception is that the president, as the chief executive, has sole authority over executive agencies. In fact, Congress also claims ownership because it is the source of each agency's programs and funding. One presidential appointee asked a congressional committee whether it had a problem with his plans to reduce an agency's programs. The committee chair replied, "No, you have the problem, because if you touch that bureau I'll cut your job out of the budget."[29]

The most substantial control that Congress exerts over the bureaucracy is through its "power of the purse." Congress has constitutional authority over spending; it decides how much money will be appropriated for agency programs. Without funding, a program simply does not exist, regardless of how important the agency believes it is. Congress can also void an administrative decision through legislation that instructs the agency to follow a different course of action. In addition, Congress can exert control by taking authority away from the bureaucracy. In 1978, as a first step in what would become a decades-long wave of deregulation, Congress passed the Airline Deregulation Act, which took away the Civil Aeronautics Board's authority to set airfares and gave it to the airlines.

Congress also has control through its oversight function, which involves monitoring the bureaucracy's work to ensure its compliance with legislative intent.[30] If an agency steps out of line, Congress can call hearings to ask tough questions and, if necessary, take legislative action to correct the problem. Bureaucrats are required by law to appear before Congress when asked to do so, and the mere possibility of being grilled by a congressional panel can lead administrators to stay in line. The effect is not altogether positive. Bureaucrats are sometimes reluctant to try innovative approaches out of a fear that particular members of Congress will disapprove.[31]

Nevertheless, Congress lacks the time and expertise to define in detail how programs should be run.[32] Accordingly, Congress has delegated much of its oversight responsibility to the Government Accountability Office (GAO). At an earlier time, the GAO's role was limited largely to keeping track of agency spending. The GAO now also monitors whether agencies are implementing policies in the way that Congress intended. When the GAO finds a problem with an agency's handling of a program, it notifies the appropriate congressional committees, which can then take corrective action.

Oversight cannot correct mistakes or abuses that have already occurred. Recognizing this limit, Congress has devised ways to constrain the bureaucracy *before* it acts. The simplest method is to draft laws that contain specific instructions on how they are to be implemented by the bureaucracy. In doing so, Congress limits administrators' options. *Sunset provisions* are another restrictive device. These provisions establish specific dates when all or part of a law will expire unless extended by Congress. Sunset provisions are a method of countering the bureaucracy's reluctance to give up outdated programs. However, because members of Congress usually want the programs they create to last, most bills do not include a sunset provision.

Accountability through the Courts

The bureaucracy is also overseen by the judiciary. Legally, the bureaucracy derives its authority from acts of Congress, and an injured party can bring suit against an agency on the grounds that it has failed to carry out a law properly.

If the court agrees, the agency must change its policy.[33] In 1999, for example, a federal court approved a settlement in favor of African American farmers who demonstrated that the Department of Agriculture had systematically favored white farmers in granting federal farm loans.[34]

Nevertheless, the courts tend to support administrators if their actions are at least somewhat consistent with the law they are administering. The Supreme Court has held that agencies can apply any reasonable interpretation of statutes unless Congress has stipulated something to the contrary.[35] This position reflects the Court's recognition that administrators must have discretionary authority if they are to operate effectively and that the federal courts would be overloaded with cases if petitioners could challenge every administrative rule they disliked.

Accountability within the Bureaucracy Itself

Recognition of the difficulty of ensuring adequate accountability of the bureaucracy through the presidency, Congress, and the courts has led to the development of mechanisms of accountability within the bureaucracy itself. Four of these mechanisms—the Senior Executive Service, administrative law judges, whistleblowing, and demographic representativeness—are particularly noteworthy.

Senior Executive Service   The agency point of view within the bureaucracy is partly a result of career patterns. Most civil servants work in the same agency throughout their time in government service. As they acquire the skills and knowledge associated with a particular agency, they rise through its ranks and derive job satisfaction and security from supporting its mission.

Recognizing that the bureaucracy's employment system encourages an agency point of view, Congress in 1978 established the **Senior Executive Service (SES).** The SES represents a compromise between a president-led bureaucracy and an expert one.[36] The SES consists of roughly 7,000 top-level career civil servants who qualify through a competitive process to receive a higher salary than their peers but, in return, can be assigned by the president to any position within the bureaucracy. Unlike the president's regular appointees, SES bureaucrats cannot be fired; if the president relieves them of their job, they have "fallback rights" to their former rank in the regular civil service.

The SES has been less successful in practice than its proponents anticipated. A study found that most SES employees are assigned to agencies that match their policy expertise, which is usually the same agency in which they have spent their career. Their value rests in significant part on their knowledge of its programs and to locate them elsewhere would diminish that value. Said a former senior executive: "I got promoted because I became an expert in the policies in that area, not because I'm such a great executive who can go anywhere and do anything."[37]

Administrative Law Judges   Every day, bureaucrats make tens of thousands of decisions affecting individuals. Occasionally, an individual will believe that he or she was unfairly disadvantaged by a bureaucrat's decision and will contest it. Such disputes are usually handled by an **administrative law judge.** Administrative law judges are charged with protecting individuals from arbitrary, prejudicial, or incorrect decisions by an agency. They are empowered to administer oaths, seek evidence, take testimony, make factual and legal determinations, and render decisions. However, they operate through a less formal process than do regular federal judges. Administrative law hearings usually take place in an office or meeting room rather than a courtroom, and administrative law judges do not wear a robe or sit on a high bench. The system is designed to provide a less formal, less expensive, and faster method of resolving administrative disputes than would be the case if they were handled through the regular federal courts. Under some circumstances, the decision of an administrative law judge can be appealed to such a court, although this seldom occurs.

Whistleblowing   Although the bureaucratic corruption that is commonplace in some countries is rare in the United States, a certain amount of fraud and abuse is inevitable in any large bureaucracy. One way to limit such practices is **whistleblowing**—encouraging employees to report misconduct by their superiors. To reassure whistleblowers, Congress enacted the Whistleblower Protection Act, which protects them from retaliation by their superiors and gives them a financial reward when their information results in substantial savings to government.

Nevertheless, whistleblowing is not for the fainthearted. Many federal employees are reluctant to report instances of mismanagement because they fear retaliation. Their superiors might claim that they are malcontents or liars and find ways to ruin their careers. A case in point is Bunnatine Greenhouse who filed a complaint alleging that the U.S. Army Corps of Engineers was greatly overpaying a contractor because it had accepted the contractor's multiyear no-bid cost estimates rather than conducting its own assessment. Her complaint was ignored by the Corps of Engineers and she was demoted, stripped of her top-secret security clearance, and subjected to on-the-job harassment after she took her complaint to Congress. In 2011, more than six years after her initial complaint, she was vindicated when a U.S. district court ruled in her favor. Greenhouse said she hoped that her experience would prompt lawmakers to give whistleblowers "the legal rights that they need."[38]

Demographic Representativeness   Although the bureaucracy is an unrepresentative institution in the sense that its officials are not elected, it can

Employees who report misconduct by their superiors are known as whistleblowers. Although they're protected by law, they can become the target of reprisals by the superiors whose misconduct they report. (©Tupungato/Shutterstock)

be representative in the demographic sense. This concept was endorsed in 1961 by the President's Commission on Equal Employment Opportunity, which was created by President John F. Kennedy. The commission concluded that if civil servants were more demographically representative of the general public, they would treat the various groups and interests in society more fairly.[39]

The federal government has made progress in improving the employment status of women and, to a lesser extent, minorities. If all employees are taken into account, the federal bureaucracy comes reasonably close to being representative of the nation's population. Moreover, women and minorities are better represented among the top ranks of administrators than they are in Congress or the judiciary. Nevertheless, the bureaucracy is not demographically representative at the top level. The highest-ranking federal employees are those in the Senior Executive Service (SES). About three in every five such employees are male and about four in every five are white (see Figure 13-6). However, the SES is far more representative today than four decades ago, when white males accounted for roughly 9 out of 10 SES employees.

In any case, **demographic representativeness** is only a partial answer to the problem of bureaucratic accountability. Careerists in the defense and welfare agencies, for example, have similar demographic backgrounds but differ markedly in their policy views. Each group believes that the goals of its agency should be a top priority. In this sense, agency loyalty trumps demographics. Once in an agency, civil servants—regardless of demographic background—tend to become advocates for its programs.

figure 13-6   COMPOSITION OF THE SENIOR EXECUTIVE SERVICE (SES), BY SEX AND RACE IN 1982 AND 2014.

Source: Office of Personnel Management, 2017.

SUMMARY

Bureaucracy is a method of organizing people and work, based on the principles of hierarchical authority, job specialization, and formalized rules. As a form of organization, bureaucracy is the most efficient means of getting people to work together on tasks of great magnitude and complexity. It is also a form of organization that is prone to waste and rigidity, which is why efforts are always being made to reform it.

The United States could not be governed without a large federal bureaucracy. The day-to-day work of the federal government, from mail delivery to provision of Social Security to international diplomacy, is done by federal agencies. Federal employees work in roughly four hundred major agencies, including cabinet departments, independent agencies, regulatory agencies, government corporations, and presidential commissions. Yet the bureaucracy is more than simply an administrative giant. Administrators have discretion when making policy decisions. In the process of implementing policy, they make important policy and political choices.

Administrative agencies operate within budgets established by the president and Congress, and they participate in the budgetary process. The process begins with the president's budget instructions, conveyed through OMB, to the agencies. They then develop their budgets, which are consolidated and sent by the president to Congress, where the House and Senate budget and appropriations committees do the bulk of the work, including holding hearings involving agency heads. Throughout, Congress, the president, and the agencies seek to promote their respective budgetary goals. Once the annual budget has been passed by the House and the Senate and signed by the president, it takes effect on October 1, the starting date of the federal government's fiscal year.

Administrators are actively engaged in politics and policymaking. The fragmentation of power and the pluralism of the American political system result in a contentious policy process, which leads government agencies to compete for power and resources. Accordingly, civil servants tend to have an agency point of view: they seek to advance their agency's programs and to repel attempts by others to weaken them. In promoting their agencies, civil servants rely on their policy expertise, the backing of their clientele groups, and the support of the president and Congress.

Administrators are not elected by the people they serve, yet they wield substantial independent power. Because of this, the bureaucracy's accountability is a central issue. The major checks on the bureaucracy occur through the president, Congress, and the courts. The president has some power to reorganize the bureaucracy and the authority to appoint the political head of each agency. The president also has management tools (such as the executive budget) that can be used to limit administrators' discretion. Congress has influence on bureaucratic agencies through its authorization and funding powers and through various devices (including enabling provisions, sunset provisions, and oversight hearings) that can increase administrators' accountability. The judiciary's role in ensuring the bureaucracy's accountability is smaller than that of the elected branches, but the courts have the authority to force agencies to act in accordance with legislative intent, established procedures, and constitutionally guaranteed rights. Internal checks on the bureaucracy—the Senior Executive Service, administrative law judges, whistleblowing, and demographic representativeness—are also mechanisms for holding the bureaucracy accountable.

©gangliu10/Getty Images

CRITICAL THINKING ZONE

KEY TERMS

administrative law judge (*p. 426*)

agency point of view (*p. 413*)

budgetary process (*p. 408*)

bureaucracy (*p. 399*)

bureaucratic accountability (*p. 420*)

cabinet (executive) departments (*p. 402*)

clientele groups (*p. 416*)

demographic representativeness (*p. 427*)

formalized rules (*p. 400*)

government corporations (*p. 404*)

hierarchical authority (*p. 399*)

independent agencies (*p. 404*)

job specialization (*p. 400*)

merit system (*p. 406*)

neutral competence (*p. 406*)

patronage system (*p. 406*)

policy implementation (*p. 411*)
presidential commissions (*p. 404*)
regulatory agencies (*p. 404*)
rule-making (*p. 412*)

Senior Executive Service (SES)
 (*p. 425*)
spoils system (*p. 406*)
whistleblowing (*p. 426*)

Applying the Elements of Critical Thinking

Conceptualizing: Explain what is meant by *agency point of view*. Why do bureaucrats tend to have an agency point of view?

Synthesizing: Contrast the patronage system and the merit system as methods of hiring government employees.

Analyzing: What are the major sources of bureaucrats' power? What mechanisms for controlling that power are available to the president and Congress?

Extra Credit

A Book Worth Reading: Charles T. Goodsell, *The New Case for Bureaucracy* (Washington, D.C.: CQ Press, 2014). A well-written book by a scholar who documents the effectiveness and importance of the federal bureaucracy.

A Website Worth Visiting: www.whistleblower.org. The Government Accountability Project is a nonpartisan organization devoted to protecting and encouraging whistleblowers, in the private sector as well as the public sector.

Participate!

If you are considering a semester or summer internship, you might want to look into working for a federal, state, or local agency. Compared with legislative interns, executive interns are more likely to get paid and to be given significant duties. (Many legislative interns spend the bulk of their time answering phones or responding to mail.) Internship information can often be obtained through an agency's website. You should apply as early as possible; some agencies have application deadlines.

You might consider a career in government. President John F. Kennedy said that government is "the highest calling." A study by Harvard's Kennedy School of Government found that public-sector managers get more intrinsic satisfaction from their work, which focuses on improving public life, than do private-sector managers. For people who want to pursue a government career, a first step is often a master's degree program in public administration or public policy. Many of these programs require only a year of study after the bachelor's degree. For an entry-level employee with a master's degree rather than a bachelor's degree, the initial salary is 40 percent higher. Appointees with master's degrees enter the civil service at a higher rank (GS-9 rather than GS-5) and are placed in positions that entail greater responsibility than those assigned to newly hired appointees with bachelor's degrees. Those who enter the civil service at the higher rank also are more likely to advance to top positions as their careers develop.

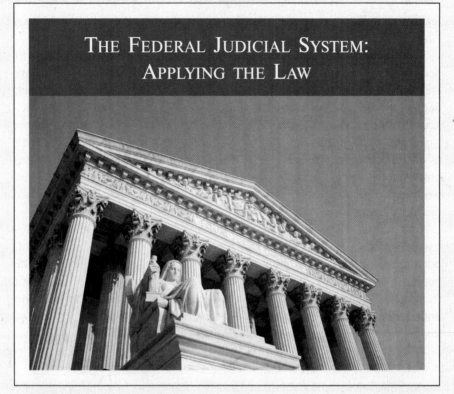

THE FEDERAL JUDICIAL SYSTEM: APPLYING THE LAW

©Pixtal/agefotostock

66 It is emphatically the province and duty of the judicial department to say what the law is. Those who apply the rule to particular cases, must of necessity expound and interpret that rule. If two laws conflict with each other, the courts must decide on the operation of each. 99

JOHN MARSHALL[1]

Through its ruling in *Obergefell v. Hodges* (2015), the Supreme Court by a 5–4 vote legalized same-sex marriage in all states. At issue in the case was whether the Fourteenth Amendment's due process and equal-protection clauses prevent states from banning marriages between individuals of the same sex.

The Supreme Court's majority concluded that a ban on same-sex marriage violated the Fourteenth Amendment. The Court said that "The Constitution promises liberty to all within its reach, a liberty that includes certain specific rights that allow persons, within a lawful realm, to define and express their identity. . . . [Same-sex couples] ask for equal dignity in the eyes of the law. The Constitution grants them that right." Regarding the issue of whether state legislatures have the power to ban such marriages, the Court held that "fundamental rights may not be submitted to a vote. . . ."[2]

The Court's same-sex marriage ruling illustrates three key points about court decisions. First, the judiciary is an important policymaking body. Some of its rulings are as consequential as a law of Congress or an executive order of the president. Second, the judiciary has considerable discretion in its rulings. The *Obergefell* decision was not based on any straightforward reading of the law or else the justices would not have divided 5–4 on the ruling. Third, the judiciary is a political as well as a legal institution. The same-sex marriage ruling was a product of contending political forces and was decided by political appointees. Four of the five justices who voted to allow same-sex marriage were appointed to the Court by a Democratic president. Of the four justices who dissented, all were Republican appointees.

This chapter describes the federal judiciary. Like the executive and legislative branches, the judiciary is an independent branch of the U.S. government, but unlike the other two branches, its top officials are not elected by the people. The judiciary is not a democratic institution, and its role is different from and, in some ways, more controversial than the roles of the executive and legislative branches. This chapter explores this issue in the process of discussing the following main points:

- *The federal judiciary includes the Supreme Court of the United States, which functions mainly as an appellate court; courts of appeals, which hear appeals; and the district courts, which hold trials.* Each state has a court system of its own, which for the most part is independent of supervision by the federal courts.

- *Judicial decisions are constrained by applicable constitutional law, statutory and administrative law, and precedent.* Nevertheless, political factors have a major influence on judicial appointments and decisions; judges are political officials as well as legal ones.

- *The judiciary has become an increasingly powerful policymaking body in recent decades, raising the question of the judiciary's proper role in a democracy.* The philosophies of judicial restraint and judicial activism provide different answers to this question.

THE FEDERAL JUDICIAL SYSTEM

The Constitution establishes the judiciary as a separate and independent branch of the federal government. The Constitution provides for the Supreme Court of the United States but gives Congress the power to determine the number and types of lower federal courts.

All federal judges are nominated and appointed to office by the president, subject to confirmation by majority vote in the Senate. The Constitution places

Pictured here is the chamber where the Supreme Court hears oral arguments on the cases before it. Oral argument is the most visible aspect of the Court's work, but it is less important than the written briefs that the contending parties submit and the judicial conference where the justices meet privately to vote on each case. (*Source:* Photographs in the Carol M. Highsmith Archive, Library of Congress, Prints and Photographs Division [LC-DIG-highsm-12515])

no age, residency, or citizenship requirements on the office of federal judge, unlike the office of president, senator, or representative. Nor does the Constitution require judges to have legal training, though by tradition they do. Once seated on the bench, as specified in the Constitution, they "hold their offices during good behavior." This has meant, in effect, that federal judges serve until they die or retire voluntarily. No Supreme Court justice and only a handful of lower-court judges have been removed through impeachment and conviction by Congress, the method of early removal specified by the Constitution.

Alexander Hamilton argued forcefully for life tenure for federal judges in *Federalist* No. 78. Responding to arguments by Anti-Federalists that life-appointed judges would be a threat to the republic, Hamilton argued that the judicial branch would be the weakest of the three branches. Whereas congressional power rests on spending authority ("the power of the purse") and presidential power rests on control of military force ("the power of the sword"), judicial power rests on what Hamilton called "judgment"–the reasonableness and fairness of its decisions. The best way to ensure that judicial decisions meet this standard, Hamilton claimed, is to grant life tenure to federal judges so that they are free of all allegiances except to the rule of law.

The Supreme Court of the United States

The Supreme Court of the United States is the nation's highest court. It has nine members—the chief justice and eight associate justices. The chief justice presides over the Court but has the same voting power as each of the other justices.

Article III of the Constitution grants the Supreme Court both original and appellate jurisdiction. A court's **jurisdiction** is its authority to hear cases of a particular type. **Original jurisdiction** is the authority to be the first court to hear a case. The Supreme Court's original jurisdiction includes legal disputes involving foreign diplomats and cases in which the opposing parties are state governments. The Court has convened as a court of original jurisdiction only a few hundred times in its history and has seldom done so in recent decades. One of the rarities was *South Carolina v. North Carolina* (2010), which involved a dispute between the two states over the distribution of water in the Catawba River, which flows through both states.[3]

The Supreme Court does its most important work as an appellate court. **Appellate jurisdiction** is the authority to review cases that have already been heard in lower courts and are appealed to a higher court by the losing party. These higher courts are called *appeals courts* or *appellate courts.* Appellate courts do not retry cases; rather, they determine whether a trial court in hearing a case has applied the law properly. The Supreme Court's appellate jurisdiction extends to cases arising under the Constitution, federal law and regulations, and treaties. The Court also hears appeals involving legal controversies that cross state or national boundaries. Article III of the Constitution gives Congress the power to create "exceptions" to the Supreme Court's appellate jurisdiction, whereas its original jurisdiction cannot be altered by Congress.

Selecting and Deciding Cases

Nearly all cases that reach the Supreme Court do so after the losing party in a lower court asks the Court to hear its case. If at least four of the justices agree to do so, the Court issues a **writ of certiorari,** which is a request to the lower court to submit to the Supreme Court a record of the case. Each year roughly 8,000 parties apply for certiorari, but the Court grants certiorari to fewer than one hundred cases (see Figure 14-1).[4]

The Supreme Court seldom accepts a routine case, even if the justices believe that a lower court made a mistake. The Court's job is not to correct the errors of other courts but to resolve substantial legal issues. The Court's own guidelines say that there must be "compelling reasons" for accepting a case, which include resolving issues that are being decided inconsistently by the lower courts, correcting serious departures from accepted standards of justice, settling key questions of federal law, and reviewing lower-court rulings that conflict with a previous Supreme

Number of cases each year

Appealed   8,000

Accepted 85

figure 14-1 THE SUPREME COURT'S DOCKET

The Supreme Court accepts only a small fraction of the roughly 8,000 cases appealed to it each year. The Court normally agrees to hear only those cases that have broad legal significance. (*Source:* Supreme Court of the United States. Figures based on yearly average for 1990–2018 period)

Court decision. When the Court does accept a case, chances are that most of the justices disagree with the lower court's ruling. About three-fourths of Supreme Court decisions reverse the lower court's judgment.[5]

During a Supreme Court hearing, the attorney for each side presents its oral argument, which typically is limited to 30 minutes.[6] Each side also provides the Court a written *brief,* which contains its fuller argument. The oral session is followed by the *judicial conference,* which is attended only by the nine justices and in which they discuss and vote on the case. The conference's proceedings are secret, which allows the justices to speak freely about a case and to change their minds as the discussion progresses.[7]

Issuing Decisions and Opinions

After a case has been decided, the Court issues its ruling, which consists of a decision and one or more opinions. The **decision** indicates which party won the case. The most important part of the ruling, however, is the **opinion,** which explains the legal basis for the decision. In the landmark *Brown v. Board of Education* opinion, for instance, the Court held that government-sponsored school segregation was unconstitutional because it violated the Fourteenth Amendment guarantee of equal protection under the law to all citizens (see discussion in Chapter 5). This opinion became the legal basis on which public schools throughout the South were ordered by lower courts to end their policy of racial segregation.

When a majority of the justices agree on the legal basis of a decision, the result is a **majority opinion.** In some cases there is no majority opinion because, although a majority of the justices agree on the decision, they disagree on the legal basis for it. The result in such cases is a **plurality opinion,** which presents the view held by most of the justices who vote with the winning side. Another type of opinion is a **concurring opinion,** a separate view written by a justice who votes with the majority but disagrees with all or part of its reasoning. The final type is a **dissenting opinion;** in it, a justice (or justices) on the losing side explains the reasons for disagreeing with the majority position.

When part of the majority, the chief justice decides which justice will write the majority opinion. Otherwise, the senior justice in the majority picks the author. The justice who writes the Court's majority opinion has the responsibility to express accurately the majority's reasoning. The vote on a case is not considered final until the opinion is written and agreed upon, so give-and-take can occur during the writing stage. In rare instances, the writing stage has produced a change in the Court's decision. In *Lee v. Weisman* (1992), a case involving prayer at a public school graduation, Justice Anthony Kennedy originally sided with the four justices who said the prayer was permissible. While writing the 5–4 majority opinion, Kennedy found that he could not make a persuasive case for allowing it. He switched sides, resulting in a 5–4 majority the other way.

Other Federal Courts

The Supreme Court's position at the top of the judicial system gives it unrivaled importance. Nevertheless, the Supreme Court is not the only court that matters. Judge Jerome Frank once wrote of the "upper-court myth," which is the view that lower courts dutifully follow the rulings handed down by the courts above them.[8] The reality is different, as the following discussion explains.

U.S. District Courts   The lowest federal courts are the district courts (see Figure 14-2). There are 94 federal district courts altogether—at least 1 in every state and as many as 4 in the most populous states. Each district includes several judges, who number roughly eight hundred in all. The federal district courts are the chief trial courts of the federal system. Virtually all criminal and civil cases arising under federal law are argued first in the district courts. They are the only courts in the federal system where the two sides present their case to a jury for a verdict. Nearly all cases at this level are presided over by a single judge.

Lower federal courts rely on and follow Supreme Court decisions in their own rulings. The Supreme Court reiterated this requirement in a 1982 case, *Hutto v. Davis:* "Unless we wish anarchy to prevail within the federal judicial system, a precedent of this Court must be followed by the lower federal courts no matter how misguided the judges of those courts may think it to be."[9] However, the idea that lower courts are rigidly bound to Supreme Court rulings is part of the upper-court myth. The facts of a case before a district court are seldom identical to those of a case settled by the Supreme Court. The lower-court judge must decide whether a different legal judgment is appropriate. As well, ambiguities or unaddressed issues in Supreme Court rulings give lower courts some flexibility in deciding cases.

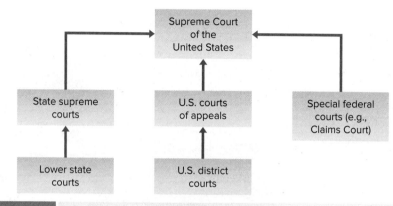

figure 14-2   THE FEDERAL JUDICIAL SYSTEM

The simplified diagram shows the relationships among the various levels of federal courts and between state and federal courts. The losing party in a case can appeal a lower-court decision to the court at the next highest level, as the arrows indicate. Decisions normally cannot be moved from state courts to federal courts unless they raise a U.S. constitutional issue, such as whether a defendant's right to a fair trial has been violated.

Another indication of the significant role of district court judges is that most federal cases end with the district court's decision. Typically, the losing party decides not to appeal the decision to a higher court.

U.S. Courts of Appeals   Cases appealed from district courts go to federal courts of appeals, which are the second level of the federal court system. Courts of appeals do not use juries. Ordinarily, no new evidence is submitted in an appealed case. Instead, appellate courts base their decision on a review of the lower court's records. Appellate judges act as overseers, reviewing trial court decisions and correcting what they consider to be legal errors.

The United States has 13 courts of appeals. Eleven of them have jurisdiction over a "circuit" made up of the district courts in anywhere from three to nine states (see Figure 14-3). Of the remaining two, one has jurisdiction over the District of Columbia (the D.C. "circuit") and the other (the U.S. Court of Appeals for the Federal Circuit) has jurisdiction over appeals involving patents and international trade, regardless of the circuit in which they arise. Between 4 and 26 judges sit on each court of appeals, but each case usually is heard by a panel of 3 judges. On rare occasions, all the judges of a court of appeals sit as a body (*en banc*) in order to resolve difficult controversies, typically ones that have resulted in conflicting decisions within the same circuit. Each circuit is monitored by a Supreme Court justice, who typically takes the lead in reviewing appeals originating in that circuit. Conflict or inconsistency in how the different circuits are applying a law can lead the Supreme Court to review such cases.

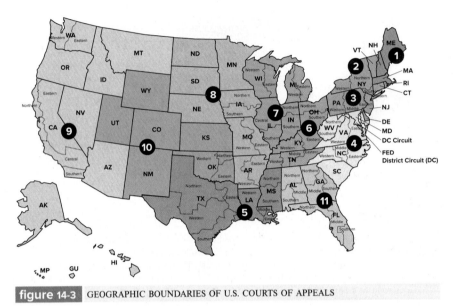

figure 14-3   GEOGRAPHIC BOUNDARIES OF U.S. COURTS OF APPEALS

The United States has 13 courts of appeals, each of which serves a "circuit." Eleven of these circuit courts serve anywhere from three to nine states, as the map shows. The other two are located in the District of Columbia: the Court of Appeals for the District of Columbia and the Court of Appeals for the Federal Circuit, which specializes in appeals involving patents and international trade. Within each circuit are federal trial courts, most of which are district courts. Each state has at least one district court within its boundaries. Larger states, such as California (which has four district courts, as can be seen on the map), have more than one. (*Source:* Administrative Office of the U.S. Courts.)

Courts of appeals offer the only real hope of reversal for most appellants, because the Supreme Court hears so few cases. The Supreme Court reviews less than 1 percent of the cases heard by federal appeals courts.*

The State Courts

The American states are separate governments within the U.S. political system. The Tenth Amendment protects each state in its sovereignty, and each state has its own court system. Like the federal courts, state court systems have trial courts at the bottom level and appellate courts at the top.

Each state decides for itself the structure of its courts and the method of selecting judges. In some states the governor appoints judges, but in most

---

*In addition to the Supreme Court, the courts of appeals, and the district courts, the federal judiciary includes a few specialty courts. Among them are the U.S. Claims Court, which hears cases in which the U.S. government is being sued for damages; the U.S. Court of International Trade, which handles cases involving appeals of U.S. Customs Office rulings; and the U.S. Court of Military Appeals, which hears appeals of military courts-martial. Some federal agencies and commissions also have judicial powers (for example, the issuing of fines), and their decisions can be appealed to a federal court of appeals.

states judges are elected to office. The most common form involves competitive elections of either a partisan or a nonpartisan nature. Other states use a mixed system called the *merit plan* (also called the "Missouri Plan" because Missouri was the first state to use it), under which the governor appoints a judge from a short list of acceptable candidates provided by a judicial selection commission. At the first scheduled election after the selected judge has served for a year, the voters by a simple "yes" or "no" vote decide whether the judge should be allowed to stay in office (see "How the 50 States Differ").

Besides the upper-court myth, there exists a "federal court myth," which holds that the federal judiciary is the most significant part of the judicial system and that state courts play a subordinate role. This view is also inaccurate. More than 95 percent of the nation's legal cases are decided by state or local courts. Most cases arising under *criminal law* (from shoplifting to murder) and most cases arising under *civil law* (such as divorces and business disputes) are defined by state laws or by local ordinances, which are derived from state laws.*

Moreover, nearly all cases that originate in state or local courts also end there. The federal courts do not come into the picture because the case does not involve a federal issue. The losing party in a divorce suit, for example, cannot appeal the decision to federal court because no federal law is involved. In most state criminal cases, there is also no federal issue, unless state authorities are alleged to have violated a right protected by the U.S. Constitution, such as the right of the accused to remain silent (see Chapter 4). In such instances, an individual convicted in a state court, after exhausting the avenues of appeal in the state system, can appeal to a federal court. If the federal court accepts the appeal, it ordinarily confines itself to the federal aspects of the case, such as whether the defendant's constitutional rights were in fact violated.

---

*Laws fall into three broad categories—procedural, civil, and criminal. Procedural law refers to rules that govern the legal process. In some cases, these rules apply to government, as in the example of the obligation of police to inform suspects of their right to an attorney. In other cases, the rules apply to private parties. For example, in some states, a homeowner cannot take an insurance company to court over a policy claim without first having that claim heard, and possibly resolved, by an arbitration board. Civil law governs relations with and between private parties as when a person injured in an accident sues the other party for monetary damages. Marriage, divorce, business contracts, and property ownership are examples of relations covered by civil law. The losing party in a civil suit might be ordered to pay or otherwise compensate the other party but would not face jail unless he or she refuses to comply with a court order, which can be a punishable offense. Government can also be a party to a civil suit, as when the IRS sues a taxpayer in a dispute over how much the taxpayer owes the government. Criminal law deals with acts that government defines as illegal, which can result in a fine, imprisonment, or other punishment. Murder, assault, and drunk driving are examples of acts covered by criminal law. The government is always a party to a criminal law case; the other party is the individual alleged to have broken the law. (Legal relationships between government and private parties, whether criminal or civil, are defined as public law. The term private law is used to refer to the legal rights and relationships between private parties.)

HOW THE 50 STATES DIFFER

CRITICAL THINKING THROUGH COMPARISONS

Principal Methods of Selecting State Judges

The states use a variety of methods for selecting the judges on their highest court, including the merit system (also known as the Missouri Plan), election, and political appointment. The states that appoint judges grant this power to the governor, except in Virginia, Connecticut, and South Carolina, where the legislature makes the choice.

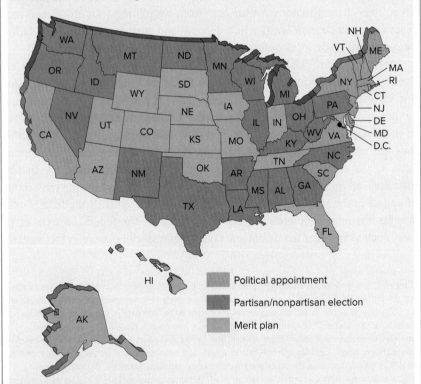

■ Political appointment

■ Partisan/nonpartisan election

■ Merit plan

Source: The Council of State Governments.

Q: What might explain why several states in the middle of the nation use the merit plan for selecting judges?

A: The merit plan originated in the state of Missouri. Innovations in one state sometimes spread to adjacent states with similar political cultures.

However, issues traditionally within the jurisdiction of the states can become federal issues through the rulings of federal courts. In its *Obergefell* (2015) ruling, for example, the Supreme Court invalidated state laws prohibiting marriage between same-sex couples. In such instances, because valid federal law supersedes conflicting state law, state courts are required to uphold the Supreme Court's ruling. Alabama chief justice Roy Moore was suspended from his post in 2016 for instructing the state's probate judges to deny marriage licenses to same-sex couples.[10] (Moore then ran and lost as the Republican nominee in the 2017 Alabama U.S. Senate election.)

FEDERAL COURT APPOINTEES

Appointments to the federal courts are controlled by the president, who selects the nominees, and by the Senate, which confirms or rejects them. The quiet dignity of the courtroom gives the impression that the judiciary is as far removed from the world of politics as a governmental institution can possibly be. In reality, federal judges and justices bring their political views with them to the courtroom and have opportunities to promote their beliefs through the cases they decide. Not surprisingly, the process by which federal judges are appointed is a partisan one.

Supreme Court Nominees

A Supreme Court appointment is a significant opportunity for a president.[11] Most justices retain their positions for many years, enabling presidents to influence judicial policy through their appointments long after they have left office. The careers of some Supreme Court justices provide dramatic testimony to the enduring nature of judicial appointments. For example, Franklin D. Roosevelt appointed William O. Douglas to the Supreme Court in 1939, and for 30 years after Roosevelt's death in 1945, Douglas remained a strong liberal influence on the Court.

Presidents usually appoint jurists who have a compatible political philosophy. Although Supreme Court justices are free to make their own decisions, their legal positions can usually be predicted from their background. A study by judicial scholar Robert Scigliano found that about three of every four appointees have behaved on the Supreme Court approximately as presidents could have expected.[12] Of course, a president has no guarantee that a nominee will actually do so. Justices Earl Warren and William Brennan, for example, proved to be more liberal than President Dwight D. Eisenhower had anticipated. Asked whether he had made any mistakes as president, Eisenhower replied, "Yes, two, and they are both sitting on the Supreme Court."[13]

The importance of Supreme Court appointments has not been lost on the justices. They have sometimes timed their departure from the Court so that their replacement will be nominated by a like-minded president. Thurgood Marshall, the first black justice, failed in his effort to do so. Marshall's health was in decline while Ronald Reagan was president, and he hated the idea of being replaced by a conservative justice. Marshall told his law clerk, "If I die when that man's president, I want you to just prop me up and keep me voting."[14] As it happened, Marshall outlived the Reagan presidency but resigned due to illness when Reagan's successor George H. W. Bush, also a Republican, was in office. Bush chose Clarence Thomas, the second black justice, to replace Marshall. Marshall was one of the most liberal justices ever to serve on the Court, while Thomas has been one of the Court's most conservative justices ever.

Although presidents seek nominees who share their political philosophy, they also must take into account a nominee's acceptability to others. Every nominee is scrutinized closely by the legal community, interested groups, and the media; must undergo an extensive background check by the FBI; and then must gain the approval of a Senate majority. Within the Senate, the key body is the Judiciary Committee, whose members have responsibility for conducting hearings on judicial nominees and recommending their confirmation or rejection by the full Senate. In 2016, following the sudden death of Justice Antonin Scalia, the Senate's Republican majority immediately announced that it would not call hearings on Democratic president Barack Obama's nominee, Merrick Garland. This action enabled Donald Trump to fill the seat with Neil Gorsuch upon becoming president in 2017. (An open seat on the Supreme Court creates the possibility that the vote in a case will be 4–4. When a tie occurs, the decision of the lower court is upheld.)

Shown here is Brett Kavanaugh testifying before the Senate Judiciary Committee during a hearing on his nomination to a seat on the Supreme Court. The Senate proceedings were the most heated in memory and included allegations of sexual misconduct when Kavanaugh was in high school and college. He was confirmed on a 50–48 Senate vote. (©Win McNamee/Getty Images)

Nearly 20 percent of presidential nominees to the Supreme Court have been rejected by the Senate on grounds of judicial qualification, political views, personal ethics, or partisanship. Most of these rejections occurred before 1900, and partisan politics was the usual reason. Today a nominee with strong professional and ethical credentials is less likely to be blocked for partisan reasons alone. Garland was the first one since Robert Bork, whose 1987 nomination by President Reagan was rejected because of Senate Democrats' opposition to his conservative judicial philosophy. The likelihood that a nominee will be blocked on the basis of partisanship has diminished. In 2017, the Republican-controlled Senate abolished the use of the filibuster as a way to prevent a Supreme Court nominee from taking a seat on the Court. The most recent appointee to the Supreme Court, Brett Kavanaugh, would not have been seated without the change. His nomination was clouded by allegations of sexual misconduct and was bitterly contested. He was confirmed by a 50–48 margin. If the filibuster had still been in place, his confirmation would have required 60 votes.

Lower-Court Nominees

The president typically delegates to the deputy attorney general the task of identifying nominees for lower-court positions, a process that includes seeking recommendations from U.S. senators of the president's party, and sometimes House members as well.

Presidents typically nominate members of their own political party. More than 90 percent of recent district and appeals court nominees have come from the president's party.[15] A constraint on these appointments is the fact that nominees must be confirmed by the Senate. Senators from the opposing party will try to derail any nominee who they perceive as holding extreme judicial views. They sometimes succeed, although their ability to do so diminished after the Senate abolished the filibustering of judicial nominees.

Although presidents are not as personally involved in selecting lower-court nominees as in naming potential Supreme Court justices, lower-court appointments are collectively significant. A president who serves two terms can shape the federal judiciary for years to come. By the time he left office, Democrat Barack Obama had appointed about a third of the seated federal judges. Republican George W. Bush appointed a similar number during his eight years in office.

Judges' partisan backgrounds influence their decisions. A study of the voting records of appellate court judges, for example, found that Democratic appointees were more likely than Republican appointees to side with defendants who claim the government violated their civil liberties.[16] Such tendencies should not be taken to mean that federal judges engage in blatant partisanship on the bench. Most lower-court cases are clear-cut enough that judges don't have much leeway in how they interpret the law. In addition, judges typically prize their judicial independence. They are officers of a separate branch of government and are secure in their tenure, factors that diminish the influence of partisanship on their decisions. However, analysts worry that the situation is changing. Some recent judicial nominees have been chosen more on the basis of their fidelity to partisan principles than for their legal qualifications, raising the question of whether they will apply those principles when deciding cases.[17]

Personal Backgrounds of Judicial Appointees

White males are overrepresented on the federal bench, just as they dominate in Congress and at the top levels of the executive branch. However, women and minority-group members have made substantial gains in recent decades, largely through appointment by Democratic presidents. Women and minority-group members are key Democratic constituencies, and Democratic presidents have responded accordingly when filling vacancies on the federal bench. Since 1993, the first year of Bill Clinton's presidency, women have made up roughly a third of the judicial appointees of Democratic presidents, compared with a sixth for Republican presidents. In terms of the appointment of minorities as federal judges, the difference is equally pronounced, with Democratic presidents having appointed roughly twice as many. Donald Trump's initial appointees were one-sided even by comparison with his most recent Republican predecessor, George W. Bush. Fewer than one-tenth of Trump's judicial appointees during his first year in office were minority-group members (see Figure 14-4).

In the past few decades, the Supreme Court has also become more demographically representative. Of the current Supreme Court justices, three are

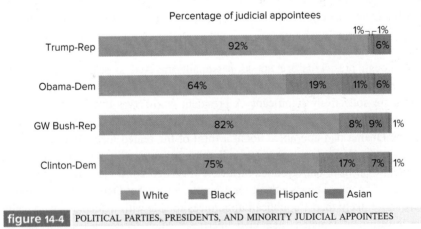

Percentage of judicial appointees

	White	Black	Hispanic	Asian
Trump-Rep	92%	6%	1%	1%
Obama-Dem	64%	19%	11%	6%
GW Bush-Rep	82%	8%	9%	1%
Clinton-Dem	75%	17%	7%	1%

figure 14-4 POLITICAL PARTIES, PRESIDENTS, AND MINORITY JUDICIAL APPOINTEES

Reflecting differences in their parties' coalitions, recent Republican and Democratic presidents have differed markedly in the percentage of minority-group members they have appointed to the federal bench. (*Source:* Alliance for Justice, 2018. Figures for past presidents are based on all confirmed nominees. For Trump, figures based on judicial nominations during first year in office.)

women (Ruth Bader Ginsburg, Sonia Sotomayor, and Elena Kagan) and two are minority-group members (Clarence Thomas and Sotomayor). The historical pattern is different. Until 1916, when Louis D. Brandeis was appointed to the Court, no Jewish justice had ever served. Prior to the 20th century, only one Catholic, Roger Taney, had served on the Court. Thurgood Marshall in 1967 was the first black justice, and Sandra Day O'Connor in 1981 was the first woman justice. Antonin Scalia in 1986 was the Court's first justice of Italian descent. Sotomayor, who was appointed in 2009, is the first Hispanic justice.

In one respect, however, the Supreme Court is less diverse than in the past. Elective office (particularly a seat in the U.S. Senate) was once a common route to the Supreme Court, but recent appointees have come overwhelmingly from the appellate courts (see Table 14-1). The assumption is that such individuals have the type of experience best suited to the duties of a Supreme Court justice. Not all observers agree. They note that many of the leading justices of the past, including John Marshall and Earl Warren, had political rather than legal backgrounds. They contend that, because Supreme Court decisions have political as well as legal implications, the Court would be better served if some of the justices had high-level political experience.

table 14-1	JUSTICES OF THE SUPREME COURT		
Justice	Year of Appointment	Nominating President	Position before Appointment
Clarence Thomas	1991	G. H. W. Bush	Judge, D.C. Circuit Court of Appeals
Ruth Bader Ginsburg	1993	Clinton	Judge, D.C. Circuit Court of Appeals
Stephen Breyer	1994	Clinton	Judge, 1st Circuit Court of Appeals
John Roberts Jr.	2005	G. W. Bush	Judge, D.C. Circuit Court of Appeals
Samuel Alito Jr.	2006	G. W. Bush	Judge, 3rd Circuit Court of Appeals
Sonia Sotomayor	2009	Obama	Judge, 2nd Circuit Court of Appeals
Elena Kagan	2010	Obama	Solicitor general of the United States
Neil Gorsuch	2017	Trump	Judge, 10th Circuit Court of Appeals
Brett Kavanaugh	2018	Trump	Judge, D.C. Circuit Court of Appeals

The Nature of Judicial Decision Making

Unlike the president or members of Congress, federal judges make their decisions within the context of a legal system. Yet, they are also political officials: they constitute one of three coequal branches of the national government. As a result, their decisions are both legal and political in nature.

Legal Influences on Judicial Decisions

Article III of the Constitution bars a federal court from issuing a decision except in response to a case presented to it. This restriction is a substantial one. For one thing, it limits judges to issues that arise from actual legal disputes. As federal judge David Bazelon noted, a judge "can't wake up one morning and simply decide to give a helpful little push to a school system, a mental hospital, or the local housing agency."[18]

The facts of a particular case also limit judicial action. The **facts** of a case are the relevant circumstances of a legal dispute or offense. In the case of a person accused of murder, for example, key facts would include evidence about the crime and whether the rights of the accused had been upheld by police. A judge must handle a murder case as a murder case, applying to it the laws that define murder and the penalties for it. A murder case cannot be used as an occasion for a judge to pronounce judgment on free speech rights or campaign finance laws.

The law is also a major constraint on the courts. Although a president or Congress can make almost any decision that is politically acceptable, the judiciary must work within the limits of the law. When asked by a friend to "do justice," Justice Oliver Wendell Holmes Jr. said that he was bound to follow the law rather than his personal sense of right and wrong.[19]

The judiciary works within the context of three main sources of law: the Constitution, legislative statutes, and legal precedents (see Table 14-2). The Constitution of the United States is the nation's highest law, and judges and justices are sworn to uphold it. When a case raises a constitutional issue, a court has the duty to apply the Constitution to it. For example, the Constitution prohibits the states from printing their own currency. If a state decided that it would do so anyway, a federal judge would be obligated to rule against the practice.

The large majority of cases that arise in courts involve issues of statutory and administrative law rather than constitutional law. *Statutory law* is legislative (statute) law. *Administrative law* is based on statutory law but is set by government agencies rather than by legislatures. Administrative law consists of the rules, regulations, and judgments that agencies make in the process of implementing and enforcing statutory law. All federal courts are bound by federal statutory and administrative laws, as well as by treaties, and judges must work within the confines of these laws. A company that is charged with violating an air pollution

table 14-2	SOURCES OF LAW THAT CONSTRAIN THE DECISIONS OF THE FEDERAL JUDICIARY

U.S. Constitution: The federal courts are bound by the provisions of the U.S. Constitution. The sparseness of its wording, however, requires the Constitution to be applied in the light of present circumstances. Thus, judges are accorded some degree of discretion in their constitutional judgments.

Statutory law: The federal courts are constrained by statutes and by administrative regulations derived from the provisions of statutes. Many laws, however, are somewhat vague in their provisions and often have unanticipated applications. As a result, judges have some freedom in deciding cases based on statutes.

Precedent: Federal courts tend to follow precedent (or *stare decisis*), which is a legal principle developed through earlier court decisions. Because times change and not all cases have a clear precedent, judges have some discretion in their evaluation of the way earlier cases apply to a current case.

law, for example, will be judged within the context of that law—what it permits and what it prohibits, and what penalties apply if the company is found to have broken the law. In most cases, the law or regulation is clear enough that when the facts of the case are determined, the decision is fairly straightforward.

The U.S. legal system developed from the English common-law tradition, which includes the principle that a court's decision on a case should be consistent with **precedent,** a term that refers to previous court rulings on similar cases. Deference to precedent gives predictability to the application of law. Government has an obligation to make clear what its laws are and how they are being applied. If courts routinely ignored how similar cases had been decided in the past, they would create confusion and uncertainty about what is lawful and what is not. A business firm that is seeking to comply with environmental protection laws, for example, can develop company policies that will keep the company safely within the law if court decisions in this area are consistent. If courts routinely ignored precedent, a firm could unintentionally engage in an activity that a court might conclude was unlawful.

Although judges are required to follow the Constitution, statutes, and precedent, the law is not always a precise guide, with the result that judges often have leeway in their rulings.[20] The Constitution, for example, is a sparsely worded document and must be adapted to new and changing situations. The judiciary also has no choice at times but to impose meaning on statutory law. Statutes are typically more detailed in their provisions than is the Constitution, but Congress cannot always anticipate the specific applications of a legislative act and often defines statutory provisions in general terms. The judiciary is then required to determine what the language means in the context of a specific case. Precedent is even less precise as a guide to decisions in that precedent is specific to

Federal judges have less discretion in their decisions than do members of Congress or the president. They act within the constraint of existing laws, which serve to guide and justify their decisions. Shown here are law books containing statutes that can bind judicial rulings. (©jjphotos/Shutterstock)

particular cases. A new case may differ in important ways from its closest precedent or rest at the intersection of conflicting precedents. In such instances, a judge must determine which precedent, if any, applies to the case at hand.

When hearing a case involving statutory law or administrative regulation, judges will often try to determine whether the meaning of the statute or regulation can be determined by common sense (the "plain meaning rule"). The question for the judge is what the law or regulation was intended to protect. Sometimes the courts will study the legislative record to determine what Congress had in mind when enacting a law. An example is a case that involved the question of whether employment protection for those with disabilities should be extended to include nearsighted people. In this instance, it was ruled that they were not protected by the legislation. If nearsighted people were to be classified as "disabled," then half of the American public would be considered disabled, which clearly was not what Congress had in mind.

The Supreme Court's ruling in *Faragher v. City of Boca Raton* (1998), involving sexual harassment in the workplace, illustrates the ambiguity that can exist in the law. The Court developed its ruling in the context of the antidiscrimination provisions of the 1964 Civil Rights Act. However, the act itself contains no description of, or even reference to, job-related sexual harassment. Yet the act does prohibit workplace discrimination, and the Court was unwilling to dismiss sexual harassment as an irrelevant form of job-related discrimination. The Court concluded that sexual harassment on the job is in fact among the types of job-related discrimination prohibited by the Civil Rights Act.[21] In this instance, the Court was "making" law. It was deciding how legislation enacted by Congress applied to behavior that Congress had not specifically addressed when it wrote the legislation.

Political Influences on Judicial Decisions

When judges have leeway in deciding a case, political influences can affect their decisions. These influences come from both inside and outside the judicial system.

Inside the Court: Judges' Political Beliefs   Although the judiciary symbolizes John Adams's description of the U.S. political system as "a government of laws, and not of men," court rulings are not simply an extension of the laws. They are also influenced by the political beliefs of the men and women who sit on the federal bench.[22] Changes in the Supreme Court's membership, for example, can bring about a change in its position (see "Party Polarization: Has Polarization Reached into the Supreme Court?"). Samuel Alito's appointment to the Court in 2006 produced that kind of change. Although the justice he replaced, Sandra Day O'Connor, usually voted with the Court's four most conservative justices, she sometimes switched sides. Voting with the Court's four most liberal justices, she cast the deciding vote, for example, in a 2003 case that upheld the limits on campaign spending by corporations contained in the Bipartisan Campaign Reform Act of 2002 (also known as the McCain-Feingold Act).[23] In contrast, Alito cast the deciding vote when the law was challenged again in 2010 in the *Citizens United* case. In that ruling, the Supreme Court struck down the limitation on campaign spending by corporations.[24]

Studies by political scientists Jeffrey Segal and Harold Spaeth show that justices tend to vote in line with their political background. Segal and Spaeth examined thousands of non-unanimous Court decisions, looking at the extent to which each justice voted on the same side or the opposite side from each of the other justices. Clear patterns emerged, such as the tendency of Republican appointees Antonin Scalia and Clarence Thomas to vote the same way and opposite that of Democratic appointees Stephen Breyer and Ruth Bader Ginsburg. Compared with Democratic appointees to the Court, Republican appointees were more likely to side with employers rather than with employees, with law enforcement officials rather than with the criminally accused, with corporations rather than with unions, and with government rather than with those claiming discrimination. Segal and Spaeth conclude that the "[policy] preferences of the justices go a long way toward explaining their decisions."[25]

PARTY POLARIZATION	Conflicting Ideas

Has Polarization Reached into the Supreme Court?

University of Chicago law professor William Landes and federal appellate judge Richard Posner, who was appointed to the bench in the 1980s by President Reagan, examined the voting records of the 43 Supreme Court justices who had sat on the Court between 1937 and 2008. For each case heard by the Court during this period, Landes and Posner assessed whether a vote could be said to favor the liberal or the conservative side. For example, in cases alleging that the government had violated a criminal defendant's constitutional rights, a vote in favor of the government would be considered conservative and a vote in favor of the defendant would be considered liberal. Then, using all the votes cast by each justice, Landes and Posner ranked the 43 justices from the justice who voted most consistently in the conservative direction to the justice who voted most consistently in the liberal direction. According to their analysis, here is the rank ordering of the 10 most conservative and 10 most liberal Supreme Court justices since 1937 (with the president who appointed the justice in parentheses):

Ten Most Conservative	Ten Most Liberal
1. Clarence Thomas (G. H. W. Bush)	1. Thurgood Marshall (Johnson)
2. William Rehnquist (Nixon)	2. William O. Douglas (Roosevelt)
3. Antonin Scalia (Reagan)	3. Frank Murphy (Roosevelt)
4. John Roberts (G. W. Bush)	4. Wiley Blount Rutledge (Roosevelt)
5. Samuel Alito (G. W. Bush)	5. Arthur Goldberg (Johnson)
6. Warren Burger (Nixon)	6. William Brennan (Eisenhower)
7. Sandra Day O'Connor (Reagan)	7. Hugo Black (Roosevelt)
8. Lewis Powell (Nixon)	8. Earl Warren (Eisenhower)
9. Charles Whittaker (Eisenhower)	9. Ruth Bader Ginsburg (Clinton)
10. Anthony Kennedy (Reagan)	10. Benjamin Cardozo (Hoover)

Q: Is there anything in the rankings that would suggest today's party polarization has reached into the Supreme Court?

Continued

A: Three of the most conservative justices of the past 80 years are currently on the Court (Thomas, Roberts, and Alito). They tend to vote together on cases, forming what Court observers have labeled the institution's "conservative bloc." It might be noted that all three were appointed by Republican presidents, as were the other seven most conservative justices. Three of the most liberal justices (Brennan, Warren, and Cardozo) were appointed by Republican presidents. Given the current level of partisanship, the likelihood is near zero today that a Republican president would appoint a justice who turned out to vote regularly on the liberal side or that a Democratic president would appoint a justice who turned out to vote regularly on the conservative side.

It is true, of course, that disputes that reach the Supreme Court are anything but clear-cut. If they were, they would have been settled in the lower federal courts. It is also true that Supreme Court justices have less leeway in making their decisions than elected officials have in making their choices. Justices operate within the confines of established laws and legal principles, which constrain their choices. The fact that Republican appointees to the Supreme Court are more likely than Democratic appointees to side with law enforcement officials than with the criminally accused does not mean that they invariably do so or that they are unmindful of legal restraints on law enforcement officials. In *United States v. Jones* (2012), for example, the Supreme Court unanimously held that law enforcement officials had exceeded their authority under the law by placing a GPS tracking device on a suspect's car without first obtaining a search warrant from a judge (see Chapter 4). Nevertheless, when viewed as a whole, Supreme Court decisions are unquestionably a mix of law and politics.

Outside the Court: The Public, Interest Groups, and Elected Officials
The courts can and do make unpopular decisions. In the long run, however, judicial decisions must be seen as fair if they are to be obeyed. In other words, the judiciary cannot routinely ignore the expectations of the general public, interest groups, and elected officials.

Judges are less responsive to public opinion than are elected officials as a result of the fact that, once appointed to office, they hold the position indefinitely. Early in his tenure as chief justice, John Roberts said: "I think the most important thing for the public to understand is that we are not a political branch of government. They don't elect us. If they don't like what we're doing, it's more or less just too bad."[26] Nevertheless, the Supreme Court in some

Even though the Supreme Court tried to temper the public response to its 1954 *Brown v. Board of Education* decision by ruling that desegregation of public schools should proceed with "all deliberate speed" rather than immediately or on a fixed timetable, the delay in implementation did little to quell the anger of many white southerners. Shown here is one of the many billboards in the South that called for the impeachment of Chief Justice Earl Warren. (©AP Photo)

instances has tempered its rulings in an effort to get public support or reduce public resistance. The Supreme Court usually stays close enough to public opinion to reduce the likelihood of outright defiance of its decisions.[27] In the 1954 *Brown* case, for example, the justices, recognizing that school desegregation would be an explosive issue in the South, required only that desegregation take place "with all deliberate speed" rather than immediately or on a fixed timetable.

Interest groups also have an influence on the judiciary. Groups petition the White House and Congress to appoint judges and justices who share their outlook on legal disputes. More directly, they submit *amicus curiae* ("friend of the court") briefs to make their positions known on court cases (see Chapter 9) and they file lawsuits to advance their policy goals. Groups that rely on a judicial strategy pick their cases carefully, choosing those that offer the greatest chance of success. They also carefully pick the courts in which they file their lawsuits, knowing that some judges will be more sympathetic than others to their argument. In fact, some groups rely almost entirely on legal action, knowing they have a better chance of success in the courts than in Congress or the White House. The American Civil Liberties Union (ACLU), for example, has filed hundreds of lawsuits over the years on issues of individual rights, including suits aimed at protecting the privacy of information stored on cellphones and computers.

F   A   K   E
or
F   A   C   T

Detecting Misinformation

Would Democracy Work Better If Presidents Could Ignore the Courts?

In America's system of divided powers, courts sometimes overturn the policies of elected officials. In President Trump's early weeks in office, for example, federal judges struck down his ban on immigration from six Muslim-dominated nations. A Public Policy Polling (PPP) survey found that two-

©moodboard/Getty Images

fifths of those polled said they trusted Trump more than judges to know what's best for America. When asked whether democracy would work better if a president could override judges' decisions, 25 percent said it would work better.[30]

Is that claim fact, or is it fake?

If a president could override or ignore the judgment of courts, it would imperil America's democracy. The United States was founded on the principle that the highest authority is the law and not the desires of those in power. "A government of laws and not of men" is how John Adams stated the principle.

No principle is more basic or more important. If elected leaders could decide for themselves the limits of the law, it would not be long before the United States had a leader who would act without restraint. Throughout history, that's been the path to authoritarian rule, where those in power trample on the legitimate rights and interests of those who dissent.

Americans' commitment to rule by law is strong, but it has been weakening. Over the past two decades, the number of Americans saying democracy might not be the best system of government has nearly doubled. One in every six Americans now holds that opinion.[31] To counter that belief, Americans need to vigorously express their support for the rule of law. It's their best protection against tyrannical government.

Elected officials also have ways of influencing the courts. Congress can rewrite legislation that it feels the judiciary has misinterpreted. Meanwhile, the president is responsible for enforcing court decisions and has some influence over the cases that come before the courts. During President Trump's first year in office, for example, the Justice Department pursued only a third as many civil rights lawsuits as the Justice Department averaged each year during the Obama administration.[28]

Judicial appointments offer the president and Congress their biggest opportunity to influence the courts. As a result of the party polarization that has worked its way into the nation's politics, the judicial appointment process has become increasingly contentious. Democratic and Republican lawmakers alike recognize the power of the courts to determine policy in areas such as affirmative action and environmental protection, and each party's lawmakers have been determined to confirm judicial appointees whose policy views align with their own. They have been joined in these efforts by interest groups on both sides of the partisan divide. In the case of Supreme Court appointments, there have even been televised advertising campaigns supporting or opposing nominees. In *Electing Justices,* political scientist Richard Davis shows that the Supreme Court appointments are now conducted more like political campaigns than like the dignified process the writers of the Constitution envisioned.[29]

JUDICIAL POWER AND DEMOCRATIC GOVERNMENT

Federal judges are unelected officials with lifetime appointments, which places them beyond the reach of the voters. Because the United States has a constitutional system that places limits on the power of the majority, the judiciary has a legitimate role in the system. Yet court decisions reflect in part the personal political beliefs of the judges. A basic question is how far judges should go in substituting their judgments for those of elected officials.

This power is most dramatically evident when courts declare a law to be unconstitutional (see "How the U.S. Differs"). This power, called **judicial review,** was first asserted by the Supreme Court in *Marbury v. Madison* (1803), when the Court rebuked both Congress and the president (see Chapter 2). In such instances, unelected judges substitute their judgment for that of the people's elected representatives. In these instances, their judgment is nearly always the final word. The difficulty of amending the Constitution (approval by two-thirds majorities in the House and Senate and by three-fourths of the states) makes it an impracticable means of reversing Supreme Court decisions. The Sixteenth Amendment, which grants the federal government the power to levy income taxes, is one of the few times that a Supreme Court decision has been reversed through constitutional amendment.

The judiciary's power has been a source of controversy throughout the nation's history, but the debate has seldom been livelier than during recent decades. The sheer number of legal disputes is among the reasons. Federal cases have increased sharply in number over the past half century as Americans have increasingly turned to the courts to settle their disputes. The judiciary at times has acted almost legislatively by addressing broad social issues, such as abortion, busing, affirmative action, church-state relations, campaign finance, and prison reform. During the 1990s, for example, the prison systems in

HOW THE U.S. DIFFERS
CRITICAL THINKING THROUGH COMPARISONS

Judicial Power

The U.S. Supreme Court has the power of judicial review. It's the most formidable tool available to a court. In applying it, a court is substituting its judgment for that of another institution, basically telling the institution that its action is a violation of the Constitution and, accordingly, is null and void. The Supreme Court is not alone in having the power of judicial review. In fact, the highest court of most democracies has it. Yet, many observers have argued that the U.S. Supreme Court is the world's most powerful court.

Q: Why is the U.S. Supreme Court more powerful than the highest court in most democracies?

A: The main reason is the U.S. system of divided and limited power. Few democracies divide power as thoroughly as does the United States, which splits it among three branches and also between the national and state levels. As well, the U.S. system grants individuals a broad range of rights that are protected from infringement by government. Each of these features of the American system is a source of constitutional dispute. What's the dividing line between legislative and executive power? Between national and state power? Between individual rights and the power of government? The Supreme Court has the final say on all these questions. As Charles Evans Hughes, a former chief justice, noted: "We live under a constitution, but the Constitution is what the judges say it is."

42 states were operating under federal court orders that mandated improvements in health care or reductions in overcrowding. Through such actions the judiciary has restricted the policymaking authority of the states, has narrowed legislative discretion, and has made judicial action an effective political strategy for some groups.[32]

The judiciary has become more extensively involved in policymaking for many of the same reasons that Congress and the president have been thrust into new policy areas. Social and economic changes have required government to play a larger role in society, and this development has generated a seemingly endless series of new legal controversies. Environmental pollution, for example, was not a major issue until the 1960s. Since then, it has been the subject of countless court cases.

What is the proper role of an unelected judiciary in a system rooted in the principle of majority rule? How far should judges go in substituting their judgment for that of the people's elected representatives? There are competing schools of thought on this issue, none of which is definitive. The Constitution is silent on the question of how it should be interpreted, which has left the judiciary's proper role open to dispute. Nevertheless, a brief review of two of the major competing theories is instructive.

Judicial Restraint versus Judicial Activism

A long-standing debate over the judiciary's proper role has pitted the advocates of judicial restraint against the advocates of judicial activism. This debate centers on the degree to which judges should defer to precedent and the policy decisions of elected officials.

The doctrine of **judicial restraint** holds that policy decisions in nearly every instance should be decided by elected lawmakers and not by appointed judges. The role of the judge is to apply the law rather than create it. Advocates of judicial restraint say that when judges substitute their views for those of elected representatives, they undermine the fundamental principle of self-government—the right of the majority, through its elected representatives, to determine how they will be governed.[33] Underlying this argument is the idea that policy is the result of conflicts between contending interests and that elected representatives, because they have to deal directly with these interests, are better positioned than judges to determine how these conflicts should be resolved.

In contrast, the doctrine of **judicial activism** holds that judges should actively interpret the Constitution, statutes, and precedents in light of fundamental principles and should intervene when elected representatives fail to uphold these principles. Although advocates of judicial activism acknowledge the importance of deference to majority rule, they claim that the courts should not blindly uphold the decisions of elected officials when core principles—such as liberty, equality, and self-government—are at issue. They also contend that precedent should be respected only if based on legal reasoning that is as sound today as it was when the precedent was established.[34]

Over its history, the Supreme Court has had strong proponents of each doctrine. Chief Justice John Marshall was an avowed activist who used the Court to enlarge the judiciary's power and to promote the national government (see Chapters 2 and 3). Judicial review—the most substantial form of judicial power—is not granted explicitly by the Constitution but was claimed through Marshall's opinion in *Marbury v. Madison.*

Associate Justice Oliver Wendell Holmes Jr. was Marshall's philosophical opposite. One of the nation's most influential jurists, Holmes argued that the judiciary should defer to the elected branches unless they blatantly over-step their authority.[35] An example of judicial restraint is the Supreme Court's 2012 ruling upholding the individual mandate provision of the

John Marshall presided over the Supreme Court during the nation's formative years. A judicial activist, he worked through court rulings to strengthen the power of the national government and bolster the Court as an independent and coequal branch of government. Marshall is the longest-serving chief justice in the nation's history. He was on the Court from 1801 to 1835, which spanned the administrations of six presidents. (©Art Reserve/Alamy)

health care reform bill enacted by Congress in 2010. The Court's majority creatively invoked Congress's taxing power in order to uphold the provision (see Chapter 3). "Because the Constitution permits such a tax, it is not our role to forbid it, or to pass upon its wisdom or fairness," said the Court's majority.[36]

Although judicial activism is sometimes associated with liberal justices, history indicates it has also been practiced by conservative justices. During the period between the Civil War and the Great Depression, the Supreme Court was dominated by conservatives and had an activist agenda, striking down most state and congressional legislation aimed at economic regulation (see Chapter 3). In the period after World War II, the Court was again in an activist mode, but this time in a different direction. Dominated by liberal justices, the Court struck down numerous state statutes in the course of expanding fair-trial rights and civil rights (see Chapters 4 and 5).

In recent years, the conservative-dominated Supreme Court has been an activist court. In the past two decades, the Supreme Court has struck down more acts of Congress than were invalidated during the previous half century.[37] An example is the Court's 2010 *Citizens United* ruling (see "Case Study: Citizens United"). In deciding that corporations and unions could spend freely on election campaigns, the Court overturned congressional action, thus substituting its judgment for that of elected officials. The ruling also overturned precedent—in earlier cases, the Court had held that Congress could regulate election spending by corporations and unions.

What Is the Judiciary's Proper Role?

The debate between advocates of judicial restraint and activism is a normative one. There is no conclusive way of settling the issue because the Constitution does not specify the method by which judges should arrive at their decisions.

Nevertheless, the debates are important because they address the fundamental question of the role of judges in a governing system based on the often-conflicting concepts of majority rule and individual rights. The United States is a constitutional democracy that recognizes both the power of the majority to rule and the claim of the minority to protection of its rights and interests. The judiciary was not established as the nation's final authority on all things relating to the use of political power. Yet the judiciary was established as a coequal branch of government charged with responsibility for protecting individual rights and limiting political authority. The question of how far the courts should go in asserting their authority is one that every student of government should ponder.

<table>
<tr><td>C A S E
S T U D Y
</td><td><h2>Politics in Action</h2></td></tr>
</table>

Citizens United

The Supreme Court concluded in the *Citizens United* case that Congress had overstepped its constitutional authority, ruling that spending restrictions infringed on the free-speech rights of corporations and unions. Writing for the majority, Justice Anthony Kennedy said: "If the First Amendment has any force, it prohibits Congress from fining or jailing citizens, or asso-

> 310   OCTOBER TERM, 2009
>
>   Syllabus
>
> CITIZENS UNITED *v.* FEDERAL ELECTION
>   COMMISSION
>
> APPEAL FROM THE UNITED STATES DISTRICT COURT FOR THE
>   DISTRICT OF COLUMBIA
>
> No. 08–205. Argued March 24, 2009—Reargued September 9, 2009—
>   Decided January 21, 2010
>
> As amended by § 203 of the Bipartisan Campaign Reform Act of 2002
> (BCRA), federal law prohibits corporations and unions from using their
> general treasury funds to make independent expenditures for speech
> that is an "electioneering communication" or for speech that expressly
> advocates the election or defeat of a candidate. 2 U. S. C. § 441b. An
> electioneering communication is "any broadcast, cable, or satellite com-
> munication" that "refers to a clearly identified candidate for Federal
> office" and is made within 30 days of a primary election, § 434(f)(3)(A),
> and that is "publicly distributed," 11 CFR § 100.29(a)(2), which in "the
> case of a candidate for nomination for President . . . means" that
>
> *Source:* Supreme Court of the United States

ciations of citizens, for simply engaging in political speech." The Court's minority dissented, arguing that corporations and unions are not what the framers had in mind in when referring to "the people" in the First Amendment.

In deciding *Citizens United*, the Supreme Court's nine justices split 5–4. All five justices (Roberts, Alito, Kennedy, Scalia, and Thomas) who claimed the First Amendment allowed for unlimited campaign spending by corporations and unions were appointed to the Court by Republican presidents. The four justices (Breyer, Ginsberg, Sotomayor, and Stevens) who claimed Congress had the power to regulate spending by these organizations were Democratic appointees with the exception of Stevens, who had been appointed to the Court three decades earlier by President Gerald Ford, a moderate Republican.

Q: What factors account for the fact that the justices' partisan backgrounds influence some of the decisions they make?

ASK YOURSELF: What types of cases reach the Supreme Court? Do they tend to be clear-cut cases where the law at issue has unmistakable meaning? Or do they tend to be cases where the law at issue has vague or ambiguous meaning and thus is subject to different interpretations? Does the First Amendment protect only individuals, or does it also protect corporations? Does the First Amendment's guarantee of "freedom of speech" include the freedom to spend unlimited amounts of money in a campaign? Is the spending of "money" a form of "protected speech"?

SUMMARY

At the lowest level of the federal judicial system are the district courts, where most federal cases begin. Above them are the federal courts of appeals, which review cases appealed from the lower courts. The U.S. Supreme Court is the nation's highest court. Each state has its own court system, consisting of trial courts at the bottom and one or two appellate levels at the top. Cases originating in state courts ordinarily cannot be appealed to the federal courts unless a federal issue is involved, and then the federal courts can choose to rule only on the federal aspects of the case. Federal judges at all levels are nominated by the president, and if confirmed by the Senate, they are appointed by the president to the office. Once on the federal bench, they serve until they die, retire, or are removed by impeachment and conviction.

The Supreme Court is unquestionably the most important court in the country. The legal principles it establishes are binding on lower courts, and its capacity to define the law is enhanced by the control it exercises over the cases it hears. However, it is inaccurate to assume that lower courts are inconsequential (the upper-court myth). Lower courts have considerable discretion, and the great majority of their decisions are not reviewed by a higher court. It is also inaccurate to assume that federal courts are far more significant than state courts (the federal court myth).

The courts have less discretionary authority than elected institutions do. The judiciary's positions are constrained by the facts of a case and by the laws as defined through the Constitution, legal precedent, and statutes (and government regulations derived from statutes). Yet existing legal guidelines are seldom so precise that judges have no choice in their decisions. As a result, political influences have a strong impact on the judiciary. It responds to national conditions, public opinion, interest groups, and elected officials, particularly the president and members of Congress. Another political influence on the judiciary is the personal beliefs of judges, who have individual preferences that affect how they decide issues that come before the courts. It's not surprising that partisan politics plays a significant role in judicial appointments.

In recent decades, as the Supreme Court has crossed into areas traditionally left to lawmaking majorities, the issue of judicial power has become more pressing, which has prompted claims and counterclaims about the judiciary's proper role. Advocates of judicial restraint claim that the justices' personal values are inadequate justification for exceeding the proper judicial role; they argue that the Constitution entrusts broad issues of the public good to elected institutions and that the courts should be exceptionally deferential to their judgment. Judicial activists counter that the courts were established as an independent branch and should seek to protect and advance fundamental constitutional principles even when such action conflicts with the policies adopted by elected institutions.

©gangliu10/Getty Images

CRITICAL THINKING ZONE

KEY TERMS

appellate jurisdiction (*p. 434*)

concurring opinion (*p. 435*)

decision (*p. 435*)

dissenting opinion (*p. 435*)

facts (of a court case) (*p. 446*)

judicial activism (*p. 456*)

judicial restraint (*p. 456*)

judicial review (*p. 454*)

jurisdiction (of a court) (*p. 434*)

majority opinion (*p. 435*)

opinion (of a court) (*p. 435*)

original jurisdiction (*p. 434*)

plurality opinion (*p. 435*)

precedent (*p. 447*)

writ of certiorari (*p. 434*)

APPLYING THE ELEMENTS OF CRITICAL THINKING

Conceptualizing: Define *majority opinion, concurring opinion,* and *dissenting opinion* in the context of Supreme Court decision making. What role is the majority opinion expected to play in decisions made by lower-court judges?

Synthesizing: Contrast the doctrines of judicial restraint and judicial activism.

Analyzing: Explain the influence of politics on the selection of Supreme Court justices and on the decisions the justices make. In comparison with lower-court judges, why would Supreme Court justices be expected to let their political beliefs play a greater role in their decisions? (Consider here the nature of the cases heard by the Supreme Court.)

EXTRA CREDIT

A Book Worth Reading: Jeffrey Toobin, *The Nine: Inside the Secret World of the Supreme Court* (New York: Anchor, 2008). Winner of the J. Anthony Lewis Book Prize, this book by a noted journalist provides a riveting look at the inside workings of the Supreme Court.

A Website Worth Visiting: www.law.cornell.edu. The Cornell University Legal Information Institute's website includes the full versions of historic and recent Supreme Court decisions, updates on cases before the Court, and links to state constitutions and other material.

PARTICIPATE!

The right to a jury trial is one of the oldest features—dating to the colonial period—
of the American political experience. Jury trials also offer the average citizen a rare
opportunity to be part of the governing structure. Yet Americans increasingly shirk
jury duty. When summoned, many of them find all sorts of reasons why they should
be excused from jury duty. In some areas of the country, the avoidance rate exceeds
50 percent. Some citizens even give up their right to vote because they know that
jurors in their area are selected from names on voter registration lists. There are
reasons, however, to look upon jury duty as an opportunity as well as a
responsibility. Studies indicate that citizens come away from the jury experience with
a fuller appreciation of the justice system. Jurors acquire an understanding of the
serious responsibility handed to them when asked to decide on someone's guilt or
innocence. The legal standard in American courts—"guilty beyond a reasonable
doubt"—is a solemn one. The fairness of the jury system also requires full
participation by the community. Studies show that jurors' life experiences can affect
the decisions they reach. If everyone on a jury is from the same background and
one that is different from the defendant's, the odds of a wrongful verdict increase.
"A jury of one's peers" should mean just that—a jury of individuals who, collectively,
represent the range of groups in the community. If you are called to serve on a jury,
you should answer the call. You would want nothing less from others if you, a
family member, or a friend were the person on trial.

15
CHAPTER

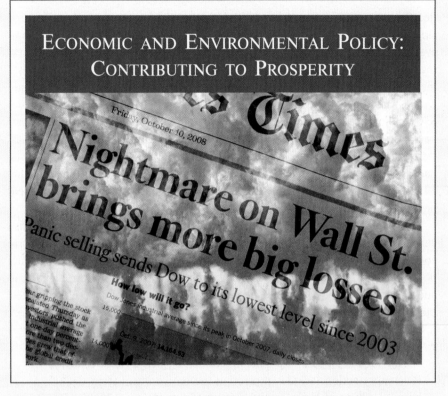

ECONOMIC AND ENVIRONMENTAL POLICY:
CONTRIBUTING TO PROSPERITY

©Alan Crosthwaite/Alamy

❝ We the People of the United States, in Order to . . . insure domestic Tranquility.**❞**

PREAMBLE, U.S. CONSTITUTION

The economy was in turmoil. The housing market was collapsing from the inability of homeowners with subprime adjustable-rate mortgages to make their monthly payments. Then, on September 15, 2008, after its stock had dropped precipitously, Lehman Brothers, one of the nation's oldest and largest commercial banks, went out of business. Its bankruptcy sent shock waves through Wall Street—the Dow Jones Industrial Average plunged 500 points, followed soon thereafter by an even larger one-day drop. Was the United States headed for an economic meltdown that would rival the Great Depression of the 1930s?

Although some pundits suggested another Great Depression might be in the offing, few economists predicted as much, and for good reason. When the Great Depression began in 1929, there were no government programs in place to stabilize and stimulate the economy. Back then, panic had swept through society, accelerating the downturn. Businesses cut back on production, investors

463

fled the stock market, depositors withdrew their bank savings, and consumers slowed their spending—all of which fueled the downward spiral. In 2008, however, government programs were in place to protect depositors' savings, slow the drop in home and stock prices, and steady the economy through adjustments in interest rates and government spending. Among the government initiatives was the Troubled Asset Relief Program (TARP) of 2008, which made $700 billion available to bolster shaky financial institutions. By 2010, job loss had lessened, the financial markets were beginning to stabilize, and businesses were starting to recover. The turnaround was slower than many economists had predicted, but government intervention had helped prevent a repeat of the 1930s, when unemployment rose to as high as 25 percent and never dropped below 10 percent.

This chapter examines economic and environmental policy. As was discussed in Chapter 1, public policy is a decision by government to follow a course of action designed to produce a particular result. In this vein, economic policy aims to promote and regulate economic interests and, through fiscal and monetary actions, to foster economic growth and stability. This chapter presents the following main ideas:

- *Through regulation, the U.S. government imposes restraints on business activity for the purpose of promoting economic efficiency and equity.* Regulatory action includes protecting the environment from the harmful effects of business and consumer activity.

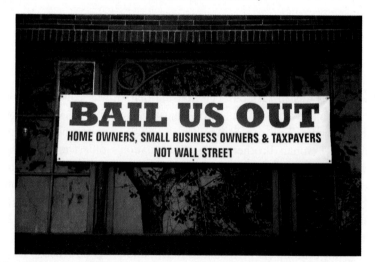

The federal government's efforts to lessen the impact of the 2008 economic recession were not popular with everyone. The bailout of troubled financial institutions was heavily criticized, but economists concluded that it prevented a much worse economic downturn. (©Karin Hildebrand Lau/Shutterstock)

- *Through promotion, the U.S. government helps private interests achieve their economic goals.* Business, in particular, benefits from the government's promotional efforts, including, for example, tax breaks and loans.

- *Through its taxing and spending decisions (fiscal policy), the U.S. government seeks to generate a level of economic supply and demand that will maintain economic prosperity.* Fiscal policy can be conducted through the use of either demand-side or supply-side tools.

- *Through its money supply decisions (monetary policy), the U.S. government—through the Federal Reserve System ("the Fed")—seeks to maintain a level of inflation consistent with sustained, controllable economic growth.*

GOVERNMENT AS REGULATOR OF THE ECONOMY

An **economy** is a system of production and consumption of goods and services that are allocated through exchange. When a shopper selects an item at a store, and pays for it with cash or a credit card, the transaction is one of the millions of exchanges that make up the economy.

In *The Wealth of Nations* (1776), Adam Smith advanced the doctrine of **laissez-faire economics,** which holds that private firms should be free to make their own production decisions. Smith reasoned that firms will produce a good when there is a demand for it (that is, when people are willing and able to buy it). Smith argued that the profit motive is the "invisible hand" that guides supply decisions in a capitalist system. He acknowledged that laissez-faire capitalism has limits. Certain areas of the economy, such as roadways, are natural monopolies and are better handled by government than by private firms. Government is also needed to impose order on private transactions by regulating banking, currency, and contracts. Otherwise, Smith argued, the economy should be left largely in private hands.

Although laissez-faire economics prevailed in the United States during the 19th century, government was not sidelined completely. Through the Pacific Railways Act of 1862, for example, Congress authorized the issuance of government bonds and the use of public lands to build the transcontinental railroad, which, though operated by private firms, was subject to government regulation. Nevertheless, it was not until the 1930s Great Depression that government assumed a broad economic role. Today, the United States has what is called a *mixed economy.* Although the economy operates mainly through private transactions, government plays a significant role. New prescription drugs, for example, cannot be marketed until they've been tested and the Food and Drug Administration (FDA) has certified them as safe and effective. The U.S. government even owns some industries (for example, the Tennessee Valley Authority, which produces electricity). Nevertheless, in comparison, say, with

table 15-1	THE MAIN OBJECTIVES OF REGULATORY POLICY	
Objective	Definition	Representative Actions by Government
Efficiency	Fulfillment of society's needs with as few of its resources as possible. The greater the output for a given input, the greater the efficiency.	Preventing restraint of trade; requiring producers to pay the costs of environmental damage; regulating business only when justified on a cost-benefit basis.
Equity	Ensuring that the outcome of an economic transaction is fair to each party.	Requiring firms to treat workers and consumers fairly.

the Scandinavian countries, where government provides health care to all citizens and controls several major industries, including the airlines, the United States relies more heavily on free-market mechanisms.

One way the U.S. government participates in the economy is through the **regulation** of privately owned businesses.[1] U.S. firms are not free to act as they please but instead operate within the limit of government regulation, which is designed to promote economic *efficiency* and *equity* (see Table 15-1).

Efficiency through Government Intervention

Economic efficiency results when the output of goods and services is the highest possible given the amount of input (such as labor and material) used to produce it.[2] Efficiency means that society is getting as many goods and services as possible from the resources used in producing them.

Promoting Competition   Adam Smith and other classical economists argued that the free market is the optimal means of achieving efficiency. In producing goods and services, firms will try to use as few resources as possible in order to keep their prices low, which will make their products more attractive to consumers. To compete, less-efficient producers will have to cut their production costs or face the loss of customers to lower-priced competitors.

Markets are not always competitive, however. If a producer can acquire a monopoly on a particular product or conspires with other producers to fix the price of the product at an artificially high level, the producer does not have to be concerned with efficiency. Consumers who need a product will have no choice but to pay the seller's price. Price fixing was prevalent in the United States in the late 19th century when large trusts came to dominate many areas

This 1914 cartoon shows railroad companies petitioning the Interstate Commerce Commission (depicted as Uncle Sam) for permission to raise their rates. The first federal regulatory agency, the ICC was created by Congress in 1887 to regulate the railroads to stop them from gouging their customers on routes where they had a monopoly. The ghost in the background is that of William Henry Vanderbilt, the richest of the railroad tycoons. (*Source*: Library of Congress, Prints and Photographs Division [LC-DIG-ppmsca-28030])

of the economy, including the oil, railroad, and sugar industries. Railroad companies, for example, had no competition on short routes and charged such high rates that many farmers went broke because of the cost of shipping their crops to markets. In 1887, Congress enacted the Interstate Commerce Act, which created the Interstate Commerce Commission (ICC) and assigned it responsibility for regulating railroad practices, including shipping rates.

The goal of such regulatory activity is to improve efficiency by restoring market competition or by placing a limit on what monopolies can charge for goods and services. Business competition today is overseen by a wide range of federal agencies, including the Federal Trade Commission (FTC). In 2016, the FTC blocked, for a second time, an attempted merger of Office Depot and Staples, saying "it would lead to higher prices" for office supplies. By contrast, the government allows concentrated ownership in industries, such as oil and automobiles, where the capital costs are so high that small firms cannot hope to compete.[3] Government acceptance of corporate giants also reflects the fact that market competition is no longer simply an issue of domestic firms. For example, the major U.S. automakers—Chrysler, Ford, and General Motors— compete for customers not only with each other but also with Asian and European auto manufacturers, such as Honda and BMW.

Deregulation and Underregulation   Although government regulation is intended to increase economic efficiency, it can have the opposite effect if it unnecessarily increases the cost of doing business.[4] Firms have to devote work hours to monitor and implement government regulations. These costs are efficient to the degree that they produce corresponding benefits. Yet if government places excessive regulatory burdens on firms, they waste resources in the process of complying. The result of overregulation is higher-priced goods that are more expensive for consumers and less competitive in the domestic and global markets.

To curb overregulation, Congress in 1995 enacted legislation that prohibits administrators in some instances from issuing a regulation unless they can show that its benefits outweigh its costs. A more concerted response is **deregulation**—the rescinding of regulations already in force for the purpose of improving efficiency. This process began in 1977 with passage of the Airline Deregulation Act, which eliminated the requirement that airlines provide service to smaller-sized cities and gave them the authority to set ticket prices (before then, the prices were set by a government agency). The change had its intended effect. Competition between airlines increased on routes between larger-sized cities, resulting in cheaper airfares on these routes. Congress followed airline deregulation with partial deregulation of, among others, the trucking, banking, energy, and communications industries.

Deregulation can be carried too far.[5] Freed of regulatory restrictions, firms can engage in reckless or unethical practices. Such was the case with the subprime mortgage crisis that struck in 2008 (see "Case Study: The Subprime Mortgage Crisis"). Mortgage firms had lured marginally qualified home buyers by offering low interest rates and small down payments. When the economy weakened, many homeowners defaulted on their mortgages, precipitating the 2008 financial crisis. In 2010, Congress responded by enacting the most substantial regulation of financial institutions since the New Deal era. Designed to curb the abuses that contributed to the financial crisis, the Dodd-Frank Wall Street Reform and Consumer Protection Act empowers government to oversee financial activities more closely. It also created a new federal agency, the Consumer Financial Protection Bureau, to protect consumers from exploitation by credit card companies, lending institutions, and other creditors.

| C A S E |
| S T U D Y |

Politics in Action

The Subprime Mortgage Crisis

"Moral hazard" is a justification for government regulation.

Economist Paul Krugman describes moral hazard as the situation in which "one person makes the decision about how much risk to take, while someone else bears the cost if things go badly."

Few developments illustrate the problem more clearly than the subprime home mortgage crisis that triggered the near collapse of America's financial sector in 2008. A decade earlier, financial regulations had been reduced to allow banks to grant mortgages to a wider range of borrowers. Banks jumped at the chance. By 2006, as the figure

©Ryan McVay/Getty Images

indicates, a third of mortgages were being given to people with weak or unconfirmed credit records. Banks had leveraged their assets at roughly 30 to 1—up from the previous level of 12 to 1—in an effort to make ever larger profits from home lending. This put the entire housing industry at risk if the economy went into a severe downturn and homeowners were unable to keep up with their mortgages, which is exactly what happened in 2007-2008. Banks found themselves in possession of millions of abandoned houses, rather than the billions of dollars in mortgage payments they had expected to collect each month.

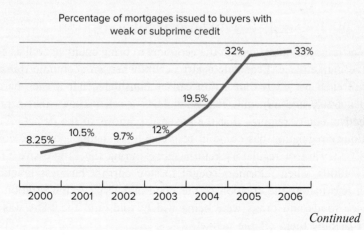

Percentage of mortgages issued to buyers with weak or subprime credit

8.25%   10.5%   9.7%   12%   19.5%   32%   33%

2000   2001   2002   2003   2004   2005   2006

Continued

So who saved the banks when the crisis threatened them with collapse? It was the American taxpayers. Congress stepped in with hundreds of billions of dollars in loans to keep Bank of America, Citibank, and other major banks from going bankrupt. They were considered "too big to fail." If they went down, they could have taken the entire economy with them. Yet, it was their risky investment strategies that put them on the verge of bankruptcy. They took the risk, and another party—the taxpayers—bore the costs, which is the precise definition of "moral hazard."

Q: Are there circumstances in which "too big to fail" is sensible public policy? What's the best way to prevent the problem from happening in the first place?

ASK YOURSELF: Would you bail out a bank if its collapse would have a domino effect, taking down other businesses with it? If you would, then the bank is too big to be allowed to fail because the consequences would be unacceptable. In terms of preventing the problem, do you trust banks to regulate themselves? Or do you think strict government regulation is necessary to prevent banks from engaging in too many high-risk investments?

The crisis in America's financial system demonstrates that the issue of business regulation is not a simple question of whether or not to regulate. Too much regulation can burden firms with excessive implementation costs, whereas too little regulation can give firms the leeway to engage in risky or unethical practices. Either too little or too much regulation can result in economic inefficiency.

Equity through Government Intervention

The government intervenes in the economy to bring equity as well as efficiency to the marketplace. **Economic equity** occurs when an economic transaction is fair to each party.[6] A transaction can be considered fair if each party enters into it freely and ethically. For example, if a seller knows that a product is defective, equity requires that the buyer also knows of the defect.

Equity regulation has come in response to changing economic conditions. The first wave of regulatory reform came during the Progressive Era of the early 1900s, when reformers sought to stop corrupt business practices. One such reform was the creation of the Food and Drug Administration in 1907. Unsafe foods and drugs were being widely sold, and the FDA was charged with keeping them off the market.

The second wave of equity regulation came during the 1930s Great Depression, when New Deal reformers sought to restrict destructive business practices. The Securities and Exchange Act of 1934, for example, aimed to protect investors from dishonest or imprudent stock and bond brokers. The New Deal also provided greater equity for organized labor. The Fair Labor Standards Act of 1938, for example, required employers to pay workers a minimum wage.

The third wave of regulatory reforms came in the 1960s and 1970s and sought to promote environmental protection, consumer protection, and worker safety. Ten federal agencies, including the Consumer Product Safety Commission and the Environmental Protection Agency, were established to curtail harmful business activity. Among the products declared to be unsafe in the 1960s and 1970s were cigarettes, leaded paint, and leaded gasoline.

This regulatory activity has had a remarkable effect. Take cigarettes, for example. Beginning in the 1960s, the federal government required cigarette manufacturers to put warning labels about the dangers of smoking on cigarette packs. At the time, more than 40 percent of American adults were cigarette smokers. Today that figure is 20 percent. As the number of smokers has declined, so has the incidence of lung cancer, emphysema, and other smoking-related ailments. A Yale University study estimated that 8 million lives have been saved in the United States through anti-tobacco regulation.[7] How many lives is that? That's twice the number of all the people currently living in Boston, San Francisco, Seattle, Dallas, Atlanta, and Minneapolis combined.

The Politics of Regulatory Policy

Although business firms fought the Progressive Era and New Deal reforms, their opposition diminished gradually when they came to realize that they could influence the new regulatory agencies. Because the agencies were charged with overseeing particular industries, such as banking or pharmaceuticals, a regulated industry could develop a close relationship with its associated agency. Pharmaceutical firms, for example, cultivated a relationship with the FDA that at times has served their interest. In the 1990s, for instance, drug companies convinced the FDA to streamline its drug-safety reviews in order to speed the marketing of new drugs.[8] One fast-tracked drug, Vioxx, had to be taken off the market in 2004 after it was found to cause strokes and heart attacks.

The third wave of regulatory reforms of the 1960s and 1970s differed from the Progressive and New Deal reforms in their structure. Most of the regulatory agencies established in the third wave were granted a broader mandate than those created earlier. They have responsibility not for a single industry but for firms of all types, and their responsibilities cover a wide range of activities. The Environmental Protection Agency (EPA), for example, is charged with regulating environmental pollution of almost any kind by almost any firm. Because newer agencies such as the EPA deal with so many industries, no single industry can easily influence their decisions.

Most of the older agencies, including the Federal Communications Commission (FCC) and the Securities and Exchange Commission (SEC), are run by a commission whose members are nominated by the president and serve fixed terms but cannot be removed by the president during their term of office, which is a reason they sometimes get too friendly with the industries they regulate. Most of the newer agencies, including the EPA, are headed by a single director who can be removed from office at the president's discretion. As a result, the newer agencies tend to be more responsive to the president than to the firms they oversee.

As in other policy areas, Republican and Democratic lawmakers are divided over the issue of regulation. Although lawmakers of both parties acknowledge the need to regulate business, the Republican Party has stronger ties to business and its lawmakers lean toward less strict regulation. The 2010 Dodd-Frank Act that tightened restrictions on financial institutions was enacted along party lines, with nearly every congressional Democrat voting in favor of the bill and nearly every congressional Republican voting against it. In 2017, with the Republicans now in control of the presidency, the Senate, and the House, Republican lawmakers sought to loosen provisions of the Dodd-Frank Act. One effort was the 2018 Economic Growth, Regulatory Relief, and Consumer Protection Act, which relaxed the regulation of small banks and, to a lesser degree, of large banks like Bank of America and Citigroup. Another was the Trump Administration's change of a rule that had required financial advisers to act "in the best interests of the client," which meant, for example, the recommending of securities that had low transaction fees. Under the change, a financial adviser could recommend securities with high fees as long as the fee was disclosed.

GOVERNMENT AS PROTECTOR OF THE ENVIRONMENT

The full costs of business activity are not always borne by producers and consumers. Take, for example, a company whose industrial wastes seep into an ocean bay. The price that consumers pay for the company's products does not reflect the cost to society of the pollution—for example, its impact on the beaches, reefs, and shellfish. **Externalities** is the term that economists use to describe these unpaid costs.

Before the 1960s, the federal government did not require firms to pay to reduce externalities. The publication in 1962 of Rachel Carson's *Silent Spring*

Environmental laws and regulations have led to greatly reduced levels of air and water pollution. Shown on the left is a photo of Los Angeles from the time when yellowish-gray polluted air ("smog") regularly hung over the city. On the right is a photo of today's Los Angeles. (smog: ©Daniel Stein/Getty Images; clear: ©ekash/Getty Images)

helped to launch the environmental movement.[9] Written at a time when the author was dying of breast cancer, *Silent Spring* exposed the threat to birds and animals of pesticides such as DDT. Carson's appearance at a Senate hearing contributed to legislative action that produced the 1963 Clean Air Act and the 1965 Water Quality Act—the first major federal laws aimed at protecting the environment from human-made pollution. Firms would be required to install antipollution devices in order to reduce their harmful air and water emissions.

Environmental Protection

The Environmental Protection Agency was created in 1970. Proposed by Republican president Richard Nixon and enacted by the Democratic-controlled Congress, the EPA was given responsibility for enforcing the nation's environmental laws, including the levying of fines and sanctions on firms that violate them.

Environmental regulation has led to dramatic improvements in air and water quality. Pollution levels today are far below their levels of the 1960s, when yellowish-gray fog ("smog") hung over cities like Los Angeles and New York and when bodies of water like the Potomac River and Lake Erie were open sewers. In the past five decades, toxic waste emissions have been halved, hundreds of polluted lakes and rivers have been revitalized, energy efficiency has increased, food supplies have been made safer, and urban air pollution has declined by 60 percent.[10]

Climate Change and Energy Policy

No environmental issue receives more attention today than does global warming. The earth's temperature level has been rising, and the rate of increase has accelerated since the mid-1970s (see Figure 15-1). The National Oceanic and

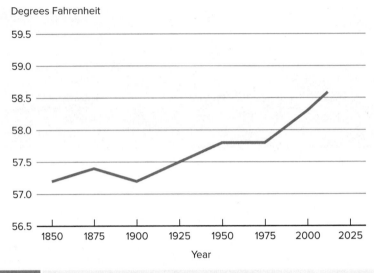

figure 15-1   AVERAGE TEMPERATURE OF THE EARTH'S SURFACE

The average surface temperature of the earth has risen substantially in the past century and has done so at an accelerating pace in the past three decades. (*Source:* National Weather Service, Great Britain, 2018)

Atmospheric Administration has been measuring annual temperatures for nearly 150 years. Six of the globe's warmest years on record have occurred since 2010.[11] Scientists theorize that the temperature rise is attributable to emissions from oil, coal, and other carbon-based fuels, and they say that dire consequences—including water shortages, rising sea levels, and extreme heat waves—will result unless carbon emissions are curbed.

U.S. policymakers have responded in varying ways to these claims. Some policymakers believe climate change is a large problem that needs to be addressed urgently. Others say that a substantial response should be delayed until the consequences of climate change are more clearly understood. Still others say that the remedies for climate change, such as requiring companies to reduce their carbon emissions, would slow economic growth to an unacceptable level. And still others have challenged the scientific consensus, saying that the evidence for the climate change thesis is faulty or inconclusive.

The United States has lagged behind most Western countries, including Germany, France, and Great Britain, in reducing its greenhouse gas emissions. The reasons are several, including policy disagreement and the structure of the U.S. political system. The division of power between the president, the House, and the Senate makes it difficult to garner the support necessary to implement costly regulatory policies. In 2015, at the United Nations Climate Change Conference in Paris, the participating countries, including the United States, unanimously agreed to "reduce their carbon emissions as soon as possible" through voluntary policies. Upon becoming president in 2017, Donald Trump, a skeptic of climate change theory, withdrew the United States from the Paris accord, making it the only nation that's not part of the agreement.

The issue of climate change is confounded by the fact that no single nation can solve the problem on its own. When carbon emissions get into the atmosphere, they affect conditions elsewhere. The problem is also confounded by the rapid expansion of the economies of China, India, and other developing nations, which has contributed to the increase in carbon emissions. Developing countries say they should not bear most of the burden of curbing global warming, arguing that the problem stems from decades-long carbon emissions by the industrialized nations, including the United States. In turn, fully industrialized countries have argued that recent increases in carbon emissions are coming largely from developing countries and that the problem cannot be solved unless they rein in their emissions (see "How the U.S. Differs").

GOVERNMENT AS PROMOTER OF ECONOMIC INTERESTS

Congress in 1789 gave a boost to the nation's shipping industry by imposing a tariff on goods brought into the United States on foreign ships, which prompted importers to make greater use of American ships. Since that first favor, the U.S. government has provided thousands of direct and indirect benefits to economic interests. The following sections describe some of these benefits.

Promoting Business

Business firms are not opposed to government regulation as such. They object only to regulatory policies that harm their interests. At various times and in different ways, as in the case of the FDA and pharmaceutical firms, some regulatory agencies have sided with the very industries they are supposed to regulate in the public interest.

Loans and tax breaks are other ways that government promotes business interests. Firms receive loan guarantees, direct loans, tax credits for capital investments, and tax deductions for capital depreciation. However, the most significant contribution that government makes to business is in the traditional services it provides, such as education, transportation, and defense. Colleges and universities, which receive substantial funding from federal and state governments, furnish business with most of its professional and technical workforce and with much of the basic research that goes into product development. The nation's roadways, waterways, and airports are other public-sector

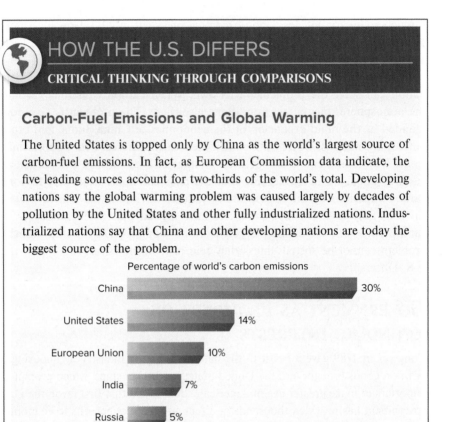

CRITICAL THINKING THROUGH COMPARISONS

Carbon-Fuel Emissions and Global Warming

The United States is topped only by China as the world's largest source of carbon-fuel emissions. In fact, as European Commission data indicate, the five leading sources account for two-thirds of the world's total. Developing nations say the global warming problem was caused largely by decades of pollution by the United States and other fully industrialized nations. Industrialized nations say that China and other developing nations are today the biggest source of the problem.

Percentage of world's carbon emissions

China	30%
United States	14%
European Union	10%
India	7%
Russia	5%

Q: Why might it make sense to place most of the burden for reducing carbon-fuel emissions on nations with developing economies, such as China and India?

A: Carbon emissions in developing countries are increasing at the fastest rate. Advanced industrialized nations such as the United States and Germany could assist them by providing the financial subsidies and technology needed to create clean-energy economies.

contributions without which business could not function. In short, America's business has no bigger booster than government.

Promoting Labor

Laissez-faire thinking dominated government's approach to labor well into the 20th century. Union activity was held by the courts to be illegal because it interfered with the rights of business. Government hostility toward labor included the use of police and soldiers to break up strikes. In 1914 in Ludlow,

Colorado, state militia attacked a tent colony of striking miners and their families, killing 19, including 11 children.

The 1930s Great Depression brought about a change in labor's position. The National Labor Relations Act of 1935, for example, gave workers the right to bargain collectively and prohibited business from disrupting union activities or discriminating against union employees. Government support for labor now also includes minimum-wage and maximum-work-hour guarantees, unemployment benefits, safer and more healthful working conditions, and nondiscriminatory hiring practices. Although the federal government's support of labor extends beyond these examples, its support is much less extensive than its support of business.

Labor has been the target of policies that have weakened its position. Slightly more than half of the states, for example, have right-to-work laws that give workers in a unionized workplace the option of not joining the union. They get the benefit of union-negotiated contracts but don't contribute dues to the union.

In a major 2018 decision, the U.S. Supreme Court in a 5-4 vote dealt unions a sharp blow by ruling that public-sector unions can no longer collect mandatory dues. Most union members today work in the public sector. The 2018 ruling reversed a 1977 ruling that held public-sector workers could be required to pay union dues because they benefit from the collective bargaining agreements negotiated by their unions. In overturning precedent, the Court held that the mandatory requirement violated members' First Amendment rights because the dues could be used by their union to support policy positions that the member found objectionable.[12]

A major contribution that government makes to economic interests–particularly business, but also labor and agriculture–is through public colleges and universities. Supported in significant part by taxpayer dollars, they provide research and workforce training of benefit to economic interests, which otherwise would have to pay these costs themselves. Shown here is a campus scene of the University of Texas at San Antonio. (Courtesy of The University of Texas at San Antonio)

Promoting Agriculture

Government support for agriculture has a long history. The Homestead Act of 1862, for example, opened government-owned lands to settlement. The federal government provided 160 acres of land free to any family that staked a claim, built a house, and farmed the land for five years.

Government programs today provide billions of dollars of assistance annually to farmers, small and large. Federal payments account for more than a fifth of net agricultural income, making America's farmers among the most heavily subsidized in the world. This assistance is intended in part to reduce the market risks associated with farming. Weather, global conditions, and other factors can radically affect crop and livestock prices from one year to the next, and federal subsidies give a degree of stability to farmers' income.

FISCAL POLICY AS AN ECONOMIC TOOL

Before the 1930s, prevailing economic theory held that the economy was self-regulating, that it would correct itself after a downturn. The greatest economic collapse in the nation's history—the Great Depression of the 1930s—shattered that idea. The economy did not recover on its own, but instead continued to decline. President Franklin D. Roosevelt's spending and job programs, which stimulated the economy and put Americans back to work, ushered in the modern era.[13] Today, government is expected to intervene when the economy dips.

The government's efforts to maintain a thriving economy occur in part through its taxing and spending decisions, which together are referred to as its **fiscal policy.** Through changes in its level of spending and taxation, government can stimulate or slow the economy.

Demand-Side Policy

Fiscal policy has its origins in the early 20th-century economic theories of John Maynard Keynes. Noting that employers tend to cut their production and workforce when the economy begins to weaken, Keynes challenged the traditional idea that government should also cut back on its spending. Keynes argued that a downturn could be shortened only if government compensates for the slowdown in private spending by increasing its spending level. In doing so, the government pumps money into the economy, which stimulates consumer spending, which in turn stimulates business production and creates jobs, thereby hastening the economic recovery.[14]

Keynesian theory holds that the level of the government's response should be commensurate with the severity of the downturn. During an **economic**

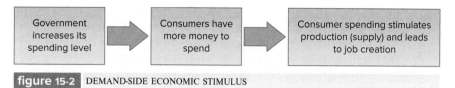

figure 15-2   DEMAND-SIDE ECONOMIC STIMULUS

When the economy is sluggish, demand-side economics holds that government should increase its spending in order to boost consumer spending (demand), which will create jobs and stimulate production (supply).

depression—an exceptionally steep and sustained decline in the economy—the government should engage in massive new spending programs to speed the recovery. During an **economic recession,** which is a more common but less-severe downturn, government spending should also be increased but by a lesser amount.

Keynes's theory is based on **demand-side economics.** It emphasizes the consumer "demand" component of the supply–demand relationship (see Figure 15-2). When the economy is sluggish, the government, by increasing its spending, places additional money in consumers' hands. With more money in their pockets, consumers spend more, which boosts "demand" for products, prompting firms to retain or hire workers to produce the goods and services. This line of reasoning was behind the $787 billion economic stimulus bill that Congress passed in 2009 as a means of combating the steep economic slide precipitated by the near collapse of the financial markets. The legislation included, for example, funding for construction projects and an extension of unemployment benefits.

Although demand-side policy is typically applied during an economic downturn, it can also be used to slow down the economy during an inflationary period—when prices are rising rapidly. By cutting back on its spending, government places less money in consumers' hands, helping to slow the rise in prices.

Supply-Side Policy

Demand-side stimulation has been the preferred policy of Democratic lawmakers. Lower-income Americans are a core Democratic constituency and are usually the most deeply affected by rising unemployment. Accordingly, Democratic leaders have typically responded to a sluggish economy with increased government spending (demand-side fiscal policy), which offers direct help to the unemployed and stimulates consumption. The $787 billion economic stimulus bill passed by Congress in 2009 was a Democratic bill. No House Republican and only three Senate Republicans voted for it.

HOW THE 50 STATES DIFFER

CRITICAL THINKING THROUGH COMPARISONS

Federal Taxes and Benefits: Winners and Losers

Fiscal policy (the federal government's taxing and spending policies) varies in its effect on the states, as data from the Tax Foundation indicate. The biggest loser is New Jersey, whose taxpayers get back in federal spending in their state only $0.61 for every dollar they pay in federal taxes. The biggest winners are New Mexico and Mississippi, whose taxpayers get back $2.03 and $2.02, respectively, in federal spending in their states for every dollar they pay in federal taxes.

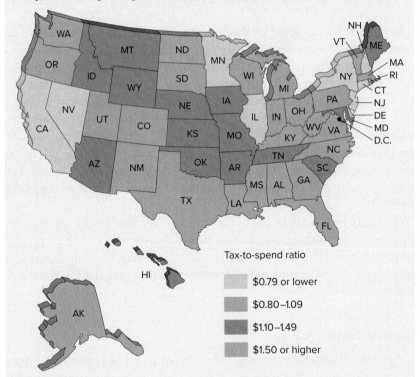

Tax-to-spend ratio

- $0.79 or lower
- $0.80–1.09
- $1.10–1.49
- $1.50 or higher

Q: Why are many of the "losers" in the Northeast?

A: The federal taxes that originate in a state reflect its wealth, and states in the Northeast are wealthier than most states. Because of this, they also get less federal assistance for programs designed to help lower-income people and areas. Finally, most federal lands and military installations—sources of federal money—lie outside the Northeast.

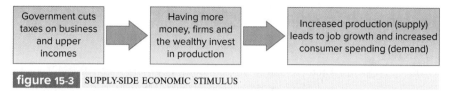

| Government cuts taxes on business and upper incomes | ➡ | Having more money, firms and the wealthy invest in production | ➡ | Increased production (supply) leads to job growth and increased consumer spending (demand) |

figure 15-3 SUPPLY-SIDE ECONOMIC STIMULUS

When the economy is sluggish, supply-side economics holds that government should cut taxes on business and wealthy taxpayers in order to boost investment in production (supply), which will create jobs and increase consumer spending (demand).

Republican Party leaders are more likely to see an economic downturn through the lens of business firms. Republicans have typically resisted large spending increases because government has to borrow the money, which creates upward pressure on interest rates, including the rates that business firms have to pay for loans.

A fiscal policy alternative to demand-side stimulation preferred by Republicans is **supply-side economics**, which emphasizes the production side of the supply–demand equation. Supply-side policies were a cornerstone of the Reagan and Bush administrations' response to slowing economic growth.[15] Rather than relying on government spending programs to boost consumer spending, Republican presidents Reagan and Bush turned to large tax cuts for companies and upper-income taxpayers as a means of stimulating business activity. The assumption of supply-side theory is that, if firms and wealthier individuals have more money on hand, they will invest it in production (supply), which will boost employment and consumer spending (see Figure 15-3). In the case of the Bush tax cuts, the tax savings to Americans in the top 1 percent of income was $54,493 per year, compared with an average of $67 for those in the bottom 20 percent and $611 for those in the middle 20 percent.[16]

Fiscal Policy: Practical and Political Limits

Both demand-side policy and supply-side policy have risks as well as rewards. Although they can serve to stimulate the economy, they come at a cost—large budget deficits and a rising level of national debt.

High levels of government spending or deep cuts in taxes result in a **budget deficit**—in which the federal government spends more in a year than it receives in tax and other revenues. The shortfall increases the **national debt,** which is the total cumulative amount the federal government owes to its creditors (see Figure 15-4). In recent years the government has spent far more than it has received in taxes. In 2018, for example, the federal government's budget deficit was roughly $800 billion, meaning that it borrowed about a sixth of what it spent. The U.S. government has not had a **balanced budget** (in which revenues

PARTY POLARIZATION	**Conflicting Ideas**

Taxes

There is barely an economic issue on which Republican and Democratic lawmakers now agree. It was not always that way. Through the 1970s, Republicans and Democrats often came together on such issues. An example is the Federal-Aid Highway Act of 1956, which led to the building of the nation's interstate highway system. Proposed by Republican president Dwight D. Eisenhower, it was backed by an overwhelming bipartisan majority in Congress.

This bipartisan spirit began to unravel in the 1980s when Republican president Ronald Reagan, despite Democratic opposition, got Congress to cut taxes on upper incomes. The divide over tax policy has persisted, with Republicans pushing for lower taxes overall, and on higher-income taxpayers particularly, and Democrats pushing for higher taxes on the wealthy and reduced taxes on lower-income individuals.

The difference between the parties was evident in passage of the 2017 Tax Cuts and Jobs Act. The Senate vote divided strictly along party lines, with every Republican voting for it and every Democrat voting against it. In the House, nearly all the Republicans supported it while every Democrat opposed it. The bill reflected the Republicans' philosophy. It included a substantial cut in individual tax rates, with higher-income taxpayers getting the largest reduction in terms of dollars, and a large cut—from 35 percent to 21 percent—in the corporate tax rate.

Q: What's your view on tax policy? Do you side with supply-side Republicans who argue that taxes on high-income taxpayers should be kept low so that they will invest the extra income, thereby contributing to economic growth? Or do you side with Democratic lawmakers who argue that tax cuts should be targeted for the less well off, because they are more likely to spend the extra dollars, thereby giving the economy a boost?

are equal to government expenditures) since the late 1990s. Projections indicate that high deficits will continue far into the future, adding to the national debt, which already exceeds $21 trillion. The U.S. government spends an enormous amount each year—currently about $300 billion—just to pay the interest on the debt. That amount exceeds the combined annual federal spending on the Departments of Education, Labor, Transportation, and Housing and Urban Development.[17]

Increase in national debt during time in
office (trillions of dollars)

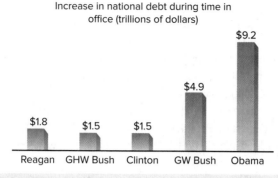

				$9.2
Reagan	GHW Bush	Clinton	GW Bush	Obama
$1.8	$1.5	$1.5	$4.9	

figure 15-4   INCREASE IN NATIONAL DEBT UNDER RECENT PRESIDENTS

The national debt, which is the total cumulative amount the federal government owes to its creditors, jumped under Presidents Bush and Obama, owing to overly steep tax cuts, wars in the Middle East, and the severe economic downturn that began in 2008. (*Source:* Federal Reserve.)

| F A K E |
| or |
| F A C T |

Detecting Misinformation

Would Eliminating Foreign Aid Balance the Budget?

A recent poll asked Americans for their "best guess" of the percentage of the federal budget spent on foreign aid. On average, respondents estimated it at 26 percent of the total budget. One in five who ventured a guess estimated it at 40 percent or higher.[18] A large number of Americans believe that eliminating foreign aid would produce enough savings to balance the federal budget.[19]

©Chris Warham/Alamy

Is that claim fact, or is it fake?

The actual level of spending on foreign aid is less than 1 percent of the federal budget. And much of this spending is not actual dollars but instead is in the form of foodstuffs and military hardware produced by American firms and sent overseas. Foreign aid spending is tiny by comparison with some spending categories. The largest category is health care, which includes Medicare and Medicaid. It accounts for roughly 28 percent of federal spending. Social Security is the second largest category, accounting for about 24 percent of spending. Third is defense spending, at roughly 17 percent. If lawmakers were to seek ways to balance the budget, cutting foreign aid wouldn't have much effect. The only realistic way to balance the budget would be through a combination of tax increases and spending cuts in areas where the federal government spends heavily.

Each political party blames the other party for the fiscal problem but, in truth, both parties have contributed to it. When the Democrats have been in power, they've sponsored increases in domestic spending, sometimes on a large scale, as in the case of the $787 billion stimulus package that the Democratic-controlled Congress passed in 2009 in response to the economic downturn of the previous year. When Republicans have been in power, they've adopted tax reductions and military spending increases. In 2017, for example, the Republican-controlled Congress with the backing of President Trump passed the 2017 Tax Cuts and Jobs Act, which will add roughly $1.5 trillion to the national debt over the next decade.

MONETARY POLICY AS AN ECONOMIC TOOL

Fiscal policy is not the only instrument of economic management available to government. A second is **monetary policy,** which is based on adjustments in the amount of money in circulation. Monetarists, as economists who emphasize monetary policy are called, contend that the money supply is the key to sustaining a healthy economy. Their leading theorist, the American economist Milton Friedman, held that supply and demand are best controlled by manipulating the money supply.[20] Too much money in circulation contributes to inflation because too many dollars are chasing too few goods, which drives up prices. Too little money in circulation results in a slowing economy and rising unemployment, because consumers lack the ready cash and easy credit required to maintain spending levels. Monetarists believe in increasing the money

Pictured here are the two most influential economists of the 20th century. On the left is Milton Friedman, who pioneered the theory of monetary policy. On the right is John Maynard Keynes, who devised fiscal policy theory. (left: ©Financial Times/ullstein bild/Getty Images; right: ©Keystone-France/Gamma-Keystone/Getty Images)

supply when the economy needs a boost and decreasing the supply when it needs to be slowed down.

The Fed

Control over the money supply rests not with the president or Congress but with the Federal Reserve System ("the Fed"). Created by the Federal Reserve Act of 1913, the Fed is directed by a board of governors whose seven members serve for 14 years, except for the chair and vice chair, who serve 4-year terms. All members are appointed by the president with the approval of the Senate. The Fed is a "bankers' bank." It does not have "customers" as do other banks. Instead, it assists and regulates all national banks and those state banks that chose to become members of the Federal Reserve System—about 6,000 banks in all.

The Fed has several tools by which to add or subtract money from the economy, seeking a balance that will permit steady growth without causing an unacceptable level of inflation (see Table 15-2). One method the Fed uses is to raise or lower the percentage of funds that member banks are required to hold in reserve—meaning they cannot loan or invest these funds. When the Fed raises the reserve rate, member banks are required to keep more of their money out of circulation, thereby reducing the money supply. When it lowers the reserve rate, the Fed allows banks to release more of their money for loans to consumers and firms. During the 2008 subprime mortgage crisis, the Fed reduced the reserve rate several times so that member banks would have more money available to deal with the shortfall resulting from failed mortgages.

A second and more publicly visible way in which the Fed affects the money supply is by lowering or raising the interest rate that member banks pay when they borrow money from the Federal Reserve. When the Fed raises the interest rate for banks, they in turn raise the rate they charge their customers for new loans, which discourages borrowing, thereby reducing the amount of money

table 15-2	MONETARY POLICY: A SUMMARY OF THE FED'S POLICY TOOLS
Reserve Rate	Amount of their assets that member banks must keep on hand. The rate can be lowered to increase the money supply or raised to decrease it.
Interest Rate	Interest rate charged to member banks when they borrow from the Fed. The rate can be lowered to increase the money supply or raised to decrease it.
Buying of Securities	By buying securities, the Fed gives money to the seller, which increases the money supply. By selling securities, the Fed receives money from the buyer, which decreases the money supply.

entering the economy. Conversely, when the Fed lowers the interest rate on its loans to member banks, they are able to lower the rate they charge customers for their loans, which leads to additional borrowing by firms and consumers, resulting in an increase in the money supply. As the economy slowed in 2008, for example, the Fed dropped the interest rate by several percentage points, enabling member banks to lower their rates, making loans more affordable.

There is also a third mechanism that the Fed routinely uses—the buying and selling of government securities. When it sells government securities in exchange for cash, the Fed is taking that money out of circulation, thereby reducing the money supply. By contrast, when it buys government securities, the Fed is putting the money used to purchase the securities into private hands to be spent or invested, thus stimulating the economy.

The severity of the 2008 economic downturn, which has been labeled the Great Recession, prompted the Fed to unleash a controversial fourth mechanism. Known as *quantitative easing (QE)*, it came into use after the Fed had lowered interest rates almost to the point of zero and therefore could not lower them further as a means of injecting money into the economy. So it turned to quantitative easing, It began to purchase the assets of member banks, such as their mortgage-backed securities. The goal was to take risky securities off the banks' hands in return for money that they could loan out to firms and consumers at historically low rates. Eventually, the Fed spent more than $3 trillion on quantitative easing, which is more money than is generated in a full year by the economy of every country on earth except the United States, China, Japan, and Germany. Never in the country's history has so much money been pumped into the economy.

Where did the Fed come up with this vast amount of money? For all practical purposes, it created the money out of paper. The Fed is the nation's central bank and essentially has the power to print money, and keep printing it. And that's what it did from 2009 until it stopped in 2014. The spending had the effect of strengthening financial institutions by relieving them of questionable assets while giving them cash that they could lend out, thereby increasing the money supply.

Quantitative easing is considered a tool of "last resort," to be used only when other tools have reached the point where they are no longer effective.[21] If too much money is pumped into the economy, it will eventually trigger a sharp rise in inflation.

The Fed and Control of Inflation

Although the meltdown of financial markets in 2008 placed the Fed in the role of trying to stimulate the economy, a sluggish economy is not the only problem the Fed is expected to address. Another is **inflation**—an increase in the price of goods and services. Before the late 1960s, inflation was a minor problem, rising by less than 4 percent annually. However, inflation jumped during the last years of the Vietnam War and remained high throughout the 1970s, reaching a postwar high of 13 percent in 1979. The impact was substantial. Prices were rising but personal income was stagnant. Many Americans were forced to cut back on basics, such as food purchases and medical care. Borrowing rates skyrocketed. The interest rate on business loans and home mortgages topped 15 percent—up from 5 percent a few years earlier.

To fight inflation, the Fed applies policies exactly the opposite of those used to fight an economic downturn. By increasing interest and reserve rates and by selling government securities, the Fed takes money out of the economy, which has the effect of reducing economic demand. As demand weakens, the price of goods and services drops, thereby easing inflationary pressures. Since late 2015, the Fed has been slowly raising interest rates to dampen the inflationary pressure expected from the large amount of money pumped into the economy in response to the 2008 economic downturn.

The Politics of the Fed

Compared with fiscal policy, monetary policy can be implemented more quickly. The Fed can adjust interest and reserve rates on short notice, thus providing the economy with a psychological boost to go along with the actual effect of a change in the money supply. In contrast, changes in fiscal policy usually take months to implement. Congressional action is relatively slow, and new taxing and spending programs ordinarily require a preparation period before they can be put into effect. In early 2010, a full year after Congress passed the $787 billion economic stimulus bill, half of the money had not yet been spent. The greater flexibility of monetary policy is a reason the Fed has emerged as the institution that has primary responsibility for keeping the U.S. economy on a steady course.[22]

When the Fed was created in 1913, no one imagined that it would have such a prominent role. Economists had not yet "invented" the theory of monetary policy. All that has changed, which has raised questions about the power the Fed wields. One concern is the issue of representation: Whose interests should the Fed serve—those of the public as a whole or those of the banking sector? The Fed is not a wholly impartial body. Although it makes decisions in the context of economic theories and projections, it is a "bankers' bank" and as such tends to be protective of financial institutions. In 2008, the Fed provided emergency loans to keep banking institutions, including Citibank and JPMorgan Chase, from bankruptcy. The Fed justified its intervention by saying that the financial markets might otherwise have collapsed, adversely affecting

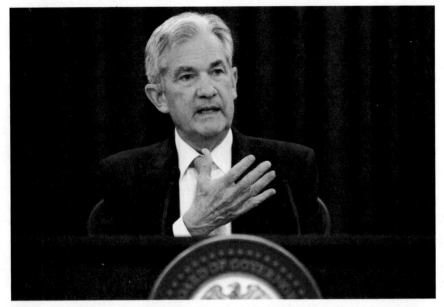

Jerome "Jay" Powell was appointed by President Donald Trump to chair the Federal Reserve in 2018. Unlike other recent chairs, who were trained economists, Powell previously worked as an attorney and investment banker. The chair of the Fed has been called the second most powerful official in Washington. (©Michael Reynolds/EPA-EFE/REX/Shutterstock)

every American. Taxpayers saw it differently. Polls indicated that most Americans opposed the use of taxpayer money to bail out banks.[23]

Another question about the Fed is the issue of its accountability. Should the Fed, an unelected body, have so much power? Though appointed by the president, members of the Federal Reserve Board are not subject to removal. They serve for fixed terms and are relatively insulated from political pressure. The Fed's policies are not always popular with elected officials. Some members of Congress, for example, were sharply critical of the Fed's bank bailout.

Regardless, the Fed is part of the new way of thinking about the federal government's role in the economy that emerged during the Great Depression of the 1930s. Roosevelt's New Deal permanently changed how policymakers thought about the government and the economy. Through its economic management and regulatory activities, the government has assumed an ongoing role in managing the economy. The overall result has been impressive. Although the American economy has suffered from economic downturns during the roughly three-quarters of a century in which the U.S. government has played a significant policy role, none of them has matched the severity of the depressions of earlier periods. (The economic policies of the federal government in the areas of social welfare and national security are discussed in Chapters 16 and 17.)

SUMMARY

Although private enterprise is the main force in the American economic system, the federal government plays a significant role through its policies to regulate, promote, and stimulate the economy.

Regulatory policy is designed to achieve efficiency and equity, which require the government to intervene, for example, to maintain competitive trade practices (an efficiency goal) and to protect vulnerable parties in economic transactions (an equity goal). Many of the regulatory decisions of the federal government, particularly those of older agencies (such as the Food and Drug Administration), are made largely in the context of group politics. Business lobbies have an especially strong influence on the regulatory policies that affect them. In general, newer regulatory agencies (such as the Environmental Protection Agency) have policy responsibilities that are broader in scope and apply to a larger number of firms than those of the older agencies. As a result, the policy decisions of the newer agencies are more often made in the context of party politics. Republican administrations are less vigorous in their regulation of business than are Democratic administrations.

Business is the major beneficiary of the federal government's efforts to promote economic interests. A large number of these programs, including those that provide loans and research grants, are designed to assist business firms, which are also protected from failure through measures such as tariffs and favorable tax laws. Labor, for its part, obtains government assistance through laws covering areas such as worker safety, the minimum wage, and collective bargaining. Yet America's individualistic culture tends to put labor at a disadvantage, keeping it less powerful than business in its dealings with the government. Agriculture is another economic sector that depends substantially on government's help, particularly in the form of income stabilization programs such as crop insurance subsidies.

The U.S. government pursues policies that are designed to protect and conserve the environment. A few decades ago, the environment was not a policy priority. Today, there are many programs in this area, and the public has become an active participant in efforts to conserve resources and prevent exploitation of the environment. The continuing challenge is to find a proper balance between the nation's natural environment, its economic growth, and its energy needs.

Through its fiscal and monetary policies, Washington attempts to maintain a strong and stable economy—one characterized by high productivity, high employment, and low inflation. Fiscal policy is based on government decisions in regard to spending and taxing, which are aimed at either stimulating a weak economy or dampening an overheated (inflationary) economy. Fiscal policy is worked out through Congress and the president and consequently is responsive to political influences. Democratic lawmakers typically prefer demand-side fiscal policy, which relies on increased government spending as a way to put more money in consumers' pockets. When they spend the money, it stimulates business production and job growth. Republican lawmakers typically prefer supply-side fiscal policy, which relies on tax cuts for business and high-income taxpayers. They are expected to invest much of their extra income in business activity, resulting in an increase in jobs and consumer spending.

Monetary policy is based on the money supply and works through the Federal Reserve System, which is headed by a board whose members hold office for fixed terms. The Fed, as the Federal Reserve is commonly called, has become the primary instrument for managing the economy. It can affect the amount of money circulating in the economy by raising or lowering the interest rate that banks are charged for borrowing from the Fed, by raising or lowering the percentage of their funds (reserve rate) that member banks are required to keep on hand, and by buying and selling securities.

©gangliu10/Getty Images

CRITICAL THINKING ZONE

KEY TERMS

balanced budget (*p. 481*)
budget deficit (*p. 481*)
demand-side economics (*p. 479*)
deregulation (*p. 468*)
economic depression (*p. 478*)
economic efficiency (*p. 466*)
economic equity (*p. 470*)
economic recession (*p. 479*)
economy (*p. 465*)

externalities (*p. 472*)
fiscal policy (*p. 478*)
inflation (*p. 486*)
laissez-faire economics (*p. 465*)
monetary policy (*p. 484*)
national debt (*p. 481*)
regulation (*p. 466*)
supply-side economics (*p. 481*)

APPLYING THE ELEMENTS OF CRITICAL THINKING

Conceptualizing: Define *economic efficiency* and *economic equity*. Provide an example of a regulatory policy aimed at achieving economic efficiency. Also provide one that has economic equity as its goal.

Synthesizing: Contrast demand-side economics and supply-side economics in terms of theory, government policy, and partisan politics.

Analyzing: What are the tools of monetary policy? How are they applied to deal with an economic recession? How are they applied to deal with high inflation?

Extra Credit

A Book Worth Reading: Milton Friedman, *Capitalism and Freedom* (Chicago: University of Chicago Press, 2002). First published in 1962, this classic by the Nobel Prize–winning economist provides a defense of free markets that argues against Keynesian economics, which at the time was the prevailing approach to managing the economy.

A Website Worth Visiting: **www.ftc.gov** The website of the Federal Trade Commission, one of the older regulatory agencies, has information on pending disputes. The site gives the reader a sense of how the regulatory process works in practice.

Participate!

The environment is a policy area in which individual citizens can make a difference by reducing waste and pollution. If you have a car, you will burn significantly less fuel if you drive and accelerate more slowly. Choosing a fuel-efficient car, keeping your car properly tuned, walking rather than driving short distances to stores, and living closer to work or school are other ways to cut gas consumption. In your residence, the simplest steps are to use lights sparingly and keep the thermostat lower during cold periods and higher during hot periods. Smaller but meaningful savings can be achieved through simple things such as using low-flow shower heads and replacing incandescent bulbs with LED bulbs, which require less energy and last longer. Even a change in eating habits can make a difference. Frozen convenience foods are wasteful of energy. They are cooked, frozen, and then cooked again—not to mention the resources used up in packaging. Fresh foods are more nutritious and less wasteful. And if you prefer bottled water to tap water, consider using a water filter system instead. Nearly all of the cost of bottled water is due to the plastic container, which is a nonbiodegradable petroleum product. The recycling of paper, plastics, and bottles also conserves natural resources. However, the recycling process uses energy. By cutting back on the use of recyclables and by recycling those you do use, you will contribute twice to a cleaner environment.

16
CHAPTER

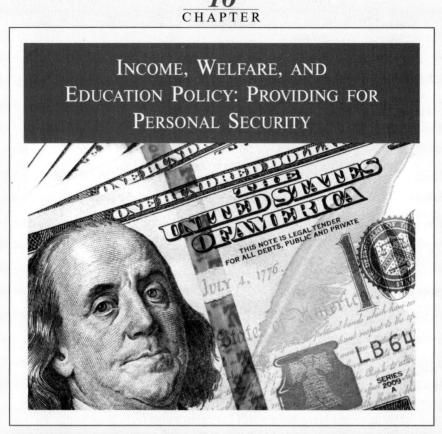

INCOME, WELFARE, AND EDUCATION POLICY: PROVIDING FOR PERSONAL SECURITY

❝We the People of the United States, in Order to . . . promote the general Welfare.**❞**

PREAMBLE, U.S. CONSTITUTION

At issue in the dispute was the 2017 Tax Cuts and Jobs Bill, the first major tax overhaul in nearly two decades. Senator Bernie Sanders (I-Vt.) called it a "farce." Senator Ron Wyden (D-Ore.) called it "an unpopular, deficit exploding corporate giveaway . . . .This is the ultimate betrayal of the middle class." House minority whip Steny Hoyer (D-Tex.) said: "Today, 227 Republicans voted to raise taxes on 36 million middle-class households and to add at least $1.7 trillion to our national debt, all in order to provide massive tax breaks to the top one percent. This is not tax reform; it doesn't even merit being called a tax cut."

Republicans had a different view. Senate majority leader Mitch McConnell (R-Ky.) said the bill "tells middle class Americans 'we heard you.'" John Curtis (R-Utah) said that the legislation helped "families by simplifying the tax code, making American businesses more competitive, and by generating hundreds of thousands of American jobs and producing real economic growth." Senator Tim Scott (R-S.C.) exclaimed, "This is a monumental moment that marks a clear win for the American people."

At the writing of the Constitution, James Madison noted that no issue is more likely to provoke conflict than the question of how society's resources are distributed.[1] And indeed, a host of government policies, including taxes, touch directly or indirectly on the distribution of resources and have rarely been resolved without a partisan fight. This chapter examines three such policy areas: income policy, which centers on the question of how taxes are distributed; welfare policy, which addresses how those who are economically disadvantaged are helped; and education policy, which includes the issue of how to prepare individuals for economically productive lives. The chapter covers the following main points:

- *Tax policy and market changes have contributed to America's widening income gap. Democrats and Republicans differ sharply in their tax policies and philosophies.*

- *Welfare policy has been a partisan issue, with Democrats taking the lead on government programs to alleviate economic insecurity and Republicans acting to slow down or limit these initiatives.* Social welfare programs are designed to reward and foster self-reliance or, when this is not possible, to provide benefits only to those individuals who are truly in need.

- *A prevailing principle in the United States is equality of opportunity, which in terms of policy is most evident in the area of public education.* The United States invests heavily in its public schools and colleges.

INCOME POLITICS AND POLICIES

America's middle class was once the envy of the world. The nation's economic boom after World War II had launched an unprecedented era of shared prosperity—good-paying jobs, rising levels of home ownership, growing numbers of college graduates.

The situation has changed dramatically. According to a recent Pew Research Center study, the American middle class is shrinking, numerically and financially (see Figure 16-1). In 1970, 62 percent of Americans lived in a middle-class household, defined as a household earning between two-thirds to two times the nation's median income. Americans in that category earned 61 percent of the nation's income. By 2015, however, middle-class Americans had dropped to 50 percent of the nation's population and their share of the nation's income had slipped even more, falling to 43 percent. The plight of lower-class Americans was worse. Even though they now make up a larger share of the population

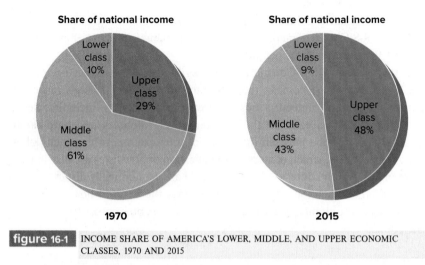

figure 16-1   INCOME SHARE OF AMERICA'S LOWER, MIDDLE, AND UPPER ECONOMIC
CLASSES, 1970 AND 2015

Between 1970 and 2015, the nation's income shifted to the upper class, such that it now gets nearly half of all income that Americans receive each year. (*Source:* Pew Research Center, 2015. Middle-income households are those whose annual household income is two-thirds to double the U.S. median household income after incomes have been adjusted for household size. In terms of 2014 U.S. dollars, this amounts to $42,000 to $126,000 annually for a household of three. Lower-income households have adjusted incomes below $42,000 while upper-income households have adjusted incomes above $126,000)

than they did in 1970, their share of the nation's income is smaller. The winners in Americans' shifting income fortunes have been those in the upper class. They now account for about a fifth of Americans, and they receive half of the nation's income, up from less than a third in 1970.

The Shifting Income Distribution

Until the 1930s Great Depression, the federal government openly sided with business and the wealthy. Efforts to organize unions and improve wages were repeatedly blocked by government action. That approach changed with Franklin D. Roosevelt's New Deal. Congress enacted pro-labor legislation that included a minimum-wage law, collective bargaining rights, and Social Security for retired workers. Congress also enacted a steeply **progressive income tax**, which is a tax where the marginal tax rate increases as income rises. The top rate was set at 79 percent on incomes above $5 million, more than three times the 24 percent rate that was in place before the Depression.

Business claimed that such policies would ruin the nation's economy, but after World War II the economy grew rapidly. As it boomed, so did workers' wages, spawning an ever larger middle class. The boom was fueled by the strength of America's manufacturing sector. The United States had emerged

The years after World War II were marked by a boom in American manufacturing. The war had devastated the factories of Europe and Japan, and the United States was producing more than half of the world's manufactured goods. Factory jobs were plentiful. Most of them paid well, and many of them included health and retirement benefits, contributing to an expanding middle class. (©Nara Archives/REX/Shutterstock)

from the war with its factories intact, whereas factories elsewhere were damaged by the war. The United States was far and away the world's leading manufacturer, which was a boon for America's factory workers.

The best-paying factory jobs were those held by union workers. Armed with collective bargaining rights, they had achieved high wages and, in some cases, employer-paid health insurance and pensions. At peak in the 1950s, a third of America's workers were unionized and in some occupations their income was a third higher than their non-union counterparts. The minimum wage also contributed to the rising standard of living, particularly for unskilled workers. It put a floor on their income and helped push up the hourly pay of those just above them on the wage scale. Social Security was also making a difference. It provided retired workers a guaranteed source of monthly income.

Equally dramatic was the impact of the GI Bill, which Congress enacted near the end of World War II. It gave military veterans cash payments for college and vocational training and provided nearly interest-free loans for home purchases and small business ventures. Before the GI Bill, college and home ownership were out of the reach of most families. By the time the original GI Bill expired, nearly 8 million veterans had participated in its education benefits, two-and-a-half million had acquired a home loan, and hundreds of thousands had received small business and farm loans.

The postwar economic boom lifted all boats. Income nearly doubled in every income category, and in the case of lower-income families, income more than doubled.[2] But the gains came to a sudden halt in the 1970s. Over the next four decades, the income of most Americans didn't increase at all (see Figure 16-2). In terms of real income, which is income adjusted for inflation, Americans in the middle fifth income category made on average roughly the same amount—$49,000—in 2010 as they did in 1970. That was true also of the next-to-bottom fifth of wage earners: they were stuck at $30,000. The bottom fifth actually went backward, from nearly $14,000 on average in real income in 1970 to $11,000 in 2010.

By contrast, the top two-fifths of Americans have experienced an increase in income. For the next-to-top fifth, income in real dollars went from about $68,000 on average in 1970 to roughly $85,000 in 2010. The top fifth did even better—their income rose over the four decades from about $102,000 a year on average in 1970 to roughly $170,000 in 2010. The biggest winners by far, however, were the top 1 percent. Their average income jumped from slightly more than $200,000 in 1970 to a million dollars in 2010.[3] Their share of national income today is at the level it was in the 1920s—an era when money was king.

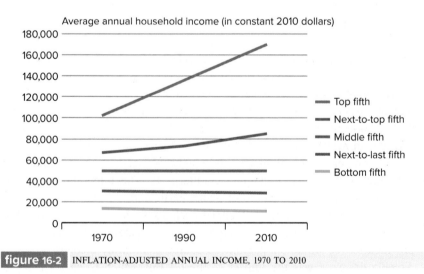

figure 16-2   INFLATION-ADJUSTED ANNUAL INCOME, 1970 TO 2010

During the 40 years beginning in 1970, the bottom 60 percent of income earners had virtually no increase in their real income, whereas those in the top 40 percent, and particularly those at the very top, had large increases in their real income. (*Source:* U.S. Census Bureau figures. Dollar amounts are expressed in 2010 dollars to eliminate the effect of inflation on changes in wages.)

Parallel Changes

Politicians and pundits regularly link income gains among top earners with wage stagnation among middle earners, as if the first explained the second. In fact, the two developments are only somewhat related. The explanation for why top earners have done so well in recent decades owes substantially to changes in tax policy, whereas wage stagnation owes chiefly to changes in the nation's job market.

Tax Policy and Income Inequality   In the period after World War II, income inequality was kept in check by tax policy. The estate tax and a high marginal tax rate on upper incomes—through 1963, the top rate never dropped below 70 percent—worked against the accumulation of large fortunes.[4] Tax policy, as economist Paul Krugman has noted, had a "compression effect."[5] The downward pressure it put on high incomes kept the gap between high earners and other Americans from growing.

The gap widened when Republican Ronald Reagan became president in 1981 and pursued supply-side economics, which is rooted in the assumption that cuts in taxes for business and high-income earners will stimulate economic growth (see Chapter 15). Under Reagan, the highest marginal tax rate dropped from 70 percent to 50 percent, and then to 28 percent. The rate was subsequently increased to 38.5 percent when Democrat Bill Clinton was president. But when Republican George W. Bush became president in 2001, he, like Reagan, pursued a supply-side economic policy that brought the rate down to 35 percent. All tax brackets got a tax cut under Bush, but the big winners were those with high incomes. The middle fifth on average paid about $1,000 less in taxes a year as a result of the Bush-era tax cuts, whereas the average was about $6,000 for those in the top fifth. But the biggest tax savings went to those in the top 1 percent. Their average tax cut—nearly $55,000 a year—was more than 50 times that of middle-income taxpayers. During the nine years the Bush-era tax cuts were in effect, the top 1 percent of taxpayers had roughly $500,000 in tax savings, compared with roughly $10,000 for middle-income taxpayers.

Even more advantageous for high earners was a cut in the **capital gains tax** (the tax individuals pay on gains in capital investments such as stocks and property) that was part of the Bush tax package. It dropped from 28 percent to 15 percent, far below the tax that Americans pay on their regular income. Although most Americans do not buy and sell stocks, a large majority of high earners do so.[6] For those in the top 1 percent, capital gains account for about a third of their pretax income.[7] That situation reflects the fact that *wealth* (the value of a person's assets, such as the property and stocks they own) is highly concentrated in the United States. The top 1 percent of households own 40 percent of all the nation's wealth, averaging more than $10 million per household. The bottom 80 percent of Americans have a mere 7 percent of the nation's wealth.[8]

The cut in the capital gains tax during the Bush era was a windfall for the top 1 percent. They received about 75 percent of the total tax savings from the cut.[9] In fact, even more than the income tax cut, the cut in the capital gains tax disproportionately helped the wealthy. A Congressional Research Service study concluded that "changes in capital gains and dividends were the largest contributor to the increase in the overall income inequality."[10]

It is important to note, however, that the income gains of America's top earners from the Reagan and Bush tax cuts did not come at the direct expense of other taxpayers. Instead, their income gains were financed through government borrowing, which means the cost was shifted to future generations. The Congressional Budget Office (CBO) estimated that the Bush tax cuts added more than $1.5 trillion to the national debt, not including interest on the borrowed money.

The recently passed 2017 Tax Cuts and Jobs Act had the same features as the Reagan and Bush tax cuts. All income categories received tax reductions, which are being funded through government borrowing. The CBO estimates that the bill will add roughly $1.7 trillion to the budget deficit over the next ten years. Like the earlier tax cuts, the 2017 cuts were tilted in favor of higher-income tax payers. According to the nonpartisan Tax Policy Center, middle-income households will see an average annual tax cut of $930 while those in the top 1 percent will get an average of $51,140 (see Figure 16-3).

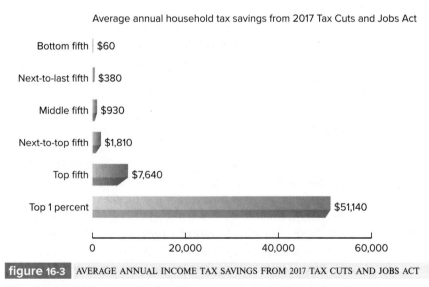

Average annual household tax savings from 2017 Tax Cuts and Jobs Act

Bottom fifth | $60

Next-to-last fifth | $380

Middle fifth | $930

Next-to-top fifth | $1,810

Top fifth | $7,640

Top 1 percent | $51,140

0   20,000   40,000   60,000

figure 16-3 AVERAGE ANNUAL INCOME TAX SAVINGS FROM 2017 TAX CUTS AND JOBS ACT

The tax cuts resulted in tax savings for all income groups, but high-income households had by far the biggest tax savings. (*Source:* Tax Policy Center, 2018.)

Economic Change and Wage Stagnation   Wage stagnation has different roots than does the widening income gap. Changes in the American economy are the main reason that lower- and middle-income workers have not realized a gain in their real income since 1970.

American goods and services after World War II accounted for roughly half of all goods being produced worldwide, which created millions of well-paying factory jobs (see Chapter 17). That situation gradually gave way to a competitive global market where U.S. manufacturers had to compete with those of Japan, Germany, Korea, and other countries. Beginning in the 1970s, the United States became a net importer—buying more goods from abroad than it was selling overseas. Factory jobs were lost in the process. That loss was accompanied by a sharp decline in union membership. Today, only about one in eight workers is a union member, and most of them work, not in the private sector, but in the public sector, such as teachers, police, and civil servants. Economist Lawrence Mishel estimates that as much as a third of the wage erosion among some categories of workers owes to the decline in private-sector unions.[11]

U.S. job growth since the 1970s has been in the service sector—areas such as banking, rental services, health care, entertainment, fast food, and housekeeping. Some service-sector employees are well paid, particularly those who work for large corporations. But there's a much larger number

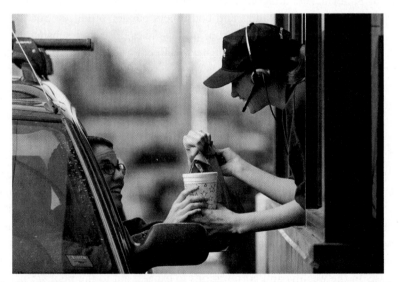

In the 1970s, manufacturing-sector jobs began to disappear as Americans increasingly purchased goods made abroad. Most of the newer American jobs are in the service sector. Many of these jobs pay lower wages and provide fewer benefits than do factory jobs. (©Photodisc/Getty Images)

of service-sector workers—such as food servers, store clerks, hotel staff, artists, lower-level administrators, and taxi drivers—who make less money than their factory counterparts.[12] In addition, service-sector jobs generate less economic activity than do factory jobs. A basic axiom of economics is that jobs generate jobs. Those who work in stores, for example, generate jobs for workers in firms that provide supplies to stores. However, manufacturing jobs generate three times as much economic activity as do retail trade jobs.[13] Auto workers are a prime example. When new cars leave the factory, they generate a wide range of economic activity—they support car dealerships, gas stations, repair shops, auto parts makers, tire makers, and more. Such jobs have been disappearing, at great cost to the financial well-being of America's workers.

In his 2016 presidential campaign, Donald Trump promised to deal with wage stagnation and low-paying jobs. Upon taking office, his efforts centered on revitalizing the nation's manufacturing sector, largely through tax incentives, reduced regulation, and trade policy. Trump withdrew the United States from the Trans-Pacific Partnership (TPP) free trade agreement, which would have reduced tariffs on trade between the United States and eleven nations bordering on the Pacific Ocean. Trump argued that TPP would result in the loss of factory jobs to the lower-wage countries that were part of the agreement. He also imposed tariffs on some products, including imported steel and aluminum, to protect U.S. manufacturers from lower-priced foreign competitors. Some U.S. lawmakers attacked these policies on the grounds that they would raise the prices that companies and consumers pay for products. But the policies, which were a sharp break from past policies, also had substantial support. What is unclear is their long-term effect. The erosion of America's manufacturing sector has taken place over decades and is the result of many factors. Whether the trend can be substantially reversed is as yet an unanswered question.

The Partisan Divide

The political parties are far apart on income policy. In Congress, Democrats have repeatedly pressed for increased taxes on the wealthy, opposed at each step by Republican lawmakers. Democrats have framed their argument in terms of fairness, while Republicans have framed their argument in terms of economic growth. Their positions are echoed by partisan voters. When a Pew Research Center poll asked Americans whether they would support a tax increase on the wealthy and corporations to expand aid to the poor, 75 percent of Democrats said they would support it, compared with 29 percent of Republicans.

If the parties are split on the issue, business groups are not. They dominate Washington lobbying (see Chapter 9) and are attentive to tax issues. As the tax cut bill was being negotiated in Congress in late 2017, business groups lobbied aggressively for its passage.[14] The U.S. Chamber of Commerce alone spent $17 million lobbying Congress during the last three months of 2017.[15] The lobbying effort by business groups paid off. They gained a large tax cut. The legislation reduced the corporate tax rate from 35 percent to 21 percent,

WELFARE POLITICS AND POLICIES

Most Americans are able to meet their housing, food, clothing, and transportation needs. But some cannot. They are the nation's poor. According to U.S. Census Bureau figures, roughly one in seven American families lives in poverty.[16] In fact, the United States has more poverty than other fully industrialized democracies. Its poverty level is twice that of France and Germany. It's also significantly higher than that of Great Britain and that of neighboring Canada.

The U.S. government uses the cost of living as the basis for calculating poverty. The **poverty line** is defined by government as the annual cost of a thrifty food budget, multiplied by three to include the cost of housing, clothes, and other necessities. Families whose income falls below that line are officially considered poor. In 2018, the poverty line for a family of four was set at an annual income of roughly $25,000. That works out to $17 per person per day to cover all of a family's needs. By the government's formula, about 45 million Americans are poor. If they could somehow join hands and form a line, it would stretch all the way from New York City to Los Angeles, and then back again.

America's poor include individuals of all ages, races, and regions, but it's concentrated among certain groups. Urban and rural dwellers have much higher poverty rates than do suburbanites. Minority-group members have a poverty rate twice that of whites. Women have a poverty rate exceeding that of men. Children are one of America's most impoverished groups. The rate of child poverty in the United States is twice the average rate of western European countries. One in every five American children—more than 10 million in total—live in poverty (see "How the 50 States Differ"). Most poor children live in families with a single parent, usually the mother. Single-parent, female-headed families are roughly five times as likely as two-income families to fall below the poverty line, a situation referred to as "the feminization of poverty."[17]

HOW THE 50 STATES DIFFER

CRITICAL THINKING THROUGH COMPARISONS

Child Poverty Rates

Based on the government-defined poverty line, about one in five American children live in poverty. However, poverty is spread unevenly among the states. At one extreme are New Mexico and Mississippi, each of which has a child poverty rate of 30 percent. At the other extreme is New Hampshire, where 8 percent of children live in poverty.

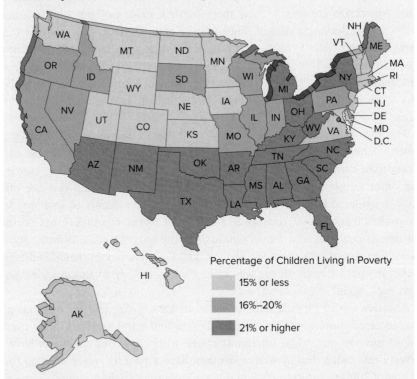

Percentage of Children Living in Poverty

- 15% or less
- 16%–20%
- 21% or higher

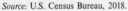

Source: U.S. Census Bureau, 2018.

Q: What might explain the difference in child poverty levels between the states?

A: States differ considerably in their natural wealth, level and type of economic activity, level of education, number of newer immigrants, and percentage of minority-group members. Each of these factors is correlated with level of child poverty.

Public Assistance Programs

Until the 1930s Great Depression, state governments had responsibility for the poor. Welfare was among the policy areas deemed reserved to the states by the Tenth Amendment and to be adequately addressed by them, even though they offered few welfare services. Individuals were expected to fend for themselves, and those unable to do so were usually supported by relatives and friends. That approach changed as a result of the Depression—a period when one in four workers couldn't find a job and another one in four had only part-time work. Income fell sharply and, as it did, so did state tax revenues. Most states were too broke to help the poor. Federal tax revenues had also declined but, unlike the states, the federal government has unlimited power to print and borrow money.

Expanding the Federal Role   During the Depression, the federal government was in the hands of officials—President Franklin D. Roosevelt and a Democratic congressional majority—who were willing to use the federal government's spending power to help the poor.[18] Republican leaders opposed their initiatives but gradually accepted the idea that the federal government had a welfare role, while arguing it should be kept as small as practicable.[19]

Most Depression-era poverty programs were meant to be temporary, such as the Works Progress Administration, which put millions of Americans to work constructing roads, public hospitals, and the like. But a few programs were designed to last. One was Supplemental Security Income (SSI), which provides federal assistance to low-income elderly people and individuals with disabilities. Another was the Aid for Dependent Children program, later renamed the Aid for Families with Dependent Children (AFDC) program, which provided financial assistance to poor single mothers—those who had little or no income by reason of the father's death or desertion.

A second wave of antipoverty programs came in the 1960s, when the federal government was again in the hands of a Democratic president, Lyndon Johnson, and a Democratic-controlled Congress. They enacted the largest set of antipoverty programs in the nation's history, including the Food Stamps program, subsidized housing, and Medicaid, which is government-paid health insurance for those of low income. These programs had broad public support. A Gallup poll at the time found that two-thirds of Americans believed that government had "a responsibility to try to do away with poverty in this country." Nevertheless, there was a clear partisan divide on the issue. When the Medicaid program came up for a vote, for example, more than 70 percent of congressional Republicans voted against it, claiming that the federal government had no business getting involved in health care.

Scholar and activist Michael Harrington called the poor "the other America," noting that Americans who live in the suburbs and other affluent areas have no idea about the scope of the nation's poverty. It's a large problem. One in seven American adults and one in five American children live in poverty. (©Lawrence Sawyer/Getty Images)

The 1960s were the high water mark of the government's antipoverty efforts. Since then, only a few major programs have been created. The largest of the newer programs is the 2010 Affordable Care Act, which, among its provisions, expanded Medicaid eligibility to those who are slightly above the poverty line and provides subsidies to enable other lower-income families to buy health insurance.[20] The legislation was enacted solely on Democratic votes. No Senate or House Republican voted for the bill.

There have also been cutbacks in welfare programs, most notably through the 1996 Welfare Reform Act (see Chapter 3). The 1996 legislation eliminated the AFDC program, which had placed no limit on how long a family could receive benefits, replacing it with the Temporary Assistance to Needy Families (TANF) program, which limits eligibility for most families to five years (see "Case Study: Welfare Reform Act of 1996"). In addition, TANF provides states with a block grant to be used to conduct training programs that will provide able-bodied adults with job skills. Developed by Republican lawmakers as a way to cut welfare rolls and costs, the 1996 act had the overwhelming support of congressional Republicans, whereas a majority of congressional Democrats voted against it.

The 1996 legislation dramatically reduced the size of the welfare rolls. Within five years of its enactment, the number of people on welfare had dropped by

50 percent. The decline was not simply the result of TANF. The American economy was expanding at a rapid rate in the late 1990s, which created millions of new jobs.[21] Nevertheless, even as the economy weakened in 2000, the number of welfare recipients continued to decline. Although the downward trend was reversed somewhat during the economic recession that began in 2008, the number of American families receiving assistance payments has dropped sharply since AFDC was replaced by TANF.

C A S E
S T U D Y

Politics in Action

Welfare Reform Act of 1996

When he ran successfully for the presidency in 1992, Bill Clinton promised "to end welfare as we know it." Democratic and Republican lawmakers alike shared his view that the welfare system—which gave people government assistance indefinitely without demanding something in return—was broken. It had the perverse effect of allowing people to go on welfare, and stay there. Nevertheless, Clinton was unable during his first two years as president—a period when his fellow Democrats controlled Congress—to get them to agree on how to fix the system.

Source: Library of Congress, Prints and Photographs Division [LC-DIG-highsm-15970]

When Republicans gained control of Congress in 1995, they quickly proposed a fix. The bill's provisions troubled many Democrats, who feared it put too many children and young mothers at risk. Clinton shared that concern but was in a weak political position. He was seeking reelection, and his unfulfilled promise to fix the welfare system was a liability. Clinton vetoed the first welfare bill passed by congressional Republicans, saying he would sign it only if it included greater protection for children. He also vetoed their second bill, insisting on more changes. Republicans came up with a few additional modifications, including increasing funding for child care for poor working mothers. When Republicans passed a third welfare bill, and made it clear there would be no more concessions, Clinton was on the spot. In the end, he signed the Republican bill. Clinton had run out

Continued

of leverage. Unlike President Johnson three decades earlier, his party did not have the numbers in Congress to give him bargaining power. And he didn't have the option of taking his case to the people—on this issue, their opinions were aligned with Republican lawmakers.

The 1996 Welfare Reform Act placed a five-year limit on welfare eligibility and requires able-bodied recipients to take job training and apply for work. The legislation has had a dramatic impact on the welfare rolls, as the accompanying figure indicates.

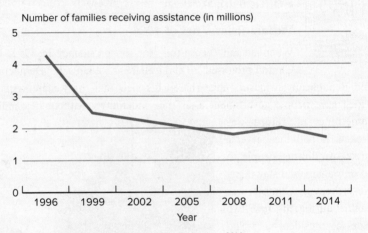

Number of families receiving assistance (in millions)

Source: U.S. Department of Health and Human Services, 2016.

Q: The 1996 legislation placed a five-year limit on eligibility for welfare assistance, although states are permitted to exempt a proportion of recipients to accommodate those who are unemployable for reasons such as health. What do you see as the advantages and disadvantages of the five-year limit?

ASK YOURSELF: What incentive to get a job or training is provided by a time-limited benefit? What are the circumstances, either personal in nature or due to the nature of the local economy, in which a time limit might hurt rather than help individuals?

Eligibility for Public Assistance   Programs such as TANF, Medicaid, and food stamps are **public assistance** programs. They are labeled as such because they're funded with general tax revenues and are available only to individuals in financial need. These programs are often referred to as "welfare" and the recipients as "welfare cases." Eligibility for these programs is established by a

means test; that is, applicants must prove that they are poor enough to qualify for the benefit. Means-tested programs are typically based on an income threshold. Those with incomes above a specified level of income are ineligible for the benefit, whereas those below the level are eligible for it.

The requirement that individuals must prove that they're poor in order to receive a benefit adds to the expense of public assistance programs. In addition to payments to recipients, the programs require local caseworkers and supervisors to determine whether applicants' income is below the designated amount and then to monitor recipients' income levels in case there's a change that would render them ineligible for the benefit (see Figure 16-4). Administrative costs account for about 10 percent of federal spending on food stamps and about 5 percent of spending on Medicaid.

Means testing is consistent with America's culture of individualism—the belief that people should be self-reliant. That belief supports the notion that public assistance should be available only to those who are able to prove they can't make it on their own. The distinctiveness of the American approach can be seen by comparing the U.S. health care system with many of those in Europe. In those cases, residents of all income levels are entitled to government-paid medical care. If they become ill, they simply go to a clinic or hospital for treatment—at government expense, no questions asked. In contrast, Americans receive government-paid health care only if they meet the eligibility criteria. Even then, to be eligible, they must apply beforehand for insurance and prove they are too poor to buy it on their own.[22]

Because of America's federal system, most public assistance programs, although funded primarily by the federal government, are administered by the states, which have a degree of control over benefits and eligibility. There is considerable variation, for example, in the amount of family assistance that states provide. Some states provide more than $600 a month, while others provide less than $300.

figure 16-4   THE WELFARE BUREAUCRACY

Because U.S. social welfare benefits are distributed on the basis of demonstrated need, a large bureaucracy is required to ascertain applicants' eligibility and to monitor whether changes in recipients' circumstances render them ineligible for further assistance.

Not all forms of public assistance involve direct cash payments to recipients. For instance, the food stamps program (formally called the Supplemental Nutrition Assistance Program, or SNAP) provides an **in-kind benefit**. Rather than cash, recipients receive cash-equivalent cards or coupons that can be used only for grocery items. On average, food stamp recipients receive the cash equivalent of about $135 a month. Some critics say that food stamps stigmatize their users by making it obvious to onlookers in the checkout line that they are "welfare cases." A more frequent criticism is that the program is too costly and that too many undeserving people receive food stamps.

Social Insurance Programs

Public assistance programs are not America's only social welfare policies. Also included are **social insurance** programs, which are based on the same pay-to-be-eligible principle as insurance. Only those individuals who pay special payroll taxes while working are eligible for the benefit. Social Security is the prime example. Established in the 1930s as part of Franklin D. Roosevelt's New Deal, it provides monthly Social Security benefits to retirees who paid Social Security taxes on their income during their working years. The current payroll tax rate on employees is 6.2 percent, with employers also required to pay a 6.2 percent tax.

When Medicaid—health care for the poor—was enacted in 1965, Congress also enacted Medicare, which is health care for retirees. Unlike Medicaid, which is a public assistance program, Medicare is a social insurance program. As is the case with Social Security, it is financed by a special tax—currently 1.45 percent—on workers' wages, with employers also paying 1.45 percent.

Social Security and Medicare are **entitlement programs**, meaning that individuals who meet the eligibility criteria are entitled to the benefit. Government cannot decide one day to cancel an entitlement program or to deny the benefit to some eligible recipients while granting it to others. In contrast to such programs, public assistance programs are not entitlement programs. The poor do not have an unqualified claim to benefits. Government can choose at will to cancel a public assistance program or change its eligibility criteria, as in the case of TANF, which reduced the length of time a family can receive assistance.

Social Security and Medicare are federal programs in their entirety. States do not administer them, or have a say in eligibility or benefits. Accordingly, recipients get the same level of benefits, regardless of where they live.

Social Security and Medicare are highly efficient programs in that they do not require a large bureaucracy to check and recheck recipients' eligibility. When workers reach the prescribed age and conditions of eligibility, they auto-

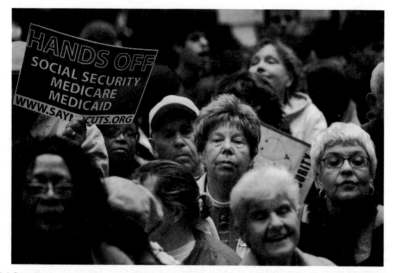

Social Security has arguably been the most successful federal program in history, giving tens of millions of older Americans a level of economic security they would otherwise not have. The fact that Social Security is funded through a special payroll tax on employees during their working years has served to protect it from political criticism and budget cuts. Social Security is a benefit that is perceived as having been "earned," and therefore deserved, by its recipients. (©Scott Olson/Getty Images)

matically qualify for the benefits. Less than 1 percent of Social Security spending is taken up by administrative costs. Medicare is more administratively complex in that it involves payments to doctors and hospitals. Even so, according to a Kaiser Family Foundation study, only about 2 percent of Medicare spending is for expenses other than patient care. In contrast, some private insurance companies—which seek to make a profit and heavily advertise their products—spend up to 20 percent on nonpatient care.[23]

Social Security and Medicare are not poverty programs in a literal sense. Recipients come from all income groups. In fact, the higher one's income while working, the larger the Social Security payment on retirement. Such individuals pay more in Social Security taxes during their working years and accordingly get a larger benefit on retirement. The average monthly benefit is about $1,200, but some recipients get less than $1,000 whereas others get more than $2,000. Nevertheless, Social Security helps keep millions of Americans out of poverty. About one-fourth of America's seniors have no significant monthly income aside from what they receive from Social Security.

The Politics of Welfare Policy

Public assistance and social insurance programs differ markedly in their level of public support (see Figure 16-5). Most Americans are convinced that Social

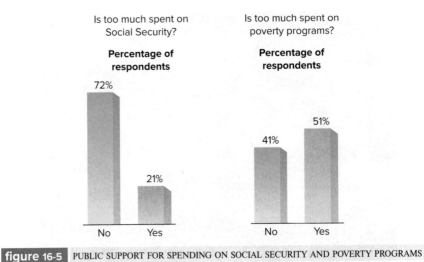

figure 16-5 PUBLIC SUPPORT FOR SPENDING ON SOCIAL SECURITY AND POVERTY PROGRAMS

Americans are much more supportive of Social Security spending than they are of antipoverty program spending. (*Sources:* CBS News poll, 2014 for Social Security data; Rasmussen poll, 2012 for poverty data.)

Security—a social insurance program—is worth the cost. At the same time, a substantial number of Americans think too much is being spent on antipoverty programs. The difference reflects America's cultural values. Social insurance programs are funded by special payroll taxes on workers and, in that sense, are widely seen as something that recipients have "earned." In contrast, public assistance programs are funded by the taxpayers as a whole and are widely seen as "handouts"—not earned and, in the minds of many, not deserved by some of the recipients.

There are, indeed, people who make no effort to hold a job and for whom public assistance is nearly a way of life.[24] Yet most poor Americans are in their situation as a result of circumstance rather than by choice. In an exhaustive poverty study, economists Signe-Mary McKernan and Caroline Ratcliffe found that most of the poor are poor only for a while, and then for reasons largely beyond their control, such as a job layoff or desertion by the father.[25] When the U.S. economy goes into a tailspin, the impact devastates many families. According to U.S. Department of Labor figures, more than 7 million Americans lost their jobs during the economic downturn that began in 2008.

Support for public assistance programs is also weakened by the widespread belief that the government spends far more on such programs than on social insurance programs. The opposite is true. Spending on Social Security and Medicare, which assist retirees regardless of their other income, is nearly double the amount spent on public assistance programs, which help only those in financial need. In fact, families in the top fifth of the income population receive more in Social Security and Medicare benefits than the government spends in total on TANF, SSI, food stamps, and housing subsidies for the poor.[26]

Nevertheless, because they don't have strong public support, public assistance programs are a political target (see "Party Polarization: Government's

| P A R T Y | **Conflicting Ideas** |
| POLARIZATION | |

Government's Social Welfare Role

The two major ways that economic benefits are distributed in America is through the economic marketplace in the form of jobs, wages, dividends, and the like and through the government in the form of programs such as Social Security, Medicaid, and food stamps. In few areas have the differences between the Republican and Democratic parties been more consistent over the years than their positions on the use of government as an instrument of economic security. Although both parties see a need for some sort of safety net for the economically vulnerable, the Democratic Party has taken the lead on extending it. Nearly every major U.S. social insurance and public assistance program was put into place by Democratic lawmakers, usually in the face of opposition from their Republican counterparts. The policy conflicts among lawmakers are aligned with how the parties' identifiers see the issue of government's role in providing assistance to those who are economically disadvantaged, as the figure indicates.

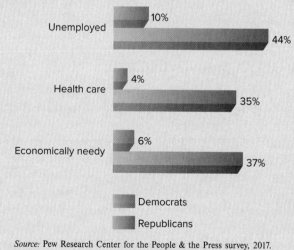

Percentage who would cut government spending on:

Unemployed — Democrats 10%, Republicans 44%

Health care — Democrats 4%, Republicans 35%

Economically needy — Democrats 6%, Republicans 37%

Democrats
Republicans

Source: Pew Research Center for the People & the Press survey, 2017.

Q: What's your opinion on how far government should go in providing economic assistance to those who are less well off?

Social Welfare Role"). In 2014, for instance, congressional Republicans sought a $40 billion reduction in the food stamp program, settling for an $8 billion cut after a threatened veto by Democratic president Barack Obama. Social Security, by contrast, has withstood partisan challenges. In 2005, President George W. Bush proposed to partially privatize Social Security—workers would have had the option of putting a portion of their Social Security tax payments into a personal retirement account. Bush was forced to back down in the face of strong resistance from senior citizens, spearheaded by AARP—a seniors' group that is one of Washington's most powerful lobbies. By contrast, poverty lobbies—groups that petition Congress on behalf of the poor—are relatively weak. Spending on Social Security has risen substantially in recent years, while spending on TANF assistance to poor families has declined.[27]

Polls over the past 50 years have repeatedly found that Americans, consistent with their cultural values, see jobs rather than public assistance as the answer to poverty. That outlook is the basis for the Earned Income Tax Credit (EITC), which was enacted in 1975 under President Gerald Ford and expanded during the presidencies of Ronald Reagan and Bill Clinton. EITC provides a refundable tax credit to low-income wage earners. Workers with sufficiently low income receive an EITC payment upon filing their taxes, with the amount varying with income level and number of dependents. The maximum yearly payment for a family with two children, for instance, is roughly $5,800. EITC is now the federal government's largest means-tested cash assistance program. According to U.S. Census Bureau calculations, the EITC lifts about a third of low-income Americans above the poverty line. EITC is a reward for working—a program that's in line with America's cultural values.

EDUCATION POLITICS AND POLICIES

Nearly all Americans endorse the principle of **equality of opportunity**—the idea that people should have a reasonable chance to succeed if they make the effort. It is a form of equality shaped by personal freedom because the outcome—personal success or personal failure—depends on what people do with their opportunities. It has been said that equality of opportunity gives individuals an equal chance to become unequal.

Equality of opportunity is an ideal. Americans do not start life on an equal footing. It was said of one successful American politician, whose father was rich and also successful in politics, that "he was born on third base and thought he hit a triple."[28] Some Americans are born into privilege, and others start life in such abject poverty that few of them escape it. Nonetheless, equality of opportunity is more than a catchphrase. It is the philosophical basis for a number of government programs, none more so than public education.

The Supreme Court has held that American children are entitled to an "adequate" education but do not have a right to an "equal" education. America's public schools differ greatly in quality primarily as a result of differences in the wealth of the communities they serve. Some public schools are overcrowded and have few facilities and little equipment. Others are very well equipped, have spacious facilities, and offer small class sizes. (©Hill Street Studios/Blend Images)

Public Education: Leveling through the Schools

During the nation's first century, the question of a free education for all children was a contentious issue. Wealthy interests feared that an educated public would challenge their political and economic power. Egalitarians, by contrast, saw free public education as a means of enabling ordinary people to get ahead. The egalitarians won out. Public schools quickly sprang up in nearly every community.[29]

Equality continues to be a guiding principle of American public education. Unlike countries that divide children even at the grade school level into different tracks that lead ultimately to different occupations, the curriculum in U.S. schools is relatively standardized. Of course, public education has never been a uniform experience for American children. During the first half of the 20th century, public schools for black children in the South were designed to keep them down, not lift them up. Today, many children in poorer neighborhoods attend overcrowded, understaffed, and underfunded public schools. The quality of education depends significantly on the wealth of the community in which the child resides. The Supreme Court has upheld this arrangement, saying that the states are obliged to give all children an "adequate" education as opposed to one that is "equal" across communities.

The uneven quality of America's public schools is a reason its students rank below Canadian and European students on standardized reading, math, and science tests (see "How the U.S. Differs"). Because U.S. neighborhoods are

HOW THE U.S. DIFFERS

CRITICAL THINKING THROUGH COMPARISONS

Education Performance

Research indicates that U.S. students score comparatively low on standardized tests. In the most recent Organization for Economic Cooperation and Development (OECD) assessment, based on 15-year-old student performance in reading, math, and science, the United States ranked 36 out of the 65 countries included, trailing nearly every Asian and western European country. The accompanying chart shows the average test score for selected countries.

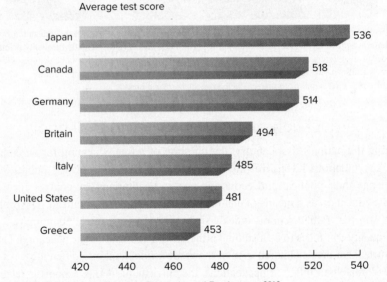

Average test score

Country	Score
Japan	536
Canada	518
Germany	514
Britain	494
Italy	485
United States	481
Greece	453

Source: Organization for Economic Cooperation and Development, 2015.

Q: Why might the United States lag behind other advanced industrialized democracies in student performance, even though it spends more heavily on public education?

A: Compared with most democracies, the United States has a relatively high proportion of non-native-speaking children, who on average do less well in school than other students. The United States also has a high level of residential segregation. Children residing in poor neighborhoods tend to perform much less well in school than do their peers.

more segregated by income than are European neighborhoods, America's poor children are more likely to go to schools where most of the other students are also poor. Moreover, because the wealth of a community affects the level of school funding, schools with a high proportion of poor students tend to have fewer resources, even though their need is greater. In fact, the best predictor of students' performance on standardized tests is the wealth of the community in which their school is located.[30]

Nevertheless, the United States through its public schools seeks to broadly educate its children. Public education was labeled "the great leveler" when it began in the early 19th century, and the tradition continues. Few countries make an equivalent spending effort. Per-pupil spending on public schools is substantially higher in the United States than it is in Europe. America's commitment to broad-based education extends to college. The United States has the world's largest system of higher education—it has roughly 4,000 two- and four-year colleges.[31] The nation's extensive education system preserves both the myth and the reality of an equal-opportunity society. The belief that success is within the reach of anyone who works for it could not be sustained if the public education system was open only to the privileged few.

The Federal Government's Role in Education Policy

Education is largely the responsibility of state and local governments, and they continue to provide roughly 90 percent of school funding. They also decide most school policies, everything from the length of the academic year to teachers' qualifications.

Historically the federal government played little part in education policy. The situation began to change after World War II when economic and social change made the public more aware of deficiencies in the nation's education system. Since the 1960s the federal government has played a larger, though still secondary, role in education policy.

Federal education programs are administered through the Department of Education, a cabinet-level agency that was created in 1979. The size of the Department of Education is an indicator of the degree to which education remains largely a state and local policy responsibility. The Department of Education is by far the smallest of the executive departments, with only 4,000 employees. The next smallest is the Department of Labor, which has four times the staff.

Federal Grants-in-Aid for Education   As part of President Johnson's War on Poverty, the federal government began in the 1960s to provide financial assistance in the education area. The 1965 Elementary and Secondary Education Act became the cornerstone of the federal government's efforts to assist public schools. The legislation authorizes funds for items such as school construction, textbooks, special education, and teacher training. Although Johnson's goal was to help schools in poorer areas, members of Congress insisted that all states and districts be eligible for some funding. As a result, the formulas for allocating the grants favor poorer school districts but not totally.

Johnson's War on Poverty also included a targeted education program— Head Start. Aimed at helping poor children at an early age, Head Start provides free preschool education to low-income children in order to help them succeed when they reach kindergarten age. However, Head Start has never been funded at a level that would allow all eligible children to participate. Today, only about 40 percent of eligible children are enrolled.

The 1965 Higher Education Act, which President Johnson signed into law at his alma mater, Texas State University, is the basis for federal assistance to institutions of higher education. Among its components are Pell Grants, federal loans to college students, and federally subsidized college work-study programs. Pell Grants account for the largest share of federal spending. Millions of college students over the years have received Pell Grants, which are reserved for students from modest- and low-income families. The federal student loan program has also helped millions of students, although it is a relatively small spending item in that most of the money is returned through loan repayment. In 2010, as a cost-saving measure, the federal government took control of the loan program. Before then, some student loans were issued by banks, which had the safety of government-insured loans while receiving a fee for handling them.

Student loans have become a major policy issue. According to Federal Reserve Bank data, state governments in the 1970s provided nearly 75 percent of the funding for public colleges, which had the effect of holding down college costs. But states in the 1980s started to cut their funding and continued to do so, such that the states now provide less than 25 percent of college funding. As a result, college costs have been shifted to students, most of whom have no choice but to rely heavily on student loans. In fact, student loan debt now exceeds credit card debt (see Figure 16-6).

The burden imposed by student loans has made it a political issue. Some Democratic candidates and lawmakers have come out in favor of cancelling some student debt and substantially reducing the interest rate on remaining student debt. They argue that the debt burden is inhibiting the advancement not only of former students but of society as a whole. Rather than using excess income to buy homes or otherwise boost the economy, former students must use it to pay off their college loans. Other Democrats and the large share of Republican candidates have opposed such ideas, arguing that the cost would

Billions of dollars

Credit card debt ▮ $784

Student loan debt ▮ $1,340

figure 16-6 STUDENT LOAN AND CREDIT CARD DEBT

In recent decades, state and local governments have reduced their spending on public colleges and universities, which has shifted a larger share of the cost to students. Student loan debt in the United States now exceeds what Americans owe on their credit cards. (*Source:* Federal Reserve Bank of New York, figures are for 2017.)

be prohibitive. They also say that the former students are getting the income benefit that comes with a college education and that it would be unfair for taxpayers, many of whom don't have a college degree, to pay the cost of unpaid loans. Given the size of the student loan debt burden, the issue is unlikely to disappear any time soon.

Partisan Conflict over Education Policy Many of the partisan and philosophical differences that affect federal welfare policy also affect federal education policy. Democrats are more inclined to find the answer to how to improve schools in increased federal spending on education, particularly in poorer communities, whereas Republicans are more inclined to look to market-like mechanisms such as achievement tests.

Partisan conflict has spilled even into policy areas largely outside the scope of federal authority. School choice is one example. Charter schools, which are publicly funded but have wider latitude than other public schools in designing curricula and picking students, are strongly championed by many Republican lawmakers. Many Democratic lawmakers have criticized charter schools on the grounds they weaken the regular public schools by siphoning away funding and top students.

Federal involvement in public school education is inherently partisan and controversial, given America's tradition of state and local control over schools. Yet lawmakers at all levels have shown from time to time that they can come together. In 2015, with majority support from Democrats and Republicans, Congress passed the Every Student Succeeds Act (ESSA) to succeed the controversial 2001 No Child Left Behind Act (NCLB), which had mandated standardized national testing and tied schools' federal funding to student test performance. ESSA also includes mandatory testing and sanctions on schools that underachieve but eliminates NCLB's "one size fits all" approach, giving states flexibility in determining the form of student testing and what constitutes underachievement. ESSA is funded through $25 billion in federal assistance each year to the states.

Detecting Misinformation

Do Citizens Who Claim to Know the Most about Policy Issues Actually Know the Most?

Misinformation involves far-fetched ideas about reality, and it is rampant in today's politics. At no time time in the history of polls have so many Americans been so misinformed on so many issues.

Some Americans express doubt whether they have their facts straight. Others do not suffer from doubt. They are convinced that they know the facts, which might lead one to conclude that the more convinced people are that they know something, the more likely they are to actually know it.

Is that claim fact, or is it fake?

©Keystone Pictures USA/Alamy

Typically, those who claim to be most knowledgeable about an issue are, in fact, the most knowledgeable. But, increasingly, those who think they're well-informed are among the most misinformed. A study found, for example, that those who are the least knowledgeable about welfare benefits are the ones who claim to know the most.[32] Another study found that those who know the least about climate-change science are the ones who think they're the most informed.[33] Such individuals typically have a strong opinion on the issue, which leads them to think they understand it, when in fact they don't. "Cognoscenti of their own bamboozlement" is how sociologist Todd Gitlin describes such individuals.[34]

THE AMERICAN WAY OF PROMOTING ECONOMIC SECURITY

All democratic societies promote economic security, but they do so in different ways and to different degrees. Economic security has a higher priority in European democracies than in the United States. European democracies have instituted programs such as government-paid health care for all citizens, compensation for all unemployed workers, and retirement benefits for all elderly citizens. As this chapter shows, the United States provides these benefits only to some citizens in each category. By contrast, the American system of higher education dwarfs those in Europe.

The differences between the European and American approaches to welfare stem from historical and cultural differences. Democracy in Europe developed in reaction to centuries of aristocratic rule, which brought the issue of economic privilege to the forefront. European democracies initiated sweeping social welfare programs and high taxes on the wealthy as ways to create greater economic equality. Social inequality was harder to root out because it was thoroughly embedded in European society, shaping everything from social manners to education. Private schools and university training were the preserve of the elite, a tradition that, though now in the past, has had a lingering effect on how Europeans think about educational opportunity.

The American experience was a different one. Democracy in America grew out of a tradition of limited government that emphasized personal liberty, which included a belief in self-reliance. This belief contributed to Americans' strong support for public education, their weak support for public assistance, and their persistent preference for low tax rates. Unlike political equality, the idea of economic equality has never captured Americans' imagination. Political scientists Stanley Feldman and John Zaller found that Americans' support for public assistance programs rests more on feelings of compassion for the poor than on an ideological commitment to economic sharing.[35] Or, as the political scientist Robert Lane expressed it, Americans have a preference for market justice, meaning that they prefer that society's material benefits be allocated largely through the economic marketplace rather than through government policies.[36] It is thus not surprising that the United States has a higher level of income inequality and poverty than do other Western democracies.

SUMMARY

The United States has several areas of policy that affect Americans' economic well-being. Tax policy is one of these policy areas. In recent decades, taxes on higher incomes and capital gains have been lowered substantially, which has contributed to a dramatic increase in income inequality. At an earlier time, a range of government policies, everything from a high tax rate on upper incomes to the GI Bill, had the opposite effect, reducing the gap between the wealthy and the rest of America.

Wage stagnation has been a persistent problem for a half century. In terms of real income, America's lower- and middle-income workers are getting roughly the same pay today as they did in 1970. Although government policy has played a part in this development, it is mainly a consequence of changes in the U.S. economy. In the period after World War II, the U.S. manufacturing sector was booming, providing millions of well-paying jobs, particularly for union workers. Since 1970, the manufacturing sector has shrunk dramatically, giving way to the service sector, where jobs on average pay less.

The United States has a complex social welfare system of multiple programs addressing specific welfare needs. Many social welfare problems are targeted for the poor. Roughly one in seven Americans fall below the government-defined poverty line, including a disproportionate number of children, female-headed families, minority-group members, and rural and inner-city dwellers. Public assistance programs, as anti-poverty programs are called, are available only to individuals who qualify for benefits by meeting the specific eligibility criteria.

Not all welfare programs are in the public assistance category. There are also social insurance programs, including Social Security and Medicare, which are funded by payroll taxes paid by potential recipients, who, in this sense, earn the benefits they later receive. Because of this arrangement, social insurance programs have broad public support. In contrast, public assistance programs are funded with general tax revenues and are targeted at individuals and families in financial need. Because of a widespread belief that many welfare recipients could get along without assistance if they tried, these programs do not have broad public support, receive only modest funding, and sharply divide the two parties. Democrats have taken the lead on government programs to alleviate economic insecurity while Republicans have sought to cut back or decentralize these initiatives.

Compared to other democracies, the United States spends more heavily on public education, a policy consistent with its cultural emphasis on equality of opportunity. That policy is evident, for example, in standardized school curricula and the nation's extensive system of public colleges and universities. Like social welfare, however, education is a partisan issue involving disputes over such issues as charter schools and spending levels.

©gangliu10/Getty Images

CRITICAL THINKING ZONE

KEY TERMS

capital gains tax (*p. 497*)
entitlement programs (*p. 508*)
equality of opportunity (*p. 512*)
in-kind benefit (*p. 508*)
means test (*p. 507*)

poverty line (*p. 501*)
progressive income tax (*p. 494*)
public assistance (*p. 506*)
social insurance (*p. 508*)

APPLYING THE ELEMENTS OF CRITICAL THINKING

Conceptualizing: The Supreme Court has held that American children are entitled to an "adequate education" but not an "equal education." Explain the difference.

Synthesizing: Contrast social insurance benefits and public assistance benefits. How do they differ in terms of how individuals qualify to get a benefit? How do they differ in terms of the level of public support they have?

Analyzing: How has U.S. social welfare policy been influenced by America's federal system of government and by Americans' belief in individualism?

EXTRA CREDIT

A Book Worth Reading: Thomas Piketty, *Capital in the Twenty First Century* (Cambridge, Mass.: Belknap Press, 2014). This award-winning bestseller explores the history of income inequality and its reemergence in extreme form in recent decades.

A Website Worth Visiting: www.journalistsresource.org Journalist's Resource, located at Harvard University's Kennedy School of Government, is dedicated to identifying the top policy-relevant research and connecting it to current issues. Many of its postings are in the areas of income, social welfare, and education policy.

PARTICIPATE!

Poverty is a contentious partisan issue. Republican and Democratic lawmakers disagree sharply on the question of how far government should go in helping the poor. By contrast, virtually all Americans—on the right and on the left—support private efforts to help low-income individuals. Numerous local religious, civic, social, and economic groups run programs for the poor, such as food kitchens and clothing drives. Also, many national organizations work locally to assist the poor. An example is Habitat for Humanity, which builds modest houses with volunteer labor and then makes them available to low-income families, who assist in the construction and receive low-interest or no-interest mortgages to pay for the cost of construction materials. Consider volunteering some of your time to a group that gives a helping hand to those in need—whether a church or a community group or a nonprofit organization like Habitat for Humanity. Habitat for Humanity has a website (https://www.habitat.org/) that makes it easy for you to volunteer.

17
CHAPTER

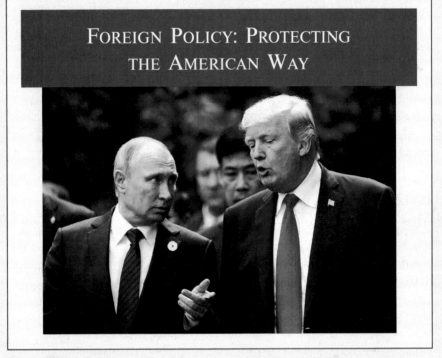

©Jorge Silva/Reuters/Newscom

❝ We the People of the United States, in Order to . . . provide for the common defence. **❞**

PREAMBLE, U.S. CONSTITUTION

One of Donald Trump's first acts as president was to withdraw the United States from the Trans-Pacific Partnership (TPP). He called the TPP "a disaster." Negotiated under President Barack Obama, the TPP was a free-trade agreement involving the United States and 11 other countries bordering the Pacific Ocean, including Japan, South Korea, Australia, Vietnam, and Chile. When Obama announced the successful negotiation of the TPP, he said it would give American workers "a fair shot to get ahead here at home, and a fair chance to compete around the world . . . so we can export more products stamped Made in America all over the world." Obama also saw the TPP as a means of countering China's growing influence in the Pacific. By strengthening economic ties with Asian countries, Obama believed that U.S. national security interests would be enhanced.

Trump had a radically different view, seeing the TPP as yet another free-trade agreement that would result in a loss of American jobs to lower-wage overseas trading partners. When he signed his executive order ending U.S. participation in the TPP, he said it was a "great thing for the American worker." Trump also claimed that his action would strengthen America's defense posture. Calling the TPP a "backdoor" through which China could gain leverage, he argued that a thriving manufacturing sector would enhance the nation's security.

As the TPP dispute illustrates, foreign policy is an issue of economic vitality as well as one of military strength. The motivation behind every nation's foreign policy is its *national interest*—what's best for the nation in terms of protecting its physical security and advancing its economic prosperity. People do not always agree on the best way to protect the national interest, but it is the central purpose of foreign policy.

Unlike other policy areas, foreign policy rests on relations with actors outside rather than within the country. As a result, the chief instruments of national security policy differ from those of domestic policy. One of these instruments is *diplomacy*—the process of negotiation between countries. The lead agency in U.S. diplomatic efforts is the Department of State, which is headed by the secretary of state and coordinates the efforts of U.S. embassies abroad, each of which is directed by a U.S. ambassador. American diplomacy also takes place through international organizations—such as the United Nations—to which the United States belongs. A second instrument of foreign policy is *military power*. The lead agency in military affairs is the Department of Defense, which is headed by the secretary of defense and oversees the

The Trans-Pacific Partnership, a free-trade agreement between the United States and 11 other Pacific-rim countries, sparked a dispute between President Barack Obama, who negotiated the pact, and President Donald Trump, who withdrew the United States from the agreement. Shown here are TPP opponents voicing their objections to the pact. (©Don Mennig/Alamy)

military services—the army, air force, navy, and marine corps. Here, too, the United States sometimes works through alliances, the most important of which is the North Atlantic Treaty Organization (NATO). NATO has nearly 30 member nations, including the United States, Canada, and most Western and Eastern European countries. A third instrument of world politics is *intelligence gathering*—the process of monitoring other countries' activities. For many reasons, but primarily because all countries pursue their self-interest, each nation keeps a watchful eye on other nations. In the United States, the task of intelligence gathering falls to specialized federal agencies including the Central Intelligence Agency (CIA) and the National Security Agency (NSA). *Economic exchange,* the fourth instrument of foreign affairs, involves both international trade and foreign aid. U.S. interests in this area are promoted by a range of U.S. agencies, such as the Agriculture, Commerce, Labor, and Treasury Departments, as well as specialty agencies such as the Federal Trade Commission. The United States also pursues its economic goals through international organizations of which it is a member, including the World Trade Organization, the World Bank, and the International Monetary Fund.

The national security policies of the United States include an extraordinary array of activities—so many, in fact, that they could not possibly be addressed adequately in an entire book, much less a single chapter. There are roughly 200 countries in the world, and the United States has relations of one kind or another—military, diplomatic, economic—with all of them. This chapter narrows the subject by concentrating on a few main ideas:

- *Since World War II, the United States has acted in the role of world leader, which has substantially affected its military, diplomatic, and economic policies.*
- *The United States maintains a high degree of defense preparedness, which requires a substantial level of defense spending and a worldwide deployment of U.S. conventional and strategic forces.*
- *Changes in the international marketplace have led to increased economic interdependence among nations, which has had a marked influence on the U.S. economy and on America's security planning.*

THE PATTERN OF U.S. FOREIGN AND DEFENSE POLICY

Before World War II, except within its own hemisphere, the United States was a mostly **isolationist** country. It was preoccupied with its internal development and intent on avoiding European entanglements. A different America emerged after World War II. It had more land, sea, and air power than any other country and more than a hundred overseas military installations. The United States had become a fully **internationalist** country—a nation deeply involved in world affairs.[1]

The Cold War and Its Lessons

Although the United States was victorious in its fight against Germany and Japan in World War II, it was not fully at peace. The global power structure was **bipolar**—the United States versus the Soviet Union. After World War II, backed by the power of the Soviet army, communists seized power in Poland, Hungary, Czechoslovakia, and other Eastern European nations.

The United States was suddenly embroiled in the **Cold War** with the Soviet Union. The two nations were not directly at war but the United States, led by President Harry S Truman, pursued a doctrine of **containment**—the notion that Soviet aggression could be stopped only by the determined use of American power.[2] This doctrine had roots in the failed efforts to appease Germany's Adolf Hitler in the years leading up to World War II. At the 1938 Munich conference, Germany was allowed to annex Czechoslovakia's Sudetenland, but it served only to whet Hitler's appetite for conquest. The "Lesson of Munich" was that totalitarian leaders could not be appeased; they had to be confronted.

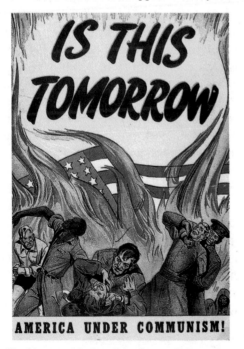

Cold War propaganda, like this poster warning of the danger of communism, contributed to a climate of opinion in the United States that led to public support for efforts to contain Soviet power. (©The Michael Barson Collection)

Containment policy led the United States to base troops in Europe and Asia and then into costly wars. When the Soviet-backed North Koreans invaded South Korea in 1950, Truman sent U.S. forces into the conflict in an attempt to stop the spread of communism in Northeast Asia. Nearly 35,000 U.S. troops lost their lives in the Korean War, which ended in stalemate. A decade later the United States was again at war. Communists were making inroads in South Vietnam, and U.S. policymakers believed that, if South Vietnam fell to the communists, so too would Laos, Cambodia, and the rest of Southeast Asia—the so-called domino theory. By the late 1960s, 550,000 Americans were fighting in South Vietnam. Although U.S. forces had military superiority, Vietnam was a guerrilla war, with no front lines and few set battles.[3] U.S. public opinion, most visibly among the young, gradually turned against the war. U.S. combat troops left Vietnam in 1973, and two years later North Vietnamese forces completed their takeover of the country. Vietnam was the most painful and costliest application of containment doctrine: 58,000 Americans lost their lives in the fighting.

America's failure in Vietnam led U.S. policymakers to reconsider the country's international role. The "Lesson of Vietnam" was that there were limits to the country's ability to assert its will in the world. President Richard Nixon proclaimed that the United States could no longer act as the free world's "Lone Ranger" and sought to reduce tensions with communist countries. In 1972, Nixon visited the People's Republic of China, the first official contact with that country since the communists seized power in 1949. Nixon also initiated the Strategic Arms Limitation Talks (SALT), which resulted in reductions in the nuclear arsenals of the United States and the Soviet Union. This spirit of cooperation lasted until the Soviet invasion of Afghanistan in 1979, which convinced U.S. leaders that the Soviet Union had not changed its ways. Ronald Reagan, elected president in 1980, called for a renewed hard line toward the Soviet Union, which he described as the "evil empire."

Although U.S. policymakers did not realize it, the Soviet Union was collapsing under the weight of its heavy defense expenditures, its isolation from Western technology, and its inefficient centralized economy. In 1989, the Soviet Union withdrew its troops from Eastern Europe. Two years later, nearly all of the Soviet republics declared their independence, marking the end of the Soviet Union as a governing entity. The bipolar power structure of the Cold War era was finished. The new structure was **unipolar**—the United States was now the world's unrivaled superpower.

Multilateralism and Its Lessons

The end of the Cold War prompted the first President Bush in 1990 to call for a "new world order." George H. W. Bush advocated **multilateralism**—the idea that major nations should act together in response to problems and crises. Included in Bush's plan was a stronger role for multinational organizations such as the United Nations and NATO.

Multilateralism defined America's response to the Iraqi invasion of Kuwait in August 1990. President Bush secured UN resolutions ordering Iraq to withdraw from Kuwait. When it failed to do so, a half-million troops, mostly American but including contingents from nearly two dozen nations, attacked Iraq. The fighting ended in four days. The Gulf operation was a military triumph, prompting President Bush to declare that the United States had "kicked the Vietnam syndrome [the legacy of America's defeat in Vietnam] once and for all." The Gulf War, however, was otherwise less successful. Believing that an overthrow of Saddam Hussein's regime would destabilize Iraq, Bush halted the hostilities after Iraqi forces retreated. Hussein remained in power but was ordered by a UN resolution to dismantle his weapons program. However, Hussein repeatedly interfered with UN inspectors' attempts to verify the status of his weapons programs, raising suspicions about his intentions.

Multilateralism carried over into Bill Clinton's administration. Confronting Serb atrocities in Bosnia—where tens of thousands of Muslims and Croats were murdered, raped, or driven from their homes—the United States and its NATO allies attacked Serb forces with air power in 1995, which culminated in a U.S.-negotiated peace agreement (the Dayton Accords) that included the deployment to Bosnia of nearly 60,000 peacekeeping troops, including 20,000 Americans. War in the Balkans flared again in 1999 when the Serbs undertook a campaign of "ethnic cleansing" in the Serbian province of Kosovo, whose population was 90 percent Albanian. When attempts at a negotiated settlement

Terrorist attacks on New York and Washington on September 11, 2001, had a profound effect on American foreign policy. They led to the invasions of Afghanistan and Iraq by the U.S. military. Although American policymakers expected a relatively quick end to the wars, U.S. forces are still fighting in those regions. (©REX/Shutterstock)

failed, NATO planes, including U.S. aircraft, attacked Serbia.[4] After nearly three months of intensive bombing, Serb president Slobodan Milošević (who died in 2006 while on trial for war crimes) pulled his troops out of Kosovo. (In 2008, Kosovo became an independent state.)

As the examples indicate, multilateralism was not a wholly successful strategy for resolving international conflicts. With the deployment of enough resources, the world's major powers showed that they could act together with some success. However, these interventions offered no guarantee of long-term success. Regional and internal conflicts typically stem from enduring ethnic, religious, factional, or national hatreds or from chronic problems such as famine, overcrowding, or government corruption. Even if these hatreds or problems can be eased momentarily, they are often too deep-seated to be settled permanently.

War on Terrorism

Upon assuming the presidency in 2001, George W. Bush rejected his father's multilateral approach to foreign policy. He announced plans to reduce America's military presence abroad. His position changed abruptly when terrorists attacked the World Trade Center and the Pentagon on September 11, 2001. In a televised address, Bush urged other nations to join the United States in a multilateral "war on terrorism."

The Afghanistan War   The first U.S. military action in the war on terrorism was an attack on Afghanistan, which commenced barely a month after the September 11 attacks. Afghanistan's Taliban-led government had granted sanctuary and training sites to the al Qaeda terrorists who carried out the attacks. Supported by troops from other NATO countries, U.S. forces quickly toppled the Taliban government but failed to capture al Qaeda leader Osama bin Laden and his top lieutenants.

The Afghan invasion marked the start of what was to become the longest war in U.S. history. The Taliban regrouped, slowly reasserting control over parts of the country. In 2011, U.S. forces succeeded in locating and killing bin Laden (he was hiding in neighboring Pakistan), but the Afghan conflict otherwise dragged on. President Obama called for the withdrawal of all U.S. combat troops by 2014 but changed his mind when the Taliban continued to pose a threat to stability in Afghanistan. Upon taking office, President Trump continued the policy of engagement, saying a "a hasty withdrawal would create a vacuum that terrorists . . . would instantly fill, just as happened before September 11th."

The Iraq War   In 2002, President George W. Bush labeled Iraq, Iran, and North Korea "the axis of evil." A few months later, he announced a new national security doctrine: the **preemptive war doctrine**.[5] Speaking at West

Point, Bush asserted that the United States would not wait until it was attacked by hostile nations. Instead, America would take "preemptive action."[6] The concept was not entirely new—U.S. officials had long maintained a right to strike first if faced with an imminent attack. What was new in the Bush Doctrine was its embrace of a first-strike option before a threat became imminent.

In the summer of 2002, Bush targeted the regime of Iraq's Saddam Hussein, claiming that it was stockpiling weapons of mass destruction (WMDs)—chemical and biological weapons, and possibly nuclear weapons—for use against U.S. interests. That October, Congress authorized the use of military force against Iraq if it did not disarm voluntarily. Despite the UN's refusal to authorize a military attack and in the face of strenuous opposition from France, Germany, and Russia, President Bush in March 2003 ordered U.S. forces to invade Iraq. British troops were also involved, but the attack was essentially an act of **unilateralism**—the situation in which one nation takes action against another state or states.[7] The Iraqi regime collapsed quickly, but the post-invasion phase was far more difficult than the Bush administration had anticipated. Age-old animosities between Sunni, Shiite, and Kurdish groups within Iraq blocked political compromise and fueled internal violence. Moreover, weapons inspectors did not find the WMDs that the Bush administration had claimed were in Iraq's possession, which undermined public support for the war.[8]

A year before leaving office, Bush announced a phased withdrawal of U.S. combat forces from Iraq. President Obama kept the timetable and the last of

Setting off a flare after refueling in midair, a U.S. Air Force F-15E heads for a combat mission. In recent years, the United States has relied primarily on air power and special operations troops in its effort to contain terrorist threats in the Middle East. (*Source:* U.S. Air Force photo by Staff Sgt. Sandra Welch)

America's combat units left Iraq in late 2011. Nearly nine years of war there had resulted in the deaths of more than 4,500 American troops and had cost nearly a trillion dollars—all with no assurance that the new Iraqi government would be on friendly terms with the United States over the long run.

The Islamic State and Syria   America's withdrawal from Iraq, in combination with a deadly civil war in Syria, created a power vacuum that spawned a radical Islamic group—the Islamic State (also known as ISIS and ISIL). From its initial base in Syria, it swept across the border into Iraq, seizing a large swath of territory that included Iraq's second-largest city, Mosul. Comprising Sunni Muslims, ISIS brutally murdered as heretics the Shiite Muslims and Christians it captured and declared its intention to establish a Caliphate—an Islamic state headed by a supreme religious and political leader. As the threat mounted, Obama ordered targeted air strikes on Islamic State forces in an effort to bolster Iraq's government, which had proven too weak and divided to counter it on its own. Obama subsequently stepped up the air attacks and deployed several hundred military advisers and special operations troops to assist Iraqi government forces.

Upon taking office, President Trump continued that policy, which helped Iraqi troops to gain the initiative. They recaptured Mosul and in late 2017 regained the last of the Islamic State strongholds in Iraq. Shortly thereafter, Islamic State forces lost the battle over their self-declared capital in Raqqa, Syria, which ended their ability to conduct large-scale combat operations. That development did not, however, mark the end of U.S. involvement in Syria. Although Trump expressed his desire "to get out of Syria," his advisers persuaded him that, if U.S. troops were withdrawn before the country was stabilized, the Islamic State could regroup, much as the Taliban had done in Afghanistan.

Even with the world's most powerful military, the United States has found it difficult to achieve success in the war against terrorism. Wars of this type do not lend themselves to quick and tidy battlefield solutions. It is one thing to defeat a conventional army in open warfare and quite another to prevail in a conflict in which the fight is not so much a battle for territory as it is a struggle for people's loyalties, especially when they harbor age-old distrust of each other, as in the case of the competing religious and ethnic groups in Afghanistan, Iraq, and Syria.

Such wars also have few boundaries. In late 2015, for example, terrorists aligned with the Islamic State murdered more than one hundred people in Paris and then nearly three dozen people in Brussels four months later. The Islamic State had developed a sophisticated, Internet-based recruiting strategy to lure disaffected Muslim youth outside the Middle East into its ranks. With the battlefield defeat of the Islamic State in Iraq and Syria, the fear now is that some of its soldiers will slip into Europe and engage in terrorist attacks there. Moreover, al Qaeda and the Islamic State have both established a military presence in other Muslim countries, including Yemen and Libya. Brian Michael Jenkins, who served as an adviser to the National Commission on Terrorism, concluded that the United States will be at war with radical Islamic terrorists "for years to come."[9]

Although terrorism and turmoil in the Middle East have dominated national attention for the past two decades, it is only one of America's foreign policy challenges. Containing the spread of nuclear weapons is another. The United States and other countries have worked together to block or retard nuclear weapon development by North Korea and Iran, but the gains might be temporary. Pakistan's nuclear arsenal is also a concern. Pakistan is a predominately Muslim country and has a large number of extremists who identify with al Qaeda and other terrorists groups. If they should somehow gain control of nuclear material, much less nuclear weapons, the threat to U.S. interests would increase sharply.

Russia and China

Russia is also of increasing concern. In 2014, Russia forcefully annexed the Crimean Peninsula, which was part of Ukraine. It then armed and encouraged separatists in their takeover of parts of eastern Ukraine, a strategy it had previously pursued in Georgia and Moldova. Russia also interceded in the Syrian civil war, providing air power and advisers in support of Syrian president Bashar Hafez al-Assad, which tipped the war in his favor. These and other actions, including efforts to disrupt elections in the United States and Europe (see "Fake or Fact: Did Russia Try to Influence the 2016 Election?"), are part of an increasingly aggressive Russian foreign policy, which seeks to reestablish Russia as a world power. "The collapse of the Soviet Union was the greatest catastrophe of the 20th century," said Russian president Vladimir Putin.[10]

China, too, is pursuing an increasingly assertive and expansionist foreign policy. It has enlarged its navy, which had been structured to protect China's territorial waters but is now being configured to operate throughout the Pacific. China launched its first aircraft carrier in 2012 and is in the process of building attack submarines and missile ships. China has also claimed huge coastal areas in the South China Sea as being within its territorial boundaries, even though by international law the areas belong to other countries, including Vietnam and the Philippines. When these countries have contested China's claims, the Chinese navy has responded with force.

F A K E *or* F A C T — Detecting Misinformation

Did Russia Try to Influence the 2016 Election?

No issue has received more attention recently than the question of Russian meddling in the 2016 U.S. presidential election. It has been the subject of congressional hearings, special investigations, and government commissions. Most Americans have concluded that Russia did meddle. A 2018 national poll found, for example, that 70 percent of respondents believed that "the Russian government tried to influence the 2016 presidential election."[11]

©Hill Street Studios/Blend Images/Glow Images

Is that claim fact, or is it fake?

Every credible investigation of the issue, including those of the CIA, FBI, NSA, and the Office of the Director of National Intelligence, has concluded that Russia did try to influence the 2016 U.S. presidential election. It's estimated that Russia employed more than 1,000 hackers, bloggers, and other Internet operatives to feed fake news and other forms of disinformation to tens of millions of Americans in an effort to influence their votes.

What's unknown is whether Russia's involvement changed the election's outcome. Some analysts have claimed that it did, but it's almost impossible to separate the influence of Russia's messages from the influence of the much larger number of messages Americans received through the news media and the candidates' own campaigns.[12]

Russia's meddling in the 2016 U.S. election is part of a larger geopolitical strategy. Russian Internet operatives have also sought to disrupt elections in Britain, France, Germany, Austria, and other European democracies. Although Russia has tried to boost support for right-wing parties, it has the broader goal of creating discord and confusion in order to create distrust in democratic institutions.[13]

Concern with China's military buildup has been magnified by its embrace of Russia after that country annexed Crimea. China was the only country to side with Russia when the UN Security Council voted to censure Russia for the Crimean takeover. The two countries subsequently signed a $400 billion deal to build a natural gas pipeline from Russia to China and then conducted joint naval exercises in the vicinity of disputed islands held by Japan. "We have powerful enemies but we don't have powerful friends, that's why we need the support of such a giant as China," said a top Russian official. In turn, China has embraced Russia, which historically has been more of an adversary than a friend. In 2018, China's foreign minister declared that his country's relationship with Russia is at "the best level in history."[14]

The optimism that followed the collapse of the Soviet Union in 1989 is today greatly diminished. Ambassador Nicholas Burns, one of America's most respected diplomats, has called today's world "the most challenging . . . for the United States since World War II."[15]

THE MILITARY DIMENSION OF NATIONAL SECURITY POLICY

Defense spending by the United States is far higher than that of any other nation. In fact, the United States accounts for roughly 35 percent of all military spending worldwide (see "How the U.S. Differs"). The U.S. defense budget is three times that of China and nine times that of Russia.

Military Power, Uses, and Capabilities

U.S. military forces are trained for different types of military action, ranging from nuclear conflict to terrorism.

Nuclear War Although the possibility of all-out nuclear war declined dramatically with the collapse of the Soviet Union, the United States retains a nuclear arsenal designed to prevent such a war. Deterrence policy is based on the concept of **mutually assured destruction (MAD)**. The assumption is that any nation will be deterred from launching a full-scale nuclear attack on the United States by the knowledge that, even if it destroyed the United States, it too would be destroyed.

America's nuclear weapons are deployed in what is called the "nuclear triad." This term refers to the three ways—by land-based missiles, submarine-based missiles, and bombers—that nuclear weapons can be launched. The triad provides a second-strike capability—that is, the ability to absorb a first-strike nuclear attack and survive with enough nuclear capacity for a massive retaliation (second strike). Since the end of the Cold War, the United States and Russia have negotiated substantial reductions in their nuclear arsenals.

A greater fear today than nuclear war with Russia is the possibility that a terrorist group or rogue nation will smuggle a nuclear device into the United States and detonate it. The technology and materials necessary to build a

HOW THE U.S. DIFFERS

CRITICAL THINKING THROUGH COMPARISONS

Worldwide Military Spending

According to the Stockholm International Peace Research Institute's annual report in 2017, the United States accounts for more than a third of worldwide military spending. China is second in military spending, but its expenditures are only a third of those of the United States. Russia spends about a ninth as much.

U.S. efforts to get European allies to bear more of the defense burden have been largely unsuccessful, although Britain, France, and Germany spend more per capita on defense than any country except the United States.

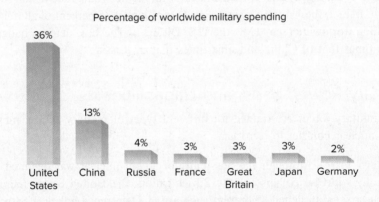

Percentage of worldwide military spending

United States	China	Russia	France	Great Britain	Japan	Germany
36%	13%	4%	3%	3%	3%	2%

Q: What do you make of the disparity in military spending between the United States and its military allies? Do you think the allies spend too little on defense, relying too heavily on the United States for their security? Or do you think the United States spends too much on defense, placing too much emphasis on military force as an instrument of foreign policy?

nuclear weapon (or to buy one clandestinely) are more readily available than ever before. Accordingly, the United States, Russia, and other nations are cooperating to halt the spread of nuclear weapons, although, as the nuclear weapons program of North Korea illustrates, the effort has not been fully successful.

Conventional War   Not since World War II has the United States fought an all-out conventional war, nor at present does it have the capacity to do so.

Such a war would require the reinstatement of the military draft and the full mobilization of the nation's industrial capacity. Instead, the U.S. armed forces are structured to be capable of fighting two medium-sized wars simultaneously, although they are currently undergoing a restructuring in response to changing military tactics.[16]

The United States today relies on an all-volunteer military force (see "How the 50 States Differ") that is second to none in its destructive power. The U.S. Navy has 11 aircraft carriers, scores of attack submarines, and hundreds of fighting and supply ships. The U.S. Air Force has thousands of high-performance aircraft, ranging from fighter jets to jumbo transport planes. The U.S. Army has roughly 500,000 regular troops and more than 300,000 Reserve and National Guard soldiers, who are supplied with tanks, artillery pieces, armored personnel carriers, and attack helicopters. This armament is doubly lethal because it is linked to sophisticated surveillance, targeting, and communication systems. No other nation has anywhere near the advanced weapons systems that the United States possesses.

Unconventional (Guerrilla) War   America's military firepower is not a large advantage in so-called unconventional wars of the type in Afghanistan. The insurgents employed guerrilla tactics including hit-and-run attacks, roadside explosive devices, and suicide bombings, as well as the killing and intimidation of civilians who sided with the Afghan government. Such tactics are extremely difficult to defend against and virtually impossible to stop by conventional means.

Unlike a conventional war, in which the measures of success are territory gained and casualties inflicted, an unconventional war requires winning the support of the people or, as it is labeled, "winning their hearts and minds." Insurgents depend on the local population for recruits, intelligence, hiding places, and food. If they can be denied access to these resources, their military capability falls dramatically. Tactically, an unconventional war is fought with small and highly mobile combat units that can seek out insurgents and provide security to local populations, while also training indigenous military and police forces to gradually assume responsibility for their nation's security.[17]

For the most part, the U.S. military is structured to fight conventional rather unconventional wars, although most of the recent conflicts have been of the second type. In response, the U.S. military has been gradually increasing its capacity to engage in unconventional warfare. It has increased the number of special operations units (such as the Army Special Forces and the Navy SEALs) and is providing its regular units with additional training in counterinsurgency warfare.

HOW THE 50 STATES DIFFER

CRITICAL THINKING THROUGH COMPARISONS

The All-Volunteer Military's Recruits

Until 1973, the United States had an active military draft. Upon reaching age 18, males were required to register for the draft. Local draft boards would then pick the draftees based on quotas that varied with the size of the local population. Accordingly, each state contributed equally to the military's manpower needs relative to its population size. Today's military is an all-volunteer force, and the states' contributions vary significantly. The accompanying map indicates the degree to which each state is over- and underrepresented in the military, as indicated by the ratio of military recruits from a state to the number of males aged 18 to 34 in that state's population. Montana has the largest number of recruits relative to its population, followed in order by Alaska, Wyoming, and Maine. Utah, Rhode Island, and Massachusetts rank lowest, in that order.

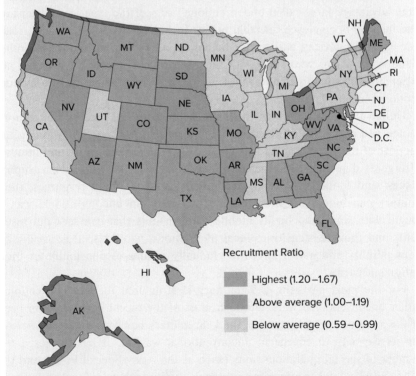

Recruitment Ratio

Highest (1.20–1.67)

Above average (1.00–1.19)

Below average (0.59–0.99)

Source: Adapted from Kane, Tim, "Who Bears the Burden? Demographic Characteristics of U.S. Military Recruits before and after 9/11," Heritage Foundation, Center for Data Analysis Report #05-08, November 7, 2005.

Continued

Q: What might explain why military recruits come disproportionately from states like Montana, Alaska, Wyoming, and Maine, as well as from the southern states?

A: According to Department of Defense data, recruits are more likely to come from rural areas, particularly areas where few well-paying jobs are available to young adults. The four states with the highest recruitment ratios have these characteristics. As for the South, higher recruitment levels have been explained in terms of its stronger military tradition and its numerous military installations. Individuals from areas near these installations, as well as the sons and daughters of military personnel, are more likely to enlist in the military. (Mississippi and Tennessee, with the South's lowest recruitment rates, have relatively few military installations.)

Transnational Terrorism   The terrorist attacks of September 11, 2001, thrust the U.S. military into a new kind of war—a war on terrorism. The United States was not prepared for a terrorist war when it was attacked in 2001. Its intelligence agencies had not focused their efforts on terrorist activity, and its military units had few linguists who spoke the terrorists' languages. Moreover, as the United States was to discover, the war on terrorism could not be waged solely through military force. Law enforcement officials would also have to play a key role, charged with locating potential terrorists and providing security at airports, major events, and other "soft" targets.

Terrorism is not by itself a new form of warfare. It has been employed in many places over the centuries, but it has become a wider threat in recent years. Historically, terrorism was a domestic problem, employed by disgruntled groups against their own government. Terrorism today has an international dimension. **Transnational terrorism** is terrorism that transcends national borders and includes attacks on nonmilitary targets.[18] When terrorists attacked the United States in 2001, or Paris in 2015, they were not seeking to take over a country. They were seeking to alter the balance of power in the Middle East by forcing Western nations to rethink their presence in the region.

America's war on terrorism is aimed at groups, such as the Islamic State, rather than nations. The Islamic State is a nonstate actor without clearly defined borders, which complicates the task of isolating and destroying it. Moreover, transnational terrorists have become adept at waging "asymmetric war," so called because they lack the strength to directly engage opposing military forces. In fighting their wars, terrorists target civilians and employ improvised weapons, including suicide bombers.

In 2015, Islamic militants armed with assault weapons entered a concert hall in Paris, killing eighty-nine people. Transnational terrorism is a new kind of warfare that transcends national boundaries and includes nonmilitary targets. (©Thierry Chesnot/Getty Images)

The Politics of National Defense

Policy elites, public opinion, and special interests all play significant roles in national defense policy. The American public usually backs the judgment of its political leaders on the use of military force. In nearly all military initiatives of the past half-century, Americans have supported the action at the outset. For example, when President Bush ordered U.S. forces to invade Iraq in 2003,[19] two-thirds of Americans supported his decision. If a war begins to seem endless, however, public support inevitably erodes.[20] A swing in public opinion against the Vietnam War forced U.S. policymakers to withdraw American troops in 1973. Public opinion on the Iraq war soured more quickly, partly because the stated reason for the war—the threat of Iraq's WMDs—proved faulty.

Although the public exerts influence on war policy, it is not informed or interested enough to affect most national security policies, which are decided largely by the president and Congress in consultation with top experts and military officers.

The defense industry also has a say in national security policy. In his 1961 farewell address, President Dwight D. Eisenhower, who had commanded U.S. forces in Europe during World War II, warned Americans against "the unwarranted influence" and "misplaced power" of what he termed "the military-industrial complex." Eisenhower was referring to the fact that national defense is big business, involving the annual expenditure of hundreds of billions of dollars.[21] As Eisenhower described it, the **military-industrial complex** has three main components: the military establishment, the arms industry, and the members of Congress from states and districts that depend heavily on the arms industry. All three benefit from a continuously high level of defense spending. In 2018, Congress approved a $300 billion increase in defense spending spread over the next two years with the goal of upgrading the nation's military capacity and replacing equipment that had been degraded by the fighting in the Middle East.

THE ECONOMIC DIMENSION OF NATIONAL SECURITY POLICY

National security is more than an issue of military might. It is also a question of maintaining a strong position in the global economy. Geographically, the world has three major economic centers. One is the United States, which produces roughly a fifth of the world's goods and services. Another center, accounting for about a fourth of the world's economy, is the European Union (EU), which contains most European countries, including Germany and France. The third center is the Pacific Rim, anchored by the economies of Japan and China, which together account for more than a fifth of the world's economy.

On at least one dimension, the United States is the weakest of the three economic centers. Its trade deficit is easily the world's largest. The United States imports substantially more goods and services than it exports. In fact, the United States has not had a trade surplus since 1975, and its annual deficit has exceeded $300 billion every year in the past decade.

In other ways, however, the United States is easily the strongest of the three centers. According to the Switzerland-based World Economic Forum, the United States is economically more competitive than its major rivals. The United States owes this position to several factors, including its technological innovation, financial institutions, and extensive higher education system.[22] The U.S. economy is also the most diversified of the three. In addition to its industrial base, the United States has a strong agricultural sector and abundant natural resources. Its vast fertile plains and advanced farming methods have made it the world's leading agricultural producer. The United States ranks among the top three countries worldwide in production of wheat, corn, soybeans, peanuts, cotton, eggs, cattle, and pigs. As for natural resources, the United States ranks among the top five nations in, among other minerals, deposits of copper, zinc, coal, gold, iron ore, and magnesium.[23]

In recent years, as a result of changes in technology, the United States has also surged to the top in terms of oil and natural gas production. Although the United States continues to import about a fourth of its oil, mainly from Canada and Latin America, it is the only one of the three economic centers that has the capacity to be "energy independent" in the sense that, if necessary, it could meet its energy needs from domestic resources alone.

Nevertheless, the United States does not have the option of "going it alone" economically. To meet Americans' production and consumption needs, the country depends on other countries' raw materials, finished goods, markets, and capital. This imperative requires the United States to exert global economic influence. The efforts of the United States in the world economy include foreign trade, foreign assistance, and global economic security.

Foreign Trade

After World War II, the United States helped enact a global trading system with itself at the center. The U.S. dollar had become the leading currency of international trade, replacing the English pound, which held that position for more than a century. World War II had weakened Britain's global economic position and elevated that of the United States, which quickly asserted its dominance. A key initiative was the European Recovery Plan, better known as the Marshall Plan. It included an unprecedented amount of aid (more than $100 billion in today's dollars) for the postwar rebuilding of Europe. Apart from enabling the countries of Western Europe to better confront the perceived Soviet threat, the Marshall Plan served America's economic needs. Wartime production had lifted the United States out of the Great Depression, but the immediate postwar period was marked by a recession and renewed fears of hard times. A rebuilt Western Europe would become a much-needed market for American products. In the early 1950s, the United States was producing nearly as many goods and services as the entire rest of the world and was by far the world's biggest exporter.[24]

That advantage was unsustainable. As the European and Japanese economies strengthened, they increasingly looked to sell their goods in foreign markets. America's trading partners had become its trading rivals. In the 1970s, the U.S. balance of trade was leveling out. Each year since then, the United States has had a negative balance-of-trade, consuming more goods from abroad than it has shipped overseas (see Figure 17-1).

By the 1980s, the American and world economies had changed fundamentally from what they were in the years immediately after World War II. **Economic globalization**—a term that describes the increased interdependence of nations' economies—was under way. There was vastly more market competition between

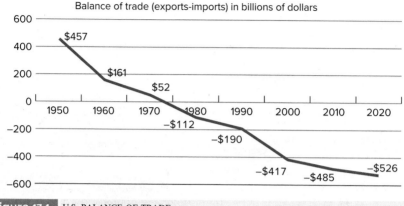

figure 17-1 U.S. BALANCE OF TRADE

After World War II, the United States had a trade surplus. In recent years, as in every year since 1975, the United States has had a trade deficit, meaning that its imports have exceeded its exports. (*Source:* U.S. Bureau of Economic Analysis, 2018. Figures are constant 2010 U.S. dollars. Figure for 2020 based on projections.)

countries, and business practices had evolved. Large U.S. firms had become *multinational corporations* (or *transnational corporations*), with operations in several countries. A firm could be headquartered in New York with its factories in Thailand, giving it the best of both worlds: access to management skills and finance in New York and access to low-wage workers in Thailand.

Free Trade vs. Protectionism   Although global trade was expanding, it was limited by **tariffs**–the taxes that countries levy on goods shipped in from another country. Even if a firm could manufacture a product more cheaply in one country, it would be prohibitively expensive in another country if that country levied a hefty tariff on the product. To deal with the problem, firms began lobbying Congress for agreements with other countries based on the principle of **free trade**–trade based on greatly reduced or no tariffs. They quickly gained the backing of a traditional ally, Republican leaders in Washington. "The freer the flow of world trade," said President Ronald Reagan, "the stronger the tides of human progress." Developments elsewhere added to the momentum behind free trade. European nations were on a path to economic integration–a passport-free Europe with few tariffs. Trade between European countries would increase, with American products losing out unless tariff reductions could be achieved. Economists contributed to the free-trade momentum. Their economic models indicated that free trade would result in a net gain to the U.S. economy.[25] Free trade would lead to a loss of jobs but that cost would be more than offset by the availability to American consumers of lower-priced goods, everything from clothing to television sets.

Nations' economies are increasingly interdependent. A sector of the American economy that has benefited from the change is agriculture. The United States is the world's leader in the production of livestock and grain, much of which is shipped to overseas markets. (©Orientaly/Shutterstock)

The first major free-trade agreement was the 1993 North American Free Trade Agreement, commonly known as NAFTA. It established a largely free market between the United States, Canada, and Mexico. The pact was negotiated by Republican President George H. W. Bush, but he had left office before Congress could vote on it. After studying the issue, Bill Clinton, his Democratic successor, chose to back NAFTA and submitted it to Congress. It passed with the support of more than 70 percent of Republican Senate and House members, even though less than 50 percent of Democrats in each chamber voted for it.[26]

To a member of Congress, free trade is often a question of its impact on their constituency. Although most members of Congress say they support free trade in principle, they don't always do so when confronted with an actual trade agreement. If it will harm a major interest in their district or state, they sometimes opt for **protectionism**—the use of tariffs or other trade barriers to protect the domestic interest from foreign competitors. With their ties to labor, Democratic lawmakers tend to be more protectionist because of the threat that free trade poses to jobs. Organized labor itself had come out strongly against NAFTA, believing that American jobs and companies would be lost to lower-cost Mexican workers and firms.

The political lines that surfaced during the NAFTA debate came to the fore again in 2011 when Congress took up the issue of bilateral free-trade agreements with Panama, Colombia, and Korea, which were negotiated under Republican president George W. Bush and recommended to Congress by Democratic president Barack Obama. Republican lawmakers provided the votes necessary for passage. The 2011 United States–Colombia Free Trade Agreement, for example, passed Congress with the support of 96 percent of Republicans and only 25 percent of Democrats.

Donald Trump's "America First" Policy   In his inaugural address, Donald Trump said the era of multilateral free-trade agreements was over. "From this moment on, it's going to be America First. Every decision on trade . . . will be made to benefit American workers and American families. We must protect our borders from the ravages of other countries making our products, stealing our companies, and destroying our jobs. Protection will lead to great prosperity and strength."

After taking office, he withdrew the United States from the twelve-nation Trans-Pacific Partnership (TPP) trade agreement. He then renegotiated NAFTA. The new trade agreement was finalized in 2018, and the name was changed to the United States-Mexico-Canada Agreement (USMCA). Trump also targeted trade with China, saying that China was stealing intellectual property, subsidizing its industries, and manipulating its currency, all for the purpose of gaining a trade advantage on the United States (see "Case Study: Trade with China"). He imposed tariffs on steel, aluminum, and other goods imported from China.

It's too early to know how far Trump's "America First" agenda will be pursued, or whether it will have a positive effect on the trade balance. Trump has said he's not interested in starting a trade war and might even bring the United States back into the TPP if the other countries involved "offered us a deal that I can't refuse." He has also endorsed the idea of tariff-free trade with countries in the European Union (EU). What's clear, however, is that Trump's trade policy is a departure from the ones pursued by other American presidents since World War II.

C A S E **S T U D Y**	**Politics in Action**

Trade with China

The United States and China are major trading partners, but their trading relationship is imbalanced. The United States imports far more goods from China than it exports to China. In the past decade, America's trade deficit with China has increased more than 30-fold,

Continued

surpassing $250 billion annually. The United States has provided China with a marketplace for its goods, which has helped fuel China's economic growth. In turn, China has provided the United States with inexpensive goods, which has satisfied the demands of America's consumers and kept inflation

©Dmitry Kalinovsky/Shutterstock

in check. Nevertheless, the trade deficit with China is a growing concern. The United States has pressured China to increase the value of its currency (the yuan, also called the renminbi), which would increase the price of the goods it exports for sale, thereby making American goods more competitive with those produced in China.

Most economists see trade with China as a net benefit. The dollar amount of the savings to American consumers from lower-priced Chinese-made goods is greater than the dollar-amount of the wages U.S. workers would receive if they were manufacturing the goods.

Members of Congress vary in their view of trade with China, depending largely on the nature of the constituency they represent. Representatives from industrialized states, for example, are usually less supportive than those from more rural states. As it happens, although the United States imports a lot of factory goods from China, the United States exports a lot of agricultural goods to China.

As part of his "America First" policy, President Trump has targeted China on the question of trade, imposing tariffs (taxes) on some of its imports, while China has responded with tariffs on U.S. goods, including agricultural products.

Q: Why might, or might not, the United States have an interest in maintaining a strong trade relationship with China?

ASK YOURSELF: What are the effects of trade with China on America's consumers and workers? Which sectors of the American economy are helped or hurt by trade with China? Does trade with China diminish the likelihood that the two countries would engage in military confrontation? Does it make it easier for them to engage in diplomacy?

Assisting Developing Nations

Since World War II, the United States has been the top source of aid to developing countries. Although the United States still contributes the most in terms of total dollars, Canada and European countries now spend more on a per-capita basis than does the United States. America's fiscal problems, and its costly wars in Iraq and Afghanistan, have weakened its ability to strengthen its position in the world through the use of foreign aid. Public opinion is also an obstacle to increased foreign aid spending. Most Americans believe the United States is already spending too much on foreign aid. Contributions include direct foreign aid and also indirect assistance through international organizations, such as the International Monetary Fund (IMF) and the World Bank, which were created by the United States and Great Britain at the Bretton Woods Conference near the end of World War II. The IMF makes short-term loans to keep countries experiencing temporary problems from collapsing economically or resorting to destructive practices such as the unrestricted printing of paper money. For its part, the World Bank makes long-term development loans to poor countries for capital investment projects such as dams, highways, and factories.

As the United States has cut back on foreign aid spending, China has stepped up its spending. Through loans and grants, China is spending heavily on infrastructure and commercial projects in scores of countries in Africa, South America, and Asia. It is also pursuing mining and drilling projects in many of these countries, seeking to secure the raw materials needed to sustain its economic growth. In a sense, China is following a path laid out by the United States after World War II, when it pursued a similar strategy as a means of expanding its global influence.

Protecting International Commerce

Although many Americans believe the nation's armed forces have a strictly military purpose, they also have an economic purpose: protecting international commerce. Trade depends on the free flow of goods, which requires open sea, air, and land routes. After World War II, the United States took the lead in this area and has maintained it, most visibly through its naval presence. The U.S. Navy patrols every major shipping lane, including the Persian Gulf, through which much of the world's oil flows, and the South China Sea, which is the shortest shipping route from Europe, the Middle East, and Africa to Pacific nations. An indicator of America's sea power is its fleet of aircraft carriers. The United States has 11 carriers, 1 in reserve, and 1 under construction. No other country has more than two.

PARTY POLARIZATION

Conflicting Ideas

Hard Power or Soft Power?

Until the Vietnam War, there was little partisan difference in Americans' views on national security. A bipartisan consensus prevailed with Republicans and Democrats alike convinced of the need to contain Soviet communism, by force if necessary. America's defeat in Vietnam disrupted the consensus. Since then, nearly every American conflict has been supported more strongly by Republicans than by Democrats, who have placed more emphasis on diplomacy, economic sanctions, and foreign aid as the means of protecting U.S. interests. Harvard's Joseph Nye, who served in national security positions in the Carter and Clinton administrations, coined the term **soft power** to describe this approach, contrasting it with the use of military force, which he characterized as hard power.

The difference between Republicans and Democrats is one of degree rather than of kind. Democrats and Republicans alike recognize that military action, diplomacy, economic sanctions, and foreign aid all have a part to play in protecting the United States. Nevertheless, there are partisan differences when it comes to the instruments of national security policy, as indicated by recent polls that have asked Americans which programs they would prefer to cut as a means of reducing the federal budget deficit.

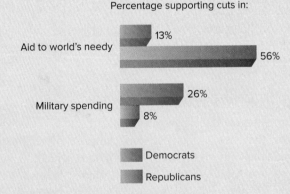

Percentage supporting cuts in:

Aid to world's needy — 13% / 56%

Military spending — 26% / 8%

Democrats
Republicans

Source: Pew Research Center survey, April 6, 2017.

Q: Where do you stand on the question of the relative use of hard power and soft power as instruments of national security policy? Why do you think Republicans and Democrats differ in their opinions on foreign aid and military spending?

As these examples illustrate, the new global economy poses risks as well as benefits to the United States. After World War II, the U.S. economy accounted for nearly half of the world's economic output, and the United States was in a position to nearly define the terms of its economic relations with other countries. Today, it operates in a global economy marked by mutual dependence. The United States depends on the economic health of other nations, just as they depend on the health of the American economy. Thus, just as the United States today faces a set of nearly unprecedented military challenges around the globe, so too is it confronting a set of nearly unprecedented economic ones. In the end, its national security will rest on its ability to respond effectively to both challenges.

The economic role of naval power has come into prominence in the past few years as China has flexed its power by laying claim to islands in the South China Sea off the coasts of Vietnam and the Philippines. The area surrounding the islands has untapped oil reserves, which China has claimed, while also claiming the right to keep foreign shipping out of the islands' territorial waters. The United States has refused to recognize the claims and has sent ships through the disputed wars and conducted joint naval exercises, including in 2012 a naval exercise with its onetime adversary, Vietnam.

The U.S. role in protecting international commerce goes far beyond the projection of military power, most notably in its efforts to strengthen global financial markets. The importance of this effort became apparent in the global economic downturn of 2008, when financial institutions worldwide teetered on the edge of failure.[27] In response, U.S. policymakers subjected America's leading banks to a "stress test" to determine their ability to withstand defaults on the debt they are owed. Banks that failed the test were provided government loans to protect them from such defaults. U.S. policymakers encouraged and assisted other nations to do the same, recognizing that major financial institutions operate around the globe and that the collapse of even one of them could send the world economy in a downward spiral.

SUMMARY

The chief instruments of national security policy are diplomacy, military force, economic exchange, and intelligence gathering. These are exercised through specialized agencies of the U.S. government that are largely responsive to presidential leadership, such as the Departments of State and Defense. National security policy has also relied on international organizations, such as the United Nations and the World Trade Organization, that are responsive to the global concerns of major nations.

From 1945 to 1990, U.S. foreign and defense policies were dominated by a concern with the Soviet Union. During most of this period, the United States pursued a policy of containment based on the premise that the Soviet Union was an aggressor nation bent on global conquest. Containment policy led the United States to enter into wars in Korea and Vietnam and to maintain a large defense establishment.

A first response to the end of the Cold War period was multilateralism—the idea that major nations could achieve common goals by working together, including the use of force to restrain regional conflicts. The interventions in the Persian Gulf and the Balkans during the 1990s are examples. They demonstrated that major nations can intervene with some success in global hot spots but also showed that the ethnic, religious, and national conflicts that fuel these conflicts are not easily resolved.

The terrorist attacks on the World Trade Center and the Pentagon in 2001 led to broad changes in national security organization and strategy. Increased defense and homeland security spending has been coupled with a partial reorganization of U.S. intelligence, law enforcement, and immigration agencies, as well as new laws affecting the scope of their activities. However, the defining moment of the post–September 11 period was America's invasion of Iraq in 2003, which was rooted in President George W. Bush's preemptive war doctrine and his willingness to commit the United States to unilateral action. America's inability to create a stable regime in Iraq, in conjunction with Syria's civil war, gave rise to the Islamic State, which became a primary target of U.S. military action.

In recent decades, the United States has increasingly taken economic factors into account in its national security considerations. This has meant, for example, that trade has played a larger part in defining relationships between the United States and other countries. The trading system that the United States helped erect after World War II has given way to one that is global in scale and more competitive. Changes in communication, transportation, and computing have altered the way large corporations operate, and as businesses have changed their practices, nations have had to adapt. The changes include the emergence of regional and international economic structures, such as the European Union and NAFTA. Nevertheless, nations naturally compete for economic advantage, including access to natural resources; accordingly, trade is a source of conflict as well as a source of cooperation.

©gangliu10/Getty Images

CRITICAL THINKING ZONE

Key Terms

bipolar (power structure) (*p. 525*)
Cold War (*p. 525*)
containment (*p. 525*)

economic globalization (*p. 540*)
free trade (*p. 541*)
internationalist (*p. 525*)

isolationist (*p. 524*)
military-industrial complex (*p. 539*)
multilateralism (*p. 526*)
mutually assured destruction
  (MAD) (*p. 533*)
preemptive war doctrine (*p. 528*)

protectionism (*p. 542*)
soft power (*p. 546*)
tariffs (*p. 541*)
transnational terrorism (*p. 537*)
unilateralism (*p. 529*)
unipolar (power structure) (*p. 526*)

APPLYING THE ELEMENTS OF CRITICAL THINKING

Conceptualizing: Explain the difference between a bipolar international power structure and a unipolar one. With which one is containment doctrine associated?

Synthesizing: Contrast free trade and protectionism as approaches to global trade and competition. Identify policies associated with each approach.

Analyzing: Two objectives of U.S. foreign policy are defense security and economic security. What are the mechanisms for pursuing each of these objectives?

EXTRA CREDIT

A Book Worth Reading: Joseph Nye, *Presidential Leadership and the Creation of the American Era* (Princeton, N.J.: Princeton University Press, 2013). An insightful look at the role various U.S. presidents have played in shaping the nation's place in the world. The author's earlier award-winning book, *Soft Power,* helped change the way policymakers think about foreign policy.

A Website Worth Visiting: **www.cfr.org** The Council on Foreign Relations brings together foreign policy leaders, analysts, scholars, and others in order to promote a better understanding of international issues. Its website includes foreign policy reports, assessments, speeches, and other information.

PARTICIPATE!

In his 1961 inaugural address, President John F. Kennedy said, "Ask not what your country can do for you. Ask what you can do for your country." Kennedy called America's young people to service on behalf of their country. His call was not just a call to military service. One of Kennedy's early initiatives, the Peace Corps, offered Americans the opportunity to apply their skills to development projects in other countries. Under Kennedy's successor, President Lyndon Johnson, a domestic version of the Peace Corps—Volunteers in Service to America (VISTA)—was established. Before the military draft ended in 1973, male Americans were expected to serve their country. Not all did so, but millions served in the army, navy, air force, or marine corps. Since the end of the draft, Congress has from time to time considered establishing a national service that would require every young American man and woman to serve the country in one way or another for a set period of time. However, you do not need an act of Congress if you want to serve your country. A range of alternatives are available, including the all-volunteer military, the Peace Corps, and AmeriCorps (a network of local, state, and national service programs).

The Constitution of the United States of America[1]

We the People of the United States, in Order to form a more perfect Union, establish Justice, insure domestic Tranquility, provide for the common defence, promote the general Welfare, and secure the Blessings of Liberty to ourselves and our Posterity, do ordain and establish this CONSTITUTION for the United States of America.

ARTICLE I

Section 1

All legislative Powers herein granted shall be vested in a Congress of the United States, which shall consist of a Senate and House of Representatives.

Section 2

The House of Representatives shall be composed of Members chosen every second Year by the People of the several States, and the Electors in each State shall have the Qualifications requisite for Electors of the most numerous Branch of the State Legislature.

No Person shall be a Representative who shall not have attained to the Age of twenty-five Years, and been seven Years a Citizen of the United States, and who shall not, when elected, be an Inhabitant of that State in which he shall be chosen.

[Representatives and direct Taxes[2] shall be apportioned among the several States which may be included within this Union, according to their respective Numbers, which shall be determined by adding to the whole Number of free Persons, including those bound to Service for a Term of Years, and excluding Indians not taxed, three fifths of all other Persons.][3] The actual Enumeration shall be made within three Years after the first Meeting of the Congress of the United States, and within every subsequent Term of ten Years, in such Manner as they shall by Law direct. The Number of Representatives shall not exceed one for every thirty Thousand, but each State shall have at Least one Representative; and until such enumeration shall be made, the State of New Hampshire shall be entitled to chuse three, Massachusetts eight, Rhode-Island and Providence Plantations one, Connecticut five, New York six, New Jersey four, Pennsylvania eight, Delaware one, Maryland six, Virginia ten, North Carolina five, South Carolina five, and Georgia three.

---

[1]This version, which follows the original Constitution in capitalization and spelling, was published by the United States Department of the Interior, Office of Education, in 1935.

[2]Altered by the Sixteenth Amendment.

[3]Negated by the Fourteenth Amendment.

When vacancies happen in the Representation from any State, the Executive Authority thereof shall issue Writs of Election to fill such Vacancies.

The House of Representatives shall chuse their Speaker and other Officers; and shall have the sole Power of Impeachment.

Section 3

The Senate of the United States shall be composed of two Senators from each State, chosen by the Legislature thereof, for six Years; and each Senator shall have one Vote.

Immediately after they shall be assembled in Consequence of the first Election, they shall be divided as equally as may be into three Classes. The Seats of the Senators of the first Class shall be vacated at the Expiration of the second Year, of the second Class at the Expiration of the fourth Year, and of the third Class at the Expiration of the sixth Year, so that one-third may be chosen every second Year; and if Vacancies happen by Resignation, or otherwise, during the Recess of the Legislature of any State, the Executive thereof may make temporary Appointments until the next Meeting of the Legislature, which shall then fill such Vacancies.

No Person shall be a Senator who shall not have attained to the Age of thirty Years, and been nine Years a Citizen of the United States, and who shall not, when elected, be an Inhabitant of that State for which he shall be chosen.

The Vice President of the United States shall be President of the Senate, but shall have no vote, unless they be equally divided.

The Senate shall chuse their other Officers, and also a President pro tempore, in the absence of the Vice President, or when he shall exercise the Office of President of the United States.

The Senate shall have the sole Power to try all Impeachments. When sitting for that purpose they shall be on Oath or Affirmation. When the President of the United States is tried, the Chief Justice shall preside: And no person shall be convicted without the Concurrence of two thirds of the Members present.

Judgment in Cases of Impeachment shall not extend further than to removal from Office, and disqualification to hold and enjoy any Office of honor, Trust, or Profit under the United States: but the Party convicted shall nevertheless be liable and subject to Indictment, Trial, Judgment and Punishment, according to Law.

Section 4

The Times, Place and Manner of holding Elections for Senators and Representatives, shall be prescribed in each State by the Legislature thereof; but the Congress may at any time by Law make or alter such Regulations, except as to the Places of Chusing Senators.

The Congress shall assemble at least once in every Year, and such Meeting shall be on the first Monday in December, unless they shall by Law appoint a different Day.

Section 5

Each House shall be the Judge of the Elections, Returns and Qualifications of its own Members, and a Majority of each shall constitute a Quorum to do Business; but a smaller number may adjourn from day to day, and may be authorized to compel the Attendance of absent Members, in such Manner, and under such Penalties, as each House may provide.

Each House may determine the Rules of its Proceedings, punish its Members for disorderly Behaviour, and, with the Concurrence of two thirds, expel a Member.

Each House shall keep a Journal of its Proceedings, and from time to time publish the same, excepting such Parts as may in their Judgment require Secrecy; and the Yeas and Nays of the Members of either House on any question shall, at the Desire of one fifth of those Present, be entered on the Journal.

Neither House, during the Session of Congress, shall, without the Consent of the other, adjourn for more than three days, nor to any other Place than that in which the two Houses shall be sitting.

Section 6

The Senators and Representatives shall receive a Compensation for their Services, to be ascertained by Law, and paid out of the Treasury of the United States. They shall in all Cases, except Treason, Felony, and Breach of the Peace, be privileged from Arrest during their Attendance at the Session of their respective Houses, and in going to and returning from the same; and for any Speech or Debate in either House, they shall not be questioned in any other Place.

No Senator or Representative shall, during the Time for which he was elected, be appointed to any civil Office under the Authority of the United States, which shall have been created, or the Emoluments whereof shall have been increased, during such time; and no Person holding any Office under the United States shall be a Member of either House during his continuance in Office.

Section 7

All Bills for raising Revenue shall originate in the House of Representatives; but the Senate may propose or concur with Amendments as on other bills.

Every Bill which shall have passed the House of Representatives and the Senate, shall, before it becomes a Law, be presented to the President of the United States; if he approve he shall sign it, but if not he shall return it, with his Objections, to that House in which it shall have originated, who shall enter the Objections at large on their Journal, and proceed to reconsider it. If after such Reconsideration two thirds of that House shall agree to pass the bill, it shall be sent, together with the objections, to the other House, by which it shall likewise be reconsidered, and if approved by two thirds of that House, it shall become a Law. But in all such Cases the Votes of both Houses shall be determined by Yeas and Nays, and the Names of the Persons voting for and against the Bill shall be entered on the Journal of each House respectively. If any Bill shall not be returned by the President within ten Days (Sundays excepted) after it shall have been presented to him, the Same shall be a Law, in like Manner as if he had signed it, unless the Congress by their Adjournment prevent its Return, in which Case it shall not be a Law.

Every Order, Resolution, or Vote to which the Concurrence of the Senate and House of Representatives may be necessary (except on a question of Adjournment) shall be presented to the President of the United States; and before the Same shall take Effect, shall be approved by him, or being disapproved by him, shall be repassed by two thirds of the Senate and House of Representatives, according to the Rules and Limitations prescribed in the Case of a Bill.

Section 8

The Congress shall have Power To lay and collect Taxes, Duties, Imposts and Excises, to pay the Debts and provide for the common Defence and general Welfare of the United States; but all Duties, Imposts and Excises shall be uniform throughout the United States;

To borrow money on the credit of the United States;

To regulate Commerce with foreign Nations, and among the several States, and with the Indian Tribes;

To establish a uniform rule of Naturalization, and uniform Laws on the subject of Bankruptcies throughout the United States;

To coin Money, regulate the Value thereof, and of foreign Coin, and fix the Standard of Weights and Measures;

To provide for the Punishment of counterfeiting the Securities and current Coin of the United States;

To establish Post Offices and post Roads;

To promote the Progress of Science and useful Arts, by securing for limited Times to Authors and Inventors the exclusive Right to their respective Writings and Discoveries;

To constitute Tribunals inferior to the Supreme Court;

To define and punish Piracies and Felonies committed on the high Seas, and Offenses against the Law of Nations;

To declare War, grant Letters of Marque and Reprisal, and make Rules concerning Captures on Land and Water;

To raise and support Armies, but no Appropriation of Money to that Use shall be for a longer Term than two Years;

To provide and maintain a Navy;

To make Rules for the Government and Regulation of the land and naval forces;

To provide for calling forth the Militia to execute the Laws of the Union, suppress Insurrections and repel Invasions;

To provide for organizing, arming, and disciplining the Militia, and for governing such Part of them as may be employed in the Service of the United States, reserving to the States respectively, the Appointment of the Officers, and the Authority of training the Militia according to the discipline prescribed by Congress;

To exercise exclusive Legislation in all Cases whatsoever, over such District (not exceeding ten Miles square) as may, by Cession of particular States, and the acceptance of Congress, become the Seat of the Government of the United States, and to exercise like Authority over all Places purchased by the Consent of the Legislature of the State in which the Same shall be, for the Erection of Forts, Magazines, Arsenals, Dock-yards, and other needful Buildings;—And

To make all Laws which shall be necessary and proper for carrying into Execution the foregoing Powers, and all other Powers vested by this Constitution in the Government of the United States, or in any Department or Officer thereof.

Section 9

The Migration or Importation of such Persons as any of the States now existing shall think proper to admit, shall not be prohibited by the Congress prior to the Year one thousand eight hundred and eight, but a tax or duty may be imposed on such Importation, not exceeding ten dollars for each Person.

The privilege of the Writ of Habeas Corpus shall not be suspended, unless when in Cases of Rebellion or Invasion the public Safety may require it.

No bill of Attainder or ex post facto Law shall be passed.

No capitation, or other direct, Tax shall be laid unless in Proportion to the Census or Enumeration herein before directed to be taken.

No Tax or Duty shall be laid on Articles exported from any State.

No Preference shall be given by any Regulation of Commerce or Revenue to the Ports of one State over those of another: nor shall Vessels bound to, or from, one State, be obliged to enter, clear, or pay Duties in another.

No Money shall be drawn from the Treasury, but in Consequence of Appropriations made by Law; and a regular Statement and Account of the Receipts and Expenditures of all public Money shall be published from time to time.

No Title of Nobility shall be granted by the United States: And no Person holding any Office of Profit or Trust under them, shall, without the Consent of the Congress, accept of any present, Emolument, Office, or Title, of any kind whatever, from any King, Prince, or foreign State.

Section 10

No State shall enter into any Treaty, Alliance, or Confederation; grant Letters of Marque and Reprisal; coin Money; emit Bills of Credit; make any Thing but gold and silver Coin a Tender in Payment of Debts; pass any Bill of Attainder, ex post facto Law, or Law impairing the Obligation of Contracts, or grant any Title of Nobility.

No State shall, without the Consent of the Congress, lay any Imposts or Duties on Imports or Exports, except what may be absolutely necessary for executing its inspection Laws; and the net Produce of all Duties and Imposts, laid by any State on Imports or Exports, shall be for the use of the Treasury of the United States; and all such Laws shall be subject to the Revision and Control of the Congress.

No state shall, without the Consent of Congress, lay any duty of Tonnage, keep Troops, or Ships of War in time of Peace, enter into any Agreement or Compact with another State, or with a foreign Power, or engage in War, unless actually invaded, or in such imminent Danger as will not admit of delay.

ARTICLE II

Section 1

The executive Power shall be vested in a President of the United States of America. He shall hold his Office during the Term of four years, and, together with the Vice President, chosen for the same Term, be elected, as follows:

Each State shall appoint, in such Manner as the Legislature thereof may direct, a Number of Electors, equal to the whole Number of Senators and Representatives to which the State may be entitled in the Congress: but no Senator or Representative, or Person holding an Office of Trust or Profit under the United States, shall be appointed an Elector.

[The Electors shall meet in their respective States, and vote by Ballot for two persons, of whom one at least shall not be an Inhabitant of the same State with themselves. And they shall make a List of all the Persons voted for, and of the Number of Votes for each; which List they shall sign and certify, and transmit sealed to the Seat of the Government of the United States, directed to the President of the Senate. The President of the Senate shall, in the Presence of the Senate and House of Representatives, open all the Certificates, and the Votes shall then be counted. The Person having the greatest Number of Votes shall be the President, if such Number be a Majority of the whole Number of Electors appointed; and if there be more than one who have such Majority, and have an equal Number of Votes, then the House of Representatives shall immediately chuse by Ballot one of them for President; and if no Person have a Majority, then from the five highest on the List the said House shall in like Manner chuse the President. But in chusing the President, the Votes shall be taken by States, the Representation from each State having one Vote; a quorum for this Purpose shall consist of a Member or Members from two-thirds of the States, and a Majority of all the States shall be necessary to a Choice. In every Case, after the Choice of the President, the Person having the greatest Number of Votes of the Electors shall be the Vice President. But if there should remain two or more who have equal votes, the Senate shall chuse from them by Ballot the Vice President.][4]

The Congress may determine the Time of chusing the Electors, and the Day on which they shall give their Votes; which Day shall be the same throughout the United States.

No person except a natural-born Citizen, or a Citizen of the United States, at the time of the Adoption of this Constitution, shall be eligible to the Office of President; neither shall any Person be eligible to that Office who shall not have attained to the Age of thirty-five years, and been fourteen Years a Resident within the United States.

In Case of the Removal of the President from Office, or of his Death, Resignation, or Inability to discharge the Powers and Duties of the said Office, the same shall devolve on the Vice President, and the Congress may by Law provide for the Case of Removal, Death, Resignation, or Inability, both of the President and Vice President, declaring what Officer shall then act as President, and such Officer shall act accordingly, until the disability be removed, or a President shall be elected.

The President shall, at stated Times, receive for his Services a Compensation, which shall neither be increased nor diminished during the Period for which he shall have been elected, and he shall not receive within that Period any other Emolument from the United States, or any of them.

Before he enter on the execution of his Office, he shall take the following Oath or Affirmation:—"I do solemnly swear (or affirm) that I will faithfully execute the Office of President of the United States, and will, to the best of my Ability, preserve, protect, and defend the Constitution of the United States."

Section 2

The President shall be Commander in Chief of the Army and Navy of the United States, and of the Militia of the several States, when called into the actual Service of the United States; he may require the Opinion, in writing, of the principal Officer in each of the executive Departments, upon any subject relating to the Duties of their respective Offices, and he shall have Power to Grant Reprieves and Pardons for Offenses against the United States, except in Cases of Impeachment.

He shall have Power, by and with the Advice and Consent of the Senate, to make Treaties, provided two-thirds of the Senators present concur; and he shall nominate, and by and with the Advice and Consent of the Senate, shall appoint Ambassadors,

---

[4]Revised by the Twelfth Amendment.

other public Ministers and Consuls, Judges of the supreme Court, and all other Officers of the United States, whose Appointments are not herein otherwise provided for, and which shall be established by Law: but the Congress may by Law vest the Appointment of such inferior Officers, as they think proper, in the President alone, in the Courts of Law, or in the Heads of Departments.

The President shall have Power to fill up all Vacancies that may happen during the Recess of the Senate, by granting Commissions which shall expire at the End of their next Session.

Section 3

He shall from time to time give to the Congress Information of the State of the Union, and recommend to their Consideration such Measures as he shall judge necessary and expedient; he may, on extraordinary occasions, convene both Houses, or either of them, and in Case of Disagreement between them, with respect to the Time of Adjournment, he may adjourn them to such Time as he shall think proper; he shall receive Ambassadors and other public Ministers; he shall take care that the Laws be faithfully executed, and shall Commission all the Officers of the United States.

Section 4

The President, Vice President and all civil Officers of the United States, shall be removed from Office on Impeachment for, and Conviction of, Treason, Bribery, or other high Crimes and Misdemeanors.

ARTICLE III

Section 1

The judicial Power of the United States, shall be vested in one supreme Court, and in such inferior Courts as the Congress may from time to time ordain and establish. The Judges, both of the supreme and inferior Courts, shall hold their Offices during good Behaviour, and shall, at stated Times, receive for their Services, a Compensation, which shall not be diminished during their Continuance in Office.

Section 2

The judicial Power shall extend to all Cases, in Law and Equity, arising under this Constitution, the Laws of the United States, and Treaties made, or which shall be made, under their Authority;—to all Cases affecting ambassadors, other public ministers and consuls;—to all cases of admiralty and maritime Jurisdiction;—to Controversies to which the United States shall be a Party;—to Controversies between two or more states;—between a State and Citizens of another State;[5]—between Citizens of different States—between Citizens of the same State claiming Lands under Grants of different States, and between a State, or the Citizens thereof, and foreign States, Citizens, or Subjects.

In all Cases affecting Ambassadors, other public Ministers and Consuls, and those in which a State shall be Party, the supreme Court shall have original Jurisdiction. In

---

[5]Qualified by the Eleventh Amendment.

all the other Cases before mentioned, the supreme Court shall have appellate Jurisdiction, both as to Law and Fact, with such Exceptions, and under such Regulations as the Congress shall make.

The trial of all Crimes, except in Cases of Impeachment, shall be by Jury; and such Trial shall be held in the State where the said Crimes shall have been committed; but when not committed within any State, the Trial shall be at such Place or Places as the Congress may by Law have directed.

Section 3

Treason against the United States, shall consist only in levying War against them, or in adhering to their Enemies, giving them Aid and Comfort. No Person shall be convicted of Treason unless on the Testimony of two Witnesses to the same overt Act, or on Confession in open Court.

The Congress shall have power to declare the Punishment of Treason, but no Attainder of Treason shall work Corruption of Blood, or Forfeiture except during the Life of the Person attainted.

ARTICLE IV

Section 1

Full Faith and Credit shall be given in each State to the public Acts, Records, and judicial Proceedings of every other State. And the Congress may by general Laws prescribe the Manner in which such Acts, Records and Proceedings shall be proved, and the Effect thereof.

Section 2

The Citizens of each State shall be entitled to all Privileges and Immunities of Citizens in the several States.

A Person charged in any State with Treason, Felony, or other Crime, who shall flee from Justice, and be found in another State, shall on demand of the executive Authority of the State from which he fled, be delivered up, to be removed to the State having Jurisdiction of the crime.

No Person held to Service or Labour in one State, under the Laws thereof, escaping into another, shall, in Consequence of any Law or Regulation therein, be discharged from such Service or Labour, but shall be delivered up on Claim of the Party to whom such Service or Labour may be due.

Section 3

New States may be admitted by the Congress into this Union; but no new State shall be formed or erected within the Jurisdiction of any other State; nor any State be formed by the Junction of two or more States, or parts of States, without the Consent of the Legislatures of the States concerned as well as of the Congress.

The Congress shall have Power to dispose of and make all needful Rules and Regulations respecting the Territory or other Property belonging to the United States; and nothing in this Constitution shall be so construed as to Prejudice any Claims of the United States, or of any particular State.

Section 4

The United States shall guarantee to every State in this Union a Republican Form of Government, and shall protect each of them against Invasion; and on Application of the Legislature, or of the Executive (when the Legislature cannot be convened) against domestic Violence.

ARTICLE V

The Congress, whenever two-thirds of both Houses shall deem it necessary, shall propose Amendments to this Constitution, or, on the Application of the Legislatures of two-thirds of the several States, shall call a Convention for proposing Amendments, which, in either Case, shall be valid to all Intents and Purposes, as part of this Constitution, when ratified by the Legislatures of three-fourths of the several States, or by Conventions in three-fourths thereof, as the one or the other Mode of Ratification may be proposed by the Congress; Provided that no Amendment which may be made prior to the Year One thousand eight hundred and eight shall in any Manner affect the first and fourth Clauses in the Ninth Section of the first Article; and that no State, without its Consent, shall be deprived of its equal Suffrage in the Senate.

ARTICLE VI

All Debts contracted and Engagements entered into, before the Adoption of this Constitution, shall be as valid against the United States under this Constitution, as under the Confederation.

This Constitution, and the Laws of the United States which shall be made in Pursuance thereof; and all Treaties made, or which shall be made, under the Authority of the United States, shall be the supreme Law of the Land; and the Judges in every State shall be bound thereby, any Thing in the Constitution or Laws of any State to the Contrary notwithstanding.

The Senators and Representatives before mentioned, and the Members of the several State Legislatures, and all executive and judicial Officers, both of the United States and of the several States, shall be bound by Oath or Affirmation to support this Constitution; but no religious Tests shall ever be required as a qualification to any Office or public Trust under the United States.

ARTICLE VII

The Ratification of the Conventions of nine States shall be sufficient for the Establishment of this Constitution between the States so ratifying the same.

Done in Convention by the Unanimous Consent of the States present the Seventeenth Day of September in the Year of our Lord one thousand seven hundred and Eighty seven, and of the Independence of the United States of America the Twelfth. In Witness whereof We have hereunto subscribed our Names.[6]

---

[6]These are the full names of the signers, which in some cases are not the signatures on the document.

George Washington
President and deputy from
  Virginia

New Hampshire
John Langdon
Nicholas Gilman

Massachusetts
Nathaniel Gorham
Rufus King

Connecticut
William Samuel Johnson
Roger Sherman

New York
Alexander Hamilton

New Jersey
William Livingston
David Brearley
William Paterson
Jonathan Dayton

Pennsylvania
Benjamin Franklin
Thomas Mifflin
Robert Morris
George Clymer
Thomas FitzSimmons
Jared Ingersoll
James Wilson
Gouverneur Morris

Delaware
George Read
Gunning Bedford, Jr.
John Dickinson
Richard Bassett
Jacob Broom

Maryland
James McHenry
Daniel of St. Thomas
  Jenifer
Daniel Carroll

Virginia
John Blair
James Madison, Jr.

North Carolina
William Blount
Richard Dobbs Spaight
Hugh Williamson

South Carolina
John Rutledge
Charles Cotesworth
  Pinckney
Charles Pinckney
Pierce Butler

Georgia
William Few
Abraham Baldwin

Articles in Addition to, and Amendment of, the Constitution of the United States of America, Proposed by Congress, and Ratified by the Legislatures of the Several States, Pursuant to the Fifth Article of the Original Constitution[7].

AMENDMENT I

Congress shall make no law respecting an establishment of religion, or prohibiting the free exercise thereof; or abridging the freedom of speech, or of the press; or the right of the people peaceably to assemble, and to petition the Government for a redress of grievances.

AMENDMENT II

A well regulated Militia, being necessary to the security of a free State, the right of the people to keep and bear Arms shall not be infringed.

---

[7]This heading appears only in the joint resolution submitting the first ten amendments, which are collectively known as the Bill of Rights. They were ratified on December 15, 1791.

Amendment III

No Soldier shall, in time of peace, be quartered in any house, without the consent of the Owner, nor in time of war, but in a manner to be prescribed by law.

Amendment IV

The right of the people to be secure in their persons, houses, papers, and effects, against unreasonable searches and seizures, shall not be violated, and no Warrants shall issue, but upon probable cause, supported by Oath or affirmation, and particularly describing the place to be searched, and the persons or things to be seized.

Amendment V

No person shall be held to answer for a capital or otherwise infamous crime, unless on a presentment or indictment of a Grand Jury, except in cases arising in the land or naval forces, or in the Militia, when in actual service in time of War or public danger; nor shall any person be subject for the same offence to be twice put in jeopardy of life or limb; nor shall be compelled in any criminal case to be a witness against himself, nor be deprived of life, liberty, or property, without due process of law; nor shall private property be taken for public use, without just compensation.

Amendment VI

In all criminal prosecutions, the accused shall enjoy the right to a speedy and public trial, by an impartial jury of the State and district wherein the crime shall have been committed, which district shall have been previously ascertained by law, and to be informed of the nature and cause of the accusation; to be confronted with the witnesses against him; to have compulsory process for obtaining witnesses in his favour, and to have the Assistance of Counsel for his defence.

Amendment VII

In suits at common law, where the value in controversy shall exceed twenty dollars, the right of trial by jury shall be preserved, and no fact tried by a jury, shall be otherwise reexamined in any Court of the United States, than according to the rules of the common law.

Amendment VIII

Excessive bail shall not be required, nor excessive fines imposed, nor cruel and unusual punishments inflicted.

Amendment IX

The enumeration of the Constitution, of certain rights, shall not be construed to deny or disparage others retained by the people.

Amendment X

The powers not delegated to the United States by the Constitution, nor prohibited by it to the States, are reserved to the States respectively, or to the people.

Amendment XI [1795]

The Judicial power of the United States shall not be construed to extend to any suit in law or equity, commenced or prosecuted against one of the United States by Citizens of another State, or by Citizens or Subjects of any Foreign State.

Amendment XII [1804]

The Electors shall meet in their respective States and vote by ballot for President and Vice-President, one of whom, at least, shall not be an inhabitant of the same State with themselves; they shall name in their ballots the person voted for as President, and in distinct ballots the person voted for as Vice-President, and they shall make distinct lists of all persons voted for as President, and of all persons voted for as Vice-President, and of the number of votes for each, which lists they shall sign and certify, and transmit sealed to the seat of the government of the United States, directed to the President of the Senate;—The President of the Senate shall, in the presence of the Senate and House of Representatives, open all the certificates and the votes shall then be counted;—The person having the greatest number of votes for President, shall be the President, if such number be a majority of the whole number of Electors appointed; and if no person have such majority, then from the persons having the highest numbers not exceeding three on the list of those voted for as President, the House of Representatives shall choose immediately, by ballot, the President. But in choosing the President, the votes shall be taken by states, the representation from each state having one vote; a quorum for this purpose shall consist of a member or members from two-thirds of the states, and a majority of all the states shall be necessary to a choice. And if the House of Representatives shall not choose a President whenever the right of choice shall devolve upon them, before the fourth day of March next following, then the Vice-President shall act as President, as in the case of the death or other constitutional disability of the President.—The person having the greatest number of votes as Vice-President, shall be the Vice-President, if such number be a majority of the whole number of Electors appointed, and if no person have a majority, then from the two highest numbers on the list, the Senate shall choose the Vice-President; a quorum for the purpose shall consist of two-thirds of the whole number of Senators, and majority of the whole number shall be necessary to a choice. But no person constitutionally ineligible to the office of President shall be eligible to that of Vice-President of the United States.

Amendment XIII [1865]

Section 1

Neither slavery nor involuntary servitude, except as a punishment for crime whereof the party shall have been duly convicted, shall exist within the United States, or any place subject to their jurisdiction.

Section 2

Congress shall have power to enforce this article by appropriate legislation.

AMENDMENT XIV [1868]

Section 1

All persons born or naturalized in the United States, and subject to the jurisdiction thereof, are citizens of the United States and of the State wherein they reside. No State shall abridge the privileges or immunities of citizens of the United States; nor shall any State deprive any person of life, liberty, or property, without due process of law; nor deny to any person within its jurisdiction the equal protection of the laws.

Section 2

Representatives shall be apportioned among the several States according to their respective numbers, counting the whole number of persons in each State, excluding Indians not taxed. But when the right to vote at any election for the choice of electors for President and Vice-President of the United States, Representatives in Congress, the Executive and Judicial officers of a State, or the members of the Legislature thereof, is denied to any of the male inhabitants of such State, being twenty-one years of age, and citizens of the United States, or in any way abridged, except for participation in rebellion, or other crime, the basis of representation therein shall be reduced in the proportion which the number of such male citizens shall bear to the whole number of male citizens twenty-one years of age in such State.

Section 3

No person shall be a Senator or Representative in Congress, or elector of President and Vice-President, or hold any office, civil or military, under the United States, or under any State, who, having previously taken an oath, as a member of Congress, or as an officer of the United States, or as a member of any State legislature, or as an executive or judicial officer of any State, to support the Constitution of the United States, shall have engaged in insurrection or rebellion against the same, or given aid or comfort to the enemies thereof. But Congress may by a vote of two-thirds of each House, remove such disability.

Section 4

The validity of the public debt of the United States, authorized by law, including debts incurred for payment of pensions and bounties for services in suppressing insurrection or rebellion, shall not be questioned. But neither the United States nor any State shall assume or pay any debts or obligation incurred in aid of insurrection or rebellion against the United States, or any claim for the loss or emancipation of any slave; but all such debts, obligations, and claims shall be held illegal and void.

Section 5

The Congress shall have the power to enforce, by appropriate legislation, the provisions of this article.

AMENDMENT XV [1870]

Section 1

The right of citizens of the United States to vote shall not be denied or abridged by the United States or by any State on account of race, color, or previous condition of servitude.

Section 2

The Congress shall have power to enforce this article by appropriate legislation.

AMENDMENT XVI [1913]

The Congress shall have power to lay and collect taxes on incomes, from whatever source derived, without apportionment among the several States, and without regard to any census or enumeration.

AMENDMENT XVII [1913]

The Senate of the United States shall be composed of two Senators from each State, elected by the people thereof, for six years; and each Senator shall have one vote. The electors in each State shall have the qualifications requisite for electors of the most numerous branch of the State legislatures.

When vacancies happen in the representation of any State in the Senate, the executive authority of such State shall issue writs of election to fill such vacancies: Provided, That the legislature of any State may empower the executive thereof to make temporary appointments until the people fill the vacancies by election as the legislature may direct.

This Amendment shall not be so construed as to affect the election or term of any Senator chosen before it becomes valid as part of the Constitution.

AMENDMENT XVIII [1919]

Section 1

After one year from the ratification of this article the manufacture, sale, or transportation of intoxicating liquors within, the importation thereof into, or the exportation thereof from the United States and all territory subject to the jurisdiction thereof for beverage purposes is hereby prohibited.

Section 2

The Congress and the several States shall have concurrent power to enforce this article by appropriate legislation.

Section 3

This article shall be inoperative unless it shall have been ratified as an Amendment to the Constitution by the legislatures of the several States, as provided in the Constitution, within seven years from the date of the submission hereof to the States by the Congress.

AMENDMENT XIX [1920]

The right of citizens of the United States to vote shall not be denied or abridged by the United States or by any State on account of sex.

Congress shall have power to enforce this article by appropriate legislation.

AMENDMENT XX [1933]

Section 1

The terms of the President and Vice-President shall end at noon on the 20th day of January, and the terms of Senators and Representatives at noon on the 3d day of January, of the years in which such terms would have ended if this article had not been ratified; and the terms of their successors shall then begin.

Section 2

The Congress shall assemble at least once in every year, and such meeting shall begin at noon on the 3d day of January, unless they shall by law appoint a different day.

Section 3

If, at the time fixed for the beginning of the term of the President, the President elect shall have died, the Vice-President elect shall become President. If a President shall not have been chosen before the time fixed for the beginning of his term or if the President elect shall have failed to qualify, then the Vice-President elect shall act as President until a President shall have qualified; and the Congress may by law provide for the case wherein neither a President elect nor a Vice-President elect shall have qualified, declaring who shall then act as President, or the manner in which one who is to act shall be selected, and such person shall act accordingly until a President or Vice-President shall have qualified.

Section 4

The Congress may by law provide for the case of the death of any of the persons from whom the House of Representatives may choose a President whenever the right of choice shall have devolved upon them, and for the case of the death of any of the persons from whom the Senate may choose a Vice-President whenever the right of choice shall have devolved upon them.

Section 5

Sections 1 and 2 shall take effect on the 15th day of October following the ratification of this article.

Section 6

This article shall be inoperative unless it shall have been ratified as an amendment to the Constitution by the legislatures of three-fourths of the several States within seven years from the date of its submission.

AMENDMENT XXI [1933]

Section 1

The eighteenth article of amendment to the Constitution of the United States is hereby repealed.

Section 2

The transportation or importation into any State, Territory, or possession of the United States for delivery or use therein of intoxicating liquors, in violation of the laws thereof, is hereby prohibited.

Section 3

This article shall be inoperative unless it shall have been ratified as an amendment to the Constitution by conventions in the several States, as provided in the Constitution, within seven years from the date of the submission hereof to the States by the Congress.

AMENDMENT XXII [1951]

No person shall be elected to the office of the President more than twice, and no person who has held the office of President, or acted as President, for more than two years of a term to which some other person was elected President shall be elected to the office of the President more than once.

But this Article shall not apply to any person holding the office of President when this Article was proposed by the Congress, and shall not prevent any person who may be holding the office of President, or acting as President, during the term within which this Article becomes operative from holding the office of President or acting as President during the remainder of such term.

This article shall be inoperative unless it shall have been ratified as an amendment to the Constitution by the legislatures of three-fourths of the several states within seven years from the date of its submission to the states by the Congress.

AMENDMENT XXIII [1961]

Section 1

The District constituting the seat of Government of the United States shall appoint in such manner as the Congress may direct:

A number of electors of President and Vice-President equal to the whole number of Senators and Representatives in Congress to which the District would be entitled if it were a State, but in no event more than the least populous State; they shall be in addition to those appointed by the States, but they shall be considered, for the purposes of the election of President and Vice-President, to be electors appointed by a State; and they shall meet in the District and perform such duties as provided by the twelfth article of Amendment.

Section 2

The Congress shall have power to enforce this article by appropriate legislation.

AMENDMENT XXIV [1964]

Section 1

The right of citizens of the United States to vote in any primary or other election for President or Vice President, for electors for President or Vice President, or for Senator or Representative in Congress, shall not be denied or abridged by the United States or any state by reason of failure to pay any poll tax or other tax.

Section 2

The Congress shall have the power to enforce this article by appropriate legislation.

AMENDMENT XXV [1967]

Section 1

In case of the removal of the President from office or of his death or resignation, the Vice President shall become President.

Section 2

Whenever there is a vacancy in the office of the Vice President, the President shall nominate a Vice President who shall take office upon confirmation by a majority vote of both Houses of Congress.

Section 3

Whenever the President transmits to the President Pro Tempore of the Senate and the Speaker of the House of Representatives his written declaration that he is unable to discharge the powers and duties of his office, and until he transmits to them a written declaration to the contrary, such powers and duties shall be discharged by the Vice President as Acting President.

Section 4

Whenever the Vice President and a majority of either the principal officers of the executive departments or of such other body as Congress may by law provide, transmit to the President Pro Tempore of the Senate and the Speaker of the House of Representatives their written declaration that the President is unable to discharge the powers and duties of his office, the Vice President shall immediately assume the powers and duties of the office as Acting President.

Thereafter, when the President transmits to the President Pro Tempore of the Senate and the Speaker of the House of Representatives his written declaration that no inability exists, he shall resume the powers and duties of his office unless the Vice

President and a majority of either the principal officers of the executive departments or of such other body as Congress may by law provide, transmit within four days to the President Pro Tempore of the Senate and the Speaker of the House of Representatives their written declaration that the President is unable to discharge the powers and duties of his office. Thereupon Congress shall decide the issue, assembling within forty-eight hours for that purpose if not in session. If the Congress, within twenty-one days after receipt of the latter written declaration, or, if Congress is not in session, within twenty-one days after Congress is required to assemble, determines by two-thirds vote of both Houses that the President is unable to discharge the powers and duties of his office, the Vice President shall continue to discharge the same as Acting President; otherwise, the President shall resume the powers and duties of his office.

AMENDMENT XXVI [1971]

Section 1

The right of citizens of the United States, who are eighteen years of age or older, to vote shall not be denied or abridged by the United States or by any State on account of age.

Section 2

The Congress shall have the power to enforce this article by appropriate legislation.

AMENDMENT XXVII [1992]

No law varying the compensation for the service of Senators and Representatives shall take effect until an election of Representatives shall have intervened.

GLOSSARY

administrative law judge An official who presides at a trial-like administrative hearing to settle a dispute between an agency and someone adversely affected by a decision of that agency.

affirmative action Refers to programs designed to ensure that women, minorities, and other traditionally disadvantaged groups have full and equal opportunities in employment, education, and other areas of life.

agency point of view The tendency of bureaucrats to place the interests of their agency ahead of other interests and ahead of the priorities sought by the president or Congress.

agenda setting The power of the media through news coverage to focus the public's attention and concern on particular events, problems, issues, personalities, and so on.

agents of socialization Those agents, such as the family and the media, that have significant impact on citizens' political socialization.

alienation A feeling of personal powerlessness that includes the notion that government does not care about the opinions of people like oneself.

Anti-Federalists A term used to describe opponents of the Constitution during the debate over ratification.

apathy A feeling of personal disinterest in or lack of concern with politics.

appellate jurisdiction The authority of a given court to review cases that have already been tried in lower courts and are appealed to it by the losing party; such a court is called an appeals court or appellate court. (See also **original jurisdiction**.)

authoritarian government A form of government in which those in power openly repress their opponents in order to stay in power.

authority The recognized right of officials to exercise power as a result of the positions they hold. (See also **power**.)

balanced budget The situation in which the government's tax and other revenues for the year are roughly equal to its expenditures.

bicameral legislature A legislature that has two chambers (the House and the Senate, in the case of the United States).

bill A proposed law (legislative act) within Congress or another legislature. (See also **law**.)

Bill of Rights The first 10 amendments to the Constitution. They include rights such as freedom of speech and religion and due process protections (for example, the right to a jury trial) for persons accused of crimes.

bipolar (power structure) A power structure dominated by two powers only, as in the case of the United States and the Soviet Union during the Cold War.

block grants Federal grants-in-aid that permit state and local officials to decide how the money will be spent within a general area, such as education or health. (See also **categorical grants**.)

budget deficit The situation in which the government's expenditures exceed its tax and other revenues.

budgetary process The process through which annual federal spending and revenue determinations are made.

bureaucracy A system of organization and control based on the principles of hierarchical authority, job specialization, and formalized rules. (See also **formalized rules; hierarchical authority; job specialization**.)

bureaucratic accountability The degree to which bureaucrats are held accountable for the power they exercise.

cabinet A group consisting of the heads of the (cabinet) executive departments, who are appointed by the president, subject to confirmation by the Senate. The cabinet was once the main advisory body to the president but no longer plays this role. (See also **cabinet [executive] departments**.)

cabinet (executive) departments The major administrative organizations within the federal executive bureaucracy, each of which is headed by a secretary or, in the case of Justice, the attorney general. Each department has responsibility for a major function of the federal government, such as defense, agriculture, or justice. (See also **independent agencies.**)

candidate-centered campaigns Election campaigns and other political processes in which candidates, not political parties, have most of the initiative and influence. (See also **party-centered campaigns.**)

capital-gains tax The tax that individuals pay on money gained from the sale of a capital asset, such as property or stocks.

categorical grants Federal grants-in-aid to states and localities that can be used only for designated projects. (See also **block grants.**)

checks and balances The elaborate system of divided spheres of authority provided by the U.S. Constitution as a means of controlling the power of government. The separation of powers among the branches of the national government, federalism, and the different methods of selecting national officers are all part of this system.

citizens' (noneconomic) groups Organized interests formed by individuals drawn together by opportunities to promote a cause in which they believe but that does not provide them significant individual economic benefits. (See also **economic groups; interest group.**)

civic duty The belief of an individual that civic and political participation is a responsibility of citizenship.

civil liberties The fundamental individual rights of a free society, such as freedom of speech and the right to a jury trial, which in the United States are protected by the Bill of Rights.

clear-and-present-danger test A test devised by the Supreme Court in 1919 to define the limits of free speech in the context of national security. According to the test, government cannot abridge political expression unless it presents a clear and present danger to the nation's security.

clientele groups Special interest groups that benefit directly from the activities of a particular bureaucratic agency and therefore are strong advocates of the agency.

cloture A parliamentary maneuver that, if a three-fifths majority votes for it, limits Senate debate to 30 hours and has the effect of defeating a filibuster. (See also **filibuster.**)

Cold War The lengthy period after World War II when the United States and the USSR were not engaged in actual combat (a "hot war") but were nonetheless locked in a state of deep-seated hostility.

collective (public) goods Benefits that are offered by groups (usually citizens' groups) as an incentive for membership but that are nondivisible (such as a clean environment) and therefore are available to nonmembers as well as members of the particular group. (See also **free-rider problem; private [individual] goods.**)

commerce clause The authority granted Congress in Article I, Section 8 of the Constitution "to regulate commerce" among the states.

common-carrier function The media's function as an open channel through which political leaders can communicate with the public. (See also **partisan function; signaling [signaler] function; watchdog function.**)

concurring opinion A separate opinion written by a Supreme Court justice who votes with the majority in the decision on a case but who disagrees with the reasoning. (See also **dissenting opinion; majority opinion; plurality opinion.**)

confederacy A governmental system in which sovereignty is vested entirely in subnational (state) governments. (See also **federalism; unitary system.**)

conference committee A temporary committee that is formed to bargain over the differences in the House and Senate versions of a bill. A conference committee's members are usually appointed from the House and Senate standing committees that originally worked on the bill.

constituency The people residing within the geographic area represented by an elected official.

constitution The fundamental law that defines how a government will legitimately operate.

constitutional democratic republic A government that is constitutional in its provisions for minority rights and rule by law; democratic in its provisions for majority influence through elections; and a republic in its mix of deliberative institutions, which check and balance each other.

constitutionalism The idea that there are lawful limits on the power of government.

containment A doctrine, developed after World War II, based on the assumptions that the Soviet Union was an aggressor nation and that only a determined United States could block Soviet territorial ambitions.

cooperative federalism The situation in which the national, state, and local levels work together to solve problems.

corporate power The power that corporations exercise in their effort to influence government and maintain control of the workplace.

critical thinking Reflective thinking focused on deciding what can reasonably be believed and then using this information to make judgments.

cultural (social) conservatives Those who believe government power should be used to uphold traditional values. (See also **economic liberals; economic conservatives; cultural [social] liberals; libertarian; populist.**)

cultural (social) liberals Those who believe it is not government's role to buttress traditional values at the expense of unconventional or new values. (See also **economic liberals; economic conservatives; cultural [social] conservatives; libertarian; populist.**)

de facto discrimination Discrimination on the basis of race, sex, religion, ethnicity, and the like that results from social, economic, and cultural biases and conditions. (See also **de jure discrimination.**)

de jure discrimination Discrimination on the basis of race, sex, religion, ethnicity, and the like that results from a law. (See also **de facto discrimination.**)

decision A vote of the Supreme Court in a particular case that indicates which party the justices side with and by how large a margin.

delegate Elected representative whose obligation is to act in accordance with the expressed wishes of the people he or she represents. (See also **trustee.**)

demand-side economics A form of fiscal policy that emphasizes "demand" (consumer spending). Government can use increased spending or tax cuts to place more money in consumers' hands and thereby increase demand. (See also **fiscal policy; supply-side economics.**)

democracy A form of government in which the people govern, either directly or through elected representatives.

demographic representativeness The idea that the bureaucracy will be more responsive to the public if its employees at all levels are demographically representative of the population as a whole.

denials of power A constitutional means of limiting governmental action by listing those powers that government is expressly prohibited from using.

deregulation The rescinding of excessive government regulations for the purpose of improving economic efficiency.

devolution The passing down of authority from the national government to the state and local governments.

direction (of an opinion) An opinion dimension that refers to whether people have a pro or con opinion on an issue.

dissenting opinion The opinion of a justice in a Supreme Court case that explains his or her reasons for disagreeing with the majority's decision. (See also **concurring opinion; majority opinion; plurality opinion.**)

dual federalism A doctrine based on the idea that a precise separation of national power and state power is both possible and desirable.

due process clause (of the Fourteenth Amendment) The clause of the Constitution that has been used by the judiciary to apply Bill of Rights protections to the actions of state governments.

economic conservatives Those who believe government tries to do too many things that should be left to private interests and economic markets. (See also **economic liberals; cultural [social] liberals; cultural [social] conservatives; libertarian; populist.**)

economic depression A very severe and sustained economic downturn. Depressions are rare in the United States: The last one was in the 1930s.

economic efficiency An economic principle holding that firms should fulfill as many of society's needs as possible while using as few of its resources as possible. The greater the output (production) for a given input (for example, an hour of labor), the more efficient the process.

economic equity The situation in which the outcome of an economic transaction is fair to each party. An outcome can usually be considered fair if each party enters into a transaction freely and is not unknowingly at a disadvantage.

economic globalization The increased interdependence of nations' economies. The change is a result of technological, transportation, and communication advances that have enabled firms to deploy their resources across the globe.

economic groups Interest groups that are organized primarily for economic reasons but that engage in political activity in order to seek favorable policies from government. (See also **citizens' [noneconomic] groups; interest group.**)

economic liberals Those who believe government should do more to assist people who have difficulty meeting their economic needs on their own. (See also **economic conservatives; cultural [social] liberals; cultural [social] conservatives; libertarian; populist.**)

economic recession A moderate but sustained downturn in the economy. Recessions are part of the economy's normal cycle of ups and downs.

economy A system for the exchange of goods and services between the producers of those goods and services and the consumers of them.

Electoral College An unofficial term that refers to the electors who cast the states' electoral votes.

electoral votes The method of voting used to choose the U.S. president. Each state has the same number of electoral votes as it has members in Congress (House and Senate combined). By tradition, electoral voting is tied to a state's popular voting. The candidate with the most popular votes in a state (or, in a few states, the most votes in a congressional district) receives its electoral votes.

elitism The notion that wealthy and well-connected individuals exercise power over certain areas of public policy.

entitlement program Any of a number of individual benefit programs, such as Social Security, that require government to provide a designated benefit to any person who meets the legally defined criteria for eligibility.

enumerated (expressed) powers The 17 powers granted to the national government under Article I, Section 8 of the Constitution. These powers include taxation and the regulation of commerce as well as the authority to provide for the national defense.

equal rights (civil rights) The right of every person to equal protection under the laws and equal access to society's opportunities and public facilities.

equal-protection clause A clause of the Fourteenth Amendment that forbids any state to deny equal protection of the laws to any individual within its jurisdiction.

equality The notion that all individuals are equal in their moral worth and are thereby entitled to equal treatment under the law.

equality of opportunity The idea that all individuals should be given an equal chance to succeed on their own.

establishment clause The First Amendment provision stating that government may not favor one religion over another or favor religion over no religion, and prohibiting Congress from passing laws respecting the establishment of religion.

exclusionary rule The legal principle that government is prohibited from using in trials evidence that was obtained by unconstitutional means (for example, illegal search and seizure).

externalities Burdens that society incurs when firms fail to pay the full costs of production. An example of an externality is the pollution that results when corporations dump industrial wastes into lakes and rivers.

facts (of a court case) The relevant circumstances of a legal dispute or offense as determined by a trial court. The facts of a case are crucial because they help determine which law or laws are applicable in the case.

federalism A governmental system in which authority is divided between two sovereign levels of government: national and regional. (See also **confederacy; unitary system.**)

Federalists A term used to describe supporters of the Constitution during the debate over ratification.

filibuster A procedural tactic in the U.S. Senate whereby a minority of legislators prevents a bill from coming to a vote by holding the floor and talking until the majority gives in and the bill is withdrawn from consideration. (See also **cloture.**)

fiscal federalism A term that refers to the expenditure of federal funds on programs run in part through states and localities.

fiscal policy A tool of economic management by which government can attempt to maintain a stable economy through its taxing and spending policies. (See also **demand-side economics; monetary policy; supply-side economics.**)

formalized rules A basic principle of bureaucracy that refers to the standardized procedures and established regulations by which a bureaucracy conducts its operations. (See also **bureaucracy.**)

framing The process by which the media play up certain aspects of a situation while downplaying other aspects, thereby providing a particular interpretation of the situation.

free trade The condition in which tariffs and other barriers to trade between nations are kept to a minimum.

free-exercise clause A First Amendment provision that prohibits the government from interfering with the practice of religion.

free-market system An economic system based on the idea that government should interfere with economic transactions as little as possible. Free enterprise and self-reliance are the collective and individual principles that underpin free markets.

free-rider problem The situation in which the benefits offered by a group to its members are also available to nonmembers. The incentive to join the group and to promote its cause is reduced because nonmembers (free riders) receive the benefits (for example, a cleaner environment) without having to pay any of the group's costs. (See also **collective [public] goods.**)

freedom of expression Americans' freedom to communicate their views, the foundation of which is the First Amendment rights of freedom of conscience, speech, press, assembly, and petition.

gender gap The tendency of white women and men to differ in their political attitudes and voting preferences.

gerrymandering The process by which the party in power draws election district boundaries in a way that enhances the reelection prospects of its candidates.

good faith exception The legal principle that otherwise excludable evidence can be admitted in trial if police believed they were following proper procedures.

government corporations Government bodies, such as the U.S. Postal Service and Amtrak, that are similar to private corporations in that they charge for their services but differ in that they receive federal funding to help defray expenses. Their directors are appointed by the president with Senate approval.

grants of power The method of limiting the U.S. government by confining its scope of authority to those powers expressly granted in the Constitution.

grants-in-aid Federal cash payments to states and localities for programs they administer.

grassroots party A political party organized at the level of the voters and dependent on their support for its strength.

Great Compromise The agreement of the constitutional convention to create a two-chamber Congress with the House apportioned by population and the Senate apportioned equally by state.

hard money Campaign funds given directly to candidates to spend as they choose.

hierarchical authority A basic principle of bureaucracy that refers to the chain of command within an organization whereby officials and units have control over those below them. (See also **bureaucracy.**)

high-choice media system A media system in which audiences have such a wide range of choices that they can largely control the type of information to which they are exposed.

honeymoon period The president's first months in office, a time when Congress, the press, and the public are more inclined than usual to support presidential initiatives.

ideology A general belief about the role and purpose of government.

imminent lawless action test A legal test that says government cannot lawfully suppress advocacy that promotes lawless action unless such advocacy is aimed at producing, and is likely to produce, imminent lawless action.

implied powers The federal government's constitutional authority (through the "necessary and proper" clause) to take action that is not expressly authorized by the Constitution but that supports actions that are so authorized. (See also **"necessary and proper" clause [elastic clause].**)

in-kind benefit A government benefit that is a cash equivalent, such as food stamps or rent vouchers. This form of benefit ensures that recipients will use public assistance in a specified way.

inalienable (natural) rights Those rights that persons theoretically possessed in the state of nature, prior to the formation of governments. These rights, including those of life, liberty, and property, are considered inherent and as such are inalienable. Since government is established by people, government has the responsibility to preserve these rights.

incumbent The current holder of a particular public office.

independent agencies Bureaucratic agencies that are similar to cabinet departments but usually have a narrower area of responsibility. Each such agency is headed by a presidential appointee who is not a cabinet member. An example is the National Aeronautics and Space Administration.

individualism The idea that people should take the initiative, be self-sufficient, and accumulate the material advantages necessary for their well-being.

inevitable discovery exception The legal principle that otherwise excludable evidence can be admitted in trial if police would eventually have discovered the evidence by other means.

inflation A general increase in the average level of prices of goods and services.

inside lobbying Direct communication between organized interests and policymakers, which is based on the assumed value of close ("inside") contacts with policymakers.

intensity (of an opinion) An opinion dimension that refers to how strongly people feel about an issue.

interest group Any organization that actively seeks to influence public policy. (See also **citizens' [noneconomic] groups; economic groups.**)

internationalist The view that the country should involve itself deeply in world affairs (See also **isolationist.**)

invisible primary The critical period before the first presidential primaries and caucuses when the candidates compete for the public support, media attention, and financial contributions that can spell the difference between winning and losing once the voting begins.

iron triangle A small and informal but relatively stable group of well-positioned legislators, executives, and lobbyists who seek to promote policies beneficial to a particular interest. (See also **issue network.**)

isolationist The view that the country should deliberately avoid a large role in world affairs and instead concentrate on domestic concerns (See also **internationalist.**)

issue network An informal and relatively open network of public officials and lobbyists who come together in response to a proposed policy in an area of interest to each of them. Unlike an iron triangle, an issue network disbands after the issue is resolved. (See also **iron triangle.**)

job specialization A basic principle of bureaucracy holding that the responsibilities of each job position should be defined explicitly and that a precise division of labor within the organization should be maintained. (See also **bureaucracy.**)

judicial activism The doctrine that the courts should develop new legal principles when judges see a compelling need, even if this action places them in conflict with precedent or the policy decisions of elected officials. (See also **judicial restraint.**)

judicial restraint The doctrine that the judiciary should broadly defer to precedent and the judgment of legislatures. The doctrine claims that the job of judges is to work within the confines of laws set down by tradition and lawmaking majorities. (See also **judicial activism.**)

judicial review The power of courts to decide whether a governmental institution has acted within its constitutional powers and, if not, to declare its action null and void.

jurisdiction (of a congressional committee) The policy area in which a particular congressional committee is authorized to act.

jurisdiction (of a court) A given court's authority to hear cases of a particular kind. Jurisdiction may be original or appellate. (See also **appellate jurisdiction; original jurisdiction.**)

laissez-faire economics A classic economic philosophy holding that owners of business should be allowed to make their own production and distribution decisions without government regulation or control.

law (as enacted by Congress) A legislative proposal, or bill, that is passed by both the House and the Senate and is not vetoed by the president. (See also **bill.**)

lawmaking function The authority (of a legislature) to make the laws necessary to carry out the government's powers. (See also **oversight function; representation function.**)

legal action The use of courts of law as a means by which individuals protect their rights and settle their conflicts.

Lemon test A three-part test to determine whether a law relating to religion is valid under the religious establishment clause. To be valid, a law must have a secure purpose, serve neither to advance nor inhibit religion, and avoid excessive government entanglement with religion.

libel Publication of false material that damages a person's reputation.

libertarian The term to describe those who believe government tries to do too many things that should be left to firms and markets, and who oppose government as an instrument for upholding traditional values. (See also **economic liberals; economic conservatives; cultural [social] liberals; cultural [social] conservatives; populist.**)

liberty The principle that individuals should be free to act and think as they choose, provided they do not infringe unreasonably on the rights and freedoms of others.

limited government A government that is subject to strict limits on its lawful uses of power and, hence, on its ability to deprive people of their liberty.

linkage institution An institution that serves to connect citizens with government. Linkage institutions include elections, political parties, interest groups, and the media.

lobbying The process by which interest group members or lobbyists attempt to influence public policy through contacts with public officials.

majoritarianism The idea that the majority prevails not only in elections but also in determining policy.

majority opinion A court opinion that results when a majority of the justices is in agreement on the legal basis of the decision. (See also **concurring opinion; dissenting opinion; plurality opinion.**)

means test The requirement that applicants for public assistance must demonstrate they are poor in order to be eligible for the assistance. (See also **public assistance.**)

median voter theorem The theory that parties in a two-party system can maximize their vote by locating themselves at the position of the median voter—the voter whose preferences are exactly in the middle.

merit system An approach to managing the bureaucracy whereby people are appointed to government positions on the basis of either competitive examinations or special qualifications, such as professional training. (See also **patronage system.**)

midterm election The congressional election that occurs midway through the president's term of office.

military-industrial complex The three components (the military establishment, the industries that manufacture weapons, and the members of Congress from states and districts that depend heavily on the arms industry) that mutually benefit from a high level of defense spending.

momentum (in campaigns) A strong showing by a candidate in early presidential nominating contests, which leads to a buildup of public support for the candidate.

monetary policy A tool of economic management based on manipulation of the amount of money in circulation. (See also **fiscal policy.**)

money chase A term used to describe the fact that U.S. campaigns are very expensive and candidates must spend a great amount of time raising funds in order to compete successfully.

multilateralism The situation in which nations act together in response to problems and crises.

multiparty system A system in which three or more political parties have the capacity to gain control of government separately or in coalition.

mutually assured destruction (MAD) The assumption that any nation will be deterred from launching a full-scale nuclear attack on the United States by the knowledge that, even if it destroyed the United States, it too would be destroyed.

national debt The total cumulative amount that the U.S. government owes to creditors.

nationalization The process by which authority in the American federal system has shifted gradually from the states to the national government.

"necessary and proper" clause (elastic clause) The authority granted Congress in Article I, Section 8 of the Constitution "to make all laws which shall be necessary and proper" for the implementation of its enumerated powers. (See also **implied powers.**)

neutral competence The administrative objective of a merit-based bureaucracy. Such a bureaucracy should be "competent" in the sense that its employees are hired and retained on the basis of their expertise and "neutral" in the sense that it operates by objective standards rather than partisan ones.

New Jersey (small-state) Plan A constitutional proposal for a strengthened Congress but one in which each state would have a single vote, thus granting a small state the same legislative power as a larger state.

news The news media's version of reality, usually with an emphasis on timely, dramatic, and compelling events and developments.

news media (press) Print, broadcast, cable, and Internet organizations that are in the news-reporting business.

nomination The designation of a particular individual to run as a political party's candidate (its "nominee") in the general election.

objective journalism A model of news reporting that is based on the communication of "facts" rather than opinions and that is "fair" in that it presents all sides of partisan debate. (See also **partisan press.**)

open party caucuses Meetings at which a party's candidates for nomination are voted on and that are open to all the party's rank-and-file voters who want to attend.

open-seat election An election in which there is no incumbent in the race.

opinion (of a court) A court's written explanation of its decision, which serves to inform others of the legal basis for the decision. Supreme Court opinions are expected to guide the decisions of lower courts. (See also **concurring opinion; dissenting opinion; majority opinion; plurality opinion.**)

original jurisdiction The authority of a given court to be the first court to hear a case. (See also **appellate jurisdiction.**)

outside lobbying A form of lobbying in which an interest group seeks to use public pressure as a means of influencing officials.

oversight function A supervisory activity of Congress that centers on its constitutional responsibility to see that the executive carries out the laws faithfully. (See also **lawmaking function; representation function.**)

packaging (of a candidate) A term of modern campaigning that refers to the process of recasting a candidate's record into an appealing image.

partisan function Efforts by media actors to influence public response to a particular party, leader, issue, or viewpoint.

partisan press Newspapers and other communication media that openly support a political party and whose news tends to follow the party line. (See also **objective journalism.**)

party caucus A group that consists of a party's members in the House or Senate and that serves to elect the party's leadership, set policy goals, and plan party strategy.

party coalition The groups and interests that support a political party.

party competition A process in which conflict over society's goals is transformed by political parties into electoral competition in which the winner gains the power to govern.

party identification The personal sense of loyalty that an individual may feel toward a particular political party. (See also **party realignment.**)

party leaders Members of the House and Senate who are chosen by the Democratic or Republican caucus in each chamber to represent the party's interests in that chamber and who give some central direction to the chamber's work.

party organizations The party organizational units at national, state, and local levels; their influence has decreased over time because of many factors. (See also **candidate-centered campaigns; party-centered campaigns; primary election.**)

party (partisan) polarization The condition in which opinions and actions in response to political issues and situations divide substantially along political party lines.

party realignment An election or set of elections in which the electorate responds strongly to an extraordinarily powerful issue that has disrupted the established political order. A realignment has a lasting impact on public policy, popular support for the parties, and the composition of the party coalitions. (See also **party identification.**)

party unity The degree to which a party's House or Senate members act as a unified group to exert collective control over legislative action.

party-centered campaigns Election campaigns and other political processes in which political parties, not individual candidates, hold most of the initiative and influence. (See also **candidate-centered campaigns.**)

patronage system An approach to managing the bureaucracy whereby people are appointed to important government positions as a reward for political services they have rendered and because of their partisan loyalty. (See also **merit system; spoils system.**)

plain view exception The legal principle that otherwise excludable evidence can be admitted in trial if discovered in plain sight in the process of arresting a suspect for another infraction.

pluralism A theory of American politics that holds that society's interests are substantially represented through the activities of groups.

plurality (winner-take-all) system An electoral system in which the candidate who gets the most votes (the plurality) in an election district is elected to office from that district.

plurality opinion A court opinion that results when a majority of justices agrees on a decision in a case but does not agree on the legal basis for the decision. In this instance, the legal position held by most of the justices on the winning side is called a plurality opinion. (See also **concurring opinion; dissenting opinion; majority opinion.**)

policy implementation The primary function of the bureaucracy; it refers to the process of carrying out the authoritative decisions of Congress, the president, and the courts.

political action committee (PAC) The organization through which an interest group raises and distributes funds for election purposes. By law, the funds must be raised through voluntary contributions.

political culture The characteristic and deep-seated beliefs of a particular people.

political (social) movements Active and sustained efforts to achieve social and political change by groups of people who feel that government has not been properly responsive to their concerns.

political participation Involvement in activities intended to influence public policy and leadership, such as voting, joining political groups, contacting elected officials, demonstrating for political causes, and giving money to political candidates.

political party An ongoing coalition of interests joined together to try to get their candidates for public office elected under a common label.

political science The systematic study of government and politics.

political socialization The learning process by which people acquire their political opinions, beliefs, and values.

politics The process through which a society settles its conflicts.

population In a public opinion poll, the people (for example, the citizens of a nation) whose opinions are being estimated through interviews with a sample of these people.

populist The term to describe those who believe government should do more to assist people who have difficulty meeting their economic needs and who look to government to uphold traditional values. (See also **economic liberals; economic conservatives; cultural [social] liberals; cultural [social] conservatives; libertarian.**)

pork (pork-barrel spending) Spending whose tangible benefits are targeted at a particular legislator's constituency.

poverty line As defined by the federal government, the annual cost of a thrifty food budget for an urban family of four, multiplied by three to allow also for the cost of housing, clothes, and other expenses. Families below the poverty line are considered poor and are eligible for certain forms of public assistance.

power The ability of persons or institutions to control policy. (See also **authority.**)

precedent A judicial decision that serves as a rule for settling subsequent cases of a similar nature.

preemptive war doctrine The idea, espoused by President George W. Bush, that the United States could attack a potentially threatening nation even if the threat had not yet reached a serious and immediate level.

presidential approval ratings A measure of the degree to which the public approves or disapproves of the president's performance in office.

presidential commissions Organizations within the bureaucracy that are headed by commissioners appointed by the president. An example is the Commission on Civil Rights.

primary election (direct primary) A form of election in which voters choose a party's nominees for public office. In most states, eligibility to vote in a primary election is limited to voters who designated themselves as party members when they registered to vote.

prior restraint Government prohibition of speech or publication before the fact, which is presumed by the courts to be unconstitutional unless the justification for it is overwhelming.

private (individual) goods Benefits that a group (most often an economic group) can grant directly and exclusively to individual members of the group. (See also **collective [public] goods.**)

procedural due process The constitutional requirement that government must follow proper legal procedures before a person can be legitimately punished for an alleged offense.

progressive income tax A tax on personal income in which the tax rate increases as income increases; in other words, the tax rate is higher for higher income levels.

proportional representation system A form of representation in which seats in the legislature are allocated proportionally according to each political party's share of the popular vote. This system enables smaller parties to compete successfully for seats. (See also **single-member districts.**)

protectionism The placing of the immediate interests of domestic producers (through, for example, protective tariffs) above that of free trade between nations.

public assistance A term that refers to social welfare programs funded through general tax revenues and available only to those in financial need. Eligibility for such a program is established by a means test. (See also **means test; social insurance.**)

public opinion The politically relevant opinions held by ordinary citizens that they express openly.

public opinion poll A device for measuring public opinion whereby a relatively small number of individuals (the sample) is interviewed for the purpose of estimating the opinions of a whole community (the population). (See also **sample.**)

public policies Decisions by government to pursue particular courses of action.

reapportionment The reallocation of House seats among states after each census as a result of population changes.

reasonable-basis test A test applied by courts to laws that treat individuals unequally. Such a law may be deemed constitutional if its purpose is held to be "reasonably" related to a legitimate government interest.

redistricting The process of altering election districts in order to make them as nearly equal in population as possible. Redistricting takes place every 10 years, after each population census.

registration The practice of placing citizens' names on an official list of voters before they are eligible to exercise their right to vote.

regulation A term that refers to government restrictions on the economic practices of private firms.

regulatory agencies Administrative units, such as the Securities and Exchange Commission (SEC) and the Environmental Protection Agency (EPA), that have responsibility for monitoring and regulating ongoing economic activities and regulating industrial pollution, respectively.

representation function The responsibility of a legislature to represent various interests in society. (See also **lawmaking function; oversight function.**)

representative government A government in which the people govern through the selection of their representatives.

republic A form of government in which the people's representatives decide policy through institutions structured in ways that foster deliberation, slow the progress of decision making, and operate within restraints that protect individual liberty. To the framers, the Constitution's separation of powers and other limits on power were defining features of a republican form of government, as opposed to a democratic form, which places no limits on the majority.

reserved powers The powers granted to the states under the Tenth Amendment to the Constitution.

right of privacy A right implied by the freedoms in the Bill of Rights that grants individuals a degree of personal privacy upon which government cannot lawfully intrude. The right gives individuals a level of free choice in areas such as reproduction and intimate relations.

rule-making The process by which bureaucratic agencies develop and make known the details on how legislation will be implemented. Rule-making is a main source of bureaucratic power.

salience (of an opinion) An opinion dimension that refers to how highly people rank an issue relative to other issues.

sample In a public opinion poll, the relatively small number of individuals who are interviewed for the purpose of estimating the opinions of an entire population. (See also **public opinion poll.**)

sampling error A measure of the accuracy of a public opinion poll; mainly a function of sample size and usually expressed in percentage terms.

selective incorporation The process by which certain of the rights (for example, freedom of speech) contained in the Bill of Rights become applicable through the Fourteenth Amendment to actions by the state governments.

self-government The principle that the people are the ultimate source and proper beneficiary of governing authority; in practice, a government based on majority rule.

Senior Executive Service (SES) Top-level career civil servants who qualify through a competitive process to receive higher salaries than their peers but who can be assigned or transferred by order of the president.

seniority A member of Congress's consecutive years of service on a particular committee.

separated institutions sharing power The principle that, as a way to limit government, its powers should be divided among separate branches, each of which also shares in the power of the others as a means of checking and balancing them. The result is that no one branch can exercise power decisively without the support or acquiescence of the others.

separation of powers The division of the powers of government among separate institutions or branches.

service strategy Use of personal staff by members of Congress to perform services for constituents in order to gain their support in future elections.

signaling (signaler) function The responsibility of the media to alert the public to important developments as soon as possible after they happen or are discovered. (See also **common-carrier function; partisan function; watchdog function.**)

single-member districts The form of representation in which only the candidate who gets the most votes in a district wins office. (See also **proportional representation system.**)

slander Spoken falsehoods that damage a person's reputation.

social capital The sum of the face-to-face interactions among citizens in a society.

social contract A voluntary agreement by individuals to form a government that is then obligated to work within the confines of that agreement.

social insurance Social welfare programs are based on the "insurance" concept, requiring that individuals pay into the program in order to be eligible to receive funds from it. An example is Social Security for retired people. (See also **public assistance.**)

soft power An approach that places emphasis on diplomacy, economic sanctions, and foreign aid as the means of protecting U.S. interests, in contrast with the use of military force, or *hard power*.

sovereignty The supreme (or ultimate) authority to govern within a certain geographic area.

spoils system The practice of granting public office to individuals in return for political favors they have rendered. (See also **patronage system**.)

standing committees Permanent congressional committees with responsibility for a particular area of public policy. An example is the Senate Foreign Relations Committee.

stewardship theory A theory that argues for a strong, assertive presidential role, with presidential authority limited only at points specifically prohibited by law. (See also **Whig theory**.)

strict-scrutiny test A test applied by courts to laws that attempt a racial or an ethnic classification. In effect, the strict-scrutiny test eliminates race or ethnicity as legal classification when it places minority-group members at a disadvantage. (See also **suspect classifications**.)

suffrage The right to vote.

super PACs Election committees that are unrestricted in their fundraising and spending as long as they do not coordinate their campaign efforts with that of a candidate.

supply-side economics A form of fiscal policy that emphasizes "supply" (production). An example of supply-side economics would be a tax cut for business. (See also **demand-side economics; fiscal policy**.)

supremacy clause Article VI of the Constitution, which makes national law supreme over state law when the national government is acting within its constitutional limits.

suspect classifications Legal classifications, such as race and national origin, that have invidious discrimination as their purpose and therefore are unconstitutional. (See also **strict-scrutiny test**.)

symbolic speech Action (for example, the waving or burning of a flag) for the purpose of expressing a political opinion.

tariffs The taxes that a country levies on goods shipped into it from other countries.

Three-Fifths Compromise A compromise worked out at the 1787 convention between northern states and southern states. Each slave was to be counted as three-fifths of a person for purposes of federal taxation and congressional apportionment (number of seats in the House of Representative).

transnational terrorism Terrorism that transcends national borders and often targets people and locations other than the ones directly at issue.

trustee Elected representative whose obligation is to act in accordance with his or her own conscience as to what policies are in the best interests of the public. (See also **delegate**.)

two-party system A system in which only two political parties have a real chance of acquiring control of the government.

tyranny of the majority The potential of a majority to monopolize power for its own gain and to the detriment of minority rights and interests.

unilateralism The situation in which one nation takes action against another state or states.

unipolar (power structure) A power structure dominated by a single powerful actor, as in the case of the United States after the collapse of the Soviet Union.

unit rule The rule that grants all of a state's electoral votes to the candidate who receives most of the popular votes in the state.

unitary system A governmental system in which the national government alone has sovereign (ultimate) authority. (See also **confederacy; federalism**.)

veto The president's rejection of a bill, thereby keeping it from becoming law unless Congress overrides the veto.

Virginia (large-state) Plan A constitutional proposal for a strong Congress with two chambers, both of which would be based on numerical representation, thus granting more power to the larger states.

voter turnout The proportion of persons of voting age who actually vote in a given election.

watchdog function The accepted responsibility of the media to protect the public from incompetent or corrupt officials by standing ready to expose any official who violates accepted legal, ethical, or performance standards. (See also **common-carrier function; partisan function; signaling [signaler] function.**)

Whig theory A theory that prevailed in the nineteenth century and held that the presidency was a limited or restrained office whose occupant was confined to expressly granted constitutional authority. (See also **stewardship theory.**)

whistleblowing An internal check on the bureaucracy whereby employees report instances of mismanagement that they observe.

White House Office (WHO) A subunit of the Executive Office of the President, the White House Office is the core of the presidential staff system in that it includes the president's closest and most trusted personal advisers.

writ of certiorari Permission granted by a higher court to allow a losing party in a legal case to bring the case before it for a ruling; when such a writ is requested of the U.S. Supreme Court, four of the Court's nine justices must agree to accept the case before it is granted certiorari.

NOTES

CHAPTER ONE

[1] John Stuart Mill, *On Liberty,* ed. Michael B. Mathias and Daniel Kolak (New York: Longman, 2006), 43.

[2] Faiz Siddiqui and Susan Svrluga, "N.C. man told police he went to D.C. pizzeria with gun to investigate conspiracy theory," *Washington Post,* December 5, 2016. https://www.washingtonpost.com/news/local/wp/2016/12/04/d-c-police-respond-to-report-of-a-man-with-a-gun-at-comet-ping-pong-restaurant/?utm_term=.c1b46f58145a

[3] Kathy Frankovic, "Belief in Conspiracies Depends Largely on Political Identity," *YouGov,* December, 27 2016, https://today.yougov.com/news/2016/12/27/belief-conspiracies-largely-depends-political-iden/

[4] American Council of Trustees and Alumni, "A Crisis in Civic Education," 2016, https://www.goacta.org/images/download/A_Crisis_in_Civic_Education.pdf.

[5] Given the increase in polls in recent years, it could be argued that the greater incidence of misinformation in recent years is a methodological artifact. That explanation, however, ignores the recent changes in the information system and in politics and society that foster a heightened level of misinformation.

[6] FBI statistics for 2005–2105 for actual crime trend. Gallup poll, 2015, for what the public believes the trend has been.

[7] Tim Marcin, "Trump Won the Popular Vote, Nearly Half His Voters, Republicans Falsely Believe: Poll," *Newsweek,* July 26, 2017, http://www.newsweek.com/trump-won-popular-vote-half-voters-believe-poll-642284.

[8] Elise Viebeck, "Poll: Four in 10 Believe in Obama Healthcare Law 'Death Panels'," *The Hill,* September, 26, 2012, http://thehill.com/policy/healthcare/258753-poll-four-in-10-believe-in-health-law-death-panels.

[9] YouGov poll, March 4–5, 2013.

[10] Glenn Kessler, "No, China Does Not Hold More Than 50 Percent of U.S. Debt," *Washington Post,* December 29, 2014, https://www.washingtonpost.com/news/fact-checker/wp/2014/12/29/no-china-does-not-hold-more-than-50-percent-of-u-s-debt/.

[11] "Social Security," *Gallup,* October, 2015, http://news.gallup.com/poll/1693/social-security.aspx.

[12] Political scientists agree on the public's low level of information but disagree on the severity of the problem. Some have interpreted the evidence as indicating widespread political ignorance. Others have argued that survey questions that test respondents on their factual information are a flawed indicator of the public's political awareness. It is safe to conclude, however, that policy awareness is not the public's strong suit. For opposing views on the question of how much the public knows, see Bruce Ackerman and James Fishkin, *Deliberation Day* (New Haven, CT.: Yale University Press, 2004), 5, and Christopher Achen and Larry Bartels, *Democracy for Realists: Why Elections Do Not Produce Responsive Government* (Princeton, NJ: Princeton University Press, 2016).

[13] James David Barber, "Characters in the Campaign," in *Race for the Presidency,* ed. James David Barber, (Englewood Cliffs, N.J.: Prentice-Hall, 1978), 181.

[14] Stephen Engelberg, "Open Your Mind," *American Journalism Review,* March 1999.

[15] Scott Althaus, "Free Falls, High Dives, and the Future of Democratic Accountability." In *The Politics of News/The News of Politics, 2nd ed.* Doris Graber, Denis McQuail, and Pippa Norris, eds. (Washington, D.C.: Congressional Quarterly Press, 2007), 185.

[16] Mark Bauerlein, *The Dumbest Generation* (New York: Penguin, 2008), 28.

[17] John Stuart Mill, *On Liberty*, eds. Michael B. Mathias and Daniel Kolak (New York: Longman, 2006), 35.

[18] Craig Silverman and Jeremy Singer-Vine, "Most Americans Who See Fake News Believe It, New Survey Says," *BuzzFeedNews,* December 6, 2016. https://www.buzzfeed.com/craigsilverman/fake-news-survey?utm_term=.ydDv9710w#.ybgmW1LKD

[19] Ipsos poll, conducted for *BuzzFeed News,* December 2016. https://www.buzzfeed.com/

craigsilverman/fake-news-survey?utm_term=.
yalDJemVa#.kwLvOnxa5

[20]Josh Pasek, Gaurav Sood, and Jon A. Krosnick, "Misinformed About the Affordable Care Act? Leveraging Certainty to Assess the Prevalence of Misperceptions," *Journal of Communication* 60 (2015): 660-673; see also, Matthew Levendusky, *Clearer cues, more consistent voters. Political Behavior,* (Chicago, IL: University of Chicago Press, 2009), 111–131; Rune Slothuus and Claes H. de Vreese, "Political parties, motivated reasoning, and issue framing effects," *The Journal of Politics* 72, no. 3 (2009): 630–645.

[21]Derek Thompson, "Where Did All the Workers Go? 60 Years of Economic Change in 1 Graph," *The Atlantic,* January 26, 2012, https://www. theatlantic.com/business/archive/2012/01/ where-did-all-the-workers-go-60-years-of-economic-change-in-1-graph/252018/.

[22]See, for example, Raymond Nickerson, "Confirmation Bias: A Ubiquitous Phenomenon in Many Guises," *Review of General Psychology* 2 (1998): 175–220.

[23]Kathy Francovic, "Belief in Conspiracies Largely Depends on Political Identity," *YouGov,* December 2016, https://today.yougov.com/ news/2016/12/27/belief-conspiracies-largely-depends-political-iden/.

[24]Ben Smith, "More Than Half of Democrats Believed Bush Knew," *Politico,* April 22, 2011, http://www.politico.com/blogs/ben-smith/2011/04/more-than-half-of-democrats-believed-bush-knew-035224.

[25]Kurt Anderson, "How America Lost Its Mind," *The Atlantic,* September 2017, https:// www.theatlantic.com/magazine/archive/2017/09/how-america-lost-its-mind/534231/.

[26]"What You Know Depends on What You Watch," *Farleigh Dickinson University's Public Mind Poll,* May 2012, http://publicmind.fdu. edu/2012/confirmed/. At the bottom in terms of knowledge were regular consumers of talk radio and cable outlets that feature talk shows.

[27]See Michael Foley, *American Credo: The Place of Ideas in American Politics* (New York: Oxford University Press, 2007).

[28]James Bryce, *The American Commonwealth,* vol. 2 (New York: Macmillan, 1960), 247–54. First published in 1900.

[29]Bryce, *The American Commonwealth,* 132.

[30]Louis Hartz, *The Liberal Tradition in America* (New York: Harcourt, Brace, 1952), 12.

[31]Alexis de Tocqueville, *Democracy in America,* vol. 2 (New York: Vintage Classics, 1990), 89.

[32]Bryce, *The American Commonwealth,* 182.

[33]T. J. Mathews & Anne K. Driscoll, "Trends in Infant Mortality in the United States, 2005–2014," Centers for Disease Control, March 2017, https://www.cdc.gov/nchs/products/databriefs/ db279.htm.

[34]Quoted in Ralph Volney Harlow, *The Growth of the United States,* vol. 2 (New York: Henry Holt, 1943), 497.

[35]Pew Research Center poll, April, 2015.

[36]Michelangelo Landgrave and Alex Nowrasteh, "Criminal Immigrants: Their Numbers, Demographics, and Countries of Origin," Cato Institute, March 15, 2017. https://www.cato. org/publications/immigration-reform-bulletin/ criminal-immigrants-their-numbers-demographics-countries

[37]*Tinker v. Colwell,* 193 U.S. 473 (1904).

[38]Martin Luther King Jr., speech at civil rights march on Washington, August 28, 1963.

[39]William Watts and Lloyd A. Free, eds., *The State of the Nation* (New York: University Books, Potomac Associates, 1967), 131.

[40]Harold D. Lasswell, *Politics: Who Gets What, When, How* (New York: McGraw-Hill, 1936).

[41]Russell Hardin, *Liberalism, Constitutionalism, and Democracy* (New York: Oxford University Press, 1999).

[42]Foucault's phrasing was a deliberate inversion of von Clausewitz's famous line, "War is politics by other means." Foucault is not the only writer who has applied this inversion.

[43]Bin Liang and Hong Lu, "Internet Development, Censorship, and Cyber Crimes in China," *Journal of Contemporary Criminal Justice* 26 (2010): 103–20.

[44]Adam Przworski and José María Maravall, eds., *Democracy and the Rule of Law* (New York: Cambridge University Press, 2003).

[45]See Robert Dahl, *On Democracy* (New Haven, Conn.: Yale University Press, 2000).

[46]Washington Post-ABC News poll June 2-4, 2017.

[47]Seymour Martin Lipset, *American Exceptionalism: A Double-Edged Sword* (New York: Norton, 1996), 37.

[48]*Gideon v. Wainwright,* 372 U.S. 335 (1963).

[49]Figures are for 2014.

[50]See William G. Domhoff, *Who Rules America? Challenges to Corporate and Class Dominance,* 7th ed. (New York: McGraw-Hill, 2013).

[51]C. Wright Mills, *The Power Elite* (New York: Oxford University Press, 1965).

[52]See Joseph A. Schumpeter, *Capitalism, Socialism and Democracy* (New York: Harper, 1975).

[53]E. E. Schattschneider, *Two Hundred Million Americans in Search of a Government* (New York: Holt, Reinhart and Winston, 1969), 42.

CHAPTER TWO

[1]Quoted in Charles S. Hyneman, "Republican Government in America," in George J. Graham Jr. and Scarlett G. Graham, eds., *Founding Principles of American Government,* rev. ed. (Chatham, N.J.: Chatham House, 1984), 19.

[2]See John Harmon McElroy, *American Beliefs: What Keeps a Big Country and a Diverse People United* (Chicago: I. R. Dee, 1999).

[3]See Russell Hardin, *Liberalism, Constitutionalism, and Democracy* (New York: Oxford University Press, 1999); A. John Simmons, *The Lockean Theory of Rights* (Princeton, N.J.: Princeton University Press, 1994).

[4]Thomas Hobbes, *Leviathan* (1651).

[5]John Locke, *Second Treatise on Civil Government* (1690).

[6]Quoted in "The Constitution and Slavery," Digital History website, December 1, 2003.

[7]Speech of Melancton Smith at the New York Constitutional Ratifying Convention, June 20, 1788. http://teachingamericanhistory.org/library/document/melancton-smith-new-york-ratifying-convention/

[8]Gaillard Hunt, ed., *The Writings of James Madison,* New York: Putnam, 1904, 274.

[9]See Vincent Ostrom, *The Political Theory of a Compound Republic: Designing the American Experiment* (Lanham, Md.: Lexington Books, 2007).

[10]See *Federalist* Nos. 47 and 48.

[11]Richard Neustadt, *Presidential Power* (New York: Macmillan, 1986), 33.

[12]Henry J. Abraham, *The Judicial Process,* 6th ed. (New York: Oxford University Press, 1993), 320–22.

[13]*Marbury v. Madison,* 1 Cranch 137 (1803).

[14]Martin Diamond, *The Founding of the Democratic Republic* (Itasca, Ill.: Peacock, 1981), 62–71.

[15]*Federalist* No. 10.

[16]Leslie F. Goldstein, "Judicial Review and Democratic Theory: Guardian Democracy vs. Representative Democracy," *Western Political Quarterly* 40 (1987): 391–412.

[17]See Douglas Bradburn, *The Citizenship Revolution: Politics and the Creation of the American Union 1774-1804* (Charlottesville: University of Virginia Press, 2009).

[18]Benjamin Ginsberg, *The Consequences of Consent* (New York: Random House, 1982), 22.

[19]Robert Dahl, *Pluralist Democracy in the United States* (Chicago: Rand McNally, 1967), 92.

[20]This interpretation is taken from Walter Lippmann, *Public Opinion* (New York: Free Press, 1965), 178–79.

[21]Michael McGeer, *A Fierce Discontent: The Rise and Fall of the Progressive Movement in America, 1870-1920* (New York: Free Press, 2005).

[22]Charles S. Beard, *An Economic Interpretation of the Constitution* (New York: Macmillan, 1941). First published in 1913.

[23]John M. Scheb and John M. Scheb II, *Introduction to the American Legal System* (Clifton Park, N.Y.: Delmar Cengage Learning System, 2001), 6.

[24]See Randall G. Holcombe, *From Liberty to Democracy* (Ann Arbor: University of Michigan Press, 2002).

CHAPTER THREE

[1]Woodrow Wilson, *Constitutional Government in the United States.* New York: Columbia University Press, 1908, 173.

[2]*Printz v. United States*, 521 U.S. 898 (1997).

[3]*National Federation of Independent Business v. Sebelius*, 567 U.S. 510 (2012); see also, *South Dakota v. Dole*, 483 U.S. 203 (1987).

[4]See Samuel Beer, *To Make a Nation* (Cambridge, Ma: The Belknap Press of Harvard, 1984).

[5]Antifederalist No. 9. This essay appeared in the *Independent Gazetteer* on October 17, 1787, under the pen name "Montezuma."

[6]Alison L. LaCroix, *The Ideological Origins of American Federalism* (Cambridge, Mass.: Harvard University Press, 2010).

[7]The process by which authority in the American federal system has shifted gradually from the states to the national government.

[8]*McCulloch v. Maryland,* 4 Wheaton 316 (1819).

[9]*Gibbons v. Ogden,* 22 Wheaton 1 (1824). [22 U.S. 1 (1824)].

[10]Oliver Wendell Holmes Jr., *Collected Legal Papers* (New York: Harcourt, Brace, 1920), 295–96.

[11]See John C. Calhoun, *The Works of John C. Calhoun* (New York: Russell & Russell, 1968).

[12]*Dred Scott v. Sanford,* 19 Howard 393 (1857).

[13]*U.S. v. Cruikshank,* 92 U.S. 452 (1876).

[14]*Slaughter-House Cases,* 16 Wallace 36 (1873); *Civil Rights Cases,* 109 U.S. 3 (1883).

[15]*Plessy v. Ferguson,* 163 U.S. 537 (1896).

[16]See, for example, Douglas A. Blackmon, *Slavery by Another Name: The Re-Enslavement of Black America from the Civil War to World War II* (New York: Anchor Books, 2009).

[17]*Santa Clara County v. Southern Pacific Railroad Co.,* 118 U.S. 394 (1886).

[18]*U.S. v. E. C. Knight Co.,* 156 U.S. 1 (1895).

[19]*Hammer v. Dagenhart,* 247 U.S. 251 (1918).

[20]*Lochner v. New York,* 198 U.S. 25 (1905).

[21]Alfred H. Kelly, Winifred A. Harbison, and Herman Belz, *The American Constitution,* 7th ed. (New York: Norton, 1991), 529; but also see Kimberley Johnson, *Governing the American State: Congress and the New Federalism, 1877–1929* (Princeton, N.J.: Princeton University Press, 2006).

[22]James E. Anderson, *The Emergence of the Modern Regulatory State* (Washington, D.C.: Public Affairs Press, 1962), 2–3.

[23]*Schechter Poultry Corp. v. United States,* 295 U.S. 495 (1935).

[24]*NLRB v. Jones and Laughlin Steel,* 301 U.S. 1 (1937).

[25]*American Power and Light v. Securities and Exchange Commission,* 329 U.S. 90 (1946).

[26]Louis Fisher, *American Constitutional Law,* 6th ed. (Durham, N.C.: Carolina Academic Press, 2005), 390.

[27]*North American Company v. Securities and Exchange Commission,* 327 U.S. 686 (1946).

[28]*United States v. Butler,* 297 U.S. 1 (1936).

[29]As will be discussed in Chapter 5, the Supreme Court also altered the constitutional doctrine of federalism in the area of civil rights. The two-race system upheld in the *Plessy* decision was struck down in 1954 as a violation of the Fourteenth Amendment's equal protection clause.

[30]See Thomas Anton, *American Federalism and Public Policy* (Philadelphia: Temple University Press, 1989).

[31]Morton Grodzins, *The American System: A New View of Government in the United States* (Chicago: Rand McNally, 1966).

[32]John D. Nugent, *Safeguarding Federalism: How States Protect Their Interests in National Policymaking* (Norman: University of Oklahoma Press, 2009).

[33]Rosella Levaggi, *Fiscal Federalism and Grants-in-Aid* (Brookfield, Vt.: Avebury, 1991).

[34]Beth Fouhy, "GOP Governors Press Congress to Pass Stimulus Bill," *Associated Press wire story,* January 31, 2009.

[35]Timothy J. Conlan, *From New Federalism to Devolution* (Washington, D.C.: Brookings Institution, 1998).

[36]The Supreme Court played a role in devolution by retreating somewhat from its New Deal-era ruling that Congress's commerce power is "as broad as the needs of the nation." In *United States v. Lopez* (1995), the Court cited the Tenth Amendment in striking down a federal law banning the possession of guns within a thousand feet of a school. The Court ruled that the ban had "nothing to do with commerce, or any sort of economic activity." The Court then applied the Eleventh Amendment (which protects a state from being sued in federal court by a private citizen without its consent) to limit Congress's authority. In *Kimmel v. Board of Regents* (2000), the Court held that state government employees cannot sue their state for violating federal age-discrimination policies. The Court ruled that states have the authority to decide the retirement age of their own employees.

[37]Andrew W. Dobelstein, *Politics, Economics, and Public Welfare* (Englewood Cliffs, N.J.: Prentice-Hall, 1980), 5.

[38]Lloyd A. Free and Hadley Cantril, *The Political Beliefs of Americans* (New York: Simon & Schuster, 1968), 21.

[39]Survey for the Times Mirror Center for the People and the Press by Princeton Survey Research Associates, July 12–27, 1994.

CHAPTER FOUR

[1]Julian P. Boyd, ed., *The Papers of Thomas Jefferson,* vol. 12 (Princeton, N.J.: Princeton University Press, 1955), 440.

[2]*United States v. Jones,* No. 10-1250 (2012).

[3]*Barron v. Baltimore,* 32 U.S. (7 Pet.) 243 (1833).

[4]*Gitlow v. New York,* 268 U.S. 652, 1925.

[5]*Fiske v. Kansas,* 274 U.S. 30 (1927); *Near v. Minnesota,* 283 U.S. 697 (1931); *Hamilton v. Regents, U. of California,* 293 U.S. 245 (1934); *DeJonge v. Oregon,* 299 U.S. 253 (1937).

[6]*Near v. Minnesota,* 283 U.S. 697 (1931).

[7]*Mapp v. Ohio,* 367 U.S. 643 (1961).

[8]*Gideon v. Wainright,* 372 U.S. 335 (1963).

[9]*Malloy v. Hogan,* 378 U.S. 1 (1964).

[10]*Miranda v. Arizona,* 384 U.S. 436 (1966); see also *Escobedo v. Illinois,* 378 U.S. 478 (1964).

[11]*Pointer v. Texas,* 380 U.S. 400 (1965).

[12]*Klopfer v. North Carolina,* 386 U.S. 213 (1967).

[13]*Duncan v. Louisiana,* 391 U.S. 145 (1968).

[14]*Benton v. Maryland,* 395 U.S. 784 (1969).

[15]Although the Supreme Court has categorically excluded child pornography from First Amendment protection, it has struggled otherwise to develop a legal test for determining whether sexual material is obscene. It has said that such material must be of a "particularly offensive type" and must be perceived as such by a "reasonable person," but in practice the Court has had trouble applying that standard, or any other, in determining the sexually explicit material that adults are not allowed to produce, see, or possess.

[16]*Schenck v. United States,* 249 U.S. 47 (1919).

[17]*Dennis v. United States,* 341 U.S. 494, 1951.

[18]See, for example, *Yates v. United States,* 354 U.S. 298 (1957); *Noto v. United States,* 367 U.S. 290 (1961); *Scales v. United States,* 367 U.S. 203 (1961).

[19]*Brandenburg v. Ohio,* 395 U.S. 444 (1969).

[20]*R.A.V. v. St. Paul,* No. 90-7675 (1992).

[21]*Wisconsin v. Mitchell,* No. 92-515 (1993).

[22]*Snyder v. Phelps,* No. 09-7571 (2011).

[23]*Texas v. Johnson,* 109 S. Ct. 2544, 1989.

[24]*National Socialist Party v. Skokie,* 432 U.S. 43 (1977).

[25]*Forsyth County v. Nationalist Movement,* No. 91-538 (1992).

[26]*New York Times Co. v. United States,* 403 U.S. 713 (1971).

[27]*Nebraska Press Assn. v. Stuart,* 427 U.S. 539 (1976).

[28]*Milkovich v. Lorain Journal,* 497 U.S. 1 (1990); see also *Masson v. The New Yorker,* No. 89-1799 (1991).

[29]*New York Times Co. v. Sullivan,* 376 U.S. 254 (1964).

[30]*Engel v. Vitale,* 370 U.S. 421 (1962).

[31]*Abington School District v. Schempp,* 374 U.S. 203 (1963).

[32]*Wallace v. Jaffree,* 472 U.S. 38 (1985).

[33]*Van Orden v. Perry,* No. 03-1500 (2005).

[34]Ibid.

[35]*Lemon v. Kurtzman,* 403 U.S. 602 (1971).

[36]*Board of Regents v. Allen,* 392 U.S. 236 (1968).

[37]*Zelman v. Simmons-Harris,* No. 00-1751 (2002); see also *Locke v. Davey,* No. 02-1315 (2004).

[38]*Burwell v. Hobby Lobby Stores,* No. 13-354 (2014).

[39]*Masterpiece Cakeshop v. Colorado Civil Rights Commission,* No. 16-111 (2018).

[40]*Edwards v. Aguillard,* 487 U.S. 578 (1987).

[41]*District of Columbia v. Heller,* 554 U.S. 570, 2008.

[42]*McDonald v. Chicago,* 561 U.S. 3025 (2010).

[43]*Griswold v. Connecticut,* 381 U.S. 479, 1965.

[44]*Roe v. Wade,* 401 U.S. 113 (1973).

[45]*Webster v. Reproductive Health Services,* 492 U.S. 490 (1989); see also *Rust v. Sullivan,* No. 89-1391 (1991).

[46]*Planned Parenthood v. Casey,* No. 91-744 (1992).

[47]*Gonzales v. Carhart,* 550 U.S. 124 (2007)

[48]*Whole Woman's Health v. Hellerstedt,* No. 15-274, 2016.

[49]*Bowers v. Hardwick,* 478 U.S. 186 (1986).

[50]*Lawrence v. Texas,* 539 U.S. 558 (2003).

[51]*McNabb v. United States,* 318 U.S. 332 (1943).

[52]The structure and content of the discussion that follows on arrest, search, interrogation, formal charge, trial, appeal, and punishment is informed by Walter F. Murphy and Michael N. Danielson, *Robert K. Carr and Marver H. Bernstein's American Democracy* (Hinsdale, Ill.: Dryden Press, 1977), 465–74.

[53]David Fellman, *The Defendant's Rights Today* Madison: University of Wisconsin Press, 1979, 256.

[54]*Kyllo v. United States,* No. 99-8508 (2001), 533 U.S. 27 (2010).

[55]*Riley v. California,* No. 13-132, 2014.

[56]*Carpenter v. United States,* No. 16-402 (2018).

[57]*Board of Education of Independent School District No. 92 of Pottawatomie County v. Earls,* No. 01-332 (2002).

[58]*Michigan v. Sitz,* No. 88-1897 (1990).

[59]*Indianapolis v. Edmund,* No. 99-1030 (2001).

[60]*Miranda v. Arizona,* 384 U.S. 436 (1966).

[61]*Missouri v. Siebert,* 542 U.S. 600 (2004).

[62]*Johnson v. Zerbst,* 304 U.S. 458 (1938).

[63] *Gideon v. Wainwright,* 372 U.S. 335 (1963).

[64] *Batson v. Kentucky,* 476 U.S. 79 (1986).

[65] *Witherspoon v. Illinois,* 391 U.S. 510 (1968).

[66] *Weeks v. United States,* 232 U.S. 383, 1914.

[67] *United States v. Leon,* 468 U.S. 897 (1984).

[68] *Nix v. Williams,* 467 U.S. 431, 1984.

[69] *Whren v. United States,* 517 U.S. 806 (1996).

[70] *Horton v. California,* 496 U.S. 128 (1990).

[71] *Lockyer v. Andrade,* No. 01-1127 (2003); see also *Ewing v. California,* No. 01-6978 (2003).

[72] *Atkins v. Virginia,* No. 01-8452 (2002).

[73] *Montgomery v. Louisiana,* No. 14-280 (2016).

[74] *Townsend v. Sain,* 372 U.S. 293 (1963).

[75] *Williams v. Taylor,* No. 99-6615 (2000).

[76] See, for example, National Institute of Justice, "Racial Profiling and Traffic Stops," January 10, 2013, www.nij.gov/topics/law-enforcement/legitimacy/pages/traffic-stops.aspx.

[77] Charles Lane, "In Terror War, 2nd Track for Suspects," *The Washington Post,* December 1, 2001, A1.

[78] *Korematsu v. United States,* 323 U.S. 214 (1944).

[79] *Rasul v. Bush,* No. 03-334 (2004); *al-Odah v. United States,* No. 03-343 (2004).

[80] *Hamdi v. Rumsfeld,* No. 03-6696, 2004.

[81] *Hamdan v. Rumsfeld,* No. 05-184 (2006).

[82] See Alpheus T. Mason, *The Supreme Court: Palladium of Freedom* (Ann Arbor: University of Michigan Press, 1962); see also Jeffrey Rosen, *The Most Democratic Branch: How the Courts Serve America* (New York: Oxford University Press, 2006).

CHAPTER FIVE

[1] Abraham Lincoln, "Speech on the Dred Scott Decision," Springfield, Illinois, June 26, 1857.

[2] *The Washington Post* wire story, May 14, 1991.

[3] Robert Nisbet, "Public Opinion versus Popular Opinion," *Public Interest* 41 (1975): 171.

[4] *Plessy v. Ferguson,* 163 U.S. 537 (1896).

[5] Ada Lois Sipuel Fisher, Danney Gable, and Robert Henry, *A Matter of Black and White: The Autobiography of Ada Lois Sipuel Fisher* (Norman: University of Oklahoma Press, 1996).

[6] *Brown v. Board of Education* of Topeka, 347 U.S. 483, 1954

[7] *Swann v. Charlotte-Mecklenburg County Board of Education,* 402 U.S. 1 (1971).

[8] Christopher Jencks and Meredith Phillips, eds., *The Black-White Test Score Gap* (Washington, D.C.: Brookings Institution, 1998).

[9] *Milliken v. Bradley,* 418 U.S. 717 (1974).

[10] *Parents Involved in Community Schools v. Seattle,* No. 05-908551 U.S. 701 (2007); *Meredith, Custodial Parent and Next Friend of McDonald v. Jefferson County Board of Education,* No. 05-915548 U.S. 938 (2007).

[11] Grover J. "Russ" Whitehurst, Richard V. Reeves, and Edward Rodrigues, "Segregation, Race, and Charter Schools," Center on Children and Families, Brookings Institution, October 2016, pp. 23-26.

[12] *Loving v. Virginia,* 388 U.S. 1 (1967).

[13] *Craig v. Boren,* 429 U.S. 190 (1976).

[14] *Rostker v. Goldberg,* 453 U.S. 57 (1980).

[15] *United States v. Virginia,* 518 U.S. 515 (1996), No. 94-1941 (1996).

[16] NBC/Marist poll, December 2014.

[17] "Findings," Stanford Open Policing Project, 2018. https://openpolicing.stanford.edu/findings/

[18] "Criminal Justice Facts," Sentencing Project, 2018. https://www.sentencingproject.org/criminal-justice-facts/

[19] National Office of Drug Control Policy, U.S. Department of Justice, 1997.

[20] Michael J. Klarman, *From Jim Crow to Civil Rights: The Supreme Court and the Struggle for Racial Equality* (New York: Oxford University Press, 2004), 236.

[21] *Smith v. Allwright,* 321 U.S. 649 (1944).

[22] *Oregon v. Mitchell,* 400 U.S. 112 (1970).

[23] *Shelby County v. Holder,* No. 12-96 (2013).

[24] *Cooper v. Harris,* 136 S. Ct. 2512 (2017).

[25] See Manny Fernandez, "Study Finds Disparities in Mortgages by Race," *The New York Times,* October 15, 2007; see also U.S. Conference of Mayors report, 1998; Survey by Federal Financial Institutions Examination Council, 1998.

[26] "Public Backs Affirmative Action, But Not Minority Preferences," Pew Research Center report, June 2, 2009, Web release.

[27] *University of California Regents v. Bakke,* 438 U.S. 265 (1978).

[28] *Adarand v. Peña,* 515 U.S. 200 (1995). This decision reversed an earlier ruling, *Fullilove v. Klutnick,* 448 U.S. 448 (1980).

[29] *Grutter v. Bollinger,* 539 U.S. 306 (2003).

[30] *Fisher v. University of Texas,* No. 14-981 (2016).

[31] See, for example, Gloria J. Browne-Marshall, *Race, Law, and American Society: 1607 to Present* (New York: Routledge, 2007).

[32]Douglas A. Blackmon, *Slavery by Another Name: The Re-enslavement of Black America from the Civil War to World War II* (New York: Anchor Books, 2009).

[33]Eric J. Sundquist, *King's Dream: The Legacy of Martin Luther King's "I Have a Dream" Speech* (New Haven, Conn.: Yale University Press, 2009).

[34]See, for example, Alejandro Del Carmen, *Racial Profiling in America* (Upper Saddle River, N.J.: Prentice-Hall, 2007).

[35]Sentencing Project, "Report of The Sentencing Project to the United Nations Human Rights Committee Regarding Racial Disparities in the United States Criminal Justice System," August 2013. http://sentencingproject.org/wp-content/uploads/2015/12/Race-and-Justice-Shadow-Report-ICCPR.pdf.

[36]See Keith Reeves, *Voting Hopes or Fears?* (New York: Oxford University Press, 1997); Tali Mendelberg, *The Race Card* (Princeton, N.J.: Princeton University Press, 2001); Juliet Eilperin, "What's Changed for African Americans since 1963, by the Numbers," *Washington Post*, August 22, 2013.

[37]See Kathleen S. Sullivan, *Women and Rights Discourse in Nineteenth-Century America* (Baltimore, Md.: Johns Hopkins University Press, 2007).

[38]*Tinker v. Colwell,* 193 U.S. 473 (1904).

[39]See Jane Mansbridge, *Why We Lost the ERA* (Chicago: University of Chicago Press, 1986).

[40]U.S. Department of Education, National Center for Education Statistics, 2017.

[41]See Sara M. Evans and Barbara Nelson, *Wage Justice* (Chicago: University of Chicago Press, 1989).

[42]Jennifer L. Lawless and Richard L. Fox, *It Takes a Candidate: Why Women Don't Run for Office* (New York: Cambridge University Press, 2005).

[43]Marshall Ganz, *Why David Sometimes Wins: Leadership, Organization and Strategy in the California Farm Worker Movement* (New York: Oxford University Press, 2009).

[44]Fox News poll, September 2017.

[45]Eric C. Henson et al., *The State of the Native Nations: Conditions under U.S. Policies of Self-Determination* (New York: Oxford University Press, 2007).

[46]See David E. Wilkins, *American Indian Politics and the American Political System* (Lanham, Md.: Rowman & Littlefield, 2006).

[47]William Evans and Julie Topoleski, *The Social and Economic Impact of Native American Casinos,* NBER Working Paper No. 9198 (Cambridge, Mass.: National Bureau of Economic Research, September 2002).

[48]W. Dale Mason, "Tribes and States: A New Era in Intergovernmental Affairs," *Publius* 28 (1998): 129.

[49]Data from U.S. Census Bureau, 2018, and Office of Minority Health, U.S. Department of Health and Human Services, 2018.

[50]*Lau v. Nichols,* 414 U.S. 563 (1974).

[51]See Timothy P. Fong, *Contemporary Asian American Experience: Beyond the Model Minority* (Upper Saddle River, N.J.: Prentice-Hall, 2009).

[52]Scott Jaschik, "The Numbers and the Arguments on Asian Admissions," *Inside Higher Ed*, August 7, 2017 . https://www.insidehighered.com/admissions/article/2017/08/07/look-data-and-arguments-about-asian-americans-and-admissions-elite

[53]Stefanie K. Johnson and Thomas Sy, "Why Aren't There More Asian Americans in Leadership Positions?," *Harvard Business Review*, December 19, 2016. https://hbr.org/2016/12/why-arent-there-more-asian-americans-in-leadership-positions

[54]See Gordon Chang, ed., *Asian Americans and Politics* (Stanford, Calif.: Stanford University Press, 2001).

[55]*Kimel v. Florida Board of Regents,* No. 98-791528 U.S. 62 (2000); but see *CBOCS West, Inc. v. Humphries,* No. 06-1431553 U.S. 442 (2008).

[56]*Board of Trustees of the University of Alabama v. Garrett,* No. 99-1240 (2002); *Tennessee v. Lane,* No. 02-1667541 U.S. 509 (2004).

[57]*Obergefell v. Hodges,* 576 U.S. No. 14-556 (2015).

[58]Gunnar Myrdal, *An American Dilemma: The Negro Problem and Modern Democracy* (New York: Harper, 1944).

[59]See Joe R. Feagin, *The White Racial Frame: Centuries of Racial Framing and Counter-Framing* (New York: Routledge, 2009).

CHAPTER SIX

[1]Bryce, James, *The American Commonwealth*, vol. 2, (Indianapolis, Ind.: Liberty Fund, 1995, 225. First published in 1888).

[2]Quinnipiac University poll, February 2018.

[3]Noelle-Neumann, Elisabeth, *The Spiral of Silence*, 2d ed., (Chicago: University of Chicago Press, 1993, ch. 1).

[4]See, for example, Dean R. Hoge and Teresa L. Ankney, "Occupations and Attitudes of Student Activists Ten Years Later," *Journal of Youth and Adolescence* 11 (1982): 365.

[5]See Herbert Asher, *Polling and the Public*, 7th ed. (Washington, D.C.: CQ Press, 2007).

[6]NBC/Wall Street Journal poll, January 17, 2018.

[7]"If polls say people want gun control, why doesn't Congress just pass it?" *Associated Press*, March 7, 2018. https://wtop.com/national/2018/03/if-polls-say-people-want-gun-control-why-doesnt-congress-just-pass-it/

[8]Seth Stevens-Davidowitz, *Everybody Lies: Big Data, New Data, and What the Internet Can Tell Us about Who We Really Are* (New York: Dey St., 2017), 7–9.

[9]Morning Consult/Politico poll, August 2017

[10]Pew Research Center polls, July 2015 and August 2016.

[11]Bradley Jones, "Support for free trade agreements rebounds modestly, but wide partisan differences remain," Pew Research Center, April 25, 2017. http://www.pewresearch.org/fact-tank/2017/04/25/support-for-free-trade-agreements-rebounds-modestly-but-wide-partisan-differences-remain/

[12]Herbert Hyman, *Political Socialization* (Glencoe, Ill.: Free Press, 1959), 51.

[13]M. Kent Jennings and Richard G. Niemi, *Generations and Politics* (Princeton, N.J.: Princeton University Press, 1981).

[14]See Orit Ichilov, *Political Socialization, Citizenship Education, and Democracy* (New York: Teachers College Press, 1990).

[15]See, however, Dietram A. Scheufele, Matthew C. Nisbet, and Dominique Brossard, "Pathways to Political Participation: Religion, Communication Contexts, and Mass Media," *International Journal of Public Opinion Research* 15 (Autumn 2003): 300–24; Michele F. Margolis, *From Politics to the Pews* (Chicago: University of Chicago Press, 2018).

[16]Noelle-Neumann, *Spiral of Silence*.

[17]Walter Lippmann, *Public Opinion* (New York: Free Press, 1965), ch. 1.

[18]Thomas E. Patterson, *The Vanishing Voter* (New York: Knopf, 2003), 89–90.

[19]Jon Western, *Selling Intervention and War: The Presidency, the Media, and the American Public* (Baltimore, Md.: Johns Hopkins University Press, 2005); see also Wojtek Mackiewicz Wolfe, *Winning the War of Words:* *Selling the War on Terror from Afghanistan to Iraq* (Westport, Conn.: Praeger, 2008).

[20]See, for example, Kristi Andersen, *The Creation of a Democratic Majority, 1928–1936* (Chicago: University of Chicago Press, 1979).

[21]Ronald J. Inglehart, "How much should we worry?" *Journal of Democracy*, 27 (2016): 18. http://pscourses.ucsd.edu/ps200b/Inglehart%20How%20Much%20SHould%20we%20Worry.pdf

[22]Washington Post poll, 2002.

[23]Washington Post-University of Maryland poll, October 2017.

[24]See Angus Campbell, Philip Converse, Warren Miller, and Donald Stokes, *The American Voter* (New York: Wiley, 1960), chs. 3 and 4.

[25]Martin P. Wattenberg, *Where Have All the Voters Gone?* (Cambridge, Mass.: Harvard University Press, 2002).

[26]Meghan McCarthy, "Republican Voters Remain Loyal to Trump in First National Poll After Video," *Morning Consult*, October 9, 2016, https://morningconsult.com/2016/10/09/republican-voters-remain-loyal-trump-first-national-poll-video/.

[27]Ariel Edwards-Levy, "Trump Voters Believe Sex Allegations against Weinstein, But Not against Trump," *HuffPost*, October 20, 2017. https://www.huffingtonpost.com/entry/trump-voters-weinstein-poll_us_59ea11c9e4b0f9d35bca3fd9

[28]Donald Green, Bradley Palmquist, and Eric Schickler, *Partisan Hearts and Minds* (New Haven, Conn.: Yale University Press, 2002).

[29]Daniel Bell, *The End of Ideology* (New York: Collier, 1961), 67.

[30]Daniel Boorstin, *The Genius of American Politics* (Chicago: University of Chicago Press, 1953).

[31]Some scholars define ideology in a stricter way, arguing that it can be said to exist only when an individual has a consistent pattern of opinions across a broad range of specific issues. By this definition, most Americans don't have an ideology. This conception is analytically useful in some situations, but it blunts the discussion of general belief tendencies in the public as a whole, which is the purpose here.

[32]"Ku Klux Klan," *History*, undated. Downloaded January 2, 2018. http://www.history.com/topics/ku-klux-klan

[33]Kenneth D. Wald, *Religion and Politics in the United States* (Lanham, Md.: Rowman & Littlefield, 2003); Robert D. Putnam and David E. Campbell, *American Grace: How Religion*

Divides and Unites Us (New York: Simon & Schuster, 2012).

[34]"Changing Attitudes on Gay Marriage, Pew Research Center, June 26, 2017. http://www.pewforum.org/fact-sheet/changing-attitudes-on-gay-marriage/

[35]Arlie Russell Hochschild, *Strangers in Their Own Land* (New York: The New Press, 2016).

[36]Ibid.

[37]Lois Duke Whitaker, ed., *Voting the Gender Gap* (Urbana: University of Illinois Press, 2008).

[38]Yuval Feinstein, "The Rise and Decline of 'Gender Gaps' in Support for Military Action: United States, 1986–2011," *Gender & Society* 13 (2017): 618–655.

[39]Pew Research Center poll, June 2017.

[40]Andrew Sullivan, "America Wasn't Built for Humans," *New York Magazine*, September 19, 2017. http://nymag.com/daily/intelligencer/2017/09/can-democracy-survive-tribalism.html

[41]Christopher Achen and Larry Bartels, *Democracy for Realists: Why Elections Do Not Produce Responsive Government* (Princeton, NJ: Princeton University Press, 2016).

[42]George Gallup, "Polls and the Political Process - Past, Present, and Future," *Public Opinion Quarterly* 40 (1965): 547–548.

[43]Clinton Rossiter and James Lare, *The Essential Lippmann: A Political Philosophy for Liberal Democracy* (Cambridge, MA: Harvard University Press, 1982), 99.

[44]Robert J. Samuelson, "What If We're to Blame? Public Opinion and Muddled Policies," *The Washington Post*, November 1, 2006.

[45]Ezra Klein, "The Budget Myth That Just Won't Die: Americans Still Think 28 Percent of the Budget Goes to Foreign Aid," *The Washington Post*, November 7, 2013; Bianca DiJulio, Jamie Firth, and Mollyann Brodie, "Data Note: Americans' Views on the U.S. Role in Global Health," *Kaiser Family Foundation*, January 23, 2015.

[46]See Bruce Ackerman and James Fishkin, *Deliberation Day* (New Haven, Conn.: Yale University Press, 2004), 5; Christopher Achen and Larry Bartels, *Democracy for Realists: Why Elections Do Not Produce Responsive Government* (Princeton, NJ: Princeton University Press, 2016).

[47]See R. Michael Alvarez and John Brehm, *Hard Choices, Easy Answers* (Princeton, N.J.: Princeton University Press, 2002); see also

Samuel L. Popkin, *The Reasoning Voter* (Chicago: University of Chicago Press, 1991).

[48]Robert S. Erikson, Michael B. MacKuen, and James A. Stimson, *The Macro Polity* (New York: Cambridge University Press, 2008), xxi.

[49]Vincent Hutchings, *Public Opinion and Democratic Accountability: How Citizens Learn about Politics* (Princeton, N.J.: Princeton University Press, 2005).

[50]See, for example, Sidney Verba and Norman H. Nie, *Participation in America: Political Democracy and Social Equality* (New York: Harper & Row, 1972), 332.

[51]Martin Gilens and Benjamin I. Page, "Testing Theories of American Politics: Elites, Interest Groups, and Average Citizens," *Perspectives on Politics* 12 (2014): 564–81.

[52]Noam Chomsky and Edward S. Herman, *Manufacturing Consent: The Political Economy of the Mass Media* (New York: Pantheon, 2002); see also William Domhoff, *Who Rules America?* 5th ed. (New York: McGraw-Hill, 2005).

[53]Robert D. Benford and David A. Snow, "Framing Processes and Social Movements," *Annual Review of Sociology* 40 (2000): 611–39.

[54]Scott McClellan, *What Happened: Inside the Bush White House and Washington's Culture of Deception* (New York: Public Affairs, 2008).

[55]James Druckman and Lawrence Jacobs, *Who Governs? Presidents, Public Opinion, and Manipulation* (Chicago: University of Chicago Press, 2015).

[56]V. O. Key Jr., *Public Opinion and American Democracy* (New York: Knopf, 1964).

[57]The Editors, "Notes from the Editors," *Monthly Review* 50 (1999). https://monthlyreview.org/1999/03/01/mr-050-10-1999-03_0/

[58]Quoted in Anthony King, "Running Scared," *The Atlantic*, January 1997.

[59]David Mayhew, *Congress: The Electoral Connection* (New Haven, Conn.: Yale University Press, 2004), 5.

[60]Anthony King, *Running Scared* (New York: Free Press, 1999).

[61]David A. Fahrenthold, Rosalind S. Helderman and Jenna Portnoy, "What Went Wrong for Eric Cantor," *The Washington Post*, June 11, 2014, https://www.washingtonpost.com/politics/what-went-wrong-for-eric-cantor/2014/06/11/0be7c02c-f180-11e3-914c-1fbd0614e2d4_story.html.

[62]See, for example, Benjamin I. Page and Robert Y. Shapiro, "Effects of Public Opinion

on Policy," *American Political Science Review* 77 (March 1983): 178; Richard Sobel, *The Impact of Public Opinion on U.S. Foreign Policy* (New York: Oxford University Press, 2001); James Stimson, *Tides of Consent: How Public Opinion Shapes American Politics* (New York: Cambridge University Press, 2004); Jeff Manza and Fay Lomax Cook, "A Democratic Polity: Three Views of Policy Responsiveness to Public Opinion in the United States," *American Politics Research* 30 (2002): 630–67; John W. Kingdon, *Agendas, Alternatives, and Public Policies*, 2d ed. (New York: Longman, 2003), 148–49.

CHAPTER SEVEN

[1] Walter Lippmann, *Public Opinion* (New York: Free Press, 1965), 36.

[2] Quoted in Ralph Volney Harlow, *The Growth of the United States* (New York: Henry Holt, 1943), 312.

[3] See Mark N. Franklin, *Voter Turnout and the Dynamics of Electoral Competition in Established Democracies since 1945* (New York: Cambridge University Press, 2004).

[4] Thomas E. Patterson, *The Vanishing Voter* (New York: Knopf, 2002), 134.

[5] Ibid.

[6] Russell Dalton, "The Myth of the Disengaged American," Web publication of the Comparative Study of Electoral Systems, October 2005, 2.

[7] *Crawford et al. v. Marion County Election Board et al.,* No. 07-21 (2008).

[8] Michael Wines and Alan Blinder, "Voter ID Laws Take a Beating in U.S. Courts," *New York Times,* July 30, 2016, p. 1.

[9] Ivor Crewe, "Electoral Participation," in David Butler, Howard R. Penniman, and Austin Ranney, eds., *Democracy at the Polls* (Washington, D.C.: American Enterprise Institute, 1981), 251–53.

[10] Richard Boyd, "Decline of U.S. Voter Turnout," *American Politics Quarterly* 9 (April 1981): 142.

[11] Kevin McSpadden, "You Now Have a Shorter Attention Span Than a Goldfish," *Time,* May 14, 2015. http://time.com/3858309/attention-spans-goldfish/

[12] Patterson, *Vanishing Voter*, 135.

[13] For an overview of minority group voting in the 2016 election, see William H. Frey, "Census shows pervasive decline in 2016 minority voter turnout," Brookings Institution, May 18, 2017. https://www.brookings.edu/blog/the-avenue/2017/05/18/census-shows-pervasive-decline-in-2016-minority-voter-turnout/

[14] Russell J. Dalton, "The Myth of the Disengaged American," CSES Report, October 25, 2005.

[15] Clare Foran, "Bernie Sanders's Big Money," *The Atlantic*, March 2016.

[16] Quoted in Ken Thomas, "Sanders Campaign Endorsed by MoveOn.org," Associated Press wire story, January 12, 2016.

[17] U.S. Department of Labor statistics, 2016.

[18] Dalton, "Myth of the Disengaged American," 2.

[19] See Benjamin Ginsberg, *The Consequences of Consent* (New York: Random House, 1982), ch. 2.

[20] See, for example, Charles J. Stewart, Craig Allen Smith, and Robert E. Denton Jr., *Persuasion and Social Movements*, 5th ed. (Long Grove, Ill.: Waveland Press, 2007).

[21] Sidney Tarrow, *Power in Movement* (New York: Cambridge University Press, 1998).

[22] William Watts and Lloyd A. Free, eds., *The State of the Nation* (New York: University Books, Potomac Associates, 1967), 97.

[23] Sidney Verba and Norman Nie, *Participation in America* (New York: Harper & Row, 1972), 131.

[24] Larry M. Bartels, *Unequal Democracy*, 2nd ed. (Princeton, NJ: Princeton University Press, 2016).

CHAPTER EIGHT

[1] E. E. Schattschneider, *Party Government* (New York: Rinehart, 1942), 1.

[2] See John Aldrich, *Why Parties? The Origin and Transformation of Political Parties in America* (Chicago: University of Chicago Press, 1995); L. Sandy Maisel, *American Political Parties and Elections* (New York: Oxford University Press, 2007).

[3] E. E. Schattschneider, *The Semisovereign People: A Realist's View of Democracy in America* (New York: Holt, Rinehart & Winston, 1961), 140.

[4] Thomas E. Patterson, *The Vanishing Voter* (New York: Knopf, 2002), ch. 2.

[5] See Richard P. McCormick, *The Second American Party System: Party Formation in the Jacksonian Era* (Chapel Hill: University of North Carolina Press, 1966).

[6] Alexis de Tocqueville, *Democracy in America (1835–1840),* eds. J. P. Mayer and A. P. Kerr (Garden City, N.Y.: Doubleday/Anchor, 1969), 60.

[7]Aldrich, *Why Parties?* 151.

[8]Kristi Andersen, *The Creation of a Democratic Majority, 1928-1936* (Chicago: University of Chicago Press, 1979).

[9]See Kevin Phillips, *The Emerging Republican Majority* (New Rochelle, N.Y.: Arlington House, 1969).

[10]See Arthur C. Paulson, *Electoral Realignment and the Outlook for American Democracy* (Boston: Northeastern University Press, 2006).

[11]Richard M. Scammon and Ben J. Wattenberg, *The Real Majority* (New York: Coward-McCann, 1970).

[12]James E. Campbell, *Polarized: Making Sense of a Divided America.* (Princeton, NJ: Princeton University Press, 2016).

[13]See, for example, Salil D. Benegal and Lyle A. Scruggs, "Correcting misinformation about climate change," *Climate Change,* 147 (2018): 1–20. https://link.springer.com/journal/10584

[14]Lewis L. Gould, *Grand Old Party* (New York: Random House, 2003); but also see Jacob S. Hacker and Paul Pierson, *Off Center: The Republican Revolution and the Erosion of American Democracy* (New Haven, Conn.: Yale University Press, 2006).

[15]Lydia Saad, "Republicans', Dems' Abortion Views Grow More Polarized," Gallup, http://news.gallup.com/poll/126374/republicans-dems-abortion-views-grow-polarized.aspx.

[16]Lydia Saad, "US Abortion Attitudes Stable; No Consensus on Legality," *Gallup,* May, 2017. http://www.gallup.com/poll/211901/abortion-attitudes-stable-noconsensus-legality.aspx.

[17]Riley E. Dunlap, "Climate-Change Views: Republican-Democratic Gaps Expand," *Gallup,* May, http://news.gallup.com/poll/107569/climatechange-views-republicandemocratic-gaps-expand.aspx; Lydia Saad and Jeffrey Jones, "U.S. Concern About Global Warming at Eight-Year High," *Gallup,* March, 2016, http://news.gallup.com/poll/190010/concern-global-warming-eight-year-high.aspx.

[18]Art Swift, "In U.S., Support for Assault Weapons Ban at Record Low," *Gallup,* October, 2016, http://news.gallup.com/poll/196658/support-assault-weapons-ban-record-low.aspx.

[19]Congress data based on work of Keith Poole and Howard Rosenthal. See, https://voteviewblog.com/

[20]See Duncan Black, "On the Rationale of Group Decision-Making," *Journal of Political Economy* 56 (1948): 23–24; Anthony Downs, *An Economic Theory of Democracy* (New York: HarperCollins, 1957).

[21]Jocelyn Kiley, "In polarized era, fewer Americans hold a mix of conservative and liberal views," Pew Research Center, October 27, 2017. http://www.pewresearch.org/fact-tank/2017/10/23/in-polarized-era-fewer-americans-hold-a-mix-of-conservative-and-liberal-views/?utm_source=Pew+Research+Center&utm_campaign=0abc6f17c9-EMAIL_CAMPAIGN_2017_10_26&utm_medium=email&utm_term=0_3e953b9b70-0abc6f17c9-400267813

[22]Bill Bishop, *The Big Sort: Why the Clustering of Like-Minded America is Tearing Us Apart* (New York: Houghton Mifflin, 2008); Alan A. Abramowitz, "U.S. Senate Elections in a Polarized Era," in Burdett A. Loomis, ed., *The U.S. Senate: From Deliberation to Dysfunction* (Washington, DC: CQ Press, 2011): 27–48.

[23]2016 election exit polls.

[24]Daniel Cox and Robert Jones, "America's Changing Religious Identity," PRRI, September 6, 2017. https://www.prri.org/research/american-religious-landscape-christian-religiously-unaffiliated/

[25]American National Election Studies (ANES) surveys, 2000-2016 elections.

[26]John Green, Mark Rozell, and William Clyde Wilcox, eds., *The Christian Right in American Politics* (Washington, D.C.: Georgetown University Press, 2003).

[27]See John B. Judis and Ruy Teixeira, *The Emerging Democratic Majority* (New York: Scribner, 2002).

[28]James G. Gimpel, "Latinos and the 2002 Election: Republicans Do Well When Latinos Stay Home," Center for Immigration Studies, University of Maryland, January 2003, https://cis.org/Latinos-and-2002-Election; see also Jorge Ramos, *The Latino Wave: How Hispanics Are Transforming Politics in America* (New York: Harper Paperbacks, 2005); F. Chris Garcia and Gabriel Sanchez, *Hispanics and the U.S. Political System: Moving into the Mainstream* (Upper Saddle River, N.J.: Prentice-Hall, 2007).

[29]See, for example, Public Religion Research Institute survey, November 6–10, 2015.

[30]2016 presidential election exit polls

[31]See Lois Duke Whitaker, ed., *Voting the Gender Gap* (Urbana: University of Illinois

Press, 2008); Karen M. Kaufmann, "The Gender Gap," *PS: Political Science & Politics,* July 2006, pp. 447–53.

[32]Micah L. Sifrey, *Spoiling for a Fight: Third-Party Politics in America* (New York: Routledge, 2003).

[33]Daniel A. Mazmanian, *Third Parties in Presidential Elections* (Washington, D.C.: Brookings Institution, 1984), 143–44.

[34]Lewis L. Gould, *Four Hats in the Ring: The 1912 Election and the Birth of Modern American Politics* (Lawrence: University Press of Kansas, 2008).

[35]See Lawrence Goodwyn, *The Populist Movement* (New York: Oxford University Press, 1978).

[36]See, for example, Eli Watkins, "How Gary Johnson and Jill Stein helped elect Donald Trump," *CNN,* November 25, 2016. https://www.cnn.com/2016/11/10/politics/gary-johnson-jill-stein-spoiler/index.html

[37]See Anthony King, *Running Scared* (New York: Free Press, 1997); but see James E. Campbell, *The American Campaign: U.S. Presidential Campaigns and the National Vote* (College Station: Texas A&M Press, 2008).

[38]See Paul S. Herrnson and John C. Green, eds., *Responsible Partisanship* (Lawrence: University Press of Kansas, 2003).

[39]See Marjorie Randon Hershey, *Party Politics in America,* 17th ed. (New York: Routledge, 2017).

[40]See, Paul S. Herrnson, "The Roles of Party Organizations, Party-Connected Committees, and Party Allies in Elections," *The Journal of Politics* 71 (2009): 1207–1224

[41]Federal Election Commission, 2018.

[42]Kathleen Hall Jamieson, *Packaging The Presidency: A History and Criticism of Presidential Campaign Advertising,* 3rd ed. (New York: Oxford University Press, 1996).

[43]Darrell M. West, *Air Wars: Television Advertising in Election Campaigns, 1952–2004,* 6th ed. (Washington, D.C.: CQ Press, 2013).

[44]See, R. Douglas Arnold, *Congress, the Press, and Political Accountability* (Princeton, NJ: Princeton University Press, 2013).

[45]Thomas E. Patterson, "News Coverage of the 2016 General Election: How the Press Failed the Voters," Shorenstein Center on Media, Politics and Public Policy," Harvard Kennedy School, Harvard University, Cambridge, MA, December 7, 2016. https://shorensteincenter.org/news-coverage-2016-general-election/

[46]Quoted by Nancy Gibbs in her Theodore H. White Lecture, Harvard Kennedy School, November 15, 2017.

[47]Quoted in Andrew Gripp, "Is Television Ruining Our Political Discourse?" *IVN,* September 26, 2015. https://andrewgripp.wordpress.com/2015/09/26/is-television-ruining-our-political-discourse/

[48]Jennifer Stromer-Galley, *Presidential Campaigning in the Internet Age* (New York: Oxford University Press, 2014).

[49]Joseph Napolitan, *The Election Game and How to Win It* (New York: Doubleday, 1972); for a contemporary look at the campaigning process, see D. Sunshine Hillygus and Todd G. Shields, *The Persuadable Voter: Wedge Issues in Presidential Campaigns* (Princeton, N.J.: Princeton University Press, 2008).

[50]Federal Election Commission projection, 2018.

[51]Federal Election Commission, 2018.

[52]David B. Magleby, J. Quin Monson, and Kelly D. Patterson, eds., *Dancing without Partners: How Candidates, Parties and Interest Groups Interact in the New Campaign Finance Environment* (Provo, Utah: Brigham Young University Press, 2005).

[53]Federal Election Commission, 2018.

[54]Emmett H. Buell Jr. and Lee Sigelman, *Attack Politics: Negativity in Presidential Campaigns since 1960* (Lawrence: University Press of Kansas, 2008). For opposing views on the effect of negative advertising, see Stephen Ansolabehere and Shanto Iyengar, *Going Negative* (New York: Free Press, 1995); and John Geer, *In Defense of Negativity* (Chicago: University of Chicago Press, 2006).

[55]Darrell M. West, *Air Wars: Television Advertising in Election Campaigns, 1952–2004,* 6th ed. (Washington, D.C.: CQ Press, 2013), 140–46.

[56]See, for example, Robert Farley, "Romney's Solar Flareout," FactCheck.org, June 1, 2012, http://factcheck.org/2012/06/romneys-solar-flareout/.

[57]John Sides and Lynn Vavreck, "What Really Decided the 2012 Election, in 10 Graphs," *The Washington Post,* October 14, 2013.

[58]Brad Lockerbie, *Do Voters Look to the Future?* (Albany: State University of New York Press, 2009).

CHAPTER NINE

[1] Schattschneider, E. E., *The Semisovereign People: A Realist's View of Democracy in America*, (New York: Holt, Rinehart & Winston, 1960), 35.

[2] Megan R. Wilson, "Analysis: More than 6,000 lobbyists have worked on taxes in 2017," *The Hill*, December 1, 2017. http://thehill.com/business-a-lobbying/business-a-lobbying/362796-analysis-more-than-6000-lobbyists-have-worked-on

[3] Anthony J. Nownes, *Total Lobbying: What Lobbyists Want (and How They Try to Get It)* (New York: Cambridge University Press, 2006).

[4] See Matthew J. Burbank, Ronald J. Hrebenar, and Robert C. Benedict, *Parties, Interest Groups, and Political Campaigns* (Boulder, Colo.: Paradigm Publishers, 2008).

[5] Alexis de Tocqueville, *Democracy in America (1835-1840)*, eds. J. P. Mayer and A. P. Kerr (Garden City, N.Y.: Doubleday/Anchor, 1969), bk. 2, ch. 4.

[6] Theodoric Meyer, "Lobbyists prepare for battle royal over tax breaks," *Politico*, September 27, 2017. https://www.politico.com/story/2017/09/27/lobbyists-tax-break-battles-243237

[7] Kay Lehman Schlozman and John T. Tierney, *Organized Interests and American Democracy* (New York: Harper & Row, 1986), 54; see also Jeffrey M. Berry and Clyde Wilcox, *The Interest Group Society*, 5th ed. (New York: Longman, 2008).

[8] Herring, E. Pendleton, *Group Representation before Congress*, (Washington, D.C.: Brookings Institution, 1929), 78.

[9] U.S. Bureau of Labor Statistics, 2018.

[10] See Jack L. Walker, *Mobilizing Interest Groups in America* (Ann Arbor: University of Michigan Press, 1991).

[11] Christopher J. Bosso, "The Color of Money: Environmental Groups and the Pathologies of Fund Raising," in Allan J. Cigler and Burdett Loomis, eds., *Interest Group Politics*, 4th ed. (Washington, D.C.: CQ Press, 1995), 101-3.

[12] See Nownes, *Total Lobbying*. The author is indebted to Professor Anthony Nownes of the University of Tennessee for the observations contained in this paragraph.

[13] Arbitron Radio Research and Corporation for Public Broadcasting Financial Reports, 2015.

[14] Mancur Olson, *The Logic of Collective Action*, rev. ed. (Cambridge, Mass.: Harvard University Press, 1971), 64.

[15] Theda Skocpol, *Diminished Democracy* (Norman: University of Oklahoma Press, 2003).

[16] Olson, *Logic of Collective Action*, 147.

[17] Dylan Matthews and Alexia Fernandez Campbell, "The numbers are in, and the House Republican tax bill raises taxes on over a quarter of Americans," *Vox*, November 8, 2017. https://www.vox.com/policy-and-politics/2017/11/6/16614540/house-republican-tax-plan-paul-ryan-tax-policy-center

[18] Ibid.

[19] Jeffrey N. Birnbaum, "Washington's Power 25: Which Pressure Groups Are Best at Manipulating the Laws We Live By?" *Fortune*, December 8, 1997.

[20] Frank R. Baumgartner, Jeffrey M. Berry, Marie Hojnacki, David C. Kimball, and Beth L. Leech, *Lobbying and Policy Change: Who Wins, Who Loses, and Why* (Chicago: University of Chicago Press, 2009).

[21] Norman J. Ornstein and Shirley Elder, *Interest Groups, Lobbying, and Policymaking* (Washington, D.C.: CQ Press, 1978), 82-86.

[22] See Paul S. Herrnson, Ronald G. Shaiko, and Clyde Wilcox, *The Interest Group Connection: Electioneering, Lobbying, and Policymaking in Washington*, 2d ed. (Washington, D.C.: CQ Press, 2004).

[23] Quoted in a National Journal excerpt in Patterson, Thomas E., *The American Democracy*, 9th ed., (New York: McGraw-Hill, 2009), 245b.

[24] See John Mark Hansen, *Gaining Access* (Chicago: Chicago University Press, 1991); Bruce Wolpe and Bertram Levine, *Lobbying Congress* (Washington, D.C.: CQ Press, 1996).

[25] Center for Responsive Politics data, 2018. https://www.opensecrets.org/lobby/

[26] Bara Vaida, "K-Street Paradox: $1.3 Million Per Hour," *The National Journal*, March 13, 2010.

[27] Quoted in Ornstein and Elder, *Interest Groups, Lobbying, and Policymaking*, 77.

[28] Steve Reinberg, "Debate Builds over Drug Companies' Fees to FDA," *The Washington Post*, April 13, 2007, www.washington-post.com/wp-dyn/content/article/2007/04/13/AR2007041301449.html.

[29] Paul J. Quirk, *Industry Influence in Federal Regulatory Agencies* (Princeton, N.J.: Princeton

University Press, 1981); John E. Chubb, *Interest Groups and the Bureaucracy: The Politics of Energy* (Stanford, Calif.: Stanford University Press, 1983), 200–201.

[30]Lee Epstein and C. K. Rowland, "Interest Groups in the Courts," *American Political Science Review* 85 (1991): 205–17.

[31]Richard Davis, *Electing Justice: Fixing the Supreme Court Nomination Process* (New York: Oxford University Press, 2005).

[32]Niv M. Sultan, "Defense sector contributions locked in on committee members," *OpenSecrets. org,* March 2, 2017. https://www.opensecrets. org/news/2017/03/defense-sector-contributions/

[33]Hugh Heclo, "Issue Networks and the Executive Establishment," in Anthony King, ed., *The New American Political System* (Washington, D.C.: American Enterprise Institute, 1978), 87–124.

[34]Ornstein, Norman J., and Elder, Shirley, *Interest Groups, Lobbying, and Policymaking,* Washington, D.C.: CQ Press, 1978, 88–93.

[35]Public Citizen, "Why the Lobbying Disclosure Act Needs to Be Broadened to Include Grass-Roots Lobbying," Congress Watch, www.cleanupwashington.org/policy/page.cfm?id=7861&SectionID=108&SubSecID=1009&SecID=1407.

[36]See, for example, Gallup poll of January, 2018.

[37]Mike Spies and Ashley Balcerzak, "The NRA Placed Big Bets on the 2016 Election, and Won Almost All of Them," *OpenSecrets.org,* November 9, 2016. https://www.opensecrets.org/news/2016/11/the-nra-placed-big-bets-on-the-2016-election-and-won-almost-all-of-them/

[38]Quoted in Mark Green, "Political PAC-Man," *The New Republic,* December 13, 1982, 20; see also Richard Skinner, *More Than Money: Interest Group Action in Congressional Elections* (Lanham, Md.: Rowman & Littlefield, 2006); Mark J. Rozell, Clyde Wilcox, and David Madland, *Interest Groups in American Campaigns,* 2d ed. (Washington, D.C.: CQ Press, 2005).

[39]Jacob Pramuk, "AARP warns Republicans it has 'strong opposition' to Obamacare replacement bill," *CNBC,* May 25, 2017. https://www.cnbc.com/2017/05/25/aarp-has-strong-opposition-on-a-health-bill-that-slams-seniors.html

[40]Federal Election Commission data, 2017.

[41]Quoted in Larry Sabato, *PAC Power: Inside the World of Political Action Committees* (New York: Norton, 1984), 72.

[42]*Citizens United v. Federal Election Commission,* 558 U.S. 50 (2010).

[43]Bernie Sanders, "Overturn Citizens United," *U.S. News & World Report,* January 13, 2012, www.usnews.com/debate-club/are-super-pacs-harming-us-politics/overturn-citizens-united.

[44]Smith, Bradley, "Super PACs Level the Playing Field," *U.S. News & World Report,* January 13, 2012, www.usnews.com/debate-club/are-super-pacs-harming-us-politics/super-pacs-level-the-playing-field.

[45]Jack L. Walker, *Mobilizing Interest Groups in America* (Ann Arbor: University of Michigan Press, 1991), 112.

[46]Theodore J. Lowi, *The End of Liberalism: The Second Republic of the United States* (New York: Norton, 1979).

[47]Larry Bartels, *Unequal Democracy: The Political Economy of the New Gilded Age* (Princeton, N.J.: Princeton University Press, 2008).

[48]Martin Gilens and Benjamin I. Page, "Testing Theories of American Politics: Elites, Interest Groups, and Average Citizens," *Perspectives on Politics* 12 (2104) 564–581. http://citeseerx.ist.psu.edu/viewdoc/download;jsessionid=37EDA24D1D5DA87AEB950CEFE63883FF?doi=10.1.1.668.8647&rep=rep1&type=pdf

[49]See, for example, James A. Stimson, *Tides of Consent: How Public Opinion Shapes American Politics* (New York: Cambridge University Press, 2004).

CHAPTER TEN

[1]Theodore H. White, *The Making of the President, 1972,* (New York: Bantam Books, 1973), 327

[2]See Bill Kovach and Tom Rosenstiel, *The Elements of Journalism* (New York: Three Rivers Press, 2001).

[3]See Rodger Streitmatter, *Mightier Than the Sword: How the News Media Have Shaped American History* (Westport, Conn.: Praeger Publishers, 2008).

[4]Frank Luther Mott, *American Journalism, a History: 1690-1960* (New York: Macmillan, 1962), 114-15; see also Si Sheppard, *The Partisan Press: A History of Media Bias in the United States* (Jefferson, N.C.: McFarland, 2007).

[5]Edwin Emery, *The Press and America: An Interpretive History of the Mass Media* (Englewood Cliffs, N.J.: Prentice-Hall, 1977), 350.

[6]Quoted in Mott, *American Journalism,* 529.

[7]Quoted in David Halberstam, *The Powers That Be* (New York: Knopf, 1979), 208-9.

[8]Nancy Kranich, "The Information Commons," Brennan Center for Justice, New York University School of Law, 2004. https://www.aaup.org/sites/default/files/files/InformationCommons.pdf

[9]See, for example, Thomas E. Patterson and Robert D. McClure, *The Unseeing Eye* (New York: Putnam, 1976).

[10]For reasons that are not fully understood, conservatives have a much stronger preference for partisan talk show. According to both polling and ratings data, conservative talk show hosts dominate the partisan talk show sector. They attract roughly 90 percent of the partisan talk show audience.

[11]William Cole, ed., *The Most of A. J. Liebling* (New York: Simon, 1963), 7.

[12]See, for example, J. Sonia Huang and Wei-Ching Wang, "Application of the Long Tail Economy to the Online News Market," *Journal of Media Economics,* 27 (2014): 158-176.

[13]Matthew Hindman, *The Myth of Digital Democracy* (Princeton, NJ: Princeton University Press, 2009), 90-91.

[14]Douglas A. McIntyre, "Breitbart Audience Steady at 83 Million," *24/7 Wall Street,* September 30, 2017. https://247wallst.com/media/2017/09/30/breitbart-audience-steady-at-83-million/

[15]Zach Exley, "Black Pigeon Speaks: The Anatomy of the Worldview of an Alt-Right YouTuber," Shorenstein Center on Media, Politics, and Public Policy, Harvard Kennedy School, Harvard University, June 28, 2017. https://shorensteincenter.org/anatomy-of-alt-right-youtuber/

[16]Kathryn Watson, "Russian Bots Still Interfering in U.S. Politics after Election, Says Expert Witness," CBS News, March 30, 2017, https://www.cbsnews.com/news/russian-bots-still-interfering-in-u-s-politics-after-election-expert/.

[17]Kathleen Hall Jamieson and Karlyn Kohrs Campbell, *The Interplay of Influence,* rev. ed. (Boston: Wadsworth, 2005), 4.

[18]Donald Shaw and Maxwell McCombs, *The Emergence of American Political Issues: The Agenda-Setting Function of the Press* (St. Paul, Minn.: West Publishing, 1977).

[19]Cohen, Bernard C., *The Press and Foreign Policy,* (Princeton, N.J.: Princeton University Press, 1963), 13.

[20]Thomas E. Patterson, *The American Democracy,* 5th ed. (New York: McGraw-Hill, 2001), 309-10.

[21]See Kathleen Hall Jamieson, *Eloquence in an Electronic Age* (New York: Oxford University Press, 1988), 42.

[22]Thomas E. Patterson, "News Coverage of Donald Trump's First 100 Days," Shorenstein Center on Media, Politics and Public Policy," Harvard Kennedy School, Harvard University, Cambridge, MA, May 18, 2017. https://shorensteincenter.org/news-coverage-donald-trumps-first-100-days/

[23]Greg Prince, "Trump's Tweets Are Seen by Less Than One Percent of His Followers, Social Media Expert Claims," *Newsweek,* January 3, 2018, http://www.newsweek.com/trump-tweets-one-percent-mainstream-media-769207.

[24]Stephen J. Farnsworth and S. Robert Lichter, *The Mediated Presidency: Television News and Presidential Governance* (Lanham, Md.: Rowman & Littlefield, 2006).

[25]Kiku Adatto, *Sound Bite Democracy,* Joan Shorenstein Center on the Press, Politics, and Public Policy, Research Paper R-2, Harvard University, June 1990.

[26]Center for Media and Public Affairs studies, available at www.cmpa.com/studies.

[27]Robert Entman, "Framing: Towards Clarification of a Fractured Paradigm," in Denis McQuail, ed., *McQuail's Reader in Mass Communication Theory* (London: Sage Publications, 2002), 391-92.

[28]Thomas E. Patterson, *Out of Order* (New York: Knopf, 1993), 84.

[29]The classic study of priming is Shanto Iyengar, Mark Peters, and Donald Kinder, "Experimental Demonstrations of the "Not-So-Minimal" Consequences of Television News Programs," *The American Political Science Review* 76 (1982): 848-858.

[30]Ibid.

[31]See, for example, Joseph N. Cappella and Kathleen Hall Jamieson, *Spiral of Cynicism* (New York: Oxford University Press, 1997), 159.

[32]Amy Chozickmay, "Emails Add to Hillary Clinton's Central Problem: Voters Just Don't Trust Her," *The New York Times,* May 25, 2016, www.nytimes.com/2016/05/26/us/politics/hillary-clinton-emails-campaign-trust.html.

[33]Nicholas Confessore and Daisuke Wakabayashi, "Russians Spun American Rage Into a Weapon," *New York Times,* October 10, 2017.

[34]Sarah Sobieraj and Jeffrey M. Berry, "From Incivility to Outrage: Political Discourse in Blogs, Talk Radio, and Cable News," *Political Communication* 28(2011): 27.

[35]Ibid, 27–28.

[36]Ibid, 30.

[37]Zach Exley, "Black Pigeon Speaks: The Anatomy of the Worldview of an Alt-Right YouTuber," Shorenstein Center on Media, Politics, and Public Policy, Harvard Kennedy School, Harvard University, June 28, 2017. https://shorensteincenter.org/anatomy-of-alt-right-youtuber/

[38]See, for example, Thomas E. Patterson, News Coverage of Donald Trump's First 100 Days, Shorenstein Center on Media, Politics and Public Policy, Harvard Kennedy School, Harvard University, Cambridge, MA, May 18, 2017. https://shorensteincenter.org/news-coverage-donald-trumps-first-100-days/

[39]Bernard Goldberg, *Bias: A CBS Insider Exposes How the Media Distort News* (New York: Harper Paperbacks, 2003).

[40]David D'Alessio and Mike Allen, "Media Bias in Presidential Elections: A Meta-Analysis," *Journal of Communication* 50 (2000):133–56.

[41]Matthew Gentzkow and Jesse M. Shapiro, "What Drives Media Slant? Evidence from U.S. Daily Newspapers," *Econometrica,* 78 (2010), 35–71.

[42]Thomas E. Patterson, News Coverage of the 2016 General Election: How the Press Failed the Voters, Shorenstein Center on Media, Politics and Public Policy, Harvard Kennedy School, Harvard University, Cambridge, MA, December 7, 2016. https://shorensteincenter.org/news-coverage-2016-general-election/

[43]Michael Robinson, "Public Affairs Television and the Growth of Political Malaise," *American Political Science Review* 70 (1976): 409–32.

[44]Mark Rozell, "Press Coverage of Congress," in Thomas Mann and Norman Ornstein, eds., *Congress, the Press, and the Public* (Washington, D.C.: American Enterprise Institute and Brookings Institution, 1994), 109.

[45]Robinson, "Public Affairs Television and the Growth of Political Malaise."

[46]The press's negativity and sensationalism have had another effect as well. They have damaged the press's credibility. According to a 2007 survey conducted by the Center for Public Leadership at Harvard University's John F. Kennedy School of Government, the press has the lowest public confidence rating of any major U.S. institution.

[47]Quoted in Stephen Bates, *Realigning Journalism with Democracy: The Hutchins Commission, Its Times, and Ours* (Washington, D.C.: The Annenberg Washington Program of Northwestern University, 1995), 11.

[48]Thomas E. Patterson, "Doing Well and Doing Good," Report of the Joan Shorenstein Center on the Press, Politics, and Public Policy, Kennedy School of Government, Harvard University, December 2000, 3, http://www.hks.harvard.edu/presspol/publications/reports/soft_news_and_critical_journalism_2000.pdf.

[49]Patterson, "Doing Well and Doing Good," 3–5. See also Michele Weldon, *Everyman News: The Changing American Front Page* (Columbus: University of Missouri Press, 2007), 37; Walter C. Dean and Atiba Pertilla, "I-Teams and 'Eye Candy': The Reality of Local TV News," in Tom Rosensteil, Marion Just, Todd L. Belt, Atiba Pertilla, Walter Dean, and Dante Chinni, eds., *We Interrupt This Newscast* (New York: Cambridge University Press, 2007), 31–35; Matthew Robert Kerbel, *If It Bleeds It Leads* (New York: Basic Books, 2000).

[50]Content in this paragraph derived from Clive Irving, "The Secret of CNN's Turnaround Flight: MH 370," *The Daily Beast,* March 6, 2016, http://www.thedailybeast.com/the-secret-of-cnns-turnaround-flight-mh370.

[51]Franklin Foer, *World Without Mind: The Existential Threat of Big Tech* (New York: Penguin Press, 2017), 147. Reference to the number of users is from CrowdTangle's website.

[52]Mark Thompson, *Enough Said: What's Gone Wrong with the Language of Politics* (New York: St. Martin's Press, 2016), 106.

[53]Franklin Foer, *World Without Mind: The Existential Threat of Big Tech* (New York: Penguin Press, 2017), 139.

[54]Ben Sherlock, "Study Shows Talk Show Hosts Made 1,060 Jokes about Trump in His First

100 Days," *BlastingNews,* July 5, 2017, https://uk.blastingnews.com/showbiz-tv/2017/05/study-shows-talk-show-hosts-made-1060-jokes-about-trump-in-his-first-100-days-001679651.html.

[55]Marcus Prior, *Post-Broadcast Democracy* (New York: Cambridge University Press, 2007).

[56]Martin J. Wattenberg, *Is Voting for Young People?* (New York: Pearson Longman, 2008), 32.

[57]Editor and Publisher Yearbook data for 1975.

[58]Arbitron data for television news; Editor and Publisher Yearbook data for newspapers.

[59]"Daily time spent reading newspapers per capita in the United States from 2010 to 2018 (in minutes)," Statista. Downloaded October 24, 2017: https://www.statista.com/statistics/186934/us-newspaper-reading-habits-since-2002/

[60]Ryan Chittum, "Print Newspapers Still Dominate Readers' Attention: Another look at how much time is spent reading newspapers online and in print," *Columbia Journalism Review,* undated. Downloaded on October 31, 2017, http://archives.cjr.org/the_audit/newspapers_time_spent.php

[61]Steve Sternberg, "Will All TV Median Ages Soon Be Over 50?" *MediaPost,* April 30, 2015. https://www.mediapost.com/publications/article/248728/will-all-tv-median-ages-soon-be-over-50.html?edition=

[62]See, for example, Thomas E. Patterson, *The Mass Media Election* (New York: Praeger, 1980), 159–165.

[63]Filipe R. Campante and Daniel Hojman, "Media and Polarization," Faculty Research Working Paper Series, Harvard Kennedy School, December 2009. file:///C:/Users/tpatters/Downloads/RWP10-002-Campante-Hojman%20(1).pdf

[64]Duncan J. Watts and David M. Rothschild. "Don't blame the election on fake news. Blame it on the media," *Columbia Journalism Review,* December 5, 2017. https://www.cjr.org/analysis/fake-news-media-election-trump.php

[65]See, for example, Thomas E. Patterson, Out of Order (New York: Knopf, 1993): 53–93; Bruce Buchanan, *Renewing Presidential Politics* (Lanham, MD: Rowman & Littlefield, 1996), 149; Regina G. Lawrence and Melody Rose, *Hillary Clinton's Race for the White House:* *Gender Politics and the Media on the Campaign Trail* (Boulder, CO: Lynne Rienner Publishers, 2009),183.

[66]Thomas E. Patterson, "Of Polls, Mountains: U.S. Journalists and Their Use of Election Surveys," *Public Opinion Quarterly* 69 (2005): 716–24.

[67]Tom Rosenstiel, Carl Gottlieb, Lee Ann Brady, "Time of Peril for TV News," Project for Excellence in Journalism, 2000.

[68]Postman, Neil, *Amusing Ourselves to Death: Public Discourse in the Age of Show Business,* New York: Viking, 1985, 106.

[69]Paul Starr, "Governing in the Age of Fox News," *The Atlantic,* January/February 2010. https://www.theatlantic.com/magazine/archive/2010/01/governing-in-the-age-of-fox-news/307838/; Natalie Jomini Stroud, "Media Use and Political Predispositions: Revisiting the Concept of Selective Exposure," *Political Behavior* 30 (2008): 341–66.

[70]Pew Research Center polls, various dates.

[71]Jeffrey Gottfried, Michael Barthel, and Amy Mitchell, "Trump, Clinton Voters Divided in Their Main Source for Election News," Pew Research Center, January 18, 2017. http://www.journalism.org/2017/01/18/trump-clinton-voters-divided-in-their-main-source-for-election-news/

[72]Ibid.

[73]Kathleen Hall Jamieson and Joseph N. Cappella, *Echo Chamber* (New York: Oxford University Press, 2008), 232; various Pew Research Center survyes.

[74]Klein, Ezra, "Unpopular Mandate," *The New Yorker,* June 25, 2012, 33.

[75]"Partisanship and Political Animosity in 2016," Pew Research Center, June 2016. http://www.people-press.org/2016/06/22/partisanship-and-political-animosity-in-2016/

[76]Daniel Cox and Robert P. Jones, "Merry Christmas" vs. "Happy Holidays": Republicans and Democrats are Polar Opposites," PRRI, December 19, 2016. https://www.prri.org/research/poll-post-election-holiday-war-christmas/

[77]Diana Mutz, *In-Your-Face Politics* (Princeton, NJ: Princeton University Press, 2015).

[78]Kathleen Hall Jamieson and Joseph N. Cappella, *Echo Chamber* (New York: Oxford University Press, 2010), 195–98.

[79]Carmen Stavrositu, "Selective Exposure," in Kerric Harvey, ed., *Encyclopedia of Social Media and Politics,* (Thousand Oaks, CA: Sage Publications, 2014): 1117–1119.

[80]See, for example, Matthew Levendusky, *How Partisan Media Polarize America* (Chicago: University of Chicago Press, 2013).

[81]Michael J. Robinson, "Public Affairs Television and the Growth of Political Malaise," *American Political Science Review* 70 (1973): 409–432.

[82]Wattenberg, Martin P., *Is Voting for Young People?*, (New York: Pearson Longman, 2008), 32.

[83]See David T. Z. Mindich, *Tuned Out: Why Americans under 40 Don't Follow the News* (New York: Oxford University Press, 2005).

[84]Thomas E. Patterson, "Young People and News," Report of the Joan Shorenstein Center on the Press, Politics, and Public Policy, Kennedy School of Government, Harvard University, July 2007, 19–21, http://www.hks.harvard.edu/presspol/research/carnegie-knight/young_people_and_news_2007.pdf.

[85]Wattenberg, *Is Voting for Young People?* 75–80.

[86]Thomas E. Patterson, book manuscript in draft, 2018.

[87]Nielsen Company audience report, 2017.

[88]Herbert A. Simon, "Designing Organizations for an Information-Rich World," in Martin Greenberger, ed., *Computers, Communication, and the Public Interest* (Baltimore, Md.: Johns Hopkins University Press, 1971), 40–41.

[89]Quoted in Steve Lohr, "The Smartphone's Rapid Rise from Gadget to Tool to Necessity," *New York Times,* June 10, 2009, B1.

[90]Kenneth Burke, "How Many Texts Do People Send Every Day?" *Text Request,* May 18, 2016, https://www.textrequest.com/blog/many-texts-people-send-per-day/.

[91]"Interview: Sherry Turkle," *Frontline,* February 2, 2010; see also Sherry Turkle, *Alone Together* (New York: Basic Books, 2011).

CHAPTER ELEVEN

[1]Roger H. Davidson and Walter J. Oleszek, *Congress and Its Members,* 10th ed. (Washington, D.C.: CQ Press, 2008), 4.

[2] See Paul S. Herrnson, *Congressional Elections: Campaigning at Home and in Washington,* 7th ed. (Washington, D.C.: CQ Press, 2012).

[3]See Gary C. Jacobson, *The Politics of Congressional Elections,* 8th ed. (New York: Longman, 2012).

[4]David Mayhew, *Congress: The Electoral Connection* (New Haven, Conn.: Yale University Press, 2004), 5.

[5]Bruce Cain, John Ferejohn, and Morris P. Fiorina, *The Personal Vote* (Cambridge, Mass.: Harvard University Press, 1987).

[6]Information provided by Clerk of the House.

[7]Lara E. Chausow, R. Eric Peterson, and Amber Hope Wilhelm, "Senate Staff Levels in Member, Committee, Leadership, and Other Offices, 1977–2014," Congressional Research Service, March 19, 2015, https://www.scribd.com/doc/315590129/Senate-Staff-Levels-in-Member-Committee-Leadership-And-Other-Offices-1977-2014.

[8]"Total Number of MPs, Peers and Staff," House of Commons Library, October 3, 2016. House of Commons members who hold leadership positions have larger staffs than the three people of the typical member.

[9]Edward Sidlow, *Challenging the Incumbent: An Underdog's Undertaking* (Washington, D.C.: CQ Press, 2003); David C. W. Parker, *The Power of Money in Congressional Campaigns, 1880–2006* (Norman: University of Oklahoma Press, 2008). See also Marian Currinder, *Money in the House: Campaign Funds and Congressional Party Politics* (Boulder, Colo.: Westview Press, 2008).

[10]Federal Election Commission preliminary data, 2018.

[11]OpenSecrets.org data, 2018.

[12]Jennifer Babson and Kelly St. John, "Momentum Helps GOP Collect Record Amounts from PACs," *Congressional Quarterly Weekly Report,* December 3, 1994, 3456.

[13]*Gill v. Whitford*, No. 16-1161 (2018).

[14]Bill Bishop, *The Big Sort: Why the Clustering of Like-Minded America Is Tearing Us Apart* (New York: Houghton Mifflin, 2008).

[15]Jesse Sussell and James A. Thomson, "Are Changing Constituencies Driving Rising Polarization in the U.S. House of Representatives," Rand Corporation, 2015. https://www.rand.org/pubs/research_reports/RR896.html. See also, Thomas E. Mann, "Polarizing the House of Representatives: How Much Does Gerrymandering Matter?" in Pietro S. Nivola and David W. Brady, eds., *Red and Blue Nation? Characteristics and Causes of America's Polarized Politics,* Vol. 1 (Washington, D.C.: Brookings Institution Press, 2006).

[16]Quoted in "A Tale of Myths and Measures: Who Is Truly Vulnerable?" *Congressional*

Quarterly Weekly Report, December 4, 1993, 7; see also Dennis F. Thompson, *Ethics in Congress* (Washington, D.C.: Brookings Institution, 1995).

[17]James E. Campbell, *The Presidential Pulse of Congressional Elections* (Lexington: University Press of Kentucky, 1993).

[18]Robert Erikson, "The Puzzle of Midterm Losses," *Journal of Politics* 50 (November 1988): 1011–29.

[19]See Eric D. Lawrence, Forrest Maltzman, and Steven S. Smith, "Who Wins? Party Effects in Legislative Voting," *Legislative Studies Quarterly* 31 (2006): 33–69; Elaine C. Kamarck, "Increasing Turnout in Congressional Primaries," Brookings Institution, July 2014, p. 10, https://www.brookings.edu/wp-content/uploads/2016/06/KamarckIncreasing-Turnout-in-Congressional-Primaries72614.pdf.

[20]Sean M. Theriault, *Party Polarization in Congress* (New York: Cambridge University Press, 2008); Barry C. Burden, "Candidate Positions in U.S. Congressional Elections," *British Journal of Political Science* 34 (2004): 211–227.

[21]Linda L. Fowler and Robert D. McClure, *Political Ambition* (New Haven, Conn.: Yale University Press, 1989).

[22]See, for example, Avery Anapol, "Poll: Dems lead by 15 points on generic House ballot," *The Hill,* March 1, 2018. http://thehill.com/homenews/house/376272-poll-dems-lead-by-15-points-on-generic-house-ballot

[23]*Congressional Quarterly Weekly Report,* various dates.

[24]Cited in Ryan Lizza, "The Obama Memos," *The New Yorker,* January 30, 2012, 36.

[25]Steven Smith, *Party Influence in Congress* (New York: Cambridge University Press, 2007); Barbara Sinclair, *Party Wars: Polarization and the Politics of National Policy Making* (Norman: University of Oklahoma Press, 2006).

[26]Danielle Thomsen, *Opting Out of Congress* (New York: Cambridge University Press, 2017).

[27]Elaina Plott, "Paul Ryan Pledges: No Immigration Reform under Obama," *National Review,* October 27, 2015. https://www.nationalreview.com/2015/10/paul-ryan-promises-no-immigration-reform-obama-administration/

[28]Quoted in Stephen E. Frantzich and Claude Berube, *Congress: Games and Strategies* (Lanham, MD: Rowman & Littlefield, 2009), 159.

[29]Quoted in Jonathan Rauch, "How American Politics Went Insane," *The Atlantic,* July/August 2016, https://www.theatlantic.com/magazine/archive/2016/07/how-american-politics-went-insane/485570/.

[30]Randall Strahan, *Leading Representatives: The Agency of Leaders in the Politics of the U.S. House* (Baltimore, Md.: Johns Hopkins University Press, 2007); David King, *Turf Wars* (Chicago: University of Chicago Press, 1997).

[31]See Stephen E. Frantzich and Steven E. Schier, *Congress: Games and Strategies* (Dubuque, Iowa: Brown & Benchmark, 1995), 127.

[32]See Gerald S. Strom, *The Logic of Lawmaking* (Baltimore, Md.: Johns Hopkins University Press, 1990).

[33]See Barbara Sinclair, *Unorthodox Lawmaking: New Legislative Processes in the U.S. Congress,* 3d ed. (Washington, D.C.: CQ Press, 2007).

[34]See Jon R. Bond and Richard Fleisher, eds., *Polarized Politics: Congress and the President in a Partisan Era* (Washington, D.C.: CQ Press, 2000).

[35]See Gary Orfield, *Congressional Power: Congress and Social Change* (New York: Harcourt Brace Jovanovich, 1975).

[36]James L. Sundquist, "Congress and the President: Enemies or Partners?" in Lawrence C. Dodd and Bruce I. Oppenheimer, eds., *Congress Reconsidered* (New York: Praeger, 1977), 240.

[37]Barry C. Burden, *Personal Roots of Representation* (Princeton, N.J.: Princeton University Press, 2007).

[38]Keith Krehbiel, "Are Congressional Committees Composed of Preference Outliers?" *American Political Science Review* 84 (1990): 149–64; Richard L. Hall and Bernard Grofman, "The Committee Assignment Process and the Conditional Nature of Committee Bias," *American Political Science Review* 84 (1990): 1149–66.

[39]See, for example, Alan Abramowitz, *The Disappearing Center: Engaged Citizens, Polarization and American Democracy* (New Haven, CT: Yale University Press, 2011).

[40]Fareed Zakaria, "Why Political Polarization Has Gone Wild in America (and What to Do About It)," *CNN World,* July 24, 2011; Frances E. Lee, *Beyond Ideology: Politics, Principles, and Partisanship in the U.S. Senate* (Chicago: University of Chicago Press, 2009).

[41]Frances E. Lee, *Insecure Majorities: Congress and the Perpetual Campaign* (Chicago: University of Chicago Press, 2016), 200–3.

[42]Quoted in ibid, 139.

[43]Joel A. Aberbach and Mark A. Peterson, eds., *The Executive Branch* (New York: Oxford University Press, 2005), 534–35.

[44]Joel Aberback, *Keeping a Watchful Eye* (Washington, D.C.: Brookings Institution, 1990); David Rosenbloom, *Building a Congress Centered Public Administration* (Tuscaloosa: University of Alabama Press, 2001).

[45]Lauren Carroll," *PolitiFact,* July 6, 2017. http://www.politifact.com/truth-o-meter/article/2017/jul/06/17-intelligence-organizations-or-four-either-way-r/

[46]Pew Research Center, "Beyond Distrust: How Americans View Their Government," November 23, 2015, http://www.people-press.org/2015/11/23/beyond-distrust-how-americans-view-their-government/.

[47]John R. Hibbing and Elizabeth Theiss-Morse, *Stealth Democracy: Americans' Belief about How Government Should Work* (New York: Cambridge University Press, 2002).

CHAPTER TWELVE

[1]Woodrow Wilson, *Constitutional Government in the United States,* New York: Columbia University Press, 1908, 67.

[2]Rebecca Ballhaus, "Trump Defends West Wing Turnover: 'I Like Conflict,'" *Wall Street Journal,* March 6, 2018, https://www.wsj.com/articles/trump-defends-west-wing-turnover-i-like-conflict-1520375738.

[3]James W. Davis, *The American Presidency* (New York: Harper & Row, 1987), 13; Sidney Milkis and Michael Nelson, *The American Presidency: Origins and Development,* 1790–2007, 7th ed. (Washington, D.C.: CQ Press, 2015); see also Bruce Ackerman, *The Failure of the Founding Fathers* (Cambridge, Mass.: Belknap Press of Harvard University Press, 2005).

[4]See Barry M. Blechman and Stephen S. Kaplan, *Force without War* (Washington, D.C.: Brookings Institution, 1978); Arthur M. Schlesinger Jr., *War and the American Presidency* (New York: Norton, 2004).

[5]James Bryce, *The American Commonwealth* (New York: Commonwealth Edition, 1908), 230.

[6]Quoted in Wilfred E. Binkley, *President and Congress,* 3d ed. (New York: Vintage, 1962), 142.

[7]Peri E. Arnold, *Remaking the Presidency* (Lawrence: University Press of Kansas, 2009).

[8]Roosevelt, Theodore, *An Autobiography,* (New York: Scribner, 1931), 383.

[9]See Richard M. Pious, *The American Presidency* (New York: Basic Books, 1979), 83.

[10]Truman, Harry S, *Years of Trial and Hope,* (New York: Signet, 1956), 535.

[11]Erwin C. Hargrove, *The Effective Presidency: Lessons on Leadership from John F. Kennedy to George W. Bush* (Boulder, Colo.: Paradigm, 2007).

[12]Quoted in Richard J. Ellis, *The Development of the American Presidency* (New York: Routledge, 2015), 194.

[13]See Thomas S. Langston, *The Cold War Presidency: A Documentary History* (Washington, D.C.: CQ Press, 2006).

[14]See Garry Willis, *Bomb Power: The Modern Presidency and the National Security State* (New York: Penguin Press, 2010).

[15]Quoted in Duncan Watts, *The American Presidency,* (Edinburgh, Scotland: University of Edinburgh Press, 2009), 104

[16]James W. Ceaser, *Presidential Selection: Theory and Development* (Princeton, N.J.: Princeton University Press, 1979).

[17]John S. Jackson and William J. Crotty, *The Politics of Presidential Selection* (New York: Longman, 2001).

[18]William Mayer, *The Front-Loading Problem in Presidential Nominations* (Washington, D.C.: Brookings Institution Press, 2004).

[19]See Thomas E. Patterson, *The Vanishing Voter* (New York: Knopf, 2003), 120.

[20]"Jill Stein: Democratic Spoiler Or Scapegoat?" *FiveThirtyEight,* December 7, 2016. https://fivethirtyeight.com/features/jill-stein-democratic-spoiler-or-scapegoat/

[21]See Roderick P. Hart, *Seducing America: How Television Charms the Modern Voter* (Thousand Oaks, Calif.: Sage, 1998).

[22]See, for example, Ezra Klein, "Hillary Clinton's 3 debate performances left the Trump campaign in ruins," *Vox,* October 19, 2016. https://www.vox.com/policy-and-politics/2016/10/19/13340828/hillary-clinton-debate-trump-won

[23]OpenSecrets.org data, 2018.

[24]Thomas E. Patterson, "News Coverage of the 2016 General Election: How the Press Failed the Voters," Shorenstein Center on Media, Politics and Public Policy," Harvard Kennedy School, Harvard University, Cambridge, MA, December 7, 2016. https://shorensteincenter.org/news-coverage-2016-general-election/

[25]Quoted in Stephen J. Wayne, *Road to the White House,* 1992 (New York: St. Martin's Press, 1992), 143; but see Jody C. Baumgartner, *The American Vice Presidency Reconsidered* (Westport, Conn.: Praeger, 2006).

[26]John P. Burke, *The Institutionalized Presidency* (Baltimore, Md.: Johns Hopkins University Press, 1992); Charles E. Walcott and Karen M. Hult, *Governing the White House* (Lawrence: University Press of Kansas, 1995).

[27]See Jeffrey E. Cohen, *The Politics of the United States Cabinet* (Pittsburgh, Pa.: University of Pittsburgh Press, 1988); Shirley Anne Warshaw, *Powersharing: White House–Cabinet Relations in the Modern Presidency* (Albany: State University of New York Press, 1995).

[28]James Pfiffner, *The Modern Presidency* (New York: St. Martin's Press, 1994), 123; James Pfiffner, "Recruiting Executive Branch Leaders: The Office of Presidential Personnel," Brookings Institution, Spring 2001, www.brookings.edu/research/articles/2001/03/spring-governance-pfiffner.

[29]Quoted in James MacGregor Burns, "Our Super-Government—Can We Control It?" *The New York Times,* April 24, 1949, 32.

[30]See Paul C. Light, *Thickening Government: Federal Hierarchy and the Diffusion of Accountability* (Washington, D.C.: Brookings Institution, 1995).

[31]Glenn Thrush, "Locked in the Cabinet," *Politico Magazine,* November 2013. www.politico.com/magazine/story/2013/11/locked-in-the-cabinet-99374.html#.VE7Txlfsp-0.

[32]David Goetsch, *Effective Leadership* (Upper Saddle River, N.J.: Prentice-Hall, 2004).

[33]Stephen Skowronek, *Presidential Leadership in Political Time* (Lawrence: University of Kansas Press, 2008).

[34]Quoted in Emmet John Hughes, *The Ordeal of Power: A Political Memoir of the Eisenhower Years* (New York: Athenaeum 1963), 124.

[35]Erwin Hargrove, *The Power of the Modern Presidency* (New York: Knopf, 1974); see also John H. Kessel, *Presidents, the Presidency, and the Political Environment* (Washington, D.C.: CQ Press, 2001); Skowronek, *Presidential Leadership in Political Time.*

[36]James P. Pfiffner, *The Strategic Presidency: Hitting the Ground Running,* 2d ed. (Chicago: Dorsey Press, 1996).

[37]Aaron Wildavsky, "The Two Presidencies," *Trans-Action,* December 1966, 7.

[38]Pfiffner, *Modern Presidency,* ch. 6.

[39]*United States v. Belmont,* 57 U.S. 758 (1937).

[40]Robert DiClerico, *The American President,* 6th ed. (Englewood Cliffs, N.J.: Prentice-Hall, 1999), 47.

[41]Quoted in Antonio Thompson and Christos Frentzos, *The Routledge Handbook of American Military and Diplomatic History* (New York: Routledge, 2013), 301.

[42]Thomas P. (Tip) O'Neill, with William Novak, *Man of the House: The Life and Political Memoirs of Speaker Tip O'Neill* (New York: Random House, 1987), 297.

[43]Charles O. Jones, *The Presidency in a Separated System* (Washington, D.C.: Brookings Institution, 2005).

[44]Quoted in Ryan Lizza, "The Obama Memos," *The New Yorker,* January 30, 2012, 44.

[45]Richard E. Neustadt, *Presidential Power and the Modern Presidents* (New York: Free Press, 1990), 71–72.

[46]Ibid., 33.

[47]"Trump Divided, Conquered in First Year in Office," *Roll Call,* undated, downloaded March 18, 2018. https://www.rollcall.com/news/politics/trump-divided-conquered-first-year

[48]Quoted in Lizza, "The Obama Memos," 49.

[49]Charles O. Jones, *The President in a Separated System* (Washington, D.C.: Brookings Institution, 2005), 173.

[50]John E. Mueller, "Presidential Popularity from Truman to Johnson," *American Political Science Review* 64 (March 1970): 18–34; Kathleen Frankovic, "Public Opinion in the 1992 Campaign," in Gerald M. Pomper, ed., *The Election of 1992* (Chatham, N.J.: Chatham House, 1993); Chris J. Dolan, *The Presidency and Economic Policy* (Lanham, Md.: Rowman & Littlefield, 2007).

[51]Samuel Kernell, *Going Public: New Strategies of Presidential Leadership,* 3d ed. (Washington, D.C.: CQ Press, 1997), 1; see also Robert M. Eisinger, *The Evolution of Presidential Polling* (New York: Cambridge University Press, 2003); Stephen J. Farnsworth and S. Robert Lichter, *Mediated Presidency: Television News & Presidential Governance* (Lanham, Md.: Rowman & Littlefield, 2005).

[52]Thomas E. Patterson, "News Coverage of Donald Trump's First 100 Days," Shorenstein Center on Media, Politics and Public Policy," Harvard Kennedy School, Harvard University, Cambridge, MA, May 18, 2017.

https://shorensteincenter.org/news-coverage-donald-trumps-first-100-days/

[53]Michael Wolff, *Fire and Fury: Inside the Trump White House* (New York: Henry Holt, 2018).

[54]Amy Mitchell, Jeffrey Gottfried, Galen Stocking, Katerina Eva Matsa, and Elizabeth Grieco, "Covering President Trump in a Polarized Media Environment," Pew Research Center, October 2, 2017, http://www.journalism.org/2017/10/02/covering-president-trump-in-a-polarized-media-environment/.

[55]Glenn Kessler and Meg Kelly, "President Trump made 2,140 false or misleading claims in his first year," *Washington Post,* January 20, 2018. https://www.washingtonpost.com/news/fact-checker/wp/2018/01/20/president-trump-made-2140-false-or-misleading-claims-in-his-first-year/?utm_term=.c2f5bab7d97f

[56]Hugh Heclo, "Introduction: The Presidential Illusion," in Hugh Heclo and Lester M. Salamon, eds., *The Illusion of Presidential Government* (Boulder, Colo.: Westview Press, 1981), 2.

[57]Theodore J. Lowi, *The "Personal" Presidency: Power Invested, Promise Unfulfilled* (Ithaca, N.Y.: Cornell University Press, 1985).

CHAPTER THIRTEEN

[1]Max Weber, *Economy and Society,* (New York: Bedminster Press, 1968), 223. Translated and edited by Guenther Roth and Claus Wittich. Originally published in 1921.

[2]Reason-Rupe poll, July 2014.

[3]Weber, *Economy and Society,* 23.

[4]See Mark Sauter and James Carafano, *Homeland Security* (New York: McGraw-Hill, 2005).

[5]Office of Personnel Management data, 2016.

[6]Gregory A. Huber, *The Craft of Bureaucratic Neutrality: Interests and Influence in Governmental Regulation of Occupational Safety* (New York: Cambridge University Press, 2007); Herbert Kaufman, "Emerging Conflicts in the Doctrine of Public Administration," *American Political Science Review* 50 (December 1956): 1060.

[7]See Allen Schick, *The Federal Budget: Politics, Policy, Process,* 3d ed. (Washington, D.C.: Brookings Institution, 2007).

[8]Zeeshan Aleem, "Trump wants to gut the State Department by 25 percent," *Vox,* February 12, 2018. https://www.vox.com/policy-and-politics/2018/2/12/17004372/trump-budget-state-department-defense-cuts

[9]See Cornelius M. Kerwin, *Rulemaking,* 3d ed. (Washington, D.C.: CQ Press, 2003); Daniel E. Hall, *Administrative Law: Bureaucracy in a Democracy* (Upper Saddle River, N.J.: Prentice-Hall, 2005).

[10]Steven Kelman, "Occupational Safety and Health Administration," in James Q. Wilson, ed., *The Politics of Regulation* (New York: Basic Books, 1980), 239–40.

[11]See Hugh Heclo, *A Government of Strangers* (Washington, D.C.: Brookings Institution, 1977), 117–18.

[12]Quoted in Aaron Wildavsky, *The Politics of the Budgetary Process,* 4th ed. (Boston: Little, Brown, 1984), 19; see also Dennis D. Riley, *Bureaucracy and the Policy Process: Keeping the Promises* (Lanham, Md.: Rowman & Littlefield, 2005).

[13]Joel D. Aberbach and Bert A. Rockman, "Clashing Beliefs within the Executive Branch," *American Political Science Review* 70 (June 1976): 461.

[14]Norton E. Long, "Power and Administration," *Public Administration Review* 10 (Autumn 1949): 269; Joel D. Aberbach and Bert A. Rockman, *In the Web of Politics* (Washington, D.C.: Brookings Institution, 2000).

[15]See B. Guy Peters, *The Politics of Bureaucracy,* 5th ed. (New York: Routledge, 2001).

[16]Ibid, 118.

[17]See B. Dan Wood and Richard W. Waterman, *Bureaucratic Dynamics* (Boulder, Colo.: Westview Press, 1994); Edward C. Page and Bill Jenkins, *Policy Bureaucracy: Government with a Cast of Thousands* (New York: Oxford University Press, 2005).

[18]See, for example, Ed Blazina, "Transit leaders lobby Congress to restore federal grants for new projects," *Pittsburgh Post-Gazette,* March 19, 2018. http://www.post-gazette.com/news/transportation/2018/03/19/American-Public-Transportation-Association-federal-grants-cut-by-Trump-lobby-Congress-bus-rapid-transit/stories/201803190141

[19]Long, "Power and Administration," 269; see also John Mark Hansen, *Gaining Access* (Chicago: University of Chicago Press, 1991).

[20]Goodsell, Charles T., *The Case for Bureaucracy,* 2d ed., (Chatham, N.J.: Chatham House, 1985), 55–60.

[21]William T. Gormley Jr. and Steven J. Balla, *Bureaucracy and Democracy* (Washington, D.C.: CQ Press, 2003); Kevin B. Smith, *Public Administration: Power and Politics in the Fourth*

Branch of Government (New York: Oxford University Press, 2006).

[22]James P. Pfiffner, "The National Performance Review in Perspective," working paper 94-4, Institute of Public Policy, George Mason University, 1994, 2.

[23]Ibid., 12.

[24]Kaufman, "Emerging Conflicts," 1062.

[25]Charles Perrow, "Disaster after 9/11: The Department of Homeland Security and the Intelligence Reorganization," *Homeland Security Affairs* 2 (2006), http://calhoun.nps.edu/handle/10945/25072.

[26]Environmental Integrity Project data, February, 2018. http://www.environmentalintegrity.org/news/civil-penalties-decline-under-trump-administration/

[27]Heclo, *Government of Strangers*, 104.

[28]William F. West, "The Administrative Presidency as Reactive Oversight: Implications for Positive and Normative Theory," *Public Administration Review* 75 (2015): 523–33.

[29]Ibid., 225.

[30]See Joel D. Aberbach, *Keeping a Watchful Eye* (Washington, D.C.: Brookings Institution, 1990).

[31]Douglas A. Van Belle and Kenneth M. Mash, *A Novel Approach to Politics* (Washington, D.C.: CQ Press, 2006).

[32]See Donald Kettl, *Deficit Politics* (New York: Macmillan, 1992).

[33]David Rosenbloom, "The Evolution of the Administrative State, and Transformations of Administrative Law," in David Rosenbloom and Richard Schwartz, eds., *Handbook of Regulation and Administrative Law* (New York: Marcel Dekker, 1994), 3–36.

[34]*Pigeford v. Veneman,* U.S. District Court for the District of Columbia, Civil Action No. 97-1978 (1999).

[35]See *Vermont Yankee Nuclear Power Corp. v. National Resources Defense Council,* Inc., 435 U.S. 519 (1978); *Chevron v. National Resources Defense Council,* 467 U.S. 837 (1984); *Heckler v. Chaney,* 470 U.S. 821 (1985); but see *FDA v. Brown & Williamson Tobacco Co.,* 529 U.S. 120 (2000).

[36]See Mark W. Huddleston, "The Carter Civil Service Reforms," *Political Science Quarterly* (Winter 1981–82): 607–22.

[37]Ed O'Keefe, "Senior Executive Service Needs Overhaul, Outside Study Finds," *The Washington Post,* August 20, 2009.

[38]Joe Davidson, "Whistleblower 'Bunny' Greenhouse Wins Settlement Near $1 Million,"

The Washington Post, July 26, 2011, www.washingtonpost.com/blogs/federal-eye/post/whistleblower-bunny-greenhouse-wins-settlement-near-1-million/2011/04/15/gIQANfFAbI_blog.html.

[39]See Brian J. Cook, *Bureaucracy and Self-Government* (Baltimore, Md.: Johns Hopkins University Press, 1996).

CHAPTER FOURTEEN

[1]*Marbury v. Madison,* 5 U.S. 137 (1803).

[2]*Obergefell v. Hodges,* No 14-556 (2015).

[3]*South Carolina v. North Carolina* 558 U.S. 256 (2010).

[4]Supreme Court of the United States data. https://www.supremecourt.gov/about/justicecaseload.aspx

[5]Henry Glick, *Courts, Politics, and Justice,* 3d ed. (New York: McGraw-Hill, 1993), 120.

[6]Timothy R. Johnson, Paul Wahlbeck, and James Spriggs, "The Influence of Oral Arguments on the U.S. Supreme Court," *American Political Science Review* 100 (2006): 99–113.

[7]Lawrence Baum, *The Supreme Court,* 8th ed. (Washington, D.C.: CQ Press, 2003), 120.

[8]From a letter to the author by Frank Schwartz of Beaver College; this section reflects substantially Professor Schwartz's recommendations to the author, as does the later section that addresses the federal court myth.

[9]*Hutto v. Davis,* 370 U.S. 256, 1982.

[10]*Obergefell v. Hodges,* No. 14-556 (2015).

[11]See Richard Davis, *Electing Justices* (New York: Oxford University Press, 2005).

[12]Robert Scigliano, *The Supreme Court and the Presidency* (New York: Free Press, 1971), 146; see also Lee Epstein and Jack Knight, *The Choices Justices Make* (Washington, D.C.: CQ Press, 1998); Stefanie A. Lundquist, David A. Yalof, and John A. Clark, "The Impact of Presidential Appointments to the Supreme Court: Cohesive and Divisive Voting within Presidential Blocs," *Political Research Quarterly* 53 (2000): 795–814.

[13]Quoted in Baum, *Supreme Court,* 37.

[14]Quoted in Kermit L. Hall and Kevin T. McGuire, *The Judicial Branch* (New York: Oxford University Press, 2005), 77.

[15]See Virginia A. Hettinger et al., *Judging on a Collegial Court: Influences on Federal Appellate Decision Making* (Charlottesville: University of Virginia Press, 2006).

[16]John Gottschall, "Reagan's Appointments to the U.S. Courts of Appeals," *Judicature* 48 (1986): 54.

[17]See, for example, "Politicization in the Federal Judiciary and Its Effect on the Federal Judicial Function," *New York University Journal of Legislation & Public Policy* 19 (2017). https://papers.ssrn.com/sol3/papers.cfm?abstract_id=2995008

[18]Quoted in Louis Fisher, *American Constitutional Law.* (New York: McGraw-Hill, 1990), 5.

[19]Quoted in Charles P. Curtis, *Law and Large as Life* (New York: Simon & Schuster, 1959), 156–57.

[20]See Lee Epstein and Jack Knight, *The Choices Justices Make* (New York: Longman, 1995); Thomas G. Hansford and James F. Spriggs II, *The Politics of Precedent on the Supreme Court* (Princeton, N.J.: Princeton University Press, 2006).

[21]*Faragher v. City of Boca Raton,* No. 97-282 (1998).

[22]John Schmidhauser, *The Supreme Court* (New York: Holt, Rinehart & Winston, 1964), 6.

[23]*McConnell v. Federal Election Commission,* 540 U.S. 93 (2003).

[24]*Citizens United v. Federal Election Commission,* 558 U.S. 310 (2010).

[25]Jeffrey A. Segal and Harold J. Spaeth, *The Supreme Court and the Attitudinal Model Revisited* (New York: Cambridge University Press, 2002), 404.

[26]Brian Lamb, Susan Swain, and Mark Farkas *The Supreme Court.* (New York: Public Affairs, 2010), 6.

[27]Stephen L. Wasby, *The Supreme Court in the Federal Judicial System,* 4th ed. (Chicago: Nelson-Hall, 1993), 53.

[28]Rob Arthur, "Trump's Justice Department isn't enforcing civil rights," *Vice News,* February 23, 2018. https://news.vice.com/en_us/article/wj44y4/trumps-justice-department-isnt-enforcing-civil-rights

[29]Davis, *Electing Justices.*

[30]Public Policy Polling survey, February 2017.

[31]Sean Illing, "20 of America's top political scientists gathered to discuss our democracy: They're scared," *Vox,* October 13, 2017. https://www.vox.com/2017/10/13/16431502/america-democracy-decline-liberalism

[32]Ross Sandler and David Schoenbrod, *Democracy by Decree* (New Haven, Conn.: Yale University Press, 2003).

[33]See, Antonin Scalia, *A Matter of Interpretation* (Princeton, N.J.: Princeton University Press, 1997).

[34]See Stephen Breyer, "Our Democratic Constitution," James Madison Lecture, New York University Law School, New York, October 22, 2001.

[35]Henry J. Abraham, "The Judicial Function under the Constitution," *News for Teachers of Political Science* 41 (Spring 1984): 14.

[36]*National Federation of Independent Business v. Sebelius,* No. 11-393 (2012).

CHAPTER FIFTEEN

[1]Marc Allen Eisner, Jeffrey Worsham, and Evan J. Rinquist, *Contemporary Regulatory Policy* (Boulder, Colo.: Lynne Rienner, 2006).

[2]The section titled "Efficiency through Government Intervention" relies substantially on Alan Stone, *Regulation and Its Alternatives* (Washington, D.C.: CQ Press, 1982).

[3]See Marc Allen Eisner, *Regulatory Politics in Transition,* 2d ed. (Baltimore, Md.: Johns Hopkins University Press, 2000).

[4]See Richard A. Harris and Sidney M. Milkis, *The Politics of Regulatory Change* (New York: Oxford University Press, 1996).

[5]Lawrence E. Mitchell, *Corporate Irresponsibility* (New Haven, Conn.: Yale University Press, 2003).

[6]H. Peyton Young, *Equity: In Theory and Practice* (Princeton, N.J.: Princeton University Press, 1995).

[7]Michael Greenwood, "8 Million Lives Saved since Surgeon General's Tobacco Warning 50 Years Ago," *YaleNews,* January 7, 2014, http://news.yale.edu/2014/01/07/8-million-lives-saved-surgeon-general-s-tobacco-warning-50-years-ago.

[8]Board on Population Health and Public Health Practice, *The Future of Drug Safety: Promoting and Protecting the Health of the Public* (Washington, D.C.: National Academies Press, 2007).

[9]Rachel Carson, *Silent Spring* (Boston: Houghton Mifflin, 1962); see also Lester R. Brown, *Plan B2.0: Rescuing a Planet under Stress and a Civilization in Trouble* (New York: Norton, 2006).

[10]See Walter A. Rosenbaum, *Environmental Politics and Policy,* 10th ed. (Washington, D.C.: CQ Press, 2016); Norman J. Vig and Michael E. Kraft, eds., *Environmental Policy: New Directions for the Twenty-First Century* (Washington, D.C.: CQ Press, 2003).

[11]"Global Climate Report - Annual 2017," National Oceanic and Atmospheric Administration. https://www.ncdc.noaa.gov/sotc/global/201713

[12]*Janus v. American Federation of State, County and Municipal Employees,* No. 16-1466 (2018).

[13]Elliot A. Rosen, *Roosevelt, the Great Depression, and the Economics of Recovery* (Charlottesville: University of Virginia Press, 2007).

[14]See Robert Lekachman, *The Age of Keynes* (New York: Random House, 1966); see also Richard Kopke, Geoffrey M. B. Tootell, and Robert K. Trist, eds., *The Macroeconomics of Fiscal Policy* (Cambridge, Mass.: MIT Press, 2006).

[15]See Bruce Bartlett, *Reaganomics: Supply-Side Economics* (Westport, Conn.: Arlington House, 1981).

[16]Paul Krugman, "Hey, Lucky Duckies," *The New York Times,* December 3, 2002, A31.

[17]"The Cost of Rising Interest Rates," Committee for a Responsible Federal Budget, December 14, 2016. http://www.crfb.org/papers/cost-rising-interest-rates

[18]Bianca DiJulio, Jamie Firth, and Mollyann Brodie, "Data Note: Americans' Views On The U.S. Role In Global Health," *Kaiser Family Foundation,* Jan 23, 2015. http://www.kff.org/global-health-policy/poll-finding/data-note-americans-views-on-the-u-s-role-in-global-health/

[19]"As Sequester Deadline Looms, Little Support for Cutting Most Programs," Pew Research Center, February 22, 2013, http://www.people-press.org/2013/02/22/as-sequester-deadline-looms-little-support-for-cutting-most-programs/.

[20]Alan O. Ebenstein, *Milton Friedman: A Biography* (New York: Palgrave Macmillan, 2007).

[21]Edward Hadas and Hugh Dixon, "Quantitative Easing: A Therapy of Last Resort," *The New York Times,* January 1, 2009, www.nytimes.com/2009/01/11/business/worldbusiness/11iht-views12.1.19248009.html.

[22]Martin Mayer, *FED: The Inside Story of How the World's Most Powerful Financial Institution Drives the Markets* (New York: Free Press, 2001).

[23]See, for example, Gallup poll, March 24–27, 2008. http://news.gallup.com/poll/106114/six-oppose-wall-street-bailouts.aspx

CHAPTER SIXTEEN

[1]*Federalist* No. 10.

[2]Chad Stone, Danilo Trisi, Arloc Sherman, and Roderick Taylor, "A Guide to Statistical Trends in Income Inequality," Center on Budget & Policy Priorities, August 29, 2018. https://www.cbpp.org/research/poverty-and-inequality/a-guide-to-statistics-on-historical-trends-in-income-inequality

[3]U.S. Census Bureau, 2016.

[4]Emmanuel Saez and Thomas Piketty, "Income Inequality in the United States: 1913–1998," *Quarterly Journal of Economics* 118 (2003): 1–39.

[5]Paul Krugman, *The Conscience of a Liberal* (New York: Norton, 2007), 7–8.

[6]David Kocieniewski, "Since 1980s, the Kindest of Tax Cuts for the Rich," *The New York Times,* January 18, 2012.

[7]Andrew Flowers, "The Top 1 Percent Earns a Lot from Cashing In on Investments," *FiveThirtyEight,* January 20, 2015, http://fivethirtyeight.com/datalab/the-top-1-percent-earns-a-lot-from-cashing-in-on-investments/.

[8]Kathleen Elkins, "80% of Americans Own an Unbelievably Small Portion of the Country's Wealth," *Business Insider,* June 15, 2015, www.businessinsider.com/inequality-in-the-us-is-much-more-extreme-than-you-think-2015-6.

[9]Adam Looney and Kevin B. Moore, "Changes in the Distribution of After-Tax Wealth: Has Income Tax Policy Increased Wealth Inequality?" Federal Reserve Board, Washington, D.C., 2015.

[10]Thomas L. Hungerford, "Changes in the Distribution of Income among Tax Filers between 1996 and 2006: The Role of Labor Income, Capital Income, and Tax Policy," Congressional Research Service, December 29, 2011, Washington, D.C.

[11]Lawrence Mishel, "Unions, Inequality, and Faltering Middle-Class Wages," Economic Policy Institute, August 29, 2012, www.epi.org/publication/ib342-unions-inequality-faltering-middle-class/.

[12]Katie Sanders, "Rattner: Manufacturing Wages Today in America Lower Than Average Wages in the Economy as a Whole,'" *Punditfact,* March 30, 2014, www.politifact.com/punditfact/statements/2014/mar/30/steven-rattner/rattner-manufacturing-wages-today-america-lower-av/.

[13]Stephen Gold, "The Competitive Edge: Manufacturing's Multiplier Effect—It's Bigger Than You Think," *Industry Week,* September 2, 2014, www.industryweek.com/global-economy/competitive-edge-manufacturings-multiplier-effect-its-bigger-you-think.

[14]Kenneth P. Vogel and Jim Tankersley, "With Billions at Stake in Tax Debate, Lobbyists Played Hardball," *New York Times,* December 15, 2017. https://www.nytimes.com/2017/12/15/us/politics/lobbyists-tax-overhaul-congress.html?mtrref=www.google.com&auth=login-email

[15]Ben Brody, "Business Groups Spent Big on Lobbying During the Tax Overhaul," *Bloomberg News,* January 23, 2018. https://www.bloomberg.com/news/articles/2018-01-23/tax-bill-prompts-business-to-pay-heavily-for-lobbying-campaigns

[16]"Census Shows 1 in 2 People Are Poor or Low-Income," *USA Today,* December 15, 2011, http://usatoday30.usatoday.com/news/nation/story/2011-12-15/poor-census-low-income/51944034/1.

[17]See Felicia Ann Kornbluh, *The Battle for Welfare Rights: Politics and Poverty in Modern America* (Philadelphia: University of Pennsylvania Press, 2007).

[18]V. O. Key Jr., *The Responsible Electorate* (Cambridge, Mass.: Belknap Press of Harvard University, 1966), 43.

[19]Everett Carll Ladd, *American Political Parties* (New York: Norton, 1970), 205.

[20]The Affordable Care Act was not strictly an antipoverty program, though it had provisions aimed at helping low-income people. The legislation's larger goal was to increase health insurance coverage primarily through mandates on companies and individuals. Most companies with more than 200 employees are now required to provide their employees with health insurance, and most companies with 50 to 200 employees must provide insurance or pay a tax penalty. Individual Americans initially faced a tax penalty if they didn't have health insurance. In 2017, the Republican-controlled Congress eliminated that requirement.

[21]See Jason DeParle, *American Dream: Three Women, Ten Kids, and a Nation's Drive to End Welfare* (New York: Penguin, 2005).

[22]Alberto Alesina and Edward Glaeser, *Fighting Poverty in the U.S. and Europe* (New York: Oxford University Press, 2006).

[23]Kaiser Family Foundation, "A Primer on Medicare Financing," January 31, 2011, http://kff.org/health-reform/issue-brief/a-primer-on-medicare-financing/.

[24]Charles Murray, *Losing Ground: American Social Policy, 1950-1980* (New York: Basic Books, 1984).

[25]Signe-Mary McKernan and Caroline Ratcliffe, "Events That Trigger Poverty Entries and Exits," *Social Science Quarterly* 86 (2005): 1146-69.

[26]See Christopher Howard, *The Welfare State Nobody Knows* (Princeton, N.J.: Princeton University Press, 2006).

[27]Mark Byrnes, "U.S. Spending on Social Welfare Programs Is Way Up, But Far Less Of It Goes to the Poorest," *CityLab,* May 19, 2014.

https://www.citylab.com/equity/2014/05/us-spending-on-social-welfare-programs-is-way-up-but-far-less-of-it-goes-to-the-poorest/371124/

[28]Said of George H. W. Bush at the 1988 Democratic Convention. The quote is variously attributed to Ann Richards or Jim Hightower.

[29]For a history of public education, see Joel H. Spring, *The American School 1642-2004* (New York: McGraw-Hill, 2008).

[30]*The 2012 Kids Count Data Book: State Trends in Child Well-Being,* a report of the Annie E. Casey Foundation, July 25, 2012, www.aecf.org/resources/the-2012-kids-count-data-book/.

[31]Based on Organization for Economic Cooperation and Development (OECD) data, 2006; see Douglas S. Reed, *On Equal Terms: The Constitutional Politics of Educational Opportunity* (Princeton, N.J.: Princeton University Press, 2003).

[32]James H. Kuklinski, Paul J. Quirk, Jennifer Jerit, David Schwieder, and Robert F. Rich, "Misinformation and the Currency of Democratic Citizenship," *Journal of Politics,* 62 (2000): 790-816.

[33]Anthony Leiserowitz, Edward Maibach, Connie Roser-Renouf, and Jay D. Hmielowski, "Politics & Global Warming: Democrats, Republicans, Independents, and the Tea Party," Yale Project on Climate Change Communication, Yale University and George Mason University, New Haven, CT, 2011. http://environment.yale.edu/climate/files/PoliticsGlobalWarming2011.pdf

[34]Quoted in Kathleen Hall Jamieson and Paul Waldman, *The Press Effect: Politicians, Journalists, and the Stories That Shape the Political World.* (New York: Oxford University Press, 2002), 167.

[35]Stanley Feldman and John Zaller, "The Political Culture of Ambivalence: Ideological Responses to the Welfare State," *American Journal of Political Science* 36 (1992): 268-307.

[36]Robert E. Lane, "Market Justice, Political Justice," *American Political Science Review* 80 (June 1986): 383-402.

CHAPTER SEVENTEEN

[1]See Douglas T. Stuart, *Creating the National Security State* (Princeton, N.J.: Princeton University Press, 2008).

[2]See Mr. X. (George Kennan), "The Sources of Soviet Conduct," *Foreign Affairs* 25 (July 1947): 566-82.

[3]David M. Barrett, *Uncertain Warriors: Lyndon Johnson and His Vietnam Advisors* (Lawrence: University Press of Kansas, 1993); see also Stanley Karnow, *Vietnam: A History* (New York: Penguin, 1983).

[4]See Dag Henriksen, *NATO's Gamble* (Annapolis, Md.: Naval Institute Press, 2007).

[5]See Ron Susskind, *The One-Percent Solution* (New York: Simon & Schuster, 2007).

[6]West Point speech, June 1, 2002; for an opposing view, see Gary Hart, *The Shield and the Cloak: The Security of the Commons* (New York: Oxford University Press, 2006).

[7]Nick Ritchie, *The Political Road to War with Iraq: Bush, 9/11 and the Drive to Overthrow Saddam* (New York: Routledge, 2007).

[8]Pew Research Center for the People and the Press, "Public Attitudes toward the War in Iraq: 2003–2008," March 19, 2008, http://pewresearch.org/pubs/770/iraq-war-five-year-anniversary.

[9]Brian Michael Jenkins, "Fifteen Years On, Where Are We in the 'War on Terror'?" *Counter Terrorism Center Sentinel* 9 (2016), https://ctc.usma.edu/fifteen-years-on-where-are-we-in-the-war-on-terror/.

[10]Quoted in Jeffrey A. Engel, "Putin wants to make Russia great again," *DallasNews,* October 5, 2017. https://www.dallasnews.com/opinion/commentary/2017/10/05/putin-wants-make-russia-great

[11]Quinnipiac University poll, March 6, 2018, https://poll.qu.edu/national/release-detail?ReleaseID=2526.

[12]See Nate Silver, "How Much Did Russian Interference Affect the 2016 Election? It's Hard to Say," *FiveThirtyEight,* February 16, 2018, https://fivethirtyeight.com/features/how-much-did-russian-interference-affect-the-2016-election/.

[13]Congressional testimony of former Director of National Intelligence James Clapper, May 8, 2017.

[14]Cristina Maza, "Russia and China Are Closer Than Ever Before, Beijing Says," *Newsweek,* April 6, 2018, http://www.newsweek.com/russia-and-china-are-closer-ever-beijing-says-it-launches-trade-war-trump-875304.

[15]Remarks of Nicholas Burns, World Affairs Council, Washington, D.C., June 23, 2011.

[16]Statement of the U.S. Secretary of Defense Leon Panetta, January 26, 2012.

[17]Thomas Rid and Thomas A. Keaney, eds., *Understanding Counterinsurgency Warfare* (New York: Routledge, 2010).

[18]See Richard Pearlstein, *Fatal Torture? Transnational Terrorism and the New Global Disorder* (Austin: University of Texas Press, 2004), 15–23.

[19]See Ofira Seliktar, *The Politics of Intelligence and American Wars with Iraq* (New York: Palgrave Macmillan, 2008).

[20]John Mueller, "Trends in Popular Support for the Wars in Korea and Vietnam," *American Political Science Review* 65 (June 1971): 358–75; see also John Mueller, "The Iraq Syndrome," *Foreign Affairs* (November/December 2005).

[21]George C. Wilson, *This War Really Matters: Inside the Fight for Defense Dollars* (Washington, D.C.: CQ Press, 2000).

[22]*The World Competitiveness Yearbook* (Lausanne, Switzerland: International Institute for Management Development, 2008).

[23]U.S. government data, various agencies, 2008.

[24]William H. Branson, *Trends in U.S. International Trade and Investment since World War II,* NBER Working Paper No. 469 (Cambridge, Mass.: National Bureau of Economic Research, April 1980).

[25]Robert Whaples, "Do Economists Agree on Anything? Yes!," *The Economists' Voice* 3 (2006): 1–6.

[26]The formal international institution that oversees trade agreements and international trade rules is the World Trade Organization (WTO), which was created in 1995 and of which the United States is a founding member. The WTO today includes more than 160 nations. The WTO's mission is to promote global free trade through reductions in tariffs, protections for intellectual property (copyrights and patents), and other policies. Trade disputes among WTO members are settled by arbitration panels, which consist of representatives from the member nations. Under WTO rules, an arbitration panel's ruling, once approved by the WTO's full membership, is binding on the countries involved in the dispute.

[27]Paola Subacchi and Stephen Pickford, *Legitimacy vs. Effectiveness for the G20: A Dynamic Approach to Global Economic Governance,* Chatham House Briefing Paper (Royal Institute of International Affairs, London, England, October 2011), 2.

INDEX

n = note

Effective, efficient studying.

Connect helps you be more productive with your study time and get better grades using tools like SmartBook, which highlights key concepts and creates a personalized study plan. Connect sets you up for success, so you walk into class with confidence and walk out with better grades.

©Shutterstock/wavebreakmedia

> " I really liked this app—it made it easy to study when you don't have your textbook in front of you. "
>
> - Jordan Cunningham,
> Eastern Washington University

Study anytime, anywhere.

Download the free ReadAnywhere app and access your online eBook when it's convenient, even if you're offline. And since the app automatically syncs with your eBook in Connect, all of your notes are available every time you open it. Find out more at **www.mheducation.com/readanywhere**

No surprises.

The Connect Calendar and Reports tools keep you on track with the work you need to get done and your assignment scores. Life gets busy; Connect tools help you keep learning through it all.

	13		14
		Chapter 11 Quiz	
Chapter 12 Quiz			
Chapter 13 Evidence of Evolution		Chapter 11 DNA Technology	
		Chapter 7 Quiz	
		Chapter 7 DNA Structure and Gene...	
		and 7 more...	

Learning for everyone.

McGraw-Hill works directly with Accessibility Services Departments and faculty to meet the learning needs of all students. Please contact your Accessibility Services office and ask them to email accessibility@mheducation.com, or visit **www.mheducation.com/about/accessibility.html** for more information.